PRENTICE-HALL

Grammar and Composition

SERIES CONSULTANTS

Grade 6

Joleen Johnson
Curriculum Writer, Office of
Secondary Instruction
San Bernardino City Unified Schools
San Bernardino, California

Grade 7

Ellen G. Manhire
English Consultant Coordinator
Fresno, California

Grade 8

Elizabeth A. Nace
Supervisor, Language Arts
Akron, Ohio

Grade 9

Jerry Reynolds
Supervisor, Language Arts
Rochester, Minnesota

Grade 10

Marlene Corbett
Chairperson, Department of English
Charlotte, North Carolina

Grade 11

Gilbert Hunt
Chairperson, Department of English
Manchester, Connecticut

Grade 12

Margherite LaPota
Curriculum Specialist
Tulsa, Oklahoma

CRITIC READERS

Hugh B. Cassell
Jefferson County Public Schools
Louisville, KY

Mary Demarest
St. Mary's Dominican High School
New Orleans, LA

Judy Luehm Junecko
Leesburg High School
Leesburg, FL

Ruth E. Loeffler
Norman High School
Norman, OK

D. Gay Masters
Salem-Keizer Public Schools
Salem, OR

Laura Moyer
Gloversville High School
Gloversville, NY

Avis Satterfield
Virgil I. Grissom High School
Huntsville, AL

Bonnie Scott
St. Augustine High School
St. Augustine, FL

Margie M. Spencer
S. R. Butler High School
Huntsville, AL

Jeanne Bussiere-Stephens
Phillips Academy
Andover, MA

Marvin Zimmerman
Little Rock School District
Little Rock, AR

PRENTICE-HALL

Grammar and Composition

SERIES AUTHORS

Gary Forlini **Senior Author**
Pelham High School, Pelham, New York

Mary Beth Bauer Harris County Department of Education,
Houston, Texas

Lawrence Biener Locust Valley Junior-Senior High School,
Locust Valley, New York

Linda Capo Pelham Junior High School,
Pelham, New York

Karen Moore Kenyon Saratoga High School,
Saratoga, California

Darla H. Shaw Ridgefield School System,
Ridgefield, Connecticut

Zenobia Verner University of Houston,
Houston, Texas

Prentice-Hall, Inc., Englewood Cliffs, New Jersey

SUPPLEMENTARY MATERIALS

Annotated Teacher's Edition
Teacher's Resource Book
Practice Book
Computer Exercise Bank
Writing Model Transparencies

Acknowledgments: page 831

PRENTICE-HALL **Grammar and Composition**
Third Edition

ISBN 0-13-697749-9

10 9 8 7 6 5 4 3

Prentice-Hall of Australia, Pty. Ltd., *Sydney*
Prentice-Hall Canada Inc., *Toronto*
Prentice-Hall Hispanoamericana, S.A., *Mexico*
Prentice-Hall of India Private Ltd., *New Delhi*
Prentice-Hall International (UK) Limited, *London*
Prentice-Hall of Japan, Inc., *Tokyo*
Prentice-Hall of Southeast Asia Pte. Ltd., *Singapore*
Editora Prentice-Hall do Brasil Ltda., *Rio de Janeiro*

Contents

Grammar   Usage   Mechanics

5

7

Composition and Allied Skills

IV Composition–The Writer's Techniques

14

17

VIII   Speaking and Listening   795

36   Speaking and Listening Skills   796

Nouns and Pronouns

Chapter 1 is the first of five chapters on the *parts of speech,* the eight basic categories of English words. Two of these parts of speech name things. *Nouns* are the actual names of things. *Pronouns* are words used in place of nouns.

1.1 Nouns

The word *noun* comes from the Latin word *nomen,* which means "name."

A noun is the name of a person, place, or thing.

Nouns as Names

Naming people and places is reasonably simple. Naming things is somewhat more complex.

Nouns name things that can be seen and touched as well as those that can not be seen and touched.

The chart at the top of page 21 lists nouns that name people, places, and things. Pay special attention to the various types of things nouns name. As you can see at the end of the chart, among the things nouns can name are ideas, actions, conditions, and qualities.

People			
Uncle Mike	Catherine	neighbor	boys
Places			
Canada	library	garden	city
Things			

Things You Can See and Touch		Ideas and Actions		Conditions and Qualities	
worm	trees	justice	rebellion	joy	illness
store	bicycles	peace	election	beauty	bravery

NOTE ABOUT COLLECTIVE NOUNS: Nouns that name *groups* of people or things form a special category. These nouns are known as *collective nouns.* (See Section 13.1 for rules about using these nouns.)

EXAMPLES: audience   crowd   group

committee   family   herd

EXERCISE A: Identifying Nouns as People, Places, or Things. Write the two nouns in each group. Then label each pair as *people, places,* or *things.*

EXAMPLE: tree   funny   dandelion

tree   dandelion   (things)

1. able   baby   musician
2. rabbit   really   chair
3. prison   mountainside   write
4. misery   rusty   success
5. only   forest   swamp
6. sailor   tiny   explorer
7. tame   table   dog
8. destroy   dentist   mayor
9. rock   clever   pie
10. beach   pasture   foolish
11. carry   courage   freedom
12. lion   kindly   kite

13. conductor   do   woman
14. grim   king   president
15. bedroom   school   rough
16. jolly   desk   thought
17. construction   pain   pretty
18. hunter   nurse   into
19. pelican   shouted   honor
20. plaza   library   ill

Compound Nouns

Nouns are not always only one word. A name such as Uncle Mike is a noun. So are other words that must stand together to name a person, place, or thing.

A compound noun is a noun that is made up of more than one word.

As the following chart shows, *compound nouns* are written in several different ways.

TYPES OF COMPOUND NOUNS		
Separated	**Hyphenated**	**Combined**
bubble bath	daughter-in-law	shipwreck
station wagon	hand-me-down	handstand

Historically, most compound nouns begin as separate words. Over a long period of time, more and more people start to hyphenate the words. Finally, many compound nouns come to be written as one word. If you are not sure how to spell a compound noun, check a dictionary. If the compound noun you are looking for is *not* entered in the dictionary, you can safely spell it as separate words.

EXERCISE B: Recognizing Compound Nouns. Write the compound noun or compound nouns in each sentence.

EXAMPLE: Last weekend Jane received an invitation to visit her grandparents.

weekend   grandparents

(1) As soon as she arrived at the airport, Jane became excited about her first flight alone. (2) Once the ticket agent had given her a boarding pass, she kissed her parents, went on board, and fastened her seatbelt. (3) Shortly after takeoff, the flight attendant brought her a soft drink. (4) Later, the passengers lunched on meat loaf, string beans, and fruit salad. (5) Soon she heard the landing gear come down and returned her tray-table to its correct position. (6) In a few minutes, she felt the gentle bump of touch-down.

(7) Inside the terminal next to the runway, her grandmother and grandfather were waiting for her. (8) A slight mix-up over her suitcases was soon solved. (9) With the help of a porter, they carried the luggage to the station wagon. (10) Jane couldn't believe her luck as she watched the beautiful scenery along the freeway on the way into town.

Common and Proper Nouns

All nouns can be divided into two groups: *common nouns* and *proper nouns*.

A common noun names any one of a class of people, places, or things.

A proper noun names a specific person, place, or thing.

As you can see in the following chart, proper nouns always begin with a capital letter.

Common Nouns	Proper Nouns
writer	Mark Twain, Emily Dickinson
country	United States, Kenya
building	White House, Monticello

EXERCISE C: Distinguishing Between Common and Proper Nouns. Write the one proper noun in each group, adding the necessary capitalization.

EXAMPLE: planet   neptune   star

        Neptune

1. town   village   smithville
2. black beauty   horse   pony
3. state   region   texas
4. river   nile   stream
5. landmark   memorial   washington monument
6. whitman   poet   writer
7. french   people   language
8. dog   puppy   lassie
9. paris   capital   city
10. country   nation   italy

DEVELOPING WRITING SKILLS: Writing Sentences with Nouns. Use the following instructions to write five sentences of your own.

EXAMPLE: Write a sentence about flowers that includes two common nouns.

They planted pansies and marigolds.

1. Write a sentence about sports that includes one proper noun and one compound common noun.
2. Write a sentence about animals that includes two common nouns.
3. Write a sentence about an interesting place that includes one compound proper noun and two common nouns.
4. Write a sentence about your school that contains one compound proper noun and one proper noun.
5. Write a sentence about music that includes one compound proper noun and two common nouns.

1.2 Pronouns

You would probably never say, "Michael said Michael lost Michael's watch." Once you had clearly identified Michael as the person you were talking about, repeating the noun *Michael* would sound awkward. Instead, you would probably say, "Michael said he lost his watch." The words *he* and *his* are called *pronouns*. They stand for the noun *Michael*.

Pronouns are words that stand for nouns or for words that take the place of nouns.

24

Antecedents of Pronouns

Pronouns get their meaning from the words they stand for. These words are called *antecedents*.

Antecedents are nouns (or words that take the place of nouns) for which pronouns stand.

The word *antecedent* comes from a Latin word meaning "to go before." An antecedent usually appears before its pronoun.

In the following examples, the arrows point from pronouns to their antecedents. In the first sentence the pronouns *he* and *his* stand for the noun *Michael,* their antecedent. In the second, the pronouns *they* and *their* stand for the noun *Levines,* their antecedent. In the third, the pronoun *it* stands for an entire group of words that takes the place of a noun. This group of words is the antecedent of the pronoun *it.*

EXAMPLES: Michael said *he* lost *his* watch.

When the Levines moved, *they* gave *their* pets to neighbors.

Caring for bees can be rewarding, but *it* requires a certain amount of bravery.

Antecedents do not always appear before their pronouns, however. Sometimes, an antecedent *follows* its pronoun.

EXAMPLES: Because of *its* climate, Tulsa is my favorite city.

All of my answers were correct.

There are several kinds of pronouns. Most of them have specific antecedents, but a few do not.

EXERCISE A: Recognizing Antecedents. Write the antecedent of each underlined pronoun.

EXAMPLE: Did Amy write <u>both</u> of the letters?

letters

1. <u>Some</u> of the children are afraid of mice.

25

2. Andrea usually brings <u>her</u> lunch to school.
3. <u>This</u> is not the record I ordered.
4. The horse has broken out of <u>its</u> stall.
5. Frank asked <u>his</u> father to help build the fire.
6. The explorers loaded supplies into <u>their</u> boat.
7. The Joneses enjoyed <u>themselves</u> at the picnic.
8. Did Joe bring <u>his</u> camera?
9. The boat with the red sail is the <u>one</u> that won.
10. The twins ordered strawberry milkshakes to drink with <u>their</u> lunches.

Personal Pronouns

The most common pronouns are those that you use to refer to yourself and the people and things around you. These pronouns are called *personal pronouns*.

Personal pronouns refer to (1) the person speaking, (2) the person spoken to, or (3) the person, place, or thing spoken about.

Personal pronouns that refer to the person speaking are called *first-person pronouns*. Those that refer to the person spoken to are called *second-person pronouns*. Those that stand for the name of the person, place, or thing spoken about are called *third-person pronouns*.

PERSONAL PRONOUNS		
	Singular	Plural
First Person	I, me, my, mine	we, us, our, ours
Second Person	you, your, yours	you, your, yours
Third Person	he, him, his she, her, hers it, its	they, them, their, theirs

The following examples contain a number of personal pronouns. In the first example, the antecedent is the person speaking; in the second it is the person spoken to; and in the third it is the people spoken about.

26

FIRST PERSON: *I* left *my* book at school.

SECOND PERSON: If *you* come to the party, don't forget to bring
                 your bathing suit.

THIRD PERSON: The girls took *their* tickets with *them*.

EXERCISE B: Identifying Personal Pronouns. Write each
sentence, underlining the two personal pronouns in each.
Then draw an arrow from each personal pronoun to its
antecedent.

EXAMPLE: Liz handed *her* brother *his* coat.

1. Alice asked Henry if he had brought his bike.
2. Paul baked his parents a cake for their party.
3. The twins took their skis with them.
4. Jody put down her pencil when she was finished.
5. Dad helped the Grants select their new piano and move it
   into the house.
6. The fans rose to their feet when they realized that the ball
   had gone over the fence.
7. The movie doesn't live up to its ads, but it does have an
   exciting ending.
8. Tracy enjoyed her trip and was sorry when it was over.
9. Ned decided he would order cake since it looked so good.
10. Ellen helped her brother find his baseball.

Reflexive and Intensive Pronouns

The ending *-self* or *-selves* can be added to some personal
pronouns to form *reflexive* and *intensive pronouns*.

> A reflexive pronoun ends in *-self* or *-selves* and
> adds information to a sentence by pointing
> back to a noun or pronoun earlier in the
> sentence.

> An intensive pronoun ends in *-self* or *-selves*
> and simply adds emphasis to a noun or pro-
> noun in the same sentence.

The following chart lists the eight reflexive and intensive pronouns used in English.

REFLEXIVE AND INTENSIVE PRONOUNS		
	Singular	**Plural**
First Person	myself	ourselves
Second Person	yourself	yourselves
Third Person	himself, herself, itself	themselves

A reflexive pronoun always adds information to a sentence. In the examples below, *herself* tells who was helped to some turkey and *themselves* tells for whom the milk was poured.

REFLEXIVE: Joy helped *herself* to some turkey.

They poured *themselves* some milk.

An intensive pronoun, on the other hand, simply adds emphasis. If you omit an intensive pronoun, the sentence will still contain the same basic information

INTENSIVE: The mayor *herself* attended the meeting.

An intensive pronoun usually comes directly after its antecedent, but not always.

INTENSIVE: Frank fixed the refrigerator *himself*.

EXERCISE C: Distinguishing Between Reflexive and Intensive Pronouns. Write the reflexive or intensive pronoun in each sentence. Then label each as *reflexive* or *intensive*.

EXAMPLE: The wind itself blew the door shut.

itself   (intensive)

1. I myself have never questioned Janet's loyalty. in
2. We all enjoyed ourselves at the picnic. reflex
3. The author described the plot to us herself. in
4. Helen wallpapered her bedroom herself. in
5. The governor himself answered our questions. in
6. Paul kept telling himself he wasn't afraid. reflex
7. The children went to the park by themselves. in
8. The guests helped themselves from the heaping platters. reflex

28

9. Pete had a hard time defending himself. reflex
10. Rita found herself the only one left. reflex

Demonstrative, Relative, and Interrogative Pronouns

Another group of pronouns can be used to direct attention, relate ideas, or ask questions.

Demonstrative Pronouns. *Demonstrative pronouns* help specify one of many different people, places, or things.

> Demonstrative pronouns direct attention to specific people, places, or things.

The following chart lists the four demonstrative pronouns.

DEMONSTRATIVE PRONOUNS	
Singular	**Plural**
this, that	these, those

Demonstrative pronouns may come before or after their antecedents.

BEFORE: *This* is the person we want to hire.

Are *those* the boots you like best?

AFTER: Of all the books in the library, *that* is my favorite.

We also need cinnamon and salt. *These* are essential.

Relative Pronouns. *Relative pronouns* relate clauses. (See Chapter 8 for more details about clauses.)

> A relative pronoun begins a subordinate clause and connects it to another idea in the sentence.

The chart below lists the five relative pronouns.

RELATIVE PRONOUNS				
that	which	who	whom	whose

The following examples show the way relative pronouns are used in sentences.

Independent Clause	Subordinate Clause
Keith made the play	*that* won the game.
I sold my radio,	*which* was very old.
Louisa is the player	*who* pitched first
Phil is the debater	*whom* the judges chose.
We visited Grandmother,	*whose* house is quite small.

Interrogative Pronouns. Most relative pronouns can also be used as *interrogative pronouns*.

An interrogative pronoun is used to begin a question.

The following chart lists the five interrogative pronouns.

INTERROGATIVE PRONOUNS				
what	which	who	whom	whose

An interrogative pronoun may or may not have a specific antecedent. In the following, only *which* has an antecedent.

EXAMPLES: *What* do you mean?

Which of the vegetables do you want?

Who will go with me to the park?

EXERCISE D: Recognizing Demonstrative, Relative, and Interrogative Pronouns. Write the pronoun in each sentence. Then label each as *demonstrative, relative,* or *interrogative.*

EXAMPLE: Alice chose the book that Paul wanted.

     that (relative)

  1. Which of the candidates is more likely to win? I

2. Ralph was the person who told Lisa. R
3. What will happen next? I
4. This is a book by the same author. D
5. Who was elected to represent the class? I
6. Jake has a pen pal who lives in New Guinea. R
7. Is that the jacket with the broken zipper? D
8. What is Paul having for dinner? I
9. Darryl's aunt is the lawyer who won the case. R
10. These are the tomatoes from Mom's garden. D

Indefinite Pronouns

Indefinite pronouns resemble interrogative pronouns in that they often lack specific antecedents.

> Indefinite pronouns refer to people, places, or things, often without specifying which ones.

The following chart lists the indefinite pronouns.

INDEFINITE PRONOUNS			
Singular		**Plural**	**Singular or Plural**
another	much	both	all
anybody	neither	few	any
anyone	nobody	many	more
anything	no one	others	most
each	nothing	several	none
either	one		some
everybody	other		
everyone	somebody		
everything	someone		
little	something		

The following examples show indefinite pronouns both with and without specific antecedents.

SPECIFIC ANTECEDENTS: *Some* of the students were late.

Of the choices, *none* were great.

NO SPECIFIC ANTECEDENTS: *Everyone* ate *something*.

EXERCISE E: Identifying Indefinite Pronouns. Write the indefinite pronoun or indefinite pronouns in each sentence.

EXAMPLE: Most of us know something about insects.

Most   something

(1) Although animals throughout the animal kingdom are adaptable, none have shown greater ability to adapt than insects. (2) Everyone knows that insects thrive in hot and humid jungle regions, but did you know that some also live in frozen polar regions? (3) Deserts, caves, lakes, and mountains provide homes for still others. (4) Few, however, are found in the earth's oceans. (5) Scientists have already identified more of these small creatures than the average person would guess— over 800,000 different kinds. (6) No one is sure, but it seems likely that many remain to be discovered. (7) Some of the scientists who study insects estimate that there may be up to ten million kinds still to be identified. (8) All have six legs, three main body parts, and external skeletons that have helped them to survive. (9) One has a wingspread of about ten inches; another is only about one-hundredth of an inch long. (10) Their great numbers and variety seem to have equipped insects with the ability to survive almost anything.

DEVELOPING WRITING SKILLS: Writing Sentences with Pronouns. Use the following instructions to write five sentences of your own.

EXAMPLE: Write a sentence that includes a personal pronoun and a reflexive pronoun.

I invited myself to dinner.

1. Write a sentence that includes two personal pronouns.
2. Write a sentence that includes a personal pronoun and an intensive pronoun.
3. Write a sentence that includes a demonstrative pronoun followed by the word *is*.
4. Write a sentence that includes a personal pronoun and a relative pronoun.
5. Write a sentence that includes an interrogative pronoun or an indefinite pronoun, followed by the word *of*.

Skills Review and Writing Workshop

Nouns and Pronouns

CHECKING YOUR SKILLS

Write the two nouns or pronouns in each sentence.

(1) Libraries can be fascinating places. (2) Everyone expects to find books there. (3) However, if a person explores further, surprises may emerge. (4) There may be a collection of intriguing, old records. (5) There may be historical documents about the local area. (6) There may be elaborate displays covering current topics. (7) Libraries exist to serve people. (8) Dedicated bookworms already know this quite well. (9) Too often, others miss the point. (10) They miss an opportunity to be royally entertained.

USING GRAMMAR SKILLS IN WRITING
Writing a Television Review

Professional writers know that vivid, specific nouns and clear pronouns can add a great deal to their writing. Imagine you are writing a brief review of a new television program for a national magazine. Your review will be read by millions of viewers. Follow the steps below to write a review that is both clear and interesting.

Prewriting: Choose a new television program and decide whether you think it will succeed or fail. Think of at least three reasons that support your opinion. Consider other similar programs from past years. Why did they succeed of fail? Will your program succeed or fail for similar reasons?

Writing: Begin with your verdict. Then add your reasons, placing the most important one last, since readers are most likely to remember the last reason you give.

Revising: First look at your nouns and pronouns and change any that could be clearer or more interesting. Then read the entire review, looking for other improvements you can make. After you have revised, proofread carefully.

33

2

Verbs

The *verb* is perhaps the most important part of speech in English. Without it there would be no sentences.

A verb is a word that expresses time while showing an action, a condition, or the fact that something exists.

If you say, "Jack *runs* daily," the verb *runs* shows an action. If you say, "Morris *will be* sorry," the verb *will be* shows a condition. If you say, "Jane *was* here," the verb *was* expresses existence.

The next two sections will discuss the two main kinds of verbs—*action verbs* and *linking verbs*. The third section will show how these verbs are often used with another kind of verb—*helping verbs*.

2.1 Action Verbs

Sit, throw, and *jump* are all *action verbs*.

An action verb is a verb that tells what action someone or something is performing.

Someone is performing an action if you say, "Marcella walks slowly." *Something* is performing an action if you say, "Lightning struck the tree." The person or thing that performs the action is called the *subject* of the verb. The verb *walks* tells what the subject *Marcella* does, and the verb *struck* tells what the subject *lightning* did.

Visible and Mental Actions

Walks and *struck* are easy to recognize as action verbs. The actions they show are visible. Action verbs, however, may also represent mental activities—actions that are not easily seen.

> Action verbs show mental action as well as visible action.

The following are all action verbs, even though the action being performed in the last two is not visible.

VISIBLE ACTION: We *picked* two bushels of apples.

   The flag *flutters* in the breeze.

MENTAL ACTION: Ann *remembers* you.

   I *believe* it.

The verbs in the following chart are other examples of verbs that show visible and mental action.

Visible Action		Mental Action	
write	run	think	learn
cry	follow	worry	hope

Even visible actions may not seem visible at first. When a person *rests*, *holds*, or *waits*, it may seem that no action is going on. But these are all action verbs.

EXERCISE A: Recognizing Action Verbs. Write the action verb in each sentence. Then label each as *visible* or *mental*.

EXAMPLE: Sarah attended the concert.

   attended   (visible)

1. The posse drove the bank robbers out of town.
2. I learned that song in kindergarten.
3. Some people worry about everything.
4. A nurse held the baby up to the nursery window.
5. Mom jogs two miles every morning.
6. The secretary filed the letter in the wrong drawer.
7. Paul often sleeps for twelve hours straight.
8. Our dog chased the squirrel up the tree.

9. We appreciated Elena's kindness.
10. The mayor wondered about the voters' reaction.

Transitive and Intransitive Verbs

An action verb can be *transitive* or *intransitive*.

> **An action verb is transitive if it directs action toward someone or something named in the same sentence.**

> **An action verb is intransitive if it does not direct action toward someone or something named in the same sentence.**

The receiver of the action of a transitive verb is called the *object* of the verb. In the following sentence, *books* is the object of *dropped*.

TRANSITIVE: Pat *dropped* her books.

Intransitive verbs, however, have no objects. The action is not directed toward anyone or anything.

INTRANSITIVE: The temperature *fell* quickly.

Transitive or Intransitive? To determine whether a verb used in a sentence is transitive or intransitive, ask *Whom?* or *What?* after the verb. If you can find the answer in the sentence, the verb is transitive. If you cannot find the answer, the verb is intransitive.

Transitive	Intransitive
Felipe *met* him at school.	Alice *left* after dinner.
Met *whom?*	Left *what?*
him	no answer

Both Transitive and Intransitive. Most action verbs can be transitive in one sentence and intransitive in another.

TRANSITIVE: Bill *reads* science fiction.
INTRANSITIVE: Bill *reads* every night before going to bed.

36

A few action verbs, however, have only transitive or intransitive uses. If you are in doubt about whether a verb should have an object, consult a dictionary.

EXERCISE B: Distinguishing Between Transitive and Intransitive Verbs. Write the action verb in each sentence. Then label each as *transitive* or *intransitive*.

EXAMPLE: The puppy growled at me.

growled   (intransitive)

1. Who called?
2. Someone ate my sandwich.
3. Mark reads the dictionary for pleasure.
4. Icicles hung from the roof.
5. Kelly often reads until bedtime.
6. We saw Grandma last night.
7. Sheila searched frantically for her umbrella.
8. The campers feared the bears.
9. A guide directed us back to our hotel.
10. The fans shouted their approval.
11. Eric shouted to his friend.
12. We crawled carefully under the fence.
13. The raindrops danced on the pavement.
14. A stray dog followed us home from the park.
15. The campers pitched their tent near the brook.
16. Helen pitched for nine straight innings.
17. Portia walks her dog before school every morning.
18. The speaker walked to the front of the platform.
19. We waited for three hours at the station.
20. The king offered a reward for the missing jewels.

DEVELOPING WRITING SKILLS: Writing Sentences with Action Verbs. Use each of the following verbs in two sentences of your own, first as a transitive verb, then as an intransitive verb.

EXAMPLE: write

Tom writes short stories.
He writes for an hour each day.

1. run   2. drop   3. play   4. finish   5. read

2.2 Linking Verbs

Linking verbs do not show action. Though small in number, these verbs are very widely used.

> A linking verb is a verb that connects a word at or near the beginning of a sentence with a word at or near the end.

A linking verb helps one word in a sentence name or describe the condition of another word in the sentence.

Forms of *Be*

The linking verb that is used most often is *be*.

> In English the most common linking verb is some form of the verb *be*.

Notice how the forms of *be—is, are,* and *was*—connect words at the beginning of the following sentences with words at the end.

EXAMPLES: Doris *is* the winner.

The losers *are* we.

He *was* glad.

The following chart lists the many forms of the verb *be*.

THE FORMS OF *BE*			
am	am being	can be	have been
are	are being	could be	has been
is	is being	may be	had been
was	was being	might be	could have been
were	were being	must be	may have been
		shall be	might have been
		should be	must have been
		will be	shall have been
		would be	should have been
			will have been
			would have been

NOTE ABOUT VERBS EXPRESSING EXISTENCE: The verb *be* is not always used as a linking verb. Sometimes it simply expresses existence, generally by showing where something is located.

EXAMPLES: The teapot *should be* in the kitchen.

Here *is* your ticket.

EXERCISE A: Recognizing Forms of *Be* Used as Linking Verbs. Write each sentence, underlining the linking verb. Then draw a double-headed arrow to show which words are linked by the verb.

EXAMPLE: Ms. Hughes *was* happy about the promotion.

1. Helena is our new president.
2. Both candidates were certain of victory.
3. The patient was a man with great courage.
4. I am nervous about the interview.
5. The play was a huge success.
6. The Homans are our new neighbors.
7. The governor is always considerate of her staff.
8. The press was critical of the mayor's plan.
9. I am always the last person in line.
10. The score was lopsided almost from the kick-off.

Other Linking Verbs

Verbs other than *be* may also be used as linking verbs.

Other verbs may be used in the same way as *be* to link two parts of a sentence.

OTHER LINKING VERBS					
appear	feel	look	seem	sound	taste
become	grow	remain	smell	stay	turn

In the examples on page 40, you can see how these verbs act as linking verbs by helping words at the end of the sentences name or describe the place and thing named at the beginning.

EXAMPLES: The empty house *remained* a wreck.

The milk *smells* sour.

EXERCISE B: Identifying Other Linking Verbs. Write each of the following sentences, underlining the linking verb. Then draw a double-headed arrow to show which words are linked by the verb.

EXAMPLE: Seán *felt* better after his nap.

1. The book became a classic.
2. Erica sounded happy about the results.
3. Peter Pan stayed a child all of his life.
4. Everyone feels a little lonely at times.
5. The bill became law despite the President's veto.
6. The boys remained good friends all their lives.
7. That style looks good on you.
8. The weather turned suddenly colder during the night.
9. The smaller car seemed more attractive.
10. The child grew sleepy after a long day at the beach.

Linking Verb or Action Verb?

Most of the verbs in the chart on page 39 can be used as either linking verbs or action verbs. To determine whether a verb is being used as a linking verb or as an action verb in a sentence, you can substitute *am, are,* or *is* for the verb. If the substituted verb makes sense and connects two words, then the original verb is being used as a linking verb in that sentence. If the substituted verb makes the sentence illogical or fails to connect two words, then the original verb is an action verb.

Am, are, or *is* will make sense when substituted for another linking verb in a sentence.

Notice in the chart at the top of page 41 how each of the verbs has been tested to see whether it is an action or a linking verb. Notice also that each linking verb connects two words in the sentence.

Linking Verbs	Action Verbs
The pears *taste* sweet.	I *taste* the red pepper.
The pears *are* sweet?	I *am* the red pepper?
linking	not linking
Father *appears* angry.	The singer *appears* nightly.
Father *is* angry?	The singer *is* nightly?
linking	not linking
The runner *grew* tired.	He *grew* a beard.
The runner *is* tired?	He *is* a beard?
linking	not linking

EXERCISE C: Distinguishing Between Linking Verbs and Action Verbs. Write the verb in each sentence. Then label each as *linking* or *action*.

EXAMPLE: The baby gently felt the kitten's fur.

      felt (action)

1. The kiss turned the handsome prince into an ugly frog.
2. The vegetables tasted salty.
3. Archie tasted the snails after a little hesitation.
4. Fred smelled the flowers.
5. The star always grows nervous before a performance.
6. The bridge looked sturdy enough.
7. The crowd became restless.
8. The grass turned brown during the drought.
9. This milk smells sour.
10. Dad stayed at home with the children.
11. The guard sounded the alarm.
12. The groundhog appeared on schedule.
13. The detective looked closely at the fingerprints.
14. The two remained friends through the years.
15. The candidate appeared confident during the campaign.
16. Two tourists remained in the museum.
17. We all felt cooler after a dip in the ocean.
18. Our neighbor grows magnificent roses.
19. The troops stayed loyal to the general during the battle.
20. Sharon sounds happy about her job.

DEVELOPING WRITING SKILLS: **Writing Sentences with Linking and Action Verbs.** Use each verb in two sentences of your own, first as a linking verb, then as an action verb.

EXAMPLE: remain

> Even after eating, the boys remained hungry.
> Three students remained in the gym.

1. turn   2. look   3. sound   4. taste   5. feel

2.3 Helping Verbs

Often a single verb is formed from as many as four words. *Helping verbs* may be added to a verb such as *sung* to make a *verb phrase* such as *had sung* or *should have been sung*.

Helping verbs are verbs that can be added to another verb to make a single verb phrase.

Recognizing Helping Verbs

Learning the forms of *be* in the chart on page 38 and the other verbs that can be used as helping verbs will help you recognize helping verbs in sentences.

Any of the many forms of *be* as well as some other verbs can be used as helping verbs.

Besides *be*, the verbs below can be used as helping verbs.

HELPING VERBS OTHER THAN THE FORMS OF *BE*			
do	have	shall	can
does	has	should	could
did	had	will	may
		would	might
			must

Verb phrases are created by the addition of helping verbs to other verbs. The following chart lists six examples, but the possibilities are almost endless.

VERB PHRASES	
Helping Verbs	**Verbs**
am	talking
did	play
can	write
will be	studying
should have	seen
might have been	considered

Helping verbs are sometimes called *auxiliary verbs* or *auxiliaries* because they add meaning to other verbs. Notice how using helping verbs can change the meaning of a sentence.

WITHOUT HELPING VERBS: They *sing* in the morning.

WITH HELPING VERBS: They *will sing* in the morning.

They *might sing* in the morning.

EXERCISE A: Supplying Helping Verbs. Write each sentence, adding one helping verb for each blank.

EXAMPLE: Al _____ _____ waiting for me.

Al will be waiting for me.

1. Judd _____ written a poem about growing up.
2. _____ you finished your homework?
3. I still _____ not found my record album.
4. The governor _____ _____ speaking.
5. The party _____ _____ ended by now.
6. _____ Ellie ever visited San Francisco?
7. Gary _____ not _____ told you that.
8. The game _____ not _____ delayed.
9. When _____ the furniture _____ delivered?
10. Janet _____ not _____ _____ chosen.

Finding Helping Verbs in Sentences

As you can see in Exercise A, verb phrases are often interrupted by other words.

Other words may sometimes separate helping verbs from key verbs in sentences.

The following examples show the words of a verb phrase together and verb phrases interrupted by other words.

WORDS TOGETHER: They *will be staying* overnight.

WORDS SEPARATED: They *will* definitely not *be going* with us.

Have you and the others *met* our friends?

EXERCISE B: Locating Helping Verbs. Write the verb phrase in each sentence. Include all helping verbs but do not include any words that interrupt the verb phrase.

EXAMPLE: Most of the earth has been explored thoroughly.

has been explored

(1) Explorers have been faced with many obstacles. (2) They may spend days looking for a shallow place in a river to cross safely. (3) Canyons and ravines can often not be crossed at all. (4) Instead, people must travel long distances around them. (5) Mountain ranges have always presented a challenge. (6) Explorers must search for a pass through them. (7) Some explorers searching for mountain passes have been killed by storms, severe cold, or landslides. (8) Desert heat can also be dangerous. (9) Even insects can be a hazard. (10) Would you explore the few areas that remain?

DEVELOPING WRITING SKILLS: Writing Sentences with Helping Verbs. Use the following instructions to write five sentences of your own.

EXAMPLE: Use the verb phrase *has seen* in a question.

Has Liz seen that movie yet?

1. Interrupt the verb phrase *can be fixed* with the word *not*.
2. Use the verb phrase *does work* in a question.
3. Interrupt the verb phrase *should have started* with the words *never really*.
4. Interrupt the verb phrase *must have been running* with the word *definitely*.
5. Use the verb phrase *will succeed* in a question.

Skills Review and Writing Workshop

Verbs

CHECKING YOUR SKILLS

Write the verb or verbs in each sentence.

(1) Scientists have discovered many interesting facts about bats. (2) These creatures are the only flying mammals in the world. (3) Bats are not blind, as many people think. (4) They actually see pretty well. (5) Some female bats help each other to care for their young. (6) Bats also play an important role as pollinators of various plants. (7) Colonies of bats live together in caves, and some bats stand sentry duty. (8) If danger approaches, these bats sound the alarm. (9) Bats use sonar to capture insects. (10) Generally, bats will not harm humans.

USING GRAMMAR SKILLS IN WRITING
Writing a Letter to the Editor

Authors realize that effective verbs can bring their prose to life. Imagine that you have just moved into your community from another part of the country. Write an effective letter to the editor of your school newspaper describing your first impressions. Follow the steps below to write a letter that will interest other students.

Prewriting: Consider your overall impression of your community as a place to live. Select a few general characteristics about your community that seem to make it stand out. Think of specific examples to support your general statements.

Writing: Begin with your overall impression. Then describe each characteristic and give a specific example. Leave the most important characteristic until last.

Revising: First look at your verbs and make sure they are all used correctly. Change any verbs that could be more vivid. After you have revised, proofread carefully.

Chapter 3

Adjectives and Adverbs

Often a noun cannot express the exact meaning you have in mind. Imagine, for example, a witness to a robbery who reports, "The thieves fled in a car." "What kind of car?" an investigating police officer might ask. If the witness were to answer, "They drove off in a *battered, green, two-door* car," the officer would have a picture of the car. Words that sharpen or adjust the meaning of nouns are called *adjectives*.

Another part of speech works in much the same way to make the meaning of verbs more precise. For example, the officer might have asked the witness "Did the car go *left* or *right*?" These words are called *adverbs*. Adverbs can also be used to make the meaning of adjectives and other adverbs more precise.

This chapter will present both adjectives and adverbs. Together, these two parts of speech are known as *modifiers*. Used carefully, they can improve your sentences greatly.

3.1 Adjectives

Whenever you are asked to describe something—your favorite city, your best friend, or the worst meal you ever ate—you are likely to give an answer that is filled with *adjectives*.

An adjective is a word used to describe a noun or pronoun or to give a noun or pronoun a more specific meaning.

The process by which an adjective describes a word or makes it more specific is called *modification*.

The Process of Modification

To *modify* means to "change slightly." An adjective modifies meaning by answering any of four questions about a noun or pronoun.

Adjectives answer the question *What kind? Which one? How many?* or *How much?* about the nouns and pronouns they modify.

Following are adjectives answering each of these questions.

What Kind?	
red house	*silver* jewelry
sick child	*cool* water

Which One?	
third chance	*any* piece
this hat	*those* apples

How Many?	
six flowers	*several* reasons
both answers	*few* letters

How Much?	
enough space	*more* energy
no rain	*little* effort

An adjective usually comes before the noun it modifies. It may, however, also come after the noun.

BEFORE THE NOUN: The *sick* child lay in bed.

AFTER THE NOUN: The child, *sick* with fever, lay in bed.

An adjective generally comes after a pronoun it modifies, usually directly after a linking verb such as *is, was, look,* or *seemed*. It may, however, also come before the pronoun.

47

AFTER THE PRONOUN: She was *sick* for a week.

BEFORE THE PRONOUN: *Sick* in bed, he was very bored.

Any number of adjectives can modify the same word.

EXAMPLE: A string of *red, yellow,* and *blue* beads was among
the gifts given to the new baby.

EXERCISE A: Recognizing Words Modified by Adjectives. Write the word modified by each underlined adjective.

EXAMPLE: In the green meadow stood an ugly, old ram.

meadow   ram   ram

1. A strange creature crept out of the murky water.
2. A steady diet of any food will not provide sufficient nutrients.
3. The winner, weary but happy, gave us a broad grin.
4. The big game was played on a raw, cold day.
5. A long drive lined with stately, old oaks lead to an old mansion.
6. Many people watched as a new record was set.
7. You were generous to give me the larger piece.
8. Alice wasted the first wish because she had not given the matter enough thought.
9. Dana tried a third time, and then she was successful.
10. The pale and wintry sun gave little warmth.

Articles

Three adjectives—*the, a,* and *an*—are called *articles. The* is called the *definite article. A* and *an* are called *indefinite articles.*

The definite article, *the,* indicates that the noun it modifies refers to a specific person, place, or thing.

The indefinite articles, *a* and *an,* indicate that the nouns they modify refer to any one of a class of people, places, or things.

In the examples below, definite articles are used to refer to a *specific* catcher, face mask, and essay.

DEFINITE: *The* catcher wore *the* face mask.

Give me *the* essay that you think I would enjoy.

When using an indefinite article you must choose between *a* and *an*. *A* is used before consonant sounds; *an* is used before vowel sounds. Notice that the emphasis is on sound. The letter *h* is a consonant, but it may *sound* like a consonant or a vowel. *O* and *u* are vowels, but they may sound like vowels or consonants.

Consonant Sounds	Vowel Sounds
a *b*aseball	an *a*pple
a *h*istory lesson (*h* sound)	an *h*onest man (no *h* sound)
a *o*ne-horse town (*w* sound)	an *o*nly child (*o* sound)
a *u*nion (*y* sound)	an *u*gly hat (*u* sound)

EXERCISE B: Using Definite and Indefinite Articles.
Write the article needed to complete each sentence.

EXAMPLE: I had (indefinite) apple for dessert.

              an

1. Joey studied hard for (definite) exam.
2. Alison is (indefinite) one-woman band.
3. That book has (indefinite) unusual title.
4. Did you find (definite) car keys?
5. Grandma always keeps (definite) cookie jar full.
6. June will give us (indefinite) honest answer.
7. Dad fixed us (indefinite) omelet for lunch.
8. (definite) agent showed us several houses.
9. We stayed in (indefinite) hotel just outside town.
10. Liz had brought (indefinite) umbrella.

Nouns Used as Adjectives

Articles and descriptive words such as *sick, green,* or *ugly* are not the only kinds of words that can act as adjectives. In fact, nouns themselves may sometimes be used as adjectives before other nouns.

A noun used as an adjective answers the question *What kind?* or *Which one?* about a noun that follows it.

The chart below shows examples of nouns used as adjectives.

Nouns	Used as Adjective
guitar	*guitar* music (*What kind* of music?)
evening	*evening* meal (*Which* meal?)

EXERCISE C: Identifying Nouns Used as Adjectives. Write the noun or nouns that are used as adjectives in each sentence. Make sure each one modifies another noun.

EXAMPLE: Good family members should be careful shoppers.

        family

(1) When you go to the grocery store, do you look for a breakfast cereal, fruit drink, or soap powder with a famous name? (2) If so, you probably pay more than you would if you bought another household product.

(3) Name brands—products with well-known names—are sold across the country. (4) As a result, name brands are usually more costly than regional products, which are sold in a limited area. (5) Producers of national brands know the value of package design and spend money to give products shelf appeal. (6) Television, radio, and magazine advertisements add to the price of household goods. (7) So do the recipe ideas and premium offers that often accompany food products.

(8) A cheaper alternative is the house brand offered by supermarket chains. (9) House brands are specially made for the chain in enormous quantities. (10) Savings in promotional and package costs are passed on to the consumer.

Proper and Compound Adjectives

In addition to the types of adjectives already mentioned, there are *proper* and *compound adjectives*.

50

Proper Adjectives. *Proper adjectives* can be simply proper nouns. Others are formed from proper nouns.

A proper adjective is a proper noun used as an adjective or an adjective formed from a proper noun.

When proper nouns are used as adjectives, the form of the proper noun is not changed, as shown in the following chart.

Proper Nouns	Used as Proper Adjectives
Alcott	*Alcott* novel (*What kind* of novel?)
Chicago	*Chicago* storm (*What kind* of storm?)

However, when an adjective is formed from a proper noun, the form of the proper noun is changed, as shown below.

Proper Nouns	Proper Adjectives Formed from Proper Nouns
Jefferson	*Jeffersonian* democracy (*What kind* of democracy?)
Mexico	*Mexican* art (*What kind* of art?)

Proper adjectives generally begin with a capital letter.

Compound Adjectives. Adjectives made up of more than one word are called *compound adjectives*.

A compound adjective is an adjective that is made up of more than one word.

Compound adjectives are usually written as hyphenated words. In a few cases, they are written as combined words.

Hyphenated	Combined
far-off land	*farsighted* leader
hard-shell crab	*hardhearted* neighbor

Consult a dictionary whenever you are in doubt about the spelling of a compound adjective.

EXERCISE D: Recognizing Proper and Compound Adjectives. Write the proper and compound adjectives in each sentence.

EXAMPLE: German shepherds make high-spirited pets.

German   high-spirited

(1) From the days of the Egyptian and Mesopotamian empires, people have valued dogs because many of their senses are much stronger than ours. (2) A dog's sense of smell is keen, as can be seen in the fugitive-hunting activities of the bloodhound. (3) A dog's sense of hearing is acute, especially for high-pitched sounds. (4) Though dogs are nearsighted and colorblind, their eyes can detect the slightest movement.

(5) In far-off days, dogs first served people as hunters. (6) Mesopotamian records from 3000 B.C. describe greyhound-like dogs. (7) Labrador retrievers, Irish setters, and Russian wolfhounds are a few descendants of early hunters. (8) Work dogs also have a long-lived history. (9) German shepherds, English collies, and Siberian huskies belong to the hard-working group. (10) Today, most breeds, such as the Yorkshire terrier, the Mexican chihuahua, and the French poodle, are kept mainly for companionship.

DEVELOPING WRITING SKILLS: Writing Sentences with Adjectives. Write each sentence, adding one or more adjectives. Include at least one noun used as an adjective, one proper adjective, and one compound adjective.

EXAMPLE: The team won a game.

The basketball team won a tournament game.

1. We moved the table out under the tree.
2. The house on our street has a fence around it.
3. We had food for dinner.
4. The child played with the ball.
5. The driver couldn't read the sign.
6. The actor granted the reporter an interview.
7. We stopped at a drugstore to ask for directions.
8. A drink tastes good in this weather.
9. The skiers wore mittens and parkas.
10. Our class saw a movie.

Pronouns Used as Adjectives 3.2

The previous section presented descriptive adjectives such as *green*, articles, nouns used as adjectives, proper adjectives, and compound adjectives. This section will discuss pronouns that can be used as adjectives.

A pronoun is used as an adjective if it modifies a noun.

Possessive Pronouns or Adjectives

Seven of the personal pronouns can be considered both pronouns and adjectives. *My, your, his, her, its, our,* and *their* can be thought of as pronouns because they have antecedents. They can also be thought of as adjectives because they modify nouns by answering the question *Which one*?

A personal pronoun that can be used as an adjective answers the question *Which one*? about a noun that follows it.

Notice that the following personal pronoun has an antecedent and modifies a noun.

ANTECEDENT   WORD MODIFIED

EXAMPLE: Our friend *Ellen* left *her* new *umbrella* here.

The possessive forms of personal pronouns may be labeled either *possessive pronouns* or *possessive adjectives*. Whatever the label, the key word is *possessive*.

EXERCISE A: Recognizing Personal Pronouns That Act as Adjectives. Write the possessive pronoun or adjective in each of the following sentences, followed by the word it modifies.

EXAMPLE: The lion paced restlessly up and down in its cage.

    its cage

1. Have you asked your parents for permission to go to the movies?
2. Stan offered his help to the motorist stranded by the side of the road.

53

3. All of the players carried their helmets.
4. After the game Tess and her friends waited for the bus.
5. Our grandparents are coming to visit us next week.
6. She helped me with my homework.
7. The dog wagged its tail at us.
8. Jed and Michael rode their bicycles to school.
9. The baby robin fell from its nest during the storm.
10. Please put the books back on their shelves.

Demonstrative, Interrogative, and Indefinite Adjectives

As you have seen, seven personal pronouns act as pronouns and adjectives at the same time. Certain other pronouns can act as either pronouns or adjectives.

A demonstrative, interrogative, or indefinite pronoun becomes an adjective if it answers the question *Which one? How many?* or *How much?* about a noun that follows it.

Demonstrative Adjectives. All four of the demonstrative pronouns—*this, that, these,* and *those*—can be used as adjectives. When demonstrative pronouns are used as adjectives, they are called *demonstrative adjectives.* Remember, *demonstrative* means "pointing out."

PRONOUN: He sent me *these.*

ADJECTIVE: He sent me *these* flowers.

Interrogative Adjectives. Only three of the interrogative pronouns—*which, what,* and *whose*—can be used as adjectives. When used as adjectives, they are called *interrogative adjectives.* Remember, *interrogative* means "asking."

PRONOUN: *Which* did she see?

ADJECTIVE: *Which* movie did she see?

Indefinite Adjectives. Many of the indefinite pronouns can also be used as adjectives. When used as adjectives, they are called *indefinite adjectives.* The chart at the top of page 55 shows which can be used to modify singular nouns and which can be used to modify plural nouns.

INDEFINITE ADJECTIVES			
Singular	**Plural**	**Singular or Plural**	
another	both	all	most
each	few	any	other
either	many	more	some
neither	several		

EXAMPLES: *Each* boy brought *several* friends.

They needed *more* fruit and *more* flowers.

EXERCISE B: Recognizing Other Pronouns Used as Adjectives. Write the pronouns used as adjectives. Label each as *demonstrative, interrogative,* or *indefinite.*

EXAMPLE: Did you catch all of these trout?

these   (demonstrative)

1. Some students still have tickets for the game.
2. Which sport is Judy trying out for?
3. All citizens have a duty to vote.
4. What subject do you like best?
5. Are these sunglasses yours or mine?
6. We visited several museums last summer.
7. Each teacher must hand in a written report.
8. That car seldom starts easily on cold mornings.
9. Whose trumpet did you borrow?
10. Please mail those letters.

DEVELOPING WRITING SKILLS: Writing Sentences with Pronouns Used as Adjectives. Use each pronoun as an adjective in a sentence of your own. Then draw an arrow from each pronoun to the word it modifies.

EXAMPLE: both

Julie wore both sweaters.

1. each	3. this	5. which	7. my	9. some
2. its	4. that	6. whose	8. their	10. most

3.3 Adverbs

Adverbs add meaning to three parts of speech.

An adverb is a word that modifies a verb, an adjective, or another adverb.

Adverbs answer certain questions about words they modify.

Adverbs Modifying Verbs

Adverbs can add meaning to verbs in many different ways.

An adverb modifying a verb answers the questions *Where? When? In what manner?* or *To what extent?*

Adverbs can also be placed in many different positions. As shown in the chart, they can come after or before a verb or verb phrase or even between the words in a verb phrase.

ADVERBS MODIFYING VERBS	
Where?	
fell *below*	move *aside*
went *there*	climbs *down*
When?	
arrived *today*	left *early*
should have spoken *before*	begins *then*
In What Manner?	
happily ran	will end *abruptly*
danced *awkwardly*	had been sung *loudly*
To What Extent?	
partly understands	wash *completely*
have *not* completed	*hardly* would have known

EXERCISE A: Recognizing Adverbs That Modify Verbs.
Make four columns as shown in the example. Then place the adverb in each sentence in the correct column.

56

EXAMPLE: We have almost finished our work.

<u>Where?</u>   <u>When?</u>   <u>In What Manner?</u>   <u>To What Extent?</u>
                                              almost

1. The pork chops are being served now.
2. The child behaved badly at the circus.
3. Several guests arrived late.
4. Julia beat the eggs briskly.
5. Have any of the tomatoes ripened completely?
6. You'll find the package inside.
7. Our neighbors are moving away.
8. Ted bravely answered the question.
9. The patient has fully recovered from surgery.
10. Jason finished the test early.
11. The pianist performed brilliantly.
12. I will meet you there.
13. The new mayor spoke confidently about the future of the city.
14. Yesterday I forgot my lab notebook.
15. The leaves rustled softly.
16. The wind scattered the papers everywhere.
17. The sky darkened overhead.
18. Did you water the plants today?
19. We scarcely had time to eat.
20. Amy approached the crowd cautiously.

Adverbs Modifying Adjectives

Many adjectives can be made more meaningful by adding adverbs.

An adverb modifying an adjective answers only one question: *To what extent?*

When an adverb modifies an adjective, it usually comes directly before the adjective, as shown in the examples in the following chart.

ADVERBS MODIFYING ADJECTIVES	
very glad	*almost* ready
absolutely wrong	*entirely* grateful

57

EXAMPLE: This soup is extremely hot.

        extremely hot

1. That child seems unusually bright.
2. Are you nearly ready for the party?
3. The road was barely visible through the dense fog.
4. Your answer is partially correct.
5. The candidate was thoroughly upset by the question.
6. Lisa looked extremely pale.
7. The auditorium was almost full on opening night.
8. The doctors remained somewhat hopeful.
9. A very sharp noise woke us at three a.m.
10. I was especially happy to see Gladys.

Adverbs Modifying Other Adverbs

Sometimes adverbs are used to sharpen the meaning of other adverbs.

An adverb modifying another adverb answers just one question: *To what extent?*

An adverb modifying another adverb generally comes directly before the adverb it modifies. In the following examples, *very* modifies *quickly*, *almost* modifies *over*, *not* modifies *completely*, and *only* modifies *just*.

ADVERBS MODIFYING ADVERBS	
moved *very quickly*	*not completely* wrong
climbed *almost over*	*only just* recognizable

EXERCISE C: Recognizing Adverbs That Modify Other Adverbs. Write the adverb that modifies another adverb in each sentence, followed by the adverb it modifies.

EXAMPLE: The movie ended too quickly.

        too quickly

1. The flood waters spread very rapidly.
2. The train arrived unusually late.
3. The horse ran surprisingly fast.
4. The dog moved somewhat closer to the squirrel.
5. The turtle moved more quickly than we had expected.
6. Arnold just barely finished in time.
7. Clare speaks more clearly than her brother.
8. The cookies are almost completely gone.
9. The jury reached its verdict unexpectedly soon.
10. Please move the couch farther forward.

Adverb or Adjective?

Some words can be either adverbs or adjectives, depending on how they are used.

Remember that an adverb modifies a verb, an adjective, or another adverb; an adjective modifies a noun or a pronoun.

Notice in the examples below that both adverbs modify verbs. Both adjectives, on the other hand, modify nouns.

ADVERB: I awoke *early*.

ADJECTIVE: I had an *early* class.

ADVERB: I studied *hard*.

ADJECTIVE: It was a *hard* test.

Most adverbs or adjectives cannot be so easily interchanged. Adverbs and adjectives generally take different forms. Many adverbs, for example, are formed by adding -*ly* to an adjective.

Adjectives	Adverbs with -*ly* Endings
gentle hands	handle *gently*
bright paint	painted *brightly*

Do not, however, think that all words ending in -*ly* are adverbs. Some are adjectives formed by adding -*ly* to a noun.

59

Nouns	Adjectives with -ly Endings
a head of *curls*	*curly* hair
a close *friend*	*friendly* neighbors

Never identify a word as an adverb simply because it ends in -*ly*. Check to see if it modifies a verb, adjective, or adverb.

EXERCISE D: Distinguishing Between Adverbs and Adjectives. Identify each underlined word as an *adverb* or *adjective*.

EXAMPLE: Agnes looks <u>exceptionally</u> happy today.

adverb

1. I spoke too <u>hastily</u>.
3. Faith always avoids <u>early</u> classes.
3. Jesse seems like a very <u>friendly</u> person.
4. The lawyer argued her case <u>convincingly</u>.
5. Alice took the <u>late</u> bus back to Minneapolis.
6. Many of the guests stayed very <u>late</u>.
7. Sid offered me a little <u>brotherly</u> advice.
8. Yesterday's game was a <u>close</u> one.
9. Christine is <u>extremely</u> athletic.
10. Mr. Hawkes gave us a <u>neighborly</u> wave.
11. This <u>past</u> year has been a busy one.
12. My French teacher lives <u>close</u> to the school.
13. We waited <u>eagerly</u> for the election results.
14. A butterfly just flew <u>past</u>.
15. Lancelot's <u>courtly</u> gesture pleased King Arthur.
16. The cyclists began at a <u>leisurely</u> speed.
17. The audience applauded <u>enthusiastically</u>.
18. Sedwick's punishment was <u>only</u> fair.
19. Her <u>stately</u> appearance on stage surprised us all.
20. The President <u>openly</u> admitted his mistake.

EXERCISE E: Using Adverbs in Sentences. Write each sentence, adding one adverb for each blank.

EXAMPLE: The story of Helen Keller's life is _____ inspiring.

The story of Helen Keller's life is truly inspiring.

(1) Illness _____ destroyed Helen Keller's sight and hearing when she was eighteen months old. (2) For _____ five years, she lived in a dark, silent world, shrieking _____ when she was unhappy or wanted something. (3) Her father _____ hired Anne Sullivan to teach Helen. (4) _____ , Anne managed to establish contact with Helen. (5) She spelled words _____ on Helen's hand with her fingers. (6) Helen _____ made the connection between the words spelled on her hand and the things the words stood for. (7) Her progress _____ became _____ rapid. (8) She _____ learned how to speak _____ _____ . (9) With Anne Sullivan to interpret the lectures, Helen _____ completed her degree at Radcliffe College in 1904. (10) For the rest of her life, Helen worked _____ _____ to improve conditions for other blind and deaf-blind people.

DEVELOPING WRITING SKILLS: Using Adverbs to Add Interest. Write each sentence, adding one or more adverbs. Include at least one adverb that modifies an adjective and one adverb that modifies another adverb.

EXAMPLE: Kim listened.

Kim listened very carefully.

1. The horse ran.
2. A small child cried.
3. Jack becomes angry.
4. The team played.
5. The family has been happy.
6. The movie began.
7. Horace writes.
8. Practical jokes are cruel.
9. The plane landed.
10. Amanda plays the piano.

Skills Review and Writing Workshop

Adjectives and Adverbs

CHECKING YOUR SKILLS

Write the adjectives and adverbs in the following sentences.

(1) Ghost towns are dusty relics of our past. (2) These old towns tell the stories of so many men and women who came to seek their fortunes. (3) Houses had been built rapidly. (4) Along the main street stood a general store and a large hotel. (5) Saloons rang out nightly with shrill laughter and loud piano music. (6) Miners walked proudly down the sidewalks, because their pockets were bulging with gold. (7) Then, the gold would suddenly disappear in the mines. (8) The town quickly emptied, as people went elsewhere. (9) Buildings were empty and silent. (10) Today, only the memories remain. 3

USING GRAMMAR SKILLS IN WRITING
Creating a Myth

Writing is colorless and lifeless without descriptive adjectives and adverbs. Imagine that you are living centuries ago, before the development of science. Create a colorful myth to explain a scientific event, such as the changing of the seasons. Follow the steps below.

Prewriting: Choose a natural event of particular interest to you. Think of a step-by-step series of incidents that might explain the event. Have these incidents tell a story with a surprise ending.

Writing: Start by naming the event that you are going to explain. Then describe the story, step-by-step, until you reach the surprise ending.

Revising: Look over your writing and change any adjectives or adverbs that could be more effective. Put in additional adjectives and adverbs in places where your writing might be more descriptive. After you have revised, proofread carefully.

4

Jake notes!

Prepositions, Conjunctions, and Interjections

Three parts of speech act as relaters, joiners, and attention-getters in sentences. They are *prepositions*, *conjunctions*, and *interjections*.

Prepositions 4.1

Prepositions, such as *at, by, in, on,* and *with,* play an important role in English. They are used to relate words.

A preposition is a word that relates a noun or pronoun that appears with it to another word in the sentence.

Words Used as Prepositions

Different prepositions can affect the entire meaning of a sentence by changing the way the words relate to each other.

The choice of preposition affects the way the other words in a sentence relate to each other.

63

In the examples below, a variety of prepositions are used to relate *tree* to *flew* and *garden* to *flowers*.

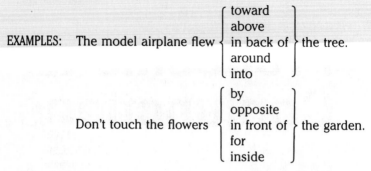

EXAMPLES: The model airplane flew { toward / above / in back of / around / into } the tree.

Don't touch the flowers { by / opposite / in front of / for / inside } the garden.

The following chart lists fifty-five of the most common English prepositions.

FREQUENTLY USED PREPOSITIONS				
about	behind	down	off	till
above	below	during	on	to
across	beneath	except	onto	toward
after	beside	for	opposite	under
against	besides	from	out	underneath
along	between	in	outside	until
amid	beyond	inside	over	up
among	but	into	past	upon
around	by	like	since	with
at	concerning	near	through	within
before	despite	of	throughout	without

Although most prepositions are single words, a few prepositions are made up of two or three words. These prepositions are called *compound prepositions*.

COMPOUND PREPOSITIONS			
according to	because of	in place of	next to
ahead of	by means of	in regard to	on account of
apart from	in addition to	in spite of	out of
aside from	in back of	instead of	owing to
as of	in front of	in view of	prior to

EXERCISE A: Recognizing Prepositions. Write each sentence, replacing the given preposition with a new one that makes sense. *mental exercise*

EXAMPLE: The reporter stood in front of the candidate.

The reporter stood behind the candidate.

1. Please put this under the counter.
2. The child played outside the pool.
3. I'd like my pizza with anchovies.
4. The secret service rode ahead of the President.
5. I finished my homework after dinner.
6. We carried the packages into the house.
7. The runners raced up the hill.
8. The senator spoke prior to the press conference.
9. The branch fell onto the woodpile.
10. The child ran from its mother.

Prepositional Phrases

Prepositions are almost always followed by nouns or pronouns.

A prepositional phrase is a group of words that includes a preposition and a noun or pronoun.

The noun or pronoun generally found after a preposition is called the *object of the preposition*.

PREPOSITIONAL PHRASES	
Prepositions	**Objects of the Prepositions**
near	*me*
before	the *storm*
according to	*her*

Most *prepositional phrases* contain two or three words. However, they may be much longer, depending on the number of words modifying the object and the length of the preposition.

EXAMPLES: *near* the tall, gently swaying *trees*

on account of the *rain*

on paper for grade

Write the prepositional phrase or prepositional phrases in each sentence. The number at the end of each sentence tells how many prepositional phrases the sentence has.

EXAMPLE: Please hand me the book with the red cover.   (1)

with the red cover

1. Very little could be seen through the fog.   (1)
2. In spite of his low test scores, he was admitted to the program.   (2)
3. The children dropped their mittens into the muddy creek.   (1)
4. The squirrels chased each other around the park.   (1)
5. The huge dog dragged his master along the path.   (1)
6. Cars and trucks streamed across the bridge during the rush hour.   (2)
7. You will find the beach house next to the pier and in back of the parking lot.   (2)
8. For three years she traveled the same road.   (1)
9. They hiked in the Rocky Mountains for two weeks.   (2)
10. Every morning, he passes by on roller skates.   (1)

Preposition or Adverb?

Many words that can be prepositions can also be adverbs, depending on how they are used.

Remember that prepositions always have objects. Adverbs do not.

If a word that can be used either as a preposition or as an adverb has an object, it will be a preposition.

PREPOSITION: The bird flew *out* the *window*.
ADVERB: We went *out*.

PREPOSITION: We play *behind* the *school*.
ADVERB: Leave your worries *behind* when you go on vacation.

For a word to act as a preposition, it must be part of a prepositional phrase. The preposition must have an object. In the examples above, only the first and the third sentences show prepositions with objects.

on paper for grade

EXERCISE C: Distinguishing Between Prepositions and Adverbs. Label each underlined word as a *preposition* or *adverb*.

EXAMPLE: The car was rusted <u>underneath</u> in three places.

adverb

1. Please take your coat <u>off</u> the table.
2. After I sent the letter <u>off</u>, I remembered the stamp.
3. The crowd would not allow him <u>through</u>.
4. Alicia skied easily <u>through</u> the dense pine trees.
5. Three beautiful boats sank slowly <u>in</u> the waves.
6. Although the space was tight, Dave fit his car <u>in</u>.
7. The crew went <u>below</u> after they heard the order.
8. <u>Below</u> the surface, I saw green and blue fish.
9. Entering the apartment, she turned the radio <u>on</u> to catch the news.
10. Bill enjoys water skiing <u>on</u> one ski.

DEVELOPING WRITING SKILLS: Writing Sentences with Prepositions. Use each prepositional phrase in a sentence of your own.

EXAMPLE: before school

I usually do my homework in the morning before school.

1. into the water
2. above the clouds
3. except one student
4. toward my house
5. until next Saturday
6. in addition to soccer
7. outside the window
8. without any fear
9. in front of the post office
10. in spite of the rain

Conjunctions and Interjections 4.2

The last two parts of speech are *conjunctions* and *interjections*. Of the two, conjunctions are more important.

Different Kinds of Conjunctions

Prepositions simply relate different words, but *conjunctions* make a direct connection between words.

A conjunction is a word used to connect other words or groups of words.

Three main kinds of conjunctions are *coordinating conjunctions, correlative conjunctions,* and *subordinating conjunctions*.

Coordinating Conjunctions. *Coordinating conjunctions* connect similar kinds of words or similar groups of words.

COORDINATING CONJUNCTIONS						
and	but	for	nor	or	so	yet

Below are some of the uses of coordinating conjunctions.

WITH NOUNS: My sister *and* brother ran the program.

WITH ADJECTIVES: She wore a simple *yet* elegant dress.

WITH VERBS: The dog barked *but* wagged his tail.

WITH PREPOSITIONAL PHRASES: Put the packages on the table *or* in the closet.

WITH COMPLETE IDEAS: Bob left early, *so* I left with him.

Correlative Conjunctions. *Correlative conjunctions* also connect similar words or groups of words. However, they always appear in pairs.

CORRELATIVE CONJUNCTIONS		
both . . . and either . . . or	neither . . . nor not only . . . but also	whether . . . or

Below are a few of the uses of correlative conjunctions.

WITH NOUNS: He lost *both* the necklace *and* the ring.

WITH NOUNS AND PRONOUNS: *Neither* Don *nor* she will go.

WITH ADVERBS: Jean finished the sketch *not only* effortlessly *but also* masterfully.

68

Subordinating Conjunctions. *Subordinating conjunctions* connect two complete ideas by making one of the ideas subordinate to the other. To *subordinate* means to "place below another in rank or importance."

FREQUENTLY USED SUBORDINATING CONJUNCTIONS

after	before	till
although	even though	unless
as	if	until
as if	in order that	when
as long as	since	whenever
as soon as	so that	where
as though	than	wherever
because	though	while

Notice that the subordinating conjunction always comes just before the subordinate idea.

EXAMPLES:

MAIN IDEA SUBORDINATE IDEA
I go to museums *whenever* I get a chance.

SUBORDINATE IDEA MAIN IDEA
As soon as we turned our backs, the cat jumped up onto the table.

Subordinating Conjunction or Preposition? *After, before, since, till,* and *until* can be subordinating conjunctions or prepositions, depending on how they are used. In the first example below, *until* is a subordinating conjunction because it connects two complete ideas. In the second example, *until* is the first word in a prepositional phrase.

SUBORDINATING CONJUNCTION: *Until* you straighten up your room, you may not go out.

PREPOSITION: *Until* yesterday, Jim didn't even know my name.

EXERCISE A: Identifying Conjunctions. Write the conjunction in each sentence. Then label each as *coordinating, correlative,* or *subordinating.*

EXAMPLE: As the rain ended, a rainbow appeared.

As   (subordinating)

69

1. Either Elizabeth or Susanne would make a good class president.
2. Janet will never agree to that plan, nor will she support anyone who does.
3. When the bus was late, Carlos became impatient.
4. The pilot of the airplane waited until he received the signal for takeoff.
5. You must either leave for the movies immediately or forget about going.
6. Wherever the child went, she left cookie crumbs.
7. The runner was exhausted but happy.
8. Sandy ate not only her own dinner but also mine.
9. We waited for hours, yet no one came.
10. You will have to call after lunch because she is in a meeting now.
11. Both Kevin and Jennifer are working on the ticket committee.
12. As soon as he heard about the sale, he rushed to the department store.
13. Would you rather have a hot dog or a hamburger?
14. Neither the tomatoes nor the peppers are ripe yet.
15. If you hear of a part-time job, please let me know.
16. Would you please set the table for dinner while I finish the salad.
17. We had to take a detour because the bridge had been washed out.
18. The town has cleaned up Jones Park, so it is now a safe place to play.
19. We all went out for pizza after we finished painting the house.
20. The visiting team played hard and well.

Conjunctive Adverbs

When an adverb is used to connect other words, it is called a *conjunctive adverb*.

A conjunctive adverb is an adverb that acts as a conjunction to connect complete ideas.

Conjunctive adverbs are often used as *transitions*. Transitions serve as bridges between different ideas.

70

FREQUENTLY USED CONJUNCTIVE ADVERBS		
accordingly	finally	nevertheless
again	furthermore	otherwise
also	however	then
besides	indeed	therefore
consequently	moreover	thus

The following examples show how conjunctive adverbs can be used to make transitions between different ideas.

EXAMPLES: Maureen would have come with us; *however*, she had a project to finish.

I arrived late; *furthermore*, I forgot my books.

EXERCISE B: Recognizing Conjunctive Adverbs. Read each sentence to see whether or not it has a conjunctive adverb. If it does, write the conjunctive adverb. If it does not, rewrite the sentence to include a conjunctive adverb.

EXAMPLE: Eat your breakfast; go to school.

Eat your breakfast; then, go to school.

1. Several accidents have occurred on that ride; nevertheless, people wait in line for their turn on it.
2. I saw that movie; however, I did not enjoy it.
3. The train arrived late; we missed the concert.
4. The book was exciting; I read it all evening.
5. Her car broke down; consequently, she had to walk home.
6. Finish your dinner; you will have no dessert.
7. Al is reliable; moreover, he is never late.
8. The fans waited for hours; finally, the star arrived.
9. Your appointment was at 6:00; you arrived at 7:00.
10. We ran out of gas; we had a flat tire.

Interjections

Interjections are used to express emotion.

An interjection is a word that expresses feeling or emotion and functions independently of a sentence.

71

Interjections, such as *aha, alas, darn, golly, goodness, hurray, oh, tsk, well,* or *whew* express different feelings or emotions. Several different emotions are being expressed by other interjections below. Because interjections are unrelated to any other words in the sentences, they are set off from the other words by exclamation marks or commas.

PAIN: *Ouch!* That burns.   CONTEMPT: *Ah,* go away.

JOY: *Wow!* This is great!   HESITANCY: Do you, *uh,* believe that?

Though common in speech, interjections should be used sparingly in writing.

EXERCISE C: Supplying Interjections. Write each sentence, adding an interjection that shows the indicated emotion.

EXAMPLE: (weariness)   This has been a long day.

Whew! This has been a long day.

1. (annoyance)   I lost my keys.
2. (surprise)   I was hoping for that.
3. (pain)   I stubbed my toe.
4. (delight)   What a beautiful cake you made.
5. (disappointment)   It's starting to rain.

DEVELOPING WRITING SKILLS: Using Conjunctions and Conjunctive Adverbs to Combine Sentences. Turn each pair of sentences into a single sentence by using the kind of conjunction or conjunctive adverb indicated.

EXAMPLE: I keep fit. I swim every day. (subordinating conjunction)

I keep fit because I swim every day.

1. The team practiced hard all week. They did not win the match.   (coordinating conjunction)
2. We yanked the door open. Jody stumbled out. (coordinating conjunction)
3. I will go. I will stay.   (correlative conjunction)
4. He insisted on driving. He had never driven a truck before.   (subordinating conjunction)
5. It rained. The game was canceled.   (conjunctive adverb)

72

Skills Review and Writing Workshop

Prepositions, Conjunctions, and Interjections

test tomorrow

CHECKING YOUR SKILLS

Write and identify the prepositions, conjunctions, and interjections in these sentences.

(1) In India, people eat a variety of foods. (2) Along the river valleys in India, rice grows abundantly. (3) It is the main ingredient in many Indian dishes. (4) Indians enjoy rice with spicy chicken dishes or vegetables. (5) Throughout warm countries, spicy foods are very popular because they help people feel cooler. (6) Both saffron and cumin are spices used with many Indian dishes. (7) Whenever they can, Indians eat yogurt with their meals. (8) Alas, many people in our country have not yet tasted Indian food. (9) Many cities now have restaurants where Indian food is served. (10) For many people in our country, Indian dishes are available.

USING GRAMMAR SKILLS IN WRITING
Writing an Eyewitness Account

Prepositions, conjunctions, and interjections help writing flow smoothly. Suppose you could go back in time, participate in a historical event, and change its outcome. Write a smooth eyewitness account of the event by following the steps below.

Prewriting: Select an important historical event and think about the sequence of things that happened to you while participating in it. What historical figures did you meet? How did you change the events?

Writing: Describe the time and place where the event occurred. Explain what you did in chronological order, ending with how you altered the outcome.

Revising: Look over your prepositions, conjunctions, and interjections to make sure they were used effectively. After you have revised, proofread carefully.

Reviewing Parts of Speech

Chapter 5 reviews the parts of speech. Knowing them can help you in the study of sentence parts that begins in Chapter 6.

5.1 Words as Different Parts of Speech

English is a very flexible language. The same word may often be used as several different parts of speech.

Identifying Parts of Speech

To identify the parts of speech, remember the following rule.

The way a word is used in a sentence determines what part of speech it is.

Notice how the use of the word *outside* changes from an adverb to a preposition in the following sentence.

EXAMPLE: We went *outside* to see the damage *outside* the school.

The charts on the next two pages can help you review the parts of speech. Note especially the questions in the middle.
Nouns and Pronouns. A noun names a person, place, or thing. A pronoun stands for a noun.

Parts of Speech	Questions to Ask Yourself	Examples
Noun	Does the word name a person, place, or thing?	*Fran* will go to *Paris* in the *spring*.
Pronoun	Does the word stand for a noun?	*He* wants *some* of *this*.

Verbs. Verbs show action, condition, or existence.

Part of Speech	Questions to Ask Yourself	Examples
Verb	Does the word tell what someone or something did?	We *sang* a song.
	Does the word connect one word with another word that identifies or describes it?	Bob *was* the leader. I *am* sleepy.
	Does the word tell where someone or something is located?	The tools *were* there.

Adjectives and Adverbs. Adjectives modify nouns or pronouns. Adverbs modify verbs, adjectives, or other adverbs.

Parts of Speech	Questions to Ask Yourself	Examples
Adjective	Does the word tell what kind, which one, how many, or how much?	*Cowboy* hats are on sale *this* week for *thirty* dollars.
Adverb	Does the word tell where, when, in what manner, or to what extent?	Come *here*. Turn in your paper *now*. He ran *slowly*. She is *almost* finished.

Prepositions, Conjunctions, and Interjections. A preposition relates a noun or pronoun that appears with it to another word in the sentence. A conjunction connects words or groups of words. An interjection expresses feeling or emotion and is not related to any other words in the sentence.

Parts of Speech	Questions to Ask Yourself	Examples
Preposition	Is the word part of a phrase that includes a noun or pronoun?	The car raced *down* the street. The parakeet flew *out of* its cage.
Conjunction	Does the word connect other words in the sentence?	*Neither* the radio *nor* the television works. We watched *as* the sun set behind the mountains.
Interjection	Does the word express feeling or emotion and function independently of the sentence?	*Oops!* I dropped your ice cream.

Now use the questions in the middle columns of the charts on pages 75 and 76 to identify the parts of speech of the following italicized words.

EXAMPLE: Her little brother traded two *soggy* potato chips for three *oatmeal* cookies.

You might begin by asking: Is *soggy* a noun? Does the word name a person, place, or thing? No. Is *soggy* a pronoun? Does the word stand for a noun? No. Is it an adjective? Does the word tell what kind, which one, how many, or how much? Yes. It tells what kind of potato chips; therefore, *soggy* is an adjective.

The second italicized word, *oatmeal*, looks like a noun. In this sentence, however, does it name a person, place, or thing? No. *Oatmeal* tells what kind of cookies. Thus, in this case, *oatmeal* is an adjective.

EXERCISE A: Identifying Nouns, Verbs, and Adjectives.
Identify each underlined word as a *noun, verb,* or *adjective.*

EXAMPLE: Did you go to the <u>book</u> sale at the library?

          adjective

1. The second act of the <u>play</u> seemed very long.
2. Those children <u>play</u> well together.
3. Angie's <u>play</u> house was built by her grandfather.
4. The train will <u>round</u> the curve in just a minute.
5. That <u>round</u> table looks lovely there.
6. The doctor completed her <u>rounds</u> this morning.
7. We could not <u>book</u> reservations for next week.
8. Ms. Jones has written a <u>book</u> about ferns.
9. <u>Yellow</u> roses are my favorite flower.
10. That paper will <u>yellow</u> with age.

EXERCISE B: Identifying Adjectives, Adverbs, Prepositions, and Conjunctions. Identify each underlined word as an *adjective, adverb, preposition,* or *conjunction.*

1. Jerry repented of his <u>past</u> mistakes.
2. Turn right just <u>past</u> the library.
3. While we waited, several buses drove <u>past</u>.
4. The Holts stopped by <u>before</u> they left on vacation.
5. Where shall we meet <u>before</u> the game?
6. Have you ever heard that song <u>before</u>?
7. Always follow <u>through</u> after you swing.
8. The baseball went <u>through</u> the window.
9. We sat around the campfire <u>after</u> dinner.
10. The gardener raked the yard <u>after</u> he trimmed the shrubs.

EXERCISE C: Identifying All Eight Parts of Speech. Identify the part of speech of each underlined word.

The (1) <u>cold</u> passed reluctantly from the earth and the retiring fogs revealed an army stretched out on the hills, resting. As the landscape changed from brown to green, the army awakened, and began to tremble with eagerness at the noise or rumors. It (2) <u>cast</u> its eyes upon the roads, which were growing from long troughs of (3) <u>liquid</u> mud to proper thoroughfares. A

77

river, amber-tinted in the shadow of its banks, purled at the army's feet; and at night, when the (4) <u>stream</u> had become of a sorrowful blackness, (5) <u>one</u> could see (6) <u>across</u> it the (7) <u>red</u>, eyelike (8) <u>gleam</u> of hostile camp fires set in the low brows of (9) <u>distant</u> hills.

There was a youthful (10) <u>private</u> who listened with eager ears to the words of the tall soldier and to the varied comments of his comrades. After receiving a (11) <u>fill</u> of discussions concerning (12) <u>marches</u> and (13) <u>attacks</u>, he went to his hut and crawled through an intricate hole that served it as a door. He (14) <u>wished</u> to be alone (15) <u>with</u> some new thoughts that had (16) <u>lately</u> come to him.

He lay down on a wide bunk that stretched across the end of a room. In the other end, (17) <u>cracker</u> boxes were made to serve as furniture. They were grouped (18) <u>about</u> the fireplace. A picture from an illustrated (19) <u>weekly</u> was upon the (20) <u>log</u> walls, and three rifles were paralleled on pegs. Equipment hung on handy projections and some (21) <u>tin</u> dishes lay upon a small pile of firewood. A folded tent was serving as a roof. The sunlight, (22) <u>without</u>, beating upon it, made it glow a light (23) <u>yellow</u> shade. A small window (24) <u>shot</u> an oblique square of whiter light upon the cluttered floor. The smoke from the fire at times neglected the (25) <u>clay</u> chimney and wreathed into the room, and this flimsy chimney of clay and sticks made endless threats to set ablaze the whole establishment.—Stephen Crane

DEVELOPING WRITING SKILLS: Using Words as Different Parts of Speech. Use each word in two sentences of your own, first as one part of speech, then as another.

EXAMPLE: rain

The rain clouds hid the sun.
Two inches of rain fell yesterday.

1. smile   2. over   3. inside   4. care   5. brown

Skills Review and Writing Workshop

Reviewing Parts of Speech

CHECKING YOUR SKILLS

Identify the part of speech of each underlined word in the following paragraph.

Our climate is (1) <u>gradually</u> growing warmer. The (2) <u>warmer</u> temperatures are caused by increased levels (3) <u>of</u> carbon dioxide in our atmosphere. Heat (4) <u>enters</u> our atmosphere from the sun. The carbon dioxide traps the (5) <u>heat</u> (6) <u>and</u> prevents (7) <u>it</u> from leaving. Scientists call this (8) <u>warming</u> of the atmosphere the "greenhouse effect." Temperatures are expected to increase up to 5° over the next century. (9) <u>This</u> might cause melting ice at the poles. Flooding would occur in coastal regions (10) <u>because</u> the sea level would have risen.

USING GRAMMAR SKILLS IN WRITING
Writing a Restaurant Review

It is important to use each part of speech correctly to communicate successfully with your reader. Suppose you are writing a short review of a fast-food restaurant for a newspaper in your community. Follow the steps below to write a review that communicates your viewpoints successfully.

Prewriting: Select a restaurant where you have eaten recently. Think about the quality of the meal, the atmosphere, the service. Would you eat there again? How would you rate this restaurant?

Writing: Begin with your rating of the restaurant. Support your rating by describing the food, the atmosphere and the service.

Revising: First, look at all the parts of speech and change any that could be clearer or more effective. After you have revised, proofread carefully.

Chapter 6

Basic Sentence Parts and Patterns

Every sentence in the English language, if it communicates clearly, follows certain basic patterns that can be described in grammatical terms. This chapter will explore some of the basic patterns, giving you a better understanding of the variety of expression that you have at your command.

6.1 The Sentence

In order to develop a true understanding of sentences, you must be able to recognize the difference between a complete sentence and a sentence part. As you will see in the following section, sentence parts may make sense in conversation, but they often lead to confusion in writing.

Complete Subjects and Predicates

Every *sentence* has two main parts.

> **A sentence is a group of words with two main parts: a complete subject and a complete predicate. Together these parts express a complete thought.**

The chart below shows the two main parts of three complete sentences. In each sentence the *complete subject* includes a noun or pronoun that names the person, place, or thing that the sentence is about. Each *complete predicate* includes a verb that tells something about the complete subject.

Complete Subjects	Complete Predicates
Several pilots from various countries	have vanished in or near the Bermuda Triangle.
The Bermuda Triangle, the area in question,	lies between Florida, Bermuda, and Puerto Rico.
The *U.S.S. Cyclops*	disappeared there in 1918.

As you can see in the following examples, the complete subject or complete predicate can consist of several words or just one word.

EXAMPLES: He|wandered around in search of his wallet.
     COMPLETE |COMPLETE
      SUBJECT |PREDICATE

The butterfly with the golden wings| landed.
     COMPLETE| COMPLETE
      SUBJECT| PREDICATE

EXERCISE A: Recognizing Complete Subjects and Predicates. Make two columns as shown in the example. Then write each complete subject in the first column and each complete predicate in the second column.

EXAMPLE: Complete Subject   Complete Predicate
    The tall pine trees   swayed in the wind.

1. The car swerved away from the child.
2. My favorite radio station plays all of the hit songs.
3. Grandfather Kim owns an art gallery in Chicago.
4. Mexico City was built on a lake.
5. The evening news summarizes the day's events.
6. Shakespeare's father was a glove maker.
7. Computers process information very quickly.
8. My older brother has a telephone shaped like Mickey Mouse.

9. The bags of coins were placed in an armored truck.
10. Damascus, the capital of Syria, has been continuously inhabited for over four thousand years.

Sentence or Fragment?

Not every group of words forms a sentence. Some are merely *fragments*.

A fragment is a group of words that does not express a complete thought.

Notice in the following examples that each fragment is only part of a complete sentence.

Fragments	Complete Sentences
The Colosseum in Rome.	The Colosseum in Rome was begun by Nero's successor.
Believed Atlantis lay somewhere west of Gibraltar.	The Greek philosopher Plato believed Atlantis lay somewhere west of Gibraltar.

Fragments in Conversation. In conversation, it is possible to use fragments and still express a complete thought. The context of the conversation, your facial expressions and gestures, and the volume and tone of your voice all add to what is said.

Notice the mixture of sentences and fragments in the following conversation.

SENTENCE: "What made the bombers disappear in the Bermuda Triangle?"

FRAGMENT: "Possibly storms."

SENTENCE: "Are storms the only possibility?"

FRAGMENT: "Or sudden changes in the air currents."

SENTENCE: "What happened to the planes?"

FRAGMENT: "Don't know."

SENTENCE: "When did they disappear?"

FRAGMENT: "In December of 1945."

82

Fragments in Writing. In writing, ideas usually must be stated fully and clearly in complete grammatical sentences. If either the complete subject or the complete predicate or parts of both are missing, the reader may be hopelessly confused. Unless you are representing speech in your writing, avoid using fragments.

EXERCISE B: Distinguishing Between Sentences and Fragments. Identify each item as a *sentence* or *fragment*.

EXAMPLE: Worked for many hours. *GOOD PAPER*

fragment

1. In the woods almost until dawn.
2. A few inches of snow.
3. The grizzly bear needs large territories undisturbed by people.
4. Have been unusually high because of the very heavy rains this season.
5. Herds of thousands of caribou.
6. Haste makes waste.
7. Dived in search of food.
8. Cousteau believes artificial islands could be built off the coast.
9. About a great white shark, one of the largest ones ever caught.
10. Cougars have become increasingly rare.
11. Is the last frontier.
12. There he sat, totally content.
13. In the day in order to hunt at night.
14. Ice-covered Mount McKinley in Alaska attracts many tourists.
15. Wolves, jaguars, and grizzly bears once numerous in North America.
16. Bored dogs need things to do, such as tricks.
17. Skeletons of old paddle-wheeled boats.
18. Without a tie and jacket.
19. The Roman Emperor Hadrian's plans for the Pantheon in Rome and Thomas Jefferson's Rotunda at the University of Virginia.
20. For two hundred years after the founding of the Olympic Games in 776 B.C.

Fragments as Sentence Parts

If you study the fragments in this section, you will see that some fragments are really the complete subjects of sentences. Others are the complete predicates. Still other fragments are neither complete subjects nor complete predicates.

To turn fragments into sentences, add whatever sentence parts are needed to express a complete thought.

If a fragment is a complete subject, turn it into a sentence by adding a complete predicate. If a fragment is a complete predicate, turn it into a sentence by adding a complete subject. When a fragment is neither a complete subject nor a complete predicate, add the missing words from both the complete subject and complete predicate to make a sentence.

These three different kinds of fragments, along with words needed to change them into complete sentences, are shown below.

FRAGMENT: Storms in the Bermuda Triangle. (complete subject only)

SENTENCE: Storms in the Bermuda Triangle may have been responsible for the disappearance of ships and planes. (complete predicate added)

FRAGMENT: Tells about the disappearances. (complete predicate only)

SENTENCE: This book tells about the disappearances. (complete subject added)

FRAGMENT: In December of 1945. (neither complete subject nor complete predicate)

SENTENCE: Five U.S. bombers disappeared in the Bermuda Triangle in December of 1945. (complete subject and complete predicate added)

EXERCISE C: Identifying Fragments as Sentence Parts.
Identify each fragment in Exercise B as a *complete subject, complete predicate,* or *neither.*

EXAMPLE: Worked for many hours.

complete predicate

DEVELOPING WRITING SKILLS: Using Fragments to Make Sentences. Combine each of the ten complete subjects on the left with one of the ten complete predicates on the right to make ten logical sentences.

EXAMPLE: The umpire at yesterday's game.   Told me to watch my temper.

The umpire at yesterday's game told me to watch my temper.

1. His Roman costume. *E*
2. The children.
3. The girl with butterflies in her stomach.
4. The curious horse.
5. The boy with the confused expression.
6. Lemon jello inside empty eggshells.
7. Their cousins coming for dinner.
8. The man standing on the corner.
9. Her long, pointed putty nose.
10. Her friends at the slumber party.

A Took the wrong bus.
B Stuck to the stage.
C Wandered into the tack room.
D Can fool people.
E Was tangled in the stage scenery.
F Put sugar at the bottom of her sleeping bag.
G Was wearing his shirt inside out.
H Scored a goal for the opposing team.
I Thought the raccoon was a ghost.
J Spoke to the flag instead of to the class.

Subjects and Verbs 6.2

Just being able to tell whether a sentence has both of the two main sentence parts—a complete subject and a complete predicate—is not enough to give you a full understanding of the way sentences work. In this section, you will take a closer look at these sentence parts.

Simple Subjects and Predicates

Every complete subject and complete predicate contains a word or group of words that is essential to the sentence.

85

> The simple subject is the essential noun, pro-
> noun, or group of words acting as a noun that
> cannot be left out of the complete subject.
>
> The simple predicate is the essential verb or
> verb phrase that cannot be left out of the com-
> plete predicate.

In the following examples, notice how all of the other words in the complete subject describe or add details to the *simple subject*. Similarly, all of the other words in the complete predicate either modify the *simple predicate* or help it complete the meaning of the sentence.

EXAMPLES:

         SIMPLE   SIMPLE
         SUBJECT   PREDICATE
The *balloon* in the sky *floated* aimlessly.
      COMPLETE COMPLETE
      SUBJECT   PREDICATE

     SIMPLE   SIMPLE
     SUBJECT PREDICATE
Sick in bed, *she had missed* the class trip.
    COMPLETE COMPLETE
    SUBJECT   PREDICATE

SIMPLE   SIMPLE
SUBJECT   PREDICATE
Visitors from Italy definitely *will be* there.
    COMPLETE COMPLETE
    SUBJECT   PREDICATE

NOTE ABOUT SIMPLE SUBJECTS: The simple subject is never the object of a preposition.

EXAMPLE: Two of Broadway's most popular stars will appear in the film.

Two is the simple subject of the sentence. *Stars* is the object of the preposition *of*.

EXERCISE A: Recognizing Simple Subjects and Predicates. Write each sentence, drawing a line between the complete subject and complete predicate. Then underline each simple subject once and each simple predicate twice.

EXAMPLE: A <u>friend</u> of mine | <u>plays</u> chess with me.

1. A sixteen-year-old girl from California gave the best dramatic interpretation.
2. A muddy dog of unknown breed ran away with Bernard's lunch.
3. Her friends at school helped her get a job.
4. The weary commuters were angry about the delay.
5. The freshman with the most unusual hat won the contest.
6. The boxes under the sink are empty.
7. The frightened witnesses wrote reports for the police.
8. The speaker caught his fishing pole on the light fixture.
9. Students going on the trip left early this morning.
10. The forward with the knee brace made ten baskets.

Focusing on Subjects and Verbs

As you may know, the simple subject of a sentence is generally referred to as the *subject* and the simple predicate is generally referred to as the *verb*.

If you can quickly find the subjects and verbs in the sentences you write, you can more easily check to be sure that your sentences are clear and grammatically correct. It will also help you understand what you read.

Being able to locate subjects and verbs quickly in sentences will help you determine that a sentence is clear and grammatically correct.

Some people find it easier to find the subject first, then the verb. The steps in the following chart can help.

FINDING THE SUBJECT FIRST
1. First, find the subject by asking, "What word is the sentence telling something about?"
2. Then, try to find the verb by asking, "What did the subject *do*?" The answer to this question will be an action verb.
3. If no word answers the second question, look for a linking verb or a verb that expresses existence.

The examples at the top of the next page show how these steps can be used to find first the subjects and then the verbs in sentences.

EXAMPLES: The bee flew into the dog's mouth.

> *Subject:* bee
> *Question:* What did the bee *do*?
> *Answer:* flew

The cabin is only a shack in the forest.

> *Subject:* cabin
> *Question:* What did the cabin *do*?
> *Answer:* Because there is no answer, you will need to look for another kind of verb—*is*.

If it is easier for you to find the verb first, use the following steps instead.

FINDING THE VERB FIRST

1. First, find the verb and its auxiliaries, if any, by looking for an action verb or a linking verb.
2. When you have found the verb, ask *Who?* or *What?* before the verb. The answer will be the subject.

The following examples show how steps for finding verbs first can be applied.

EXAMPLES: Kit ran quickly to first base.

> *Verb:* ran
> *Question:* *Who* ran?
> *Answer:* Kit

This book is admired for its plot.

> *Verb:* is admired
> *Question:* *What* is admired?
> *Answer:* book

EXERCISE B: Finding Subjects and Verbs. Write each subject and verb, underlining the subject once and the verb twice.

EXAMPLE: Many people visit the Grand Canyon.

> <u>people</u> <u>visit</u>

(1) A <u>tourist</u> <u>gets</u> a spectacular view at the Grand Canyon. (2) Curious <u>visitors</u> <u>can take</u> nature walks along the trails on the edge of the canyon. (3) <u>Hikers</u> may <u>want</u> to venture down the steep trails into the canyon. (4) However, the crumbling <u>walls</u> of the canyon's sides <u>make</u> mountain climbing dangerous. (5) A guided mule <u>trip is</u> a safer way to see the canyon. (6) <u>Trips</u> down the Colorado River also <u>enable</u> tourists to see the canyon from the inside.

(7) <u>Tourists</u> <u>can</u> also <u>take</u> a helicopter or an airplane ride over the canyon. (8) From the helicopter or plane, <u>passengers</u> <u>can see</u> the different branches of the canyon. (9) The <u>aircraft</u> <u>can fly</u> into the canyon for a closer view of the river and rock formations. (10) With all of these approaches, <u>tourists</u> <u>can see</u> the canyon from above, from the inside, or from the edge.

DEVELOPING WRITING SKILLS: Using Subjects and Verbs to Write Sentences. Use each subject and verb in a sentence of your own.

EXAMPLE: robins   chirped

> In the nest baby robins chirped for food.

1. truck   is stopping
2. girl   jumped
3. steak   shriveled
4. wind   was shrieking
5. radio   blared

6. lawnmower   charged
7. train   is wobbling
8. water   feels
9. waiter   dropped
10. newscaster   hiccupped

Compound Subjects and Verbs   6.3

A sentence such as *Jerry went home* has just one subject and just one verb. Many sentences, however, have more than one subject or verb.

Compound Subjects

Some sentences have two or more subjects.

A compound subject is two or more subjects that have the same verb and are joined by a conjunction such as *and* or *or*.

In each of the following examples, the parts of the *compound subject* are underlined once and the verb twice.

EXAMPLES: <u>You</u> and <u>she</u> <u>must take</u> your tests tomorrow.

Either the <u>duck</u> or the <u>drake</u> <u>will rescue</u> the poor ducklings.

<u>Snow</u>, <u>ice</u>, and <u>flooding</u> <u>made</u> the roads treacherous.

EXERCISE A: Recognizing Compound Subjects. Write the nouns that make up each compound subject.

EXAMPLE: The windows and doors are locked.

windows   doors

1. Both flowers and perfume cause her to sneeze.
2. David and Marie both failed to win the prize.
3. Neither pets nor pianos are allowed in the apartment.
4. Lettuce, tomatoes, peppers, and cucumbers grew in the garden.
5. Hurricanes and tornadoes cause much damage to property every year.
6. Louise, Yolanda, and Audrey will plan the menu.
7. Citizen band radios and power lawnmowers are two of the favorite gadgets of many Americans.
8. Basketball, football, and track attract the most spectators at their school.
9. Large bushes and a grove of trees hide their yard from the street.
10. From the cliff, seals, otters, and seagulls could be seen.

Compound Verbs

Just as a sentence can have a compound subject, it can also have a *compound verb*.

A compound verb is two or more verbs that have the same subject and are joined by a conjunction such as *and* or *or*.

In the examples at the top of the next page, each subject is underlined once and the parts of the compound verb twice.

EXAMPLES: The <u>logs</u> in the fire <u>hissed</u> and <u>crackled</u>.

<u>I</u> neither <u>want</u> your help nor <u>need</u> it.

The little <u>children</u> <u>hopped</u>, <u>skipped</u>, and <u>jumped</u> about the meadow.

Sometimes a sentence has both a compound subject and a compound verb.

EXAMPLE: The <u>boys</u> and <u>girls</u> <u>danced</u> and <u>listened</u> to records for hours.

EXERCISE B: Recognizing Compound Verbs. Write the verbs that make up each compound verb.

EXAMPLE: I studied hard and passed the test.

studied   passed

1. The car suddenly <u>skidded</u> on the ice and <u>hit</u> the curb.
2. Winds <u>howled</u> through the night but <u>died down</u> at dawn.
3. Hercules <u>lifted</u> Antaeus from the ground and <u>crushed</u> him.
4. Sports medicine <u>is</u> a relatively new field and <u>offers</u> many opportunities for careers.
5. The duck <u>waddled</u> down the bank, <u>splashed</u> into the water, and <u>paddled</u> to safety.
6. My brother and I <u>built</u> a rowboat in 1979 and <u>used</u> it on the lake the next year.
7. We <u>washed</u> the dishes and <u>put</u> them away.
8. He <u>survived</u> the war but <u>died</u> soon after.
9. The Romans <u>erected</u> buildings in brick and then <u>faced</u> them with marble.
10. We <u>rehearsed</u> the play for three weeks, <u>had</u> a dress rehearsal, and then <u>gave</u> a performance.

DEVELOPING WRITING SKILLS: Writing Sentences with Compound Subjects and Verbs. Use the following items to write ten sentences of your own. Use the first three items as compound subjects, the next three as compound verbs, and the last four as compound subjects and verbs.

EXAMPLE: dog   squirrel

Our dog and a squirrel raced around the yard.

91

1. jumper   sprinter
2. beaches   restaurants
3. guitarist   drummer   composer
4. stamped   screamed
5. dribbled   tossed
6. nods   smiles
7. orchestra   conductor   bowed   disappeared
8. horses   riders   galloped   trotted
9. clown   acrobat   stumbled   fell   rose
10. vans   trucks   cost   carry

6.4 Hard-to-Find Subjects

Basic methods for finding the subject and verb of a sentence were given in Section 6.2. This section presents ways of finding subjects that are hard to find or that appear to be missing.

Subjects in Orders and Directions

In most sentences that give orders or directions, the subject is understood rather than actually stated.

In sentences that give orders or directions, the subject is understood to be *you*.

In the following chart, sentences are given with and without the understood *you*. In the second example, the subject is still understood to be *you* even though the sentence contains a *noun of direct address*—that is, the name of the person being addressed.

Orders or Directions	With Understood Words Added
After beating the eggs, pour them into a skillet.	After beating the eggs, [you] pour them into a skillet.
Michael, come here.	Michael, [you] come here.

EXERCISE A: Finding Subjects in Orders or Directions. Write each sentence, inserting the understood subject.

EXAMPLE: During your break, take the dog out.

During your break, [you] take the dog out.

1. After school, come straight home.
2. Joanne, give me a quarter.
3. Now tell me what happened.
4. When using that machine, always wear safety goggles.
5. Sue, order me a milkshake, please.
6. After class, meet me at the library.
7. Pete, during takeoff, keep your seatbelt fastened.
8. Before leaving, pack a good lunch.
9. Dad, turn left at the end of the exit ramp.
10. When filling out that form, use ink.

Subjects in Questions

In most sentences the subject comes before the verb. However, in some sentences, including many sentences that ask questions, the subject comes after the verb. Such sentences are said to be *inverted*.

In questions the subject often follows the verb.

Questions that are in inverted order will generally begin with a verb, with a helping verb, or with one of the following words: *how, what, when, where, which, who, whose,* or *why*. The following examples show all three types of inverted questions. The subjects are underlined once and the verbs or verb phrases twice. In the last two examples, notice that the subject comes between the parts of a verb phrase.

VERB FIRST: Is dinner ready?

HELPING VERB FIRST: Are you working here?

ADVERB FIRST: When will you leave?

To find the subject in questions with inverted order, mentally rephrase the question as a statement. This will place the subject in the normal position before the verb. Then follow the same steps that you would to find any other subject and verb.

The chart at the top of the next page shows three questions that have been reworded as statements.

Questions	Reworded as Statements
<u>Is</u> <u>dinner</u> ready?	<u>Dinner</u> <u>is</u> ready.
<u>Are</u> <u>you</u> <u>working</u> here?	<u>You</u> <u>are working</u> here.
When <u>will</u> <u>you</u> <u>leave</u>?	<u>You</u> <u>will leave</u> when.

NOTE ABOUT QUESTIONS: Not all questions are in inverted order. Sometimes, questions beginning with an adjective or pronoun are in the usual subject-verb order.

EXAMPLES: Which <u>record</u> <u>is playing</u>?

Who <u>is going</u> on the field trip?

EXERCISE B: **Finding Subjects in Questions.** Write the subject of each sentence.

EXAMPLE: Where did they spend their last winter vacation?

they

1. Have <u>you</u> seen the new horror movie?
2. When will <u>Sally</u> be home?
3. <u>Who</u> baked this cake?
4. About what will <u>Andy</u> write?
5. Are the final <u>reports</u> complete?
6. Is the <u>story</u> ready for publication?
7. Why hasn't <u>Judy</u> answered my note?
8. What did <u>Jack</u> wear to the game?
9. Has <u>Joyce</u> finished her term paper yet?
10. Which <u>team</u> won the championship?

Subjects in Sentences Beginning with *There* or *Here*

Other inverted sentences begin with the word *there* or *here*.

The subject of a sentence is never *there* or *here*.

In sentences that begin with the word *there* or *here*, the subject will usually be found after the verb. In each of the following three examples, *there* and *here* are adverbs. Each of them answers the question *Where?* and modifies the verb in the sentence.

EXAMPLES: There <u>is</u> your <u>train</u> to Kansas City.

Here <u>are</u> the <u>pictures</u> of the wedding.

There <u>goes</u> the <u>senator</u>.

Like inverted questions, sentences beginning with *there* or *here* can usually be rephrased mentally in order to place the subject in the normal position before the verb. All you need to do is make a logical sentence that does not begin with *there* or *here* out of the words given in the sentence. Then follow the same steps that you would for finding any subject in a sentence.

Sentences Beginning with *There* or *Here*	Reworded with Subjects Before Verbs
There <u>is</u> your <u>train</u> to Kansas City.	Your <u>train</u> to Kansas City <u>is</u> there.
Here <u>are</u> the <u>pictures</u> of the wedding.	The <u>pictures</u> of the wedding <u>are</u> here.
There <u>goes</u> the <u>senator</u>.	The <u>senator</u> <u>goes</u> there.

In some sentences you may find that the word *there* is used just to get the sentence started. In these situations, *there* is *not* an adverb modifying the verb. Instead, it just fills out the sentence. When the word *there* is used simply to fill out a sentence, it is called an *expletive*.

EXAMPLES: There <u>were</u> four misspelled <u>words</u> in the article.

There <u>are</u> two <u>reasons</u> for her resignation.

Rephrasing a sentence to place the subject first is not always possible when *there* is used as an expletive. The important thing to remember is that *there* will never be the subject. To find the subject in a sentence that cannot be rephrased, drop the word *there* and ask *Who?* or *What?* before the verb.

Sentences with Expletive *There*	Questions for Finding Subject
There <u>were</u> four misspelled <u>words</u> in the article.	*Question: What* were? *Answer:* words
There <u>are</u> two <u>reasons</u> for her resignation.	*Question: What* are? *Answer:* reasons

NOTE ABOUT INVERTED SENTENCES: Some sentences beginning with *there* or *here* are not inverted but are in normal word order.

EXAMPLE: There <u>they are</u>.

EXERCISE C: Finding Subjects in Sentences Beginning with *There* or *Here*. Write the subject of each sentence.

EXAMPLE: Here she is.

she

1. There are your keys on the table.
2. Here comes the bus.
3. There was no excuse for his behavior.
4. There goes the kite into the tree.
5. Here is your pizza with mushrooms and extra cheese.
6. There is the rest of the strawberry pie.
7. There are last week's papers.
8. Here are the poppy-seed rolls from the bakery.
9. There went my sister in her new car.
10. There were only three seeds left in the birdfeeder.

Subjects in Sentences Inverted for Emphasis

Occasionally, sentences are inverted to draw attention to the last words in the sentence.

In some sentences the subject is placed after the verb in order to receive greater emphasis.

In the following example, notice how the order of the words creates suspense by leading up to the subject, *eagle*.

EXAMPLE: High on the cliff overlooking the rugged landscape
<u>was</u> an <u>eagle</u>.

This sentence can be mentally rephrased in normal subject-verb order.

Inverted Word Order for Emphasis	Reworded with Subject Before Verb
High on the cliff overlooking the rugged landscape <u>was</u> an <u>eagle</u>.	An <u>eagle</u> <u>was</u> high on the cliff overlooking the rugged landscape.

EXERCISE D: Finding Subjects in Inverted Sentences.
Write the subject of each sentence.

EXAMPLE: In her hand was the missing letter.

letter

1. After the rain came a beautiful rainbow.
2. All about us rang the bells of the village's three churches.
3. To the south rose the snow-covered peaks of a lofty mountain.
4. Ahead of the couple ran four noisy children.
5. All around them lay the scattered leaves.
6. With their safe arrival came a feeling of great happiness and relief.
7. Among the people in the crowd were our neighbors.
8. Beside the fire sat an old man.
9. On a raft floating down the river were their treasured possessions.
10. From the distance came the sound of thunder.

DEVELOPING WRITING SKILLS: Writing Sentences with Hard-to-Find Subjects. Write four sentences of your own. The first sentence should give an order; the second should ask a question; the third should be an inverted sentence that begins with *there* or *here;* and the fourth sentence should be inverted for emphasis.

EXAMPLE: Lisa, leave right away.

97

6.5 Direct Objects

In addition to a verb, the complete predicate of a sentence often contains a *complement*.

A complement is a word or group of words that completes the meaning of the predicate of a sentence.

It is, of course, possible to have a complete sentence with just a subject and verb. However, most of the sentences you read and write will contain one or more complements that are needed to complete the meaning of the sentence.

Different kinds of complements will be presented here and in the next two sections. This section discusses one of the most important complements, the *direct object*.

The Direct Object

Direct objects are generally found after action verbs.

A direct object is a noun or pronoun that receives the action of a transitive action verb.

You can determine if a word is a direct object by asking *Whom?* or *What?* after an action verb. In the following examples, the subjects are underlined once, the action verbs twice, and the direct objects are boxed and labeled. Notice how each direct object answers the question *Whom?* or *What?*

EXAMPLES: The <u>hailstorm</u> <u><u>bombarded</u></u> the ⟦picnickers.⟧ `DO`

(Bombarded *whom?*   *Answer:* picnickers)

The <u>workers</u> <u><u>are repaving</u></u> the ⟦road.⟧ `DO`

(Are repaving *what?*   *Answer:* road)

Not all action verbs have direct objects. Transitive action verbs do. Intransitive action verbs do not. Since some action verbs can be either transitive or intransitive, knowing that a verb is an action verb will not tell you whether or not it has a direct object. You will always need to ask the question *Whom?* or *What?* after the verb to see if there is a direct object.

98

EXAMPLES: Joshua <u>won</u> the $\overset{\text{DO}}{\boxed{\text{contest.}}}$

(Won *what?*   *Answer:* contest)

<u>Paula</u> <u>won</u> yesterday.

(Won *what?*   *Answer:* There is none, so there is no direct object.)

NOTE ABOUT DIRECT OBJECTS IN QUESTIONS: When a question is inverted, the direct object is sometimes located near the beginning of the sentence, before the verb. To find the direct object in an inverted question, reword the question as a statement.

QUESTION: Which <u>bus</u> <u>should</u> <u>I</u> <u>take</u>?

REWORDED AS A STATEMENT: <u>I</u> <u>should take</u> which $\overset{\text{DO}}{\boxed{\text{bus.}}}$

EXERCISE A: Recognizing Direct Objects. Write the direct object in each sentence.

EXAMPLE: Most people own umbrellas.

umbrellas

(1) Umbrellas have a long history. (2) Even the ancient Egyptians used them. (3) The umbrella symbolized royal and religious power to the Egyptians. (4) Assyrian tablets from 1350 B.C. show an umbrella-shaded king. (5) The early Greeks also used the umbrella symbol. (6) Religious festivals and parades featured it prominently. (7) The later Greeks used the umbrella shape more practically. (8) They invented the sunshade. (9) They even developed a sunshade hat. (10) Later still, the Romans used parasols.

Compound Direct Objects

Like subjects and verbs in sentences, direct objects can be compound.

A compound direct object is two or more nouns or pronouns that receive the action of the same transitive verb.

99

If a sentence contains a *compound direct object*, asking the question *Whom?* or *What?* after the verb will lead to two or more answers.

EXAMPLES:
$$\text{The } \underline{\text{hailstorm}} \underline{\text{bombarded}} \overset{\text{DO}}{\boxed{\text{Linda}}} \text{ and } \overset{\text{DO}}{\boxed{\text{Hal.}}}$$
(Bombarded *whom?* *Answer:* Linda and Hal)

$$\text{The } \underline{\text{workers}} \underline{\text{are repaving}} \text{ the } \overset{\text{DO}}{\boxed{\text{road}}} \text{ and } \overset{\text{DO}}{\boxed{\text{alley.}}}$$
(Are repaving *what?* *Answer:* road and alley)

EXERCISE B: Recognizing Compound Direct Objects. Write the nouns or pronouns that make up each compound direct object.

EXAMPLE: Maggie knitted a hat and mittens.

       hat   mittens

1. Don't forget the hammer and nails.
2. Mike bought a new jacket, shirt, and trousers.
3. The fire destroyed both the main house and the barn.
4. Who invited Joan and Jack?
5. That factory produces cars and trucks.
6. The baby doesn't eat fruit or cereal yet.
7. Which shrubs and bushes did the gardener trim?
8. The recipe requires cinnamon and sugar.
9. The waiter overlooked you and me.
10. Mom planted cabbage, tomatoes, lettuce, and peppers.

Direct Object or Object of a Preposition?

Do not confuse a direct object with the object of a preposition.

A direct object is never the noun or pronoun at the end of a prepositional phrase.

The first example on page 101 contains a direct object only. The second contains a direct object and a prepositional phrase. The third contains a prepositional phrase only.

EXAMPLES: They <u>bought</u> a dilapidated Victorian $\boxed{\text{mansion.}}$

DO

(Bought *what?*   *Answer:* mansion)

DO   PREP PHRASE

They <u>restored</u> the $\boxed{\text{downstairs}}$ of the mansion.

(Restored *what?*   *Answer:* downstairs)

PREP PHRASE

Soon, <u>they</u> <u>moved</u> into the mansion.

(Moved *what?*   *Answer:* none)

EXERCISE C: Distinguishing Between Direct Objects and Objects of Prepositions. Write the direct object in each sentence. If a sentence does not have one, write *none*.

EXAMPLE: People have used umbrellas for a long time.

umbrellas

(1) The word *umbrella* has come to us from the Romans. (2) The Latin word *umbra* translates into our word *shade*. (3) The Romans used umbrellas for protection against the sun. (4) People often carried them to chariot races. (5) Romans sometimes dyed the umbrellas with the colors of their favorite chariot team. (6) Eventually umbrellas at chariot races caused a public uproar. (7) They often blocked the view of other spectators. (8) The Roman emperor Domitian finally settled the dispute about umbrellas. (9) By his decree only sunshade hats could be used at the public games. (10) No one with an umbrella could attend the games.

DEVELOPING WRITING SKILLS: Writing Sentences with Direct Objects. Use each subject and verb to write a sentence with a direct object. Then circle each direct object.

EXAMPLE: kittens   played

The kittens played (tag) with each other.

1. police   will escort
2. truck   dented
3. Mr. Lopez   described
4. elephant   trampled
5. water   ruined
6. Eileen   organized
7. Craig   should have won
8. grasshoppers   destroy
9. detectives   found
10. noise   shook

101

6.6 Indirect Objects and Objective Complements

Once you have found a direct object in a sentence, you can look further to see if the sentence also has one of two other kinds of complements. Both *indirect objects* and *objective complements* are found only in sentences with direct objects.

The Indirect Object

In addition to a verb and direct object, the complete predicate of a sentence may contain an *indirect object*.

An indirect object is a noun or pronoun that appears with a direct object and names the person or thing that something is given to or done for.

A sentence cannot have an indirect object unless it has a direct object. You can tell if a word is an indirect object by finding the direct object and asking *To or for whom* or *to or for what?* after the action verb. In the following examples, subjects are underlined once, verbs twice, and direct and indirect objects are boxed and labeled. Note that indirect objects generally come before direct objects.

EXAMPLES: I bought my parents an anniversary present.
(Bought *for whom? Answer:* parents)

Lucinda gave her room a fresh coat of paint.
(Gave *to what? Answer:* room)

EXERCISE A: Recognizing Indirect Objects. Write the indirect object in each sentence.

EXAMPLE: He gave me his old tennis racquet.
me

1. He told his parents the news.
2. Greg ordered us seconds.
3. The receptionist gave the messenger an envelope.

4. The sitter read Paul two stories at bedtime.
5. I lent Amanda my pink sweater.
6. Ms. Hall showed us slides of Venice.
7. Who sent you these flowers?
8. Sandy hasn't written me a letter for weeks.
9. Mom left the painters a note.
10. Mr. Poirot teaches his students French.

Compound Indirect Objects

Like subjects, verbs, and direct objects, indirect objects can be compound.

A compound indirect object is two or more nouns or pronouns that appear with a direct object and name the people or things that something is given to or done for.

If a sentence has a *compound indirect object,* the question *To or for whom?* or *to or for what?* after the verb will give you two or more answers.

EXAMPLES:
               IO   IO   DO
I bought my mother and father a present.
(Bought *for whom?*   Answer: mother and father)

                IO   IO   DO
She gave her room and the hall a last glance.
(Gave *to what?*   Answer: room and hall)

EXERCISE B: Recognizing Compound Indirect Objects. Write the nouns or pronouns acting as indirect objects in each sentence. Then circle the nouns or pronouns that make up each compound indirect object.

EXAMPLE: We wrote Sue and Al letters about our trip.
       (Sue Al)

(1) Bart showed us the route for the trip. (2) Mr. Perkins rented Joyce and me bikes. (3) My mother packed us a snack. (4) I had already given the group the other food supplies. (5) I had also given Helen and Max the sleeping bags. (6) Our families wished us a pleasant trip. (7) At the

campsite Bart showed Helen, Joyce, and Max the best way to make a fire. (8) We cooked ourselves a fine meal. (9) No one left the raccoons and other animals even a nibble. (10) Then Joyce told us ghost stories around the campfire.

Indirect Object or Object of a Preposition?

Do not confuse indirect objects with objects of prepositions.

An indirect object never follows the word *to* or *for* in a sentence.

In the first of the following examples, *conductor* is an indirect object. In the second, however, conductor is the object of the preposition *to*.

INDIRECT OBJECT: I gave the |conductor| our |tickets.|

OBJECT OF A PREPOSITION: I gave our |tickets| to the conductor.

EXERCISE C: Distinguishing Between Indirect Objects and Objects of Prepositions. In the following sentences, change each indirect object into a prepositional phrase. Change each prepositional phrase that you can into an indirect object.

EXAMPLE: Janet left a message for you.

Janet left you a message.

1. Last night at the restaurant, the chef prepared a special dessert for us.
2. The sitter handed the baby the rattle.
3. The realtor showed us four apartments.
4. Alex sold his farm to the county.
5. Did you bring some ice cream for the children?
6. The police offered Jake a reward.
7. Grace promised a new bike to Jessica.
8. Please save me some dessert.
9. The librarian read the children a story about an elephant named Babar.
10. The defendant told the judge his story.

104

The Objective Complement

Indirect objects generally come before direct objects. Complements called *objective complements* generally come after direct objects and give additional information about them.

An objective complement is an adjective or noun that appears with a direct object and describes or renames it.

To find an objective complement, say the verb and the direct object and then ask *What?*

EXAMPLES: She painted her room green.
$$\overset{DO}{room} \quad \overset{OC}{green}$$

(Painted room *what?* *Answer:* green)

The coach appointed David captain of the team.

(Appointed David *what?* *Answer:* captain)

EXERCISE D: Recognizing Objective Complements. Write the objective complement in each sentence.

EXAMPLE: The movie made him very sad.

sad

1. The third-period class nominated him treasurer.
2. The continuous rain made them depressed.
3. The cousins called their talented uncle a wizard.
4. The actor dyed his blond hair red.
5. My parents' rules sometimes make me angry.
6. Washington appointed John Jay the first Chief Justice.
7. Their new record made them an overnight success.
8. The jury found the defendant guilty.
9. The president appointed Perkins director.
10. The school board voted Ms. Limirez supervisor.

DEVELOPING WRITING SKILLS: Using Indirect Objects to Combine Sentences. Turn each pair of sentences into a single sentence with an indirect object.

EXAMPLE: I bought the album. I bought it for Mark.

I bought Mark the album.

1. The sitter prepared a snack. He prepared it for Paul.
2. The waiter served my order. He served it to Ann.
3. I made a macrame belt. I made it for my mother.
4. The realtor rented the apartment. She rented it to us.
5. The principal gave an award. He gave it to our class.

DEVELOPING WRITING SKILLS: Writing Sentences with Objective Complements. Use each subject and verb to write a sentence with a direct object and an objective complement.

EXAMPLE: students   find

Some students find math difficult.

1. critic   called
2. rides   make
3. Amy   colored

4. class   voted
5. teacher   appointed

6.7 Subject Complements

The last two sections were about complements that help complete the meaning of sentences with transitive action verbs. Sentences with linking verbs contain a different kind of complement: a *subject complement.*

A subject complement is a noun, pronoun, or adjective that appears with a linking verb and tells something about the subject of the sentence.

A subject complement will almost always be found *after* a linking verb. The two kinds of subject complements are known as *predicate nominatives* and *predicate adjectives.*

The Predicate Nominative

The word *nominative* comes from the same Latin word (meaning "name") that the words *noun* and *pronoun* do.

A predicate nominative is a noun or pronoun that appears with a linking verb and renames, identifies, or explains the subject of the sentence.

In a sentence with a *predicate nominative,* the linking verb acts as an equal sign between the subject and the predicate nominative. They refer to the same person or thing.

In the examples, subjects are underlined once, linking verbs twice, and predicate nominatives are boxed and labeled.

EXAMPLES:　The painting of Toledo is a PN masterpiece.

　　　　　(*Masterpiece* renames *painting*.)

　　　　　The new captain of the team will be PN Sue.

　　　　　(*Sue* renames *captain*.)

　　　　　Their first choice was PN you.

　　　　　(*You* identifies *choice*.)

EXERCISE A: Recognizing Predicate Nominatives. Write the predicate nominative in each sentence.

EXAMPLE:　Carl is my brother.

　　　　　brother

1. Hawkins remained the best player on the team.
2. Some people stay children throughout their lives.
3. The first speaker was I.
4. Which of those records is a classic?
5. A hamburger seemed the safest thing to order.
6. The puppies in the corner are the ones for sale.
7. Our state senator may soon become governor.
8. The special today is broiled swordfish.
9. The girls have remained friends for years.
10. Ellen appears the strongest candidate.

The Predicate Adjective

The other kind of subject complement is called a *predicate adjective.*

A predicate adjective is an adjective that appears with a linking verb and describes the subject of the sentence.

107

In each of the following examples, you can see that the linking verb links the subject to a word that describes the subject. These descriptive words are called predicate adjectives.

EXAMPLES: The air smelled smoky.
$$\text{PA}$$

(*Smoky* describes *air*.)

The raging fire seemed impossible to control.
$$\text{PA}$$

(*Impossible* describes *fire*.)

EXERCISE B: Recognizing Predicate Adjectives. Write the predicate adjective in each sentence.

EXAMPLE: Jean seems tired this afternoon.

tired

1. The flowers smell heavenly.
2. I look awful in that shade of green.
3. Some of the cheese is moldy.
4. The pineapple tasted delicious.
5. The music sounds better from farther away.
6. The sky became cloudy toward evening.
7. I felt angry after our argument.
8. The weather remained hot all week.
9. The team's fans became more unhappy with each new setback.
10. The children grew tan from the summer sun.

Compound Subject Complements

Like other parts of a sentence, subject complements may be compound.

A compound predicate nominative is two or more nouns or pronouns that appear with a linking verb and rename the subject of the sentence.

A compound predicate adjective is two or more adjectives that appear with a linking verb and describe the subject of the sentence.

EXAMPLES: The contest <u>winners</u> <u>are</u> [Rita] and [Daniel.] (PN, PN)

(*Rita* and *Daniel* identify *winners*.)

The <u>waves</u> <u>seemed</u> [powerful] and [dangerous.] (PA, PA)

(*Powerful* and *dangerous* describe *waves*.)

EXERCISE C: Recognizing Compound Subject Complements.

Write the nouns or adjectives that make up each compound subject complement. Then label each compound complement as a *predicate nominative* or *predicate adjective*.

EXAMPLE: The museum is beautiful and interesting.

beautiful   interesting   (predicate adjective)

(1) The most frequent visitors to the museum are foreign visitors or other out-of-towners. (2) The museum's treasures are mainly furniture and paintings. (3) Its collection grows larger and better every year. (4) The paintings are old and valuable. (5) Most of them are pastels, watercolors, or oils. (6) The majority of paintings are Dutch or Italian. (7) The museum's furnishing are graceful and elegant. (8) The most interesting pieces in the foyer are a colonial table, a Philadelphia clock, and a silver lamp. (9) Other museum highlights are its beautiful rugs and its formal gardens. (10) The museum is free to the public and open daily except holidays.

DEVELOPING WRITING SKILLS: Writing Sentences with Subject Complements.

Use each subject and verb to write a sentence with the kind of subject complement indicated.

EXAMPLE: Liz   seems   (predicate adjective)

Liz seems excited about the trip.

1. friends   are   (compound predicate nominative)
2. dogs   became   (predicate adjective)
3. baby   grew   (compound predicate adjective)
4. Eric   became   (predicate nominative)
5. singer   was   (predicate nominative)
6. leaves   turned   (compound predicate adjective)
7. vegetables   are   (compound predicate nominative)

8. guests   looked   (predicate adjective)
9. voice   sounded   (predicate adjective)
10. Agnes   remained   (predicate nominative)

6.8 Basic Sentence Patterns

All sentences follow patterns. The most basic pattern in English is a *subject* followed by a *verb*. If you say, "The baby cried loudly," you are using the S-V pattern. The subject is *baby* and the verb is *cried*. The other words are modifiers.

Five Basic Patterns with Complements

Sentences with complements follow certain patterns.

In the English language, subjects, verbs, and complements follow five basic sentence patterns.

The following charts show the way complements are generally used in sentences. Subjects are underlined once, verbs twice. Complements are boxed and labeled.

Patterns with Transitive Verbs. Direct objects usually follow transitive action verbs. Indirect objects or objective complements may also follow them. Three basic patterns are used for sentences that contain transitive action verbs.

Patterns	Examples
S-AV-DO	Brian oaked an apple [pie]. (DO) Their team defeated [ours]. (DO)
S-AV-IO-DO	Sue handed [me] (IO) the [book]. (DO)
S-AV-DO-OC	We painted the [doghouse] (DO) [pink]. (OC) I call my little [brother] (DO) [Skeezix]. (OC)

Patterns with Linking Verbs. Linking verbs are generally followed by subject complements. Two basic patterns are used for sentences that contain linking verbs. The following chart shows both patterns—one for predicate nominatives and one for predicate adjectives.

Patterns	Examples
S-LV-PN	My favorite <u>meal</u> <u>is</u> spaghetti. [PN]
	The <u>mayor</u> <u>was</u> he. [PN]
S-LV-PA	The setting <u>sun</u> <u>was</u> bright red. [PA]
	I <u>feel</u> silly today. [PA]

Compound Patterns. Any of the basic sentence patterns may be expanded by using compound sentence parts.

Patterns	Examples
S-S-LV-PA-PA	<u>Pat</u> and <u>Amy</u> <u>are</u> tall [PA] and thin. [PA]
S-S-AV-DO-DO-DO	<u>Father</u> and <u>I</u> <u>cooked</u> eggs, [DO] pancakes, [DO] and sausage. [DO]

EXERCISE A: Recognizing the Parts of Basic Sentence Patterns. Write each sentence, underlining the subject once and the verb twice. Then circle each complement.

EXAMPLE: <u>Edna</u> <u>sent</u> (Tom) and (me) a (present.)

1. The coach named Jill captain.
2. This soup tastes too salty.
3. The farmer sold us fresh corn and beans.
4. Bill and Tom sound angry.
5. Albert is a lawyer in San Francisco.

111

6. Julie carefully wrote, revised, and typed her report.
7. The committee from Northbrook High School will be visiting our school.
8. My favorite seasons are spring and fall.
9. They painted the barn red.
10. Mr. Evans sent Susanne and me a thank-you note.

EXERCISE B: Recognizing Basic Sentence Patterns.
Write the pattern of each sentence in Exercise A, using the abbreviations in the charts.

EXAMPLE: Edna sent Tom and me a present.

         S-AV-IO-IO-DO

DEVELOPING WRITING SKILLS: Writing Sentences with a Variety of Patterns. Use each pattern in a sentence of your own. Then underline each subject once, underline each verb twice, and circle each complement.

EXAMPLE: S-LV-PN

         Fred is an excellent musician.

1. S-AV-DO
2. S-AV-DO-OC
3. S-LV-PA
4. S-S-AV-IO-DO-DO
5. S-LV-PN

6. S-LV-PA-PA
7. S-S-AV-DO-DO-DO
8. S-LV-PN-PN
9. S-S-AV-DO-OC-OC
10. S-AV-IO-IO-DO

6.9 Diagraming Basic Sentence Parts

Diagraming is a visual means of helping you understand how all the different parts of a sentence relate to each other. Diagraming allows you to see a sentence, not as a string of separate words, but as several groups of words arranged in a logical pattern.

Subjects, Verbs, and Modifiers

In a diagram the subject and verb are placed on a horizontal line with the subject on the left and the verb on the right. A vertical line separates the subject from the predicate. The following example shows how to diagram a subject and verb.

EXAMPLE: Jonathan sneezed.
S   V

Jonathan	sneezed

Adjectives and adverbs are placed on slanted lines directly below the words they modify.

EXAMPLE: The weary hikers were walking very slowly.
ADJ ADJ   ADV ADV

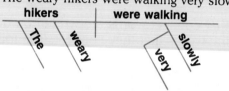

A sentence whose subject is understood to be *you* is diagramed in the usual way with parentheses around the subject. Inverted sentences are also diagramed in the usual way. The capital letter tells you which word begins the sentence.

EXAMPLES: ORDER: Come here.   QUESTION: Was she there?

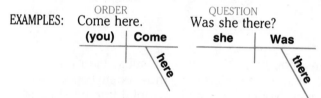

If *there* or *here* at the beginning of a sentence is an adverb, it is diagramed in the usual way. Often, however, *there* is used just to get the sentence started. When that is the case, the word is an expletive. Interjections are also expletives. The following examples show how to diagram expletives.

EXAMPLES: EXP: There was an accident.   INT: Hooray, we won!

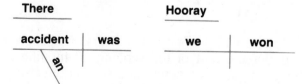

113

EXERCISE A: Diagraming Subjects, Verbs, and Modifiers. Correctly diagram each sentence.

1. Sit down.
2. The weary runner suddenly sprinted ahead.
3. Your exceptionally studious friend thinks very quickly.
4. There was no test given today.
5. Goodness, Sandy signs very poorly.

Adding Conjunctions

Conjunctions that connect words are written on dotted lines drawn between the words that they connect. The following example shows where to place conjunctions that connect adjectives and adverbs.

EXAMPLE: The black and tan dog barked loudly and constantly.

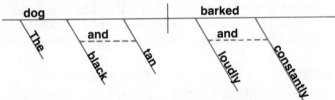

Conjunctions that connect compound subjects or compound verbs are also placed on dotted lines drawn between the words that they connect. Notice how the horizontal line must be split when a sentence has a compound subject or a compound verb.

EXAMPLE: Jean and I neither dance nor sing.

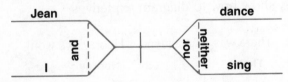

In sentences with compound subjects or verbs, a modifier is placed under the part of the sentence it modifies. If a word modifies both parts of a compound subject or verb, it is placed under the main line of the diagram.

114

EXAMPLE: My older sister and younger brother left early but
arrived late.

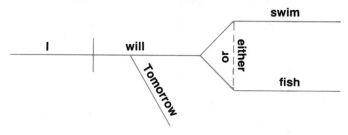

If each part of a compound verb has its own helping verb, each helping verb is placed on the line with its verb. If compound verbs share a helping verb, however, the helping verb is placed on the main line of the diagram.

EXAMPLE: Tomorrow I will either swim or fish.

EXERCISE B: Diagraming Sentences with Conjunctions.
Correctly diagram each sentence.

1. Ferns and palms were everywhere.
2. He can stay but should go.
3. Kim and Ian were leaving now but returning later.
4. The eighteen boys and girls waited quietly.
5. Very agile and highly skilled acrobats tumbled about.

Complements

The following diagrams show how to add direct objects and indirect objects to sentence diagrams.

EXAMPLES: Bill plays chess.   I told Joan a story.

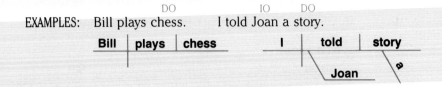

The next diagram shows where to place an objective complement.

EXAMPLE: Our class elected Beth Green treasurer.

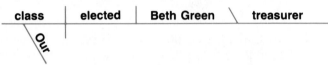

Predicate nominatives and predicate adjectives are diagramed in a similar way.

EXAMPLES: Sean is an actor.   He is talented.

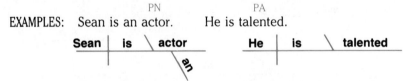

Compound complements are diagramed by splitting the lines on which they are placed and adding on dotted lines any conjunctions that connect them.

EXAMPLE: We gave Ann and Ed some crackers and cheese.

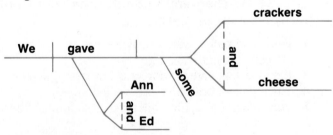

EXERCISE C: Diagraming Complements. Correctly diagram each sentence.

    1. Several urgent calls distracted the doctor.

116

2. Cathy wrote her name and her new address.
3. I bought my mother and my sister beautiful designer scarves.
4. The dance committee selected Alan Stavinsky chairperson.
5. The happy parents named one twin Christopher and the other twin Christine.
6. That is it!
7. The fog grew deeper and more mysterious.
8. The Chinese cooking tasted strange but delicious.
9. The largest airplane was silver and blue.
10. The coin was very old but still shiny.

DEVELOPING WRITING SKILLS: Writing and Diagraming Sentences with a Variety of Patterns. Use each pattern to write a sentence of your own. Then correctly diagram each sentence. Keep your sentences simple, but be sure to include appropriate adjectives and adverbs.

EXAMPLE: Subject–Action Verb–Action Verb

Our neighbors packed up and moved away.

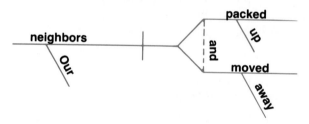

1. Subject–Action Verb–Direct Object
2. Subject–Subject–Action Verb–Indirect Object–Direct Object
3. Subject–Action Verb–Direct Object–Objective Complement
4. Subject–Linking Verb–Predicate Nominative
5. Subject–Linking Verb–Predicate Adjective–Predicate Adjective

Skills Review and Writing Workshop

Basic Sentence Parts and Patterns

CHECKING YOUR SKILLS

Identify each underlined word as a *subject, verb, direct object, indirect object, objective complement, predicate nominative,* or *predicate adjective.*

(1) The <u>Incas</u> ruled a mighty <u>empire</u> in South America centuries ago. (2) From Colombia to Chile <u>stretched</u> the <u>empire</u> of the Incas. (3) They made their <u>capital</u> <u>Cuzco</u>, which is in Peru. (4) A vast road system gave the <u>Incas</u> the <u>ability</u> to communicate and trade with all parts of their land. (5) <u>Agriculture</u> was the main <u>occupation</u> of the people. (6) Incas grew <u>corn</u>, potatoes, and other <u>crops</u> in terraces along the hillsides. (7) Incan buildings <u>were</u> <u>magnificent</u>. (8) <u>Ruins</u> of some of these buildings still <u>stand</u> at the city of Machu Picchu in the Andes Mountains. (9) This once proud <u>empire</u>, however, no longer <u>exists</u>. (10) Spanish <u>soldiers</u> and <u>explorers</u> conquered the Incas in the sixteenth century.

USING GRAMMAR SKILLS IN WRITING
Writing Advertising Copy

By writing clear, concise sentences, writers can keep their readers involved and interested. Suppose you work for an advertising firm and have to write an advertisement for a product. Write an advertisement by following these steps.

Prewriting: Select a product that you have used recently, or make up one. Consider how to persuade people to try the product. How will it benefit people? How much will it cost to buy? How does it compare to similar products?

Writing: Describe the most important benefit first in order to catch your reader's attention immediately. Then add the other information about the product.

Revising: Make sure your sentences are clear, concise, and interesting. Change any words that could be more vivid and descriptive. After you have revised, proofread carefully.

7

Phrases

Previous chapters in this unit have focused on the parts of speech and the basic parts of a sentence: the subject, the predicate, and the different parts of the predicate. This chapter will present another grammatical structure, the *phrase*.

A phrase is a group of words, without a subject and verb, that functions in a sentence as one part of speech.

This chapter will explore the ways several different kinds of phrases can be used to add variety and meaning to sentences. The first section will cover the type of phrase with which you are probably most familiar, the *prepositional phrase*.

Prepositional Phrases   7.1

A *prepositional phrase* was defined earlier as a group of words made up of a preposition and a noun or pronoun, called the object of the preposition. *By the lake, out of gas,* and *with brown eyes* are all examples of prepositional phrases. Prepositions may also have compound objects. *For Maria and me* and *to the kitchen, hallway, or living room* are examples of prepositions followed by compound objects. (See Section 4.1 to review prepositions.)

Prepositional phrases function either as adjectives by modifying nouns and pronouns or as adverbs by modifying verbs, adjectives, and adverbs. Like one-word adjectives and adverbs, they add important details to sentences.

Adjective Phrases

When acting as an adjective, a prepositional phrase is called an *adjective phrase*.

An adjective phrase is a prepositional phrase that modifies a noun or pronoun by telling what kind or which one.

From the following, you can see that an adjective phrase serves basically the same purpose that an adjective does.

Adjectives	Adjective Phrases
The *masked* man frightened the children.	The man *with a mask* frightened the children.
The *cartoon* caption made me chuckle.	The caption *on the cartoon* made me chuckle.
The *striped* umbrella is on the table.	The umbrella *with stripes* is on the table.

A prepositional phrase is an adjective phrase if it answers one of the adjective questions: *What kind?* or *Which one?* For the first of the above sentences with adjective phrases, the question to ask would be *Which one?* Since the phrase *with a mask* answers it, you know the phrase is an adjective.

Adjective phrases generally modify nouns functioning as subjects, direct objects, indirect objects, or predicate nominatives.

MODIFYING A SUBJECT: The hotel *on the beach* was crowded.

MODIFYING A DIRECT OBJECT: Rob bought a car *with power brakes*.

MODIFYING AN INDIRECT OBJECT: He gives students *with high marks* less homework.

MODIFYING A PREDICATE NOMINATIVE: Every morning her alarm clock was the whistle *of a train*.

120

Occasionally, an adjective phrase may also be used to modify the object of the preposition of another prepositional phrase.

EXAMPLE: The law student had originally hoped to rent the two

large rooms *at the back of the house.*

The adjective phrase *at the back* modifies *rooms*. The adjective phrase *of the house* describes *back*.

At other times more than one adjective phrase may be used to modify the same noun.

EXAMPLE: The carton *of milk in the sun* has turned sour.

Both of the adjective phrases in this sentence modify *carton* by telling which one.

EXERCISE A: Identifying Adjective Phrases. Write each sentence, underlining the adjective phrase or adjective phrases in each. Then draw an arrow from each phrase to the word it modifies.

EXAMPLE: Their house in the mountains is spectacular.

1. The price of the car was much too high.
2. Put that box of books down here.
3. My sister is the one in the yellow sweater.
4. The house on the corner of our street needs paint.
5. The cry of the wounded animal haunted us.
6. This is another book by the same author.
7. The shapes of the two objects are very similar.
8. Something in the corner of the room moved.
9. Did you close the window behind the couch?
10. I enjoyed your article about Mr. Hill.
11. Mary Elizabeth is playing the part of the nurse in the ninth-grade play.
12. Maisie made all of the plans for the surprise party.
13. When did your cousin from Indiana visit you?
14. The supports for the railing on the front porch are weak.
15. I saw the painting of the clown with the flower in his hat.
16. The trouble between Jerry and me ended our friendship.
17. I made that pot with the enamel finish and straight sides.

121

18. The horse jumped the fence around the field behind the barn.
19. Paul has always been the tallest one in his class.
20. Irene accepted an invitation from the Johnsons for dinner.

Adverb Phrases

When a prepositional phrase functions as an adverb it is called an *adverb phrase*.

An adverb phrase is a prepositional phrase that modifies a verb, adjective, or adverb by pointing out where, when, in what manner, or to what extent.

The following examples show that adverb phrases can serve basically the same purposes that adverbs do.

Adverbs	Adverb Phrases
The team played *well*.	The team played *with great skill*.
The Cardinals played *here*.	The Cardinals played *at Spartan Stadium*.
The game lasted *forever*.	The game lasted *into the thirteenth inning*.

A prepositonal phrase is an adverb phrase if it answers one of the adverb questions: *Where? When? In what manner?* or *To what extent?* For the first of the above sentences with adverb phrases, you might ask the question *Played in what manner?* The phrase *with great skill* answers this question, so the phrase is an adverb.

While an adjective phrase almost always comes directly after the word it modifies, an adverb phrase can be separated from the word it modifies by being located elsewhere.

EXAMPLES: Our band marched *in the parade*.

Cathy lost her sweater *at the parade*.

After the parade we walked home.

122

Like single-word adverbs, adverb phrases can modify verbs, adjectives, and adverbs.

MODIFYING A VERB: The skater skimmed *over the glassy ice*.

MODIFYING AN ADJECTIVE: Mary was unhappy *with her job*.

MODIFYING AN ADVERB: We arrived late *for dinner*.

Two or more adverb phrases may also be used to modify the same word.

EXAMPLE: *On Saturdays* my cousin works *at the garage*.

EXERCISE B: Identifying Adverb Phrases. Write each sentence, underlining the adverb phrase or adverb phrases in each. Then draw an arrow from each phrase to the word it modifies.

EXAMPLE: After school we went to the soccer game.

1. Simmer the stew over low heat.
2. The coach is always tougher on newcomers.
3. Louis delivered their anniversary present to the wrong house.
4. Lightning hit the barn during the storm.
5. The frightened squirrel ran across the roof and jumped into the tree.
6. Allie swam away from us.
7. The couple sailed their boat around the world.
8. They returned before dark.
9. The flood waters rose over the breakwater and onto the roadway.
10. Run into the backyard and take the lawnmower out of the rain.
11. With great skill the pilot banked the plane toward the left.
12. This book is different from other mysteries.
13. Sharon spoke with great feeling and confidence.
14. The tourists followed the guide through the museum.
15. We arrived early for the party.
16. The committee is eager for volunteers.

17. That author often writes about marine life.
18. All the guests were happy for the bride and groom.
19. She appears in movies and on television.
20. The child moved closer to his mother.

DEVELOPING WRITING SKILLS: Writing Sentences with Adjective and Adverb Phrases. Use the following instructions to write ten sentences of your own. Then underline each indicated phrase and draw an arrow from it to the word it modifies.

EXAMPLE: Use of *red roses* as an adjective phrase.

On Friday she received a bouquet of red roses.

1. Use *under the rock* as an adjective phrase.
2. Use *for five years* an an adverb phrase.
3. Use *before half time* as an adverb phrase.
4. Use *of the trees* as an adjective phrase.
5. Use *after class* as an adverb phrase.
6. Use *between the towns* as an adjective phrase.
7. Use *across the river* as an adverb phrase.
8. Use *to the puzzle* as an adjective phrase.
9. Use *in a three-piece suit* as an adjective phrase.
10. Use *to the music* as an adverb phrase.

7.2 Appositives and Appositive Phrases

Appositives, like adjective phrases, are used to develop the meaning of nouns and certain pronouns.

Appositives

A word *in apposition* is "placed next to" another word.

An appositive is a noun or pronoun placed next to another noun or pronoun to identify, rename, or explain it.

Notice in the following chart that each of the *appositives* follows immediately after the word it identifies, renames, or explains.

124

APPOSITIVES

Tony's car, a *sedan,* ran out of gas on the bridge.

He, a *friend,* should understand my feelings.

Her hobby, *graphology,* is the study of handwriting.

Notice also that the appositives in the chart above are set off by commas. The commas indicate that these appositives are not essential to the basic meaning of the sentences. The appositives could be dropped without changing the meaning of the sentences.

In the following examples, however, the appositives are not set off by commas because they are needed to define the nouns that come before them. The appositives could not be dropped from the sentences without taking away a very important part of the sentences' meaning.

EXAMPLE: The famous baseball player *Lou Gehrig* played for the New York Yankees from 1923 to 1939.

I heard the famous violinist *Itzhak Perlman* play.

EXERCISE A: Identifying Appositives. Write the appositive in each sentence. Then write the word or words each appositive renames.

EXAMPLE: This book, a novel, is extremely fast-paced.

novel   book

1. Mr. Smith, a lawyer, is away on vacation.
2. My sister Alice is a medical student.
3. Our house, a saltbox, is typical of colonial New England architecture.
4. The reporter, Ms. Hughes, confirmed the story.
5. John Greenleaf Whittier wrote the poem "Snowbound."
6. My favorite teacher, Ms. Jenkins, will retire next year.
7. The artist Mary Cassatt painted mothers and their children.
8. Dad's special dessert, cheesecake, won a blue ribbon.
9. The poet Shelley drowned in a boating accident.
10. Ed ordered his favorite dinner, pizza.

125

Appositive Phrases

When an appositive has its own modifiers, it forms an appositive phrase.

An appositive phrase is a noun or pronoun with modifiers, placed next to a noun or pronoun to add information and details.

The modifiers added to make an *appositive phrase* can be adjectives, adjective phrases, or other groups of words acting as adjectives.

APPOSITIVE PHRASES

The dog, *a large Saint Bernard,* crushed the flowers in the garden.

The horrible smoke, *a blend of burnt rubber and industrial fumes,* made her choke.

Sean handed in his report, *a ten-page paper on the Russian Revolution.*

In the first of the sentences above, the appositive *Saint Bernard* is modified by the article *a* and the adjective *large;* together they form the appositive phrase. In the second sentence, the appositive *blend* is modified by the article *a* and the adjective phrase *of burnt rubber and industrial fumes.* In the third sentence, the appositive *paper* is modified by an article, an adjective, and an adjective phrase.

Both appositives and appositive phrases can accompany almost any noun or pronoun used in a sentence. Following are some of the many possibilities.

WITH A SUBJECT: An aviator, *the pilot of a World War II Spitfire,* explained the structure of the plane to us.

WITH A DIRECT OBJECT: The disc jockey introduced her special guest, *a popular guitarist.*

WITH AN INDIRECT OBJECT: Bob gave Julia, *his favorite aunt,* a ticket to the concert.

WITH AN OBJECTIVE COMPLEMENT: At the meeting, they named her treasurer, *an important position*.

WITH A PREDICATE NOMINATIVE: Franklin's Fortune is a deserted mining camp, *a ghost town*.

WITH THE OBJECT OF A PREPOSITION: The closets of the house, *an old mansion*, were empty.

In addition to identifying, renaming, and explaining other words, appositives and appositive phrases also make it possible for a writer to put more information into one sentence.

TWO SENTENCES: The road was the scene of many accidents. It was a congested expressway.

COMBINED: The road, *a congested expressway*, was the scene of many accidents.

TWO SENTENCES: Yosemite National Park is a natural wonder. It attracts thousands of tourists each year.

COMBINED: Yosemite National Park, *a natural wonder*, attracts thousands of tourists each year.

EXERCISE B: Identifying Appositive Phrases. Write the appositive phrase in each sentence. Then write the word or words each appositive phrase renames.

EXAMPLE: Our new pet, a frisky puppy, loves to play.

   a frisky puppy   pet

1. They hope to win the prize, a trip for two to Hawaii.
2. Mrs. Konevich fixed the car, an old station wagon.
3. Shelley's sister, a track star at UCLA, runs three miles daily.
4. He took her to a movie, a comedy about army life.
5. Two boys, friends of ours, gave us a ride.
6. The youngest player, a pitcher on the second team, received an award at the dinner.
7. We gave Mrs. Hunt, our noisy neighbor, a warning.
8. Amy's father, a federal court judge, will be the speaker.
9. Chess, her favorite game, can take hours to play.
10. He is an artist, a genius with a paint brush.

Compound Appositives

An appositive or an appositive phrase may be compound.

A compound appositive is two or more appositives or appositive phrases connected by a conjunction and used to identify the same noun or pronoun.

The following examples show *compound appositives*.

EXAMPLES: His vacation, *a weekend in California* and *a week in Mexico*, thoroughly relaxed him.

Their horses, *Thoroughbreds, Arabians,* and *two Tennessee walking horses,* were all champions.

EXERCISE C: Identifying Compound Appositives. Write each sentence, underlining each part of each compound appositive. Then draw an arrow from each part to the word or words it renames.

EXAMPLE: Viewing ocean creatures, fish and other animals, is one reason that underwater diving is popular.

(1) As early as 4500 B.C., people were diving in the ocean to bring up food, both fish and plants. (2) Early Greek and Roman divers also dived to retrieve the ocean's riches, pearls, sponges, and shells. (3) The most common diving method, skin diving or breath-hold diving, has been practiced the longest. (4) Skin diving, a very simple type of diving and a popular form of recreation today, requires little or no equipment. (5) The basic equipment, fins, masks, and snorkels, is easy to use. (6) Years ago, divers used natural equipment, hollow reeds for snorkels and tortoise shells for goggles. (7) Now, however, this equipment is made from more modern materials, glass and plastic. (8) In 1943, two Frenchmen, Cousteau and Gagnan, developed practical independent breathing equipment. (9) Improved equipment gives today's divers great advantages, more mobility and increased time under water. (10) Today, divers often use special gear, compressed-air tanks and wet suits, which allows them to swim underwater for long periods.

DEVELOPING WRITING SKILLS: **Using Appositives and Appositive Phrases to Combine Sentences.** Turn each pair of sentences into one with an appositive or appositive phrase.

EXAMPLE: Sam typed his paper. It was a book report.

Sam typed his paper, a book report.

1. The book was published in many languages. It was an autobiography.
2. A neighbor's tree became the graveyard for their colorful kite. The kite was a large dragon with a silver tail.
3. Candice completed the race in spite of her injury. She had a twisted ankle.
4. The memorial honors the people who died while in service during World War II. It is a simple, symbolic structure made of white stone.
5. Mount Shasta towers thousands of feet above the surrounding valleys and plateaus. The mountain is a volcano.

Participles and Participial Phrases   7.3

Sometimes certain forms of verbs are used not as verbs but as other parts of speech. Verb forms used as other parts of speech are called *verbals*.

Verbals may be used alone or in phrases. Like verbs, they can have complements or be modified in different ways.

This section will cover the verbal known as the *participle*.

Participles

A *participle* is a verbal that is used as an adjective.

A participle is a form of a verb that can act as an adjective.

Participles fall into two groups: *present participles* and *past participles*. You can identify these two different kinds of participles by their endings. Present participles end in *-ing (dancing, playing, waiting)*. Past participles generally end in *-ed (danced, played, waited)* but may also have irregular endings such a *-t* or *-en (burnt, spoken)*. (See Section 11.1 for lists of irregular verb endings.)

129

The following chart shows how these two types of participles are used as adjectives in sentences.

Present Participles	Past Participles
A *whining* sound came from the engine of the car.	The *cracked* ice looked like slivers of glass.
Smiling, the official shook my hand.	*Disgusted*, Len walked away without saying goodbye.

Notice how participles answer the questions for adjectives, *What kind?* or *Which one?*

EXAMPLES: A *whining* sound came from the engine of the car.
(*What kind* of sound?   *Answer:* a *whining* sound.

The *frozen* pipe needs to be repaired.
(*Which* pipe?   *Answer:* the *frozen* pipe)

EXERCISE A: Identifying Participles Write the participle in each sentence. Then label each as *present* or *past*.

EXAMPLE: The frightened cat ran up a tree.
frightened   (past)

1. The howling coyotes woke the neighborhood.
2. Raoul brought the injured hawk to a veterinarian.
3. The child gave his mother a crumbling cookie.
4. Stumbling, Nicole dropped her books in the hall.
5. A falling star streaked across the clear sky.
6. The frozen ice cream was too hard to eat.
7. The disappointed team vowed to practice harder.
8. Hurt, Vivian ate lunch by herself.
9. Howard turned off the blaring radio.
10. The torn tent was no protection against the wind.

Verb or Participle?

Since verbs often have endings such as *-ing* and *-ed,* you will have to be careful not to confuse them with participles acting as adjectives.

A verb shows an action, a condition, or the fact that something exists. A participle acting as an adjective modifies a noun or pronoun.

The same word can be used as a verb and as a participle.

Verbs	Participles
The train was *chugging* down the track.	The *chugging* train puffed down the track.
The directions *confused* her.	*Confused,* she could not follow the directions.

EXERCISE B: Distinguishing Between Verbs and Participles. Identify each underlined word as a *verb* or *participle*. If the word is used as a participle, also write the word it modifies.

EXAMPLE: The cat <u>frightened</u> the bird.

   verb

1. The train is <u>arriving</u> on Track 7.
2. Reporters interviewed the <u>arriving</u> delegation.
3. My little brother loves <u>frozen</u> yogurt.
4. Usually, by this time of year, the pond has <u>frozen</u>.
5. The theatrical company has been <u>touring</u> major cities.
6. The <u>touring</u> company will perform here next week.
7. The Baskins are <u>moving</u> to Toronto.
8. The <u>moving</u> truck arrived an hour late.
9. Have the police recovered the <u>stolen</u> jewels?
10. Someone has <u>stolen</u> a valuable painting from the museum.

Participial Phrases

Because participles are forms of verbs, they can be expanded with modifiers and complements.

A participial phrase is a participle modified by an adverb or adverb phrase or accompanied by a complement. The entire phrase acts as an adjective.

131

Notice the different ways participles can be expanded.

PARTICIPIAL PHRASES

Swimming leisurely, we didn't notice the dolphin approach.

Frightened by its sudden appearance, I yelled, "Shark!"

The lifeguard, *using her megaphone,* told us not to panic.

In the above chart, an adverb modifies *swimming,* an adverb phrase modifies *frightened,* and *using* gains a direct object.

Placement. A participial phrase can usually be placed either before or after the word it modifies.

EXAMPLES: *Munching hay,* the elephant looked content.

The elephant, *munching hay,* looked content.

Punctuation. The participial phrases you have seen so far have been set off by commas. However, when a participial phrase distinguishes one person, place, or thing from others, it is not set off by commas. In the following example, *wearing the blue sweater* is essential to the meaning of the sentence. It distinguishes one boy from others. Thus, no commas are used.

EXAMPLE: The boy *wearing the blue sweater* is my brother.

Used to Combine Sentences. Participial phrases can often be used to combine information from two sentences into one sentence. The following examples show ways in which participial phrases can be used to unite separate sentences.

TWO SENTENCES: We picked up the injured bird. We could see it had a broken wing.

COMBINED: *Picking up the injured bird,* we could see it had a broken wing.

TWO SENTENCES: The President shook hands with people in the crowd. He barely made his way to the car.

COMBINED: *Shaking hands with people in the crowd,* the President barely made his way to the car.

132

EXERCISE C: Recognizing Participial Phrases. Write each sentence, underlining the participial phrase. Then draw an arrow from each participial phrase to the word it modifies.

EXAMPLE: Frightened by the cat, the bird flew away.

1. Our house, shaded by trees, stays cool in the summer.
2. Kicking stones, the children ran down the street.
3. They boarded the subway packed with people.
4. Frightened by the smoke, they called the fire department.
5. Ms. Foley served a pie steaming from the oven.
6. The commuters, stuck in traffic, were impatient.
7. In the summer the sun, beating on the roads, melts the tar.
8. He ordered a sundae dripping with hot fudge.
9. Thinking quickly, she took her foot off the accelerator.
10. Whirling on one skate, the skater executed a perfect turn.

DEVELOPING WRITING SKILLS: Using Participial Phrases to Combine Sentences. Turn each pair of sentences into one with a participial phrase. Then underline each participial phrase and draw an arrow from it to the word it modifies.

EXAMPLE: The palms sway in the wind. They are like dancers.

Swaying in the wind, the palms are like dancers.

1. The tollbooth would not accept the coins. It buzzed.
2. The soft music flows out of the restaurant. It invites passers-by to enter.
3. The outrigger canoe sprayed water onto the faces of the crew. It raced along the top of the waves.
4. The telephone poles had been snapped by the hurricane. They hung dangerously over the road.
5. Dolores placed her shot carefully. She hit the ball to her opponent's backhand.
6. Al swims every day. He is an excellent swimmer.
7. The tires were worn out. They needed to be replaced.
8. The celery was chopped into small pieces. It added texture to the salad.
9. The jet soars high above the clouds. It is flying to Paris.
10. The band members wore their new uniforms. They played and marched with more confidence than usual.

133

EXAMPLE: Use *paint* as a past participle.

A picture painted on wet plaster is called a fresco.

1. Use *write* as a present participle.
2. Use *laugh* as a present participle.
3. Use *cook* as a past participle.
4. Use *stamp* as a past participle.
5. Use *amuse* as a present participle.

7.4 Gerunds and Gerund Phrases

Many of the nouns you use are actually forms of verbs called *gerunds*.

Gerunds

You will find that *gerunds* are somewhat easier to identify than participles.

A gerund is a form of a verb that acts as a noun.

You need only to remember two things to identify a gerund. Gerunds always end in *-ing,* and they always act as nouns. The following chart shows the many different positions gerunds can take in a sentence.

GERUNDS

Subject: *Dancing* helps a person lose weight.

Direct Object: On their vacation, the Rezendes discovered *snorkeling*.

Indirect Object: His performance gives *acting* a bad name.

Predicate Nominative: One relaxing exercise is *swimming*.

Object of a Preposition: After three hours, Steve was tired of *studying*.

Appositive: I have a new hobby, *cooking*.

EXERCISE A: Identifying Gerunds. Write the gerund or gerunds in each sentence. Label each one as a *subject, direct object, indirect object, predicate nominative, object of a preposition,* or *appositive*.

EXAMPLE: Swimming is her favorite activity.

Swimming   (subject)

1. She expanded her vocabulary by reading.
2. At the age of five, Winston began acting.
3. Dribbling requires coordination and dexterity.
4. On summer nights, the family enjoys picnicking.
5. One of Lenore's hobbies is sewing.
6. The parakeet's main pastime, chirping, prevents loneliness.
7. Loving is trusting.
8. Stephanie loved excitement and dancing.
9. Weeding has improved the appearance of the yard.
10. The team excelled in batting and running.

Verb, Participle, or Gerund?

If you remember that a gerund is always a noun, you should have no problem telling a gerund from a verb or a participle.

Words ending in *-ing* that act as nouns are gerunds. They do not have helping verbs nor do they act as adjectives.

The following examples of a verb, a participle, and a gerund demonstrate the difference between them.

Verb	Participle	Gerund
I am *walking* home.	Carol, *walking* to school, saw an owl.	*Walking* can be fun.

EXERCISE B: Distinguishing Between Verbs, Participles, and Gerunds. Identify each underlined word as a *verb, participle,* or *gerund*.

EXAMPLE: The girls are <u>swimming</u> in the lake.

verb

135

1. The <u>losing</u> team put up a good fight.
2. No one enjoys <u>losing</u>.
3. The home team was <u>losing</u> at the half.
4. The contractors are <u>painting</u> the exterior today.
5. <u>Painting</u> is more than a hobby to Chuck.
6. Have you seen my <u>painting</u> clothes?
7. Our <u>meeting</u> at the station was a surprise.
8. Hayes was a member of the delegation <u>meeting</u> the plane.
9. You will be <u>meeting</u> many new people at camp.
10. Why are you <u>reading</u> that book?

Gerund Phrases

A gerund, like a participle, may be part of a phrase.

A gerund phrase is a gerund with modifiers or a complement, all acting together as a noun.

Notice the many ways gerunds can be expanded into phrases.

GERUND PHRASES
The loud, irregular snoring annoyed him.
Waiting for the bus exhausted her patience.
Vicky's morning routine includes *showering leisurely*.
Their parents forbade *shouting in the house*.
His favorite pastime is *leaving her mysterious notes*.
Denise's greatest accomplishment was *becoming president*.
They ran into the house without *removing their muddy shoes*.

In the first two sentences the gerunds *snoring* and *waiting* are modified by adjectives and an adjective phrase. In the next two, the gerunds are modified by an adverb and an adverb phrase. In the last three, the gerunds have complements.

NOTE ABOUT GERUNDS AND POSSESSIVE PRONOUNS: Always use the possessive form of a personal pronoun before a gerund.

INCORRECT: Mr. Avery disliked *him smirking*.

CORRECT: Mr. Avery disliked *his smirking*.

EXERCISE C: Identifying Gerund Phrases. Write the gerund phrase or gerund phrases in each sentence. Label each one as a *subject, direct object, predicate nominative,* or *object of a preposition*.

EXAMPLE: During our vacation last summer, we all enjoyed swimming in the lake.

swimming in the lake   (direct object)

1. The pilot of a hang glider generally takes off by running down a hill.
2. Holly's favorite activity is climbing mountains in state parks.
3. Thousands of spectators showed their interest by following the pro golfers around the course.
4. After one night of mosquito attacks the Percivals regretted camping by the river.
5. In the 1800's some miners made as much as $5,000 in a few days of panning gold.
6. Flying an airplane in bad weather requires extensive training.
7. Running out of gas is a horrible experience.
8. Some body surfers use styrofoam boards for riding the waves.
9. Going to bed late and getting up early may lead to exhaustion.
10. Given the choice between hearing a story and playing a game, the children chose hearing a story.

DEVELOPING WRITING SKILLS: Writing Sentences with Gerund Phrases. Use the following instructions to write five sentences with gerund phrases. Then underline the gerund phrase in each.

EXAMPLE: Use *sneezing* as a subject.

Her violent sneezing startled me.

1. Use *staring* as a subject.
2. Use *joking* as a predicate nominative.
3. Use *driving* as the object of a preposition.
4. Use *whispering* as a direct object.
5. Use *sliding* as a direct object.

7.5 Infinitives and Infinitive Phrases

A third kind of verbal, in addition to the participle and the gerund, is the *infinitive*.

Infinitives

Like gerunds, infinitives can be nouns. But unlike gerunds, infinitives can also be adjectives and adverbs.

An infinitive is a form of a verb that generally appears with the word *to* and acts as a noun, adjective, or adverb.

The following chart shows infinitives acting as nouns, adjectives, and adverbs.

INFINITIVES
Subject: To *apologize* takes courage and humility.
Direct Object: Alone and frightened, she wanted *to survive.*
Predicate Nominative: Their response was *to economize.*
Object of a Preposition: He had no choice except *to relent.*
Appositive: His goal, *to travel,* was never realized.
Adjective: The director of the camp is the person *to notify.*
Adverbs: She worked *to improve.*
Afraid *to speak,* he looked at his shoes.

EXERCISE A: Identifying Infinitives. Write the infinitive in each sentence. Then label each as a *noun, adjective,* or *adverb.*

EXAMPLE: My friend started to laugh.

   to laugh   (noun)

1. He wanted to protest.
2. Her only thought was to win.
3. She had no alternative except to drive.

4. Eager to succeed, he studied every night.
5. The ghost town to visit is on a deserted road.
6. Rob likes to swim.
7. Nadine told me what book to read.
8. To write takes more time than I have.
9. That is the most economical car to buy.
10. The bus to take stops only at major towns.

Prepositional Phrase or Infinitive?

You should take care not to confuse a prepositional phrase beginning with *to* with an infinitive.

A prepositional phrase always ends with a noun or pronoun. An infinitive always ends with a verb.

Notice the difference in the following examples.

Prepositional Phrase	Infinitive
We went *to the movies* last week.	I didn't want the movie *to end*.

EXERCISE B: Distinguishing Between Prepositional Phrases and Infinitives. Write the prepositional phrase or infinitive beginning with *to* in each sentence. Then label each as a *prepositional phrase* or *infinitive.*

EXAMPLE: He had an essay to write.

　　　　　to write   (infinitive)

1. Because the music was so loud, Pat found it hard to study.
2. To win was our only desire.
3. Have you ever been to Seattle?
4. My sister likes to ski.
5. When do we go back to school?
6. My grandparents are coming to visit.
7. Who phones in the message about the lost children to headquarters?
8. Have you shown her the pictures of your trip to Alaska?
9. Is it time to go?
10. Our neighbors have gone to Europe.

Infinitive Phrases

Like participles and gerunds, infinitives can be used to form phrases.

An infinitive phrase is an infinitive with modifiers, complements, or a subject, all acting together as a single part of speech.

The following chart shows the many different ways infinitives can be expanded into phrases.

INFINITIVE PHRASES
Professional dancers need *to practice daily*.
To stroll along the boardwalk at sunset is relaxing.
Jill uses her microscope *to magnify blood cells*.
I need *Donna to show me the way*.

In the first sentence, the infinitive is modified by an adverb. In the second sentence, the infinitive is modified by two adverb phrases. In the third sentence, the infinitive has a direct object. In the last sentence, the infinitive has a subject and two complements, a direct object and an indirect object.

NOTE ABOUT INFINITIVES WITHOUT *To*: Infinitives do not always include the word *to*. When an infinitive follows one of the eight verbs listed below, the *to* is generally omitted.

dare	help	make	see
hear	let	please	watch

EXAMPLES: I don't dare *leave* home without my medicine.

I heard them *sing* a song.

She helped me *rake* the leaves.

Let's *go* to the movies.

We made the dog *sit* still for the photographer.

Please *stand* here.

I saw the dog *steal* the cheese from the platter.

From the beach he watched the storm *approach*.

140

EXERCISE C: Identifying Infinitive Phrases. Write the infinitive phrase or infinitive phrases in each sentence. Label each one as a *subject, direct object, predicate nominative, object of a preposition, adjective,* or *adverb.*

EXAMPLE: To become an astronaut requires special training.

> To become an astronaut   (subject)

(1) To carry out their missions, astronauts undergo years of preparation. (2) At first only experienced pilots were able to become astronauts. (3) They needed to have a degree in engineering, physical science, or mathematics. (4) Since 1965 "mission specialists" have been recruited to perform scientific experiments. (5) They also needed to complete flight training. (6) To prepare for missions, astronauts study subjects ranging from rocket engines to geology. (7) Astronauts use full-size spacecraft models and simulators (devices that reproduce conditions of space flight) to train for missions. (8) Astronauts have no choice but to work hard. (9) We admire their ability to succeed at difficult tasks. (10) They make us feel proud of their accomplishments.

DEVELOPING WRITING SKILLS: Writing Sentences with Infinitive Phrases. Use the following instructions to write five sentences with infinitive phrases. Then underline the infinitive phrase in each.

EXAMPLE: Use *to help* as a direct object.

> He wanted <u>to help the lost child</u>.

1. Use *to change* as a predicate nominative.
2. Use *to challenge* as an adjective.
3. Use *to paint* as a subject.
4. Use *to refuse* as an object of a preposition.
5. Use *to leap* as a direct object.

Diagraming Phrases 7.6

The diagrams in this section will show how prepositional phrases, appositives, appositive phrases, verbals, and verbal phrases can be added to sentence diagrams.

141

Prepositional Phrases

A prepositional phrase can act as either an adjective or an adverb in a sentence. In a diagram an adjective phrase is placed directly below the noun or pronoun it modifies. An adverb phrase is placed directly below the verb, adjective, or adverb it modifies. The preposition is placed on a slanted line with its object on a horizontal line below the slanted line. Any adjectives that modify the object of the preposition are placed on slanted lines below the horizontal line.

EXAMPLE: The woman *with the large hat* went *into the store*.

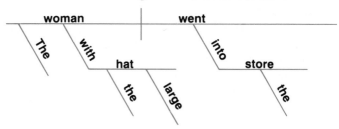

The first example below shows how to diagram a prepositional phrase that modifies the object of another prepositional phrase. The other example shows how to diagram a prepositional phrase that modifies an adjective or an adverb.

EXAMPLES: I ate pizza *with mushrooms on it*. The rain started yesterday *after lunch*.

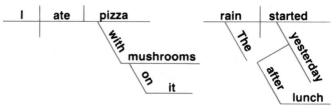

A prepositional phrase with a compound object is diagramed in the same way other compound sentence parts are diagramed. The diagram at the top of the next page is an example of a sentence containing a prepositional phrase with a compound object.

142

EXAMPLE: I eat whole-wheat bread *with breakfast and lunch*.

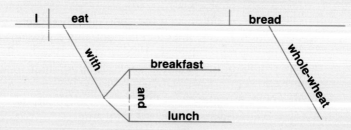

EXERCISE A: **Diagraming Prepositional Phrases.** Correctly diagram each sentence.

1. Mark is working at the radio station.
2. You may take the television to your room.
3. The boy on the bench played in the first half.
4. She runs for exercise.
5. The roof of the old house on the corner collapsed.

Appositives and Appositive Phrases

To diagram an appositive, place it in parentheses beside the noun or pronoun it identifies, renames, or explains. Any adjectives or adjective phrases included in an appositive phrase are placed directly beneath the appositive.

EXAMPLE: Blue whales, *the largest animals in the world,* are rare.

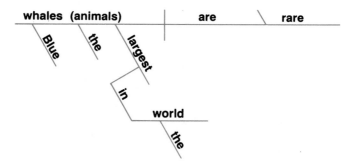

143

EXERCISE B: Diagraming Appositives and Appositive Phrases. Correctly diagram each sentence.

1. The governor announced the appointee, his wife!
2. Give Colonel Grey, the commandant, this message.
3. That is our representative, Miss Hoyt.
4. The results of the exam, the Scholastic Aptitude Test, have arrived.
5. My uncle, a bachelor for fifty years, finally married.

Participles and Participial Phrases

Participles function as adjectives. Thus, in a diagram, they are placed directly beneath the nouns or pronouns they modify. Participles are placed partly on a slanted line and partly on a horizontal line extending from the slanted line. Any adverbs or adverb phrases included in a particular phrase are placed directly beneath the horizontal line. When a participle has a complement, it is placed on the horizontal line with the participle and separated from it by a short vertical line.

EXAMPLE: *Carefully following the instructions,* Karen assembled the model airplane.
PARTICIPIAL PHRASE

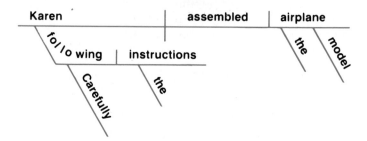

EXERCISE C: Diagraming Participles and Participial Phrases. Correctly diagram each sentence.

1. Laughing, she turned toward me.
2. Carefully detailed reports will be available.
3. Exhausted, we finally reached our destination.

4. My grandmother, speaking in low tones, continued the bedtime story.
5. Closing the door, I heard the kettle whistling on the stove.

Gerunds and Gerund Phrases

Because gerunds act as nouns, they can be subjects, complements, objects of prepositions, or appositives. When a gerund acts as a subject, direct object, or predicate nominative, it is placed on a pedestal above the main horizontal line of the diagram. Notice in the following diagram the stepped line on which all gerunds are written. Notice also that any modifiers and complements that are part of a gerund phrase are added to the diagram in the usual way.

GERUND PHRASE
EXAMPLE: We will not allow *your reading comics in class*.

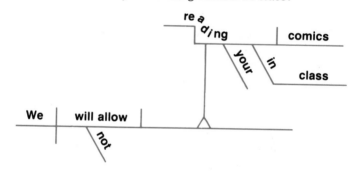

When a gerund acts as an indirect object or an object of a preposition, it is placed on a line slanting down from the main horizontal line.

GERUND
EXAMPLE: His performance gives *acting* a bad name.

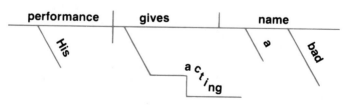

145

Diagraming Gerunds and Gerund Phrases.
Correctly diagram each sentence.

1. Exercising can be a form of relaxation.
2. By exercising, you can improve your physical fitness.
3. Exercise is a way of dealing with some diseases.
4. Being in good physical condition contributes to good emotional health.
5. Exercise is performing activities for your health.

Infinitives and Infinitive Phrases

Infinitives can act as nouns, adjectives, or adverbs. An infinitive acting as a noun is generally diagramed on a pedestal as is a gerund, but the line on which the infinitive is written is simpler. Modifiers included in an infinitive phrase are added to a diagram in the usual way. Complements are also added in the usual way.

EXAMPLE:
    INFINITIVE PHRASE
    To leave early was his goal.

When an infinitive phrase has a subject, it is added to the left on a horizontal line.

EXAMPLE:
    INFINITIVE PHRASE
    I want *you to pay me the ten dollars*.

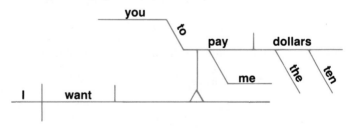

An infinitive used as an adjective or adverb is diagramed in much the same way as a prepositional phrase.

146

EXAMPLE: He will be happy *to drive*.

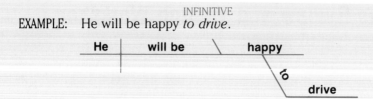

If an infinitive does not include the word *to*, add the word *to* to the sentence diagram but place it in parentheses.

INFINITIVE PHRASE

EXAMPLE: They watched *the ship sail into the harbor*.

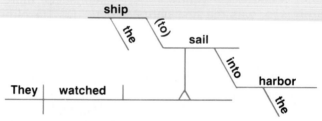

EXERCISE E: Diagraming Infinitives and Infinitive Phrases. Correctly diagram each sentence.

1. This is the road to take.
2. Our goal is to drive across the continent.
3. To pack the car is our next job.
4. My father wants me to study German.
5. We saw Bernstein conduct three symphonies.

DEVELOPING WRITING SKILLS: Writing and Diagraming Sentences with Phrases. Use the following instructions to write five sentences of your own. Then correctly diagram each sentence.

EXAMPLE: Write a sentence that includes a participial phrase.

Blowing his whistle, the referee called a foul.

1. Write a sentence that includes an adjective phrase.
2. Write a sentence that includes an adverb phrase.
3. Write a sentence that includes an appositive.
4. Write a sentence that includes a gerund.
5. Write a sentence that includes an infinitive phrase.

Skills Review and Writing Workshop

Phrases

CHECKING YOUR SKILLS

Write the phrase in each sentence and identify it as a *prepositional, appositive, participial, gerund,* or *infinitive* phrase.

(1) National parks have been created to preserve America's natural beauty. (2) Yellowstone, established more than a century ago, was the first national park. (3) Traveling there is an unforgettable experience. (4) You can see the geyser Old Faithful shoot hot water skyward. (5) Mt. Whitney is located in California's Sequoia National Park. (6) This is also the home of the giant sequoia trees. (7) Crater Lake was created by a volcano. (8) To see the lake, you must visit southern Oregon. (9) Entering Grand Teton National Park, you will observe a beautiful mountain range. (10) Hiking there is fun.

USING GRAMMAR SKILLS IN WRITING

In writing, phrases can add information to your sentences and make them more powerful. Suppose you are a political candidate writing a speech on a topic of national importance. Write a brief, powerful speech by following these steps.

Prewriting: Choose a topic and take a position on it. List three reasons for supporting that position and two arguments to use against people who would oppose your position.

Writing: Begin by stating your position. Then explain your reasons, placing the most important one last. Finally, address those who would oppose your position.

Revising: Look at your phrases to make sure they are used correctly and effectively. Then look for other improvements to be made. After you have revised, proofread carefully.

8

Clauses

Like the phrase, the sentence part known as the *clause* can add interest to your writing.

A clause is a group of words with its own subject and verb.

There are two basic kinds of clauses: *independent clauses* and *subordinate clauses.*

An independent clause can stand by itself as a complete sentence.

Independent clauses can be used in several different ways. The sentence *The boy maneuvered his bicycle around the parked cars* is an example of an independent clause standing alone. *Flora won first prize, and her cousin won second prize* is an example of one independent clause added to another. *He missed us because he woke up late* is an example of an independent clause followed by a subordinate clause. Notice that each independent clause could be written by itself as a complete sentence.

Subordinate clauses differ from independent clauses because they do not express complete thoughts by themselves. Although each subordinate clause has a subject and verb, none expresses a complete thought or can stand by itself as a sentence. Each subordinate clause works with an independent clause to form a complete idea.

A subordinate clause cannot stand by itself as a complete sentence; it can only be part of a sentence.

In the sentence *Flora, who won first prize, is thrilled,* the subordinate clause is *who won first prize.* It appears in the middle of the independent clause *Flora is thrilled. Because he woke up late, he missed us* is a sentence that contains the subordinate clause *because he woke up late.* It appears at the beginning of the sentence, before the independent clause. *They have decided that you should study more* also contains a subordinate clause, *that you should study more.* It appears at the end of the sentence, following the independent clause.

There are three different kinds of subordinate clauses: *adjective, adverb,* and *noun.* The next several sections explain how these different kinds of clauses can help you express more interesting and complex ideas in your writing.

8.1 Adjective Clauses

Adjective clauses add detail to sentences by acting as adjectives.

An adjective clause is a subordinate clause that modifies a noun or pronoun by telling what kind or which one.

The Adjective Clause

Adjective clauses usually begin with one of the *relative pronouns: that, which, who, whom,* or *whose.* (See Section 1.2 for a discussion of relative pronouns.) Sometimes, however, adjective clauses may begin with a *relative adverb,* such as *before, since, when, where,* or *why.* These words are called "relative" pronouns and adverbs because they "relate" a clause to the word it modifies.

Adjective clauses begin with relative pronouns or relative adverbs.

In the chart at the top of the next page, each adjective clause is italicized. The arrows indicate the noun or pronoun that each clause modifies. Notice that the first two clauses begin with relative pronouns. The last two sentences begin with relative adverbs.

ADJECTIVE CLAUSES

Our station wagon, *which lurched into a pothole,* cracked an axle.

We selected those *who were best qualified for the job.*

In the year *since I last saw you,* I have been in the hospital twice.

The sun never shines on days *when I can enjoy it.*

You can tell that these clauses are adjective clauses because they answer the questions *What kind?* and *Which one?* The first clause, for example, tells which station wagon.

Modification of Nouns and Pronouns. Like single-word adjectives or adjective phrases, adjective clauses may modify any noun or pronoun in a sentence. The following examples suggest only a few of the many possibilities.

MODIFYING A SUBJECT: The city *where I would like to live* is Florence.

MODIFYING A DIRECT OBJECT: We scolded the puppy *that chewed up the shoes.*

MODIFYING THE OBJECT OF A PREPOSITION: I wrote to my uncle *who lives in Tulsa.*

Placement in Sentences. An adjective clause must closely follow the word it modifies. If it does not, the meaning of the sentence may become unclear.

CORRECT: The person *whom you saw in the car* is my cousin.

INCORRECT: The person in the car *whom you saw* is my cousin.

Punctuation. Adjective clauses are set off by commas only when they are not essential to the meaning of a sentence. As you can see in the chart at the top of this page, only the first sentence has a clause set off with commas. The clauses in the other three sentences are essential to the meaning of those sentences.

151

Used to Combine Sentences. Adjective clauses often allow you to combine information from two sentences into one sentence. They not only add detail to sentences but also indicate the relationship between ideas.

TWO SENTENCES: Robert Lowell was a major American poet. His ancestors include the poets James Russell Lowell and Amy Lowell.

COMBINED: Robert Lowell, *whose ancestors include the poets James Russell Lowell and Amy Lowell,* was a major American poet.

EXERCISE A: Identifying Adjective Clauses. Write the adjective clause in each sentence. Then circle the relative pronoun or relative adverb in each.

EXAMPLE: The town where I live is peaceful.

(where) I live

1. I met a woman who works with your mother.
2. Have you thought of a place where we can meet?
3. Is this the person whom you saw in the library?
4. I found the book that I needed.
5. She remembers the days when there were trolley cars.
6. Did Harriet tell you the reason why she left?
7. I lost the sweater that Aunt Sue made me.
8. Have they found the girl who was lost?
9. Most people who visit the museum are impressed.
10. The pictures that I took are not ready yet.

EXERCISE B: Identifying Adjective Clauses and the Words They Modify. Write the adjective clause in each sentence. Then write the word the adjective clause modifies.

EXAMPLE: The town where she lives is hectic.

where she lives   town

1. Crocuses are usually the first flowers that bloom.
2. She works in the town where the movie was filmed.
3. The boys who play handball with me go to Central.
4. Is this the weekend that you are leaving?

152

5. The scene that reveals the heroine's secret is the best.
6. The dessert that I ordered never came.
7. Did you find all of the tools that you needed?
8. They can subpoena anyone who refuses to testify.
9. The books that you ordered will be in next week.
10. Is he the one who told you about the meeting?

Relative Pronouns

A *relative pronoun* has two functions in a sentence with an adjective clause. First, it connects the adjective clause to the word the clause modifies. Second, it acts *within the clause* as a subject, direct object, object of a preposition, or adjective.

Relative pronouns connect adjective clauses to the words they modify and act as subjects, direct objects, objects of prepositions, or adjectives in the clauses.

You can tell how a relative pronoun is being used within a clause by separating the clause from the rest of the sentence and then finding the subject and verb in the clause. Sometimes, you may have to turn the words in the clause around just as you would with a question.

THE USES OF RELATIVE PRONOUNS WITHIN CLAUSES
As a Subject
The boat *that is barely visible on the horizon* is ours.
Clause: that is barely visible on the horizon
Subject: that   *Verb:* is
Use of relative pronoun: subject
As a Direct Object
The movie *that you recommended* is no longer playing.
Clause: that you recommended
Reworded clause: you recommended that
Subject: you   *Verb:* recommended
Use of relative pronoun: direct object

As an Object of a Preposition
The person *of whom you spoke* happens to be my friend.
Clause: of whom you spoke
Reworded clause: you spoke of whom
Subject: you   *Verb:* spoke
Use of relative pronoun: object of a preposition

NOTE ABOUT UNDERSTOOD WORDS: Sometimes a relative pronoun is left out of an adjective clause. The missing word, nevertheless, is understood and still functions in the sentence.

EXAMPLES: The flowers [*that*] *she bought* made him sneeze.

The relatives [*whom*] *they visited* were cousins.

EXERCISE C: Recognizing the Uses of Relative Pronouns. Write the adjective clause in each sentence, circling the relative pronoun. Then label the use of the relative pronoun within the clause as *subject, direct object, object of a preposition,* or *adjective.*

EXAMPLE: Leonardo, who is greatly admired, was an artist.

(who) is greatly admired   (subject)

(1) Leonardo da Vinci, whose paintings are among the most famous in the world, was born in 1452 in Italy. (2) As a teenager Leonardo was apprenticed to a painter, with whom he worked for several years. (3) Later, Leonardo moved to Milan to work for a duke who needed the services of an artist. (4) There he designed artillery and planned ways to change the course of rivers, tasks that were usually the jobs of an engineer. (5) Leonardo also designed revolving stages, on which plays were performed. (6) He planned a statue of the duke's father who was shown riding a horse. (7) Leonardo also kept notebooks that contain scientific drawings and ideas for inventions. (8) In the notebooks are drawings that many consider among the first accurate ones of human anatomy. (9) In Florence, a city to which he later moved, Leonardo made sketches of his ideas. (10) These include a movable bridge, a parachute, and a flying machine that resembles a helicopter.

154

Relative Adverbs

Like a relative pronoun, a *relative adverb* connects clauses while playing a role within the adjective clause.

Relative adverbs connect adjective clauses to the words they modify and act as adverbs in the clauses.

Unlike the relative pronoun, however, the relative adverb has only one use within the clause. It acts only as an adverb.

THE USE OF RELATIVE ADVERBS WITHIN CLAUSES

The settlers cleared a plot of land *where they could build*.

Reworded clause: they could build where

Subject: they   *Verb:* could build

Use of relative adverb: adverb

EXERCISE D: Recognizing the Use of Relative Adverbs. Write the adjective clause in each sentence, circling the relative adverb. Then draw an arrow from the relative adverb to the word or words it modifies.

EXAMPLE: The street where Joyce lives is near the library.

(where) Joyce lives

1. Anna wouldn't tell us the reason why she quit.
2. In the week since the report was filed, many of the facts have been changed.
3. It was a day when we all enjoyed every minute.
4. The stands where the dignitaries would sit were draped with bunting.
5. In the twelve years since I visited Greece, I have learned to speak German.
6. Weddings are times when many people cry.
7. Dinner was served in the room where the board was meeting.
8. The doctor determined the reason why the patient's fever had risen.
9. The hour before the party began was a hectic time.
10. We finally reached the place where we had left our gear.

EXAMPLE: The letter will be mailed today. I wrote the letter.

The letter <u>that I wrote</u> will be mailed today.

1. Give this package to the person. The person is at the door.
2. Tomorrow is the day. School starts then.
3. The player struck out. He is everyone's favorite.
4. The book is about Africa. I got the book from the library.
5. The candidate has withdrawn for some reason. No one knows the reason.
6. We followed the path. The path led into the woods.
7. We all have some moments. We need to be alone then.
8. Mount Everest is a lofty mountain. Very few people have climbed it.
9. The farm has an old barn. The children like to play there.
10. The candidate spoke at length. He used a manuscript.

8.2 Adverb Clauses

In addition to acting as adjectives, subordinate clauses can act as adverbs.

Subordinate adverb clauses modify verbs, adjectives, adverbs, or verbals by telling where, when, in what manner, to what extent, under what condition, or why.

The Adverb Clause

All *adverb clauses* begin with the same part of speech.

All adverb clauses begin with subordinating conjunctions.

The chart at the top of the next page lists some of the subordinating conjunctions that are most commonly used. (See Section 4.2 for a more complete list and a review of subordinating conjunctions.)

156

SUBORDINATING CONJUNCTIONS		
after	even though	unless
although	if	until
as	in order that	when
as if	since	whenever
as long as	so that	where
because	than	wherever
before	though	while

Knowing these words can help you identify adverb clauses. In the following examples, each adverb clause is italicized. The arrows indicate the words that the clauses modify.

ADVERB CLAUSES

Wherever he travels, he collects souvenirs.

I will help you with your chemistry *whenever you ask.*

He ran *as if he had a twisted ankle.*

She ran more rapidly *than I did.*

If it rains, we will go to the museum.

Jeanette wanted to stay *because the band was good.*

Adverb clauses answer the questions adverbs answer. The first clause above tells where, the second tells when, and so on. The last two clauses are special in that they answer questions that simple adverbs can not: *Under what condition?* and *Why?*

Modification of Different Words. An adverb clause can modify a verb, adjective, adverb, or any of the three kinds of verbals.

MODIFYING A VERB: She will lose the job *unless she returns the call immediately.*

MODIFYING AN ADJECTIVE: Mother was happy *because I did well on the test.*

157

MODIFYING AN ADVERB: The storm struck sooner *than the fore-casters expected.*

MODIFYING A PARTICIPLE: Smiling *so that he wouldn't seem nervous,* Mark asked her to the dance.

MODIFYING A GERUND: Jogging *when you are not wearing the right shoes* is foolish.

MODIFYING AN INFINITIVE: They decided to stay *after the meeting ended.*

Placement in Sentences. Adverb clauses can be placed at the beginning, in the middle, or at the end of a sentence. When the clause is at the beginning or in the middle of a sentence, it is set off by commas.

EXAMPLES: *When it rains,* the river often floods.

The river, *when it rains,* often floods.

The river often floods *when it rains.*

Sometimes the position of an adverb clause can affect the meaning of the sentence. To be safe, you should generally place the clause as close as possible to the word you want it to modify. Notice in the following examples how the placement of the adverb clause changes the word that the clause modifies.

EXAMPLES: *After the meeting ended,* they decided to stay.

They decided to stay *after the meeting ended.*

Used to Combine Sentences. Like adjective clauses, adverb clauses often can be used to combine information from two sentences into one sentence.

TWO SENTENCES: We were outside. The cat broke the vase.

COMBINED: *While we were outside,* the cat broke the vase.

EXERCISE A: Identifying Adverb Clauses. Write the adverb clause in each sentence. Then circle the subordinating conjunction in each.

158

EXAMPLE: We arrived after the band had left.

(after) the band had left

1. Will you move the couch when you have time?
2. Because the music was so loud, I got a headache.
3. No one came since I forgot to mail the invitations.
4. Did you see Alex when you were in Bloomington?
5. My ride came before I had finished breakfast.
6. Even though it was raining, we enjoyed the day.
7. Mimi takes her dog wherever she goes.
8. Have you heard from James since I saw you last.
9. She stayed there until the report was finished.
10. Before you leave, please stop by my office.

EXERCISE B: **Identifying Adverb Clauses and the Words They Modify.** Write the adverb clause in each sentence. Then write the word or words the adverb clause modifies.

EXAMPLE: When I was three, I lived in Dallas.

When I was three   lived

1. I called you before I fell asleep.
2. I will not be able to finish while you are here.
3. Will you wait until I get a sweater?
4. Mom likes skating when the ice is thick.
5. Put those books where the others are.
6. The old house was quiet after the guests had left.
7. Though it was still early, many of the picnickers were leaving.
8. I feel better than I did yesterday.
9. Jay stood in the wings while he waited for his cue.
10. Daisy plans to work as soon as we leave.
11. Ed got a stomach cramp after he ate three hamburgers.
12. Everyone was happy because Jan won the election.
13. We arrived early so that we would get good seats.
14. I will be happy to dance whenever you ask.
15. Walking while she juggled three oranges, the aerialist held the audience spellbound.
16. Studying while you watch TV is a bad idea.
17. The litmus paper will change to another color if the solution is acidic.

18. Eating as if they had been starved for days, the team devoured everything in the refrigerator.
19. We decided to stop before the storm grew worse.
20. The children are angelic when they are asleep.

Elliptical Adverb Clauses

When adverb clauses beginning with *as* or *than* are used to express comparisons, words are sometimes left out. These are called *elliptical clauses*.

An elliptical clause is a clause in which the verb or subject and verb are understood but not actually stated.

The missing words in an elliptical clause still function in the sentence. In the following examples, the missing words have been added in brackets.

VERB UNDERSTOOD: I respect him more *than she* [*does*].

SUBJECT AND VERB UNDERSTOOD: I respect him more *than* [*I respect*] *her*.

When writing elliptical clauses, you should mentally add the missing words to help make sure that the sentence says what you want it to.

EXERCISE C: **Recognizing Elliptical Adverb Clauses.** Write each sentence, adding the missing words in any elliptical clause. Then underline the complete adverb clause in each sentence and circle any words you have added.

EXAMPLE: I like cake more than candy.

I like cake more than (I like) candy.

1. The other members were more restless than I.
2. We found our backpacks where we had left them.
3. The thieves acted as if no one knew their whereabouts.
4. The San Mateo Matadors are ranked higher in football than our team.
5. The actors wanted the new spotlights more than a videotape machine.

160

6. John dozed on the couch while the other guests finished the meal.
7. Mary's younger sister is as tall as she.
8. We set the alarm clock so that we would not oversleep.
9. The children feared the dentist more than the doctor.
10. The whooping crane is almost as scarce as the dinosaur.

DEVELOPING WRITING SKILLS: Using Adverb Clauses to Combine Sentences. Turn each pair of sentences into a single sentence with an adverb clause. Then underline each adverb clause.

EXAMPLE: I couldn't go to the play. I was sick in bed.

I couldn't go to the play <u>because I was sick in bed</u>.

1. The temperature in the oven was too high. The turkey was burnt outside but still raw inside.
2. Our parents were worried. We hadn't phoned them.
3. Professor Wilkes was grumpy. Someone interrupted his work.
4. We were enjoying our sailing. A storm arose.
5. I was waiting for a call about the job I wanted. I jumped every time the phone rang.
6. The store is close to my house. The library is even closer.
7. We were not ready to play. We practiced harder.
8. You finish school at 3:00. Meet me in the parking lot.
9. Our time was up. Most of us had finished the test.
10. The police had checked all the pawn shops. They found no trace of the stolen goods.

Noun Clauses 8.3

In addition to acting as adjectives and adverbs, subordinate clauses can also act as nouns.

A noun clause is a subordinate clause that acts as a noun.

The Noun Clause

A *noun clause* acts much like a single-word noun in a sentence.

161

In a sentence a noun clause may act as a subject, direct object, indirect object, predicate nominative, or object of a preposition.

The following chart shows noun clauses functioning as several different parts of sentences.

NOUN CLAUSES

Subject: Whomever you bring will be welcome.

Direct object: Carl does whatever his parents ask.

Indirect object: The teacher gave whoever presented an oral report extra credit.

Predicate nominative: The big question is whether he will be allowed to play on the team.

Object of a preposition: Hand your ticket to whoever is standing at the door.

EXERCISE A: Identifying Noun Clauses. Write the noun clause in each sentence. Then label the clause as a *subject, direct object, predicate nominative,* or *object of a preposition.*

EXAMPLE: Andy wished that they would leave.

that they would leave   (direct object)

1. No one understands why Tim is afraid of the dark.
2. Jean chose to write about how bees communicate.
3. Where the treasure is buried remains a mystery.
4. He wrote to whoever promised to write back.
5. Our biggest worry was where we would end up.
6. My sister has not decided what she wants to study.
7. That he didn't ask his neighbors to the party suggests his dislike of them.
8. The most difficult question was whether the land should be rezoned.
9. He gave whoever flattered him his friendship.
10. They consulted about who would do the job.
11. We wondered which route was shorter.
12. Her excuse was that she had lost the assignment.
13. Why he dropped the class isn't clear.
14. Whomever you hire must speak French.

15. They worried about how they would cross Death Valley.
16. She gave whatever crossed her desk a careful examination.
17. Our neighbor was angered by whoever rang his doorbell.
18. We are seldom pleased with what they tell us.
19. They always prepared whomever they invited a lavish meal.
20. That Joe won did not surprise his friends.

Introductory Words

Noun clauses often begin with the words *that, which, who, whom,* and *whose.* These are the same pronouns that can be used to begin adjective clauses. Noun clauses may also start with variants of these words: *whichever, whoever,* or *whomever.* Other noun clauses begin with the words *how, if, what, whatever, when, where, whether,* or *why.* Most of these words play roles within the noun clauses.

Introductory words may act as subjects, direct objects, objects of prepositions, adjectives, or adverbs in noun clauses, or they may simply introduce the clauses.

The examples show some roles introductory words play.

THE USE OF INTRODUCTORY WORDS WITHIN NOUN CLAUSES
Subject: Pat will agree with *whoever speaks first.*
Adverb: How you decorate reflects your personality.
Adjective: The argument raged over *whose car we should take.*
No function in clause: Your score will determine *whether you pass.*

Because so many different words may be used to introduce a noun clause, the words themselves often give no clue as to whether or not the clause is a noun clause. Thus, you must look at the clause's function in the sentence to determine if it is a noun clause. The clauses in the examples on the next page all begin with *that,* but only the first is a noun clause. It is a noun clause because it is acting as a direct object.

NOUN CLAUSE: She remembered *that she had no choice.*

ADJECTIVE CLAUSE: The card *that she received* made her laugh.

ADVERB CLAUSE: His sisters were happy *that he was there.*

NOTE ABOUT INTRODUCTORY WORDS: Sometimes the introductory word *that* is left out of a noun clause. The missing word is understood.

EXAMPLE: My mother feared [*that*] *we would arrive late.*

EXERCISE B: Recognizing the Uses of Introductory Words. Write the noun clause in each sentence, circling the introductory word. Then label the use of the introductory word in the clause as *subject, direct object, object of a preposition, adjective, adverb,* or a word with *no function.*

EXAMPLE: (Ellen) knew that she would be late.

   that she would be late   (no function)

1. Do you know whether Ms. Hall will be in today?
2. What she wanted to speak about was Judy's decision.
3. Just leave a message with whoever answers the phone.
4. Pete feared that he would forget his lines.
5. The university catalog lists which professor gives each course.
6. Whether you go or stay makes no difference.
7. Do you know whose keys these are?
8. The governor said that she would not run again.
9. The real issue is who would do a better job.
10. We began without knowing where we were headed.
11. Whoever draws the short straw must do the dishes.
12. No one told us what we were looking for.
13. The rumor is that the house is haunted.
14. Someone should have told us how he would react.
15. No one could remember where the keys were.
16. Promise me that you will not forget to write.
17. Did she tell you whether Sheila will be there?
18. When we would arrive was hard to estimate.
19. We argued about where we would eat.
20. Alicia wondered which door she should choose.

164

DEVELOPING WRITING SKILLS: Writing Sentences with Noun Clauses. Write ten sentences of your own with noun clauses. Then underline the noun clause in each and label its use in the sentence.

EXAMPLE: <u>What he wrote</u> was illegible.   (subject)

Sentences Classified by 8.4 Structure and Function

All sentences can be classified in two ways. First, they can be classified by structure—that is, by the number and types of clauses they contain. Second, they can be classified by function—that is, by whether they state ideas, ask questions, give orders, or express surprise.

The Four Structures of Sentences

There are two kind of clauses: independent and subordinate. These can be used to form four basic sentence structures: *simple, compound, complex,* and *compound-complex.*

A simple sentence consists of a single independent clause.

Although a *simple sentence* is just one independent clause with one subject and one verb, the subject, verb, or both may be compound. A simple sentence may also have modifying phrases and complements. However, it can not have a subordinate clause.

In the following simple sentences, the subjects are underlined once and the verbs twice.

ONE SUBJECT AND VERB: The <u>snow</u> <u>melted</u>.

COMPOUND SUBJECT: <u>Baseball</u> and <u>soccer</u> <u>are</u> <u>played</u>.

COMPOUND VERB: The <u>tree</u> <u>rotted</u> and <u>died</u>.

COMPOUND SUBJECT AND VERB: Neither the <u>driver</u> nor the <u>skier</u> <u>heard</u> or <u>saw</u> the other boat.

WITH PHRASES AND COMPLEMENT: Melting quickly, <u>snow</u> from the mountains <u>flooded</u> the valley.

165

A *compound sentence* is simply a combination of two or more simple sentences.

A compound sentence consists of two or more independent clauses.

The clauses in a compound sentence can be joined by a comma and a coordinating conjunction *(and, but, for, nor, or, so, yet)* or by a semicolon (;). Like a simple sentence, a compound sentence contains no subordinate clauses.

EXAMPLES: <u>Alice</u> <u>skimmed</u> the leaves from the pool, but <u>she</u>
<u>forgot</u> to add chlorine.

<u>Stan</u> <u>read</u> the book Friday; <u>he</u> <u>wrote</u> his essay today.

Subordinate clauses appear in the third type of sentence structure—*complex sentences*.

A complex sentence consists of one independent clause and one or more subordinate clauses.

The independent clause in a complex sentence is often called the *main clause* to distinguish it from the subordinate clause or clauses. The subject and verb in the independent clause are called the *subject of the sentence* and the *main verb*. Note in the second example how a subordinate clause may fall between the parts of a main clause.

EXAMPLES: MAIN CLAUSE   SUBORDINATE CLAUSE
<u>No one</u> <u>answered</u> the phone when <u>she</u> <u>called</u> us.

MAIN SUBORDINATE CLAUSE CLAUSE
The <u>letter</u> which <u>I</u> <u>had mailed</u>, never <u>arrived</u>.

In complex sentences with noun clauses, the subject of the main clause may sometimes be the subordinate clause itself.

MAIN CLAUSE
SUBORDINATE CLAUSE
EXAMPLE: That <u>I</u> <u>wanted</u> to go <u>bothered</u> them.

The last structure is the *compound-complex* structure.

A compound-complex sentence consists of two or more independent clauses and one or more subordinate clauses.

EXAMPLE: The <u>truck</u> <u>broke</u> down, and the <u>family</u> <u>walked</u> ten

INDEPENDENT CLAUSE   INDEPENDENT CLAUSE

miles because <u>no one</u> <u>passed</u> <u>who</u> <u>could rescue</u>

SUBORDINATE CLAUSE   SUBORDINATE CLAUSE

them.

EXERCISE A: Identifying the Structure of Sentences.
Identify each sentence as *simple, compound, complex,* or *compound-complex.*

EXAMPLE: I got the one that I wanted.

complex

1. We chose one way; they chose another.
2. They learned a dance with a variety of steps.
3. Whenever Angelo gets to school early, he talks to his friends.
4. The vibrations from the jet caused the vase to fall and crack.
5. The gum stuck to his face; it looked like glue.
6. Stuck to his face, the gum looked like glue.
7. The gum that stuck to his face looked like glue.
8. My uncle planned to drive to work, but he couldn't until the snowplows cleared the roads.
9. She wanted to go on the study tour, yet she could not bring herself to spend all of her savings.
10. Because Kelly forgot to water her plants, they wilted.
11. The game of football is fun, but I prefer soccer because it is safer.
12. My pet rabbit escaped through a hole in the fence.
13. Both Mom and Dad enjoy camping and fishing.
14. Hank carries his Swiss Army knife everywhere he goes.
15. Everyone I asked gave me the same answer.
16. When it started to rain, the game was called, so we went to a movie.
17. Days passed, but the survivors of the plane crash still hoped to be rescued.
18. Many drivers saw the incident on the highway, but no one reported it.
19. Everyone who knows Allen admires him.
20. The owner refuses to sell, so the land bordering the highway will not be developed.

167

The Four Functions of Sentences

In addition to classification by the number and types of clauses it contains, a sentence may be classified by function as *declarative, interrogative, imperative,* or *exclamatory.*

A declarative sentence states an idea and ends with a period.

EXAMPLES: Athena sprang fully grown from the forehead of Zeus.

Necessity is the mother of invention.

An interrogative sentence asks a question and ends with a question mark.

EXAMPLES: Which Greek goddess sprang fully grown from the forehead of Zeus?

Is necessity the mother of invention?

An imperative sentence gives an order or a direction and ends with a period or an exclamation mark.

EXAMPLES: Clean up your room.

Help!

Most imperative sentences do not contain stated subjects. Some do, however. Generally, these sentences are phrased like questions but do not have a question mark at the end.

EXAMPLES: Will you please return the letter immediately.

Would someone help with these bags, please.

An exclamatory sentence conveys strong emotion and ends with an exclamation mark.

EXAMPLES: He is still not home!

What a beautiful day it is!

Some exclamatory sentences may look like questions, but they are exclamatory if the emotions behind the words are strong.

EXAMPLES: Can you believe that!

What are you doing!

EXERCISE B: Identifying the Function of Sentences.
Identify each sentence as *declarative, interrogative, imperative,* or *exclamatory*. Then write the end mark for each sentence.

EXAMPLE: I decided to run for class president

declarative

(1) When my friends asked how they could help me campaign for class president, the answer was simple (2) "Make some posters for me" (3) Having little artistic talent, I needed all the help with posters that I could get (4) The next challenge I had to face really worried me—making a campaign speech (5) Should I talk about my previous experience as secretary of the Spanish Club (6) Perhaps I should talk about my ability to get along with my classmates (7) The day of the speech was I nervous (8) I knew what I had to do, and I repeated my task to myself again and again (9) "Go out there and convince them" (10) I guess I succeeded because when the results were announced, I was the new class president.

DEVELOPING WRITING SKILLS: Writing Sentences with Different Structures and Functions. Use the following instructions to write ten sentences of your own.

EXAMPLE: Write a compound interrogative sentence about dogs.

Should we get a poodle, or should we get a dachshund?

1. Write a simple declarative sentence about food.
2. Write a compound declarative sentence about music.
3. Write a complex declarative sentence about homework.
4. Write a compound-complex declarative sentence about politics.
5. Write a simple interrogative sentence about next weekend.
6. Write a compound interrogative sentence about a friend.
7. Write a complex interrogative sentence about the weather.
8. Write a compound-complex interrogative sentence about a sports event.
9. Write a simple imperative sentence about something that needs cleaning.
10. Write a simple exclamatory sentence about the results of the action in Sentence 9.

8.5 Diagraming Clauses

The only major difference in diagraming a sentence with more than one clause is that each clause has its own horizontal line.

Compound Sentences

To diagram a compound sentence, simply diagram each of the independent clauses separately, join the verbs with a dotted line, and write the conjunction or semicolon on the dotted line.

INDEPENDENT CLAUSE   INDEPENDENT CLAUSE

EXAMPLE: *I found his books,* and *I returned them to him.*

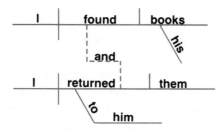

EXERCISE A: Diagraming Compound Sentences. Correctly diagram each sentence.

1. We installed insulation, and our fuel bills are much lower.
2. We can go to the beach today, or we can wait for better weather.
3. School ends soon, and Pauline has not started her paper.
4. Money can be enjoyable, but happiness is more important.
5. The chimpanzee shook the doll, and then he cuddled it in his arms.

Complex Sentences

Complex sentences contain an independent clause and one or more subordinate clauses. The subordinate clauses can be adjective clauses, adverb clauses, noun clauses, or any combination of these.

170

Adjective Clauses. The line on which an adjective clause is placed goes beneath the main line, to which it is connected by a dotted line. The dotted line extends from the noun or pronoun being modified by the clause to the relative pronoun or relative adverb in the adjective clause. The position of the relative pronoun varies depending on its function in the adjective clause. In the following diagram, the relative pronoun is the direct object in the subordinate clause.

ADJECTIVE CLAUSE

EXAMPLE: The table lamps *that you ordered* have just arrived.

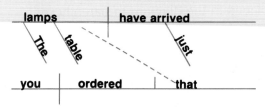

Sometimes an adjective clause may be introduced by a relative pronoun acting as an object of a preposition or as an adjective. The dotted line must be bent to connect the clauses properly. This is also true when the adjective clause is introduced by a relative adverb as the following example illustrates.

ADJECTIVE CLAUSE

EXAMPLE: We visited a laboratory *where testing was done*.

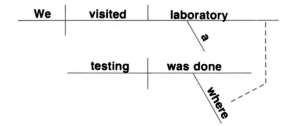

Adverb Clauses. An adverb clause is diagramed in the same way an adjective clause is, except that the subordinating conjunction is written along the dotted line. This line extends from the verb, adjective, adverb, or verbal being modified by the clause to the verb in the adverb clause.

171

EXAMPLE: Gas will be rationed *whenever a shortage occurs.*

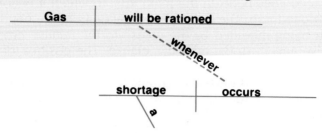

If the adverb clause is elliptical, the understood but unstated words are placed in the diagram in parentheses.

ADVERB CLAUSE

EXAMPLE: The tree in our yard is taller *than the tree in yours.*

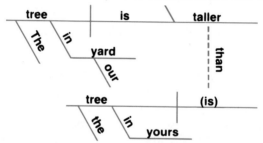

Noun Clauses. To diagram a sentence containing a noun clause, first diagram the independent clause. Then place the noun clause on a pedestal extending upwards from the position the clause fills in the independent clause. The noun clause in the following is acting as the subject of the sentence.

NOUN CLAUSE

EXAMPLE: *Whoever is responsible* will pay for the damage.

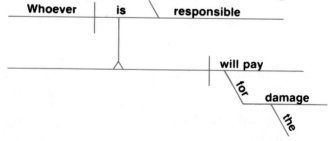

172

When the introductory word in a noun clause has no function in the clause, it is written alongside the pedestal.

NOUN CLAUSE

EXAMPLE: I wonder *whether we should wait for them.*

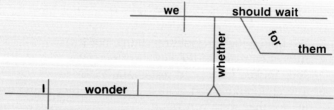

EXERCISE B: **Diagraming Complex Sentences.** Correctly diagram each sentence.

1. The restaurant that we chose is famous for its pastry.
2. When we were in New York City we toured the Stock Exchange.
3. Whatever boat we rent must accommodate six people.
4. The director was furious because the star quit the picture.
5. This chair adjusts to whatever position you desire.

Compound-Complex Sentences

When diagraming a compound-complex sentence, begin by diagraming each of the independent clauses. Then diagram each subordinate clause.

ADVERB CLAUSE   INDEPENDENT CLAUSE

EXAMPLE: *Before the play began, the audience was restless,*

INDEPENDENT CLAUSE

and *the actors were nervous.*

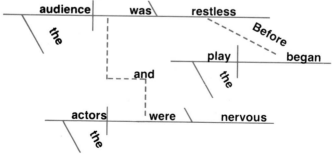

173

Diagraming Compound-Complex Sentences. Correctly diagram each sentence.

1. When their father returned, Jill set the table, and Peter poured the milk.
2. The letter that he received was short, but he read it very slowly.
3. We hoped that it would be sunny, but it was not.
4. After they reached the city, they bought a newspaper, and Judy looked for a good restaurant.
5. The children gasped at their luck when they found the wallet, for they were very poor.

DEVELOPING WRITING SKILLS: Writing and Diagraming Sentences with Clauses. Use the following instructions to write five sentences of your own. Then correctly diagram each sentence.

EXAMPLE: Write a compound-complex sentence with an adjective clause.

The sun rose suddenly, and the birds, who were singing their morning song, woke me up.

1. Write a compound sentence.
2. Write a complex sentence with an adjective clause.
3. Write a complex sentence with an adverb clause.
4. Write a complex sentence with a noun clause.
5. Write a compound-complex sentence with an adjective clause.

Skills Review and Writing Workshop

Clauses

CHECKING YOUR SKILLS

Write the clause in each sentence and identify it as either an *adjective, adverb,* or *noun* clause.

(1) Benjamin Franklin was a man who symbolized the spirit of early America. (2) Although he was born in Boston, Franklin moved to Philadelphia as a young man. (3) When he arrived there, he began working as a printer. (4) Franklin published *Poor Richard's Almanac,* the publication for which he was most famous. (5) Science was also an area that fascinated him. (6) His experiments proved that lightning was a form of electricity. (7) Many of Franklin's achievements occurred when he was an old man. (8) When Franklin was seventy, he attended the Continental Congress. (9) After the Revolutionary War started, he served as ambassador to France. (10) All Americans recognize that Franklin's contributions were important.

USING GRAMMAR SKILLS IN WRITING

Writing a Filmstrip Script

By using clauses, you can vary the structure of your sentences and add vivid details that will enhance your writing. Write a vivid and detailed filmstrip script on an easily illustrated topic.

Prewriting: Select a topic that can be illustrated with a few pictures. Plan an introduction to capture readers' attention.

Writing: Write out your introduction and make sure that all the sentences can be easily illustrated. Present your ideas on the topic. Conclude with a brief summary of these ideas.

Revising: Make sure you have varied the structure of your sentences. Look at your clauses and replace any that could be more effective. Then examine the script and make sure the sentences are clear. After you have revised, proofread carefully.

175

Chapter 9

Avoiding Sentence Errors

As you continue to study sentence structure, you should also become aware of certain common writing problems. *Fragments, run-on sentences,* and *misplaced* or *dangling modifiers* can all confuse your reader and distort your ideas.

In this chapter you will begin to apply your knowledge of grammar to the correction of these common sentence errors. You will correct fragments by writing sentences containing complete ideas. You will place end marks at the end of sentences to avoid run-ons. You will place modifiers correctly so that they will modify the words you want them to modify. By studying sentence errors, you will learn to watch for them and correct them in your own writing.

9.1 Fragments

As noted earlier, a *fragment* is only part of a sentence.

A fragment is a group of words that does not express a complete thought.

A fragment may lack a complete subject, a complete predicate, or the essential part of both. Fragments make writing feel choppy. Because they do not express complete ideas, fragments can also be confusing. The reader does not receive a complete message and, as a result, may be left wondering what was meant.

Recognizing Fragments

In most written work, a fragment is considered an error. This will be true whether it is a lengthy phrase, a subordinate clause, or a long series that does not contain a subject and a verb.

Part of a sentence should not be presented as a full sentence ending with a period or other end mark.

Fragments in the following passage are italicized. Read the passage aloud. Do the fragments sound like complete sentences?

PASSAGE WITH FRAGMENTS

Totally bored with the movie. Jane left her seat to get popcorn. She returned a few minutes later and found David sleeping in his seat. *Apparently was also bored.* Jane nudged him sharply, and he awoke with a start.

If the above passage is rewritten to contain only complete sentences, it will read more smoothly and will also make more sense.

PASSAGE WITHOUT FRAGMENTS

Totally bored with the movie, Jane left her seat to get popcorn. She returned a few minutes later and found David sleeping in his seat. He apparently was also bored. Jane nudged him sharply, and he awoke with a start.

If you find that you use sentence fragments in your writing, learn to read your work aloud. Listen to the natural pauses and stops as you read. With practice you will be able to hear where your sentences should begin and end.

EXERCISE A: Identifying Sentence Fragments. Identify each item as a *fragment* or *sentence*.

EXAMPLE: Leaving early in the morning.

       fragment

 1. A bouquet of freshly cut flowers.
 2. Will arrive between one and two o'clock.
 3. In the jar on top of the refrigerator.
 4. Swimming, skiing, or boating on the lake.
 5. That hurts.
 6. Wanting to write to you.
 7. To know her is to admire her.
 8. Broke all speed records in the last race.
 9. After you sit down, I will begin.
10. A doctor of great skill and devotion to her patients.
11. While we were swimming.
12. Please be seated.
13. Seeing my friend at the concert.
14. If the train is not late.
15. John was angry with us.
16. Because the rain has stopped.
17. Someone left a mess behind.
18. Everyone had voted.
19. Which hangs on the wall.
20. Until the next time we meet.

Correcting Fragments

The two most common kinds of fragments found in writing are phrases and subordinate clauses that are capitalized and punctuated as if they were sentences. Series fragments are also common. Often, such fragments simply need to be linked up with the words that come before or after the fragments. Sometimes, however, they will need additional words to make them into sentences.

In the next few pages, you will see how these fragments can be identified and corrected.

Phrase Fragments. A phrase is a group of words without a subject and verb. By itself, any phrase is a fragment because it does not express a complete idea.

A phrase should not be capitalized and punctuated as if it were a sentence.

A *phrase fragment* may be a noun with modifiers or a verb with modifiers and complements. It may also be a prepositional phrase or a verbal phrase. The way you correct it will depend in part on the type of fragment it is.

Sometimes, especially with prepositional and participial fragments, you can add the fragment to a nearby sentence.

PREPOSITIONAL FRAGMENT: For my uncle.

ADDED TO NEARBY SENTENCE: We chose a new tie *for my uncle.*

Other times, however, you will have to add the missing sentence parts. A noun fragment will usually need a verb or a subject and a verb.

NOUN FRAGMENT: A ten-speed bicycle.

COMPLETED SENTENCES: *A ten-speed bicycle* was first prize.

　　　　　　　　　　　She wanted *a ten-speed bicycle.*

If the noun is modified by a participial phrase, you can turn the participle into a verb by adding a helping verb.

NOUN FRAGMENT: The book written by Hemingway.

COMPLETED SENTENCE: *The book* was *written by Hemingway.*

A verb fragment will need a subject.

VERB FRAGMENT: Were standing on the porch.

COMPLETED SENTENCE: The boys *were standing on the porch.*

A prepositional fragment will need a subject and a verb.

PREPOSITIONAL FRAGMENT: Along the edge of the lake.

COMPLETED SENTENCE: We walked *along the edge of the lake.*

A participial fragment will need a subject and a verb or a subject and a helping verb.

PARTICIPIAL FRAGMENT: Painted green and yellow.

COMPLETED SENTENCES: *Painted green and yellow,* the chairs looked like new.

　　　　　　　　　　　The new chairs were *painted green and yellow.*

179

A gerund fragment will need a verb, a subject and a verb, or a subject and a helping verb.

GERUND FRAGMENT: Sweeping the porch.

COMPLETED SENTENCES: *Sweeping the porch* was her favorite household chore.

She liked *sweeping the porch*.

The old man in gray overalls was *sweeping the porch*.

An infinitive fragment will need a verb or a subject and a verb.

INFINITIVE FRAGMENT: To jog in the park.

COMPLETED SENTENCES: *To jog in the park* was her plan.

They wanted *to jog in the park*.

Clause Fragments. A clause is a group of words containing a subject and verb. An independent clause always expresses a complete thought. A subordinate clause, however, does not express a complete thought even though it has a subject and verb. A subordinate clause must be joined to an independent clause.

Clause fragments must be written as parts of complete sentences, whether you add them to nearby sentences or make up the missing parts yourself.

ADJECTIVE CLAUSE FRAGMENT: That I bought yesterday.

COMPLETED SENTENCE: Today, I will wear the coat *that I bought yesterday*.

ADVERB CLAUSE FRAGMENT: While the radio was playing.

COMPLETED SENTENCE: I wrote the lettter *while the radio was playing*.

NOUN CLAUSE FRAGMENT: Whatever you want.

COMPLETED SENTENCE: He will write *whatever you want*.

Series Fragments. Another type of fragment is a group of words in a series.

180

Words in a series should not be capitalized and punctuated as if they were a sentence.

The way you correct a *series fragment* will depend on the type of words that make up the series. For example, you must add both a subject and a verb to a series of prepositional phrases.

SERIES FRAGMENT: In the morning, at noon, and at the end of the day.

COMPLETED SENTENCE: School announcements are made *in the morning, at noon, and at the end of the day.*

EXERCISE B: Using Phrase Fragments to Write Sentences. Use each fragment in a complete sentence.

EXAMPLE: Among the clouds.

Our hot-air balloon rose higher and higher until it floated among the clouds.

1. On the front page.
2. To sing folk songs professionally.
3. Many beautiful birds.
4. Drinking from a green glass.
5. A dark, menacing cloud.
6. Can't be found anywhere.
7. During the violent storm.
8. Near the zoo.
9. Children laughing and splashing in the water.
10. Were taking too long.

EXERCISE C: Using Clause Fragments to Write Sentences. Use each fragment in a complete sentence.

1. When I awoke this morning.
2. That my class likes best.
3. Unless you practice each day.
4. If it is cold tomorrow.
5. Who waited in line.
6. Although his arm is broken.
7. While we performed on stage.

8. Which was in my pocket.
9. Where we will meet.
10. Even though the starting quarterback was injured.

EXERCISE D: Using Series Fragments to Write Sentences. Use each of the following fragments in a complete sentence.

1. Calico kittens, green parakeets, and dachshund puppies.
2. Ran, skipped, and jumped.
3. In the drawer, on the top shelf of the closet, or under the sink.
4. Deep orange, yellow, or red.
5. Slowly, methodically, and quite gracefully.
6. Never very late, never very early, but never on time.
7. Swimming, fishing, and canoeing on the river.
8. To enjoy life, to work hard, and to get into a good college.
9. Sat still, listened carefully, and tried to learn.
10. Raspberries, blueberries, and grapes.

DEVELOPING WRITING SKILLS: Correcting Fragments. Rewrite the following paragraph, using the methods you have learned to correct all fragments.

(1) In the 1920's archaeologists discovered the remains of an ancient civilization. (2) Located in the Indus Valley in Pakistan and western India. (3) The towns and villages of this civilization thrived. (4) From about 2500 B.C. until about 1700 B.C. (5) No one knows. (6) Why people abandoned those towns and villages. (7) A change in the course of a river, prolonged flooding, or attacks by invaders from the north and west. (8) Many of the people of this ancient civilization lived in small farming villages. (9) Some, however, lived in two larger towns. (10) Studying the ruins of these towns. (11) Scientists have found evidence of carefully planned communities. (12) Stone houses lined the sides of straight streets. (13) Each house had a special bathing room. (14) Which was connected to a central drainage system. (15) Buildings for storing grain. (16) Were centrally located. (17) Unlike the ruins of many other ancient cities. (18) The ruins of the Indus Valley civilization do not seem to contain large temples,

tombs, or palaces. (19) If scientists are ever able to translate the writing found on stone seals. (20) More may be learned about the Indus Valley civilization and its fate.

Run-ons 9.2

Fragments are confusing because they are missing essential parts. Another sentence error is confusing because it places too much information in a sentence. Such overcrowded sentences are called *run-on sentences,* or simply *run-ons.*

A run-on sentence is two or more complete sentences that are not properly joined or separated.

Recognizing Run-ons

There are two kinds of run-on sentences.

Run-ons are two or more independent clauses that are not separated at all or that are separated by only a comma.

One common kind of run-on sentence contains two independent clauses with no punctuation between them.

WITH NO PUNCTUATION: He sat bolt upright chills of fear ran through his body.

Another kind of run-on sentence is made up of two independent clauses with only a comma between them.

WITH ONLY A COMMA: The animals weren't hungry, they had already eaten.

It is important to reread your work to correct any run-ons. Otherwise, a reader may not be able to tell where one thought ends and the next one begins.

EXERCISE A: Identifying Run-ons. Identify each item as a *run-on* or *sentence.*

EXAMPLE: Although he disliked her, he was polite.

           sentence

183

1. Queen Mary slowly entered the huge hall in silence the crowd gathered there gazed at the woman who was about to be executed.
2. Forced onto the sidelines by his torn ligament, Jack was restless and unhappy.
3. Keats came into the house from the garden and casually threw down some paper, on it was written "Ode on a Grecian Urn."
4. Lord Rosse built a telescope in Ireland in 1845, it was often inactive because of poor Irish weather.
5. Though billions of comets circle beyond the edges of our solar system, few come close to the earth.
6. Wind and water are major causes of erosion of the soil, they constantly change the appearance of the earth's surface.
7. Shrimp eggs can survive for over one year in the desert sands, rainwater brings them to life.
8. March is the month when huge blocks of ice in the Arctic begin to melt and break up.
9. In drawings by young children, sizes and shapes of objects often look wrong.
10. Deserts turn cold at night, there is nothing to stop the heat from escaping into the atmosphere.
11. My grandmother loved *Gone with the Wind* she read it years ago.
12. Lightning turns nitrogen in the air into an oxide, it then falls with the rain and fertilizes the soil.
13. The famous Irish writer James Joyce left his native land in 1902 at various times he lived in the cities of Paris, Trieste, and Zurich.
14. For the last fifty years of his life, the poet Robinson Jeffers lived in a tower on the California coast.
15. When the bases are loaded and two players are already out, baseball is at its most exciting.
16. National Parks in this country were established to protect wildlife, preserve natural resources, and provide recreational areas.
17. Crater Lake in the state of Oregon is a unique tourist attraction, it fills a crater on top of an inactive volcano.
18. The typical sonnet has fourteen lines, ten syllables make up each line.

19. The sun's rays striking raindrops can produce a rainbow you can see it if the sun is behind you and the rain is ahead of you.
20. Roosters begin to crow at dawn, they seem to bring the farm to life.

Correcting Run-ons

There are at least five solutions to the problem of run-on sentences. The first method calls for turning the run-on into two sentences. The next two methods call for combining two independent clauses. The last two methods call for some rewriting.

Using End Marks. The simplest way to correct a run-on sentence is to place a period, question mark, or exclamation mark between the two sentences.

Use an end mark to separate run-on sentences.

When using this method, you should choose whichever end mark works best with the first sentence.

RUN-ON: Do most people like criticism I don't think so.

CORRECTED SENTENCES: Do most people like criticism? I don't think so.

RUN-ON: In 79 A.D., Mount Vesuvius erupted, Pompeii was destroyed.

CORRECTED SENTENCES: In 79 A.D., Mount Vesuvius erupted. Pompeii was destroyed.

Using Commas and Conjunctions. A comma itself cannot join two sentences, but a comma with a coordinating conjunction *(and, but, for, nor, or, so, yet)* often works well.

Use a comma and a coordinating conjunction to combine two independent clauses.

When using this method, choose whichever conjunction best expresses the idea you had in mind.

RUN-ON: The sky became dark it began to rain.

CORRECTED SENTENCE: The sky became dark, and it began to rain.

RUN-ON: You may visit the White House, you can tour the museums.

CORRECTED SENTENCE: You may visit the White House, or you can tour the museums.

Using Semicolons. When two parts of a run-on are closely related in meaning, a semicolon can be used to correct the run-on.

Use a semicolon to connect two closely related ideas.

The two sentences in each of the following run-ons are closely related because they work together to present a particular idea.

RUN-ON: The camper wasn't frightened by the bear he was terrified.

CORRECTED SENTENCES: The camper wasn't frightened by the bear; he was terrified.

RUN-ON: She swims often, water relaxes her.

CORRECTED SENTENCES: She swims often; water relaxes her.

Do not let transitions such as *however, for example,* and *moreover* fool you into writing run-on sentences. When these words are used to join two closely related sentences, a semicolon should be placed before the transition and a comma after it.

RUN-ON: Our team played hard, however we lost by a staggering margin.

CORRECTED SENTENCE: Our team played hard; however, we lost by a staggering margin.

Forming a Simple Sentence. You can often correct run-ons by adjusting the sentence structure. One way to do this is to form a simple sentence by finding some way to get one of the ideas into a phrase or to make it part of a compound subject or verb.

Rewrite run-ons to form simple sentences.

The examples on the next page show three run-ons and possible ways to correct them. In the first example, the run-on can

186

be corrected by placing some of the information in an appropriate phrase.

RUN-ON: Ms. Jenner is the coach of our cross-country team, she has placed us on a rigorous training program.

SENTENCE WITH   Ms. Jenner, *the coach of our cross-country*
APPOSITIVE PHRASE: *team,* has placed us on a rigorous training program.

In the next example, the run-on can be corrected by rewriting it as one sentence with a compound subject.

RUN-ON: Ms. Jenner often runs with us, her assistant also runs with us.

SENTENCE WITH   *Ms. Jenner and her assistant* often run
COMPOUND SUBJECT: with us.

In the last example, the run-on can be corrected by rewriting it as one sentence with a compound verb.

RUN-ON: Before the season opened, some runners bought new shoes, they also practiced regularly.

SENTENCE WITH   Before the season opened, some runners
COMPOUND VERB: bought new shoes and practiced regularly.

Forming a Complex Sentence. If the two sentences in a run-on are related to one another, they can often be rewritten as one complex sentence. The information in one of the sentences can be put into a subordinate clause.

Rewrite run-ons to form complex sentences.

Consider the two sentences in the following run-on.

RUN-ON: Some people do not go to college it costs too much.

The second sentence tells *why* some people do not go to college. With the addition of the word *because,* the second sentence becomes a subordinate clause.

SENTENCE WITH   Some people do not go to college *be-*
SUBORDINATE CLAUSE: *cause it costs too much.*

Generally, one of the clauses will obviously be the one to make into a subordinate clause. Sometimes, however, either of the sentences can be chosen.

RUN-ON: I helped wash the car, Dad did most of the work.

SENTENCES WITH   I helped wash the car *although Dad did*
SUBORDINATE CLAUSES: *most of the work.*

                         Although I helped wash the car, Dad
                         did most of the work.

EXERCISE B: **Using Punctuation and Conjunctions to Correct Run-ons.** Use an end mark, a comma and a coordinating conjunction, or a semicolon to correct each run-on. Use each method at least twice.

EXAMPLE: The cash was hidden in a rusty tin can nobody
           thought to look inside it.

           The cash was hidden in a rusty tin can, but nobody
           thought to look inside it.

1. I could hardly wait to jump in the water looked so inviting.
2. They seemed to expect me to babysit again, I wouldn't do it for any price.
3. A stray dog wandered onto the field, the outfielder tried to catch it.
4. We spent hours searching for the car keys we never found them.
5. Would you care for French dressing on your salad, would you prefer it unseasoned?
6. Everyone else was on time for the party Jason arrived an hour late.
7. The dry river basin came to life, the caked soil became green with grass.
8. We enjoyed a long afternoon of play, afterwards, everyone ate an enormous supper.
9. Helen practiced for many hours she was determined to win the prize.
10. We were very surprised when we opened the trunk of our car, a family of squirrels had moved in.

EXERCISE C: **Forming Simple and Complex Sentences to Correct Run-ons.** Form a simple or complex sentence to correct each run-on. Use each method at least four times.

EXAMPLE: The sun set, the forest was quiet.

    When the sun set, the forest was quiet.

1. Mr. Adams was a candidate for mayor, he spoke to many community organizations.
2. The iguana raced across the yard it was a family pet.
3. The snow was piled around the parked cars, it made it impossible for us to leave.
4. The child was delighted with the gift, he began to play with it right away.
5. I couldn't handle the luggage alone I had three suitcases and a small trunk.
6. My sister studies hard, she is a medical student.
7. After the flood the people along the waterfront returned home, they began to repair the damage.
8. My mother still finds time to play tennis she is a news reporter as well as a homemaker.
9. My best friend won the scholarship she is also a superb athlete.
10. The car is old and has a lot of miles on it it still runs well.

DEVELOPING WRITING SKILLS: Correcting Run-ons.
Rewrite the following paragraphs, correcting all run-ons.

(1) After flying through a dense, seemingly endless cloud bank, the shuttle plane with its pilot, co-pilot, and three nervous passengers was lost. (2) The pilot could not recognize any landmarks, the co-pilot could not recognize any either. (3) One of the passengers, a young girl, entered the pilot's cabin and asked if she could help. (4) Although worried, the pilot smiled, he was very good-natured.

(5) The girl explained that she recognized the terrain her father had taken her camping in these hills just last summer. (6) "If you turn slightly and fly over that far ridge," explained the girl, "you will see a highway. (7) Follow it west it will lead toward Pescadora."

(8) The pilot and co-pilot thanked the girl and complimented her on her keen sense of direction. (9) Their praises pleased the girl, they also gave her an idea. (10) As soon as she finished school, she would take flying lessons.

9.3 Misplaced and Dangling Modifiers

A third kind of sentence error is caused by faulty placement of modifiers within a sentence.

A modifier should be placed as close as possible to the word it modifies.

Recognizing Misplaced Modifiers

Most problems with modifiers arise when a modifier is placed too far from the word it modifies. The modifier is then called a *misplaced modifier*. When modifiers are not placed to their best advantage, the reader may be confused.

A misplaced modifier appears to modify the wrong word in a sentence.

Notice how the placement of the italicized modifier in the following sentence might cause confusion.

MISPLACED MODIFIER: *Coming in for a landing,* ground control radioed to the distressed airliner.

It seems as if ground control is coming in for a landing. In fact, that is precisely what a reader might think because the modifying phrase is placed next to the words *ground control.* The writer probably intended the phrase to modify the word *airliner.* Therefore, the phrase should have been placed closer to that word.

CORRECTED SENTENCE: Ground control radioed to the distressed airliner *coming in for a landing.*

EXERCISE A: **Recognizing Misplaced Modifiers.** Write each misplaced modifier. If a sentence is correct, write *correct*.

EXAMPLE: The baby crawled on the floor with blue overalls.

with blue overalls

1. The messenger spoke to the receptionist who delivered the package.
2. The golfer won the trophy wearing green golf shoes.

3. Our desire grew smaller to win the prize.
4. Reading the menu, Hugh decided to have steak again.
5. Finishing the dishes, we were ready to relax.
6. The kitten drank the milk that was hungry.
7. I hurried to open the gift happily surprised.
8. Sailing into port, my grandfather stood at the wheel of his beautiful new boat.
9. Soaring gracefully over the treetops, I watched the hawk disappear from view.
10. Badly frightened, the puppy cowered under the porch.

Correcting Misplaced Modifiers

A misplaced modifier is usually a prepositional phrase, a participial phrase, or an adjective clause.

Correct a misplaced modifier by moving the phrase or clause closer to the word it should logically modify.

The following examples show some of the ways that misplaced modifiers can be corrected.

MISPLACED PREPOSITIONAL PHRASE: A man leaped into the water *over the ship's rail.*

CORRECTED SENTENCE: A man leaped *over the ship's rail* into the water.

MISPLACED PARTICIPAL PHRASE: *Smashed beyond repair,* Rob saw his watch lying on the court.

CORRECTED SENTENCE: Rob saw his watch, *smashed beyond repair,* lying on the court.

MISPLACED ADJECTIVE CLAUSE: Seeing the miner and his mule approaching, the bandits loaded their rifles *that were perched atop a rock.*

CORRECTED SENTENCE: Seeing the miner and his mule approaching, the bandits *that were perched atop a rock* loaded their rifles.

191

of the following sentences, correcting each misplaced modifier. Then underline the corrected modifier and draw an arrow from it to the word it modifies.

EXAMPLE: The child ran into the house crying loudly.

Crying loudly, the child ran into the house.

1. A sundae was served to each guest, dripping with chocolate sauce.
2. Wilkins realized the mistake he had made after a few minutes.
3. The dean spoke to the boys about loitering in the principal's office.
4. We gave the scraps of meat to the dog that had been left on our plates.
5. Michelle bought an umbrella after shopping carefully with red and yellow stripes.
6. The ballad singer heard most of the songs he later sang wandering through the hill country.
7. The hunter crouched behind a tree waiting for a bear to come along with a bow and arrow.
8. Trying to catch the scent, the sheriff gave the bloodhound one of the fugitive's socks.
9. We saw many beautiful homes driving through the South.
10. Wilma put the trophies into a glass cabinet that she had won in golf tournaments.

Recognizing Dangling Modifiers

Problems also arise when a modified word seems to be missing entirely. Then the modifier is known as a *dangling modifier*. Readers are often confused by dangling modifiers.

A dangling modifier appears to modify either the wrong word or no word at all because the word it should logically modify is missing.

Reading a sentence that contains a dangling modifier can make a reader stop to guess what the missing word might be.

DANGLING MODIFIER: *Giving a party,* several balloons were blown up.

The italicized modifier should describe whoever gave the party, but no word in the sentence identifies the partygiver. Adding the missing word can correct this problem.

CORRECTED SENTENCE: *Giving a party,* they blew up several balloons.

EXERCISE C: Recognizing Dangling Modifiers. Write each dangling modifier. If a sentence is correct, write *correct.*

EXAMPLE: Carrying so many packages, the path was hard to follow.

   Carrying so many packages

1. Skating across the pond, the ice was very slick.
2. Studying for weeks, the test was easy.
3. Considering my small allowance, the tickets were expensive.
4. Writing letters at camp all afternoon, home seemed far away.
5. Finishing the dishes, we were ready to relax.
6. The roast was forgotten greeting the guests.
7. Running to catch the bus, I stumbled and almost fell.
8. Traveling for hours, we finally reached our destination, the best trout stream in the state.
9. The smell of freshly baked bread reached my nose watching television.
10. Lost in a strange city, the theater could not be found.

Correcting Dangling Modifiers

A dangling modifier is usually a participial phrase or an adverb clause.

Correct a dangling modifier by rewriting the sentence to include the missing word.

With a dangling participial phrase, the missing word can be added after the phrase, or the phrase can be rewritten as a clause. In the first corrected example on the next page, the missing word has been added after the phrase. In the second, the phrase has been expanded into a clause.

DANGLING PARTICIPIAL PHRASE: *Driving through the desert at night,* the cactuses looked eerie.

CORRECTED SENTENCES: *Driving through the desert at night,* we thought the cactuses looked eerie.

When we were driving through the desert at night, the cactuses looked eerie.

With a dangling clause, you will generally find it sufficient to make the clause itself more specific.

DANGLING ADVERB CLAUSE: *When he was three years old,* Jerry's uncle entered medical school.

CORRECTED SENTENCE: *When Jerry was three years old,* his uncle entered medical school.

EXERCISE D: Correcting Dangling Modifiers. Write each sentence, correcting the dangling modifier. Then underline the correct modifier and draw an arrow from it to the word it modifies.

EXAMPLE: Losing hope, the mountains rose in the distance.

Losing hope, we saw the mountains rise in the distance.

1. Trying to get to town quickly, the highway seemed best.
2. Jogging one morning, the solution to the problem was obvious.
3. When she was five, Paula's mother graduated from the university.
4. Wandering aimlessly in the woods, the first sight of camp was welcome.
5. Hearing of the refugees' plight, emergency funds were made available.
6. Getting up much earlier than usual, the house seemed strangely quiet.
7. When he developed measles, Dan's father called the school.
8. Absorbed in the crossword puzzle, the time passed quickly.

9. Waiting for a ride, the rain pounded down all around.
10. Sailing far from shore, a squall suddenly arose.

DEVELOPING WRITING SKILLS: Correcting Misplaced and Dangling Modifiers. Rewrite the following paragraph, correcting all misplaced or dangling modifiers.

(1) Washington Irving's stories often contain elements of fantasy. (2) In one story, Rip van Winkle slept through the whole American Revolution that Irving wrote. (3) Waking up, his rusted musket should have indicated that something unusual had happened. (4) Rip was greeted by other puzzling things strolling into town. (5) The faces of the people were all strange that he met. (6) Hanging over the door of the inn, Rip noticed George Washington's portrait. (7) King George's portrait had always hung there before. (8) Rip then looked for his old friend, the innkeeper. (9) Rip questioned an old man trying to find the innkeeper. (10) The old man replied, "He is dead these eighteen years."

Skills Review and Writing Workshop

Avoiding Sentence Errors

CHECKING YOUR SKILLS

Rewrite the following paragraph, correcting all fragments, run-ons, misplaced modifiers, and dangling modifiers.

(1) The Caribbean, one of the world's most beautiful areas. (2) You can see magnificent sunrises walking along the beach. (3) Rolling onto the shore is the emerald colored water it stretches for miles. (4) Glass bottom boats standing ready to take you out to the coral reefs. (5) There are various types of coral these include brain, finger, and staghorn. (6) Waterskiing that can be a favorite sport of many tourists. (7) Touring the marketplaces, unusual gifts are often found. (8) Which are available at reasonable prices. (9) If you're willing to do some bargaining. (10) To remember your trip, buy some postcards bring a camera to take pictures.

USING USAGE SKILLS IN WRITING
Writing Travel Information

Sentence errors make your writing much less effective, so it is important to avoid them. Imagine that you work for a vacation resort and are writing a brochure describing it. Make the brochure as effective as possible by following these steps.

Prewriting: Select a vacation spot that you have visited recently or would like to visit. Think of three or four facts about this vacation area that would be most attractive to visitors.

Writing: Begin by stating the name and location of the vacation spot and give a general description of it. Then list the three or four facts that make this area attractive, beginning with the most important one.

Revising: Check your writing and correct any sentence errors. Change any words that could be more descriptive. After you have revised, proofread carefully.

UNIT II

Usage

Chapter 10

Levels of Usage

Usage is the customary way a word or grammatical construction is used in speaking or writing. Customs differ from place to place and according to the occasion. Correct usage is language that is appropriate for the time, the place, and the occasion.

There are two main levels of usage: *standard* and *nonstandard*. Standard English is used by most educated speakers. Nonstandard English is used by certain social, regional, or ethnic groups for a variety of reasons. In this chapter you will learn to recognize these levels of usage and to know when each is appropriate or inappropriate.

10.1 The Varieties of English

Both standard and nonstandard English have more than one variation. Standard English can be either formal or informal. Nonstandard English includes dialect and slang.

Standard English

The way educated people use standard English varies according to the circumstances. The kind of standard English used in a serious speech, for example, is more likely to be *formal*, while the kind used in casual conversation among old friends is more likely to be *informal*.

Formal English is appropriate for most serious writing and speaking. It is not necessarily more difficult than informal English, but it is used with more accuracy and precision. This unit will stress formal English to help you develop a firm command of it in the many circumstances that require formal use of the language.

Formal English uses traditional standards of correctness. It is characterized by complex sentence structures and an extensive vocabulary.

Notice in the following passage that the author uses sophisticated sentence structures and words not commonly found in casual conversation.

EXAMPLE: Five score years ago, a great American, in whose symbolic shadow we stand, signed the Emancipation Proclamation. This momentous decree came as a great beacon light of hope to millions of Negro slaves who had been seared in the flames of withering injustice.—Martin Luther King, Jr.

Informal English is often used in personal letters, on television, and in casual conversation.

Informal English is conversational in tone. It uses a smaller vocabulary than formal English and generally shorter sentences.

In the following example the author uses looser grammatical constructions than would be found in formal English as well as many contractions.

EXAMPLE: I'm almost twenty now—two decades gone. I know now that I will never be a ballerina. That's not because of any conscious choice, because of anything I've done, but because of what's been negotiated.
—Joyce Maynard

EXERCISE A: Recognizing Formal and Informal English.
Label each sentence as *formal* or *informal*.

EXAMPLE: Feel free to drop by when you're in town.

informal

1. The evidence to which the lawyer referred was questionable.
2. He's mad because everyone's left him to clean up the mess.
3. The policy, prematurely implemented by the new president, failed to increase the firm's productivity.
4. Surprised and delighted, the scientist effusively thanked the assembly for the prestigious award.
5. Grab a chair and make yourself at home.
6. The kids were squabbling, so we couldn't get any rest.
7. The committee members listened with impartiality.
8. It's raining so hard we can't possibly take the boat out.
9. Those who are patient have the most tolerant dispositions.
10. We've just got to get to the beach while the sun's still out.

Nonstandard English

Nonstandard English is used by certain smaller groups of people who do not follow all the rules of standard English. The two kinds of nonstandard English you will study in this section are *dialect* and *slang.*

A nonstandard dialect is mainly spoken language used by people in a specific social, regional, or ethnic group. The vocabulary, pronunciations, and grammatical constructions of a dialect are considered nonstandard if they are not commonly used by the general population of educated people.

A nonstandard dialect is a form of English that makes use of words, pronunciations, and sentence structures not commonly used in standard English.

The following passage of dialogue is from a short story by Eudora Welty. It presents a very strong regional dialect.

EXAMPLE: So here come the young man Livvie wait for. . . .
Now I lay eyes on young man and it come to be somebody I know all the time, and been knowing since he were born in a cotton patch.—Eudora Welty

Slang includes words or expressions often understood only by certain groups of people. Musicians, for example, might refer to a musical engagement as a *gig.* Young people of the 1960's might have expressed a general approval of something by saying that it was *groovy.* Sometimes a slang word is used by a larger cross section of the population, but it rarely survives long enough to become standard English.

Slang is a nonstandard form of English that is generally colorful and expressive but short-lived.

The following is from a song of the 1960's. See if you can pick out the slang expressions in the lyrics.

EXAMPLE: We breeze up and down the street.
We get respect from the people we meet,
They make way day or night.
They know The "In" Crowd is out of sight.
—Billy Page

EXERCISE B: Recognizing Dialect and Slang. Label each sentence as *dialect* or *slang.*

EXAMPLE: He ain't fixin' to eat that there mess.

dialect

1. It was a real bummer when the cops broke up the sit-in.
2. The storm's middling bad now, but it's worse it'll be getting.
3. The dudes looked real cool decked out in punk clothes.
4. He ain't likely to git hisself hitched without his pap lets him.
5. Nobody don't know nothin' 'bout it.
6. The party was, like, groaty to the max.
7. He's been real spaced-out all morning.
8. She be doin' good, now that the fever done broke.
9. When we set eyes on the bill, we knew the place was a real clip joint.
10. I just got to ketch that train afore it's too late.

DEVELOPING WRITING SKILLS: Changing Nonstandard English into Standard English. Rewrite the ten sentences in Exercise B using formal English.

EXAMPLE: He ain't fixin' to eat that there mess.
He has no intention of eating that horrible meal.

201

Skills Review and Writing Workshop

Levels of Usage

CHECKING YOUR SKILLS

Rewrite the following sentences using standard English.

(1) We're into hanging out at the mall on Saturday. (2) Some of these malls are massive. (3) You know, sometimes heavy metal bands come to the mall and, man, their sound is awesome. (4) And, at Christmas, they have that dude Santa Claus for the kiddies. (5) My little sister always beating up on me to take her to see him. (6) Shopping at these malls is excellent. (7) I mean, like they are cool city. (8) The stores have tough threads just my style. (9) You can get some good grub, too. (10) Like, man, these malls are alright!

USING USAGE SKILLS IN WRITING
Writing a Newspaper Column

Formal English is essential for serious writing to make it accurate and precise. Suppose you are writing a column for your school newspaper and the title of your current article is: "Advice for A Freshman." Develop the column by following these steps.

Prewriting: Consider a few things you've learned that every freshman should know in order to have a satisfying year. Then think of some personal experiences to illustrate your advice.

Writing: Begin with a general statement that describes the experience of being a freshman. Then present each element of advice followed by an example, leaving the most important advice until last.

Revising: Remove any slang expressions and replace them with formal English. Then check the rest of your sentences to make sure they are clear and precise. After you have revised, proofread carefully.

Chapter 11

Verb Usage

Using verbs correctly is one of the most important language skills to acquire. Most native speakers of English automatically choose the right verb when they speak, but some verbs cause trouble. For example, someone might say, "The balloon busted" instead of "The balloon burst." Since there are many such chances to misuse verbs, you should take special care to learn the various forms of verbs.

This chapter explains how verbs are formed, how they are used to indicate time. It will also explain how verbs are used to show who is performing an action.

Verb Tenses 11.1

In speaking and writing you often need to indicate when something happens—now, yesterday, tomorrow. In English, the different *tenses* of verbs are used to show when something happens.

A tense is a form of a verb that shows the time of an action or a condition.

The Six Tenses of Verbs

Verbs have six tenses, each of which can be expressed in two different forms.

Each tense has a basic and a progressive form.

The first chart on the next page gives examples of the six tenses in their *basic forms.*

THE BASIC FORMS OF THE SIX TENSES

Present	She *writes* for a living.
Past	She *wrote* a play last year.
Future	She *will write* a book of essays next year.
Present Perfect	She *has written* for the best magazines.
Past Perfect	She *had written* her first novel by the time she was eighteen.
Future Perfect	She *will have written* two plays by July.

The second chart gives examples of the six tenses in their *progressive forms*. Note that all these forms end in *-ing*.

THE PROGRESSIVE FORMS OF THE SIX TENSES

Present Progressive	She *is writing* a letter now.
Past Progressive	She *was writing* her weekly column.
Future Progressive	She *will be writing* us soon.
Present Perfect Progressive	She *has been writing* for years.
Past Perfect Progressive	She *had been writing* speeches when her first novel was published.
Future Perfect Progressive	She *will have been writing* fiction for a decade by the end of 1985.

As you can see, the forms of a verb change in order to show present, past, and future time.

EXERCISE A: Recognizing Basic and Progressive Forms.
Identify the form of each verb as *basic* or *progressive*.

EXAMPLE: He has been swimming.

    progressive

1. He is leaving.
2. I was singing.
3. She has rested.
4. They had tried.
5. He has been waiting.
6. I will have been working.
7. He spoke.
8. They will help.
9. He had been sleeping.
10. You will have gone.

EXERCISE B: Recognizing the Six Tenses. Write the tense of each verb in Exercise A. If the tense is a progressive form, add the word *progressive*.

EXAMPLE: He has been swimming.

　　　　　present perfect progressive

The Four Principal Parts of Verbs

Tenses are formed from *principal parts* and helping verbs.

A verb has four principal parts: the present, the present participle, the past, and the past participle.

The chart below lists the principal parts of two verbs.

THE FOUR PRINCIPAL PARTS			
Present	**Present Participle**	**Past**	**Past Participle**
walk	walking	walked	walked
run	running	ran	run

The first principal part is used to form the present and future tenses. To form the present, an *-s* or *-es* is added whenever the subject is *he, she, it,* or a singular noun *(I walk, Paul runs).* To form the future tense, the helping verb *will* is added *(I will walk, Paul will run).*

The second principal part is used with various helping verbs to produce all six of the progressive forms *(I am walking, Paul was walking,* and so on).

The third principal part is used to form the past tense *(I walked, Paul ran).*

The fourth principal part is used with helping verbs for the three perfect tenses *(I have walked, Paul had run,* and so on).

EXERCISE C: Recognizing Principal Parts. Identify the principal part used to form each verb in Exercise A.

EXAMPLE: He has been swimming.

　　　　　present participle .

Regular and Irregular Verbs

The way the past and the past participle of a verb are formed determines whether the verb is *regular* or *irregular*.

Regular Verbs. Most of the verbs in the English language, including the verb *walk*, are regular.

A regular verb is one whose past and past participle are formed by adding -*ed* or -*d* to the present form.

The past and past participle of regular verbs have the same form. In the chart below, *have* is in parentheses in front of the past participle to remind you that this verb form is a past participle only if it is used with a helping verb.

Notice that the final consonant is sometimes doubled to form the present participle (ski*pp*ing) as well as the past and the past participle (ski*pp*ed). Notice also that the final *e* may be dropped in forming the present participle (typ*i*ng).

PRINCIPAL PARTS OF REGULAR VERBS			
Present	**Present Participle**	**Past**	**Past Participle**
play	playing	played	(have) played
skip	skipping	skipped	(have) skipped
type	typing	typed	(have) typed
wave	waving	waved	(have) waved

Irregular Verbs. Although most verbs are regular, a number of very common verbs, such as *run*, are irregular.

An irregular verb is one whose past and past participle are not formed by adding -*ed* or -*d* to the present form.

The past and past participle of irregular verbs are formed in various ways. The most common ways are shown in the three charts on pages 207–209. Study each chart until you are familiar with all of the principal parts. The verbs in the first two charts are relatively easy to learn because the past and past participle have the same form. The verbs in the third chart deserve special attention because the past and past participle are formed in unpredictable ways.

As you study the charts, keep in mind three problems when using irregular verbs. The first is using a principal part that is nonstandard (for example, *busted* instead of *burst*). The second is confusing the past with the past participle when they are different (for example, "she *swum*" instead of "she *swam*"). The third is spelling. Just as with regular verbs, the final consonant is sometimes doubled to form the present participle (hi*tt*ing).

**IRREGULAR VERBS WITH THE SAME
PRESENT, PAST, AND PAST PARTICIPLE**

Present	Present Participle	Past	Past Participle
bid	bidding	bid	(have) bid
burst	bursting	burst	(have) burst
cost	costing	cost	(have) cost
hit	hitting	hit	(have) hit
hurt	hurting	hurt	(have) hurt
let	letting	let	(have) let
put	putting	put	(have) put
set	setting	set	(have) set

**IRREGULAR VERBS WITH THE SAME
PAST AND PAST PARTICIPLE**

Present	Present Participle	Past	Past Participle
bind	binding	bound	(have) bound
bring	bringing	brought	(have) brought
build	building	built	(have) built
buy	buying	bought	(have) bought
catch	catching	caught	(have) caught
fight	fighting	fought	(have) fought
find	finding	found	(have) found
get	getting	got	(have) got *or* (have) gotten
hold	holding	held	(have) held
keep	keeping	kept	(have) kept
lay	laying	laid	(have) laid
lead	leading	led	(have) led
leave	leaving	left	(have) left

lose	losing	lost	(have) lost
pay	paying	paid	(have) paid
say	saying	said	(have) said
send	sending	sent	(have) sent
sit	sitting	sat	(have) sat
sleep	sleeping	slept	(have) slept
spend	spending	spent	(have) spent
spin	spinning	spun	(have) spun
stand	standing	stood	(have) stood
stick	sticking	stuck	(have) stuck
swing	swinging	swung	(have) swung
teach	teaching	taught	(have) taught
win	winning	won	(have) won
wind	winding	wound	(have) wound

IRREGULAR VERBS THAT CHANGE IN OTHER WAYS

Present	Present Participle	Past	Past Participle
arise	arising	arose	(have) arisen
begin	beginning	began	(have) begun
blow	blowing	blew	(have) blown
break	breaking	broke	(have) broken
choose	choosing	chose	(have) chosen
come	coming	came	(have) come
do	doing	did	(have) done
draw	drawing	drew	(have) drawn
drink	drinking	drank	(have) drunk
drive	driving	drove	(have) driven
eat	eating	ate	(have) eaten
fall	falling	fell	(have) fallen
fly	flying	flew	(have) flown
freeze	freezing	froze	(have) frozen
give	giving	gave	(have) given
go	going	went	(have) gone
grow	growing	grew	(have) grown
know	knowing	knew	(have) known
lie	lying	lay	(have) lain
ride	riding	rode	(have) ridden
ring	ringing	rang	(have) rung

208

rise	rising	rose	(have) risen
run	running	ran	(have) run
see	seeing	saw	(have) seen
shake	shaking	shook	(have) shaken
shrink	shrinking	shrank	(have) shrunk
sing	singing	sang	(have) sung
sink	sinking	sank	(have) sunk
speak	speaking	spoke	(have) spoken
spring	springing	sprang	(have) sprung
steal	stealing	stole	(have) stolen
swear	swearing	swore	(have) sworn
swim	swimming	swam	(have) swum
take	taking	took	(have) taken
tear	tearing	tore	(have) torn
throw	throwing	threw	(have) thrown
wear	wearing	wore	(have) worn
write	writing	wrote	(have) written

Whenever you are in doubt about the principal parts of an irregular verb, use a dictionary to check.

EXERCISE D: Learning the Principal Parts of Irregular Verbs. Write the present participle, the past, and the past participle of each verb.

EXAMPLE: throw

        throwing   threw   thrown

1. build
2. find
3. get
4. hold
5. drink
6. do
7. bring
8. burst
9. fly
10. teach
11. go
12. sing
13. catch
14. choose
15. swing
16. sit
17. eat
18. freeze
19. shrink
20. wind

EXERCISE E: Recognizing Principal Parts in Sentences. Choose the correct form of the verb in parentheses.

EXAMPLE: He (brung, brought) the wrong book to class.

        brought

1. The batter (swang, swung) hard but missed the ball.
2. Steve (drived, drove) me home.

3. Rachel (built, builded) the cabin in the woods in only two and a half months.
4. We (payed, paid) the rent a week early.
5. All around us fire crackers were (busting, bursting).
6. The used car (costed, cost) me only a little more than two hundred dollars.
7. The campers (sleeped, slept) on the ground.
8. I (layed, laid) the money on the table.
9. Our guide (leaded, led) us to a waterfall.
10. She (binded, bound) the package with string.

EXERCISE F: Correcting Principal Parts. The paragraph below contains five errors in the choice between the past and the past participle. Rewrite the paragraph, correcting the errors.

EXAMPLE: Dorothea Dix fighted for the mentally ill.

Dorothea Dix fought for the mentally ill.

(1) Dorothea Dix played a crucial role in helping the mentally ill. (2) After visiting a jail in Massachusetts in the 1840's, she seen that they led the same life as criminals. (3) Until her visit, she had not knew that the mentally ill led such miserable lives. (4) Often, they lived in unheated housing. (5) Dix knew that she had not took enough responsibility in the past. (6) She begun to visit each place in the state where the mentally ill lived. (7) After her visits, she wrote a detailed report. (8) She convinced the state to improve the treatment of the mentally ill. (9) She also fighted in other states. (10) In all, fifteen states passed laws to help the mentally ill.

Conjugating the Tenses

With the principal parts of verbs and helping verbs, you can form all of the tenses. One way to become familiar with the variety of verb forms is through *conjugation.*

A conjugation is a complete list of the singular and plural forms of a verb in a particular tense.

For each tense there are three singular forms and three plural forms that correspond to the first-, second-, and third-person forms of personal pronouns.

The charts below conjugate the verb *see.* To conjugate the six tenses in their basic forms, you need only three of the principal parts: the present *(see),* the past *(saw),* and the past participle *(seen).*

CONJUGATION OF THE BASIC FORMS OF *SEE*		
Present	**Singular**	**Plural**
First Person	I see	we see
Second Person	you see	you see
Third Person	he, she, it sees	they see
Past		
First Person	I saw	we saw
Second Person	you saw	you saw
Third Person	he, she, it saw	they saw
Future		
First Person	I will see	we will see
Second Person	you will see	you will see
Third Person	he, she, it will see	they will see
Present Perfect		
First Person	I have seen	we have seen
Second Person	you have seen	you have seen
Third Person	he, she, it has seen	they have seen
Past Perfect		
First Person	I had seen	we had seen
Second Person	you had seen	you had seen
Third Person	he, she, it had seen	they had seen
Future Perfect		
First Person	I will have seen	we will have seen
Second Person	you will have seen	you will have seen
Third Person	he, she, it will have seen	they will have seen

To conjugate the six tenses in their progressive forms, you need the present participle and a form of the verb *be*.

CONJUGATION OF THE PROGRESSIVE FORMS OF *SEE*		
Present Progressive	**Singular**	**Plural**
First Person	I am seeing	we are seeing
Second Person	you are seeing	you are seeing
Third Person	he, she, it is seeing	they are seeing
Past Progressive		
First Person	I was seeing	we were seeing
Second Person	you were seeing	you were seeing
Third Person	he, she, it was seeing	they were seeing
Future Progressive		
First Person	I will be seeing	we will be seeing
Second Person	you will be seeing	you will be seeing
Third Person	he, she, it will be seeing	they will be seeing
Present Perfect Progressive		
First Person	I have been seeing	we have been seeing
Second Person	you have been seeing	you have been seeing
Third Person	he, she, it has been seeing	they have been seeing

Past Perfect Progressive

First Person	I had been seeing	we had been seeing
Second Person	you had been seeing	you had been seeing
Third Person	he, she, it had been seeing	they had been seeing

Future Perfect Progressive

First Person	I will have been seeing	we will have been seeing
Second Person	you will have been seeing	you will have been seeing
Third Person	he, she, it will have been seeing	they will have been seeing

NOTE ABOUT *BE*: The verb *be* is highly irregular. The following conjugation of the first two tenses lists the forms.

PRESENT:	I am	we are
	you are	you are
	he, she, it is	they are
PAST:	I was	we were
	you were	you were
	he, she, it was	they were

EXERCISE G: Conjugating the Basic Forms of Verbs. Conjugate the basic forms of the four verbs below in the manner shown in the example.

EXAMPLE: spend (conjugated with *we*)

Present: we spend	Present Perfect: we have spent
Past: we spent	Past Perfect: we had spent
Future: we will spend	Future Perfect: we will have spent

1. open (conjugated with *I*)
2. move (conjugated with *you*)
3. know (conjugated with *he*)
4. run (conjugated with *they*)

213

EXERCISE H: **Conjugating the Progressive Forms of Verbs.** Conjugate the progressive forms of the four verbs below in the manner shown in the example.

EXAMPLE: spend (conjugated with *we*)

Present Progressive: we are spending
Past Progressive: we were spending
Future Progressive: we will be spending
Present Perfect Progressive: we have been spending
Past Perfect Progressive: we had been spending
Future Perfect Progressive: we will have been spending

1. walk (conjugated with *you*)   3. say (conjugated with *they*)
2. jump (conjugated with *she*)   4. leave (conjugated with *he*)

EXERCISE I: **Supplying the Correct Tense.** Write the indicated form for each verb in parentheses.

EXAMPLE: She (write—*past perfect*) the most interesting paper.

had written

1. Within seconds she (fly—*past*) into a rage.
2. My father said that he (buy—*future*) a new car next week.
3. We were surprised to learn that he (know—*past perfect*) about the report for some time.
4. The Senator said that she (travel—*future progressive*) to Finland next fall.
5. The executive was told that he (charge—*past perfect progressive*) too much to his expense account.
6. They (discover—*past*) the relic by accident.
7. Our neighbors told us that they (think—*present perfect progressive*) about retiring to a warmer climate.
8. Worried about the test, she (work—*past perfect*) all night.
9. We only (swim—*present*) when a lifeguard is on duty.
10. By the time the plane arrives, we (wait—*future perfect progressive*) for three hours

DEVELOPING WRITING SKILLS: **Using Different Tenses.** Use each verb in a sentence of your own.

EXAMPLE: Past perfect of *break*

I was afraid I had broken Mom's favorite bracelet.

1. Present perfect of *cost*
2. Past of *go*
3. Future of *freeze*
4. Present perfect progressive of *drive*
5. Past perfect of *draw*
6. Past of *hurt*
7. Past perfect progressive of *ring*
8. Future perfect progressive of *spend*
9. Present of *say*
10. Present progressive of *begin*
11. Past progressive of *enjoy*
12. Future of *substitute*
13. Past of *bid*
14. Present perfect progressive of *fight*
15. Past perfect of *throw*
16. Future of *lie*
17. Past perfect progressive of *ride*
18. Future perfect progressive of *paint*
19. Present perfect of *sing*
20. Present perfect progressive of *race*

Expressing Time Through Tense 11.2

The basic and progressive forms of the six tenses show the time of an action or condition in the present, the past, or the future.

Uses of Tense in Present Time

Two verb forms are used to point out that something is happening right now.

The present and the present progressive show present actions or conditions as well as various continuing actions or conditions.

The following chart gives an example of each of these two forms.

FORMS EXPRESSING PRESENT TIME	
Present	He walks.
Present Progressive	He is walking.

The chart at the top of the next page shows the main uses of the present.

215

USES OF THE PRESENT
Present action: There he *goes.*
Present condition: The apples *are* rotten.
Regularly occurring action: My sister *chews* her nails.
Regularly occurring condition: They *are* never ready.
Constant action: The sun *radiates* energy.
Constant condition: Human blood *is* red.

The main uses of the present progressive are to show continuing actions or conditions.

USES OF THE PRESENT PROGRESSIVE
Continuing action: He is *working* on a novel.
Continuing condition: The baby *is being* very difficult this week.

EXERCISE A: Identifying the Uses of Tense in Present Time. Identify the use of the underlined verb in each sentence, using the labels in the charts above.

EXAMPLE: Greg *plays* tennis every Saturday.

        regularly occurring action

1. I *leave* for school at 7:30 each morning.
2. Gasoline *is* a flammable liquid.
3. My friends and I *race* home from school every afternoon.
4. This entire meal *is* delicious.
5. I *hear* a television in the other room.
6. My brother *is doing* his homework now.
7. Gravity *pulls* all objects downward.
8. My father *is building* a stereo cabinet.
9. He *reads* mostly biographies.
10. My sister Judy generally *travels* to work on the train.

Uses of Tense in Past Time

Six verb forms are used to point out that something happened or began happening at some time before the present.

The six forms that express past time show actions and conditions beginning in the past.

The following chart gives each form with an example.

FORMS EXPRESSING PAST TIME	
Past	He walked.
Present Perfect	He has walked.
Past Perfect	He had walked.
Past Progressive	He was walking.
Present Perfect Progressive	He has been walking.
Past Perfect Progressive	He had been walking.

The chart below shows the ways the first form, the past, can be used. Notice that the time can be changed from indefinite to definite by such words as *yesterday* or *last week*.

USES OF THE PAST
Completed action (indefinite time): She *went* home.
Completed condition (indefinite time): I *was* sick.
Completed action (definite time): She *went* home yesterday.
Completed condition (definite time): I *was* sick last week.

Like the past, the present perfect can be used to show completed actions and conditions that took place at some indefinite time. It can also be used to show actions and conditions continuing to the present time.

USES OF THE PRESENT PERFECT
Completed action (indefinite time): He *has finished* his work.
Completed condition (indefinite time): He *has been* upset.
Action continuing to present: Sue *has waited* for two hours.
Condition continuing to present: She *has been* very sick.

The past perfect is used to show that one past action or condition took place before another.

USES OF THE PAST PERFECT

Action completed before another: I *had left* before she did.

Condition completed before another: Ken *had been* healthy before he caught pneumonia.

The three progressive forms that express past time are used to show continuous actions and conditions.

USES OF THE PROGRESSIVE FORMS
THAT EXPRESS PAST TIME

Past Progressive	*Continuous completed action:* He *was working* on a ranch that summer.
	Continuous completed condition: Mimi *was being* agreeable last week.
Present Perfect Progressive	*Action continuing to present:* Louisa *has been reading* mysteries for a month now.
Past Perfect Progressive	*Continuing action interrupted by another:* I *had been sleeping* when you called.

EXERCISE B: Using Past, Present Perfect, and Past Perfect. Choose the correct form of the verb in parentheses.

EXAMPLE: Mary (bought, has bought) a new dress yesterday.

       bought

1. Father (grew, has grown) tomatoes in our yard last year.
2. I (called, have called) her three times on Tuesday.
3. Carol (has waited, had waited) an hour before she left.
4. We (postponed, have postponed) our trip yesterday.
5. Ken (rode, has ridden) the bus to work since he moved.
6. Sue (visited, has visited) her sister at college last week.
7. I (was, have been) terribly sleepy lately.
8. My sister (has arrived, had arrived) before I did.
9. I (finished, have finished) my report at three o'clock.
10. He (has swum, had swum) across the river before I started.

EXERCISE C: Identifying the Uses of the Progressive Forms in the Past. Identify the use of each underlined verb.

218

EXAMPLE: I <u>was</u> <u>writing</u> my book report last night.

continuous completed action

1. Father <u>has</u> <u>been</u> <u>building</u> a porch behind the house.
2. My brother <u>had</u> <u>been</u> <u>going</u> to college until his accident.
3. After lunch I <u>was</u> <u>writing</u> my report on Walt Whitman.
4. Our fruit trees <u>have</u> <u>been</u> <u>growing</u> at an amazing rate.
5. I <u>was</u> <u>painting</u> my bicycle when the rain started.
6. Jan <u>was</u> <u>being</u> unusually generous last night.
7. They <u>were</u> <u>eating</u> when we arrived.
8. I <u>had</u> <u>been</u> <u>working</u> nights until I inherited the money.
9. Mary <u>has</u> <u>been</u> <u>studying</u> French for two years now.
10. Linda <u>was</u> <u>rehearsing</u> her speech this morning.

Uses of Tense in Future Time

Four verb forms are used to point out things in the future.

The four forms that express future time show future actions or conditions.

The following chart gives each form with an example.

FORMS EXPRESSING FUTURE TIME	
Future	He will walk.
Future Perfect	He will have walked.
Future Progressive	He will be walking.
Future Perfect Progressive	He will have been walking.

The uses of the two basic forms are shown below.

USES OF THE FUTURE AND THE FUTURE PERFECT	
Future	*Future action:* A frost *will damage* the crop.
	Future condition: I *will be* home tomorrow.
Future Perfect	*Future action completed before another:* I *will have left* by the time you arrive.
	Future condition completed before another: I *will have been* up for hours before you call.

Occasionally, the present is used to express ideas that can also be expressed by the future.

EXAMPLES: Her new job *begins* in June.

Her new job *will begin* in June.

The uses of the two progressive forms are illustrated below.

USES OF THE PROGRESSIVE FORMS THAT EXPRESS FUTURE TIME	
Future Progressive	*Continuing future action:* They *will be visiting* New York this fall.
Future Perfect Progressive	*Continuing future action completed before another:* When we meet next week, I *will have been practicing* tennis for a month.

Just as the present is sometimes used to express the future, the present progressive can be used instead of the future progressive.

EXAMPLES: He *is going* to a new school next September.

He *will be going* to a new school next September.

EXERCISE D: Identifying the Uses of Tense in Future Time. Identify the use of each underlined verb, using the labels above and on page 219.

EXAMPLE: She <u>will</u> <u>have</u> <u>been</u> <u>traveling</u> a full year when she comes home tomorrow.

continuing future action completed before another

1. The President <u>will</u> <u>deliver</u> a speech tonight.
2. The Kramers <u>will</u> <u>be</u> <u>vacationing</u> for two weeks.
3. Fred <u>will</u> <u>move</u> to California next summer.
4. Fred <u>will</u> <u>be</u> <u>transferring</u> to Oregon in two years.
5. By the time you reach Chicago, you <u>will</u> <u>have</u> <u>been</u> <u>driving</u> for eight hours.
6. By the time Mom gets home, I <u>will</u> <u>have</u> <u>finished</u> the dishes.
7. Tomorrow I <u>will</u> <u>be</u> <u>skiing</u> in the Alps.
8. Jane <u>will</u> <u>be</u> home on Friday.

9. If she wins tonight, she <u>will</u> <u>have</u> <u>won</u> the contest four years in a row.
10. Alex <u>will</u> <u>study</u> archaeology in college.

EXERCISE E: Using Tenses in Future Time. Write the indicated form of each verb in parentheses.

EXAMPLE: By the time we reach the summit, we (climb—*future perfect progressive*) for four hours.

will have been climbing

1. My aunt (travel—*future progressive*) in Brazil for a month.
2. The department store (open—*future*) in an hour.
3. By tomorrow, we (receive—*future perfect*) our grades.
4. I (leave—*future*) for Toronto at noon.
5. When I return from Puerto Rico in August, I (speak—*future perfect progressive*) Spanish for two months.
6. Max (open—*future progressive*) a new store in Phoenix sometime next year.
7. Before I leave, I (practice—*future perfect*) for an hour.
8. They (polish—*future perfect progressive*) their act for six months by the time they appear on stage.
9. She (recover—*future perfect*) by the time we are able to visit her next week.
10. I probably (see—*future*) you later tonight.

Shifts in Tense

Tenses allow you to indicate the sequence of events.

When showing a sequence of events, do not shift tenses unnecessarily.

This rule is particularly important when a sentence has a compound verb.

	PAST	PRESENT
INCORRECT:	He *rushed* into the house and *slams* the door.	

	PAST	PAST
CORRECT:	He *rushed* into the house and *slammed* the door.	

Tenses should also not shift unnecessarily from one sentence to the next.

221

| | PAST | | PRESENT |
INCORRECT: I *dropped* the radio. Suddenly it *begins* to play.

| | PAST | | PAST |
CORRECT: I *dropped* the radio. Suddenly it *began* to play.

Sometimes, you will need to shift tenses. Only the meaning of the sentence can tell you when you must use another tense.

| | PRESENT | PRESENT |
INCORRECT: If you *go* home, I *wait* here.

| | PRESENT | FUTURE |
CORRECT: If you *go* home, I *will wait* here.

EXERCISE F: Avoiding Unnecessary Shifts in Tense. Rewrite each sentence, correcting tense problems by changing the second verb.

EXAMPLE: Bill goes fishing whenever he got a day off.

Bill goes fishing whenever he gets a day off.

1. I sit in the hall all day and answered the phone.
2. The class had read *Hamlet* before it reads *Macbeth*.
3. Eric talked to the newcomers before I do.
4. When Grandfather arrived, the whole family greets him at the airport.
5. As soon as you find a pleasing color, I help you.
6. By the time you phoned, I will have gone to bed.
7. Stella had eaten by the time I get there.
8. He will reach his goal when he got ten more orders.
9. I will be lonely when you will be away.
10. By the time I found him, he has mailed the letter already.
11. It has been months since the day I have seen you.
12. He went below deck and cleans his bunk.
13. Sally opens the door whenever the dog barked.
14. He sailed for Paris and has arrived there two weeks later.
15. If he goes to the rally, I joined him later.
16. The game was over when we leave.
17. Our team never wins the championship, nor did our rival from across town.
18. If I am elected secretary, I will have done many things.
19. My little sister smiled at the doctor and says hello.
20. He shook my hand and asks me to sit down.

EXERCISE G: Correcting Errors in Tense. Rewrite the following paragraph, correcting unnecessary shifts in tense.

(1) An unusual feature of Quincy Market in Boston is Faneuil Hall. (2) It was built in 1742 by Peter Faneuil, who later gives it to the city. (3) Nineteen years later, it burns. (4) Soon after, however, it was rebuilt. (5) Before the Revolutionary War, it had been a theater. (6) Later, it was called "The Cradle of Liberty." (7) The name was given to it because it is the scene of many important meetings during the Revolutionary War. (8) For years the first floor was a produce market. (9) The second floor is the place for meetings. (10) It now has contained many historical paintings and is exciting to visit.

DEVELOPING WRITING SKILLS: Using the Correct Tense in Your Writing. Begin or complete each sentence with words of your own choice.

EXAMPLE: I had just fallen asleep when _____.

I had just fallen asleep when the phone rang.

1. When I opened the door, _____.
2. We were winning the game until _____.
3. _____ after I had met Marie.
4. The principal announced that _____.
5. _____ when the dog barked.
6. Although he wanted to start his own business, _____.
7. Our old truck stalls when _____.
8. _____ as soon as Liza sees her present.
9. If she can describe her lost watch, _____.
10. _____ since my aunt from Texas visited.

Active and Passive Voice 11.3

In addition to indicating time, most verbs can indicate whether the subject is performing an action or having an action performed upon it. Two different *voices* of verbs are used to show how an action is performed.

Voice is the form of a verb that shows whether the subject is performing the action.

223

Linking verbs do not show voice. Only action verbs show voice. The voice may be either *active* or *passive.*

Differences Between Active and Passive Voice

Any action verb, with or without a direct object, can be in the active voice.

A verb is active if its subject performs the action.

In the two examples below, the subjects are the performers.

ACTIVE VOICE: Laura *found* a gold bracelet.

Beth's aunt *called* yesterday.

Most action verbs can also be used in the passive voice.

A verb is passive if its action is performed upon the subject.

In a sentence with a passive verb, the performer of the action may or may not be named. In the first example below, Laura is still the performer. The word *Laura,* however, is no longer the subject, but the object of the preposition *by.* In the second example, the person who called is not identified.

PASSIVE VOICE: A gold bracelet *was found* by Laura.

Beth *was called* yesterday.

EXERCISE A: Distinguishing Between the Active and Passive Voice. Identify each verb as *active* or *passive.*

EXAMPLE: The letter was signed by the President.

passive

1. The bitter medicine was taken by my sister.
2. Delegates to the convention have been chosen by the voters.
3. We each purchased several new outfits for spring.
4. Later, the speaker wrote a letter of apology.
5. Bread crumbs were then sprinkled on the fish.
6. Many wild animals live in the forest.

7. Surgery was performed by a team of specialists.
8. Ellen grew her own fresh vegetables this summer.
9. In the winter snow covers the mountains.
10. The bad news was then given to Brad by the coach.
11. Representatives had been selected earlier by Congress.
12. Kansas City was reached by the convoy in two hours.
13. I always read the evening newspaper after dinner.
14. After a debate the report was accepted by the chairperson.
15. The President has appointed a new ambassador.
16. The jammed window was finally opened by the mechanic.
17. The four-engine jet taxied down the main runway.
18. That story is told over and over again by Grandfather.
19. She bought fresh apples, peaches, plums, and bananas.
20. The former mayor addressed the civic association last Wednesday night.

The Forms of Passive Verbs

Passive verbs have two parts.

A passive verb is made from a form of *be* plus the past participle of a transitive verb.

The tense of a passive verb is determined by the tense of the helping verb *be*. The past participle does not change.

The following chart shows a conjugation of the verb *call* in the passive voice with the pronoun *she*. Notice that there are only two progressive forms in the passive voice instead of the six in the active voice.

THE VERB *CALL* IN THE PASSIVE VOICE	
Present	she is called
Past	she was called
Future	she will be called
Present Perfect	she has been called
Past Perfect	she had been called
Future Perfect	she will have been called
Present Progressive	she is being called
Past Progressive	she was being called

EXERCISE B: Forming the Tenses of Passive Verbs.

Conjugate each verb in the passive voice, using the chart on page 225 as your model.

1. type (with *it*)
2. forgive (with *we*)
3. sell (with *it*)
4. alert (with *they*)

Using Voice Correctly

To write well, you need to know when to use the active voice and when to use the passive voice. There are no firm rules, but here are some suggestions.

Use the active voice whenever possible.

Good writing is crisp and direct. Sentences with active verbs are less wordy and more direct than those with passive verbs. Notice that both sentences below report the same information but that the active sentence is shorter and more direct.

ACTIVE VOICE: Jennifer *opened* the package.

PASSIVE VOICE: The package *was opened* by Jennifer.

There are times, however, when you may prefer to use the passive voice.

Use the passive voice to emphasize the receiver of action rather than the performer of an action.

Because of their position at the beginning of the sentence, the words before the passive verb receive slightly more emphasis than they would if they followed the verb.

PASSIVE VOICE: My best friend *was struck* by a car yesterday evening.

PASSIVE VOICE: The film's special effects *were developed* by a team of engineers.

The passive voice should also be used when there is no performer of the action.

Use the passive voice to point out the receiver of an action whenever the performer is not important or not easily identified.

EXAMPLES: The mysterious phone call *was made* at midnight.

At noon, the stadium gates *were unlocked.*

EXERCISE C: Using the Active Voice. Rewrite each of the ten sentences in Exercise A that have verbs in the passive voice. Change or add words in order to put each verb into the active voice.

EXAMPLE: The letter was signed by the President.

The President signed the letter.

EXERCISE D: Correcting Unnecessary Use of the Passive Voice. Rewrite the following paragraph, changing at least five uses of the passive voice to active.

EXAMPLE: Loch Ness *is being studied* by many scientists.

Many scientists are studying Loch Ness.

(1) For years a so-called monster has been spotted by visitors to Loch Ness in Scotland. (2) The large creature has been reported by many witnesses. (3) Do lake monsters really exist? (4) These reports have been questioned by scientists. (5) According to some Canadian scientists, the sightings may be explained by temperature inversions. (6) A temperature inversion occurs when the temperature of a body of water is much lower than the temperature of the air above it. (7) Experiments were conducted by scientists on Lake Winnipeg, Canada, during a temperature inversion. (8) Two photos of an ordinary stick floating on the lake were taken only three minutes apart. (9) The bending, or refraction, of light caused by the inversion made the stick appear to be a strangely shaped "monster." (10) These photos have been accepted by some scientists as proof that the lake monsters are really ordinary objects that appear distorted because of a temperature inversion.

DEVELOPING WRITING SKILLS: Using the Active and Passive Voice in Writing. Write five sentences describing the events that happened on your way to school this morning. Include one sentence using the passive voice. Make sure all the other sentences use the active voice.

Skills Review and Writing Workshop

Verb Usage

CHECKING YOUR SKILLS

Rewrite the following paragraph, correcting all errors in verb usage. Use the active voice throughout.

(1) Many people have say that the perfect place for future Olympic Games is Greece. (2) After all, the first games take place in Greece. (3) The site of the ancient games is still visited by tourists every year. (4) Just outside the sleepy little village of Olympia, the remains of the old temples and track still stood. (5) Arguments in favor of such a move will include the fact that Greece is a relatively neutral site. (6) Countries that have staid away from games in the past would have less reason to do so with Greece as the site. (7) Indeed, a sense of common heritage would be felt by all of the participants. (8) The weather in Greece was excellent. (9) Only one major problem has arose. (10) Olympia don't have any mountains for the winter games.

USING USAGE SKILLS IN WRITING
Writing a Sports Story

Action verbs in the active voice can make writing come alive. This is particularly true in adventure stories and in sports stories. Follow the steps below to write a sports story that combines action with a surprise ending.

Prewriting: Most sports stories are pretty typical. The only question is who will win. Imagine a sports story in which the ending is totally unexpected. List the events in sequence.

Writing: Begin by letting your audience know that something unusual is going to happen. Wait until the end, however, to let them know exactly *what* happens.

Revising: First look at your verbs. Make sure they are all used correctly and that enough of them are action verbs in the active voice. Look for other improvements you can make. After you have revised, proofread carefully.

Chapter 12

Pronoun Usage

A thousand years ago, the English language relied on different forms of nouns and pronouns to show how the words were being used in a sentence. For example, the word for dog was *hund* when it acted as a subject and *hunde* when it acted as an indirect object.

Today, English relies mainly on the position in a sentence to show how nouns are being used. Certain pronouns, however, still change form to indicate their use. This chapter will explain the correct uses of these pronoun forms.

The Cases of Pronouns 12.1

Only two parts of speech have *case*.

Case is the form of a noun or a pronoun that indicates its use in a sentence.

The Three Cases

Both nouns and pronouns have three cases.

The three cases are the nominative, the objective, and the possessive.

The chart on the next page shows how each case can be used in a sentence.

229

Case	Use in Sentence
Nominative	Subject or Predicate Nominative
Objective	Direct Object, Indirect Object, or Object of a Preposition
Possessive	To Show Ownership

The case of a noun in modern English is rarely a problem because the form changes only in the possessive case.

NOMINATIVE: The *coin* cost one hundred dollars.

OBJECTIVE: He carefully put the *coin* in a plastic envelope.

POSSESSIVE: The *coin's* value will increase over the years.

In the first example, *coin* is *nominative* because it is the subject; in the second, it is *objective* because it is the direct object. The same form is used for both cases. Only the *possessive* case of nouns requires a change in form, usually by adding an apostrophe and an *-s.*

Personal pronouns, however, often require a change of form for all three cases. The chart below shows the various forms of the personal pronouns in the three cases.

Nominative	Objective	Possessive
I	me	my, mine
you	you	your, yours
he, she, it	him, her, it	his, her, hers, its
we	us	our, ours
they	them	their, theirs

EXERCISE A: Identifying Case. Write the case of each underlined pronoun. Then write its use.

EXAMPLE: The doctor gave <u>her</u> the good news.

   objective   (indirect object)

1. After waiting an hour, <u>we</u> finally spoke to the coach.
2. Give <u>them</u> the present.
3. <u>Their</u> reply surprised the judge.
4. Betty will see <u>you</u> on Friday.

5. John waved to <u>us</u> on the way to the game.
6. There is no question that this is <u>my</u> wallet.
7. <u>They</u> accepted our explanation completely.
8. <u>Your</u> mother phoned from her office.
9. Much to <u>my</u> delight, Phil asked me to dance.
10. My mother asked for <u>her</u> help with the children.
11. General Smith gave <u>his</u> word to the troops.
12. My sister and <u>I</u> agreed to perform.
13. The chairperson is <u>she.</u>
14. The principal gave <u>us</u> a broad smile.
15. Does Father want to hear <u>our</u> reasons?
16. <u>Their</u> science project is the best in the class.
17. The winners are Joan and <u>I.</u>
18. Give your answer to <u>him</u>.
19. Dr. Smith gave <u>us</u> debaters a small pin.
20. <u>I</u> really want to visit the campus.

The Nominative Case

The nominative case is used when a personal pronoun is either a subject or a predicate nominative.

Use the nominative case for the subject of a verb.

EXAMPLES: *I* do most of the cooking in the family.

You know that *we* are friends.

If the pronoun is part of a compound subject, make sure you have used the nominative case by removing the other subject.

EXAMPLES: Father and *I* do most of the cooking.
(*I* do most of the cooking.)

She and Lenny planned to go to the concert.
(*She* planned to go to the concert.)

Use the nominative case for a predicate nominative.

A predicate nominative is the noun or pronoun that appears with a linking verb and identifies or renames the subject. If the predicate nominative is a pronoun, you may not be in the habit of using the nominative case. In informal use, people customarily use the objective case instead.

231

INFORMAL USAGE: It's *me*

The one who helped us is *him*.

In formal writing, however, you should use the nominative case.

FORMAL USAGE: It is *I*.

The one who helped us is *he*.

Take special care to use the nominative case when a pronoun is part of a compound predicate nominative. Check yourself by mentally rewording the sentence.

EXAMPLE: The losers were Denise and *I*.

(Denise and *I* were the losers.)

NOTE ABOUT APPOSITIVES: When a pronoun used as a subject or predicate nominative is followed by an appositive (a noun renaming the pronoun), you must still use the nominative case.

SUBJECT: *We* athletes need self-discipline.

PREDICATE NOMINATIVE: The decision-makers are *we* the voters.

EXERCISE B: Identifying Pronouns in the Nominative Case. Choose the pronoun in the nominative case to complete each sentence. Then write the use of the pronoun.

EXAMPLE: Greg and (me, I) are going home.

I   (subject)

1. Gary and (I, me) have been elected to the Student Council.
2. The culprits are (them, they).
3. (Us, We) boys want to go fishing together.
4. My brother and (I, me) bought six new shirts when we were in the city.
5. Charles and (he, him) left the meeting early.
6. The principal is (her, she).
7. My father and (me, I) rebuilt the engine of our neighbor's old car.
8. Our captain for two years has been (he, him).
9. (I, Me) myself will take the first watch.
10. The new members of the committee on school policies are Jerry and (her, she).

EXERCISE C: **Using Pronouns in the Nominative Case.**
Write a nominative pronoun to complete each sentence. Then write the use of the pronoun.

EXAMPLE: Jane and _____ worked late.

       I   (subject)

1. _____ are waiting for us at the station.
2. _____ is a cold and damp morning.
3. Are _____ serious about that offer?
4. The key to victory is _____ delegates from Boston.
5. _____ are hoping for an invitation to the party.
6. _____ is the uncle I love most.
7. You know that _____ is ill today.
8. I hope that _____ will go with me.
9. _____ is my oldest sister.
10. Surely _____ will accept your offer.

The Objective Case

The objective case is used when a personal pronoun is a direct object, an indirect object, or the object of a preposition.

Use the objective case for a direct object.

EXAMPLES: Fran's behavior embarrassed *me.*

           Michael's suit no longer fits *him.*

Be sure to check compounds by mentally removing one of the direct objects.

EXAMPLES: The thunderstorm frightened Don and *me.*
           (The thunderstorm frightened *me.*)

           Louise saw Frank and *her* at the dance.
           (Louise saw *her* at the dance.)

Use the objective case for an indirect object.

EXAMPLES: The berries gave *me* a stomachache.

           Dad sent *us* a post card from Paris.

If the pronoun is part of a compound, check for the proper case by mentally removing one of the indirect objects.

EXAMPLES: The berries gave my sister and *me* a stomachache.
(The berries gave *me* a stomachache.)

Dad sent my brother and *me* a post card from Paris.
(Dad sent *me* a post card from Paris.)

Use the objective case for the object of a preposition.

EXAMPLES: Sit by *me*.

I refuse to speak to *him*.

They could not understand why she had gone with *us*.

If the pronoun is in a compound object of a preposition, check the case by mentally removing one of the objects of the preposition.

EXAMPLES: Sit behind Lou and *me*.
(Sit behind *me*.)

My mother often speaks about Joe and *him*.
(My mother often speaks about *him*.)

NOTE ABOUT APPOSITIVES: If a pronoun used as a direct object, indirect object, or object of a preposition has an appositive, be sure to use the objective case just as if the pronoun were by itself.

DIRECT OBJECT: Ms. Voss patiently taught *us* new students.

INDIRECT OBJECT: They awarded *us* losers a gag prize.

OBJECT OF PREPOSITION: Summer is too short for *us* surfers.

EXERCISE D: Identifying Pronouns in the Objective Case. Choose the pronoun in the objective case to complete each sentence. Then write the use of the pronoun.

EXAMPLE: Todd invited only (us, we) boys to the party.

us (direct object)

1. This secret is just between you and (I, me).
2. He bought ice cream for Judy and (I, me).
3. Between him and (her, she) there is little choice.
4. I gave both Tommy and (she, her) a stern lecture.
5. He asked all of (us, we) girls for our opinions.

234

6. Mother wants to be fair to both him and (her, she).
7. I prepared (him, he) for the bad news.
8. Nancy gave Greg and (me, I) the cookies.
9. The test is too hard for (them, they).
10. You have one real rival in (him, he).

EXERCISE E: Using Pronouns in the Objective Case.
Write an objective pronoun to complete each sentence. Then write the use of the pronoun.

EXAMPLE: George gave _____ his old catcher's mitt.

      me   (indirect object)

1. Brenda gave _____ lots of unwanted advice.
2. The disc jockey smiled at _____ girls.
3. My father lent _____ his car.
4. Our teacher gave _____ two new baseball bats after our surprise victory.
5. With his record, can we really trust _____ ?
6. He gave _____ Little Leaguers tickets to the big game next Saturday.
7. That experience gave _____ boys a real scare.
8. Call for Elizabeth and _____ in about an hour.
9. I gave _____ different eye makeup to try.
10. I congratulated _____ and the other swimmers.

The Possessive Case

The possessive case of personal pronouns shows possession before nouns and before gerunds. It can also be used alone.

Use the possessive case before nouns to show ownership.

EXAMPLES: Mark left *his* umbrella at the library.

        Our theater group performed *Julius Caesar.*

        The lion escaped from *its* cage.

Use the possessive case before gerunds.

EXAMPLES: *Your* walking in the rain caused the fever.

        Do you mind *my* borrowing your sweater?

A common error is *"you* walking" or *"me* borrowing." Be sure to use a possessive pronoun in front of any gerund.

Use certain possessive pronouns by themselves to indicate possession.

EXAMPLES: This sweater is *mine,* not *yours.*

Is this book *his* or *hers?*

You should also notice that a possessive pronoun is never written with an apostrophe. Spellings such as *your's, our's,* and *their's* are incorrect. In addition, do not confuse a possessive pronoun with a contraction.

POSSESSIVE PRONOUN: The dog buried *its* bone.

CONTRACTION: *It's* too cold to go swimming today.

EXERCISE F: Using Pronouns in the Possessive Case. Choose the correct word in each set of parentheses.

EXAMPLE: We must give them (theirs, their's).

theirs

1. I spoke to Ralph about (his, him) chewing gum in class.
2. There is no question that this is (yours, your's).
3. Our kitten hurt (it's its) front paw.
4. The president asked for (his, his's) resignation.
5. (His, Him) speeding finally got him into trouble.
6. We told him that this is (our's, ours).
7. They want (his, him) cutting to stop immediately.
8. (They're, Their) winnings will be divided equally.
9. May I borrow (your's, yours)?
10. I feel that (its, it's) too expensive.
11. (Our, Us) singing leaves much to be desired.
12. I finally said that it was (mine's, mine).
13. (Your, You) leaving will cause much embarrassment.
14. Is it really (hers, her's)?
15. (Him, His) constant smiling cheers us all up.
16. (Your, You're) not really prepared to dance.
17. I thought he would understand (our, us) joking.
18. Mother was worried about (me, my) growing.
19. (Its, It's) really none of your business.
20. The ship veered off (its, it's) course.

EXERCISE G: Using All Three Cases. Choose the correct word in each set of parentheses.

1. My neighbor helped (he, him) with the model.
2. (Their, They're) policy is very strict.
3. The professor said that it was (she, her, her's).
4. (We, Us) girls will decorate the gym.
5. Dr. Stevenson gave (she, her) and (he, him) his blessing.
6. Our puppy wagged (its, it's) tail.
7. I waited for (they, them) while (they, them) changed clothes.
8. Can (we, us) work on (our, our's) projects now?
9. Your costume is the best of all of (them, their's).
10. Why were (he, him) and (she, her) late to class?
11. "Will you sing with (us, we) girls?" asked Mary.
12. (He, Him) and (I, me) will cook the bacon and eggs.
13. With you and (they, them) on our team, we will surely win.
14. (Your, Yours) experience will help all of (we, us) boys.
15. Between you and (I, me), I hope to win the contest.
16. (Their, They're) contributions will keep (he, him) safe.
17. My sister and (I, me) have joined (they're, their) club.
18. Ask (he, him) to show you (his, his's) identification.
19. Only (she, her) could solve the riddle.
20. Do you prefer (they, them) or (we, us) for the team?

DEVELOPING WRITING SKILLS: Writing Sentences with Nominative, Objective, and Possessive Pronouns. Use each item in a sentence of your own.

EXAMPLE: she and her brother
　　　　　　She and her brother raise tropical fish.

1. Mother and me	11. her and Bruce
2. he and I	12. the reporters and they
3. my coach and she	13. my parakeet and me
4. his friends and them	14. she and my grandfather
5. Uncle Bill and us	15. Fred and them
6. you and he	16. we golfers
7. my brother and they	17. you and him
8. your teacher and she	18. their house
9. him and his brother	19. his practicing
10. between you and me	20. him and me

237

12.2 Special Problems with Pronouns

Just as some verbs pose special usage problems, so do some pronouns. For example, would a receptionist be correct in asking, "*Whom* should I say is calling?" Would it be correct to say, "Pat is a better player than *me*"? This section will show you that each of these sentences is incorrect and will help you avoid such errors.

Using *Who* and *Whom* Correctly

Perhaps the most troublesome pronouns in the language are *who* and *whom*. To choose the correct pronoun for a sentence, you must remember the case.

Who is nominative. Whom is objective.

The chart below shows the uses of each pronoun.

Case	Pronoun	Use in Sentence
Nominative	who	Subject or Predicate Nominative
Objective	whom	Direct Object or Object of a Preposition
Possessive	whose	To Show Ownership

Since few people have problems using *whose*, the following pages will focus on the nominative and objective pronouns.

NOTE ABOUT *WHOSE*: Do not confuse the possessive pronoun *whose* with the contraction *who's*, meaning *who is*.

POSSESSIVE PRONOUN: *Whose* hat is this?

CONTRACTION: *Who's* the person in charge here?

The Nominative Case: *Who*. The nominative case is used for subjects and predicate nominatives.

Use *who* for the subject of a verb.

EXAMPLES: *Who* won this year's Pulitzer Prize for poetry?

Who will be the group leader?

238

Be sure to follow this rule when the pronoun is the subject of a subordinate clause.

EXAMPLES: I wonder *who* wrote this article.

Carlos is the guide *who* conducted the tour.

Louis is the one *who* invited us.

Both examples are complex sentences: Each has a main clause and a subordinate clause. *Who* is used because it is the subject of each subordinate clause.

You can be sure you are using the correct case of the pronoun in a complex sentence if you determine how the pronoun is used. In the following example, is the pronoun correct?

EXAMPLE: I did not know *who* left the roses.

To see if the case of the pronoun is correct, first isolate the subordinate clause. Then determine the pronoun's use in the clause. Since the pronoun in the example is acting as the subject of the verb *left,* the nominative *who* is correct.

SUBORDINATE CLAUSE: who left the roses

USE OF PRONOUN: subject

CASE FOR SUBJECTS: nominative

Use *who* for a predicate nominative.

EXAMPLE: The winner was *who?*

Be sure to follow this rule when the pronoun is the predicate nominative of a subordinate clause.

EXAMPLE: No one knew *who* the winner was.

To see if the case of the pronoun is correct, begin by isolating the subordinate clause. If the clause is inverted (as this one is), put it in the usual order. Next, determine how the pronoun is used in the clause. Since a pronoun following a linking verb must be nominative, *who* is correct as the predicate nominative.

SUBORDINATE CLAUSE: who the winner was

REWORDED CLAUSE: the winner was who

USE OF PRONOUN: predicate nominative

CASE FOR PREDICATE NOMINATIVES: nominative

The Objective Case: *Whom*. The objective case is used for direct objects and objects of prepositions.

Use *whom* for the direct object of a verb.

In the following example, *whom* is the direct object of the verb *did ask.*

EXAMPLE: *Whom* did she ask to the dance?

The objective case is also used when the pronoun acts as a direct object in a subordinate clause. In the first example below, *whom* is the direct object of the verb *meant.* In the second, *whom* is the direct object of the verb *was taking.*

EXAMPLES: I wonder *whom* he meant.

I asked him *whom* he was taking to the dance.

A subordinate clause that begins with *whom* will always be inverted. To see if the case of the pronoun is correct, put the clause in the usual order. If the pronoun is a direct object, it will follow the subject and verb when the clause is reworded. Its case should be objective.

SUBORDINATE CLAUSE: whom he was taking to the dance

REWORDED CLAUSE: he was taking whom to the dance

USE OF PRONOUN: direct object

CASE FOR DIRECT OBJECTS: objective

Use *whom* for the object of a preposition.

In both of the following examples, *whom* is the object of the preposition *with.*

EXAMPLES: With *whom* were you speaking?

Whom were you speaking with?

Be sure to follow this rule when the pronoun is part of a subordinate clause. In the first example below, the pronoun immediately follows its preposition. In the second example, however, the pronoun is separated from its preposition, *from.*

EXAMPLES: We met the writer about *whom* we had read so much.

Marie thanked the police officer *whom* she had gotten the directions from.

To check the case of the pronoun, put the clause in its usual order and determine the use of the pronoun.

SUBORDINATE CLAUSE: whom she had gotten the directions from

REWORDED CLAUSE: she had gotten the directions from whom

USE OF PRONOUN: object of a preposition

CASE FOR OBJECTS OF PREPOSITIONS: objective

Checking Case in Subordinate Clauses with Parenthetical Expressions. Parenthetical expressions such as *we believe, I suppose,* or *experts say* do not affect the case of a pronoun when they appear within a subordinate clause.

EXAMPLES: He is the one *who,* experts say, will win.

He is the one *whom,* experts say, the voters want.

NOTE ABOUT *WHOM* IN INFORMAL ENGLISH: *Whom* is becoming less common in informal English. This is especially true when an object of a preposition is separated from its preposition.

INFORMAL: *Who* did you want to speak with?

When the pronoun follows the preposition, however, you should use the objective case even in informal English.

FORMAL AND INFORMAL: With *whom* did you want to speak?

EXERCISE A: Using *Who* and *Whom* Correctly in Questions. Choose the correct pronoun in each sentence.

EXAMPLE: To (who, whom) did you give the key?

whom

1. From (who, whom) did you buy that basketball?
2. (Who, Whom) is your best friend?
3. (Whose, Who's) camera are we using tonight?
4. (Who, Whom) did you expect?
5. The committee selected (who, whom)?
6. (Who, Whom) knows how to use the copying machine?
7. With (who, whom) have you agreed to work on the project?
8. (Whose, Who's) the choice of the committee?
9. (Who, Whom) will you invite to the party?
10. (Who, Whom) spoke to you at lunch?

EXERCISE B: Using *Who* and *Whom* Correctly in Clauses.
Write the subordinate clause in each sentence. Then indicate
how *who* or *whom* is used.

EXAMPLE:　We applauded the man who rescued the cat.

who rescued the cat　(subject)

 1. He knows whom we want.
 2. They gave free tickets to the man who got there first.
 3. My mother could not imagine who would phone that late.
 4. Later, he told us who was responsible.
 5. The teacher congratulated the students who passed.
 6. This is the person whom we all admire.
 7. We talked to the dealer from whom they bought their car.
 8. She is the actress whom I most admire.
 9. We do not know whom she has chosen.
10. She is the doctor whom you should see.
11. They are the people whom we defeated.
12. Those who are here will clean the barracks.
13. Give our thanks to the man who cleaned the garage.
14. The prize will go to the one who finishes first.
15. The club will accept all who apply.
16. The guide whom they selected knew the city well.
17. My mother asked me who had won the contest.
18. The cowboys whom we met were experts with a lasso.
19. I wonder whom you expected.
20. This is the player whom I told you about.

**EXERCISE C: Using *Who* and *Whom* in Questions and
Clauses.** Choose the correct pronoun in each sentence.

EXAMPLE:　She is the candidate for (who, whom) I voted.

whom

 1. I know (who, whom) the culprit is.
 2. Can you tell us (who, whom) they really want?
 3. Fritz is the only barber (who, whom) I trust.
 4. We accept contributions from all (who, whom) will give.
 5. The girl (who, whom) you like is a friend of mine.
 6. Into (whose, who's) classroom have they gone?
 7. I met the man (who, whom), all the polls said, will win.
 8. To (who, whom) were you writing?

9. It is he with (who, whom) you should speak.
10. Take these roses to the man (who, whom) lives next door.
11. The lieutenant (who, whom) won was later promoted.
12. My father is the man (who, whom) prepared the schedule for the volunteer fire department.
13. (Who's, Whose) the student with the highest score?
14. Ask all (who, whom) are concerned to aid our cause.
15. With (who, whom) were you visiting?
16. Is she the saleswoman to (who, whom) you spoke?
17. The shortstop (who, whom) you saw at today's game is having a poor season.
18. To (who, whom) will you give the job?
19. (Who, Whom) is the teacher you want us to meet?
20. We are the ones (who, whom) are to blame.

EXERCISE D: More Work with *Who* and *Whom*. Write *who, whom, whose,* or *who's* to complete each sentence.

EXAMPLE: Give money to the student _____ most needs it.

who

1. From _____ did you get that package?
2. He is the sailor _____ we spotted earlier.
3. _____ do you expect to see in Boston?
4. _____ car do you want to borrow?
5. I want to meet the student _____ wrote this essay.
6. It is she _____ you should contact.
7. The applicant _____ is selected must be able to type.
8. Those _____ practice will play better.
9. She was a singer _____ everyone liked.
10. The principal told _____ ?
11. With _____ have you consulted about the trip?
12. _____ the technician repairing my stereo?
13. Tell us _____ , you think, will be best for the job.
14. Gladys consoled the actor _____ the director fired.
15. I know _____ wrote this report.
16. To _____ have you talked?
17. Max hired the applicant _____ I recommended.
18. _____ the drummer in the band?
19. He is the racer _____ , we believe, will finish first.
20. The speaker _____ uses pronouns correctly wins the prize.

Using Pronouns Correctly in Elliptical Clauses

Elliptical clauses are clauses in which some of the words are omitted yet understood. To shorten comparisons, for example, some words in a subordinate clause may be left out. Sometimes only a pronoun may be stated. In choosing the case of the pronoun, mentally complete the rest of the clause.

In elliptical clauses beginning with *than* or *as*, use the form of the pronoun that you would use if the clause were fully stated.

The following examples indicate that the words left out of an elliptical clause may come after or before the pronoun. The words in brackets are understood but not actually stated.

WORDS LEFT OUT AFTER PRONOUN: He is as tall as *she.*
He is as tall as she [is].

WORDS LEFT OUT BEFORE PRONOUN: She gave us fewer chores than *them.*
She gave us fewer chores than [she gave] them.

When selecting a pronoun for an elliptical clause, begin by mentally completing the clause. If the words left out would normally come after the pronoun, use a nominative pronoun (*I, we, he, she, they*) because it will be the subject of the understood verb. If the words left out would normally come before the pronoun, use an objective pronoun *(me, us, him, her, them)* because it will be the direct object of the understood verb or the object of a preposition.

Sometimes the entire meaning of the sentence depends on the case of the pronoun. Notice in the following examples how the meaning changes when *he* is changed to *him.*

NOMINATIVE PRONOUN: Fran helped us more than *he.*
Fran helped us more than he [did].

OBJECTIVE PRONOUN: Fran helped us more than *him.*
Fran helped us more than [she helped] him.

Follow the steps in the chart at the top of the next page in order to determine which case of a pronoun to use.

**STEPS FOR CHOOSING A PRONOUN
IN ELLIPTICAL CLAUSES**

---

1. Consider the pronouns you have to choose from.
2. Mentally complete the elliptical clause.
3. Make your choice based on the complete elliptical clause.

EXERCISE E: Identifying the Correct Pronoun in Elliptical Clauses. Rewrite each sentence, choosing one pronoun in parentheses and correctly completing the elliptical clause.

EXAMPLE: She is as short as (I, me).

　　　　　　She is as short as I am.

1. Beth has more experience than (I, me).
2. She writes better than (I, me).
3. He feels that he is as skilled as (she, her).
4. I have better manners than (he, him).
5. He was more seriously injured than (she, her).
6. My brother is as advanced in chemistry as (she, her).
7. Helen can type as fast as (I, me).
8. Mrs. Pratt gave me a higher grade than (he, him).
9. I worked longer last night than (he, him).
10. Find out if he earned more money than (she, her).

EXERCISE F: Using the Correct Pronoun in Elliptical Clauses. Rewrite each sentence, choosing an appropriate pronoun and completing the elliptical clause.

EXAMPLE: John studies more than _____.

　　　　　　John studies more than I do.

1. My friend Bruce is more trustworthy than _____.
2. Unfortunately, you are just as wrong as _____.
3. My grandfather is much wiser than _____.
4. The collection is more valuable to me than _____.
5. My oldest sister was always bolder than _____.
6. Jonathan eats more than _____.
7. He is less likely to get the job than _____.
8. When we were insulted, Rachel was as indignant as _____.
9. The contest is more important to him than _____.
10. She is less likely to accept advice than _____.

DEVELOPING WRITING SKILLS: Writing Sentences with *Who, Whom,* and Elliptical Clauses. Use each item in a sentence of your own.

EXAMPLE: as tall as she

My younger brother is now as tall as she.

1. stronger than I
2. whom I like best
3. more than him
4. whom I helped
5. as slow as we
6. who loses
7. happier than they
8. whom we select
9. as capable as he
10. the one who plays best
11. less than them
12. to whom you like
13. as strong as she
14. beside whom sits
15. more than us
16. who the thief is
17. as well as she
18. whom she asked
19. better than her
20. who runs the fastest

Skills Review and Writing Workshop

Pronoun Usage

CHECKING YOUR SKILLS

Rewrite the following paragraph, correcting all the errors in pronoun usage.

(1) My older sister Sarah and me spent an entire day hiking. (2) No one is a better hiker than her. (3) Its interesting to walk through the woods because there is so much to see. (4) Along the way some deer passed so close to us that there were only a few yards between we and they. (5) We had only a moment to watch them walking by before them ran off. (6) Afterward, Sarah, who swims better than me, decided to go swimming in a nearby stream. (7) Us splashing around must have scared away every animal in the area. (8) Sarah was the one to who my mother gave the sandwiches for lunch. (9) I ate all of my sandwich, but Sarah could not finish her's. (10) After lunch, us girls set off again.

USING USAGE SKILLS IN WRITING
Writing Your Autobiography

A good writer knows that pronouns must be used correctly for writing to have the desired impact. Write your autobiography, but with a difference. Make it an autobiography of yourself at age forty-five. Give the autobiography as much impact as possible by following these steps.

Prewriting: Consider the most important things that have happened in your life so far. Then think of any other things you would like to have achieved by the time you reach forty-five.

Writing: Begin with a short statement that sums up the way you feel about your life. Then present the highlights of your life chronologically.

Revising: First look at your pronouns and correct any mistakes in usage. Then read through your autobiography, looking for other improvements you could make. After you have revised, proofread carefully.

13

Agreement

When you speak, you automatically make some words agree with other words. You might say, for example, "She *talks* faster than they *talk*." You know you must add an *-s* to *talk* when the subject is *she* to make the verb agree with the subject.

Because grammatical agreement is not always obvious, you need to study some sentences more closely. In this chapter you will learn to make a subject and its verb agree as well as a pronoun and its antecedent.

13.1 Subject and Verb Agreement

To make a subject and a verb agree, make sure that both are *singular* or that both are *plural*. In this section you will learn how to distinguish between singular and plural subjects. You will also learn how to determine if the form of a verb is singular or plural.

Number: Singular and Plural

In grammar the concept of *number* is simple.

Number refers to the two forms of a word: singular and plural. Singular words indicate one; plural words indicate more than one.

Only nouns, pronouns, and verbs indicate number. The other parts of speech do not.

The Number of Nouns. The chart below lists some common nouns in their singular and plural forms.

NOUNS	
Singular	**Plural**
truck	trucks
player	players
box	boxes
watch	watches
woman	women
mouse	mice

The plurals of most nouns are formed by adding an -*s* or -*es* (player*s*, box*es*). Other nouns, however, form their plurals in special ways (wom*en*, m*ice*). If you are in doubt about the plural of a noun, consult a dictionary.

The Number of Pronouns. Many pronouns also have singular and plural forms. For example, *I, he, she,* and *it* are singular; *we* and *they* are plural; *you* can be either singular or plural.

The chart below lists these common pronouns.

PRONOUNS		
Singular	**Plural**	**Singular or Plural**
I	we	you
he, she it	they	

The Number of Verbs. The grammatical number of verbs is more complex. Like the pronoun *you,* many verbs can be singular or plural. With such verbs, the number depends on the subject.

SINGULAR: I *walk.*   *I have walked.*

PLURAL: We *walk.* We *have walked.*

For most verbs there are only two major exceptions to this rule. In the present tense and in the present perfect tense, *he, she, it,* and singular nouns have forms that are always singular.

ALWAYS SINGULAR: He *walks.* He *has walked.*

The verb *be* has a few additional special forms. In the present tense, both *I* and *he, she, it,* and singular nouns have special forms.

ALWAYS SINGULAR: I *am*.   He *is*.

In the past tense, there is a single special form that is shared by *I, he, she, it,* and singular nouns.

ALWAYS SINGULAR: I *was*.   He *was*.

The following chart lists the verb forms that are always singular as well as verbs that can be singular or plural.

VERBS	
Always Singular	**Singular or Plural**
(he, Lisa) walks	(I, you, we, they) walk
(he, Lisa) has walked	(I, you, we, they) have walked
(I) am (he, Lisa) is	(you, we, they) are
(I, he, Lisa) was	(you, we, they) were

If a verb has had an *-s* or *-es* added to it *(walk, walks)* or if it includes the words *has, am, is,* or *was,* it will be a singular verb. All other verbs will be singular or plural depending upon their subjects.

EXERCISE A: Determining the Number of Nouns, Pronouns, and Verbs. Identify each item as *singular, plural,* or *both.*

EXAMPLE: speaks

   singular

1. car	11. helps	21. we
2. lifeguards	12. is	22. tulips
3. tomatoes	13. was	23. it
4. woman	14. was plotting	24. draws
5. he	15. grow	25. could
6. lizard	16. seeks	
7. demonstrators	17. loses	
8. writes	18. has been watching	
9. soldiers	19. choose	
10. she	20. you	

Singular and Plural Subjects

Two simple rules about subject and verb agreement govern all other rules.

A singular subject must have a singular verb.

A plural subject must have a plural verb.

In the following examples, the subjects are underlined once and the verbs twice.

SINGULAR SUBJECT AND VERB: Ann always tells the truth.

I am ready for lunch now.

Jerry was playing football.

PLURAL SUBJECT AND VERB: The twins always tell the truth.

We are ready for lunch now.

My friends were playing football.

A subject must agree with its verb even when a phrase or clause comes between them.

A phrase or clause that interrupts a subject and its verb does not affect subject-verb agreement.

In the first of the following examples, the singular subject, *captain,* agrees with *stands,* a singular verb. *Guards,* the object of a preposition, does not affect the agreement. In the second example, the plural subject, *troopers,* agrees with *stand,* a plural verb. The clause that interrupts the subject and verb does not affect the agreement.

EXAMPLES: The captain of the guards stands at attention.

The troopers whom the captain put in charge of the roadblock stand on either side.

EXERCISE B: Making Subjects Agree with Their Verbs.
Choose the verb in parentheses that agrees with the subject of each sentence.

EXAMPLE: He (jog, jogs) two miles every day.

jogs

251

1. A tall tree (stands, stand) in our front yard.
2. The ships (was, were) passing the island.
3. It seems that the baby (grows, grow) an inch everyday.
4. Our blackboards (was, were) all scratched.
5. Candles (is, are) quite expensive.
6. Yesterday the newspaper (was, were) not delivered.
7. His pictures (belongs, belong) in the gallery.
8. Mr. Cody (was, were) reading poems in a dramatic voice.
9. At sunrise the ships (sails, sail) from harbor.
10. At the quarry the noises (is, are) deafening.

EXERCISE C: Making Separated Subjects and Verbs Agree. Choose the verb in parentheses that agrees with the subject of each sentence.

1. The girls on the team (has, have) arrived.
2. The bear that was thought to be roaming through the fields (was, were) spotted in the woods.
3. The representative for the townspeople (is, are) unable to appear at tonight's meeting.
4. The insects on the rubber plant (was, were) sprayed.
5. The racing yachts that arrived late (was, were) delayed by an unexpected squall.
6. The managers in our office (is, are) holding a meeting.
7. The filing cabinets that were in the storeroom (has, have) been moved to the new offices.
8. The marble from Vermont (was, were) shipped to Ohio.
9. Investigating teams from the FBI (is, are) now in the area.
10. The book on developing your own photos (was, were) helpful.

Compound Subjects

A compound subject consists of two or more subjects usually connected by *or* or *and.* A number of different rules apply to compound subjects.

Singular Subjects Joined by *Or* or *Nor*. When both parts of a compound subject connected by *or* or *nor* are singular, a singular verb is required.

Two or more singular subjects joined by *or* or *nor* must have a singular verb.

In the following example, the conjunction *or* connects two singular subjects which act as a singular compound subject. Either Beth or Sam will be the winner—not both.

EXAMPLE: <u>Beth</u> or <u>Sam</u> <u>is going</u> to win.

Plural Subjects Joined by *Or* or *Nor*. When both parts of a compound subject connected by *or* or *nor* are plural, a plural verb is required.

Two or more plural subjects joined by *or* or *nor* must have a plural verb.

EXAMPLE: The <u>girls</u> or the <u>boys</u> <u>are going</u> to win.

Subjects of Mixed Number Joined by *Or* or *Nor*. If one part of a compound subject is singular and the other is plural, the verb agrees with the subject that is closer to it.

If one or more singular subjects are joined to one or more plural subjects by *or* or *nor,* the subject closest to the verb determines agreement.

EXAMPLES: <u>Beth</u>, <u>Sam</u>, or the <u>twins</u> <u>are going</u> to win.

Either the <u>twins</u> or <u>Sam</u> <u>is going</u> to win.

Subjects Joined by *And*. Only one rule applies to compound subjects connected by *and* whether the parts of the compound subject are all singular, all plural, or mixed.

A compound subject joined by *and* is generally plural and must have a plural verb.

EXAMPLES: <u>Penny</u> and <u>Rose</u> <u>are going</u> to lose.

The <u>boys</u> and <u>girls</u> <u>are going</u> to have a rematch.

The <u>twins</u> and <u>Sam</u> <u>are going</u> to have a rematch.

There are two exceptions to the preceding rule. If the parts of the compound subject are thought of as one item, then a singular verb is needed. A singular verb is also needed if the word *every* or the word *each* precedes a compound subject.

EXAMPLES: <u>Bacon</u> and <u>eggs</u> <u>is</u> my favorite breakfast.

Every <u>boy</u> and <u>girl</u> in the class <u>does</u> volunteer work.

EXERCISE D: Making Compound Subjects Agree with Their Verbs. Choose the verb in parentheses that agrees with the subject in each sentence.

EXAMPLE: Either Kelly or Jim (play, plays) the lead role.

plays

1. The door and the window (is, are) stuck.
2. Neither Mother nor Father (has, have) phoned.
3. The dog or the cats (is, are) always howling.
4. Apples and bananas (has, have) been my favorite fruits for years.
5. Mary or Louise (belongs, belong) to the bridge club.
6. Each morning Tom or the children (buys, buy) fresh rolls at the bakery.
7. Both the man with the appliances and the plumber (has, have) arrived.
8. My son and daughter (has, have) never been so cooperative.
9. Mark and David (isn't, aren't) in the office yet.
10. Two large packages and a letter (was, were) delivered.
11. Either the children or I (walks, walk) into town for the mail.
12. Joan and Ellen (hasn't, haven't) called in a month.
13. My car or Ted's (is, are) always available.
14. His messiness and my chattering (annoys, annoy) Mother.
15. Every cup and saucer (was, were) broken in the move.
16. Rain and snow always (falls, fall) this time of year.
17. The principal or the dean (wants, want) to speak with you.
18. After dinner either Bruce or Debbie (cleans, clean) the table.
19. Sausage and peppers in tomato sauce (was, were) served with a green salad.
20. Heavy rains and high winds (has, have) hit the coast.

Confusing Subjects

Some subjects create special arrangement problems.

Hard-to-Find Subjects. Foremost among the confusing subjects are hard-to-find subjects that come after their verbs.

A subject that comes after its verb must still agree with it in number.

A sentence in which the subject comes after the verb is said to be *inverted.* The subject in the following example is *tractors.* It is plural and agrees with the plural verb *are.* Check the verb by mentally rewording the sentence so that the subject comes at the beginning.

EXAMPLE: On the top of the hill <u>are</u> two <u>tractors</u>.

(Two tractors are on top of the hill.)

The words *there* and *here* at the beginning of a sentence often signal an inverted sentence. The subject in the first of the following sentences is *orange.* It is singular and agrees with the singular verb *is.* The plural subject *oranges* in the second sentence agrees with the plural verb *are.*

EXAMPLES: There <u>is</u> only one <u>orange</u> in the basket.

There <u>are</u> still several <u>oranges</u> in the basket.

NOTE ABOUT *THERE'S* AND *HERE'S*: The contractions *there's (there is)* and *here's (here is)* contain singular verbs. They should not be used with plural subjects.

CORRECT: Here'<u>s</u> my <u>friend</u> now.

Here <u>are</u> my <u>friends</u> now.

Subjects of Linking Verbs. Subjects with linking verbs may also cause agreement problems. Do not be misled by a predicate nominative.

A linking verb must agree with its subject, regardless of the number of its predicate nominative.

Problems occur when the subject and predicate nominative are not the same in number. In the first example below, the plural subject *cars* agrees with the plural verb *are* even though the predicate nominative *reason* is singular. In the second example, the nouns are reversed: The subject is now *reason,* which agrees with the singular verb *is,* and *cars* becomes the predicate nominative.

EXAMPLES: Speeding <u>cars</u> <u>are</u> one reason for the accident rate.

One <u>reason</u> for the accident rate <u>is</u> speeding cars.

Collective Nouns. Collective nouns, such as *assembly, audience, class, club, committee, faculty, flock,* and *group,* name groups of people or things. These words can be confusing subjects since they can be either singular or plural, depending on how they are used.

A collective noun takes a singular verb when the group it names acts as a single unit.

A collective noun takes a plural verb when the group it names act as individuals with different points of view.

SINGULAR: The <u>jury</u> <u>has reached</u> a verdict.

   The <u>class</u> <u>is going</u> on a field trip today.

PLURAL: The <u>committee</u> <u>are taking</u> their seats.

   The <u>cast</u> of the play <u>are rehearsing</u> their lines.

Plural-Looking Nouns. Other confusing subjects are nouns that end in *-s* and appear to be plural but are actually singular in meaning.

Nouns that are plural in form but singular in meaning agree with singular verbs.

Some of these nouns name branches of knowledge, such as *civics, economics, physics, mathematics,* and *social studies.* Others are singular because, like collective nouns, they name single units: *molasses* (one kind of syrup), *mumps* (one disease), *news* (one body of information), and so on.

EXAMPLES: <u>Social studies</u> <u>has become</u> my favorite subject.

   <u>Measles</u> <u>is</u> a dangerous disease for unborn children.

Indefinite Pronouns. Most indefinite pronouns do not cause agreement problems because their number is usually self-evident. Review the list on page 31. Notice that some of the pronouns will always be singular: those ending in *-one (anyone, everyone, someone)* or *-body (anybody, everybody, somebody)* and those that imply one *(each, either).* Others are always plural: *both, few, many, others, several.* The rules for these indefinite pronouns are simple.

Singular indefinite pronouns take singular verbs.

Plural indefinite pronouns take plural verbs.

Do not be misled by a prepositional phrase that interrupts the subject and verb. The interrupting phrase does not affect subject-verb agreement.

ALWAYS SINGULAR: <u>One</u> of the paintings <u>is</u> missing.

<u>Everyone</u> in our class <u>has finished</u>.

<u>Either</u> of your plans <u>is</u> acceptable to me.

ALWAYS PLURAL: <u>Few</u> of the contestants <u>are</u> here yet.

<u>Both</u> of the players <u>were</u> late.

<u>Several</u> of the witnesses <u>have testified</u>.

The indefinite pronouns that cause the most problems are those that can be either singular or plural.

The pronouns *all, any, more, most, none,* and *some* usually take a singular verb if the antecedent is singular and a plural verb if it is plural.

In the first example below, the antecedent of *all* is the singular *soup;* therefore, a singular verb is used. In the second example, the antecedent is the plural *seats* and a plural verb is required.

EXAMPLES: <u>All</u> of the soup <u>was eaten</u>.

<u>All</u> of the seats <u>were taken</u>.

Titles. Do not be confused by the title of a book or other work of art when it is the subject of a verb.

A title is singular and must have a singular verb.

Though the titles in the following examples look and sound plural, they are singular and require singular verbs.

EXAMPLES: *Hard Times* <u>is</u> a novel by Charles Dickens.

Wuthering Heights <u>is</u> a famous novel by Emily Bronte.

Amounts and Measurements. Most amounts and measurements, although they appear to be plural, actually express single units or ideas.

A noun expressing an amount or measurement is usually singular and requires a singular verb.

In the first three examples below, the subjects agree with singular verbs. *Fifty cents* equals one sum of money; *twelve feet* is one measurement; and *four fifths* is one part of a total crop. In the last example, however, the subject, *half*, refers to many individual items and is, therefore, plural.

EXAMPLES: Fifty cents <u>is</u> more than enough.

            Twelve feet <u>was</u> the length of the room.

            Four fifths of the crop <u>was saved</u>.

            Half of the nails <u>were</u> useless.

EXERCISE E: Making Confusing Subjects Agree with Their Verbs. Choose the item in parentheses that agrees with the subject of each sentence.

EXAMPLE: All of the apples (is, are) rotten.

        are

1. Near the top of the closet (is, are) an old electric fan.
2. The committee (has, have) been unable to reach an agreement.
3. Rich foods (is, are) one cause of oily skin.
4. Economics (was, were) my sister's major in college.
5. (Do, Does) exotic plants thrive in this climate?
6. The group of tourists (has, have) left on the bus.
7. The jury (has, have) left their seats but will soon return.
8. He said that civics (was, were) his favorite subject.
9. (Is, Are) some of the soup still available?
10. (Here's, Here are) more volunteers for the clean-up crew.
11. The problem at the picnic (was, were) bees.
12. There (is, are) two excellent reasons for his choice.
13. Politics (was, were) one of his major interests.
14. The entire faculty (has, have) voiced their opinions.
15. (There's, There are) the captains of both teams.
16. *Green Mansions* (is, are) her favorite novel.

258

17. There (is, are) only one possible explanation.
18. Another example of the area's underdevelopment (is, are) the narrow dirt roads.
19. Mumps (is, are) a dangerous disease for adults.
20. The team (has, have) been squabbling with each other again.
21. At the top of the stairs (is, are) the two lights.
22. (Is, Are) mathematics on your program this term?
23. Here (is, are) two records I particularly like.
24. The news from the Middle East (has, have) been unsettling.
25. The assembly (has, have) voted themselves a pay increase.

EXERCISE F: More Work with Confusing Subjects. Choose the verb in parentheses that agrees with the subject of each sentence.

1. One of the girls (was, were) hurt on the soccer field.
2. Few (has, have) volunteered for the assignment.
3. Somebody in the room above (seems, seem) to be quite ill.
4. Several of the contestants (has, have) arrived.
5. Some of the food (was, were) not cooked thoroughly.
6. Four dollars (is, are) an outrageous price for the book.
7. Each of the guards (has, have) sworn allegiance.
8. Why (is, are) everyone so unhappy?
9. None of the cakes (was, were) thrown away.
10. Three fourths of the fence (was, were) installed.
11. *The Adventures of Tom Sawyer* (has, have) always been a favorite of mine.
12. One half of the report (was, were) all I could finish.
13. Three fourths of the wire (is, are) frayed.
14. Two thirds of the cartons (has, have) been opened.
15. *The Comedy of Errors* (is, are) an early Shakespeare play.
16. *Rumors* by Fleetwood Mac (is, are) a best seller.
17. Sixty cans of beans (was, were) needed for the picnic.
18. Some of the cheese (has, have) become moldy.
19. Few of the apples (is, are) ripe.
20. Not one of the masqueraders (is, are) wearing a mask.
21. *Lives of the Poets* (has, have) material on Tennyson.
22. Almost a hundred dollars in change (was, were) collected.
23. None of the students (is, are) absent.
24. Most of the money (was, were) lost.
25. Most of the galleries in the museum (was, were) closed.

EXERCISE G: Using All of the Rules of Subject and Verb Agreement. Choose the verb in parentheses that agrees with the subject of each sentence.

1. Barry and Marie (has, have) celebrated another anniversary.
2. Steak and eggs (is, are) Dad's favorite breakfast.
3. Neither my mother nor my father (is, are) at home.
4. My father or my sisters (is, are) going to pick me up.
5. The two dentists in our building (is, are) both excellent.
6. Everyone at the meeting (speaks, speak) well of Charles.
7. There (is, are) only one way we can travel there.
8. The news about the earthquakes (was, were) frightening.
9. *The Grapes of Wrath* always (moves, move) me to tears.
10. None of my suggestions (was, were) adopted at the meeting last night.
11. The man who sells fruits and vegetables (has, have) moved to another city.
12. Half of my house (hasn't, haven't) been painted yet.
13. Sixty dollars for jeans (is, are) too much.
14. Molasses (is, are) used in that recipe.
15. *Scott's Catalogue* (is, are) the bible of stamp collectors.
16. Most of the roast leg of lamb (was, were) still juicy.
17. Each of the girls (contributes, contribute) to the effort.
18. Here (is, are) three letters that must be delivered by tomorrow morning at the latest.
19. *Long Day's Journey into Night* and *The Crucible* (is, are) plays my sister studied in the upper grades.
20. No, she and I (isn't, aren't) ready to give our report to the class yet.

DEVELOPING WRITING SKILLS: Applying the Rules of Subject and Verb Agreement. Use each item at the beginning of a sentence, followed by the verb *is* or the verb *are*.

EXAMPLE: his uncle or my parents

His uncle or my parents are meeting us.

1. Michael and Judy
2. neither he nor she
3. each of the boys
4. the two cats and the dog
5. the committee
6. everyone
7. ham and eggs
8. two dollars
9. all of the cake
10. those two girls and that boy

260

Pronoun and Antecedent 13.2 Agreement

Antecedents are the nouns (or the words that take the place of nouns) for which pronouns stand. Although the word *antecedent* comes from a Latin word meaning "to go before," an antecedent in English follows its pronoun. This section will explain how pronouns agree with their antecedents.

Agreement Between Personal Pronouns and Antecedents

One rule of pronoun and antecedent agreement is the basis for almost all of the other rules.

A personal pronoun must agree with its antecedent in number, person, and gender.

As you know, the grammatical number of a pronoun indicates if it is *singular* or *plural.* The person of a pronoun indicates whether it refers to the *first person* (the one speaking), the *second person* (the one spoken to), or the *third person* (the one spoken about).

Some pronouns and nouns also indicate one of three *genders: masculine, feminine,* or *neuter.* Nouns referring to males, such as *uncle* and *boy,* are masculine. Nouns referring to females, such as *actress* and *mother,* are feminine. Nouns that do not refer to either males or females, such as *stone* and *freedom,* are neuter.

Only pronouns in the third-person singular indicate gender.

GENDER OF THIRD-PERSON SINGULAR PRONOUNS		
Masculine	**Feminine**	**Neuter**
he, him, his	she, her, hers	it, its

In the following example, the pronoun and antecedent agree completely. Both the antecedent *Charlie* and the pronoun *his* are singular, third person, and masculine.

EXAMPLE: *Charlie* gave *his* report to the teacher.

261

Agreement in Number. Making personal pronouns agree with their antecedents in number is usually a problem only when the antecedent is a compound.

Use a singular personal pronoun with two or more singular antecedents joined by *or* or *nor*.

EXAMPLE: Neither *Lisa* nor *Amy* can find *her* gloves.

Use a plural personal pronoun with two or more antecedents joined by *and*.

EXAMPLE: *Gene* and *Rita* have changed *their* plans.

Agreement in Person and Gender. Errors in agreement between personal pronouns and their antecedents often involve a shift in either person or gender.

When dealing with pronoun-antecedent agreement, take care not to shift either person or gender.

SHIFT IN PERSON:	*Jill* is studying biology, a course *you* need in order to prepare for medical school.
CORRECT:	*Jill* is studying biology, a course *she* needs in order to prepare for medical school.
SHIFT IN PERSON:	*Jill* is studying biology, a course *you* need in order to prepare for medical school.
CORRECT:	Each *nation* has *its* own culture, and our *nation* has *its* own culture, too.

Generic Masculine Pronouns. Historically, a masculine pronoun has been used to refer to a singular antecedent whose gender is not specified. Such use of the masculine pronoun is said to be *generic,* meaning it covers both the masculine and feminine genders. The use of the masculine is still correct, but many writers today prefer to avoid the generic masculine pronoun by rewriting the sentence.

When gender is not specified, use the masculine or rewrite the sentence.

EXAMPLES: A *student* should turn in *his* assignments on time.

A *student* should turn in assignments on time.

Students should turn in *their* assignments on time.

EXERCISE A: Making Personal Pronouns Agree with Their Antecedents. Write an appropriate personal pronoun to complete each sentence.

EXAMPLE: Either Mark or Bill will drive _____ car.

                        his

1. Mrs. Berger described _____ plans for the new store.
2. Carol will read _____ own report.
3. The goat shook _____ head in confusion.
4. My father gave us _____ secret recipe for muffins.
5. The city officials explained _____ reasons for the curfew.
6. Marie sealed the letter; then _____ tore it open again.
7. Neither Nancy nor Carol explained _____ position.
8. Uncle Roy sent us a package, but _____ never arrived.
9. I told John and Irene that _____ should be here by noon.
10. The nurse asked us about _____ eating habits.

Agreement with Indefinite Pronouns

When you write a sentence with both a personal pronoun and an indefinite pronoun, such as *few, one,* or *some,* you must always make sure that the two pronouns agree. This is relatively easy when both are plural.

Use a plural personal pronoun when the antecedent is a plural indefinite pronoun.

EXAMPLE: *Few* of the mice had returned to *their holes.*

The rule is also simple when both are singular.

Use a singular personal pronoun when the antecedent is a singular indefinite pronoun.

EXAMPLE: *One* of the boys lost *his* watch.

As you can see, however, with singular personal pronouns and indefinite pronouns, there must be agreement in gender as well as in number. *His* is used in the example above because the phrase after *one* specifies *boys.* If no gender is specified, you can use *his* or you can reword the sentence.

EXAMPLES: *One* of the students lost *his* watch.

                        One of the students lost a watch.

263

With an indefinite pronoun that can be either singular or plural, agreement depends on the antecedent of the indefinite pronoun. In the first example below, *some* stands for part of a *pie,* a singular noun. In the second example, *some* stands for part of the *students,* a plural noun.

EXAMPLES: *Some* of the pie has lost *its* filling.

   Some of the students are not in *their* seats.

NOTE ABOUT *EVERYBODY* AND *EVERYONE:* An exception is sometimes made for *everybody* and *everyone.* Since they mean *all,* they can be used informally with a plural personal pronoun.

INFORMAL: *Everybody* is eager to cast *their* votes.

EXERCISE B: Making Personal Pronouns Agree with Indefinite Pronouns. Choose the correct pronoun in each sentence.

EXAMPLE: All of the boys lost (his, their) money.

   their

1. Few at the conference gave (its, their) approval.
2. Every one of the boys has (his, their) instructions.
3. Each of the girls is responsible for (her, their) own room.
4. Neither of the boys agreed to ask (his, their) parents.
5. Every one of the girls agreed to ask (her, their) opinion.
6. One of the fellows will have to volunteer (his, their) time.
7. Both of my aunts sent (her, their) congratulations.
8. Several of the men volunteered (his, their) service.
9. Each of the women was given (her, their) lieutenant bars.
10. Neither of the men could remember (his, their) number.
11. Each of the ballerinas gave us (her, their) autograph.
12. All of the women refused to give (her, their) consent.
13. Several of the ships had (its, their) sails destroyed.
14. Each of the boys must pay (his, their) dues soon.
15. Some of the foods had lost (its, their) flavor.
16. Neither of the girls brought (her, their) new records.
17. Someone in the battalion has betrayed (his, their) trust.
18. Nobody in the boys' group brought (his, their) radio.
19. Each of the sales women announced (her, their) results.
20. Only one of the committees gave (its, their) consent.

Agreement with Reflexive Pronouns

A reflexive pronoun ends in *-self* or *-selves* and points back to a noun or pronoun near the beginning of the sentence, as in "*Louis* hurt *himself* while playing soccer."

A reflexive pronoun must agree with an antecedent that is clearly stated.

In the following example, the antecedent of *myself* is not clearly stated. The personal pronoun *me* should be used instead.

POOR: Our friends gave Clara and *myself* a surprise party.

CORRECT: Our friends gave Clara and *me* a surprise party.

EXERCISE C: Using Reflexive Pronouns Correctly. Rewrite each sentence, correcting the misused reflexive pronoun.

EXAMPLE: Both Todd and myself are going to the game.

            Both Todd and I are going to the game.

1. Bob and I think the best person for this job is yourself.
2. The Parkinsons and ourselves went to the opera together.
3. Neither Francine nor myself knew who left the package.
4. A guard directed the teacher and ourselves to the entrance.
5. Sal was worried that he would hurt himself or myself.
6. The only person we spoke to was yourself.
7. The results were a surprise to the doctor and ourselves.
8. The children and myself went swimming in the pool.
9. Will you tell Maria and ourselves that joke?
10. The package was for Amy and myself.

Four Special Problems in Pronoun Agreement

Careless writing can sometimes lead to sentences in which the antecedent of a personal pronoun is not clearly defined. When you use personal pronouns, make sure that they have antecedents.

A personal pronoun requires an antecedent that is either stated or clearly understood.

In the example below, there is no antecedent for the pronoun *they*. The sentence can be corrected by replacing *they* with a noun or a personal pronoun agreeing with the antecedent *story*.

POOR: The story was exciting, but *they* didn't explain what happened at the end.

CORRECT: The story was exciting, but the author didn't explain what happened at the end.

          The story was exciting, but it didn't explain what happened at the end.

You should also make sure that there is only one possible antecedent for each of the personal pronouns you use.

A personal pronoun should always refer to a single, obvious antecedent.

If a pronoun can refer to more than one antecedent, the sentence should be rewritten. In the example below, the pronoun *it* is confusing because it can refer to either *ad* or *paper*.

POOR: I saw the ad in the paper, but now I can't find *it*.

CORRECT: I saw the ad in the paper, but now I can't find the page with the ad.

          I can't find the ad that I saw in the paper.

A personal pronoun should also be close to its antecedent.

A personal pronoun should always be close enough to its antecedent to prevent confusion.

In the example below, *he* is too far away from its antecedent, *Caesar*. One solution is to replace *he* with *Caesar*. The other solution is to rewrite the passage to move the pronoun closer.

POOR: When *Caesar* entered the Senate, Brutus and the other conspirators began to crowd around. Even so, *he* did not yet sense any danger.

CORRECT: When Caesar entered the Senate, Brutus and the other conspirators began to crowd around. Even so, Caesar did not yet sense any danger.

          When Caesar entered the Senate, he did not sense any danger even as Brutus and the other conspirators began to crowd around.

A final problem involves the personal pronoun *you,* which is sometimes carelessly used in general statements.

Use the personal pronoun *you* only when the reference is truly to the reader or the listener.

In the example below, the pronoun *you* is vague and imprecise unless the reader or listener is planning a trip to Argentina.

POOR: | In Argentina *you* will find many cattle ranches.
CORRECT: | In Argentina a tourist will find many cattle ranches.

EXERCISE D: Correcting Special Problems in Pronoun Agreement. Choose the word or words in parentheses that more clearly complete each sentence.

EXAMPLE: The defendant was shocked when (they, the judge) read the verdict.

the judge

1. Going to a big city all alone often makes (you, a young person) feel more responsible.
2. Why did (they, the station) show that movie in the middle of the night?
3. William was very angry with Jonathan, but no one knew what (he, William) had said.
4. Take the books from the shelves and dust (them, the shelves) with a clean cloth.
5. In camp they expect (you, everyone) to rise early and exercise.
6. The catalog says that (you, students) must pay all fees by May.
7. He ate everything on his plate but did not even thank us for (it, the meal).
8. I liked the match, but (they, the players) were rude.
9. Debby gave Rita the news right after (she, Rita) arrived.
10. The phone call frightened her because (they, the anonymous caller) hung up.

EXERCISE E: More Work with Special Problems in Pronoun Agreement. Rewrite each sentence, correcting the error in pronoun agreement.

EXAMPLE: The road was dangerous because they had not yet cleared the snow.

The road was dangerous because it had not yet been cleared of snow.

1. When Mother shops for my sister, she is very pleased.
2. The brochure says that you must be eighteen to enlist.
3. A student must learn that homework is important to them.
4. The captain gave orders to the troops. Each man quickly took up his post. An hour later he checked to see that all was well.
5. After forgetting her lines in the show, my sister did not want to try it again.
6. The police chased the thieves until they crashed into a telephone pole.
7. When the dean spoke to Richie, he smiled.
8. When Mrs. Stevenson spoke to Alice, Alice felt that the plan was poor. Thus, she wanted another opinion.
9. Marge told Alice that she had been elected treasurer.
10. The rules say that you must take chemistry before physics.

DEVELOPING WRITING SKILLS: Making Pronouns and Antecedents Agree. Use each item as the antecedent of a personal pronoun.

EXAMPLE: each

Each of the men wore his gloves.

1. all	6. neither
2. one	7. several
3. both	8. Emily and John
4. Andrea	9. some
5. Joel	10. our neighbors

Skills Review and Writing Workshop

Agreement

CHECKING YOUR SKILLS

Correct the errors in agreement by rewriting the following paragraph.

(1) In the northern regions lays an area called the *taiga*. (2) Throughout the taiga, there is large forests of evergreen trees. (3) The evergreen tree never loses all their leaves at one time. (4) They remains green throughout the year. (5) Evergreens protect herself from insects by producing sticky gums. (6) A pine, or conifer, are an example of an evergreen. (7) All pine trees reproduce by means of seeds contained in its cones. (8) The bristlecone pine hold the record as the world's oldest living thing. (9) Sometime a forest of pine are destroyed by fire. (10) The jack pine, however, releases their seeds when heated and these grow after the fire has ended.

USING USAGE SKILLS IN WRITING
Writing About a Personal Experience

Writers who want their work to be understood follow all the rules of agreement. Write an account of your experience learning how to do something for the first time (for example, skiing). Create a polished draft by following these steps.

Prewriting: Think about how you felt before trying the new activity. Consider the steps you followed in learning how to do it. Did you feel a sense of accomplishment?

Writing: Begin by describing your feelings about doing something new. Then present your method of learning the activity in chronological order, followed by your feelings afterward.

Revising: First look at your work and correct any mistakes in agreement. Then read the entire draft looking for other improvements you can make. After you have revised, proofread carefully.

14

Adjective and Adverb Usage

Adjectives and adverbs modify other words, making the meaning more specific. They are often used for comparisons. You might say, for instance, that communication by letter is *fast*, by telegram *faster*, and by telephone *fastest*. Notice that the word *fast* changes form, depending on whether two things or more than two things are compared.

In this chapter, you will learn how to use adjectives and adverbs correctly in comparisons.

14.1 Degrees of Comparison

Often, instead of simply describing something, you may want to compare it to something else. There are three *degrees*, or forms, of adjectives and adverbs that are used to modify and make comparisons.

Most adjectives and adverbs have different forms to show degrees of comparison.

Recognizing Degrees of Comparison

In order to make comparisons, you need to know the three degrees of comparison.

The three degrees of comparison are the positive, the comparative, and the superlative.

The chart below lists the three degrees of some common adjectives and adverbs. As you can see, the *comparative* and *superlative* degrees of modifiers are formed in various ways. The adjective *high,* for example, adds an *-er* for the comparative degree and an *-est* for the superlative, while the adjective *eager* uses the words *more* and *most.*

ADJECTIVES		
Positive	**Comparative**	**Superlative**
high	higher	highest
eager	more eager	most eager
good	better	best
ADVERBS		
Positive	**Comparative**	**Superlative**
early	earlier	earliest
eagerly	more eagerly	most eagerly
well	better	best

EXERCISE A: Recognizing Positive, Comparative, and Superlative Degrees. Identify the degree of each underlined modifier.

EXAMPLE: Today's test was the <u>hardest</u> one of all.

   superlative

1. This is the <u>largest</u> room in the house.
2. Dad's health is <u>more robust</u> than it has been in years.
3. Your memory is <u>better</u> than mine.
4. The tractor moved <u>slowly</u> across the field.
5. Our house is the <u>farthest</u> one from the corner.
6. Getting medicine to the victims is <u>more urgent</u> than getting food to them.
7. Tim is the <u>shortest</u> player on the team.
8. A poet would describe the scene <u>more lyrically</u> than I.
9. His mother is <u>stricter</u> with him than mine is with me.
10. Greenwald was the <u>best-known</u> painter in the exhibition.
11. Marilyn is <u>happiest</u> when she is dancing.
12. We reminded him of his <u>important</u> responsibility.

13. My sister has been <u>more successful</u> than I.
14. The <u>finest</u> piece of jade sold for $25,000.
15. I thought the movie was <u>more interesting</u> than the book.
16. This behavior is <u>typical</u> of him.
17. She is <u>better</u> in biology than she is in math.
18. The <u>sunniest</u> day all week was Tuesday.
19. Copland's <u>most famous</u> piece is *Fanfare for the Common Man*.
20. You will feel <u>warmer</u> by the fire.

Regular Forms

Modifiers are either regular or irregular. Most regular adjectives and adverbs form their comparative and superlative degrees by one of two rules. The first rule applies to modifiers with one or two syllables.

Use -*er* or *more* to form the comparative degree and -*est* or *most* to form the superlative degree of most one- and two-syllable modifiers.

The more common method for forming the comparative and superlative degrees of one- and two-syllable modifiers is to add -*er* and -*est* to the modifier rather than to use *more* and *most*.

EXAMPLES:

slow	slower	slowest
soon	sooner	soonest
heavy	heavier	heaviest

More and *most* are used with one- and two-syllable modifiers when adding -*er* or -*est* would sound awkward. Notice that the words below would sound awkward with -*er* or -*est*.

EXAMPLES:

just	more just	most just
childish	more childish	most childish
hopeless	more hopeless	most hopeless

All adverbs that end with the suffix -*ly*, regardless of the number of syllables, form their comparative degrees with *more* and *most*.

EXAMPLES:

quickly	more quickly	most quickly
smoothly	more smoothly	most smoothly

The second rule applies to modifiers with three or more syllables.

Use *more* and *most* to form the comparative and superlative degrees of all modifiers with three or more syllables.

EXAMPLES: popular   more popular   most popular

likable   more likable   most likable

NOTE ABOUT COMPARISONS WITH *LESS* AND *LEAST:* *Less* and *least* mean the opposite of *more* and *most* and can be used to form the comparative and superlative degrees of most modifiers.

EXAMPLES: favorable   less favorable   least favorable

quickly   less quickly   least quickly

EXERCISE B: Forming Regular Comparative and Superlative Degrees. Write the comparative and the superlative form of each modifier.

EXAMPLE: large

larger   largest

1. tough
2. heavy
3. strong
4. comfortable
5. interesting

6. pretty
7. popular
8. confusing
9. frightening
10. clearly

Irregular Forms

A few adjectives and adverbs do not form their comparative and superlative degrees in any predictable manner.

Memorize the irregular comparative and superlative forms of certain adjectives and adverbs.

The most commonly used irregular modifiers are listed in the chart on the next page. Notice that some modifiers differ only in the positive degree. For instance, the modifiers *bad, badly,* and *ill* all have the same comparative and superlative forms *(worse, worst).*

IRREGULAR MODIFIERS

Positive	Comparative	Superlative
bad	worse	worst
badly	worse	worst
far (distance)	farther	farthest
far (extent)	further	furthest
good	better	best
ill	worse	worst
late	later	last *or* latest
little (amount)	less	least
many	more	most
much	more	most
well	better	best

NOTE ABOUT *BAD AND BADLY: Bad* is an adjective, not an adverb. Thus, it should *not* be used as an adverb after an action verb. It can, however, be used as an adjective after a linking verb.

INCORRECT: John played *bad.*

CORRECT: John felt *bad.*

Badly is an adverb. Thus, it should *not* be used as an adjective after a linking verb. It can, however, be used as an adverb after an action verb.

INCORRECT: Julie felt *badly.*

CORRECT: Julie played *badly.*

NOTE ABOUT *GOOD* AND *WELL:* Like *bad, good* is an adjective, not an adverb. Thus, it should *not* be used as an adverb after an action verb. It can, however, be used as an adjective after a linking verb.

INCORRECT: John played *good.*

CORRECT: John felt *good.*

Well is generally an adverb. Like *badly,* it can be used after an action verb.

CORRECT: Julie played *well.*

274

When *well* is used to mean "healthy," it is an adjective. Thus, *well* can also be used after a linking verb.

CORRECT: Julie felt *well* again after a good night's sleep.

EXERCISE C: Forming Irregular Comparative and Superlative Degrees.
Write the appropriate form of the underlined modifier to complete each sentence.

EXAMPLE: I may have <u>little</u> money, but you have _____ than I.

      less

1. Cod is a <u>good</u> fish, but Boston scrod is even _____.
2. Grandmother is <u>well</u> today, but she felt even _____ yesterday.
3. Utica is <u>farther</u> from New York City than Albany, but Ithaca is the _____ from New York City of the three.
4. Trissy did <u>badly</u> on the first three tests of the term, but her performance on the final test was the _____ of all.
5. Terry is still <u>ill</u>, but she was _____ two hours ago.
6. Billy's house is <u>far</u> from the center of town, but Tom's house is even _____ away.
7. Michael danced very <u>well</u> in the contest, but Karyn danced even _____ .
8. Although my mother's chocolate cake tastes very <u>good</u>, my grandmother's tastes much _____ .
9. Jonathan arrived <u>late</u> for the party, and Tina and Jim arrived even _____ .
10. There has been <u>much</u> talk of a tax break, but during the campaign there will be even _____ .
11. There were not <u>many</u> visitors this morning, but there will be _____ this evening.
12. I thought *The Empire Strikes Back* was <u>better</u> than *Return of the Jedi*, but *Star Wars* was the _____ of the three movies.
13. Cynthia was <u>late</u> to class; Carol was _____ .
14. The singer's first song during the concert was quite <u>good</u>, but his second was much _____ .
15. The rehearsal went <u>well</u> today, but it went _____ yesterday.
16. Penelope has <u>less</u> money than Christine, but Suzanne has the _____ money.

17. We had walked quite <u>far</u>, but we still had _____ to walk.
18. I thought the movie was <u>bad</u>, but the book was _____ .
19. Sue had <u>more</u> money than Rita, but Kay had the _____ .
20. There is <u>much</u> work today; tomorrow there will be _____ .

DEVELOPING WRITING SKILLS: Using Adjectives and Adverbs to Make Comparisons. Use each item in a sentence of your own.

EXAMPLE: most frightening

That was the most frightening movie I've ever seen.

1. hungrier
2. proudest
3. farther
4. more quickly
5. fastest
6. most foolish
7. worst
8. good
9. well (as adjective)
10. well (as adverb)
11. more nervous
12. most selfish
13. badly
14. better
15. most handsome
16. least likely
17. best
18. less reliable
19. more lively
20. funniest

14.2 Clear Comparisons

The problems you are likely to have with comparisons generally involve using the wrong degree, comparing unrelated things, or comparing something with itself.

Using Comparative and Superlative Degrees

There are two simple rules to keep in mind in order to use the correct degree of comparison.

Use the comparative degree to compare two people, places, or things.

Use the superlative degree to compare three or more people, places, or things.

276

Notice in the following examples that it is not necessary to mention specific numbers when making a comparison.

COMPARATIVE: Steve is *more intelligent* than Michael.

                The bus depot is *closer* to us than the airport.

                My notes are *more complete* than hers.

SUPERLATIVE: Sue is the *most intelligent* pupil in our class.

                The diner is the *closest* restaurant to our home.

                Of the members of my class, Teresa has the *most complete* notes.

NOTE ABOUT DOUBLE COMPARISONS: A double comparison is an error caused by using both -er and *more* to form the comparative degree or both -est and *most* to form the superlative. It can also be caused by adding any of these endings or words to an irregular modifier.

INCORRECT: Amy is *more smarter* than I.

            Jim's condition is *worser* than Jon's.

CORRECT: Amy is *smarter* than I.

            Jim's condition is *worse* than Jon's.

EXERCISE A: Using the Comparative and Superlative Degrees Correctly. Choose the correct comparative or superlative form in parentheses to complete each sentence.

EXAMPLE: He is (more, most) patient than his sister.

           more

1. Which of the twins swims (better, best)?
2. She is the (more, most) talented actress in The Thespians.
3. My sister is (hungrier, hungriest) than I.
4. Are you the (stronger, strongest) in your family?
5. He is (less, least) responsible than his older brother.
6. She was the (more, most) beautiful child I've ever seen.
7. My health is (worse, worst) today than it was yesterday.
8. Of the two, Copenhagen is the (cleaner, cleanest) city.
9. That actor is (smaller, smallest) than he appears on television.
10. Tim is (less, least) willing to cooperate than his friend.

EXERCISE B: Supplying the Comparative and Superlative Degrees. Write the appropriate comparative or superlative degree of the modifier in parentheses.

EXAMPLE: Of the two plays, *Macbeth* is (short).

          shorter

1. June 21 is the (long) day of the year.
2. The weather is (bad) today than it was yesterday.
3. Ted is the (old) of Uncle John's three sons.
4. This is the (fast) train I've ever been on.
5. Today is the (happy) day of my life.
6. Louise is (capable) than the other dentist in town.
7. Bill is the (kind) person I know.
8. Aunt Sarah is (ill) this morning than she was last night.
9. Edward speaks French (fluently) than I do.
10. Arthur's essay is the (good) in the class.
11. St. Louis is (far) from New Orleans than Memphis is.
12. Alan does (well) on English tests than I do.
13. Kim is the (young) of the three children.
14. This is the (delicious) cake I've ever eaten.
15. Your computer is (versatile) than mine.
16. Faulkner is a (difficult) novelist than Hemingway is.
17. Jill arrived (late) than Joan.
18. The living room is the (warm) room in the house.
19. I'm feeling (well) than I did yesterday.
20. This chair is (comfortable) than that one.

Balanced Comparisons

Whenever you write a comparison, you must check the sentence to make sure that the things being compared are properly balanced. Otherwise, you may compare two or more items that can not logically be compared.

Make sure that your sentences compare only items of a similar kind.

The unbalanced sentences at the top of the next page are illogical because they unintentionally compare dissimilar things. A speech cannot be compared to a person, and the tail of one dog cannot be compared to another entire dog.

UNBALANCED: *Joe's speech* was more effective than *Ken.*

CORRECT: *Joe's speech* was more effective than *Ken's.*

UNBALANCED: The *tail of a setter* is longer than a *dachshund.*

CORRECT: The *tail of a setter* is longer than a *dachshund's.*

EXERCISE C: Making Balanced Comparisons. Rewrite each sentence, correcting the unbalanced comparison.

EXAMPLE: Valerie's eyes are bluer than Annie.

             Valerie's eyes are bluer than Annie's.

1. His swimming record is better than his chief rival.
2. Dad's cooking is better than Mom.
3. The rooms in my dorm are bigger than this hotel.
4. My gloves are in poorer condition than Sandra.
5. I like Cynthia's costume better than her twin.
6. Isn't my haircut more stylish than Joan?
7. My old bike's tires are bigger than my new bike.
8. Her coin collection is more valuable than her brother.
9. Jennifer's grades are higher than Keith.
10. My brother's wardrobe is more varied than my sister.

Other and *Else* in Comparisons

Another common error in making a comparison is to compare something with itself.

When comparing one of a group with the rest of the group, make sure that your sentence contains the word *other* or the word *else*.

Adding *other* or *else* in these situations will prevent comparing something with itself. For example, since Lincoln was one U.S. president, he can not logically be compared to all U.S. presidents. He must be compared to all *other* U.S. presidents.

ILLOGICAL: Lincoln was *greater than any* U.S. president.

CORRECT: Lincoln was *greater than any other* U.S. president.

ILLOGICAL: I scored *more points than anyone* on the team.

CORRECT: I scored *more points than anyone else* on the team.

EXERCISE D: Using *Other* and *Else* in Comparisons. Rewrite each sentence, correcting the illogical comparison.

EXAMPLE: Beth is nicer than anyone in class.

Beth is nicer than anyone else in class.

1. This ice cream is better than any I've ever tasted.
2. The guitarist plays better than anyone in the band.
3. Senator Hammer's record is better than any senator's.
4. Ty Cobb hit better than any baseball player.
5. He spends more money on clothing than anyone I know.
6. Walt Whitman's style is better than that of any poet.
7. Our driveway is steeper than any on the block.
8. Susan's writing is better than any student's in the class.
9. Mother's roses won more blue ribbons than any flowers in the contest.
10. The pothole on our street is deeper than any in town.

DEVELOPING WRITING SKILLS: Writing Effective Comparisons. Use the following instructions to write five sentences of your own.

EXAMPLE: Compare the jump shots of two basketball players.

Phil's jump shot is more accurate than Bob's.

1. Compare your mother's pumpkin pie with that of your aunt.
2. Compare the performance of two different television sets.
3. Compare your last three summer vacations.
4. Compare the coverage of local news in one newspaper with that in another.
5. Compare two recent tests in one particular subject.

Skills Review and Writing Workshop

Adjective and Adverb Usage

CHECKING YOUR SKILLS

Rewrite the following paragraph, correcting all errors in adjective and adverb usage.

(1) This was the importantest interscholastic track meet of the year. (2) Of the two runners representing our school, John was the best. (3) However, he was not feeling too good today. (4) So Bill's run might be faster than John. (5) As the gun sounded, both boys started slow and fell behind the other runners. (6) Gradually, Bill picked up speed and began moving more quicker than John. (7) As the runners passed the halfway mark, Bill seemed to be running faster than anyone on the track. (8) His pace seemed very well, and only one runner was ahead of him. (9) Bill was strongest, though, and rapidly gained ground. (10) He crossed the finish line first and proved he was better than any runner out there.

USING USAGE SKILLS IN WRITING
Writing a Movie Review

Adjectives and adverbs can be effective modifiers as long as all of their forms are used correctly. Imagine you are the movie critic for the local newspaper and write an effective movie review by following these steps.

Prewriting: Choose a film you have seen recently and decide whether it was good or poor. Think of at least three reasons to support your opinion.

Writing: Begin with your verdict. Then add your reasons, placing the most important one last, since readers are most likely to remember the last reason you give.

Revising: First look at your adjectives and adverbs and make sure they are used correctly. Then read the entire review, looking for other improvements you might make. After you have revised, proofread carefully.

15

Miscellaneous Problems in Usage

This chapter discusses those usage problems that have not been presented earlier in the unit. You will learn how to form negative sentences correctly, and you will study a list of troublesome words and expressions.

15.1 Negative Sentences

Negative words, such as *not* or *never*, are used to deny or to refuse something. Hundreds of years ago, it was customary to crowd many negative words into one sentence, as in "Mary *didn't never* ask *nobody*." Today, only one negative word is needed to make the meaning negative. The sentence about Mary could be stated correctly in any of three ways: "Mary *didn't* ask anybody." Mary *never* asked anybody." "Mary asked *nobody*."

Recognizing Double Negatives

A *double negative* is the use of two negative words in a sentence when one is sufficient.

Do not write sentences with double negatives.

282

The chart below provides examples of double negatives and the two ways in which each can be corrected.

CORRECTING DOUBLE NEGATIVES	
Double Negatives	**Corrections**
I *don't* owe *no one* money.	I *don't* owe anyone money.
	I owe *no one* money.
I *haven't no* excuse.	I *haven't* any excuse.
	I have *no* excuse.
Tom *never* said *nothing*.	Tom *never* said anything.
	Tom said *nothing*.

EXERCISE A: Avoiding Double Negatives. Choose the word in parentheses that makes each sentence negative without forming a double negative.

EXAMPLE: Sue could find (none, any) of the lost coins.

   any

1. He has never done (anything, nothing) to help us.
2. I don't want (no, any) more spinach.
3. We couldn't read (none, any) of the writing in the letter.
4. Don't strike a match (anywhere, nowhere) near the gasoline.
5. I did (none, any) of the things they accused me of.
6. The children didn't eat (any, none) of their dinner.
7. No one at the party ate (any, none) of the cake.
8. Nobody said (nothing, anything) to me about a meeting.
9. We could get (nothing, anything) out of the burning house.
10. I haven't (no, any) more sentences to write.

Forming Negative Sentences Correctly

There are three common ways to form negative sentences.

Using One Negative Word. The most common way to make a statement negative is to use one negative word, such as *never, no, nobody, none, not, nothing,* or *nowhere*. Notice that each word begins with the letter *n*. The contraction *n't* with a verb can also be used to make a sentence negative.

Do not use two negative words in the same clause.

Using two of these words in the same clause will create a double negative.

DOUBLE NEGATIVE: We *don't* want *no* help from you.

CORRECT: We *don't* want any help from you.

We want *no* help from you.

Using *But* in a Negative Sense. When *but* means "only," it generally acts as a negative.

Do not use *but* in its negative sense with another negative.

DOUBLE NEGATIVE: There *wasn't but* one survivor.

CORRECT: There was *but* one survivor.

Using *Barely, Hardly,* and *Scarcely*. All three of these words are negative.

Do not use *barely, hardly,* or *scarcely* with another negative.

DOUBLE NEGATIVE: She *wasn't barely* gone when the phone rang.

CORRECT: She was *barely* gone when the phone rang.

DOUBLE NEGATIVE: We *didn't scarcely* recognize him.

DOUBLE NEGATIVE: I *couldn't hardly* see in the snowstorm.

CORRECT: I could *hardly* see in the snowstorm.

EXERCISE B: Avoiding Problems with Negatives. Choose the word in parentheses that makes each sentence negative without creating a double negative.

EXAMPLE: Jon (could, couldn't) hardly believe he'd won.

could

1. I don't want (anything, nothing).
2. Remember that I have done (anything, nothing) wrong.
3. Lila (could, couldn't) scarcely catch her breath.
4. We haven't (any, no) strong feelings about it.
5. I couldn't have (anything, nothing) for dessert.

284

6. There (were, weren't) but three choices.
7. I (can, can't) hardly believe my eyes.
8. Don't you have (anything, nothing) more exciting to read?
9. She doesn't write to me (any, no) more.
10. Luke (had, hadn't) but two days of provisions left when he was found.

EXERCISE C: Correcting Double Negatives. Rewrite each sentence, correcting the double negative.

EXAMPLE: Dad would never accept no charity.

Dad would never accept any charity.

1. I promise that I won't tell nobody.
2. Mary can't hardly read the small print.
3. My father hadn't never been to Athens.
4. I haven't but a few minutes left to work.
5. She didn't have no lunch.
6. My uncle hasn't traveled nowhere in years.
7. He couldn't barely see me in the crowd.
8. Which of you hasn't gained no weight?
9. He couldn't offer but one constructive idea.
10. They couldn't scarcely find their way out.

DEVELOPING WRITING SKILLS: Writing Negative Sentences. Use each word in a negative sentence of your own.

EXAMPLE: no

We found no money in the safe.

1. didn't
2. never
3. hardly
4. can't
5. hasn't
6. no one
7. not
8. scarcely
9. nothing
10. barely

Fifty Common Usage Problems   15.2

This section provides a list of fifty usage problems arranged in alphabetical order.

Solving Usage Problems

The following glossary presents words that are often confused because they have similar meanings or spellings. Whether you use the glossary for classroom work or for reference, you should begin by carefully reading through all the entries so that you can make distinctions between similar words that have different uses.

Study the items in this glossary, paying particular attention to similar meanings and spellings.

You will also find a few reminders about words that are nonstandard and should generally be avoided.

(1) accept, except   *Accept* is a verb meaning "to receive." *Except* is a preposition meaning "other than."

VERB: I *accept* your gift willingly.

PREPOSITION: Everyone *except* Craig was at the dance.

(2) adapt, adopt   *Adapt* means "to change." *Adopt* means "to take as one's own."

EXAMPLES: She *adapted* the piano piece to make it more appropriate for the children's concert.

The impressionable young man *adopted* his hero's style of dress.

(3) advice, advise   *Advice* is a noun meaning "opinion." *Advise* is a verb meaning "to give an opinion to."

NOUN: I asked my guidance counselor for *advice* about what courses to take next semester.

VERB: My guidance counselor *advised* me to take a science course and a foreign language.

(4) affect, effect   *Affect* is almost always a verb meaning "to influence." *Effect*, usually a noun, means "result." Occasionally, *effect* is a verb meaning "to bring about" or "to cause."

VERB: The President's speech deeply *affected* me.

NOUN: The *effects* of pollution can be deadly.

VERB: The Student Council *effected* many important changes.

286

(5) ain't   *Ain't* was originally a contraction of *am not*. It is not considered standard English. Avoid it in all writing and speaking.

NONSTANDARD: Jon *ain't* ready yet.

CORRECT: Jon *isn't* ready yet.

(6) all ready, already   The two words *all ready* are used as an adjective meaning "ready." *Already* is an adverb meaning "by or before this time" or "even now."

ADJECTIVE: I am *all ready* to leave for the airport.

ADVERB: I have *already* packed my suitcase.

(7) all right, alright   *Alright,* though it is seen more and more frequently in print, is not considered a correct spelling. Make sure that in your own writing you always use the two-word form.

NONSTANDARD: That new album is *alright*.

CORRECT: He is feeling *all right* today.

(8) all together, altogether   These two adverbs have different meanings. *All together* means "together as a group." *Altogether* means "completely" or "in all."

EXAMPLES: Let's sing the song *all together*.

The old television flickered once or twice and then broke *altogether*.

(9) among, between   *Among* and *between* are both prepositions. *Among* always implies three or more. *Between* is generally used with only two.

EXAMPLES: The dog sat down *among* the tulips.

The judges split the money *between* the two of us.

Sit here *between* your mother and me.

(10) anywhere, everywhere, nowhere, somewhere   None of these adverbs should ever end with an *-s*.

NONSTANDARD: The child lost the money *somewheres* on the playing field.

CORRECT: The child lost the money *somewhere* on the playing field.

(11) as to   *As to* is awkward. Replace it with *about*.

NONSTANDARD: I have no ideas *as to* where we should eat.

CORRECT: I have no ideas *about* where we should eat.

(12) at   Do not use *at* after *where*. Simply eliminate it.

NONSTANDARD: Can you tell me *where* to catch the bus *at?*

CORRECT: Can you tell me *where* to catch the bus?

(13) awhile, a while   *Awhile* is an adverb, which in it-self means "for a while." *A while* is an article and a noun usu-ally used after the preposition *for*.

ADVERB: Lie down *awhile* and rest.

NOUN: For *a while* he lay still without moving.

(14) because   Do not use *because* after *the reason*. Say "The reason . . . is that" or reword the sentence altogether.

NONSTANDARD: *The reason* he is sad is *because* his dog died.

CORRECT: *The reason* he is sad is *that* his dog died.

He is sad *because* his dog died.

(15) being as, being that   Avoid using both expres-sions. Use *because* or *since* instead.

NONSTANDARD: *Being as* it was so late, we went home.

Being that it was too cold, we went inside.

CORRECT: *Because* it was so late, we went home.

Since it was too cold, we went inside.

(16) beside, besides   These two prepositions have dif-ferent meanings and cannot be interchanged. *Beside* means "at the side of" or "close to." *Besides* means "in addition to."

EXAMPLES: The vegetable garden is *beside* the house.

Who is going to the concert *besides* me?

(17) bring, take   *Bring* means "to carry from a distant place to a nearer one." *Take* means "to carry from a near place to a more distant place."

EXAMPLES: *Bring* those books here, please.

Take these forms to the principal's office.

288

(18) burst, bust, busted The verb *burst* has the same present, past, and past participle. *Bust* and *busted* are non-standard forms.

NONSTANDARD: The balloon will *bust* if you poke it.

He poked the balloon and *busted* it.

CORRECT: The balloon will *burst* if you poke it.

He poked the balloon and *burst* it.

(19) can't help but Replace this nonstandard expression with *can't help* plus a gerund.

NONSTANDARD: I *can't help but feel* sorry for Jonathan after his recent misfortune.

CORRECT: I *can't help feeling* sorry for Jonathan after his recent misfortune.

(20) different from, different than *Different from* is preferred.

LESS ACCEPTABLE: My handwriting is *different than* Alice's.

PREFERRED: My handwriting is *different from* Alice's.

(21) doesn't, don't Use *doesn't* instead of *don't* with all third-person singular pronouns and nouns.

NONSTANDARD: She *don't* sing well.

The machine *don't* work.

CORRECT: She *doesn't* sing well.

The machine *doesn't* work.

(22) done *Done* is the past participle of *do*. It should always follow a helping verb.

NONSTANDARD: He *done* his homework.

CORRECT: He *has done* his homework.

(23) due to *Due to* means "caused by" and should be used only when the words *caused by* can logically be substituted.

NONSTANDARD: *Due to* a rare virus, he became seriously ill on his recent trip.

CORRECT: His illness was *due to* a rare virus he caught on his recent trip.

289

(24) due to the fact that   This phrase is unnecessarily wordy. Use *since* or *because* instead.

LESS ACCEPTABLE: *Due to the fact that* he was late, we left.

PREFERRED: *Since* he was late, we left.

(25) farther, further   *Farther* refers to distance. *Further* means "additional" or "to a greater degree or extent."

EXAMPLES: My house is *farther* away than yours.

I need *further* advice.

(26) fewer, less   Use *fewer* for things that can be counted. Use *less* for quantities that cannot be counted.

EXAMPLES: *fewer* calories, *fewer* dollars, *fewer* assignments

less sugar, *less* money, *less* homework

(27) gone, went   *Gone* is the past participle of *go*. It should be used as a verb only with a helping verb. *Went* is the past of *go* and is never used with a helping verb.

NONSTANDARD: Craig and Louise *gone* to the movies.

You really *should have went* to the party.

CORRECT: Craig and Louise *have gone* to the movies.

Craig and Louise *went* to the movies.

You really *should have gone* to the party.

(28) healthful, healthy   Things are *healthful*. People are *healthy*.

LESS ACCEPTABLE: Fresh green salads are *healthy*.

PREFERRED: Fresh green salads are *healthful*.

(29) in, into   *In* refers to position. *Into* suggests motion.

EXAMPLES: The plates are *in* the cabinet.

Let's go *into* the next room.

(30) just   When you use *just* as an adverb meaning "no more than," place it right before the word it logically modifies.

LESS ACCEPTABLE: She *just* wants one piece of candy.

PREFERRED: She wants *just* one piece of candy.

290

(31) kind of, sort of   Do not use *kind of* or *sort of* in place of *rather* or *somewhat*.

NONSTANDARD: I feel *sort of* sick.

CORRECT: I feel *somewhat* sick.

(32) lay, lie   *Lay* means "to put or set (something) down." Its principal parts—*lay, laying, laid,* and *laid*—are usually followed by a direct object. *Lie* means "to recline." Its principal parts—*lie, lying, lay,* and *lain*—are never followed by a direct object.

LAY: Please *lay* the basket on the counter.

The hens are *laying* eggs again.

Before she left, she *laid* the books on the table.

The masons have *laid* three rows of bricks so far.

LIE: If you are sick, you should *lie* down.

They are *lying* in the sunshine.

Last week he *lay* in the hammock every evening.

The children have *lain* in bed long enough.

(33) learn, teach   *Learn* means "to receive knowledge." *Teach* means "to give knowledge."

EXAMPLES: I *learned* a new word today.

Ralph *taught* us how to fix the carburetor on our old automobile.

(34) leave, let   *Leave* means "to allow to remain." *Let* means "to permit." Do not use one in place of the other.

NONSTANDARD: We must *let* the kitten alone.

CORRECT: We must *leave* the kitten alone.

NONSTANDARD: *Leave* me go!

CORRECT: *Let* me go!

(35) like, as   *Like* is a preposition meaning "similar to" or "such as." It should not be used in place of the conjunction *as*.

NONSTANDARD: She writes *like* she speaks—graciously.

CORRECT: She writes *as* she speaks—graciously.

(36) of, have   Do not use the preposition *of* in place of the verb *have*.

NONSTANDARD: I could *of* gone if I had wanted.

CORRECT: I could *have* gone if I had wanted.

(37) only   Because the position of *only* can affect the entire meaning of a sentence, be sure to place it before the word that should be modified.

EXAMPLES: *Only* Rita wanted to go bowling. (No one else wanted to go bowling.)

Rita *only* wanted to go bowling. (Rita did not want to do anything else.)

(38) raise, rise   *Raise* usually takes a direct object. *Rise* never takes a direct object.

EXAMPLES: Our landlady *raises* the rent on our apartment every year at this same time.

The hot-air balloons *rise* above the treetops.

(39) seen   *Seen* is a past participle and can be used as a verb only with a helping verb.

NONSTANDARD: We *seen* the new auditorium already.

CORRECT: We *have seen* the new auditorium already.

(40) set, sit   *Set* means "to put (something) in a certain place." Its principal parts—*set, setting, set,* and *set*—are usually followed by a direct object. *Sit* means "to be seated." Its principal parts—*sit, sitting, sat,* and *sat*—are never followed by a direct object.

SET: *Set* the peaches on the table.

He should be *setting* the table now.

They *set* the television on the corner table.

We have *set* all of the clocks to go off at seven.

SIT: I will *sit* in his place tonight.

You must have been *sitting* there for hours.

She *sat* in her office and thought about the problem.

We have *sat* in the front seats for three weeks now.

292

(41) so   *So* is a coordinating conjunction. It should be avoided when you mean "so that."

LESS ACCEPTABLE: We left early *so* we would not be late.

PREFERRED: We left early *so that* we would not be late.

(42) than, then   *Than* is used in comparisons. Do not confuse it with the adverb *then*, which usually refers to time.

EXAMPLES: Lucy is taller *than* Beverly.

I liked the movie more *than* Chuck did.

We finished shopping and *then* ate lunch.

We stayed to congratulate the winners, and *then* we went home.

(43) that, which, who   Use these relative pronouns correctly. *That* refers to things or people; *which* refers only to things; *who* refers only to people.

EXAMPLES: I lost the book *that* (or *which*) you lent me.

Please return the suitcase *that* (or *which*) you borrowed last month.

He is not the man *that* (or *who*) delivered the box.

We thanked the soldier *that* (or *who*) helped us.

(44) that there, this here   Avoid these nonstandard expressions. Simply leave out *here* and *there*.

NONSTANDARD: *That there* man is the one I saw.

This here package is for you.

CORRECT: *That* man is the one I saw.

This package is for you.

(45) their, there, they're   *Their*, a possessive pronoun, always modifies a noun. *There* can be used either as an expletive at the beginning of a sentence or as an adverb. *They're* is a contraction for *they are*.

PRONOUN: The spectators threw *their* hats into the air.

EXPLETIVE: *There* are three police officers guarding the gate.

ADVERB: The accident occurred *there*.

CONTRACTION: *They're* waiting for us at the gate.

(46) to, too, two   *To,* a preposition, begins a prepositional phrase or an infinitive. *Too,* an adverb, modifies adjectives and other abverbs. *Two* is a number.

PREPOSITION: *to* the store

INFINITIVE: *to* run

ADVERB: *too* tall, *too* quickly

NUMBER: *two* eggs, *two* dollars

(47) unique   *Unique* means "one of a kind." It should
not be used to mean "odd," "interesting," or "unusual." Such
expressions as *most unique, very unique,* and *extremely
unique* are illogical and should be avoided.

ILLOGICAL: My aunt has a *most unique* art collection.

CORRECT: My aunt has a *unique* art collection.

(48) ways   Do not use *ways,* a plural, after the article *a.*

NONSTANDARD: You still have *a* long *ways* to drive before dusk.

CORRECT: You still have *a* long *way* to drive before dusk.

(49) when, where   Do not use *when* or *where* directly
after a linking verb, and do not use *where* in place of *that.*

NONSTANDARD: An audition *is when* you can try out for a part.

A library *is where* you can find books.

We read *where* taxes are rising.

CORRECT: At an audition you can try out for a part.

A library is the place where you can find books.

We read that taxes are rising.

(50) -wise   Avoid using this suffix to create new words
for a particular situation.

LESS ACCEPTABLE: *Gradewise,* I did well last term.

PREFERRED: I received good grades last term.

EXERCISE A: **Avoiding Usage Problems 1–10.** Choose
the correct expression to complete each sentence.

EXAMPLE: The (affects, effects) of the experiment startled us.

effects

1. I can't find my glasses (anywhere, anywheres).
2. I hope you can (advice, advise) him properly.
3. Everyone visited the museum (accept, except) my father.
4. There (ain't, isn't) a dry eye in the auditorium.
5. Is everything (all right, alright) at home?
6. The horses were huddled (all together, altogether).
7. Are you (all ready, already) to go?
8. What is the (affect, effect) of the new law?
9. Pete (adapted, adopted) the machine for a particular job.
10. Your (advice, advise) was very helpful.
11. A mimosa tree grows (between, among) those two houses.
12. It is dishonest to (accept, except) bribes.
13. I've (all ready, already) seen that movie.
14. He feels (all right, alright) now.
15. The concert was (all together, altogether) delightful.
16. Mom divided the money (among, between) my brother and me.
17. Lack of sleep will (affect, effect) your athletic ability in the game tomorrow.
18. China recently (adapted, adopted) a new spelling system.
19. The medicine had an immediate (affect, effect) on the accident victim.
20. Let's go (all together, altogether) in one car.

EXERCISE B: Avoiding Usage Problems 11–20. Choose the correct expression to complete each sentence.

1. The old man stood (beside, besides) the tree.
2. (Being that, Since) you asked, I will tell you the story.
3. (Bring, Take) your empty tray over here.
4. The sergeant (burst, busted) into the room.
5. This new pen is much different (from, than) my old one.
6. I can't help (but want, wanting) to go with you.
7. I don't know where (I'm at, I am).
8. They had no suggestions (as to, about) what to do next on our vacation.
9. Practice is canceled (being as, because) the coach is sick.
10. The reason I am not going is (because, that) I am exhausted from my trip yesterday.
11. My grandparents are staying with us for (a while, awhile).
12. (Beside, Besides) me, no one saw the shooting star.
13. My sister (brought, took) me a souvenir from Jamaica.

14. Before I left, we talked (a while, awhile).
15. Who is the girl standing (beside, besides) John?
16. Mother asked me to (bring, take) the dog out.
17. His explanation is very different (from, than) hers.
18. (Being as, Since) my aunt came to visit, I have had to sleep on the sofa.
19. His cleats (burst, busted) the football.
20. (Beside, Besides) carrots, I like peas and beans.

EXERCISE C: **Avoiding Usage Problems 21–30.** Choose the correct expression to complete each sentence.

1. My brother (doesn't, don't) care much for rock music.
2. We (done, have done) our French homework already.
3. I have (fewer, less) classical records in my collection than my sister does.
4. My parents (gone, have gone) to a movie.
5. There was (fewer, less) damage after the tornado than we had expected at first.
6. (Due to, Because of) his poor record, he was dropped from the team.
7. (Doesn't, Don't) your friend care whether you borrow his new bicycle?
8. I (done, have done) all that I can for you.
9. His explanation led her to seek (farther, further) answers from other experts in the field.
10. The diver jumped (in, into) the water from the cliff.
11. I (just want, want just) one slice of pie.
12. The doctor recommended (healthy, healthful) exercise for my father after his accident.
13. The Pattersons (would have went, would have gone) to the opera tonight, but their oldest son was ill.
14. The vote was postponed (due to the fact that, because) many legislators were absent.
15. Her success has been (due to, because of) all the hard work she had done over the years.
16. Move your bicycle (in, into) the garage at night.
17. A good diet will help you stay (healthy, healthful).
18. The fog prevented us from driving any (farther, further).
19. This soup has (fewer, less) calories than the other.
20. (Doesn't, Don't) he look handsome in that new suit!

296

EXERCISE D: Avoiding Usage Problems 31–40. Choose the correct expression to complete each sentence.

1. Lester (sat, set) the book on the shelf.
2. My grandfather (learned, taught) me how to milk a cow.
3. Their singing style was (kind of, rather) unusual.
4. Will you (leave, let) me take your picture?
5. I (lay, laid) in bed and made plans for the day.
6. I should (of, have) spoken to her first.
7. I will (leave, let) you do as you please.
8. Carl (seen, has seen) that movie twice.
9. The wholesaler plans to (rise, raise) the prices again.
10. (Only eat, Eat only) what you are served.
11. Will you (learn, teach) us how to tie a square knot?
12. Dressed all in white, she looked (like, as) a bride.
13. I was (sort of, somewhat) disappointed with the movie.
14. You could (of, have) called me from the gymnasium if you knew you were going to be late.
15. The television is not working (like, as) it should.
16. The helicopter will soon (rise, raise) into the sky.
17. You should not have (lain, laid) in the sun so long.
18. The guards didn't treat the prisoners (like, as) the prisoners deserved to be treated.
19. (Let, Leave) me stay here by myself.
20. I (seen, have seen) Grandmother twice this week.

EXERCISE E: Avoiding Usage Problems 41–50. Choose the correct expression to complete each sentence.

1. The report was more amusing (than, then) informative.
2. Loretta was (to, too, two) frightened to call for help.
3. My brother turned pale and (than, then) fainted.
4. That stamp from British Guiana is (unique, very unique).
5. (This here, This) coin is over 2,300 years old.
6. (Their, There, They're) clothes were completely soaked.
7. Spring is (when, the season when) flowers bloom.
8. Ms. Campbell is the person (that, which) I met at the museum yesterday afternoon.
9. (Their, There, They're) leaving for Europe tomorrow on an extended vacation.
10. We live a long (way, ways) from town.

11. Mr. Wilson moved to the city (so, so that) he could find a better job.
12. I read (where, that) it will rain today.
13. The new principal, (who, which) came from Florida, doesn't like our cold winters.
14. Spain is (where, the country) I'd most like to visit.
14. (Weatherwise, As far as the weather is concerned), the area is very desirable.
16. I like (that there, that) suit best.
17. This is the most (unique, interesting) shell in my collection.
18. Put the package down over (their, there, they're).
19. You gave me (to, too, two) much work to do in one day.
20. The boat (that, who) rounds the lighthouse first will win.

EXERCISE F: Correcting Usage Problems. Rewrite each sentence, correcting the error in usage.

EXAMPLE: He laid in bed until noon.

He lay in bed until noon.

1. She divided the candy among her brother and sister.
2. The reason he quit his job is because he won the lottery.
3. The lake is further down the road.
4. Due to the fact that he missed two exams, he had to drop the course.
5. He can't help but tell a lie.
6. Bring all of the messages to the woman down the hall.
7. I thought it was a rather unique experience.
8. If I wanted, I could of gone to the game tonight.
9. This film is different than all the others.
10. Being as I overstayed my welcome, I decided to leave.
11. What is the affect of water pollution on our health?
12. That there candidate has an unusually strong platform.
13. She don't expect too much from us.
14. Later in the day, we went to they're house.
15. He expected to receive to records for his birthday.
16. I seen Marilyn only once since she returned.
17. My sister sort of liked him, I guess.
18. You should of refused to buy the used car at that outrageous price.

19. Lay down and get some rest.
20. She learned us all we needed to know about boating.
21. We saved our allowance so we could go to the movies.
22. Our teacher told us we needed to study the problem much farther.
23. The celebrity excepted the lovely bouquet of roses with graciousness.
24. The happy couple had just adapted the newborn baby.
25. Walter said we could catch a bus anywheres on Main Street.

DEVELOPING WRITING SKILLS: Using the Correct Expressions in Your Writing. Use each expression in a sentence of your own.

EXAMPLE: advise

Dentists advise their patients to avoid sweets.

1. different from	11. unique
2. set	12. learn
3. all right	13. seen
4. due to	14. less
5. except	15. all together
6. affected	16. as
7. altogether	17. fewer
8. burst	18. than
9. can't help	19. like
10. done	20. besides

Skills Review and Writing Workshop

Miscellaneous Problems in Usage

CHECKING YOUR SKILLS

Rewrite the following paragraph, correcting all errors in usage.

(1) Being as we had nothing better to do, we decided to go to the lake. (2) At first, nobody didn't want to drive us. (3) But my dad finally said he would due to the fact that he wasn't busy. (4) We couldn't have went far, however, when we had a flat tire. (5) The reason we had the flat is because we ran over a nail. (6) Dad didn't have a spare, so we had to bring the flat tire to a nearby service station. (7) We couldn't help but feel sorry for Dad since he didn't really want to take us to the lake anyway. (8) The attendant finally fixed the tire and adviced us to carry a spare in the future. (9) We could of gone on to the lake, but we no longer had much enthusiasm. (10) Dad drove us home, and we went too the movies instead.

USING USAGE SKILLS IN WRITING
Writing a Description

By mastering troublesome usage problems, you can improve your writing and make it more polished. Imagine that you were growing up in your community at the turn of the century. Write a polished description of it following these steps.

Prewriting: Consider how your community appeared. Think of any major events or inventions that might have affected your community. Has anyone purchased an automobile? Do you talk to your friends on the telephone?

Writing: Begin with a general description of your community. Then describe the impact of any inventions or recent events.

Revising: Look over your work and correct any errors in usage. Then look for any other improvements you might make. After you have revised, proofread carefully.

16

Capitalization and Abbreviation

You have probably already mastered the major rules of capitalization and many common abbreviations. In the next two sections, you will have a chance to review the rules you already use and to master some new rules that will make it possible for you to communicate even more clearly.

16.1 Rules for Capitalization

Visitors to the ruins of ancient Rome can view one of the earliest forms of the alphabet on stone engravings. The Roman alphabet was at first limited to capital letters. However, people eventually began to fit more on a page by using smaller rounded letters. A whole system of capital and small letters came into use, and the concept of capitalization was born.

To capitalize means to begin a word with a capital letter.

Although writers can still fit more on a page by combining capitals and small letters, there is a more important reason for capitalizing certain words today. Correctly used, capitals provide clues to the reader by signaling the start of a new sentence or by pointing out specific words within a sentence.

Capitals for Sentences

One of the most important uses of capitals is to signal the beginning of each new sentence.

Capitalize the first word in declarative, interrogative, imperative, and exclamatory sentences.

DECLARATIVE: Our company installed a new computer system.

INTERROGATIVE: Have you prepared your report yet?

IMPERATIVE: Bring the reference book to class tomorrow.

EXCLAMATORY: What an astounding turn of events!

Sometimes, especially in informal writing, only a part of the sentence is written out. The rest of it is understood. In these cases, you still must capitalize the first word.

EXAMPLES: Where?   This year?   My goodness!

Capitalization also signals the beginning of a quotation.

Capitalize the first word in a quotation if the quotation is a complete sentence.

In the following examples, each quotation is a complete sentence. In the last example, note that the full quotation consists of two complete sentences. Each of the two sentences begins with a capital.

EXAMPLES: She said, "The children are thirsty."

"The children are thirsty," she said.

"The children are thirsty," she said. "We will get them some lemonade."

When a quotation consists of one complete sentence in two parts, only one capital is required.

EXAMPLE: "The children are thirsty," she said, "because they have been playing outside in the hot sun."

In dealing with quoted material, you will occasionally have only a fragment of a quotation contained within a larger sentence. This fragment should not be capitalized.

EXAMPLE: June told us that the band performed "better than I expected."

303

Here is one more capitalization rule to keep in mind when writing sentences.

Capitalize the first word after a colon if the word begins a complete sentence.

In the first of the following examples, a capital is used for the first word of the sentence following the colon. In the second example, the first word following the colon is not capitalized because it begins a list, not a sentence.

EXAMPLES: We council members all had the same reaction: How are we going to find funds for all these suggested improvements to the park?

The members agreed on the need for some of the improvements: a new fence, a separate bicycle path, and sidewalk repairs.

NOTE ABOUT *I* AND *O*: The pronoun *I* is always capitalized, as is the poetic interjection *O*.

EXAMPLES: I came, I saw, I conquered.—Julius Caesar

O but not yet—not yet.—Zona Gale

EXERCISE A: Using Capitalization Correctly in Sentences. Copy the following sentences, adding the missing capitals. Some sentences may require more than one capital.

EXAMPLE: what a difficult mountain that was to climb!

What a difficult mountain that was to climb!

1. show me what you are holding in your hand, young man.
2. getting my school schedule worked out for next year is causing problems.
3. "every hero becomes a bore at last," observed Emerson.
4. when will dinner be ready?
5. my grandmother taught me one important lesson: giving more than 100 percent is the surest way to get ahead.
6. we found a twenty-dollar bill on the sidewalk!
7. at one time Confucius warned, "the cautious seldom err."
8. the store down the street is holding a big sale today.
9. will you go on many weekend ski trips this winter?
10. sit still while the barber finishes cutting your hair.

11. "if you would wish another to keep your secret," advised Seneca, "first keep it yourself."
12. where did you take the camera to be repaired?
13. we saw quite a feat at the circus: a young man did a high-wire act without any safety nets below him.
14. the company gave us a substantial salary increase today!
15. many people put more salt on their food than is healthful.
16. they spent yesterday buying gifts: a stuffed panda, an electric razor, and a giant rubber plant.
17. "we can stay as long as we want," she said. "they have given us permission."
18. what in the world were you thinking of?
19. "why not try," she asked, "to climb a mountain?"
20. he was afraid: he had never climbed a mountain.

Capitals for Proper Nouns

As you may recall, a proper noun names a specific person, place, or thing. One general rule governs the capitalization of proper nouns.

Capitalize all proper nouns.

Names. Consider first the names of specific people.

Capitalize each part of a person's full name.

EXAMPLES: Diana T. Cheng   B. L. Baker

Surnames (last names) that are composed of two parts are more difficult to capitalize correctly. If a last name begins with *Mc, O',* or *St.,* the next letter should also be capitalized.

EXAMPLES: McDonald   O'Keefe   St. James

In last names beginning with *de, D', la, le, Mac, van,* and *von,* capitalization varies. The only way to be sure of which letters are capitalized is to ask for a spelling of the name.

EXAMPLES: D'Arpino or D'arpino   le Blanc or Le Blanc
             MacDonald or Macdonald   van Wyck or Vanwyck

NOTE ABOUT ANIMALS: Capitalize the names of specific animals.

EXAMPLES: Lassie, the dog   Morris, the cat

Places. A second group of proper nouns, the names of specific places, must also be capitalized.

Capitalize geographical names.

According to this rule, any place that can be found on a map should be capitalized. Study the following chart for samples of different kinds of geographical names that you must capitalize.

GEOGRAPHICAL NAMES	
Streets	Bascom Avenue, Aborn Road
Towns and Cities	Evansdale, Kansas City, London
Counties	Macon County, Champaign County
States and Provinces	Vermont, Saskatchewan
Nations	United States of America, Japan
Continents	North America, Europe, Asia
Valleys and Deserts	Death Valley, the Sahara Desert
Mountains	Sierra Nevadas, Mount Everest
Sections of a Country	the Great Plains, the Northwest
Islands	the Canary Islands, Maui
Scenic Spots	the Grand Canyon, Yellowstone National Park
Rivers and Falls	the Amazon River, the Tigris, Niagara Falls
Lakes and Bays	Lake Huron, Chesapeake Bay
Seas and Oceans	South China Sea, Pacific Ocean

When a compass point names a specific area of a country, it is capitalized. It is not capitalized when it simply refers to a physical direction.

EXAMPLES: My family lives in the Northeast.

The wind came from the west.

The names of other specific places that are not ordinarily found on maps also need to be capitalized.

Capitalize the names of other special places.

306

The following chart provides examples of how to capitalize these other special places.

OTHER SPECIAL PLACES	
Monuments	the Statue of Liberty
Memorials	the John F. Kennedy Memorial
Buildings	the Empire State Building, the Theater of Fine Arts
School or Meeting Rooms (with a number, name, or letter)	Room 14, the Madison Room, Conference Room B
Celestial Bodies (except the moon, the sun, and generally the earth)	the Milky Way, Venus, the Big Dipper, Earth (only when referred to as a planet)

Other Proper Nouns. There are other rules about capitalizing proper nouns. One deals with events and times.

Capitalize the names of specific events and periods of time.

This rule covers a variety of different categories. Study the following chart to see how examples of each are capitalized.

SPECIFIC EVENTS AND TIMES	
Historical Periods	the Renaissance, the Middle Ages, the Age of Enlightenment
Historical Events	the Revolutionary War, World War II
Documents	the Declaration of Independence, the Magna Carta
Days	Tuesday, Saturday
Months	April, November
Holidays	Fourth of July, Groundhog Day, Labor Day
Religious Days	Christmas, Easter, Passover, Ramadan
Special Events	Ashland Shakespeare Festival, Parade of Roses, Boston Marathon

Although they stand for specific times of the year, seasons are not capitalized.

EXAMPLES: We visited Barbados last winter.

The spring is my favorite time of year.

The names of a number of specific groups are also capitalized, along with words used to refer to them.

Capitalize the names of various organizations, government bodies, political parties, races, nationalities, and languages.

These different categories are shown in the following chart.

SPECIFIC GROUPS AND LANGUAGES	
Clubs	Kiwanis Club, Weld Chess Club
Organizations	Red Cross, Fund for Animals
Institutions	University of Washington, Valley Hospital
Businesses	General Motors, Sears Roebuck
Government Bodies	the Congress of the United States, the Department of Transportation
Political Parties	the Republican Party, the Democratic Party, the Conservative Party
Races and Nationalities	Caucasian, Chinese, British
Languages Spoken by Different Groups	English, Dutch, Swahili, Russian

Another rule deals specifically with religious terms. Just as you capitalize the names of religious days, you must capitalize names of religious deities and holy writings.

Capitalize references to religions, deities, and religious scriptures.

Each religion has a set of sacred words referring to its particular beliefs, and these words are generally capitalized. In the chart at the top of the next page, some of the sacred words associated with religions are listed. Note that the names of the religions themselves are also capitalized.

RELIGIOUS REFERENCES	
Christianity	God, the Lord, the Father, the Son, the Holy Spirit, the Bible, books of the Bible (that is, Genesis, Revelations, and so on)
Judaism	God, the Lord, the Father, the Prophets, the Torah, the Talmud, the Midrash
Islam	Allah, the Prophet, the Koran
Hinduism	Brahma, the Bhagavad Gita, the Vedas
Buddhism	the Buddha, Mahayana, Hinayana

The only exception to the rule for capitalizing religious terms occurs when you refer to a god or goddess of ancient mythology. In these cases, the word *god* is not capitalized.

EXAMPLES: the god Zeus, the goddess Hera

NOTE ABOUT PRONOUN REFERENCES: All pronoun references made to the Judeo-Christian deity are capitalized.

EXAMPLE: Great is His love.

A number of other proper nouns not mentioned as yet also need capitalization. The following rule covers these.

Capitalize the names of other special items.

The chart provides examples of how to capitalize these items.

OTHER SPECIAL ITEMS	
Awards	the Nobel Peace Prize, the Newbery Medal
Air, Sea, Space, and Land Craft	the Concorde, the *Nautilus*, *Apollo I*, the Model T
Trademarks	Kodak Instamatic, Sony Walkman

When you use a trademark, all the words should be capitalized. If you are using only part of the trademark (the brand name), capitalize only the word that comes from the trademark.

TRADEMARK: Kodak Instamatic

BRAND NAME ALONE: Kodak camera

EXERCISE B: Capitalizing Proper Names. Copy the following sentences, adding the missing capitals.

EXAMPLE: After the sun sets, venus will be visible in the west.

After the sun sets, Venus will be visible in the west.

1. To see a play that has been running for twenty-five years, you should go to st. martin's theater in london.
2. One well-known suspension bridge is the golden gate, which spans san francisco bay.
3. Both the shoshone and the arapaho make up a part of the population of wyoming.
4. By checking a perpetual calendar, I found that benjamin franklin was born on sunday, january 17, 1706.
5. In the northeast winters are quite harsh and long.
6. Astronauts will probably visit jupiter some day.
7. The lowest point in all north america is in death valley.
8. thomas mckean, a lawyer from pennsylvania, signed the declaration of independence.
9. Some of the major airline companies are united airlines, trans world airlines, and american airlines.
10. In october, 1976, congress repealed the homestead act of 1862 since there was no longer any land available for homesteading.
11. In ancient mythology the goddess athena dispensed wisdom.
12. The kentucky derby is held annually in the spring at churchill downs.
13. A well-known race horse, secretariat, won $1,316,808.
14. The torah, the talmud, and the midrash are the sacred writings of judaism.
15. You can find out about the great smoky mountains by writing to the chamber of commerce, 505 fesslers lane, nashville, tennessee 37210.
16. I think arabic is a difficult language to master.

310

17. The nebula award is presented for outstanding works of science fiction.
18. The nuclear regulatory commission regulates all civilian uses of atomic energy.
19. The white house uses the blue room as its official reception room.
20. About one half of our national leaders have been republicans and the other half have been democrats.

Capitals for Proper Adjectives

A proper adjective is a proper noun used as an adjective or an adjective formed from a proper noun.

Capitalize most proper adjectives.

All of the proper adjectives in the following examples are capitalized.

EXAMPLES: Paris fashions

the Korean people

some Victorian chairs

Some proper adjectives, however, have been used so often that they have lost their capitals.

EXAMPLES: french fries

venetian blinds

the teddy bear

When using proper adjectives, keep in mind a few special rules. First, you must remember to capitalize brand names.

Capitalize brand names used as adjectives.

In the following examples, the brand names describe common nouns. Thus, the brand names function as adjectives.

EXAMPLES: a Xerox copy

Cheer detergent

Second, you must also pay special attention to prefixes.

Do not capitalize prefixes with proper adjectives unless the prefix refers to a nationality.

311

In the first three examples, the prefixes are correctly left uncapitalized. However, when the prefix refers to a nationality, as in the last two examples, capitals are needed.

EXAMPLES:　all-American

　　　　　　pre-Renaissance

　　　　　　pro-Mexican

　　　　　　Sino-Russian

　　　　　　Anglo-American

Third, you must pay attention to the other parts of hyphenated proper adjectives.

In a hyphenated adjective, capitalize only the proper adjective.

EXAMPLE:　French-speaking Canadians

EXERCISE C: Capitalizing Proper Adjectives. Copy the following sentences, adding the missing capitals.

EXAMPLE:　I am taking a chinese cooking course.

　　　　　　I am taking a Chinese cooking course.

1. Open-air theaters are often used for the performance of elizabethan plays.
2. Many afro-american groups have held several conferences during the past few years to discuss their heritage.
3. Large crowds at an anti-nazi rally gave the police some crowd-control problems.
4. The anglo-saxon invasion of Britain took place in the fifth and sixth centuries.
5. Some early buddhist monasteries were caves that were elegantly carved and decorated.
6. Her old kodak camera accompanied her on all her travels.
7. A sino-russian pact could have a significant effect on foreign policy.
8. Those who own pre-columbian sculptures have valuable art pieces in their possession.
9. A lovely indian woman in a sari came into the store asking for the manager.
10. The franklin d. roosevelt years were marred by World War II.

312

Capitals for Titles

To signal titles of people and titles of works clearly, you must use capitals.

Capitalize titles of people and titles of works.

Titles of People. Several rules apply to the titles of people. The first deals with titles used before names and in direct address.

Capitalize a person's title when it is followed by the person's name or when it is used in direct address.

Some of the most common titles in the English language are given below.

SOCIAL: Sir, Madam or Madame, Lord, Lady
BUSINESS: Professor, Doctor, Superintendent
RELIGIOUS: Reverend, Bishop, Father, Pope, Sister, Rabbi
MILITARY: Sergeant, Major, Lieutenant, Colonel, Admiral, General
GOVERNMENT: Mayor, Governor, President, Ambassador, Secretary of Defense

The following sentences show some of these titles in use. Notice that each title is followed by a proper name or is used in place of the person's name.

EXAMPLES: The military band directed by Major Leonard played some rousing marching tunes.

I heard that Lady Eleanor Hartley was interested in contemporary sculpture.

Where are you going, Doctor?

A special rule covers the capitalization of some titles.

Capitalize the titles of certain high government officials even when the titles are not followed by a proper name or used in direct address.

The titles of some high government officials are almost always capitalized. These include the titles of President and the Chief Justice of the United States, the Secretary of State, and the Queen of England. Notice in the following examples that these titles are often capitalized even when they do not refer to a particular person holding the office.

EXAMPLES: The visiting diplomats were presented to the Queen at a reception.

The Chief Justice is one of nine justices on the Supreme Court.

The President of the United States has a very difficult job.

Other titles may be capitalized to show special respect. They are almost never capitalized, however, unless the writer is referring to a specific person holding the office.

EXAMPLES: The Senator spoke to us at graduation.

A senator's schedule is demanding.

Titles made up of more than one word need a special rule.

Capitalize all important words in compound titles, but do not capitalize prefixes and suffixes added to titles.

In the following compound titles, notice that all words except *in* are capitalized.

EXAMPLES: Vice President

Lieutenant Governor

Commander in Chief

If a prefix or suffix is part of the title, it is not capitalized.

EXAMPLES: ex-Senator Smith

President-elect Jefferson

Another special rule covers names for relationships.

Capitalize titles showing family relationships when they refer to a specific person, unless they are preceded by a possessive noun or pronoun.

The titles in the first three of the examples at the top of the next page must be capitalized. In the last two examples, the possessives make capitals unnecessary.

314

EXAMPLES: Long ago, Grandfather Pleski played the violin.

I need a new jacket, Mother.

Did Father buy the tickets for the play?

Stan's grandmother once played the violin.

Our aunt forgot where she put the plane tickets.

The final rule for capitalizing titles of people involves abbreviated titles.

Capitalize abbreviations of titles before and after names.

BEFORE NAMES: Mr., Mrs., Dr., Rev., Hon.

AFTER NAMES: Jr., Sr., Ph.D., Esq.

See Section 16.2 for a more complete listing of these abbreviations. Here are two of these abbreviations in use.

EXAMPLES: The art professor, Dr. Lois Nelson, studied abroad.

Mark Delaney, Jr., just sold his first watercolor.

Titles of Things. Titles are given not only to people but also to things such as written works and other works of art.

Capitalize the first word and all other key words in the titles of books, periodicals, poems, stories, plays, paintings, and other works of art.

All words in a title should be capitalized except articles *(a, an, the)* and prepositions and conjunctions with fewer than five letters. These words are capitalized only when they are the first word in a title. Other parts of speech, no matter how short they may be, are always capitalized.

EXAMPLES: *The Grapes of Wrath*

"I Have a Dream"

On the Road to Victory

A Tour Through America's Museums

"Who Is Sylvia?"

When capitalizing a subtitle, use the same rule that you use for titles. Notice in the example at the top of the next page that *A* is capitalized because it is the first word in the subtitle.

EXAMPLE: *Art History: A Look at Great Masterpieces*

A second rule involves the titles of courses.

Capitalize titles of courses when the courses are language courses or when the courses are followed by a number.

EXAMPLES: French I   Chemistry 1A   Economics 313

The capital letters are dropped when school subjects are discussed in a general way and no specific course is named. Languages, however, always receive capitals.

EXAMPLE: Last year, I studied chemistry, history, and French.

EXERCISE D: Capitalizing Titles of People. Copy the following sentences, adding the missing capitals.

EXAMPLE: The recruits saluted major general carruthers.

The recruits saluted Major General Carruthers.

1. Could you direct me, sir, to this address?
2. We invited dr. and mrs. strutner to the play.
3. One of the greatest mystery writers of all time was dame agatha christie.
4. It is my great pleasure to present the president of the United States.
5. The ex-secretary of state is writing his memoirs.
6. Lieutenant governor taylor ran our state last week while governor hull was away on a business trip.
7. We expect colonel green to inspect the troops today.
8. We visited grandmother, who teaches in a small country school.
9. Please tell us, senator, how you expect to vote.
10. The reverend john hyder and father madison met to discuss some of the concerns facing their parishes.

EXERCISE E: Capitalizing Titles of Things. Copy the titles that need capitalization from the following sentences, adding the missing capitals. Underline any titles that appear in italics.

EXAMPLE: Have you read the novel *the red pony* by Steinbeck?

The Red Pony

1. *The wall street journal* is a respected newspaper that presents news from the point of view of business people.
2. The only classes they are offering that I want to take are psychology, german, and art.
3. The story "the lottery" by Shirley Jackson makes the reader contemplate some of humanity's baser instincts.
4. When registration opened, english 1A, biology 43, and all the calculus courses filled up immediately.
5. *the making of the past: the egyptian kingdoms* contains some excellent pictures of ancient tomb treasures.
6. Robert Graves based much of his novel *i, claudius* on the Roman historian Suetonius's *the lives of the caesars*.
7. Loren Eiseley's *the man who saw through time* is a collection of essays about the Elizabethan scientist Francis Bacon.
8. Edgar Allan Poe once wrote a very fine poem entitled "a dream within a dream."
9. One of Phyllis McGinley's best books for children is *the horse who lived upstairs*.
10. *measure for measure* is one of Shakespeare's lesser-known plays.

Capitals in Letters

When writing letters, you are likely to find problems with capitals only in the salutations and the closings.

Capitalize the first word and all nouns in letter salutations and the first word in letter closings.

In the following examples, you will see that all nouns are capitalized in the salutations. In each of the closings, only the first word is capitalized.

SALUTATIONS: Dear Ms. Crawford,   My dear Friend,

Ladies and Gentlemen:

CLOSINGS: Sincerely yours,   With kind regards,

EXERCISE F: Using Capitals in Letters. Copy the following letter, adding the missing capitals. Then circle each capital letter.

(handwritten: in book)

3 locust drive
mount kisco, new york 10549
december 23, 1986

(handwritten: yeah!)

chancellor louisa travis
oakville college
oakville, new york 10634

dear chancellor travis:

since norman rockwell is one of our greatest american illustrators, i would like to propose that you offer a new course listing, rockwell's art I. he has captured the hearts of all with paintings such as "after the prom," "the runaway," and "freedom from want." his collection contains pictures of famous american personalities such as general eisenhower, president john f. kennedy, and uncle sam.

e. b. browning once wrote, "do ye hear the children weeping, o my brother?" anyone who has looked at mr. rockwell's paintings knows that he has. a sensitivity toward people, their condition, their hopes, and their fears is captured in each of his works. he has enabled us to see ourselves: reflected in his dinner scenes are not just people, but our own relatives. we see grandma rodgers, uncle george, and all the others.

there is plenty of material, chancellor, to cover an entire semester course, and many books could easily be purchased as texts. thank you for considering this new course. i eagerly await your response.

sincerely yours,

l. k. claire, ph.d.

EXERCISE G: Using All Capitalization Rules. Copy the following sentences, adding the missing capitals. Underline any titles that appear in italics.

EXAMPLE: with 2,223 passengers on board, the *titanic* sailed for new york.

With 2,223 passengers on board, the Titanic sailed for New York.

(handwritten: Good paper)

(handwritten: -10 whoa)

318

1. in his play *the merchant of venice,* shakespeare wrote, "ships are but boards, sailors but men."
2. in 1912 officers of the white star ship lines would have scoffed at this since they believed that they had an unsinkable ship, the *titanic.*
3. it was a luxury liner with a swimming pool on deck g and turkish baths for the guests' enjoyment.
4. the harland and wolff shipbuilding firm in belfast had outdone themselves in creating a beautiful cruise ship.
5. as the ship left southampton, england, it was filled with english, german, swedish, russian, irish, and greek passengers and included such wealthy passengers as the astors, mr. guggenheim, and the strauss family.
6. disaster struck on a sunday evening, april 14, southwest of iceland; an iceberg tore a huge gash in the hull.
7. captain edward smith soon realized that it was only a matter of hours before the ship met a watery death in the atlantic ocean.
8. a nearby cunard liner, the *carpathia,* picked up 705 survivors, many of whom gave thanks to god for their delivery.
9. *the new york times* and other national newspapers carried headlines of the tragedy.
10. today, the steamship historical society of staten island retains maps of this famous ship, and many books, such as jack winocour's *the story of the titanic,* recount its tragic fate.

EXERCISE H: Correcting Faulty Capitalization. Copy the following sentences, correcting all of the errors in capitalization. Underline any titles that appear in italics.

EXAMPLE: i recited the Poem "the highwayman" for cousin al.

I recited the poem "The Highwayman" for Cousin Al.

1. the registration for the Conference was held in room 13, and dr. raymond parker was in charge.
2. the *Sporting and fun* Mail Order Catalog came from 31 miller avenue, rosemount, Minnesota 55105.
3. when we visited the New orleans world's fair, we could hear people all around speaking french, italian, japanese, and Spanish.

4. when the bankrupt man asked for a loan from the first National bank, it was the same as asking for the Sun, Moon, and Stars.
5. in order to finish a semester early, jack took Chemistry, German, and Psychology during Summer School.
6. we went to the same Hotel every year; the kona Village had excellent food and fine accommodations.
7. The president addressed the united nations on concerns facing the southeast Asia treaty organization.
8. During the garlic Festival in gilroy, you can get Armenian bread drenched in Garlic butter.
9. the *enterprise* docked in Hudson bay while admiral Smith came aboard for a quick Naval briefing.
10. monday, the book aunt Mabel wrote, called *Adventure At Fern ridge Lake,* goes to the printers.

DEVELOPING WRITING SKILLS: Using Capitals Correctly.
Write the following information, using your imagination where necessary.

EXAMPLE: A continent

South America

A. A military or government title
B. A friend's last name
C. A city
D. An animal's name
E. A villain on TV or in a book
F. A compass direction
G. A mountain range
H. Your favorite book
I. A brand name and product
J. A body of water
K. A high government official
L. An award

Then insert your answers into the following brief plot. Expand the plot into a story of about ten sentences. Make it exciting, and be sure to capitalize correctly.

A B from C is really an undercover agent aided by a trusty animal friend, D. AB must catch E, who is a spy. They meet F of G, where the spy is spotted casually reading H. AB finds the secret plans hidden by E in I. After bringing E across J, they are greeted by K, who gives L to AB for the successful completion of a dangerous mission.

Rules for Abbreviation 16.2

An abbreviation is simply a shortened form of a word or phrase. It usually consists of the first several letters of a word or the first letter of each word in a longer phrase.

To abbreviate means to shorten an existing word or phrase.

Abbreviations have been discovered on the earliest-known tombs, monuments, and coins. When manuscripts were still each tediously produced by hand, writers used abbreviations to save time and space. Abbreviations still allow writers to save time and space, but they must be appropriately used. Abbreviations should not become a shortcut for lazy writers who just do not want to be bothered writing the whole word or phrase out.

Some abbreviations are not permissible in formal writing but are allowed in addresses, technical writing, lists, bibliographies, or informal writing. Knowing the circumstances under which abbreviations can be used is an important responsibility for writers. You should also know the correct spelling and punctuation of abbreviations.

The rules on the following pages cover the basic aspects of abbreviation. After learning the basic rules, however, you may still need to consult a dictionary for spelling and punctuation from time to time.

Titles of People

Perhaps the most commonly used abbreviations are the social titles *Mr.* and *Mrs.*

Abbreviations of social titles before a proper name begin with a capital and end with a period.

The following abbreviations are all common social titles. They can be used before a proper name in both formal and informal writing.

SOCIAL TITLES: Mr., Mrs., Mme. (Madam or Madame)

Messrs. (plural of Mr.), Mmes. (plural of Mrs. or Mme.)

321

In the following sentences, note that each abbreviation is used with one or more proper names.

EXAMPLES: Mrs. Jackson gave a fine talk on the company stock.

Messrs. Berg and Inesco founded the business.

NOTE ABOUT *MISS* AND *MS.*: Though *Miss* is a title preceding a name, it is not an abbreviation, so no period goes at the end of it. Although it starts with a capital and ends with a period, *Ms.* is not an abbreviation of a word either. It may, however, be used before a proper name just as an abbreviation can be. It refers to either a single or a married woman.

Abbreviations of other titles used before proper names begin with a capital letter and end with a period.

The following chart shows how some of the most common of these abbreviations are formed.

ABBREVIATIONS OF COMMON TITLES					
Governmental		**Military**		**Professional**	
Supt.	Superintendent	Sgt.	Sergeant	Dr.	Doctor
Rep.	Representative	Lt.	Lieutenant	Atty.	Attorney
Sen.	Senator	Capt.	Captain	Prof.	Professor
Gov.	Governor	Lt. Col.	Lieutenant Colonel	Hon.	Honorable
Treas.	Treasurer	Col.	Colonel	Rev.	Reverend
Sec.	Secretary	Maj. Gen.	Major General	Fr.	Father
Amb.	Ambassador	Lt. Gen.	Lieutenant General	Sr.	Sister
Pres.	President	Gen.	General	Br.	Brother

These abbreviations should generally be spelled out in formal writing, especially when only the surname is given.

EXAMPLES: Ambassador Wilson rose to discuss oil imports.

She interviewed Reverend Johnson about his work.

322

There are two major exceptions. The word *Dr.* is almost always abbreviated before a proper noun just as *Mrs.* and *Mr.* are. In addition, an abbreviation is often used for the other nonreligious titles as well when the first name or initials are given.

EXAMPLES: Dr. Lopez was the surgeon who performed the delicate operation.

Prof. Julia A. Whitaker wrote a famous book on investments.

Another rule concerns titles after names.

Abbreviations of titles after a name begin with a capital letter and end with a period.

The following sentences show the use of the common titles *Jr.* and *Sr.*

EXAMPLES: Ricardo Flores, Jr., earned $200 last week.

She wrote to Eugene Munster, Sr., for a job interview.

The rule also applies to academic degrees. The most common abbreviations of these degrees and their meanings, follow.

ABBREVIATIONS OF ACADEMIC DEGREES

B.A. or A.B.	Bachelor of Arts	Ph.D.	Doctor of Philosophy
B.S. or S.B.	Bachelor of Science	D.D.	Doctor of Divinity
M.A. or A.M.	Master of Arts	D.D.S.	Doctor of Dental Surgery
M.S. or S.M.	Master of Science	M.D.	Doctor of Medicine
M.B.A.	Master of Business Administration	R.N.	Registered Nurse
M.F.A.	Master of Fine Arts	Esq.	Esquire (lawyer)

These titles can always be abbreviated after proper names, just as *Jr.* and *Sr.* are.

EXAMPLE: Rosalind Marks, Ph.D., narrated a film on investing in real estate.

EXERCISE A: Using Abbreviations with Titles. Write the abbreviation for each of the titles in the following sentences. Then rewrite the sentences in which the abbreviations can be used appropriately in formal writing, using the abbreviations.

EXAMPLE: Alan Hill, Doctor of Dental Surgery, lives next door.

D.D.S.   Alan Hill, D.D.S., lives next door.

1. With her diploma in her hand, she could officially write Ellen Garcia, Master of Arts.
2. Major General Barker plans to present several awards at a ceremony today.
3. I went to Doctor Powers when I was sick because I had confidence in him.
4. The name plate on his desk read "Derek Felton, Registered Nurse."
5. While in Washington, I visited the office of Senator Partridge.
6. Marjorie Block, Esquire, is planning a trip to Belgium and France this summer.
7. The parents planned to call their new son Tobias Halsten, Junior.
8. Father Leakins led the congregation in the Sunday morning worship.
9. Once I complete my oral examinations, I will be a Doctor of Philosophy.
10. After many years Mister Gilbert finally started his own printing business.

Geographical Terms

Abbreviations for geographical terms have become an essential part of our lives. Without abbreviations, addressing envelopes could become quite a chore.

Abbreviations for geographical terms before or after a proper noun begin with a capital letter and end with a period.

Although the abbreviations for geographical terms are seldom used in formal writing, you will find many uses for them in your personal writing. Generally, you will use several of these abbreviations when you address envelopes and packages. Any list of names and addresses you may keep is also a good place to use these abbreviations. Frequently, some of these abbreviations may be found in bibliographies. In addition, classroom notes can be taken more rapidly if you use easily recognized abbreviations whenever you can.

In the following chart are some of the most common abbreviations of geographical terms. Remember that in most cases these abbreviations should not be used in formal writing.

ABBREVIATIONS OF GEOGRAPHICAL TERMS					
Ave.	Avenue	Ft.	Fort	Prov.	Province
Bldg.	Building	Hwy.	Highway	Pt.	Point
Blk.	Block	Is.	Island	Rd.	Road
Blvd.	Boulevard	Mt.	Mountain, Mount	Rte.	Route
Co.	County	Natl.	National	Sq.	Square
Dist.	District	Pen.	Peninsula	St.	Street
Dr.	Drive	Pk.	Park, Peak	Terr.	Territory

Notice in the following examples that each abbreviation appears either before or after a proper noun. Remember also that these are examples of informal, not formal, writing.

EXAMPLES: Your friends are waiting for you at the corner of Rte. 9W and Palisade Ave.

Mt. McKinley, the highest mountain in North America, is located in Denali Natl. Pk., Alaska.

The fifty states have traditional abbreviations, which you should generally use only in lists, addresses, and informal writing. The states also have United States Postal Service abbreviations, which you should use on envelopes or packages to be mailed.

Traditional abbreviations for states begin with a capital and end with a period. The Postal Service abbreviations are all capitals with no periods.

The chart on the next page includes both traditional and U.S. Postal Service abbreviations for states.

325

STATE ABBREVIATIONS

State	Traditional	Postal Service	State	Traditional	Postal Service
Alabama	Ala.	AL	Montana	Mont.	MT
Alaska	Alaska	AK	Nebraska	Nebr.	NB
Arizona	Ariz.	AZ	Nevada	Nev.	NV
Arkansas	Ark.	AR	New Hampshire	N.H.	NH
California	Calif.	CA	New Jersey	N.J.	NJ
Colorado	Colo.	CO	New Mexico	N.M.	NM
Connecticut	Conn.	CT	New York	N.Y.	NY
Delaware	Del.	DE	North Carolina	N.C.	NC
Florida	Fla.	FL	North Dakota	N.Dak.	ND
Georgia	Ga.	GA	Ohio	O.	OH
Hawaii	Hawaii	HI	Oklahoma	Okla.	OK
Idaho	Ida.	ID	Oregon	Ore.	OR
Illinois	Ill.	IL	Pennsylvania	Pa.	PA
Indiana	Ind.	IN	Rhode Island	R.I.	RI
Iowa	Iowa	IA	South Carolina	S.C.	SC
Kansas	Kans.	KS	South Dakota	S.Dak.	SD
Kentucky	Ky.	KY	Tennessee	Tenn.	TN
Louisiana	La.	LA	Texas	Tex.	TX
Maine	Me.	ME	Utah	Utah	UT
Maryland	Md.	MD	Vermont	Vt.	VT
Massachusetts	Mass.	MA	Virginia	Va.	VA
Michigan	Mich.	MI	Washington	Wash.	WA
Minnesota	Minn.	MN	West Virginia	W.Va.	WV
Mississippi	Miss.	MS	Wisconsin	Wis.	WI
Missouri	Mo.	MO	Wyoming	Wyo.	WY

NOTE ABOUT *D.C.*: The traditional abbreviation for the District of Columbia is *D.C.*; the Postal Service abbreviation is *DC*. Use the traditional abbreviation in formal writing whenever it follows the word Washington.

EXAMPLE: Last year we visited Washington, D.C., in the spring.

EXERCISE B: Using Geographical Abbreviations. Write the abbreviation for each item in parentheses. Then rewrite the sentences in which the abbreviations can be used appropriately in formal writing, using the abbreviations.

EXAMPLE: The city of Calgary is located in Canada's Alberta (Province).

Prov.

1. The Cranston (Building) was situated right off Forbes (Highway).
2. I would like to visit the Yukon (Territory) during my summer vacation.
3. On the package that was delivered to us by mistake, we saw the following address: 1641 Saratoga (Avenue), (Mount) Rosewood, (Tennessee).
4. We took a weekend trip to visit my brother at (Fort) Bragg this year.
5. We were registered to vote in (District) 14 in San Joaquin (County).
6. I could barely read the return address: 35 Markle (Street), Wilmington, (Delaware) 19081.
7. After her election she looked for a house in Washington, (District of Columbia).
8. (Mount) Olympus was the home of the gods according to Greek mythology.
9. The store where I bought your present is in (Fort) Laredo, (Montana).
10. My friends traveled in their camper to Yellowstone (National) (Park).

Time, Dates, and Measurements

Other common abbreviations are used for time, dates, and measurements. Some of these abbreviations are used only in informal writing, while others may be used in any kind of writing. The first rule is for abbreviations for various time spans.

Abbreviations for clocked time begin with a small letter, but those for days of the week and months begin with a capital. All end with a period.

Below are abbreviations used for various time spans. They are used only in informal or technical writing.

TIME ABBREVIATIONS					
Clocked Time					
sec.	second(s)	min.	minute(s)	hr.	hour(s)
Days of the Week					
Mon.	Monday	Thurs.	Thursday	Sat.	Saturday
Tues.	Tuesday	Fri.	Friday	Sun.	Sunday
Wed.	Wednesday				
Months of the Year					
Jan.	January	May	May	Sept.	September
Feb.	February	June	June	Oct.	October
Mar.	March	July	July	Nov.	November
Apr.	April	Aug.	August	Dec.	December

Abbreviations are used for time before and after noon.

Abbreviations of time before noon and after noon are formed with either capital letters followed by periods or small letters followed by periods.

Notice that abbreviations for time before noon and after noon can be written in two different ways. In any one piece of writing, be sure to use either all capitals or all small letters. Do not mix the two styles.

ABBREVIATIONS: A.M. or a.m. (*ante meridiem,* before noon)

P.M. or p.m. (*post meridiem,* after noon)

Use these abbreviations in both formal and informal writing whenever the time of day is expressed in numerals.

EXAMPLES: The stockholders' meeting began at 10:30 A.M.

We left at 8:00 p.m., but more remained to be done.

Abbreviations are also needed to distinguish between dates before and after the birth of Christ.

Abbreviations for historical dates before and after the birth of Christ require capital letters followed by periods.

ABBREVIATIONS: B.C. (before Christ)

A.D. (*anno Domini*, in the year of the Lord)

In both formal and informal writing, use *B.C.* and *A.D.* to distinguish between dates before and after the birth of Christ when the year is expressed in numerals. *B.C.* always follows the number, *A.D.* may come after or before the number.

EXAMPLES: The city crumbled in 255 B.C.

The Roman Emperor Nero died in 68 A.D.

The philosopher wrote his treatise around A.D. 500.

In technical writing, abbreviations for measurements are often used. In both informal and technical writing, these abbreviations are used only with numerals. They are generally avoided entirely in formal writing, except for those showing degrees of temperature.

You may be most familiar with the abbreviations for traditional measurements.

For the abbreviations of traditional measurements, use small letters and periods.

In the following examples, notice that the abbreviation for *Fahrenheit* is an exception to the rule as it uses a capital.

ABBREVIATIONS:

in.	inch(es)	oz.	ounce(s)
ft.	foot, feet	lb.	pound(s)
yd.	yard(s)	pt.	pint(s)
mi.	mile(s)	qt.	quart(s)
tsp.	teaspoon(s)	gal.	gallon(s)
tbsp.	tablespoon(s)	F.	Fahrenheit

Abbreviations of metric measurements do not have periods.

For the abbreviations of metric measurements, use small letters and no periods.

In the examples at the top of the next page, notice that the abbreviations for *liter* and *Celsius* are exceptions to the rule in that capitals are used.

329

ABBREVIATIONS: mm   millimeter(s)   g   gram(s)
                 cm   centimeter(s)   kg kilogram(s)
                 m   meter(s)   L   liter(s)
                 km   kilometer(s)   C   Celsius

Even in informal writing, the abbreviations for traditional measurements and for metric measurements should be used only with numerals. Never abbreviate these units when they follow spelled-out numbers.

EXAMPLE: Our newest product on the market weighs three pounds less than our old one.

EXERCISE C: Using Abbreviations for Time, Dates, and Measurements. Write the abbreviation for each item in parentheses. Then rewrite the sentences in which the abbreviation can be used appropriately in formal writing, using the abbreviations.

EXAMPLE: We still need 10 (pounds) of potatoes.

        lb.

1. We must change our clocks tonight from 2:00 (before noon) to 3:00 (before noon).
2. The Mayan civilization dates from approximately 100 (in the year of the Lord).
3. Alexander, ruler of Macedon, died in 323 (before Christ).
4. Then add 2 (quarts) of water to the soup.
5. My parents made my curfew 11:30 (after noon).
6. My recipe calls for 3 (tablespoons) flour.
7. Our gas pumps may soon switch to (liters).
8. The long distance runner jogged 15 (miles).
9. A caterpillar measuring 2 (centimeters) came in the door.
10. The thermostat read 17° (Celsius).

Latin Expressions

In note-taking, abbreviations of Latin expressions are often used.

Use small letters and periods for abbreviations of most Latin expressions.

In formal writing write out the English equivalents, given in the following examples.

EXAMPLES:

c., ca., circ.	about (used for approximate dates)	f.	and the following (page or line)
e.g.	for example	ff.	and the following (pages or lines)
et al.	and others		
etc.	and so forth	i.e.	that is

EXERCISE D: Understanding Abbreviations of Latin Expressions. Turn each of the following into formal writing by spelling out the underlined abbreviation.

EXAMPLE: William Murray <u>et al</u>. wrote the article.

William Murray and others wrote the article.

1. For answers, check page 43 <u>ff</u>.
2. The vegetable stand has fresh corn, carrots, onions, <u>etc</u>.
3. I may take part in an activity—<u>e.g.</u>, band or tennis.
4. The dealer dated the antique table <u>circ</u>. 1721.
5. I need three volunteers, <u>i.e.</u>, three able volunteers.
6. Read page 12 <u>f</u>. before class tomorrow.
7. Lao Tse, the Chinese philosopher, was born <u>c</u>. 604 B.C.
8. A coronary thrombosis, <u>i.e.</u>, a heart attack, can be fatal.
9. I need a part-time job, <u>e.g.</u>, a paper route or babysitting.
10. The report was prepared by Barbara Brewster <u>et al</u>.

Other Abbreviations

A few other abbreviations are worth knowing.
Business Abbreviations. These follow a single rule.

An abbreviated word in a business name begins with a capital letter and ends with a period.

BUSINESS ABBREVIATIONS:

Bros.	Brothers	Co.	Company
Ltd.	Limited	Inc.	Incorporated

Use only the abbreviations *Inc.* and *Ltd.* in formal writing.
Abbreviations Pronounced Letter by Letter. A special type of abbreviation is used for names of some organizations, business firms, government agencies, and other groups and objects.

Use all capitals and no periods to abbreviate names whose abbreviations are pronounced letter by letter as if they were words.

In the following chart, notice that the abbreviations are written in capital letters and are not followed by periods.

ABBREVIATIONS FOR ORGANIZATIONS		
Organizations	AMA	American Medical Association
	OAS	Organization of American States
Business Firms	GM	General Motors
	IBM	International Business Machines
Government Agencies	FBI	Federal Bureau of Investigation
	IRS	Internal Revenue Service
Other Things	TB	Tuberculosis
	TV	Television

In formal writing, you may use any of these abbreviations as long as you first identify what they mean by using the full term once before beginning to use the abbreviation.

EXAMPLE: Officials of the United Auto Workers agreed to the contract. Members of the UAW must now approve it.

Acronyms. Other abbreviations often used for organizations are acronyms. An acronym is a word formed from the first letter (or first few letters) of a series of words. The letters are never followed by periods.

Use all capital letters and no periods for acronyms that form the names of organizations.

Notice in the following examples that the acronym is often more familiar than the full title.

ACRONYMS: NASA National Aeronautics and Space
Administration

NATO North Atlantic Treaty Organization

VISTA Volunteers in Service to America

Acronyms for organizations may be used in formal writing as long as they are sufficiently identified first.

332

EXERCISE E: Using Other Abbreviations. Write the abbreviation for each item in parentheses. Then rewrite the sentences in which the abbreviation can be used appropriately in formal writing, using the abbreviation.

EXAMPLE: I work for the (Central Intelligence Agency).

CIA   I work for the CIA.

1. Our newly formed company was called Lucien (Brothers).
2. They used an (International Business Machines) computer.
3. The (Federal Bureau of Investigation) has lots of power.
4. (Tuberculosis) is a serious disease.
5. The accounting firm is called Counting, (Incorporated).
6. (North Atlantic Treaty Organization) troops were alerted.
7. We contacted the (American Medical Association).
8. Have you considered (Volunteers in Service to America)?
9. We had Colbert's Cement (Company) put in our patio.
10. Children, please turn that (television) off.

DEVELOPING WRITING SKILLS: Using Abbreviations in Formal Writing. If the underlined items below are used correctly, write *correct*. If not, correct them. Then write a paragraph of your own, using at least five abbreviations correctly.

For over six centuries (1) B.C., people desired gold; today, they still consider it a precious metal. Our (2) Treasury Dept. keeps gold at (3) Ft. Knox in Louisville, (4)KY. It takes (5) c. six thousand (6) lb. of rock to produce one (7) ounce of gold. Whether gold is to be shipped on a (8) Mon. or a (9) Tues. in the (10) a.m. or the (11) p.m. is never revealed in order to reduce theft. To set the price of gold, the London Gold Market, generally referred to as the LGM, calls around the world from its headquarters, (12) N.M. Rothschild and Sons, Ltd., to determine the stable selling price. Crises have shut down the (13) LGM for several (14) hr., but generally gold retains its value. For instance, (15) Mr. Jay Gould managed to buy up all of the gold on the gold market once, but regulations instituted while (16) Pres. Nixon was in office prevent gold hoarding now. Some gold goes into making jewelry, (17) e.g., watches and necklaces. Some gold is used by other (18) co. in making scientific equipment, (19) etc. It seems that whatever its use, gold is worth its weight—in gold, (20) i.e.

Skills Review and Writing Workshop

Capitalization and Abbreviation

CHECKING YOUR SKILLS

Rewrite the paragraph, correcting all errors in capitalization and using only abbreviations appropriate in formal writing.

(1) For bob sax, the first day at peterson high school had not begun well. (2) Bob had not wanted to leave his old School in centerville, Ind. (3) However, his father had accepted a job at Mcgovern college and his mother had been offered a job as a reporter on *the evening chronicle,* so they had moved here in Aug. (4) The bus this a.m. had been delayed in traffic on maple St. (5) Bob's first class was biology I with mr. harris, but he couldn't find the classroom. (6) Now it was 8 a. m., and Bob was afraid of being late. (7) finally, he discovered room 302 and found a seat. (8) The girl next to him smiled and extended her hand. (9) "i am Sarah carter," she said, "And this is my first day here." (10) Perhaps tues., sept. 2, was going to be a good day for bob after all.

USING MECHANICS SKILLS IN WRITING
Writing a Character Sketch

By mastering the rules of capitalization and abbreviation, you can communicate more effectively. Write a biographical sketch entitled "The Most Unforgettable Person I Have Known," following these steps.

Prewriting: Think of a person who has deeply affected your life. Consider that person's personality characteristics. Think of the most important ways that he or she has influenced you.

Writing: Begin by describing the person, focusing on his or her most outstanding attributes. Then explain how this person has influenced you.

Revising: Correct any mistakes in capitalization and abbreviation and look for other improvements you might make. When you have finished revising, proofread carefully.

17

Punctuation

In order to prevent serious automobile accidents, drivers are required to obey various road signs. The signs tell drivers when to stop, yield, and slow down. Just as these road signs direct drivers, punctuation in a sentence directs readers.

Punctuation is a commonly accepted set of symbols used in writing to convey specific directions to the reader.

The basic punctuation marks are the period (.), question mark (?), exclamation mark (!), comma (,), semicolon (;), colon (:), quotation marks (" "), parentheses (( )), dash (—), hyphen (-), and apostrophe ('). These marks tell when to stop or pause or when to read with a questioning tone or with excitement. Punctuation may also show relationships between ideas, by either connecting them or setting them apart.

In this chapter you will look at some of the most widely accepted punctuation rules.

End Marks 17.1

End marks are what their name implies—punctuation marks that signal the end of a sentence and, sometimes, a word or phrase.

There are three end marks: the period (.), the question mark (?), and the exclamation mark (!). They usually indicate the end of a sentence.

Which end mark you use will depend on whether you are making a statement, asking a question, or conveying great excitement.

335

Uses of the Period

The period is the most commonly used end mark. Four rules govern its use. The first involves declarative sentences.

Use a period to end a declarative sentence, that is, at the end of a statement of fact or opinion.

STATEMENT OF FACT: A circle has 360 degrees.

STATEMENT OF OPINION: I think I will pass English this term.

A period is also used at the end of many directions and commands.

Use a period to end an imperative sentence, that is, at the end of a direction or command.

DIRECTION: Fold your ballot once and place it in the box.

COMMAND: Sit up straight.

Do not be confused by an indirect question included in a declarative sentence.

Use a period to end an indirect question.

An indirect question is always part of a declarative sentence. It does not require an answer.

INDIRECT QUESTION: They asked what time the polls would open.

The final use of the period is in abbreviations.

Use a period to end most abbreviations.

As noted in Section 16.2, not all abbreviations require periods. The following examples represent just a few of the many kinds of abbreviations that do end in periods.

INITIALS: J. R. Dattilo

TITLES: Mrs.   Mr.   Dr.   Capt.

PLACE NAMES: St.   Ave.   Rd.

When a sentence ends in an abbreviation with a period, it is not necessary to put a second period at the end of the sentence.

EXAMPLE: The speaker at the dinner was Richard Johnson, Jr.

Book

17.1 End Marks

EXERCISE A: Using the Period Correctly. Copy the following sentences, adding the necessary periods.

EXAMPLE: John R Carlson asked you to return his call

John R. Carlson asked you to return his call.

1. The American humorist S J Perelman was once a scriptwriter for the Marx Brothers
2. My parents wondered what grade I received on the test
3. Address the package to Mr Arthur Grover, Jr
4. I think Elizabeth Bishop is a fine modern American poet
5. She prefers the title Mrs to the title Ms
6. I asked Mrs Ramos to go with us
7. Schedule a certain amount of time for studying every day
8. Elizabeth P Peabody started the first kindergarten in the United States in 1860
9. The son of Efrem Zimbalist, Sr, a violinist, is an actor
10. Dr Elvira M Thackery spoke at the seminar

Uses of the Question Mark

For a question requiring a reply, a question mark is needed.

Use a question mark to end an interrogative sentence, that is, at the end of a direct question.

The following are direct questions requiring answers.

DIRECT QUESTIONS: Are you planning to go out tonight**?**

Who do you think will win the contest**?**

Remember, do not confuse a direct question with an indirect question. End an indirect question with a period.

Sometimes, only part of the question is written out. The rest of the question is simply understood.

Use a question mark to end an incomplete question in which the rest of the question is understood.

EXAMPLE: A sloth spends its life hanging upside down. Why**?**

A question that indicates surprise is sometimes phrased as if it were a declarative sentence. In these cases the question mark is the only clue that the sentence is a question.

Use a question mark to end a statement that is intended as a question.

EXAMPLES: Four extra guests are coming for dinner**?**

The auditorium can hold only fifty people**?**

EXERCISE B: Using the Question Mark Correctly. Some of the following sentences are direct questions and require question marks. Others are indirect questions and require periods. Copy the sentences, adding the necessary punctuation.

EXAMPLE: What was comedian Milton Berle's nickname

What was comedian Milton Berle's nickname?

1. How much money has Lucille Ball made from her television series
2. Many have wondered whether more people watched Lucille Ball or President Eisenhower's inauguration
3. How did Dinah Shore customarily end her shows
4. Who was known as Mr. Television
5. What were two of the popular TV shows that children of the fifties liked to watch
6. Before 1951 what percentage of the American public was asleep by midnight After 1951
7. Some wondered whether shows like the Steve Allen and Jack Paar talk shows were responsible for people staying up later
8. In what TV show did Mary Martin fly through the air on wires
9. In what show did audiences see Joe Friday In what role
10. During the 1953–1954 season, which show was rated first Second

Uses of the Exclamation Mark

When a period is not enough to show the emotion or importance of an idea, an exclamation mark should be used.

Use an exclamation mark to end an exclamatory sentence, that is, at the end of a statement showing strong emotion.

EXAMPLES: She won the election by only one vote!

That is absolutely incredible!

In addition to ending exclamatory sentences, the exclamation mark can sometimes be used to end an imperative sentence.

Use an exclamation mark after an imperative sentence if the command is urgent and forceful.

EXAMPLE: Watch out for the broken glass!

The exclamation mark is also often used after interjections.

Use an exclamation mark after an interjection expressing strong emotion.

EXAMPLE: Hurray! We won the state championship.

NOTE ABOUT USING EXCLAMATION MARKS: Use exclamation marks sparingly. Otherwise, they lose their effectiveness or make the writing overemotional.

OVERUSED: I heard the choir sing only yesterday! They were absolutely wonderful!! You must go to hear them!

CORRECT: I heard the choir sing only yesterday. They were absolutely wonderful! You must go to hear them.

EXERCISE C: Using the Exclamation Mark Correctly.
Copy the following items, adding the necessary exclamation marks. Then identify each use as *exclamatory, imperative,* or *interjection.*

EXAMPLE: What a terrifying movie that was

What a terrifying movie that was!   (exclamatory)

1. Our dog had fourteen puppies last night
2. There goes the thief
3. Quick Hide Mother's birthday present
4. Help me
5. We have just three minutes before the plane takes off
6. I got the highest grade on the history exam
7. Shazam Blam As Billy spoke the magic words, he felt as if he were Captain Marvel.
8. Stop that talking

339

9. Had Nancy Drew only known *exclamatory* She stood within twenty feet of the room where her father was being held prisoner.
10. It's a bird. It's a plane. No, it's Superman *declarative exclamatory*

EXERCISE D: Using End Marks Correctly. Copy the following sentences, adding the necessary end marks.

EXAMPLE: Have you ever tried to break a world record

Have you ever tried to break a world record?

1. Many people have tried hard to break world records
2. The public often asks if these records are ever verified
3. What verifications do need to be made
4. Many people scoff at those who try to shatter old records
5. What are some records that have been set By whom
6. Serge Lepage designed an amazing $1,500,000 dress
7. Linda Kurth ate twenty-three hot dogs in about three minutes
8. The man who holds the record for the longest name recently had it shortened to Wolfe + 585, Sr
9. His last name originally contained an incredible 585 letters
10. People hold records for just about everything

DEVELOPING WRITING SKILLS: Using End Marks in Your Own Writing. Choose one of the following topics and use your imagination to write a description of the scene. In your description, use each of the end marks at least once.

1. The day the UFO landed in our school cafeteria
2. I was a famous bullfighter in Spain
3. The evening of my high school class's tenth reunion
4. Shootout at the Dry Gulch Saloon
5. My earth-shattering discovery

17.2 Commas That Separate Basic Elements

A comma represents a short pause. It tells the reader to hesitate before going on. Commas also help set up relationships among parts of a sentence and make long sentences easier to read. Unfortunately, many writers have trouble using commas.

Some writers sprinkle their work with far too many commas, and others leave them out completely. Either technique leads to confusing writing.

Keep in mind two basic uses of the comma: (1) Commas can be used *to separate* similar items; (2) one or more commas can be used *to set off* a single item at the beginning, middle, or end of a sentence. Do not use a comma unless you have a comma rule in mind, and that requires knowing the rules in this section and the next one. This section gives rules for commas that separate similar elements; Section 17.3 presents rules for commas that set off added material.

Commas with Compound Sentences

A compound sentence is two or more independent clauses joined by a coordinating conjunction (*and, but, for, nor, or, so, yet*).

Use a comma before the conjunction to separate two independent clauses in a compound sentence.

COMPOUND SENTENCES: We saw many beautiful sights on our vacation, but we spent far too many hours on the road.

The weather was pleasant, yet we still did not see all we had planned.

Before putting a comma before a conjunction, be sure you have complete sentences on both sides of the conjunction. Sometimes conjunctions merely join two words, phrases, or subordinate clauses, as in the following examples. Commas are not necessary in these sentences since the conjunctions are not joining independent clauses.

COMPOUND SUBJECT: *Father* or *Mother* will drive us home.

COMPOUND VERB: They *laughed* and *sang* around the fire.

TWO PREPOSITIONAL PHRASES: We hiked *around the lake* and then *up the trail*.

TWO SUBORDINATE CLAUSES: We hiked along those trails *that the ranger suggested* or *that were clearly marked with signs*.

341

EXERCISE A: Using Commas with Compound Sentences. Write each sentence, adding the necessary commas.

EXAMPLE: I have been sending funny Valentine cards to many of my friends every year but I never place my name on them.

I have been sending funny Valentine cards to many of my friends every year, but I never place my name on them.

(1) Valentine's Day is celebrated by most Americans yet few people know the story of how the holiday first began. (2) The holiday originated in ancient Rome but the actual date of its origin is about A.D. 270. (3) According to legend Emperor Claudius II would not allow the troops of the Roman army to marry for he felt that married men made poor soldiers. (4) A priest called Valentinus took pity on two young lovers and he secretly married them against Emperor Claudius's orders. (5) Valentinus was arrested and thrown in jail and Claudius had him beheaded several months later. (6) It was from this Roman jail that the first Valentine card was sent for Valentinus supposedly cured the jailer's daughter of blindness and sent her a note signed "From Your Valentine." (7) You may want to believe this legend or you may feel that this is just a romantic tale that was concocted to explain the origin of Valentine's Day. (8) The first Valentines in America were not covered with sweet verses nor were they elaborate and lacy works of art. (9) Boys and girls of the late 1850's loved to send "Penny Dreadfuls" on Valentine's Day and they looked forward to receiving them from their friends in turn. (10) A typical Penny Dreadful might contain a message such as this one: 'Tis all in vain your fluttering lids, your curly hair, your tinted cheeks for finding you a Valentine will take at least a HUNDRED weeks!

Commas Between Items in a Series

Items in a series must be separated by commas. A series consists of three or more similar items. These items may be words, phrases, or clauses.

Use commas to separate three or more words, phrases, or clauses in a series.

The number of commas that should be used in a series is one fewer than the number of items in the series. For example, if you have a series of three items, you should use two commas; if you have a series of four items, you should use three commas; and so on.

SERIES OF WORDS:	We packed a *tent*, a *stove*, *several sleeping bags*, and *plenty of food*.
SERIES OF PHRASES:	He wanted *to walk Boston's Freedom Trail*, *to see Walden's Pond*, and *to sit on Bunker Hill*.
SERIES OF CLAUSES:	*Who the thieves are*, *when the crime was committed*, and *where the paintings have been taken* are questions the police are now trying to answer.

Consistent Commas. In each of the preceding examples notice that the last comma is placed before the conjunction joining the last two items. Many writers omit this comma except when it is needed to prevent confusion. Many other writers, however, consistently use the last comma. Placing the comma before the conjunction in almost every situation prevents confusion and makes it possible for a writer to be consistent. Notice the problem in the sentence below if a writer is trying to follow the pattern of consistently omitting the last comma. You will find it easier in your own writing if you consistently use the last comma.

CONFUSING:	The roses on the table, the aroma of fresh-baked bread and the delicate lace tablecloth all reminded her of home.
ALWAYS CLEAR:	The roses on the table, the aroma of fresh-baked bread, and the delicate lace tablecloth all reminded her of home.

Two Exceptions. There are two major exceptions concerning the use of commas between items in a series. First, when each of the items in a series is joined to the next item by a conjunction, no commas are necessary.

EXAMPLE:	My parents debated whether to gather firewood *or* set up camp *or* go exploring.

343

Second, some pairs, such as *bacon and eggs*, are naturally thought of as one item. Do not split pairs apart with commas, especially when the pair is part of a series. Note in the following example that the comma comes after the last pair, not before the last conjunction.

EXAMPLE: The boy packed *shoes and socks*, *a coat and tie*, and *a brush and comb*.

EXERCISE B: Using Commas Between Items in a Series.
Copy each sentence that needs commas, adding the necessary commas. If a sentence does not need commas, write *correct*.

EXAMPLE: The speaker was intelligent talented and poised.

The speaker was intelligent, talented, and poised.

1. The student driver nervously pressed down the accelerator turned the key and put the car in gear.
2. The flash flood raced through the narrow canyon over the flatlands and into the town's main street.
3. Mrs. Robertson offered the children peanut butter and jelly bacon and avocado or cheese and bologna sandwiches.
4. The children bowled the parents kept score and the grandparents watched.
5. He ate breakfast she read the newspaper and then they both left for work.
6. The sheepdog pushed and coaxed and prodded his stubborn charges into their pen.
7. Skiing skating and dancing burn up many calories.
8. The physician said he wanted to take some X-rays check the results and call us later in the day.
9. Did you pack a bathing suit pajamas a sweatshirt and a toothbrush?
10. The ball flew over the pitcher's head above the centerfielder's glove and into a spectator's waiting hands.

Commas Between Adjectives

Some writers become confused when two or more adjectives precede a noun. Sometimes the adjectives should be separated by commas, and sometimes not.

Use commas to separate adjectives of equal rank.

Two or more adjectives are considered equal in rank if an *and* can be placed between the adjectives without changing the meaning of the sentence. Another test is to change the order of the adjectives. If the sentence still sounds correct, then, the adjectives are of equal rank.

The adjectives in the following examples fulfill both of these requirements and need commas between them.

EXAMPLES: The *twisting, scenic* path leads to a secluded park.

The *swaying, majestic, graceful* pines surrounded our campsite.

If an *and* cannot not be placed between the adjectives or if changing their order would result in nonsense, then no commas are needed.

Do not use commas to separate adjectives that must stay in a specific order.

If you try the two tests for adjectives on the following examples, you will discover that the adjectives must stay in the exact order in which they are written if the sentences are to make sense.

EXAMPLES: *Several long* days of hiking brought us to the glacier's edge.

They kept *many old* tools in the barn.

NOTE ABOUT COMMAS WITH ADJECTIVES: Do not use a comma to separate the last adjective in a series from the noun it modifies.

INCORRECT: The twisting, scenic, path leads to a lake.

CORRECT: The twisting, scenic path leads to a lake.

EXERCISE C: Using Commas Between Adjectives. Copy the underlined adjectives in each of the following sentences, adding any necessary commas.

EXAMPLE: The surgeon was a <u>conscientious skilled</u> doctor.

conscientious, skilled

1. The <u>modern well-built</u> home looked out over the valley.
2. They offered us rides on <u>two restored</u> stagecoaches.
3. <u>Many grand oak</u> trees line the drive to the stately mansion.
4. <u>Beautiful delicate fragrant</u> wildflowers dotted the field.
5. His eyes looked out from a <u>weather-beaten wrinkled</u> face.
6. The new shoes hurt her <u>tired aching</u> feet.
7. The speaker provided a <u>brilliant educational</u> program.
8. The <u>tall English</u> woman played tennis almost every day.
9. The kit came with <u>complicated confusing</u> instructions.
10. He wore an <u>expensive suede</u> jacket.

DEVELOPING WRITING SKILLS: Using Commas in Your Own Writing. Follow the directions to write five sentences of your own containing commas that separate.

1. Write a sentence listing the foods you had for dinner last night. List the foods in a series of at least three items.
2. Write a compound sentence describing something that happened in your English class yesterday.
3. Write a sentence containing two adjectives to describe the time you had the mumps or another childhood ailment.
4. Write a compound sentence about a beautiful place you have visited. Include a series of three adjectives.
5. Write a compound sentence listing what you think are the season's three best and three worst television shows.

17.3 Commas That Set Off Added Elements

Commas can also set off—that is, isolate—certain parts of sentences. Commas used this way help show the relationship among sentence parts. In many cases you will have a choice of locations for an added sentence part. Consider, for example, the phrase *after passing once over the henhouse* and the simple sentence *The hawk began its dive*. You could add the phrase at the beginning: *After passing once over the henhouse, the hawk began its dive*. You could add the phrase in the middle: *The hawk, after passing once over the henhouse, began its dive*. Or you could add the phrase at the end: *The hawk began its dive after passing once over the henhouse*.

In the first two sentences, notice that the commas set off the added phrase from the basic sentence. One comma isolates the phrase at the beginning of the sentence; two commas isolate the phrase in the middle. In the third sentence, however, no comma is necessary since the phrase no longer seems to be extra or in the way of the subject and main verb. The sentence flows from beginning to end without the need for a pause. The idea that a sentence has a natural flow is important to keep in mind. When this flow is interrupted, commas will usually be needed.

Commas After Introductory Material

A comma is usually needed to set off introductory material from the rest of the sentence.

Use a comma after an introductory word, phrase, or clause.

To learn what types of words, phrases, and clauses make up introductory material, study the following chart.

KINDS OF INTRODUCTORY MATERIAL	
Introductory Words	*Yes,* I will be happy to stay for dinner.
	Oh, I didn't know you were here.
	Dan and Rosa, please help me with this.
	Please, I need your help now.
	Wounded, the hawk couldn't fly.
Prepositional Phrases (of four or more words)	*Over the thickly wooded hills,* the sun cast its morning rays.
Participial Phrases	*Running along the path,* the child slipped and fell.
Infinitive Phrases	*To prevent a fall,* she was walking very slowly.
Adverbial Clauses	*After we finished our long hike,* we stopped for ice cream.
	If you want to succeed in school, then you must study regularly.

An introductory prepositional phrase of two or three words does not need to be set off from the rest of the sentence.

EXAMPLE: With perfect grace the doe raised her head and stared at us.

EXERCISE A: Using Commas After Introductory Material. Write the introductory word, phrase, or clause in each sentence, adding any necessary commas.

EXAMPLE: Boys and girls welcome to the Winchester House.

Boys and girls,

(1) After you hear about Sarah Winchester you will probably agree that she was an eccentric woman. (2) Following a short and romantic courtship Sarah Pardee married William Winchester of Winchester rifles. (3) Upon her husband's death Sarah inherited twenty million dollars from his estate. (4) Fearing the ghosts of people killed by Winchester guns she felt she must build continuously to keep them from haunting her. (5) With a great deal of determination she bought an eighteen-room house and hired sixteen workmen to add rooms to it. (6) To keep the ghosts confused she had doors open into brick walls and stairs lead up into the ceiling. (7) Oh the workmen must have thought her strange, but good wages kept them building for thirty-eight years. (8) Testing their loyalty to her Mrs. Winchester occasionally had the gardeners plant her orange trees upside down. (9) When she died it took six moving vans and six weeks to empty the house. (1) Within her 160-room mansion carpenters had installed 2,000 doors and 10,000 windows.

Commas with Parenthetical Expressions

A parenthetical expression is a word or phrase that is only loosely related to the rest of a sentence. It usually adds information that is not essential to the sentence's meaning.

Use commas to set off parenthetical expressions.

The chart on the next page shows some common types of parenthetical expressions, both in the middle and at the end of sentences. Note that each of the sentences makes sense with or without the parenthetical expression.

348

KINDS OF PARENTHETICAL EXPRESSIONS	
Names of People Being Addressed	I'll start dinner, *Dad*, in a while.
	That's a handsome suit, *Mr. Jones*.
Conjunctive Adverbs	We left, *therefore*, an hour late.
	I did not catch any fish, *however*.
Common Expressions	The President was accompanied, *of course*, by secret service agents.
	He was on time, *I hope*, for work.
Contrasting Expressions	Our new car, *not the station wagon*, broke down.
	The dress is red, *not blue*.

EXERCISE B: Using Commas with Parenthetical Expressions. Copy each of the following sentences, adding the necessary commas to set off the parenthetical expressions.

EXAMPLE: It is warm enough I think to plant the tomatoes.

It is warm enough, I think, to plant the tomatoes.

1. The new plants however did not survive the frost.
2. I will vacuum Hazel if you will wash the windows.
3. He went to Harvard Law School I believe.
4. The young rascal furthermore put salt in my sugar bowl.
5. Spread lime in the garden not near the evergreens.
6. Typing your paper you know will make it easier to read.
7. The plane therefore did not arrive on time.
8. Tennis not golf is my favorite sport.
9. May I help you carry that package Mr. Goodman?
10. If it rains, the picnic will be called postponed until next week I suppose.

Commas with Nonessential Expressions

To decide when other phrases or clauses should be set off, you must learn to distinguish between *essential* and *nonessential* expressions. (The terms *restrictive* and *nonrestrictive* are sometimes used to refer to essential and nonessential expressions.)

An expression is said to be *essential* if it adds essential information to a sentence. An essential expression cannot be left out without changing the basic meaning of the sentence. A *nonessential* expression does not add essential information to a sentence. It can be left out without changing the basic meaning.

Use commas to set off nonessential expressions.

An appositive, a participial phrase, or an adjective clause can be either essential or nonessential. In the following chart, note that essential information is not set off. Nonessential items, however, are set off with two commas if they are in the middle of a sentence and one comma if they are at the end.

APPOSITIVES	
Essential	Orchard House was the childhood home of the well-known author *Louisa May Alcott*.
Nonessential	Louisa May Alcott, *the well-known author*, lived in Orchard House as a child.
	Orchard House was the childhood home of Louisa May Alcott, *the well-known author*.

PARTICIPIAL PHRASES	
Essential	The piano *now standing in the living room of Orchard House* is the one described in *Little Women*.
Nonessential	Beth's piano, *now standing in the living room of Orchard House*, is described in *Little Women*.
	In *Little Women* Alcott describes Beth's piano, *now standing in the living room of Orchard House*.

ADJECTIVE CLAUSES	
Essential	The man *who led the tour of Orchard House* knew much about its contents.
Nonessential	Mr. Hoopen, *who led us on the tour*, knew much about the contents of Orchard House.
	We were led on a tour of Orchard House by Mr. Hooper, *who knew much about its contents*.

EXERCISE C: Using Commas with Nonessential Expressions. Copy each of the following sentences, adding commas to set off all nonessential expressions.

EXAMPLE: Esmeralda our curious and friendly dog likes to explore the neighborhood.

Esmeralda, our curious and friendly dog, likes to explore the neighborhood.

1. My orthodontist who just came back from a trip to Hawaii tightened my braces.
2. The woman who was hired as a company consultant made some fine suggestions to the management.
3. The President's wife is the one boarding the plane right now.
4. Calligraphy the art of beautiful writing takes practice and skill in order for one to become proficient at it.
5. The suit worn by the model on the left probably costs a fortune.
6. The museum held the saddle of John Wayne one of the most famous Hollywood cowboys.
7. Have you ever visited the Alamo a fascinating building in Texas?
8. Yosemite Falls which drops 2,425 feet to the river below almost dries up at the end of a hot summer.
9. Joanne Lewis who happens to be my cousin writes news articles for a local television station.
10. Pélé a famous soccer player from Brazil played in the United States several years ago.

Commas with Places, Dates, and Titles

The names of places are often made up of several parts. The name of a town may be followed by the name of a county, which in turn may be followed by the name of a state. Commas are used to avoid confusion.

When a geographical name is made up of two or more parts, use a comma after each item.

In the examples at the top of the next page, note especially the final comma after the last item in the name.

EXAMPLES: We visited Rockport, Massachusetts, last July.

He returned to Bad Neustadt, Bavaria, West Germany, where he was born.

Dates are also often made up of several parts, such as months, days, and years. Commas can help avoid confusion.

When a date is made up of two or more parts, use a comma after each item except in the case of a month followed by a day.

In the following examples, notice that commas follow most of the words and numbers in the dates. No commas, however, are placed between month and days.

EXAMPLES: ~~Friday, August 1~~, is my birthday.

September 10, 1973, was my first day of school.

The museum opened on October 29, 1949, after a special ceremony.

Commas are optional if with only months and years.

EXAMPLES: In December 1979 we visited Los Angeles.

In December, 1979, we visited Los Angeles.

Titles after the name of a person can also cause confusion. Once again, commas are added.

When a name is followed by one or more titles, use a comma after the name and after each title.

EXAMPLES: Patricia Anderson, Ph.D., lectured on ecology.

John Ruiz, Jr., D.D.S., spoke about dentistry.

A similar rule is followed for special abbreviations following the names of businesses.

EXAMPLE: Prentice-Hall, Inc., published this book.

EXERCISE D: Using Commas with Places, Dates, and Titles. Copy the sentences, adding the necessary commas.

EXAMPLE: On June 9 1987 we moved to Houston Texas.

On June 9, 1987, we moved to Houston, Texas.

1. Microtec Inc. opened on the New York Stock Exchange at $14 per share.
2. The bus stopped in Texarkana on its way to Little Rock Arkansas.
3. The nurse signed her letter of resignation "Allison Evans R.N."
4. On July 4 1884 the Statue of Liberty was officially presented to the United States.
5. Is it true that your ancestors traveled from St. Louis Missouri to San Francisco California by wagon train?
6. Professor John H. Coleman Ph.D. accepted a position at another university.
7. Please cancel delivery of our newspaper from Tuesday August 8 to Sunday August 19.
8. Are Randall Knudtsen Sr. and Randall Knudtsen Jr. working for the same electronics company now?
9. The boy was an exchange student from Celle Germany.
10. The boat will stop at Bridgetown Barbados on January 11.

Other Uses of the Comma

A number of additional rules explain the use of commas in addresses, salutations and closings of letters, numbers, elliptical sentences, and quotations. There is also a general rule covering commas used to prevent misunderstandings.

First, consider the use of commas in addresses.

Use a comma after each item in an address made up of two or more parts.

In the example below, note the commas after the name, street, and city. Instead of using a comma before a ZIP code, it is customary to leave some additional space.

EXAMPLE: The return address should be A.F. Sharpe, 14 North Main Street, Fort Cobb, Oklahoma 73030.

When an address is written on an envelope, most of the commas are omitted.

EXAMPLE: A.F. Sharpe
14 North Main Street
Fort Cobb, Oklahoma   73030

Another comma rule concerns letters.

Use a comma after the salutation in a personal letter and after the closing in all letters.

SALUTATIONS: Dear Joanne,   My dearest Friend,
CLOSINGS: Sincerely,   With kind regards,

Another use for the comma is making large numbers easier to read.

With numbers of more than three digits, use a comma after every third digit from the right.

EXAMPLES: 3,421 different species
The population totaled 27,844.
764,231,519 paperclips

NOTE ABOUT COMMAS IN NUMBERS: Do not use commas in ZIP codes, telephone numbers, page numbers, serial numbers, years, or house numbers.

ZIP CODE: 10549   SERIAL NUMBER: 062 43 1495
TELEPHONE NUMBER: (210) 555–1234   YEAR: 1888
PAGE NUMBER: on page 1863   HOUSE NUMBER: 1111 Oak St.

Commas are also used to help make some elliptical sentences easier to read. In an elliptical sentence, words are left out but are understood to function in the sentence.

Use a comma to indicate the words left out of an elliptical sentence.

In the following example, the word *radiated* is left out between *man* and *poverty;* it is understood. Even with the word missing, the meaning of the sentence remains clear.

EXAMPLE: The young woman radiated wealth; the young man,
poverty.

Commas are also used to help show where direct quotations begin and end.

Use commas to set off a direct quotation from the rest of a sentence.

354

Notice in the examples below that the placement of the commas depends on the location of the non-spoken words in the sentence. For more detailed information about punctuation used with quotations, see Section 17.5.

EXAMPLES: The boy suggested, "Let's go on a picnic."

"By late morning," the boy continued, "I'd like to be on our way to the lake."

"But that's far too early," his friend protested.

The next use of the comma is particularly helpful to readers.

Use a comma to prevent a sentence from being misunderstood.

In each of the following examples, the sentences without the commas can easily be misread. Commas help readers by giving visual clues about when to pause slightly.

UNCLEAR: Whenever necessary explanations are included.

CLEAR: Whenever necessary, explanations are included.

UNCLEAR: Near the house Jack built a tool shed.

CLEAR: Near the house, Jack built a tool shed.

EXERCISE E: Using Commas in Other Situations. Copy each of the following sentences, adding the necessary commas.

EXAMPLE: Ann guessed that the jar contained 3864 jelly beans.

Ann guessed that the jar contained 3,864 jelly beans.

1. The last-known address of the Parker family was 1318 View Ridge Drive Missoula Montana.
2. Chicago is 2189 miles from Los Angeles.
3. The parents headed off to work; the children to school.
4. Regina was born on September 15 1972 in Honolulu Hawaii.
5. Outside the house looked as new as the day we bought it.
6. Someone once said "A grandparent is a child's best press agent."
7. The school's address is P.O. Box 900 Cupertino California 95014.
8. When reading the boy hears nothing around him.

355

9. "It is much easier to be critical than to be correct" Benjamin Disraeli once observed.
10. The first horse shown was an Arabian; the second a quarter horse; the third a Thoroughbred.

DEVELOPING WRITING SKILLS: Using Commas That Set Off in Your Writing. Follow the directions to write five sentences of your own containing commas that set things off.

1. Write a sentence requesting someone in your family to do something for you. Begin with the name of the person.
2. Write a sentence telling about a place you visited recently. Name the town and the state.
3. Write a sentence giving your friend your current address and telephone number.
4. Write a sentence about a hobby that you have. Use a nonessential expression in it.
5. Write about the celebration of your most recent birthday. Include the date of your birthday and the day of the week on which it fell.

17.4 The Semicolon and the Colon

The semicolon is a punctuation mark made up of a period above a comma (;). It is less final than a period, but it calls for more of a pause than a comma does. The semicolon clearly separates two clauses but allows the writer to show that these clauses are linked in some way. It offers a good means of combining ideas and avoiding the choppiness of many short sentences.

The colon is made up of one period placed directly above another (:). One good way to remember the basic purpose of the colon is to think of it as an arrow or a pointer. It instructs the reader to look straight ahead to find out more information about something just read. The additional information may be a list, a quotation, an explanation, or any of a number of other items of information.

In this section, you will first look at the basic uses of the semicolon and then turn to a detailed list of ways in which the colon can be used.

Semicolons and Independent Clauses

Semicolons are often used to join independent clauses. They should only be used in certain situations, however. The most important rule to keep in mind is the rule about conjunctions.

> Use a semicolon to join independent clauses that are not already joined by the conjunction *and, but, for, nor, or, so, or yet.*

A basic rule for commas states that when two clauses are joined by a conjunction, a comma is needed before the conjunction.

CLAUSES WITH COMMA: May celebrated her birthday with a delicious cake, and we all ate several pieces of it.

In some sentences, however, the conjunctions are omitted. In these sentences, the semicolon takes the place of the comma and the missing conjunction.

CLAUSES WITH SEMICOLON: May celebrated her birthday with a delicious cake; we all ate several pieces of it.

A semicolon should not be used between unrelated sentences. The two independent clauses must be close in meaning and structure. The clauses in the first example below are not closely related in meaning. A period, instead of a semicolon, should be used. The second example shows the semicolon used correctly to join two closely related ideas.

INCORRECT: My favorite dinner begins with a steaming bowl of pea soup; I wonder why Mother isn't home.

CORRECT: We ate until we couldn't eat another bite; we were all famished from our hike in the woods.

Occasionally, semicolons are also used to join two clauses that present a direct contrast. The clauses in the following example set up two extremes in a similar situation. Notice that even when the two clauses present a contrast the subjects of the two clauses are similar.

EXAMPLE: She loved fresh vegetables at dinner; he wanted only meat on his dinner table.

357

Semicolons may also be useful when there are three or more independent clauses in a sentence.

EXAMPLE: I cleared the table; Mark washed the dishes; Ann loaded the dishwasher.

Another rule to follow in joining clauses with semicolons involves certain key words.

Use a semicolon to join independent clauses separated by either a conjunctive adverb or a transitional expression.

Conjunctive adverbs and transitional expressions help to set up relationships between parts of a sentence. Following is a list of some of the most common conjunctive adverbs and transitional expressions.

CONJUNCTIVE ADVERBS: also, besides, consequently, furthermore, however, indeed, instead, moreover, nevertheless, otherwise, therefore, thus

TRANSITIONAL EXPRESSIONS: as a result, at this time, first, for example, for instance, in fact, on the other hand, second, that is

When these words are used to set up a relationship between two independent clauses, a semicolon is used to join the clauses. In most cases it goes in front of the conjunctive adverb or the transitional expression.

EXAMPLE: We stopped at a place where we could rest; consequently, we were slightly late in arriving home.

Be sure to place a comma after the conjunctive adverb or transitional expression since it functions in the second clause as an introductory expression.

In other sentences the transitional expression or conjunctive adverb falls in the middle or at the end of the second clause. In these situations a semicolon divides the two independent clauses, and commas are used to set off the adverb or transition.

EXAMPLE: The museum was quite a distance away; we all felt, however, that the exhibit we saw was worth the long trip.

358

EXERCISE A: Using Semicolons to Join Independent Clauses. For each sentence write the word that goes before the semicolon, the semicolon, and the word that goes after it.

EXAMPLE: A raccoon has claws its name means "scratcher."

claws; its

(1) Raccoons sometimes live in hollow trees they have also been found living in burrows made by other animals. (2) These creatures seem to be quite intelligent they can learn how to open small packages and to turn on appliances. (3) When raccoons are young, their mother provides food when they are older, they must find their own. (4) Some raccoons love fish others prefer bird and turtle eggs. (5) Raccoons can distinguish between different sounds one raccoon appears to like listening to Beethoven. (6) Raccoon litters may include only two babies they sometimes include as many as seven. (7) Some people think baby raccoons make good pets usually, however, they do not. (8) Raccoons are sometimes pests to farmers they get into the garbage cans and the poultry house. (9) Raccoons also raid garbage cans in suburban neighborhoods they sometimes make nuisances of themselves at camp sites and garbage dumps. (10) Raccoon hats were popular during frontier days raccoon coats were popular during the 1920's.

EXERCISE B: Using Semicolons and Commas to Join Clauses. Some of the following sentences are missing semicolons; some are also missing commas. Copy each sentence, making the necessary corrections.

EXAMPLE: Stocks were soaring to an all-time high in 1929 consequently people were buying more stocks.

Stocks were soaring to an all-time high in 1929; consequently, people were buying more stocks.

(1) Stockholders hoped to get rich when their stocks rose in price therefore many borrowed money to buy stocks. (2) On Black Thursday in October, 1929, stocks tumbled to forty percent of their original value as a result many people lost almost everything they owned. (3) Pandemonium broke out on the stock exchange floor fist fights, for instance, were common. (4) Frantic orders to sell came into the exchange

many orders to sell, however, could not be completed because there were no buyers. (5) Some stockholders were forced to sell their homes, businesses, and other possessions to pay back money they had borrowed; others could not pay their debts at all. (6) There were several short rallies in stock prices; nevertheless, prices generally spiraled down. (7) Some tragedies were caused by the stock market crash; in fact, the president of Union Cigar jumped to his death when his stock dropped over $100 in one day. (8) The President assured the public that business was good; many business leaders continued to buy stocks. (9) Some of the richest people did manage to survive the stock market crash; most people, however, had barely enough left to survive. (10) The collapse of the stock market almost destroyed the business world; it is a tragic lesson to people today.

Semicolons Used to Avoid Confusion

Semicolons may also be used to prevent confusion.

Consider the use of semicolons to avoid confusion when independent clauses or items in a series already contain commas.

If the clauses in a compound sentence already contain a number of commas, using a semicolon may prevent confusion.

EXAMPLE: Tim, who was taking Cooking I in school, decided to make dinner for his family; but he soon discovered that it is not easy to cook for eight picky eaters.

A comma would usually be placed in front of the word *but* when it joins two independent clauses. However, the first independent clause in the preceding example contains several commas and another comma might confuse readers. To avoid confusion, use a semicolon before the conjunction.

Items in a series may also be separated by semicolons when the items themselves contain a number of commas. The semicolons help make clear where each complete item ends.

EXAMPLE: My garden consisted of yellow squash, which were running wild along the ground; beans, which were growing faster than I could pick them; and strawberries, which were already ripe enough to eat.

EXERCISE C: Using Semicolons to Avoid Confusion.
Write the following sentences using semicolons to replace commas that might cause confusion.

EXAMPLE: Cautiously, he investigated the noise, but it was only the cat, scratching on the door.

Cautiously, he investigated the noise; but it was only the cat, scratching on the door.

1. When Martin fell, we were sure he had broken his leg, but it turned out, happily, to be just a painful sprain.
2. Mr. Franklin, my math teacher, enjoys his students, and he even invites groups over to his house for dinner.
3. We will either get the shoes from Mr. Beck, who owns the soccer shop, or we will order them from a supply house.
4. I need to cut some roses, carnations, and greenery from the garden, and after that is done, I'll make a flower arrangement for our dinner party tonight.
5. With hammers going all the time, work on the university library continues, but at the moment, it is doubtful whether the changes will be completed on time.
6. Three of my teachers are Mrs. Pizo, a history teacher, Mrs. Fox, my Spanish teacher, and Mr. Soo, my science teacher.
7. Three football players came onto the field: Greg Stern, quarterback, Dirk Ives, center, and Chuck Latter, halfback.
8. I would like to introduce you to Penny, my turtle, Tuxedo, my cat, and Heather, my dog.
9. Some people are very handy: Ben, who repairs his own car, John, who puts up shelves, and Kate, who builds bookcases.
10. You can find big amusement parks in Anaheim, California, Six Flags, Texas, and San Jose, California.

The Colon as an Introductory Device

Colons can be used to introduce a list of items.

Use a colon before a list of items following an independent clause.

Notice in the example at the top of the next page that the colon points to the list that follows. The list, in turn, provides information about the subject discussed in the opening clause.

361

EXAMPLE: The recipe requires the following ingredients: flour, sugar, eggs, baking powder, and vanilla.

Note that the initial clause before the colon is a complete independent clause. Although it may use words such as *the following* to hint that something is to come, it makes sense by itself. Never put a colon before a list that is an essential part of the sentence. Colons should not be placed between a verb and its object or between a preposition and its object.

INCORRECT: On the hike, we brought: apples, nuts, and raisins.

The snacks were made up of: apples, nuts, and raisins.

CORRECT: The snacks for the hike included a number of healthful foods: apples, nuts, and raisins.

Colons may also be used to introduce certain quotations.

Use a colon to introduce a quotation that is formal or lengthy.

The quotation below is both formal and lengthy.

QUOTATION
WITH COLON: The speaker on health foods stated: "Putting inadequately tested additives into our bodies through the foods we consume is a health risk. Every day, scientists discover that additives once thought safe contain cancer-causing agents. Removing unnecessary additives is one way to protect against possible health hazards."

The colon is a more formal mark of punctuation than the comma. Do not use it for casual quoted remarks or dialogue— even if the words quoted are longer than one sentence.

QUOTATION
WITH COMMA: My mother called out, "I want one more item. Get me the glue. I need it for the scrapbook."

Colons are always used, however, in quotations that are not preceded by a verb that shows speech (*said, explained,* or *announced,* for example). A colon always introduces these quotations regardless of their formality and length.

EXAMPLE: He watched the young gymnast on the bars: "Your technique is good, but you need more practice."

362

Another important use of the colon is to introduce a sentence that offers a summary or explanation of the sentence that comes right before it.

Use a colon to introduce a sentence that summarizes or explains the sentence before it.

The colon in the following example points to a further explanation of the initial independent clause. What follows the colon either explains or extends what has been stated just before it.

EXAMPLE: The chef concluded her speech with one important thought regarding the choice of ingredients: She said that using the freshest ingredients that can be found will always lead to a more flavorful final product.

The final use of the colon as an introductory device is to introduce a formal appositive.

Use a colon to introduce a formal appositive.

Generally, when an appositive is used in a sentence it is set off by commas from the noun or pronoun it renames.

APPOSITIVE WITH COMMAS: She did not eat the vegetables, peas, but she did eat the veal.

Sometimes, however, a writer needs to set off an appositive with more force than a comma permits. In these cases, a colon precedes the appositive.

APPOSITIVE WITH COLON: Tonight, we present a well-known and talented chef: Julia Child.

In the preceding example, the initial clause points to one item, the appositive. The colon allows for a more dramatic effect than the comma does.

EXERCISE D: Using Colons as Introductory Devices.
Read each sentence and decide where colons are required. Write the word that goes before the colon, the colon, and the word that goes after it, adding any necessary capitals. One of the sentences is already correct. For this sentence, write *correct*.

EXAMPLE: The huge metal eagle on the roof of the high school sparked my interest in my new hobby collecting weather vanes.

hobby: collecting

(1) Weather vanes were first used two thousand years ago in a mighty, noble city Athens. (2) Years later, the Pope sent out an important order a statue, or weather vane, of a rooster was to be placed on top of every Christian church. (3) The rooster-shaped weather vane had a significant purpose it was to remind church members to attend church regularly. (4) The symbol of the rooster was chosen because of Christ's prediction "I tell you Peter, the cock will not crow this day, until you three times deny that you know me." (5) As weather vanes began to be made in other shapes, those made in the shape of a banner were given a special name bannerets. (6) Only one group was entitled to use bannerets in medieval times this was the nobility. (7) In later centuries countries in which weather vanes could be found included England, France, and the United States. (8) In the United States, many different shapes of weather vanes could be seen barnyard animals, carriages, fire engines, ships, and lions, among others. (9) In the nineteenth century, weather vanes often took the shape of the following patriotic symbols flags, liberty bells, and eagles. (10) These weather vanes could be seen on the tops of a variety of buildings barns, houses, churches, schools, and government offices.

Special Uses of the Colon

The colon also has a number of other special uses. It is used to express time, to refer to volumes and pages of periodicals, to specify chapters and verses in books of the Bible, to introduce subtitles of books, to end formal openings in letters, and to signal important ideas.

Use a colon in a number of special writing situations.

The chart at the top of the next page gives examples that will show you how to use the colon in each of these special circumstances.

SPECIAL USES OF THE COLON	
Numerals Giving the Time	11:30 P.M. 6:00 A.M.
References to Periodicals (Volume: Page)	*Southern Humanities Review* XIII:203
Biblical References (Chapter: Verse)	Luke 17:19
Subtitles for Books and Magazines	*Cooking on a Nickel-and-Dime Budget: An Answer to Rising Food Costs*
Salutations in Business Letters	Dear Ms. Adams: Gentlemen:
Labels Used to Signal Important Ideas	Note: The bus leaves at ten. Warning: Do not measure the ingredients carelessly.

EXERCISE E: Using Colons in Special Writing Situations. Copy the following items, adding the necessary colons. Underline all words that appear in italics.

EXAMPLE: Warning The contents of this bottle are poisonous.

Warning: The contents of this bottle are poisonous.

1. One of my favorite stories in the Bible is Mark 4 3.
2. Dear Mr. Harrison
3. The schedule indicated that the train from Chicago should arrive at 5 38 P.M.
4. Note The following information has not yet been verified by the main office.
5. Our coach suggested that we read *Playing Team Soccer A Study in Offense and Defense Skills.*
6. My teacher suggested I check in *Business Week* 61 12 for further information for my report.
7. Dear Mrs. Phillips
8. I took out a reference book called *Rules for Writing A Guide to Better Compositions.*
9. The minister asked the congregation to turn to Exodus 6 2.
10. Are we supposed to leave at 6 15 a.m. or 6 45 a.m.?

DEVELOPING WRITING SKILLS: **Writing Sentences with Semicolons and Colons.** Write sentences illustrating each of the rules in Column A, using topics from Column B. Be sure to punctuate your sentences correctly.

Column A	Column B
1. Semicolon joining two clauses similar in meaning	insects
	swimming
	umbrellas
2. Semicolon followed by a conjunctive adverb	St. Patrick's Day
	monsters'
3. Semicolon followed by a transitional expression	current movie
	bath tubs
4. Semicolons in a series of items, each item containing internal punctuation	volleyball
	a singer
	Saturdays
	paintings
5. Colon pointing to a list of items	hair cuts
	the beach
6. Colon introducing a long or formal quotation	pinball machines
	vegetables
7. Colon introducing a sentence that summarizes or explains	vacations
	cars
	magazines
8. Colon introducing a formal appositive	Halloween
	desserts
9. Colon used to express time or to list a numerical reference	radio stations
	the President
	motorcycles
10. Colon used with a subtitle or in the opening of a business letter	school supplies
	baseball

17.5 Quotation Marks with Direct Quotations

Authors want their readers to feel the events being described in a story. They hope their characters will seem real to their readers. One of the best ways to achieve realism is to let the characters speak for themselves—in other words, to quote them directly, using direct quotations.

Since direct quotations can involve a variety of sentence patterns and punctuation in addition to quotation marks, many writers find them troublesome. The basic rules presented in this section, however, will make it easier for you to make good use of quotations.

Direct Quotations

Only the actual words of a person or character can be used in a *direct quotation*.

A direct quotation represents a person's exact speech or thoughts and is enclosed in quotation marks (" ").

EXAMPLES: She announced, "I won the spelling bee in school today!"

He thought, "You must be kidding; you're absolutely awful at spelling."

If the words presented are only an approximation of what a person actually said or thought, the result is an *indirect quotation*.

An indirect quotation reports only the general meaning of what a person said or thought and does not require quotation marks.

EXAMPLES: She announced that she had won the spelling bee at school today.

He thought that she was just kidding since she was a terrible speller.

Direct quotations can be entire sentences or they can be just words or phrases.

EXAMPLES: Rachel Carson, the well-known author of books about nature, once wrote, "The sea lies all around us. The commerce of all lands must cross it."

Writing about the sea, Rachel Carson has stressed that it is not something that we can casually ignore but rather it is something that we must be concerned about, for it "lies all around us."

As you can see in the examples at the end of the last page, when one or more complete sentences are quoted, each quoted sentence begins with a capital letter. When only part of a sentence is quoted, it begins with a small letter. An exception is made, of course, if the quoted phrase comes at the beginning of the sentence in which it is quoted.

EXAMPLE: "The commerce of all lands" makes use, in one way or another, of the worldwide network of seas, according to Rachel Carson.

EXERCISE A: Recognizing Direct Quotations. Decide whether the underlined material in each of the following items is a direct or indirect quotation. Then rewrite each direct quotation, adding necessary quotation marks and capitals.

EXAMPLE: He often thought, <u>someday I will know enough to become a poet</u>.
            He often thought, "Someday I will know enough to become a poet."

1. Christine said that <u>she would like to play badminton tomorrow afternoon</u>.

2. Each fact that a person learns is, in the words of E.L. Youman, <u>a key to other facts</u>.

3. Eleanor Roosevelt once said <u>no one can make you feel inferior without your consent</u>.

4. Carlyle once defined endurance in two precise words: <u>patience concentrated</u>.

5. After listening to a weather forecast, our coach announced that <u>there would be no practice today</u>.

6. You must know which song contains the words <u>in the dawn's early light</u>.

7. During the first lap, Andrea decided, <u>I must win today since my parents are watching</u>.

8. Later in the race, she decided that <u>they would have to be satisfied with second place this time</u>.

9. <u>A book with an unhappy ending</u> were the words he used to describe his checkbook.

10. Emerson once wrote, <u>the creation of a thousand forests is in one acorn</u>.

Introductory, Concluding, and Interrupting Expressions

Sentences in which quotations appear often include expressions such as *he said* or *she said* to indicate the speaker. These expressions can introduce, conclude, or interrupt a direct quotation. You should know how to punctuate them.

Introductory Expressions. An introductory expression can be short or can take up most of a lengthy sentence.

Use a comma or colon after an introductory expression.

For most introductory expressions, especially those that are informal and short, use a comma, as in the first of the examples below. If an introductory expression is particularly formal or a full sentence, use a colon, as in the second example.

EXAMPLES: Our teacher declared, "It's nice to be back!"

In his Valedictorian Address, Paul included these words: "This graduation signals a new beginning for us—a step into adulthood."

Concluding Expressions. An explanatory expression that comes at the end of a direct quotation will generally be short.

Use a comma, question mark, or exclamation mark after a quotation followed by a concluding expression.

In the first of the following examples, notice that a comma is used instead of a period at the end of the direct quotation. The fact that the full sentence is not yet complete makes a period here incorrect. Thus, a comma is used instead.

EXAMPLES: "Grades will come out next week," the teacher announced.

"When will you tell us what we are getting in this class?" the students asked.

"You are all getting grades!" the teacher teased.

Notice that the concluding expressions do not begin with capitals. Notice also that the quotation marks follow the punctuation marks at the end of the direct quotations.

Interrupting Expressions. Sometimes an expression interrupts a continuous quotation. In this case, you will need twice as many quotation marks as you would with an introductory or concluding expression. You will also need to consider whether the interrupted quotation is one sentence or more than one.

Use a comma after part of a quoted sentence followed by an interrupting expression. Use another comma after the expression.

As you look at the following examples, note that each quotation is one sentence. Thus, only one capital is used. Note also that the quotation marks in these sentences again follow the punctuation marks.

EXAMPLES: "You are," the substitute stated, "to continue work on your descriptive essays."

"Did the teacher tell you," one student inquired, "when they will be due?"

When a quotation is two sentences long with one complete sentence on either side of the interrupting expression, a different rule applies.

Use a comma, question mark, or exclamation mark after a quoted sentence that comes before an interrupting expression. Use a period after the expression.

In the following examples note that there are two capitals in each example since there are two full sentences in each. Notice also that as in the examples above the quotation marks follow the punctuation marks.

EXAMPLES: "I wrote for hours last night," he said. "I still, however, haven't finished my essay."

"Why couldn't you finish it?" his friend inquired. "I wrote mine last week and it took only three hours from start to finish."

EXERCISE B: Writing Direct Quotations with Introductory, Concluding, and Interrupting Expressions. Copy the following quotations, correctly punctuating and capitalizing them.

370

EXAMPLE: my mother cautioned you better be home on time
this evening

My mother cautioned, "You better be home on time
this evening."

1. Persuasively, the sales clerk added this particular radio won't be on sale much longer.
2. the park will be closed the ranger said so that we can repair the picnic area
3. that jacket looks nice on you my father said as he walked in the door
4. with growing irritation, the taxi driver asked have you decided where we are going yet
5. Henry Ward Beecher once made this important distinction between work and worry it is not work that kills me; it is worry
6. he who has imagination without learning warns Joubert has wings but no feet
7. when you get to the rodeo my cousin warned watch out for wild horses and bulls
8. don't forget june 15 his wife reminded him that's our anniversary
9. you've got to keep your eye on the ball every second instructed my coach
10. when the dance is over my date informed me we are going to go out for some pizza

EXERCISE C: More Work with Direct Quotations. Copy the following sentences, adding the necessary punctuation and capitalization.

1. Judith Guest has written to have a reason to get up in the morning, it is necessary to possess a guiding principle
2. if you have a problem I told the babysitter just call me at the number listed by the phone
3. could you drive for a while Ron asked I've been driving for hours and I'm exhausted
4. are you going asked Sharon to the party that Doug is giving this weekend
5. the doctor patted the dog's head, saying that's your last shot for awhile, Scamper

371

6. the person who mistrusts most should be trusted least notes an old Greek proverb
7. Allen whispered I think the scary part of the movie starts in about a minute
8. with the road so muddy the highway patrol officer suggested you should switch to Highway 84
9. a record was set in the last race announced the scorekeeper
10. are you willing to pay the repairman asked the 75 dollars it will take to repair this dishwasher

Quotation Marks with Other Punctuation Marks

One of the most difficult aspects of punctuating quotations is knowing whether the other punctuation marks go inside or outside the quotation marks. You have seen that in direct quotations commas and end marks that accompany the quotations go inside the quotation marks. There are times, however, when end marks come after the quotation marks. The following rules should help you master these differences.

The first rule is the most important.

Always place a comma or a period inside the final quotation mark.

EXAMPLE: "Class has started," the teacher emphatically stated. "Please turn to Chapter 4."

The second rule is also easy to remember.

Always place a semicolon or colon outside the final quotation mark.

EXAMPLES: One teacher said, "There is a rally today"; another indicated that it had been postponed.

The psychologist cited three "seasons of discontent": adolescence, middle age, and retirement.

Quotation marks with question marks or exclamation marks are more confusing since whether the punctuation is placed inside or outside the quotation marks depends not only on the sense of the quotation but also on the sense of the entire sentence.

372

Place a question mark or exclamation mark inside the final quotation mark if the end mark is part of the quotation.

Note that although the complete sentences in the following examples are declarative sentences, they end with the punctuation that is required by the sense of the quotation.

EXAMPLES: The student asked, "Did you find a math book in here last period**?**"

The student delightedly reported, "I got every question right on the quarter-final examination**!**"

When a sentence ends with a direct quotation, it may seem that you need one end mark for the quoted material and one end mark for the entire sentence. However, when the quotation must end with a question mark or an exclamation mark but the entire sentence calls for a period, the period is dropped.

INCORRECT: I heard the Dean ask, "Which one of you did this**?**".

CORRECT: I heard the Dean ask, "Which one of you did this**?**"

The order of the punctuation changes when the end mark does not go with the quotation.

Place a question mark or exclamation mark outside the final quotation mark if the end mark is not part of the quotation.

In the following examples, note that although the quotations within the sentences are declarative, the sentences themselves are not. The first sentence is a question; the second is an exclamation.

EXAMPLES: Did Mrs. Lind say, "I will not accept any papers after today"**?**

I couldn't believe that our principal actually said, "No school on Thursday"**!**

Again do not be tempted to end the sentence with two end marks when one is correct.

INCORRECT: Who said, "I need help**.**"**?**

CORRECT: Who said, "I need help"**?**

EXERCISE D: **Using Punctuation with Direct Quotations.**
One or two punctuation marks are missing in each of the following items. Rewrite the sentences, taking care to place the missing punctuation marks correctly.

EXAMPLE: "Please hand in your papers" Miss Smithson said.

"Please hand in your papers," Miss Smithson said.

1. The boys shouted, "We won the championship" *inside*
2. "When the film comes back" Jim announced, "we will set up a slide show"
3. The teacher said, "You will need to study hard for this test" he also said we should get plenty of rest the night before the test.
4. The salesperson in the shoe department asked, "Do those boots pinch your toes"
5. Carlos shouted frantically, "The man in the gray parka stole my wallet"
6. The clerk asked, "Are you certain you want just a one-way ticket"
7. My mother felt my forehead and said, "You get into bed right this minute"
8. She constantly reminded us of "the keys to success" hard work, a goal, and a little luck.
9. Did the coach say, "Be at the field at eight in the morning or at eight in the evening"
10. The garage attendant said, "Your resonator has a hole in it" however, he didn't offer to fix it.

EXERCISE E: **More Work with Punctuation.** Follow the instructions given in Exercise D.

1. I got the lead in this year's one-act play: "Roses and Wine"
2. My friend asked, "Why don't you go jogging with me in the morning before school"
3. "The plane will take off" the stewardess stated, "as soon as the fog clears a bit more"
4. The new father proudly announced, "We have a beautiful baby girl"
5. Are you certain the doctor specifically said, "Take two pills fifteen minutes before eating"

374

6. She gave us her list of "absolute travel necessities" make-up, hair dryer, and bathing suit.
7. Did Emerson say, "If a man owns land, the land owns him"
8. Angela confessed, "I should read the newspaper more"
9. "We must try harder" he said, "if we truly want to win this debate"
10. I heard him ask, "Can you tell me where a drinking fountain is"

Quotation Marks in Special Situations

At times in your writing you may need to deal with dialogue, long quotations, or quotations within quotations. Several rules exist to help you use direct quotations in these situations.

Dialogue. Dialogue is direct conversation between two or more people.

When writing dialogue, begin a new paragraph with each change of speaker.

EXAMPLE: "Mrs. Abel, I came in to talk about my quarter grade," Mark timidly stated.

Mrs. Abel encouraged him, saying, "What seems to be the problem? Do you think I made an error?"

"Well," he replied, "I had expected to get a B instead of a C."

"My records show that you got a B. I wonder what happened," mused the teacher. "Let me check and I'll get back to you if that is okay with you."

Notice that the individual sentences are punctuated according to the rules discussed earlier in this lesson. The only difference is that each time a new speaker talks a new paragraph is started.

Long Quotations. Sometimes in writing a story or research paper you may need to punctuate a quotation that continues for several paragraphs.

For quotations longer than a paragraph, put quotation marks at the beginning of each paragraph and at the end of the final paragraph.

EXAMPLE: Our counselor began by telling us about college: "You need to begin considering now what you will want in a college. A college is like a pair of shoes that you wear every day. It must fit you comfortably, must wear well, and must serve your purpose. *(No quotation mark)*

"First, consider the cost of the college you may want to attend. How much can you afford to pay? Can you get a scholarship? *(No quotation mark)*

"Second, make sure that the school offers the programs you are interested in. Some schools specialize in particular fields of study. Is this college well respected in the field you may want to major in? *(No quotation mark)*

"Finally, you should consider the school life. Are the dorms pleasant? Does the school offer activities you would enjoy? *(No quotation mark)*

"Now let me answer any questions that you may have." *(Closing quotation mark)*

Quotations Within Quotations. Till now, all of the quotation marks in this lesson have been double (" "). When a quotation comes within another quotation, you may use single quotation marks (' ') as well as double.

Use single quotation marks for a quotation within a quotation.

EXAMPLE: My mother reported, "Our Superintendent said, 'The school system is sometimes unfairly maligned.'"

Notice that both *Our* and *The* are capitalized since they both begin sentences. Also, notice that since the second quotation is at the end, both sets of quotation marks are outside the period.

Now look at this slightly different example, which contains a full sentence and a phrase. Notice that only the full sentence is capitalized. The phrase quoted within the sentence begins with a small letter.

EXAMPLE: The Superintendent of Schools continued, "Education should not be a 'process of driving a set of prejudices down your throats'; instead, it should teach you to be independent thinkers."

376

EXERCISE F: Using Quotation Marks with Dialogue and Long Quotations. The following selection includes both dialogue and a long quotation. Copy the sentences, adding quotation marks and indentations. You should have eight paragraphs when you are through.

(1) Did Mrs. Jones say that the speaker was a dog? Paul asked. (2) No. (3) She said that he would talk about prairie dogs, his friend replied. (4) Thank goodness, Paul said. (5) I didn't think a dog would be a very interesting speaker! (6) Hush now, his friend warned him. (7) I think the speaker is going to begin. (8) At that moment, the speaker began his talk: (9) Prairie dogs used to be common in the Great Plains. (10) In fact, these animals once lived in a community believed to be 100 miles wide and 250 miles long. (11) Close to 400 million prairie dogs once lived in this area. (12) Today, things are different. (13) Because prairie dogs hurt agriculture, the government destroyed many of them. (14) Unfortunately, the government's program was almost too successful. (15) Now the prairie dog is on the endangered species list. (16) If you have ever seen one of these little creatures, you know why we want to protect them. (17) They have short, brown fur and bright, inquisitive eyes. (18) They even greet one another with a gesture like a kiss. (19) Please help us collect signatures on a petition. (20) The petition asks that more reserves be set up for these animals, he concluded.

EXERCISE G: Marking Quotations Within Quotations. Each of the following sentences contains a quotation within a quotation. Copy the sentences, adding the necessary quotation marks, capitals, and other punctuation.

EXAMPLE: Mary announced Mother said dinner is ready

Mary announced, "Mother said, 'Dinner is ready.' "

1. The professor said please tell me who said humility, like darkness, reveals the heavenly lights
2. She told us remember the saying charity begins at home
3. Elsie said my favorite proverb is the one that says a bird in the hand is worth two in the bush
4. Booker T. Washington once said you can't hold a man down without staying down with him my cousin told me

5. Please keep my secret, for as you know, silence is golden my friend pleaded
6. Don't despair she said for as Allison always says the sun will rise tomorrow
7. The speaker continued remember the words of John F. Kennedy when he said the torch has been passed to a new generation
8. I told them Thomas Alva Edison once said genius is one percent inspiration and ninety-nine percent perspiration
9. A Blackfoot warrior named Crowfoot defined life by saying it is the little shadow which runs across the grass and loses itself in the sunset my mother commented
10. Our teacher said Emily Dickinson wrote that it will never come again is what makes life so sweet

DEVELOPING WRITING SKILLS: Using Quotation Marks in Writing. Choose one of the following topics or pick a topic of your own.

Protecting endangered species   Problems at the Olympics
The firing of a team manager   A forest fire

Build your chosen topic into a short scene for a melodrama. Include about fifteen sentences of dialogue. Remember, a melodrama has a villain, a hero or heroine, and an innocent person threatened by the villain. Also remember, good triumphs over evil in melodramas. Punctuate correctly and use as many different quotation rules as possible. Do not forget to indent.

17.6 Underlining and Other Uses of Quotation Marks

Titles of works and a few special items should stand out from the rest of the words on a page. To set these off, you should underline them or put quotation marks around them. Quotation marks are used in all writing and printing, but underlining is used only in handwritten and typed work. In printed materials, italics take the place of underlining.

The following section will give you rules to follow in deciding when to underline and when to use quotation marks. You will even look at special titles that require no marks at all.

Underlining

One of the major uses of underlining is for titles of long works made up of several parts, such as a novel made up of several chapters.

Underline the titles of long written works and the titles of publications that are published as a single work.

The many different items covered by this rule are found in the following chart, along with underlined examples.

WRITTEN WORKS THAT ARE UNDERLINED	
Titles of Books	<u>Exodus</u> by Leon Uris
	<u>The Collected Stories of Katherine Anne Porter</u>
Titles of Plays	<u>Measure for Measure</u> by William Shakespeare
	<u>Harvey</u> by Mary Chase
Titles of Long Poems	<u>The Waste Land</u> by T.S. Eliot
	<u>Paradise Lost</u> by John Milton
Titles of Periodicals (magazines, journals, and pamphlets)	<u>Sports Illustrated</u>
	<u>Journal of Internal Medicine</u>
	<u>Your Housepets</u>
Titles of Newspapers	<u>The New York Times</u>
	the Buffalo <u>Courier</u>

NOTE ABOUT NEWSPAPER TITLES: The part of the item that should be underlined varies from newspaper to newspaper. <u>The New York Times</u> should always be fully capitalized and underlined. Other papers, however, can usually be treated in one of two ways: the <u>Los Angeles Times</u> or the Los Angeles <u>Times</u>. Unless you know the true name, use one of these two forms consistently.

Other major works of art are also underlined.

Underline the titles of movies, TV and radio series, lengthy works of music, paintings, and sculptures.

Examples of these works of art are found in the chart below.

OTHER ARTISTIC WORKS THAT ARE UNDERLINED	
Titles of Movies	Gone with the Wind
	Casablanca
	Star Wars
Titles of Radio and TV Series	The Green Hornet
	Masterpiece Theater
	M.A.S.H.
	Family Feud
Titles of Long Musical Compositions and Record Albums (Any musical work made up of several parts, such as operas, musical comedies, symphonies, and ballets)	Rossini's The Barber of Seville
	Haydn's Surprise Symphony
	Tchaikovsky's Nutcracker Suite
	Michael Jackson's Thriller
Titles of Paintings and Sculptures	Gainsborough's The Blue Boy
	Rodin's The Thinker

The titles of individual planes, ships, space vehicles, trains, and cars are also underlined.

Underline the names of individual air, sea, space, and land craft.

AIR: Air Force One   SPACE: Explorer I

SEA: the Savannah   LAND: the Orient Express

Note also that a specific name given to a group of vehicles is not underlined.

EXAMPLE: Apollo I is just one of many Apollo spaceships.

Underlining is not restricted to titles. It is also used with certain types of words. Foreign phrases or expressions that still retain their foreign spelling and pronunciation should be underlined.

380

Underline foreign words not yet accepted into English.

EXAMPLES: At the Jewish wedding, the guests wished <u>mazel tov</u> to the new couple.

The latest <u>coup d'état</u> led to a new regime.

You may be unsure at times whether the word you want to use is still considered foreign and, thus, whether it needs to be underlined. In these cases, check a dictionary. A foreign word, if it is entered at all, will be clearly labeled.

Sometimes English words must also be underlined.

Underline numbers, symbols, letters, and words used to name themselves.

EXAMPLES: The <u>8</u> and the <u>?</u> that you wrote are almost illegible.

Remember the first <u>r</u> in <u>February</u>.

Finally, you may want to stress a particular word in a sentence.

Underline words that you wish to stress.

Since the *not* is crucial in understanding the following sentence, it is underlined.

EXAMPLE: Do <u>not</u> go near the cave.

When you use underlining to stress certain words, be careful not to underline too often since it can distract a reader.

EXERCISE A: Underlining Titles, Names, and Words.

Write each title, name, and word that requires underlining in each of the following sentences. If there are no such items in a sentence, write *correct*.

EXAMPLE: Ben Hur, starring Charleton Heston, is my all-time favorite movie.

<u>Ben Hur</u>

1. The book <u>David Copperfield</u> by Charles Dickens is considered a classic.
2. The Concert by Jan Vermeer is one of only thirty-six existing paintings by this Dutch artist.

381

3. Gemini 5 played an important role in the U.S. space program.
4. I always have trouble spelling the word occasion.
5. The works of Picasso make a valuable addition to any individual's art collection.
6. The first two sections of Lord Byron's Childe Harold, published in 1812, shocked English society and established the young poet's reputation.
7. When I walked into the room, I had a strong sense of déjà vu.
8. I like to read The New York Times and watch the TV series Meet the Press on Sunday mornings.
9. Our high school is putting on the operetta The Mikado by Gilbert and Sullivan.
10. The Empire State Building is no longer the tallest building in the world.

Quotation Marks

In general, quotation marks are used for short works and works that are part of a larger work.

Use quotation marks around the titles of short written works.

Written works that are considered short include short stories, one-act plays, short poems, essays, and articles. Works that are part of larger works include chapters of books. The following chart provides examples of each of these.

WRITTEN WORKS WITH QUOTATION MARKS	
Short Stories	"The Garden Party" by Katherine Mansfield
One-Act Plays	"The Devil and Daniel Webster" by Stephen Vincent Benét
Short Poems	"Southern Mansion" by Arna Bontemps
Titles of Essays and Articles	"A Hanging" by George Orwell "Gifts for Under $10"
Chapters of Books	"End of a Dream" from The Proud Tower by Barbara Tuchman

The titles of other short artistic works are also put in quotation marks.

Use quotation marks around the titles of episodes in a series, songs, and parts of a long musical composition.

Study the chart below to see examples of the application of this rule.

OTHER ARTISTIC WORKS WITH QUOTATION MARKS	
Titles of Episodes of a Series	"The Homecoming" from The Waltons
Titles of Songs	"When Johnny Comes Marching Home Again"
Titles of Parts of a Long Musical Composition	"Wandering by the Brookside" from Strauss's Alpine Symphony

Sometimes the title of a play or other large work that would normally be underlined is placed in quotation marks because it is mentioned as part of a collection.

Use quotation marks around the title of a work that is mentioned as part of a collection.

Antigone, a long play, would usually be underlined. However, in the following example, it is placed in quotation marks since a collection in which it is found is also named.

EXAMPLE: "Antigone" in The World's Greatest Tragedies

EXERCISE B: Using Quotation Marks with Titles. Write the titles from the following sentences, either enclosing them in quotation marks or underlining them.

EXAMPLE: We listened to Solveig's Song from Grieg's Peer Gynt Suite.

        "Solveig's Song"   Peer Gynt Suite

1. We were studying the chapter called The Character Sketch.
2. Trifles by Susan Glaspell can be found in a collection called Plays.

3. We listened to the Surprise Symphony from The Complete Symphonies of Haydn.
4. Almost everybody in California knows the song California Here I Come.
5. I read an article in Science News entitled Frog Talk: Chirp, Chuckle, and Thump.
6. Edgar Allan Poe wrote a good horror story when he wrote The Masque of the Red Death.
7. Emily Dickinson wrote an interesting poem on death called I Heard a Fly Buzz—When I Died.
8. Public Broadcasting Television showed The Prince and the Pauper on Once Upon a Classic.
9. Once More to the Lake by E. B. White is an essay that looks back to the childhood of the writer.
10. Eleanor Clark's short story Hurry, Hurry begins and ends with the activities of a poodle named de Maupassant.

Titles Without Underlining or Quotation Marks

Some titles are neither underlined nor placed in quotation marks.

Do not underline or place in quotation marks the name of the Bible, its books, divisions, or versions of other holy scriptures, such as the Koran.

EXAMPLES: The Koran sets forth the beliefs of Islam.

The class will study Genesis and Exodus during the next several months.

Certain government documents also need no punctuation.

Do not underline or place in quotation marks the titles of government charters, alliances, treaties, acts, statutes, or reports.

EXAMPLES: The Constitution of the United States

the Magna Carta

the Treaty of Versailles

the Homestead Act

EXERCISE C: Recognizing Titles That Should Not Be Underlined or Placed in Quotation Marks. Rewrite each sentence that requires underlining or quotation marks. Write *correct* if a sentence needs no changes.

EXAMPLE: Genesis is the first book of the Old Testament.

correct

1. Ovid's Metamorphoses and Virgil's Aeneid are considered two masterpieces of Roman literature.
2. Which document formally ended the Revolutionary War, the Treaty of Paris or the Treaty of Versailles?
3. Great Issues in American History, edited by Richard Hofstadter, contains the texts of many famous documents, such as the Declaration of Independence and Lincoln's Second Inaugural Address.
4. In 1766, William Pitt delivered a powerful speech before the House of Commons denouncing the Stamp Act.
5. Matthew, Mark, Luke, and John are the four major texts of the New Testament.
6. Madame Butterfly is a famous Italian opera.
7. Robert Penn Warren's book All the King's Men is about government corruption.
8. My friend received an engraved Bible on her confirmation.
9. Our Bill of Rights has stood the test of time.
10. The Fighting Angel, a novel by Pearl Buck, is set in China.

EXERCISE D: Supplying Underlining and Quotation Marks. Rewrite each sentence, adding underlining and quotation marks where needed.

EXAMPLE: Once More to the Lake by E.B. White is an essay that makes me think of my childhood days.

"Once More to the Lake" by E.B. White is an essay that makes me think of my childhood days.

1. One of the first radio shows in the 1920's was Laundryland Lyrics.
2. We took the Southwest Limited, one of the fastest trains in the United States.
3. I saw the play 1776 performed two years ago at my sister's college.

4. Joan Crawford played in the movie Our Dancing Daughters, a look at the youth of the 1920's.
5. In the one-act play Sorry Wrong Number, a woman overhears a plot to murder her.
6. When we sing in the car, we always sing A Bicycle Built for Two.
7. TV Guide is by far the magazine with the largest number of weekly subscribers.
8. Though Richard Cory is a short poem, it carries a strong message.
9. There are seven major sections in the poem The Rime of the Ancient Mariner by Coleridge.
10. The Intolerable Acts of 1774 prohibited the use of Boston Harbor until a tea tax was paid.

DEVELOPING WRITING SKILLS: Using Underlining and Quotation Marks in Your Own Writing. Write five sentences about things you enjoy. Use underlining or quotation marks for a different type of title, name, or word in each sentence.

17.7 **Dashes and Parentheses**

A writer can use three different types of punctuation marks—commas, dashes, and parentheses—to set off information that is not essential to a sentence. The comma, the weakest separator, serves to set off material that is most closely related to the main sentence. The dash (—), which is somewhat stronger, is generally used to set off material that is less closely related to the main sentence. It sets off material more distinctly than the comma does and adds emphasis to the material it sets off. Parentheses (( )), even stronger separators, are generally used for material that is least closely related to the main sentence. Unlike the dash, which adds emphasis to the material it sets off, parentheses tend to de-emphasize the material they set off.

In this section you will find a number of rules concerning the use of the dash and the parentheses. These rules will help you decide when you can best convey your meaning by using them, as well as when you should avoid them.

386

Uses of the Dash

There are three basic uses of the dash.

Use dashes to indicate an abrupt change of thought, a dramatic interrupting idea, or a summary statement.

The following chart gives examples of these three basic uses of dashes. Notice that only one dash is needed when the material falls at the end of a sentence.

USES OF THE DASH	
To indicate an abrupt change of thought	The movie involves three couples—but you probably don't want to hear the whole plot.
To set off interrupting ideas dramatically	The star—if you can call her that—will begin shooting a new TV movie soon.
	The producer—she won an Emmy last year—has promised us a hit show.
	The part of Lassie—why did the network cancel this program?—calls for an extremely well-trained dog.
To set off a summary statement	A strong cast, fine writers, and a good time slot—all of these can lead to a successful series.
	It was a spin-off of the number one comedy—this was all the critics needed to know to predict success.

Although commas are generally preferred, dashes can sometimes be useful for dealing with appositives used to rename a noun or pronoun in the sentence or for nonessential modifiers.

Use dashes to set off a nonessential appositive or modifier when it is long, when it is already punctuated, or when you want to be dramatic.

The examples at the top of the next page show nonessential appositives appropriately set off by dashes.

387

EXAMPLES: One basic problem—the fact that the station had set the show against two top-rated shows—caused its cancellation.

The three primary networks—ABC, CBS, and NBC—bring out their new shows in the fall.

One award above all others—the Emmy—signifies success to most TV performers.

When a nonessential appositive is introduced by words such as *for example* or *that is* dashes may also be used to set it off.

EXAMPLE: Situation comedies—for example, M.A.S.H.—have successfully handled controversial issues in a humorous way.

The following examples show dashes used to set off nonessential modifiers. Again, remember that commas are preferred, except in the cases listed in the rule.

EXAMPLES: James Garner—whose TV roles have included a sheriff, an ex-convict, and a private investigator—also does occasional commercials.

The series—which was actually funnier than the original movie—stayed on TV for six years.

Although dashes can be useful, you should only use them in formal writing when you have the rule clearly in mind. Too many dashes suggest a lazy writer—one who lacks the energy to choose the appropriate punctuation mark and settles for a dash.

EXERCISE A: Using the Dash. Write the following sentences, adding the necessary dashes.

EXAMPLE: Shall we pack a lunch it's such a beautiful day and go on a picnic?

Shall we pack a lunch—it's such a beautiful day—and go on a picnic?

1. Food, housing, and clothing all of these are getting more expensive.
2. Tobogganing sounds like something oh, here comes Mario.
3. We will play tennis or at least attempt to play tennis at school today.

388

4. The man underwent an emergency appendectomy the surgical removal of an appendix and is now recovering.
5. Our guest speaker who had a flat tire as he was coming here was a little late.
6. I'd like to introduce you to what did you say your name was?
7. That the plane burned huge amounts of fuel this was the concern voiced by the conservationists.
8. The Crusades there were four major ones, weren't there? were not an overwhelming success.
9. Some of the instruments the drums, guitars, and piano still need to be loaded onto the truck.
10. The parents say that their talented they use this term loosely daughter will perform in a piano recital.
11. Pencils, paper, book covers, and pens these will all be required in this course.
12. That old table which is on its last legs, to say the least was the first item sold at the flea market.
13. Feeding, exercising, and providing the necessary medical care all of these constitute important aspects of pet ownership.
14. I got Danielle a bracelet for her why, Dani, what a surprise to see you!
15. Our club raised fifty dollars more or less for the U.S. Olympic team.
16. Some horror writers for instance, Stephen King have wonderful imaginations.
17. It bothers me when you continually oh, never mind.
18. Eating, watching fireworks, and being with friends there is no better way to celebrate the Fourth of July.
19. They sent me four identical forms why, I'll never understand for the insurance claim I'm submitting.
20. Some bad habits biting your nails, grinding your teeth, and drumming your fingers seem almost impossible to break.

Uses of Parentheses

When using parentheses, you should keep two points in mind. Parentheses are the strongest separator. They also act to de-emphasize anything they set off. Thus, you should never use parentheses for an essential idea.

> **Use parentheses to set off asides and explanations only when the material is not essential or when it consists of one or more sentences.**

EXAMPLES: Actors try to empathize with **(**to share the feelings of**)** the characters they portray.

Alfred Hitchcock produced some masterful horror films **(***The Birds, Psycho,* and *Rear Window,* among others**)** that are now considered classics of the film-maker's art.

Ingrid Bergman won the Academy Award for Best Actress twice. **(**She won it for *Gaslight* in 1944 and for *Anastasia* in 1956.**)** She also won an Oscar for Best Supporting Actress.

Parentheses are also used in several situations involving numbers.

> **Use parentheses to set off numerical explanations such as dates of a person's birth and death and around numbers and letters marking a series.**

EXAMPLES: Rudolph Valentino **(**1895–1926**)** probably ranks as the most famous actor of the silent screen.

The average American spends about 16 percent of each week **(**27 hours**)** watching TV.

The movie costs one dollar and fifty cents **(**$1.50**)**.

During the summer, I read several books: **(**1**)** *The Mosquito Coast,* **(**2**)** *Growing Up,* and **(**3**)** *My Antonia.*

My favorite actors include the following: **(**a**)** Meryl Streep, **(**b**)** Dustin Hoffman, and **(**c**)** Alan Alda.

Do not overuse parentheses. Too many parentheses make it difficult for a reader to follow the flow of your ideas.

EXERCISE B: Using Parentheses. Write the following sentences, adding the necessary parentheses.

EXAMPLE: We sang the songs of Woody Guthrie 1912–1967.

We sang the songs of Woody Guthrie (1912–1967).

390

1. The lamp sale held only twice a year at Brueners usually offers some outstanding bargains.
2. The first place winner was Ronald Carmassi Italy with a world-record-breaking time.
3. We will study character development Chapter 6 in the text as it relates to this novel.
4. My grandmother 1900–1980 saw many changes occur during her lifetime.
5. Don't forget the four cans 16-ounce size of canned tomatoes.
6. The kit calls for the following tools: 1 screwdriver, 2 hammer, and 3 wrench.
7. The ice cream machine more often than not broken took my quarter and dime but didn't give me any ice cream again today.
8. The angler a fisherman who uses a hook and line pulled in a 25-pound northern pike to win the competition.
9. We listened to the last song "The Night They Drove Old Dixie Down" and then left.
10. The Dachshund Races a favorite event on Picnic Day were fun to watch.
11. The bill said she owed sixty-four dollars and ten cents $64.10.
12. Steve stifled a yawn having been up thirty-six hours straight and tried to look interested.
13. I must get some items at the store: a cleansing powder, b paper towels, and c window cleaner.
14. My paper route brings in a steady income though getting up so early is a strain.
15. She made a lot of mistakes seventeen, to be exact during rehearsal today.
16. The recipe called for six 6 tablespoons of flour.
17. Cut along the lines which should be clearly marked until you have used up all the felt.
18. Joseph Pulitzer 1847–1911 began his career as a journalist working on a St. Louis newspaper printed in German.
19. In class today Ann raised her hand quickly perhaps a little too quickly and proceeded to answer the question incorrectly.
20. The story page 84 in your books is about a man hounded by his own self-doubts.

Capitalization and Punctuation with Parentheses

There are special rules for capitalization and punctuation in sentences with parentheses.

When a phrase or declarative sentence interrupts another sentence, do not use an initial capital or end mark inside the parentheses.

EXAMPLE: The show (it began at eight) preempted my favorite program.

When a question or exclamation interrupts another sentence, use both an initial capital and an end mark inside the parentheses.

In the following examples, note especially that question marks and exclamation marks always go inside the parentheses when they are part of the item in parentheses.

EXAMPLES: *Magnum, P.I.* (Isn't that filmed in Hawaii?) is a long-running series.

Walt Disney's version of *Cinderella* (I love the scene in which the animals make Cinderella's gown!) has been criticized for distorting the original tale.

With any sentence that falls between two complete sentences, use both an initial capital and an end mark inside the parentheses.

EXAMPLE: The movie was extremely popular. (It grossed over thirty million dollars.) In fact, it was the first science fiction movie to appeal to the general public.

In a sentence with a set-off phrase, place any punctuation belonging to the main sentence after the parentheses.

EXAMPLES: When a network airs a pilot (a sample episode of a series), it checks the audience's response.

Sesame Street features a variety of puppet characters (originated by Jim Henson); it is one of the best-known educational children's series.

Will you watch the special (an all-star revue)?

392

EXERCISE C: **Capitalizing and Punctuating with Parentheses.** Write each sentence that needs punctuation or capitalization, making the necessary changes. If a sentence is already correct, write *correct*.

EXAMPLE: The flight we are taking (how I love to fly) leaves at noon.

The flight we are taking (How I love to fly!) leaves at noon.

1. I have an appointment today (right after the game)
2. Will you meet me at 716 Elm Street (the building right across from the library)
3. The dress (it was the most beautiful shade of blue) fit perfectly.
4. When we go to Seacliff Beach (a resort just south of Santa Cruz) we will have a picnic on the beach or possibly a clambake.
5. Something in the refrigerator smelled (some meat had gone bad) so I cleaned it out.
6. I watched the ants. (there was an ant hole within three feet of me) They were busy gathering crumbs from the sandwich I was trying to eat for lunch.
7. She has honey-blonde hair (do you think it is natural) and blue eyes.
8. Using the flowers (dahlias, I think) I created a lovely centerpiece.
9. The road appears to be lined with oaks. (do you think that is the right type of tree)
10. I slowly savored the pistachio ice cream (my favorite flavor) until it was gone.

DEVELOPING WRITING SKILLS: **Using Dashes and Parentheses Correctly.** Rewrite the following paragraph, correcting the error in each sentence. Then write a paragraph of your own using one set of dashes and one set of parentheses correctly.

(1) The Bermuda Triangle (An area of ocean space in the shape, roughly speaking, of a triangle) is the site of many bizarre occurrences, or so some people believe. (2) Many vehicles—planes, ships, and helicopters have disappeared in this

region. (3) One man, Larry Kusche, decided (to investigate) these reports. (4) (He was interested since he was a pilot himself). (5) The first incident he looked into occurred late in 1945; a Navy plane flew over the Atlantic Ocean and—never—returned. (6) Many crew members—fourteen, to be exact—were lost (Including the pilot, Lt. Charles Taylor). (7) The investigation revealed that the plane was not swallowed up by the sea—as some people had maintained—but had probably run out of gas and—sank. (8) Larry Kusche was also able to explain (all) of the other disappearances logically. (9) Many critics—however—remain unconvinced. (10) Thus, the mystery of the Bermuda Triangle—That part of the ocean where people and ships disappear and are never seen or heard from again—may simply be the result of our imagination, not to mention our love of intrigue.

17.8 The Hyphen

The hyphen is similar in appearance to the dash but shorter. It is used to connect some compound numbers, some prefixes and roots, and some compound words. It is also used to indicate a break in a word at the end of a line. In typewritten material, one hyphen (-) acts as a hyphen but two (--) act as a dash. In this section you will look at the rules concerning the use of the hyphen.

When to Use the Hyphen

Perhaps the most common use of the hyphen is in compound numbers.

With Numbers. Certain compound numbers require a hyphen for clarity.

Use a hyphen when writing out the numbers *twenty-one* through *ninety-nine*.

EXAMPLES: We collected *seventy-four* pounds of aluminum cans.

Twenty-four members of the club went to the tournament.

Fractions also require hyphens in certain cases.

394

Use a hyphen with fractions used as adjectives.

EXAMPLE: Sandy asked for a *one-third* reduction on the cost of the damaged luggage she received.

If a fraction is used as a noun rather than as an adjective, the hyphen is omitted.

EXAMPLE: Only *one third* of the members showed up to vote.

With Word Parts. Hyphens are also required to connect certain word parts.

Use a hyphen after a prefix that is followed by a proper noun or adjective.

The following prefixes are often used as prefixes before proper nouns: *ante-, anti-, mid-, post-, pre-, pro-,* and *un-.*

EXAMPLE: The reporters were *pro-American* in their outlook.

A hyphen is always used with three particular prefixes and one particular suffix even when they are not connected to proper nouns.

Use a hyphen in words with the prefixes *all-, ex-,* and *self-* and in words with the suffix *-elect.*

EXAMPLES: all-around   self-satisfied

ex-advisor   treasurer-elect

Make sure that a complete word follows one of the above prefixes before you use a hyphen. When a prefix is combined with only part of a word, no hyphen is needed.

INCORRECT: ex-ceed

CORRECT: exceed

With Compound Words. Hyphens are also used to connect certain compound words.

Use a hyphen to connect two or more words that are used as one word, unless the dictionary gives a contrary spelling.

Some compound nouns are written as one word without a hyphen, and some are written as separate words. The examples at the top of the next page are among those that are written with hyphens.

395

EXAMPLES: mother-in-law   great-grandfather
           a class of five-year-olds   secretary-treasurer

In addition, hyphens are used to connect certain modifiers.

Use a hyphen to connect a compound modifier that comes before a noun.

In the following examples, note that the first word or words in the modifier really modify the last word in the modifier, not the noun. Thus, they are connected to avoid confusion.

EXAMPLES: The *well-attended* program grossed over $600.

           Our *never-to-be-forgotten* marathon left us all extremely tired and sore.

When a compound modifier comes after a noun, no hyphen is needed.

BEFORE: The *after-school* meeting went well.

AFTER: We had a good meeting *after school*.

There is an exception, however. If the dictionary spells a word with a hyphen, the word must always be hyphenated, even if it follows a noun.

EXAMPLES: Some *old-fashioned* people belong to the club.

           Some of the club members are *old-fashioned*.

When dealing with compound modifiers, you must also remember this rule.

Do not use hyphens with compound modifiers that include words ending in *-ly* or with compound proper adjectives.

INCORRECT: badly-damaged   East-Asian architecture
            extremely-quick   New-England cooking

CORRECT: badly damaged   East Asian architecture
            extremely quick   New England cooking

For Clarity. Occasionally, a hyphen is needed to prevent misreading of a particular word or group of words.

Use a hyphen within a word when a combination of letters might otherwise be confusing.

396

In the first of the following examples, the hyphen is needed to prevent the confusing appearance of three l's in a row. In the second example, the hyphen is needed to distinguish a word that means "reshape" from a more common word that means "improve."

EXAMPLES:　*bell-like* instead of *belllike*

　　　　　　re-form versus *reform*

A hyphen is also sometimes needed to prevent the wrong combination of words in a reader's mind.

Use a hyphen between words to keep the reader from combining them erroneously.

EXAMPLE:　six foot-soldiers (six soldiers who are on foot)

　　　　　　six-foot soldiers (soldiers who are six feet tall)

EXERCISE A: Using Hyphens with Compound Numbers, Word Parts, and Words.

Rewrite the following paragraph, adding the necessary hyphens.

EXAMPLE:　Chocolate is my all time favorite kind of candy.

　　　　　　Chocolate is my all-time favorite kind of candy.

(1) The able bodied explorer Columbus introduced the well loved treat chocolate to Western Europe. (2) When Columbus returned from the Central American terrain with some chocolate beans, the Spanish king did not recognize their potential. (3) Hernando Cortes, however, did see the potential of the dark, bitter drink he was served by Montezuma, and he dreamed up a far fetched plan to cultivate chocolate beans in Spain. (4) This quick witted explorer had his sailors learn to cultivate the bean. (5) For over ninety nine years, Spain was the sole European producer of a thickly sweet drink they had made from the beans. (6) But other Western European nations were not left out for long. (7) They discovered the sought after secret and were soon enjoying chocolate. (8) During the post Renaissance period, chocolate was expensive, and less than one fourth of the population could afford it. (9) However, mass produced chocolate was soon available to the general public. (10) Today, chocolate is greatly loved in the United States and around the world.

397

Rules for Dividing Words at the End of the Line

In general, avoid dividing words at the end of the line whenever possible. Of course, sometimes a word must be divided. When you must divide words, use the following rules.

The most important rule for dividing words is the first one.

If a word must be divided, always divide it between syllables.

Use a dictionary when necessary to find the breaks between syllables.

EXAMPLE: The National Honor Society is an honor organization that performs services for the community.

Be sure that you place a hyphen only at the end of the first line, not at the beginning of the second line.

INCORRECT: Our club will build trails in the moun
-tains.

CORRECT: Our club will build trails in the mountains.

Also take care not to divide one-syllable words, even if they are long or sound like two-syllable words. If a one-syllable word does not fit in the space remaining on a line, leave the space open and put the word on the next line.

INCORRECT: thro-ugh   gle-amed   rhy-thm
CORRECT: through   gleamed   rhythm

There is also a rule for syllables that are one letter long.

Do not divide a word so that a single letter stands alone.

Although all of the words in the following incorrect examples are correctly broken into syllables, they should not be broken in this way at the end of a line.

INCORRECT: a-lone   read-y   e-lect
CORRECT: alone   ready   elect

You should also avoid placing *ed* alone at the beginning of a new line.

398

INCORRECT: stall-ed   CORRECT: stalled

A special rule is needed for proper nouns and adjectives.

Do not divide proper nouns and adjectives.

INCORRECT: Lou-ise   Amer-ican
CORRECT: Louise   American

Words that are already hyphenated also have a special rule.

Divide a hyphenated word only after the hyphen.

INCORRECT: Seeing the need, she made a great self-sacri-
             fice.
CORRECT: Seeing the need, she made a great self-sacrifice.

EXERCISE B: Dividing Words. If a word has been divided correctly, write *correct*. If not, rewrite the sentence, dividing the word correctly or writing it as one word if it cannot be divided.

EXAMPLE: The teacher told me that my essay was too word-
           y.
           The teacher told me that my essay was too wordy.

1. When I read the directions, I saw they were self-expla-
   natory.
2. Yesterday, we drove past countless fields of grazing cattle.
3. With Marion helping, it didn't take long to clean the ta
   -ble.
4. The high altitude in the mountains gave me a very head-
   y feeling.
5. After crossing the rickety bridge, we slowly walked down to the water's edge.
6. The three of us had an early morning meeting with Superintendent Glaros.
7. As we watched from afar, the horse and her colt galloped across the pasture.
8. Do you suppose that your invitation to Maryanne Ellins-
   worth will arrive in time?
9. The building was so badly burnt that it was unrecogniza-
   ble.

10. The man ahead of me bought a first-class ticket to New Zea-
    land.
11. Will you be well enough to attend next Friday night's foot
    -ball game?
12. The lecturer provided us with a great deal of food for tho-
    ught.
13. Next year, the county will close down one more high scho-
    ol.
14. The terrible heat finally penetrated the house's insula-
    tion.
15. Will you please give a warm welcome to the new Secretary-
    General of the United Nations?
16. My grandfather has decided that all of us should supple-
    ment our diet with vitamins.
17. When you make this coffee cake, remember to use all-pur-
    pose flour.
18. The neighbor's precious tabby cat certainly has a bad te-
    mper.
19. I will need to work quite hard next week in order to e-
    liminate enough calories from my diet.
20. Is there still any chance that they will ground the air-
    plane?

**DEVELOPING WRITING SKILLS: Using Hyphens in Your
Own Writing.** Proofread a paper you wrote recently. Circle all
the hyphens you used. Write the rule that applies to each correctly used hyphen. Correct any incorrectly used hyphens.

17.9 The Apostrophe

The apostrophe is used to show ownership and to indicate
missing letters in contractions.

Apostrophes with Possessive Nouns

Apostrophes are used with nouns to show possession or
ownership of items, ideas, and personality traits.

With Singular Nouns. The easiest possessives to form are
those formed from singular nouns.

Add an apostrophe and -s to show the possessive case of most singular nouns.

All of the following examples follow this simple rule.

EXAMPLES: The idea of the *boy* becomes the *boy's* idea.

The hat of *Mr. Harker* becomes *Mr. Harker's* hat.

The role of the *guard* becomes the *guard's* role.

The color of the *wave* becomes the *wave's* color.

When a singular noun ends in -*s*, you will still add an apostrophe and an -*s* to show the possessive case.

EXAMPLES: The games of *James* becomes *James's games.*

The anger of the *boss* becomes the *boss's* anger.

An exception is made when an apostrophe and an -*s* would make a word that already ends in -*s* difficult to pronounce. Then, just an apostrophe is added.

AWKWARD: I brought *Dickens's* book along to read.

BETTER: I brought *Dickens'* book along to read.

With Plural Nouns. The possessives of most plural nouns are also easy to form.

Add an apostrophe to show the possessive case of plural nouns ending in -s or -es.

EXAMPLES: The sands of the *beaches* becomes the *beaches'* sands.

The strokes of the *swimmers* becomes the *swimmers'* strokes.

Remember, however that not all plural nouns end in -*s* or -*es*. Another rule is needed for these nouns.

Add an apostrophe and -s to show the possessive case of plural nouns that do not end in -s or -es.

EXAMPLES: The toys of the *children* becomes the *children's* toys.

The hope of the *people* becomes the *people's* hope.

401

With Compound Nouns. The possessives of compound nouns also follow a simple basic rule.

Add an apostrophe and -s (or just an apostrophe if the word is a plural ending in -s) to the last word of a compound noun to form the possessive.

The following chart lists some of the different kinds of compound nouns that are commonly used as possessives.

POSSESSIVES OF COMPOUND NOUNS	
Names of Businesses and Organizations	Wolff and Taylor's store. the Boy Scouts' pledge University of Michigan's mascot
Titles of Rulers and Leaders	King Henry VII's reign the Queen of England's children the President of Egypt's tour
Hyphenated Compound Nouns Used to Describe People	the Secretary-Treasurer's idea her mother-in-law's purse the editor-in-chief's pencil

Sometimes, possessives of compound nouns are awkward. In these cases, reword the phrase using the preposition *of.*

AWKWARD: the actress-heiress's hounds

BETTER: the hounds of the actress-heiress

With Time, Amounts, and the Word *Sake*. Some common expressions use the possessives of time or amounts. The word *sake* is also found in possessive expressions. For these, follow the basic rules for singular and plural possessives.

To form possessives involving time, amounts, or the word *sake,* use an apostrophe and -s or just an apostrophe if the possessive is plural.

TIME:	one day's wages	five minutes' walk
AMOUNT:	one dollar's worth	five pounds' worth
SAKE:	for Heaven's sake	for Pete's sake

With the word *sake,* the *-s* after the apostrophe is often dropped.

EXAMPLES: for convenience' sake   for goodness' sake

Distinguishing Between Singular and Plural Possessives. If you have trouble deciding where to put the apostrophe or whether an *-s* is required, you may find the following two steps useful.

STEP 1:   Determine the owner of the idea, object, or personality trait. Ask yourself, "To whom does it belong?"

STEP 2:   If the answer to the question is a singular noun, follow the rule for forming singular possessives. If the answer is a plural noun, follow the rules for forming plural possessives.

In the phrase *my friends house,* ask yourself, "To whom does the house belong?" If the answer is "my friend," then the possessive is the singular *my friend's house.* If the answer is that the house belongs to "my friends," then the answer is the plural *my friends' house.*

EXERCISE A: Using Apostrophes to Make Singular Nouns Possessive. Write the underlined nouns, putting them in the possessive form.

EXAMPLE: The door of the <u>bird</u> cage was open.

bird's

1. The <u>student</u> paper discussed the book in great detail.
2. <u>Phyllis</u> hair looked good styled that way.
3. The <u>dog</u> water bowl needs to be refilled.
4. <u>Andrew</u> pet turtle wandered from his bowl sometime last night.
5. The new <u>representative</u> performance on the floor of the House of Representatives was quite impressive.
6. New courses were listed in the <u>college</u> fall catalog.
7. <u>Jim</u> coat shrank in the wash.
8. The <u>cat</u> claws need to be trimmed.
9. We read three of <u>Robert Graves</u> books.
10. A part of each <u>month</u> wages was added to our small but growing savings account.

403

EXERCISE B: Using Apostrophes to Make Plural Nouns Possessive. Write the underlined nouns, putting them into the possessive form.

EXAMPLE: The <u>members</u> dues should be paid this week.

members'

1. The <u>ladies</u> desserts came with their coffee.
2. The <u>children</u> toys were scattered all over the floor.
3. The <u>twins</u> presents were to be kept hidden until their birthday.
4. Many important issues were discussed at the <u>governors</u> conference.
5. The <u>critics</u> reviews helped boost the confidence of the actors.
6. The presidential candidate promised to uphold the <u>people</u> interests.
7. The <u>relatives</u> invitations must be mailed immediately.
8. Neat and well-written was the best way to describe the <u>women</u> tests.
9. The <u>visitors</u> suitcases had not yet been unpacked.
10. The report said that the <u>cities</u> problems continue to grow worse each year.

EXERCISE C: Using Apostrophes with Compound Nouns. Write each sentence, making the compound noun possessive.

EXAMPLE: The Red Cross lifesaving class starts next week.

The Red Cross's lifesaving class starts next week.

1. The Secretary of State home was the scene of a recent reception for foreign dignitaries.
2. Colbert and Nelson store is having a three-day sale on sandals.
3. My father-in-law hair has a streak of gray in it.
4. The police chief wife is a police officer, too.
5. The Camp Fire Girls summer program teaches children a great deal about nature.
6. The jack-in-the-box spring broke, and now the toy no longer works.
7. They just printed the poet-philosopher third book of poems about nature.

404

8. The Queen of England limousine was involved in a small collision.
9. My great-grandmother old books are quite valuable since some of them are first editions.
10. The runner-up smile told us that he wasn't too upset about losing.

Joint and Individual Ownership

Special rules are needed for possessive nouns indicating joint or individual ownership. When showing ownership you should always ask yourself, "Who owns what?" If one object or a set of objects belongs to two or more people, then you are dealing with joint ownership.

To show joint ownership, make the final noun possessive.

EXAMPLES: Sarah and Bob's books (They share the same books.)

Ron and Mark's attic (They jointly own one attic.)

If separate objects belong to different people, then you are dealing with individual ownership.

To show individual ownership, make each noun possessive.

EXAMPLES: Sarah's and Bob's books (Each one has different books.)

Ron's and Mark's attics (Each owns his own attic.)

EXERCISE D: Using Apostrophes to Show Individual or Joint Ownership. Write each sentence, adding apostrophes to show the kind of ownership indicated in parentheses.

EXAMPLE: <u>Mike</u> and <u>Sue</u> jackets are in the closet.   (individual)

Mike's and Sue's jackets are in the closet.

1. In the aftermath of the hurricane, it became apparent that the <u>husband</u> and <u>wife</u> house was damaged beyond hope of repair.   (joint)
2. The <u>prosecutor</u> and <u>defense attorney</u> opening remarks took up most of the morning.   (individual)

405

3. <u>Stacy</u> and <u>Kevin</u> teacher assigned a lengthy research paper. (joint)
4. During the party <u>Margaret</u> and <u>Matt</u> conduct was perfect. (individual)
5. The <u>drummer</u> and the <u>guitarist</u> instruments arrived safely. (individual)
6. <u>Cindy</u> and <u>Amber</u> room has just been painted and redecorated. (joint)
7. The statement showed that <u>Don</u> and <u>Hilary</u> checking account was overdrawn. (joint)
8. I would say that either <u>Carol</u> or <u>Duane</u> paper could win the essay competition. (individual)
9. <u>Sally</u> and <u>Scott</u> ice cream cones soon began to melt in the heat. (individual)
10. <u>Mrs. Tavenner</u> and <u>Ms. Wood</u> dentist will be retiring soon. (joint)

Apostrophes with Pronouns

There are many types of pronouns, but only those that show ownership are considered here. First, there are the indefinite pronouns, which are treated just as nouns are.

Use an apostrophe and an -s with indefinite pronouns to show ownership.

The following examples show how indefinite pronouns are made possessive.

EXAMPLES: another's wish   nobody's child
             anyone's game   one's country
             everybody's favorite   someone's dog
             one another's choices someone else's house

Second, there are the personal pronouns. These pronouns are not treated as nouns are.

Do not use an apostrophe with possessive forms of personal pronouns.

The following personal pronouns are already possessive: *my, mine, your, yours, his, her, hers, its, our, ours, their,* and *theirs.* Some are used as adjectives.

406

EXAMPLE: Put *your* shovel in *its* bucket.

His sandcastle is lovely.

Others are used as subjects, direct objects, and subject complements.

EXAMPLES: *Yours* has more colors in it.

He wrecked *hers*.

The shovel is *ours*.

Remember that none of the possessive pronouns needs an apostrophe to show possession.

Writers often confuse the possessive form *its* with the contraction *it's*. Remember that *its* is only used to show possession. *It's*, on the other hand, is used to indicate the contraction for *it is*.

EXAMPLES: *Its* pattern is colorful.

It's only a little hermit crab.

EXERCISE E: Using Apostrophes with Pronouns. If a sentence uses apostrophes correctly, write *correct*. If not, rewrite the sentence correcting all of the errors.

EXAMPLE: Someone's else's package was delivered to them.

Someone else's package was delivered to them.

1. Robin gave his' coconut cake to her.
2. When the coat didn't fit, he decided he had picked up another's by mistake.
3. It's my duty to fight crime whenever and wherever I find it.
4. Her's was the first car to be pulled over for routine inspection.
5. Someone's car keys have been left behind on the kitchen table.
6. Everybodys' presents were so thoughtful and generous.
7. When he was cooking the steaks, he cooked their's a little longer since they liked them well-done.
8. According to the job descriptions, emptying trash cans is nobodys' responsibility.
9. Is that your umbrella that is making that huge puddle on the floor?

407

10. Anybody elses' actions would have been suspect, but no-body doubts his word.
11. Ours is the red car parked across the street.
12. Our new furniture is here, but their's has not been delivered yet.
13. His time for the 100-yard dash was extremely fast, but hers' broke the school record.
14. My car needs it's yearly check-up.
15. Nobody else's teeth hurt as much as mine do after they have been cleaned.
16. Can you borrow his' records for the party?
17. We must not damage one's another's possessions.
18. The boat is finally all our's—free and clear!
19. Yours is some of the worst handwriting I have ever seen.
20. The meeting is not at my house; it's at yours.

Apostrophes with Contractions

A contraction is a word or phrase that is shortened by leaving out one or more letters. Contractions use apostrophes to show where letters are left out.

Use an apostrophe in a contraction to indicate the position of the missing letter or letters.

By far the most common contractions are those formed with verbs.

Contractions with Verbs. Most contractions are combinations of verbs and adverbs or of pronouns and verbs. The following list gives you an indication of some of the contractions that can be formed with verbs. This is not a complete list by any means.

COMMON CONTRACTIONS WITH VERBS		
Verbs with *not*	aren't (are not)	isn't (is not)
	can't (cannot)	shouldn't (should not)
	couldn't (could not)	wasn't (was not)
	didn't (did not)	weren't (were not)
	don't (do not)	wouldn't (would not)

Pronouns with the Verb *will*	I'll (I will) you'll (you will) he'll (he will) she'll (she will)	we'll (we will) they'll (they will) who'll (who will)
Pronouns and Nouns with the Verb *be*	I'm (I am) you're (you are) he's (he is) she's (she is) it's (it is)	we're (we are) they're (they are) mine's (mine is) who's (who is) Mary's (Mary is)
Pronouns and the Verb *would*	I'd (I would) you'd (you would) he'd (he would) she'd (she would)	we'd (we would) they'd (they would) who'd (who would)

Contractions should be used sparingly in formal writing.

INFORMAL WRITING: He's never been there.

FORMAL WRITING: He has never been there.

Contractions of Years. Another type of contraction that is sometimes used in informal writing is a contraction for the name of a year. When numbers are left out of the name of a year, an apostrophe should be used in place of the missing numbers.

EXAMPLE: the class of '86

Contractions with *o, d,* and *l.* Three special kinds of contractions begin with the letters *o, d,* and *l. 0'* is a shortened version of the longer phrase *of the. D'* in French also means *of the. L'* in French simply means *the.* These letters and an apostrophe are sometimes used with certain words and proper names.

EXAMPLES: o'clock

jack o'lantern

O'Henry (of the Henry family)

d'Angelo (of the Angelo family)

l'Ermite (the Ermite family)

409

Contractions in Dialogue. Although most contractions with verbs are avoided in formal writing, if you want written dialogue to sound realistic, you should use the contractions people commonly use.

When you write in a regional dialect or a foreign accent, you may need to use unusual contractions. In such words, insert apostrophes where a letter or letters have been removed. Try not to use too many apostrophes in dialogue, however. If overused, they can be distracting.

EXAMPLES: Sure 'preciate you doin' this.

Me thinks 'tis a fine ol' day.

EXERCISE F: Using Apostrophes with Contractions. If a contraction is underlined in the following sentences, write the two words that make it up. If two words are underlined, write the contraction they would form.

EXAMPLE: *I've* always been an Alfred Hitchcock fan.

I have

Alfred Hitchcock was a filmmaker of whom many people said, "This (1) man's a legend in his own time." The legend of Alfred Hitchcock began in England, when he produced his first film, *Pleasure Garden*. However, we (2) don't see the now famous Hitchcock style until his third film, *The Lodger*. Hitchcock moved to the United States early in his career, but he (3) did not plan to remain here. However, he and his wife (4) could not return to England considering his growing popularity here. Instead, they decided (5) they'd become residents of California. (6) It has been the movies of Alfred Hitchcock that have brought a new dimension to the horror film. His films (7) aren't just shocking; (8) they're stories that explore artistically the irrational aspects of life. In these films, (9) we've got the quality (10) we'd like to find in all films. Among the films (11) he has made in the most creative periods in his life—the (12) '30's, '40's, and '50's— (13) you'll find such thrillers as *Notorious* and *Psycho*. You (14) should not ignore these films; (15) they're classics (16) that will entertain moviegoers for years to come. We (17) shouldn't forget the contributions this man has made. One (18) thing's certain: (19) We'll never forget the thrills his (20) work's brought us.

Special Uses of the Apostrophe

Apostrophes are also used in four special kinds of plurals.

Use an apostrophe and -s to write the plurals of numbers, symbols, letters, and words used to name themselves.

EXAMPLES: three *8*'s or eight *3*'s

             two *?*'s

             Your *n*'s look like *h*'s.

             He prefaced every comment with *um*'s.

EXERCISE G: Recognizing Special Uses of the Apostrophe. Write each sentence, adding an apostrophe and an -*s* wherever necessary. Underline any items that appear in italics.

EXAMPLES: Please dot all your *i* carefully.

            Please dot all your i's carefully.

1. I cut out six *8* for my bulletin board.
2. Do you spell this word with one *c* and two *s* or two *c* and one *s*?
3. Should I put two *?* in this sentence, Miss Mellgren?
4. I had to write twenty *f* in my calligraphy class before I was able to master that letter.
5. Now that we have a new house number, we will need to buy two more *4*.
6. Five *and* and three *but* in one paragraph indicate lazy writing.
7. Have you noticed that *6* are really upside down *9*?
8. There are too many *nice* in this essay.
9. She told me to watch my *p* and *q*.
10. Make sure the *;* look different from the *:* in your paper.

DEVELOPING WRITING SKILLS: Using Apostrophes in Your Own Writing. Write a short dialogue in which two people argue over who owns one of the following objects. Use at least five apostrophes in your dialogue.

A record album   A ragged teddy bear

A 1923 penny   An overdue library book

Skills Review and Writing Workshop

Punctuation

CHECKING YOUR SKILLS

Rewrite the paragraph, correcting errors in punctuation.

(1) According to the World Book Encyclopedia, the skeleton is your bodys framework. (2) The skeleton gives shape to your body and it provides places where muscles can be attached. (3) Did you know that there are about 206 bones in your body. (4) There are sixty four bones in the arms and hands alone. (5) Bones also protect the brain the heart and the lungs. (6) The skeletal system also serves another important function it stores minerals. (7) Parts of the skeleton are joined at certain important points joints. (8) Fixed, pivot, hinge all these are types of joints. (9) To keep moving properly joints must contain enough synovial fluid to prevent friction. (10) This fluid was named by Paracelsus 1494–1541 a Swiss physician.

USING MECHANICS SKILLS IN WRITING
Writing a TV Commercial

Punctuation allows readers to clearly understand the meaning of your sentences. Imagine that you are writing a television commercial for a new product. Write a clear, interesting commercial following these steps.

Prewriting: Select a new product that you have used or make up one. Consider some of the ways you might persuade people to try the product. How will it benefit them? Think of the most effective method of presenting these benefits.

Writing: Begin by describing the most important benefits. Then add other information about the product.

Revising: Look over your punctuation and correct any mistakes. Then change any words that could be more descriptive. When you have finished revising, proofread carefully.

Chapter 18

The Writing Process

To achieve excellence in any field, there are certain prescribed steps that must be followed. If you hope to become a professional baseball pitcher, for instance, you do not simply arrive on the mound one day, toss some balls to home plate, and expect to be given a contract. Becoming a professional baseball player involves following a certain prescribed course of action.

Professional writers, too, know the value of following an established set of steps in order to excel at their work. Successful student writers have used that knowledge to help them create their own best work.

Whether you are writing a poem, a short story, or a paper on an assigned topic or on a topic of your own choosing, following certain steps will help insure excellence. The writing process can be divided into three stages: prewriting, writing the first draft, and revising.

18.1 Prewriting

The first step in the writing process is the prewriting, or planning, stage. It includes exploring ideas, choosing a topic, determining audience and purpose, deciding on a main idea, and developing and organizing supporting ideas in the most effective way possible.

414

Exploring Ideas

Writing topics can come from many sources—magazines, newspapers, books, TV, other people, and so on. Perhaps the best source for writing ideas is you. You are full of opinions, likes and dislikes, and positive and negative experiences. If you think, then you can write.

To explore ideas for writing topics, take inventory of your interests, experiences, and ideas.

In school, you are often asked to write a paper on an assigned topic. Sometimes, though, you are given the opportunity to write a paper on a topic of your own choosing. As you continue your schooling, you will probably have increasingly more opportunities to write on subjects that you have selected. Here are some techniques for generating ideas for potential writing topics.

Interview Yourself. To discover topics that interest you, ask yourself questions like the ones that are shown in the following chart.

QUESTIONS FOR INTERVIEWING YOURSELF

1. What activities do I enjoy?
2. In what areas do I have special skills and/or extensive knowledge?
3. What kinds of subjects arouse my curiosity?
4. To whom do I like to speak and about what topics?
5. To whom could I speak to learn more about topics that interest me?
6. What has happened to me in the past or is happening to me now that seems of special interest?

Free Writing. Set aside a specific amount of time or number of pages and begin writing. Write anything that comes to your mind, without editing your thoughts. Do not stop writing even if you have to repeat a word or sentence over and over until you have a fresh idea. When you are finished, set the paper aside and read it later. Decide if any ideas could be potential writing topics.

Journal Writing. Each day write thoughts, feelings, and experiences in a notebook. At the end of each week, read over your journal to find potential writing topics.

Reading and Saving. Read as much and as often as possible from a variety of sources: newspapers, magazines, books, encyclopedias, and so on. Jot down any ideas that interest you. Cut out articles from newspapers and magazines and make subject files of potential writing topics.

Clustering. Clustering is a technique that is used to narrow a broad topic into one appropriate for a short paper. Pick a topic (art, for instance), and write it in the center of a piece of paper. Think of all the words that you associate with that word (painting, sculpture, artists) and write them around that "nucleus" word. Circle each word and draw a line from that word to the nucleus word. Continue this process until you have a topic narrow enough for a short paper.

Brainstorming. Brainstorming is a way of creating or combining as many ideas as you can on a subject. It is a process you probably go through all the time, even if it is just planning a party with friends or trying to decide what to do on a day off. To brainstorm, start with any idea and build on it. Try to go in as many directions as possible. Explore all your thoughts on the subject. Don't stop to evaluate your ideas at this point. Keep the flow moving.

You can brainstorm alone or in a group. If you brainstorm alone, jot down your ideas quickly without judging them at all. If you work with a group, appoint one member as the recorder to write down ideas.

Cueing. You can use cueing devices such as the 5 W's (who, what, where, when, and why) or the alphabet to stimulate ideas. For example, to use the 5 W's choose a topic and ask yourself who, what, where, when, and why (or how) about it, just as a journalist may do when writing a news story. Here is an example of 5-W cueing:

Topic:	Cycling
Who:	Me
What:	Training
Where:	Deserted roads, away from traffic
Why:	To increase speed and endurance
When:	After school, weekends

416

Alphabet cueing is a similar process. Write down an idea about your topic for each letter of the alphabet. If you are writing about a personal experience, the list for the letter *A* might be annoyed, angry, Ann, and so forth.

The five senses of touch, taste, sight, sound and smell can also spark ideas on a topic by re-creating in your mind memories associated with each. The five senses are especially suited to cueing ideas for descriptive writing. List all the words or thoughts connected to your topic that are related to sight, then sound, and so on until you have completely covered all the senses associated with that topic.

With all of these techniques for exploring ideas, it is important not to limit your thinking. Do not stop to evaluate and select. There is nothing close-minded about prewriting. It is the time to be free in your thinking and free in your writing.

EXERCISE A: Taking Inventory. Answer the six questions under the heading "Interview Yourself" on page 415.

EXERCISE B: Free Writing. Write for ten minutes, non-stop, on any of the following topics. Do not worry about spelling or punctuation. Just keep writing. Start with general reactions and move to specific ones. Include any sights, sounds, or other details associated with the subject.

an embarrassing moment	youth (or parents) of today
a fight or conflict	a favorite place
girls' sports	the best music ever created
what I do best	life
the stars	ferocious animals
daydreams/nightmares	nature

EXERCISE C: Journal Writing. Keep a journal for a week. Describe what you do, think, see, or feel during the day. For example, try to record accurately a reaction to something someone else said, a movie or TV show, a quiet time, or a competitive sports moment.

EXERCISE D: Brainstorming. Work in a group of four or five. Appoint one person to take notes. Brainstorm ideas for a new product, something that does not yet exist, such as a car that comes when you call it. Toss out ideas for at least ten minutes without discussing their merits. Just keep the ideas flowing. Then choose one idea and, working on your own, write down why you think it would be a good product.

EXERCISE E: Cueing. Choose one of the cueing methods (5W's, alphabet, or five senses) and imagine that you have discovered part of Earth or a new planet that has never been seen by anyone else. Using the cueing method of your choice, write down words or sentences to describe this place.

Choosing and Narrowing a Topic

Now that you see how ideas can grow, you probably realize that not all ideas can be adequately covered in a short paper.

Choose a topic that can be effectively covered in the allotted amount of space.

You may be assigned a broad topic, such as bicycling, for a short paper, or you may choose that topic to develop a topic of your own. In either case, the topic of bicycling is so broad that it could take several books to cover it satisfactorily. One way to narrow such a topic is to use the clustering method described on page 416. Here is how the clustering technique could be used to narrow the topic of bicycling.

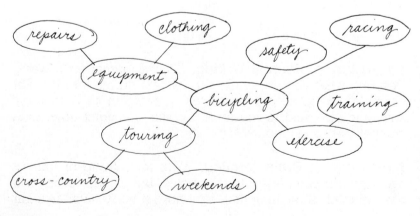

EXERCISE F: Narrowing a Topic. Below are five broad topics. Select one and use clustering to narrow the topic.

health   sports   animals   hobbies   history

EXAMPLE: animals
                      pets suitable for small apartments

Determining Audience and Purpose

How a writing topic is developed depends on whom you are writing for and what your purpose for writing is.

Determine your audience and purpose before you begin writing.

Your audience, or potential readers, might be your teacher, your classmates, or the readers of your local newspaper. Your purpose might be to inform, to persuade, or to entertain.

The chart shows audiences and purposes for topics that have been narrowed from the large topic of cycling.

Topic	Audience	Purpose
—Support for a cycling marathon	readers of local newspaper	to persuade
—tips on training	cyclists who compete	to inform
—cycling mishaps	classmates	to entertain

Identifying an audience and purpose tells you what kinds of details to include and the appropriate language to use.

EXERCISE G: Identifying Audiences and Purposes. Use your narrow topic from Exercise F and write two possible purposes and a potential audience for each purpose.

EXAMPLE: advantages of home computers

　　　　　1. Purpose: to persuade readers of the value of home computers; audience: parents of friends
　　　　　2. Purpose: to inform readers of currently available educational software; audience: teachers, parents, students

419

Developing a Main Idea and Support

Once you have chosen a topic, a purpose, and an audience, you are ready to state your main idea and gather support.

State a main idea. Then gather and organize supporting information to develop the main idea effectively.

Your main idea is the most important thought you want to leave with your readers. It can usually be stated in a sentence, which may or may not appear in your final paper.

MAIN IDEA: My cycling training program is based on the recommendations of experts and my own goals.

Knowing your main idea makes it easier to develop support for that idea. One way of finding support is to use the techniques described under Exploring Ideas on pages 415–418.

When you have gathered all your support material, it is time to decide on the best method of organization. To do this, think about your purpose and the most effective approach to achieve that purpose. For instance, if you are trying to persuade someone to see things your way, you might present your strongest argument first, in an attempt to grab your reader's attention, or you might save it for last, hoping to leave a strong impression in your reader's mind. The chart shows ways of organizing information.

ORGANIZATION OF SUPPORTING INFORMATION	
Chronological order	Information arranged in time sequence
Spatial order	Information arranged according to space relationships
Order of importance	Information arranged from least to most important or vice versa
Comparison and contrast	Information arranged according to similarities and differences between items
Developmental	Information arranged so that one point leads logically to the next

Below is a list of supporting information for a paper on training to be a cyclist. The items on the list are numbered in developmental order.

1. my goals for training
2. advantages of training
3. warm-ups
4. variation
5. aerobic conditioning
6. speed runs, gear changes
7. rest periods
8. technique tips: posture, pedaling
9. enjoyment of training and riding

EXERCISE H: Developing a Topic. Select one of the topics, one of the purposes, and one of the audiences listed below. Write a main idea about the topic. Then jot down supporting ideas for developing the topic. Finally choose a method of organization and write that down.

Topics: how to earn money, getting ready for school in the morning, the best food in town
Purposes: to inform, to entertain, to persuade
Audiences: your classmates, your family, young people ages 8–10

EXERCISE I: Prewriting. Put the ideas from this section into practice by going through the prewriting stage of the writing process. First, choose a general topic of interest to you. Then, use whatever techniques you want to narrow that topic to one suitable for a short paper. Next, determine your purpose and audience. Jot down notes about your topic, and identify the best method of organization for your topic and purpose. Number your notes according to the method of organization you chose. Add any ideas that you feel will improve your work, or delete those that will detract from it. Save your work for use later in the chapter.

DEVELOPING WRITING SKILLS: Prewriting. Choose another general topic and follow all the steps of the prewriting stage to create an outline for a short paper.

18.2 Writing

After you have a topic, a purpose, an audience, and a well-organized set of notes, you are ready to begin writing.

Writing a First Draft

A first draft is a rough stage. When you write a first draft, just get your ideas into sentences and paragraphs.

Translate your prewriting notes into sentences and paragraphs, without worrying about punctuation, spelling, grammar, or perfect sentences.

When you are writing a first draft, you have the chance to rework your ideas. As you translate your notes into sentences and paragraphs, you may want to change your approach or even your entire topic. This is the time to experiment.

Here is a first draft of a paragraph about a training program for cycling.

Training to be a top-notch bicyclist is my favorite way to spend time. It's not easy, but it definitely is worth the effort. Since I began training, strength and endurance are increasing. My personal training program is based on expert advice and my goals. To increase speed and endurance, I concentrate on developing muscles, aerobic endurance, pacing, technique, and last but not least, enjoyment.

Notice that the paragraph contains the main idea that appeared on page 420 and the first two items from the list of supporting ideas on page 421. However, the writer has reversed the order of the first two supporting ideas and has added several specific examples.

Writing a rough draft is an essential stage in the writing process. Once a draft is complete, you have something concrete on which to make improvements. Any draft can benefit from fine tuning before it becomes a polished piece of writing.

EXERCISE A: Writing a First Draft. Write a first draft of a short paper based on your notes from Exercise I on page 421. Concentrate just on getting your thoughts down on paper.

Overcoming Writer's Block

Just about the only thing that can go wrong during the writing of a first draft is writer's block. Writer's block occurs when a writer feels incapable of putting any words at all down on paper. You may experience writer's block because you have so many ideas that you do not know where to begin or because you cannot think of a single thing to write. In either case, the solution for writer's block is to keep on writing something, no matter what.

If you feel incapable of writing, write anything. Remember you can always change it later.

When you experience writer's block, try some of the prewriting techniques you learned about in the beginning of this chapter: do some free writing; talk with people and try to get interested in new ideas; read a magazine or book. Most important, do not panic. Your mind will begin to work again—everyone's does—as soon as you relax and give your thoughts a chance to flow.

EXERCISE B: Overcoming Writer's Block. Consider the techniques you learned in Exercises A through E on pages 417 and 418. Choose three of these techniques and explain why you think each one of them could help you to overcome writer's block.

DEVELOPING WRITING SKILLS: Write a first draft based on your notes and outline from Developing Writing Skills on page 421.

Revising 18.3

Revising is as essential to the writing process as prewriting and writing a first draft. During the revision process, you have a chance to think critically about your work and to further solidify your ideas. You have already made some revisions when you translated your ideas from the prewriting stage to the first draft. Now it is time to refine even further.

Revising for Sense

The first stage in the revision process involves reading your paper critically to make sure that it makes sense.

Make sure that all of the ideas in a paper support your purpose and that they are presented in a logical way with the connections between them apparent.

When you read your paper for sense, look at it objectively. Ask yourself the questions in the following chart.

REVISING FOR SENSE
1. Have I clearly stated my topic?
2. Will the main idea be clear to my readers?
3. Is there enough relevant supporting information?
4. Are the ideas presented in a logical order?
5. Are the logical connections between ideas expressed?

EXERCISE A: Revising. Revise the paragraphs below for sense.

(1) Admiral Peary discovered the North Pole. He also discovered a meteorite that weighs 31 metric tons in Melville Bay, Greenland. This was back in 1894. Meteorites are pieces of other planets that have landed on Earth. This particular meteorite was from the core of a planet, so it was about ninety percent iron. The Inuit people had been using little chips off the meteorite to make iron tips for their weapons. For a long time they had refused to tell explorers where the meteorite was. But they finally told Admiral Peary. They didn't want outsiders to know where their weapons came from. But by the time Admiral Peary reached them, they had learned that they could get weapons more easily by trading than by chipping at an iron "mountain" (that's what they called it) with stones. Peary received permission from the Inuit to take away the meteorite. It was a big job. The meteorite was lodged in permafrost. That is a type of soil that is permanently frozen. He finally got the meteorite back to New York City in 1897. Now it is in the American Museum of Natural History. You can see it if you go there.

(2) Do you know what I like about the library? It's the feeling that you could find out just about anything you wanted to know there. Our library is a neat place to spend a few hours. You can sit in a comfortable chair and get lost in a good mystery story. You can look up the phone numbers of people you know in any major city in the country. You can look at an atlas and plan a trip around the world. You can listen to records. You can just wander around the stacks discovering books that no one has taken out of the library in years. Our librarians are very helpful. My younger sister likes to go to story hour on Saturday morning. Sometimes the library has interesting films. I like the feeling of being surrounded by books. With all those books I haven't yet read, I'll never have to be bored in my life. I recommend a trip to the library for anyone who likes knowing little-known facts.

Editing for Word Choice and Sentences

The second stage in revision is often called editing.

Read your paper several times, making sure that every word is the best possible one to express your thought and that your sentences are clear and varied.

When you edit, ask yourself the questions in the chart.

EDITING WORDS AND SENTENCES
1. Does each word mean exactly what I want to say?
2. Is the language appropriate for the intended audience?
3. Is the meaning of each sentence clear?
4. Have I used a variety of sentence lengths and structures?

Following is the paper on cycling after it has been revised for sense and edited for word choice and sentences.

> ⟨Training to be a top-notch bicyclist⟩ is ~~my favorite way to~~
> ¶ Though ↓ is   is
> spend ~~time.~~ It's not easy, but it∧definitely worth the effort.
>   I have felt my   grow steadily.
> Since I began training,∧strength and endurance ~~are increasing.~~
>   the recommendations of
> My ~~personal~~ training program is based on∧expert∧advice and my

personal *maximize*
own ^goals. To increase speed and endurance, I concentrate on

power,
developing muscles, ^aerobic endurance, pacing, technique, and

t
las^but not least, enjoyment.

I take
During a week's training, I vary the types of rides ^ Some

conditioning;   *nonstop*
are focused on aerobics,^ which requires steady^pedaling on

challenging
^terrain like hills. Other rides are concentrated on speed.

and try to   *my*
For these, I look for a deserted spot,^cut seconds off^time

by   *achieved some*
^riding the same distance over and over. Once I have gained

gain,   *and riding the same run*
speed,^ I experiment with changing the gears,^^Short rests *periods of slow cycling*

help prevent exhaustion, whereas long rests cause muscles

or sluggish.
to become "cold," ^ When I train for speed, I take short rest

periods between runs.

Therefore,
Technique, of course, is vital to speed. ^ One day a week I

my
devote to developing technique. I work on my style and form,

that my
making sur^e that^ knees are bent,^ back is straight, and that

concentrate on   *ing*
I'm pedaling in concentric circles. I attempt to maintain^ a

cadence.   *e*   *series*   *runs*
steady pedaling motion. I dev^lop a run of fast series, none

e
lasting more than a minute, which will minimize^ strain and

s
With all the hard work, I never
tension.

^But I must not forget enjoyment, for that is the main

k
reason I ride. I^now I must push myself, but not too hard.

If I vary my routes, my pacing, and my techniques, riding

I focus on the overall goal
does not get monotonous. I enjoy the time and effort I put

and purpose of my rides, remembering how good
into training. I feel alive when I ride, looking forward to

I feel when I finish and my training for the day has brought
new rides and speed, so it is worth the pain.

me closer to being the cyclist I want to be

EXERCISE B: Editing for Word Choice and Sentences.
Edit the paragraphs from Exercise A on pages 424 and 425, paying particular attention to word choice and for clear and varied sentences.

EXERCISE C: Revising and Editing Your Paper.
Use the checklists on revising for sense and for editing words and sentences on pages 424 and 425 to revise and edit the paper you wrote for Exercise A on page 422.

Proofreading and Publishing

Proofreading is the final stage in the writing process. It is your chance to make sure that your paper makes the best possible impression on your audience.

Proofreading involves making final corrections in spelling, capitalization, punctuation, and grammar.

You have probably read over your work many times already. This is your last chance to read it over. Approach your paper as an actor does a part he or she has played every night for a month. Approach it anew and with vigor. Challenge yourself to come up with as many errors as you can find in it. When you proofread your paper, make a conscious effort not to read for ideas. Read only for spelling, capitalization, punctuation, and grammar. If you have to correct numerous errors, recopy your paper neatly.

Once you have your final version, you are ready to publish it. This simply means finding the best way to distribute it to your intended audience. In some cases, "publishing" will simply mean giving the paper to the teacher who asked you to write the paper. In other cases, you may submit it to the editor of your school paper or make photocopies for your family and friends.

EXERCISE D: Proofreading a Paragraph. Proofread the following paragraph carefully. Correct any errors that you find in the paragraph in grammar, spelling, punctuation, and capitalization.

   martin watch the kittens playing and thoght that he would like to join in there games the white kitten was at that moment running in circels around the gray one. Who was rollin first to it's left and than to its write in an effort to keep an eye on the white kitten. Suddenly the white kitten, pounced on the gray one. It jump up and run across the room, with the white one in close pursuit martin lauffed as the kittens chast each other aroun the room. How nice it must be to be so carefree. He thought to himself. Finally the kittens dashed out of the room Martin looks after them and turns back to the work he doing.

EXERCISE E: Proofreading Your Paper. Proofread the paper you revised for Exercise B on page 426. If necessary, recopy your paper neatly. Then think of how you want to present your work to your audience.

DEVELOPING WRITING SKILLS: Revising, Proofreading, and Publishing Your Writing. Use the checklists on page 425 to revise the rough draft you wrote for the Developing Writing Skills on page 423. Proofread your final draft and recopy it if necessary. Then, think of ways you can publish your work for your audience.

Writing Workshop: The Writing Process

ASSIGNMENT 1

Topic   Today's Senior Citizens

Form and Purpose   An essay that informs and persuades readers about an issue related to senior citizens

Audience   Readers of newspaper editorials

Length   Four to six pages

Focus   Introduce your narrowed topic and thesis statement in the first paragraph. Support your thesis with facts, details, examples, and reasons. Conclude with a reminder of your thesis and a clincher sentence.

Sources   Magazines, newspapers, television documentaries, interviews, and personal observations

Prewriting   Use the clustering technique to narrow your topic. Then research your topic, write a thesis statement, and prepare an outline.

Writing   Use your outline to write a first draft. Include footnotes if you use information from other sources.

Revising   Use the checklists on page 424 to revise, edit, and proofread your first draft.

19

The Use of Words

When you write, you should try to choose the clearest, most *precise* words you can in order to make your ideas stand out. You should also try to be *concise*, avoiding extra words that get in the way of clear communication. The ideas in the next two sections should help.

19.1 Choosing Precise Words

There are many alternative ways to express any idea. By selecting your words with care, you can make your thoughts come alive for the reader.

Using Action Words

Action is a key part of making writing come alive.

Whenever possible, use action verbs in the active voice.

Action verbs in the active voice add life to your sentences. They also make your sentences easier to understand.

Using Action Verbs. Linking verbs are necessary for expressing some ideas. Too many linking verbs, however, can make your writing dull and lifeless.

If your sentences contain too many linking verbs, you can improve them by using one or more of the following methods.

REPLACING LINKING VERBS WITH ACTION VERBS
Method 1: Change an important noun in the sentence into an action verb.
Method 2: Think of a verb that has a meaning similar to that of one of the important nouns or adjectives in the sentence.
Method 3: If no related verbs come to mind, rephrase your sentence.

In the following examples, weak linking verbs have been replaced with strong action verbs. Notice how much more direct and alive the revised sentences are.

LINKING VERB: the Curies *were* of the belief that they could create a polio vaccine.

ACTION VERB: The Curies *believed* that they could create a polio vaccine. (The noun *belief* changes into the action verb *believed*.)

LINKING VERB: The actor's poor performance *was* a disgrace to the theater company.

ACTION VERB: The actor's poor performance *humiliated* the theater company. (The action verb *humiliated* is related to the noun *disgrace*.)

LINKING VERB: She *was* happy to be asked to take part in the campaign.

ACTION VERB: Being asked to take part in the campaign *delighted* her. (An entirely new sentence expresses the same idea.)

Using the Active Voice. Besides using action verbs, you can make your writing livelier and more direct by using the active voice. Verbs in the passive voice delay what would normally be the subject until the end of the sentence or leave out the normal subject entirely, robbing the reader of useful information.

Notice how much clearer and more precise the following examples are when they are rephrased in the active voice.

PASSIVE: Dave *was followed* into a dark side street by the two sinister-looking men.

ACTIVE: The two sinister-looking men *followed* Dave into a dark side street.

PASSIVE: Money for the new theater *was raised* quickly.

ACTIVE: The committee quickly *raised* money for the new theater.

EXERCISE A: Using Action Verbs in the Active Voice.
Rewrite each sentence, replacing the underlined verb with an action verb in the active voice.

EXAMPLE: The old barn was destroyed by a wind storm.
             A wind storm destroyed the old barn.

1. A roll of twenty-dollar bills was flashed before his eyes by his friend, a braggart.
2. The shortage of heating fuel was a threat to our survival.
3. Her dog should not be permitted to pounce on people.
4. The stories were written by Edgar Allan Poe to frighten readers.
5. Cooler weather and unexpected rains were a relief to our discomfort.
6. A vote was taken by the king's council to determine who would inform the king.
7. The honking of horns is often a violation of local noise ordinances.
8. A musical was presented by the freshman class.
9. After my swim my bed was made, my room was cleaned, and my bathing suit and towel were hung on a chair.
10. The flood in the street was an obstruction to traffic.

Using Specific Words

In addition to using action verbs in the active voice, you can make your writing clearer and more precise by using the most specific words you can find.

Replacing Overly General Words. Words with specific meanings will give your readers a mental picture, let them see what you see, and help them think what you think. Use your imagination, a thesaurus or a dictionary of synonyms, and a little extra time to replace vague words with specific ones.

Choose specific rather than general words to express your ideas precisely.

Just as action verbs are stronger than linking verbs, specific action verbs are stronger than general action verbs. In the following example, a simple action verb has been replaced by a more descriptive action verb.

GENERAL: The injured quarterback *walked* back to the bench.

SPECIFIC: The injured quarterback *hobbled* back to the bench.

Generalizations about people, places, and things also leave the details up to the reader's imagination. Choose specific nouns as well as specific verbs. In the following example, notice how more specific nouns clarify the writer's thoughts.

GENERAL: *Problems* destroyed the *relationship*.

SPECIFIC: *Mistrust and jealousy* destroyed the *friendship*.

You can further sharpen the meaning of your nouns with well-chosen adjectives and specific details. Vague adjectives such as *great* and *tremendous* show your enthusiasm but they add little to your meaning. In the following example, notice how the more colorful adjective, the more specific noun, and the additional details help focus the writer's meaning.

GENERAL: *The Scarlet Letter* is an *interesting* book.

SPECIFIC: *The Scarlet Letter* is a *memorable novel, full of complex characters and dramatic situations.*

Choosing the Right Connotation. The *denotation* of a word is its literal meaning. For example, the denotation of *cabin* is its dictionary definition: "a small, one-story house built simply or crudely, as of logs." The *connotation* is a broader area of meanings that the word suggests. The connotation of the word *cabin* includes the feelings and ideas that people may associate with a cabin: kerosene lamps, the smell of pine trees, wood burning in a fireplace, wild animals, and so on.

To make your words as specific as possible, choose the words with the best connotations for your idea.

You can use your general knowledge of words, a thesaurus, a dictionary of synonyms, or the synonyms given after many words in most dictionaries to find the words with the best connotations for your idea. Consider the words *crafty, shrewd,* and *clever.* These words mean skillful and intelligent but their connotations differ. The following examples show how the connotations of a word change the meaning of a sentence.

CRAFTY: Jill was *crafty* and would sometimes imitate the voices of her three sisters. (*Crafty* has a negative connotation; it implies deception.)

SHREWD: Jill was *shrewd* and would sometimes imitate the voices of her three sisters. (*Shrewd* can also have a negative connotation, although it is not as strong as *crafty*; it implies skill in practical matters.)

CLEVER: Jill was *clever* and would sometimes imitate the voices of her three sisters. (*Clever* has a more positive connotation than the other two words; it suggests that Jill's ability is harmless and playful rather than secretive and deceptive.)

EXERCISE B: Replacing General Words. Rewrite each sentence, replacing the underlined words with more exact expressions.

EXAMPLE: He kicked off his shoes and sat in the hammock.

He kicked off his shoes and stretched out in the hammock.

1. It was funny to see the chimp walk across the floor.
2. With the engine going, the boat began to gain speed.
3. For his birthday, Anthony received presents.
4. He ate his food and then stood.
5. Angrily, the child threw insults at the gang of boys who had taken his bicycle from him.
6. My feelings for my brother grew slowly over the years.
7. When the man said that there was a fire in the building, everyone left.
8. Jeremy was happy to learn that he had won the election.
9. When a secret drawer in the old desk sprang open, Ellen saw the missing will.
10. After the ten-mile hike over rough terrain, John was tired.

434

EXERCISE C: Choosing the Best Connotations. Choose the word in parentheses that best fits the context of the sentence.

EXAMPLE: The pine trees (hovered, towered) over the cabin.

towered

1. The medicine was (important, vital) to the patient's recovery.
2. Although my pride was (maimed, hurt), I didn't show my embarrassment.
3. Except for the (solitary, single) figure in the distance, we could see no one in the vast, golden-green fields.
4. Randy (overshadowed, dominated) the conversation by talking loudly.
5. Because he has no interests of his own, Mr. Ratchet is always (prying, inquiring) into other people's business.
6. The (slender, scrawny) model displayed the latest style in skirts.
7. The constant (uproar, noise) from the party next door made it impossible to concentrate.
8. The council member refused to (move, budge) from his position on the issue.
9. According to the (list, schedule), we were supposed to be in the gym during second period.
10. The messenger (said, reported) that the opposing troops had turned and fled.

Using Vivid Words

To make your writing more interesting, strive to avoid expressions and words that are overused or worn out.

Replace overused and worn-out phrases with original expressions.

Vivid descriptions have a better chance of holding a reader's attention, and learning how to create them may help you to clarify your ideas.

Avoiding Clichés. An expression that is used often and is too familiar is called a *cliché*. In the following examples, the clichés have been rewritten. Notice that original descriptive phrases give a clearer picture than the clichés do.

CLICHÉ:	The flat tire was *the last straw* for Ryan.
REVISED:	The flat tire made Ryan explode with anger.
CLICHÉ:	For the retreat, the faculty chose a site *out in the boondocks*.
REVISED:	For the retreat, the faculty chose a site away from hamburger stands, movie theaters, and paved roads.

Avoiding Dead Metaphors. *Dead metaphors* are a particular kind of cliché. They are comparisons that have lost their power to evoke a visual image. Like other clichés, dead metaphors add nothing to your writing. Expressions such as *head honcho* and *bone of contention* weaken your writing by making it predictable.

The following examples show how to correct dead metaphors.

DEAD METAPHOR:	For years Jimmy Valentine had eluded *the long arm of the law*.
REVISED:	For years Jimmy Valentine had eluded all of the posses that had pursued him.
DEAD METAPHOR:	Pat's plan to involve more ninth graders in the broadcasting club was *rocking the boat*.
REVISED:	Pat's plan to involve more ninth graders in the broadcasting club provoked shouts of disagreement.

EXERCISE D: Using Vivid Words. Rewrite each sentence, replacing clichés and dead metaphors with original expressions.

EXAMPLE:	The principal called us on the carpet for being rude to Mr. Fowler.
	The principal severely reprimanded us for being rude to Mr. Fowler.

1. His grades took a nose dive.
2. We began our march at the crack of dawn.
3. An amusement park can be a barrel of fun.
4. Beyond a shadow of a doubt, Tom drew this.
5. When the truck backfired, I nearly jumped out of my skin.

6. Jim was as sick as a dog, so he couldn't drive us to the show.

7. Marjorie looked as cool as a cucumber when she told the bully to leave her alone, but I think she was really quaking in her boots.

8. The music from the cafeteria was coming through to the science lab as clear as a bell.

9. Although the icy cold winds whistled outside the house, inside we were as warm as toast.

10. The rock singer was a legend in her own time.

Using Words That Fit Your Tone

The words you choose often express your attitude toward your subject. For example, if you are writing about something that makes you angry, your words may reflect your anger. You may also find that your words reflect the audience for whom you are writing. For example, when you are writing a business letter, your words will probably be formal and businesslike.

The attitude that your writing reflects toward both your subject and your readers is called *tone*. Within any particular piece of writing, you should always strive for a consistent tone. Decide if you are going to be serious, amusing, friendly and informal, or businesslike and formal. Then use words that fit that tone.

Select words that maintain a consistent tone.

Just as clichés and dead metaphors can weaken your writing, so can confusing the tone by suddenly using inappropriate words. In particular, you should avoid *self-important language, flowery language, slang,* and *jargon.*

Avoiding Self-Important Language. Self-important language tries to sound impressive but winds up being merely long-winded and vague. It can ruin the tone of an otherwise clear passage.

To avoid self-important language, be careful not to overdo formality with vague, general nouns and long verbs ending in *-ate* or *-ize.* In the following example, notice that the revised passage is appropriately formal, yet it is much clearer and to the point, presenting the same information but in a much more natural way.

SELF-IMPORTANT:	*Familiarity* with the *baccalaureate require-ments* of the *higher education system* will help you to *prioritize* your *credit sequence.*
REVISED:	Finding out which courses the college requires for graduation will help you decide which ones to take first.

Avoiding Flowery Language. Good writing should contain vivid words but should never become overloaded with flowery adjectives and adverbs that try too hard to sound poetic. To avoid flowery language in your own writing, you should learn to recognize when modifiers are acting merely as useless decoration and then look for a simpler way to express your ideas.

One sentence with flowery language spoils the tone of the following description. When the passage is revised, it remains descriptive but is much more consistent in tone.

FLOWERY:	*Poor Rosalind wandered aimlessly and sadly, all alone amongst the lonely bushes and weeping trees.* Looking at the moon, she remembered her home and wept.
REVISED:	Sad and lonely, Rosalind wandered through the woods. Looking at the moon, she remembered her home and wept.

Avoiding Slang. Slang is made up of informal expressions that are popular with certain groups of people, generally for only a brief period of time. Because it is so informal, slang draws attention to itself and can disrupt the flow of your writing. Except in dialogue and casual letters to friends, you should avoid using slang when you are writing.

In the following example, the slang phrase is not consistent with the tone of the rest of the sentence. Notice that the revised passage corrects the inconsistency by replacing the slang expression with an appropriate phrase.

SLANG:	Mike's father reprimanded him for coming home three hours late; my father also *gave me grief* for coming home late.
REVISED:	Mike's father reprimanded him for coming home three hours late; my father also criticized me for coming home late.

438

Avoiding Jargon. Inappropriate technical language, called jargon, can also disrupt the tone of your writing. In addition, the use of terms limited to a narrow field may confuse general readers.

The following examples show how jargon can be eliminated so that ideas are expressed more clearly.

JARGON: The skipper let the boat *fall off* when he saw the sail *luff*.

REVISED: The skipper angled the boat away from the wind when the forward edge of the sail began to flap.

JARGON: Because the *amplitude of inertial-gravity waves is sufficiently small in the atmosphere,* they do not noticeably affect the *Rossby waves.*

REVISED: Sound waves in the atmosphere generally do not affect the movement of the air that creates our weather.

EXERCISE E: **Maintaining a Consistent Tone.** Label the type of language used in each sentence as *self-important, flowery, slang,* or *jargon.* Then rewrite each sentence, using a consistent tone appropriate for a general audience. If you do not understand the jargon, use a dictionary.

EXAMPLE: I just about blew my cool when she accused me of cheating on the exam.

(Slang) I almost lost my temper when she accused me of cheating on the exam.

1. The shimmering, silver rays of the pale, voluminous moon pierced the dim, misty haze that arose from the waters of the dark, murky swamp.
2. What a bummer it was to spend five dollars to see a movie that was a total bomb.
3. As he snuck back to the hideout, Gary kept glancing nervously over his shoulder. He was afraid he had blown his cover.
4. That editorial certainly does a number on the hypocrites who say they support conservation yet drive around in big gas guzzlers.
5. According to Sheldon's theory concerning human physique,

endomorphs will tend to exhibit greater insecurity than mesomorphs.

6. The blazing fire crackled louder and louder, and the flames leapt up toward the distant heavens. At last, the fearless firefighters brought the destructive inferno under control, quenching the towering blaze until it was just a smoldering heap of ashes.
7. Over the next few annual periods, we will need to conceptualize the necessary changes and see that they are properly effected.
8. During the interphase stage of mitosis, chromosomes duplicate to form identical sets of genes.
9. Roger says that he is flat broke.
10. Worn-out shocks cause a rough ride, while poor wheel alignment can cause tires to wear faster or even damage the suspension.

DEVELOPING WRITING SKILLS: Using Precise Words.
Rewrite the following composition, eliminating the imprecise and inappropriate expressions.

(1) When it was discovered that Jake Slattery had skipped out of Silvertown in the dead of night, suspicions were immediately aroused. (2) It was shown in a quick investigation of his bank account that the old duffer had withdrawn every last penny of his savings. (3) Even the sheriff joined in the search because Jake had recently borrowed some money from him and had given an IOU to the sheriff's daughter.

(4) It soon dawned on the townspeople that Jake had borrowed money from several people and was in debt to most of the local merchants. (5) To find the sly dude, the townspeople had a posse formed and sent out an all-points bulletin for Jake's arrest.

(6) But Jake had conspired his own escape carefully in advance. (7) Aware that he was doing a dirty deed, he had assumed an artful disguise, capable of escaping the detection of even the most careful, inquisitive observer. (8) He had also purchased a new horse in the next town. (9) By taking a seldom-used route, Jake soon cleared out of the territory, just in the nick of time! (10) Alas, terribly angry, resentful, and frustrated to the depths of their being at a monetary loss, the posse could find no trace of the bad-news guy.

440

Using Words Concisely 19.2

Unnecessary words, phrases, and clauses muddle ideas and slow readers down. Even if your ideas are vividly expressed and your sentences are grammatically correct, a wordy style can make your writing sound heavy and dull. You can avoid these traps and make your writing not only vivid but also clear and concise.

Eliminating Deadwood

Unnecessary words and phrases are called *deadwood.* Deadwood includes *empty words* that pad your sentences as well as *hedging words* that sap the strength of your writing.

Eliminate deadwood—empty words and hedging words—from your sentences.

Empty words lengthen sentences. They are often used to make writing sound important, but they actually give writing a false ring. They also delay readers and make a writer's ideas sound shallow. The following chart gives just a few examples of words that can make sentences longer than they really need to be.

EMPTY WORDS		
is a great deal of	I think that	the thing that
by way of	it is a fact that	the type of
for the reason that	it is true that	to the extent that
in my opinion	there are	what I mean is
is of the opinion that	there is	what I want is

Hedging words suggest that the writer is not sure of his or her ideas. Words such as *kind of* and *sort of* imply that the writer is afraid to take a stand. Try to make definite statements unless you *must* be indefinite. The following chart lists some of the most common hedging words.

HEDGING WORDS					
almost	it seems	kind of	rather	somewhat	sort of

441

Whenever you find yourself using deadwood, cut out the unnecessary words and rephrase your ideas as necessary. Notice how the following sentences with deadwood have been rewritten.

WITH DEADWOOD: *It is a fact that* sunspot activity affects our weather.

CONCISE: Sunspot activity affects our weather.

WITH DEADWOOD: *I think that* everyone should go to the game *for the reason that* our team needs our support.

CONCISE: Everyone should go to the game to support our team.

WITH DEADWOOD: The car wash was *kind of* a failure because only ten people came to help.

CONCISE: The car wash was a failure because only ten people came to help.

EXERCISE A: Eliminating Deadwood. Rewrite each sentence, eliminating the underlined words and rephrasing the sentence as necessary.

EXAMPLE: In the opinion of my teacher I am a good reader.

My teacher believes I am a good reader.

1. The solution to this question is an answer that is simple.
2. Johnny's feelings changed greatly in the way that he felt toward his work.
3. Wrap the crystal sort of carefully and then pack it rather neatly.
4. The thing that bothers me is that this will take hours.
5. What I mean is that he was somewhat upset about losing.
6. It is a fact that there are dozens of new families that move into Cuyloga Village each month.
7. It was with great reluctance that Samantha turned in her half-completed report.
8. There were many people in her life whom she admired.
9. The turning point of the game was the time when Harrison fumbled the ball.
10. It seems that the sky is beginning to cloud over, and it almost looks as if it's going to rain.

Avoiding Redundancy

Redundancy is the unnecessary repetition of an idea. In a redundant sentence, the writer might, for example, use a modifier that repeats the meaning of the word it modifies, as in a *written letter* (all letters are written). Like deadwood, redundancy makes writing heavy and dull.

Eliminate redundant modifiers in your sentences.

In the following sentences, the redundant words and phrases have been identified for you.

REDUNDANT: Pierre's departure left an *empty* void in her heart.

PROBLEM: A *void* is already *empty*.

CONCISE: Pierre's departure left a void in her heart.

REDUNDANT: The consensus *of opinion* in our class is that we should plan a field trip.

PROBLEM: *Consensus* means "majority opinion."

CONCISE: The consensus in our class is that we should plan a field trip.

REDUNDANT: A brown bear, large *in size,* ambled up to us.

PROBLEM: *In size* repeats the idea that *large* is a size.

CONCISE: A large brown bear ambled up to us.

EXERCISE B: Eliminating Redundancy. Rewrite each of the following sentences, eliminating the redundant word or phrase.

EXAMPLE: The twins were both similar in personality and appearance.

The twins were similar in personality and appearance.

1. To solve these problems, we must cooperate together.
2. After the play's final conclusion, the audience applauded.
3. Our new school, rectangular in shape, is low to the ground.
4. As the mixture became darker in color, it also hardened.
5. When the engine exploded, hot, boiling oil flowed in every direction.

6. His spitefully nasty remarks turned us against him.
7. I have never read a book so confusing and difficult to understand.
8. Shivering in the cold rain, the stray dog was a pitiful, sad sight.
9. University institutions of higher learning demand hard work and long hours.
10. I was unable to pack the many separate pieces of my project into my suitcase.

Simplifying Wordy Phrases and Clauses

Like deadwood and redundancy, wordy phrases and clauses can weaken your writing by causing ideas to lose their sharpness and impact.

Shorten wordy phrases and clauses when you can do so without changing the meaning of a sentence.

Many wordy phrases can be replaced by single words. Wordy clauses can sometimes be rewritten to form shorter sentence parts such as appositive and prepositional phrases.

Reducing Wordy Phrases. You can improve many sentences by replacing prepositional phrases with single adjectives, adverbs, or possessive nouns. Notice the conciseness of the following revised sentences.

WORDY: Sharon replied *in a loud voice* to every question the teacher asked.

CONCISE: Sharon replied *loudly* to every question the teacher asked.

WORDY: Many immigrants *from Spain and Portugal* have settled in New England.

CONCISE: Many *Spanish and Portuguese* immigrants have settled in New England.

WORDY: We found the hiding place *of the pirates* by nightfall.

CONCISE: We found the *pirates'* hiding place by nightfall.

Reducing Wordy Clauses. If you use many adjective clauses that begin with *which is* or *who are* or *that was,* you can probably eliminate some excess words. Simplify these clauses by dropping the subject and verb of the clause as well as other unnecessary words. In the following example, the clause becomes a participial phrase.

WORDY: She wore a medallion *that was made of pure gold*.

CONCISE: She wore a medallion *made of pure gold*.

You can shorten a wordy adjective clause to form a participial phrase, a prepositional phrase, an appositive phrase, part of a compound verb or subject complement, or a single word. Notice how the wordy clauses in the following examples are simplified.

WORDY: We finally found Matthew, *who was hiding in the attic*.

CONCISE: We finally found Matthew *hiding in the attic*.

WORDY: Quito, *which is the capital of Ecuador*, lies near the equator.

CONCISE: Quito, *the capital of Ecuador*, lies near the equator.

WORDY: Our 1920 car, *which ran faithfully for my grandparents and my parents*, finally broke down for me.

CONCISE: Our 1920 car *ran faithfully for my grandparents and my parents but* finally broke down for me.

EXERCISE C: Simplifying Wordy Phrases and Clauses.
Rewrite each of the following sentences to shorten a phrase or a clause.

EXAMPLE: The article that was in the newspaper mentioned Mother.

The newspaper article mentioned Mother.

1. Did you remember to take the socks and shirts that were in the dryer?
2. In the 1500's and 1600's, explorers from Europe claimed lands along the North American coast.
3. The statue, which is in the center of the park, commemorates an American victory in the Revolutionary War.
4. Our flight attendant, who brought our meal, also gave us pillows and headphones.

445

5. Christopher Columbus, who was the head of the expedition, sailed in the *Santa Maria*.
6. The first name of the boy is Michael.
7. Lynn cried in a desperate way when her pet fawn died.
8. At one time, Great Britain, which was the world's major colonial power, was also the leading industrial nation.
9. A band of odd-looking people appeared at the gates of the village.
10. Seedlings that are planted too early are often killed by frost.

DEVELOPING WRITING SKILLS: Writing Concise Sentences. Rewrite the following composition, making it more concise.

(1) In his costume as a clown and with his pet, which was a monkey, on his shoulder, Walter looked perfectly ridiculous. (2) He wore enormous red shoes on his feet and a puffy, frizzy wig that was red. (3) There was clown makeup on his face, and it was brightly colored in vivid, contrasting shades of yellow, red, purple, and green. (4) The way he walked, which was like a duck, was something that made us all laugh.

(5) The mistake that Walter made was bringing his pet monkey: The monkey was sort of funnier than Walter. (6) What I mean is that the monkey, who was wearing a party hat, stole the show. (7) It seems that the monkey would tip the hat that he wore every time Walter finished telling a funny joke. (8) Truly, the gesture of the monkey, as well as the look of pride on its face, made everyone roar in a hysterical way. (9) Poor Walter finally realized the fact that he had been upstaged by the monkey. (10) He vowed to change his act in a major way, to the extent that he would leave the monkey home next time.

Skills Review and Writing Workshop

The Use of Words

CHECKING YOUR SKILLS

Rewrite the following paragraph to make it more precise, concise, vivid, and consistent in tone.

(1) Mexico is an interesting country. (2) For years its rulers were the Aztec people. (3) They were conquered in the 16th century by the Spanish conquistador Herman Cortez. (4) The Spanish seemed to sort of transform the country almost overnight. (5) They had new customs, a new language, and new styles of architecture. (6) Some of the buildings they erected were as pretty as a picture. (7) A capital, Mexico City, was built by them on the site of the old Aztec capital. (8) Today Mexico City is a veritable treasure trove filled with innumerable historical relics and artistic achievements with which all travelers should familiarize themselves. (9) Visitors who do so will get a sense of the past history of Mexico. (10) Like, wow, it's a neat place to discover.

USING COMPOSITION SKILLS IN WRITING
Writing a Science Article

Writers know that they can have the greatest impact on their readers by using clear, precise words. Imagine you work for a natural science magazine. Write a short article about a natural event. Make your writing as precise, vidid, and concise as possible by following these steps.

Prewriting: Select an event that interests you, such as a thunderstorm or an eclipse. Find out about the reasons why the event occurs and the sequence it follows.

Writing: Begin with the highlight of the event to catch the reader's attention. Then describe the order in which the event occurs and the scientific reasons why it happens.

Revising: Look over your work and change any words that could be more precise or vivid. After you have revised, proofread carefully.

Chapter 20

Sentence Style

This chapter will show you several ways to improve the style of your sentences and add life to your writing. First, it will show you how to combine sentences. Then it will show you how you can maintain interest by varying the lengths, openings, and structures of your sentences. Finally, it will help you clarify the connections between your ideas.

20.1 Sentence Combining

If you rely on too many short sentences, your writing can seem choppy and disconnected. You can overcome excessive use of short sentences by combining some of them to make longer sentences.

Combining Ideas

You can correct short sentences by grouping your ideas to create longer, smoother sentences.

Combine short sentences by using compound subjects or verbs, phrase modifiers, compound sentences, complex sentences, or compound-complex sentences.

The following charts illustrate ways to combine sentences. The first chart shows how you can combine two or more short simple sentences by using a compound subject or a compound verb.

USING A COMPOUND SUBJECT OR VERB
Forming Compound Subjects
Mosquitoes bother Sam when he is out camping. Other insects also annoy him.   *Mosquitoes* and *other insects* annoy Sam when he is out camping.
Forming Compound Verbs
The audience applauded for fifteen minutes. They shouted for an encore.   The audience *applauded* for fifteen minutes and *shouted* for an encore.

You can also turn a simple sentence into a phrase—such as a prepositional phrase, an appositive phrase, or an infinitive phrase—and add it to another sentence.

TURNING A SENTENCE INTO A PHRASE
Turning a Sentence into a Prepositional Phrase
The weather-beaten house needed a good paint job. It was at the end of our block.   The weather-beaten house *at the end of our block* needed a good paint job.
Turning a Sentence into an Appositive Phrase
The prominent lawyer represented us in court. She is a close friend of the family.   The prominent lawyer, *a close friend of the family,* represented us in court.
Turning a Sentence into an Infinitive Phrase
Follow these instructions. Assemble the radio.   Follow these instructions *to assemble the radio.*

In many cases, you will want to join simple sentences by forming compound, complex, or compound-complex sentences, using coordinating or subordinating conjunctions.

449

CHANGING SENTENCE STRUCTURES

Making a Compound Sentence

Jane wanted to accept the job. Unfortunately, she had drama rehearsals after school.

Jane wanted to accept the job, *but* she had drama rehearsals after school.

Making a Complex Sentence

The volcano was going to erupt. The villagers were evacuated quickly.

Since the volcano was going to erupt, the villagers were evacuated quickly.

Making a Compound-Complex Sentence

He stared out the window. He didn't notice the change. The sky had grown suddenly very dark.

He stared out the window, *yet* he didn't notice that the sky had grown suddenly very dark.

EXERCISE: Combining Sentences. Combine the sentences in each item.

EXAMPLE: Wes and Ted bicycled about twenty-five miles a day. They stayed in youth hostels.

Wes and Ted bicycled about twenty-five miles a day and stayed in youth hostels.

1. The dazed guests stumbled out of the house. The host called the police to report the fire.
2. Last year, farmers turned the soil in the north field. Then they planted soybeans and corn.
3. The moon rose over the hills. It cast long shadows across the valley.
4. A hand is a unit of measure used to specify the height of a horse. It equals four inches.
5. At the picnic we had some special games. We had an egg toss, a pie-eating contest, a bake-off, and a three-legged race.
6. Amelia Earhart was the first woman to earn a license to fly.

450

She was also the first woman to fly across the Atlantic Ocean.

7. In 1937 Amelia Earhart attempted to fly around the world alone. Her plane disappeared in the South Pacific without a trace.

8. Tourists on the West Coast and the East Coast have recently begun to take small boats out in the ocean. They watch passing schools of whales.

9. The idea of the Frisbee originated in the 1940's. People working at a bakery used to toss tin pie plates during their lunch hour.

10. Last summer Ruth and Renee went on a long bicycle trip. They traveled for two weeks. They averaged about fifteen miles per day on hilly roads.

DEVELOPING WRITING SKILLS: Further Practice in Combining Sentences. Combine the sentences in each item. Try to use a variety of methods.

EXAMPLE: The goalie darted to the left. He almost blocked the goal.

Darting to the left, the goalie almost blocked the goal.

1. The eruption of a volcano can be destructive. Volcanic eruptions also enrich the soil and bring water up to the surface.

2. Mount Pelée is in Martinique. Kilhauea is in Hawaii. They are both active volcanoes.

3. Snow began to fall in the morning. Six inches had accumulated by evening.

4. A reporter for a newspaper is very busy. However, the city desk editor is even busier.

5. A reporter tracks down the details of a story and then writes an article. The editor must be familiar with all of the developing stories to choose which ones to print.

6. She walked down the road. She looked up into the trees. She saw a parrot.

7. A star called SS 433 puzzles astronomers. It seems to be moving both toward and away from the earth. No other star acts that way.

8. The star's apparent movement is hard to explain. It could be a neutron star. It could also be a dying star.
9. The star is 10,000 light years away. The star cannot be seen without a telescope.
10. In 1930 scientists discovered the planet we now call Pluto. Pluto was the last of the planets in our solar system to be discovered.

20.2 Varying Your Sentences

When you are writing, you should always try to vary your sentences. If all your sentences are the same length or all begin the same way, a passage may seem dull. Variety holds the reader's interest.

There are certain specific problems to watch for. If a passage is choppy, you probably have too many short simple sentences. If a passage seems to ramble, you probably have too many long compound or complex sentences. If a passage seems repetitious, you may not have varied your sentence openers and structures enough.

This section will discuss ways to avoid these problems in style and achieve variety in your writing.

Expanding Short Sentences

Short sentences are sometimes appropriate. A series of short sentences, however, will often sound choppy. The many pauses at the ends of the sentences will tire the reader.

You can overcome this problem by combining sentences. You can also expand short sentences by adding details.

Short sentences can be lengthened by adding details that develop the subject, verb, or complement.

Phrases that describe, rename, or develop your basic ideas make for longer, more interesting sentences.

Notice how the subjects, verbs, and complements of the short sentences in the following chart have been lengthened and developed with prepositional, infinitive, appositive, and participial phrases.

ADDING DETAILS TO SIMPLE SENTENCES

Developing the Subject

A plane eased away from the terminal.	A plane *bound for Europe* eased away from the terminal.

Developing the Verb

The plane accelerated.	The plane accelerated *rapidly to gain momentum for takeoff.*

Developing the Complement

The plane left the runway.	The plane left the runway, *a shrinking black ribbon bordered with flashing blue lights.*
The clouds were a cocoon.	The clouds were a cocoon *surrounding the plane with darkness.*

EXERCISE A: Adding Details to Short Sentences. Improve each sentence by adding the phrase in parentheses.

EXAMPLE: The river flooded the streets. (swollen by rain)

The river, swollen by rain, flooded the streets.

1. We must develop new sources of energy. (to provide for the future as well as the present)
2. The teller counted one-dollar bills. (slowly and tediously)
3. The bicycle rider crossed the finish line. (followed closely by an enthusiastically cheering crowd)
4. The noise came from beneath the water. (of the scuba divers salvaging the downed submarine)
5. The hikers returned. (eager to tell about their adventure)
6. Beetles and aphids can destroy gardens. (by stripping the leaves from the plants in only a few days)
7. Football is an exhausting game. (even for the cheering fans in their armchairs at home)
8. The paper was full of mistakes. (not only in spelling and punctuation, but in grammar as well)
9. My aunt went on a trip to Ireland. (originally from Dublin)
10. We headed toward the bank with our first paychecks. (with a growing sense of self-satisfaction)

Shortening Long Sentences

Just as too many short sentences can hurt the flow of a passage, so can trying to put too many ideas into a few long, rambling sentences. If most of your sentences seem long and involved, you are probably overusing compound, complex, and compound-complex sentences.

You can, however, learn to separate thoughts to make them clearer. You can break some compound or compound-complex sentences into two or more sentences to achieve variety. Sometimes you may also want to break long complex sentences into separate simple sentences, but you should remember that most complex sentences are useful in showing precise relationships between ideas. Remember also that you want to achieve variety. Not all long sentences should be divided.

Long, involved sentences can be broken into shorter, simpler sentences.

Notice how the following long compound-complex sentence seems to drag on while the thoughts become lost.

One long, involved sentence
> The snow had begun to fall early in the morning and by six o'clock that evening had accumulated to more than fifteen inches, and while the weather reports predicted fifteen more inches of snow, icy winds were blowing up to thirty miles per hour, causing huge snow drifts to form, which would trap some people in their homes for three days.

When this long sentence is broken up into several shorter sentences, the passage becomes clearer and more readable.

Shorter, more readable sentences
> The snow had begun to fall early in the morning and by six o'clock that evening had accumulated to more than fifteen inches. While the weather reports predicted fifteen more inches of snow, icy winds were blowing up to thirty miles per hour, causing huge snowdrifts to form. These drifts would trap some people in their homes for three days.

EXERCISE B: Shortening Long Sentences. Divide each long sentence into two or more shorter, clearer sentences.

454

EXAMPLE: When Jerry turned the ignition key in the car, it made a clicking noise, but the motor did not start because, as the mechanic later explained, the battery was dead.

When Jerry turned the ignition key in the car, he heard a clicking noise, but the motor did not start. As the mechanic later explained, the car's battery was dead.

1. Ants are warlike creatures, and they are natural empire builders, so they attack weaker insects to increase the numbers of their slaves and the size of their territory.

2. The boat's crew located the sound and used radar to track its course through the harbor but could not identify the sound, and whatever lurked beneath the surface circled the area for almost thirty minutes.

3. Gale-force winds buffeted the tiny seacoast village, including Judd Beere's old, single-masted sloop, which was tied to the rotting town dock, and the sloop's lines strained against rusty cleats until first one and then another gave way.

4. Helen was determined to compete in the marathon and had been training for the race for several months by exercising and running one mile each morning and five miles each afternoon.

5. The amount of energy that a specific food provides is determined by burning the food in an instrument called a calorimeter, which records the amount of heat given off by the burning food in calories, one of which is equal to the amount of heat necessary to raise temperature of one thousand grams of water 1°C.

Using Different Sentence Openers

In addition to writing sentences of varied lengths, you can improve your writing by varying your sentence openers. If all of your sentences begin the same way, with a subject, for example, your sentences will begin to sound alike even though the ideas are different. Your reader may tire of knowing exactly how each sentence will begin. By using many different sentence openers, you can hold your reader's attention.

Vary sentence openers, using one-word modifiers, phrases, and clauses.

Sentences often begin with a subject, but there are many other ways a sentence can begin. The following chart shows some of the most commonly used openers.

WAYS TO BEGIN SENTENCES
With a Subject
Subject: The *crowd* cheered the visiting diplomat.
Subject: They refused to hear our side of the issue.
With a One-Word Modifier
Adjective: Furious, the actor threw down the script.
Adverb: Swiftly, the large birds swooped down from the tree.
With a Phrase
Prepositional phrase: With great difficulty I unlocked the attic door.
Participial phrase: Trudging up the stairs, he dropped the carton of milk.
Infinitive phrase: To learn the dance routine, she practiced two hours a day.
With a Clause
Adverb clause: Because Juneau, Alaska, is surrounded by a glacial ridge, it can't be reached by car.

Notice that a sentence beginning with a subject is different in sound and even in meaning from a sentence beginning with a one-word modifier, a phrase, or a clause. *The furious actor threw down the script* differs in sound and even in meaning from *Furious, the actor threw down the script.* Experiment with all these ways of starting sentences to achieve variety.

EXERCISE C: Identifying Sentence Openers. Label each sentence opener as a *subject,* a *one-word modifier,* a *phrase,* or a *clause.*

EXAMPLE: Like a carefree seagull, the hang glider hovered over the waves.

phrase

1. When the storm ended, we inspected the barn for damage.
2. Proudly, the marchers strutted down the boulevard waving their flags.
3. The mayor feared a drop in the city's mass transit income.
4. To do somersaults on a trampoline, you need good balance.
5. Hissing loudly, the cat backed away from the curious puppy.
6. Lost, the three-year-old sat down on the curb and cried.
7. Pedro earned letters in three varsity sports.
8. In the street eighty floors below, the taxis darted to and fro like yellow bugs.
9. While Angie entertained the guests, Karl made dinner.
10. Usually, the local bus runs on schedule on weekdays.

EXERCISE D: Using Different Sentence Openers. Rewrite each sentence to make it begin with a one-word modifier, a phrase, or a clause.

EXAMPLE: You should pass the test if you review your notes.

If you review your notes, you should pass the test.

1. You should read the instructions carefully before you assemble a model.
2. Carol, insulted, turned on her heel and stalked out.
3. The cars on the highway were backed up for miles because of a jackknifed tractor-trailer.
4. The auditorium was filled with the sound of cheering at the end of the graduation ceremony.
5. The spacecraft encountered the other ship at 1300 hours.
6. The governess happily waved to Meg on the Ferris wheel.
7. See the dentist at least twice a year to check for cavities and other problems.
8. A mid-afternoon solar eclipse predictably drew hundreds of onlookers into the street.
9. Chicago was a thriving young city when the great fire erupted.
10. The actor enthusiastically campaigned for the senator.

Using Different Sentence Structures

In addition to using a variety of sentence openers, you can further improve your writing by varying the structures of your sentences.

Use a variety of sentence structures in a passage.

Too many simple sentences can make your writing monotonous. The following passage is made up entirely of simple sentences. If you read the passage aloud, you will see that repeating the same sentence structure over and over creates a predictable, lifeless rhythm.

Monotonous passage with all simple sentences

I moved from California to New Jersey. I had to adjust to a different climate. California has a much milder climate. It has less contrast between the seasons. In California you may never have to cancel a picnic. It hardly ever rains. You may not have enough water to water your lawn or wash your car. In New Jersey rain falls every season. You cannot always plan on good weather, even in the summer. The rain keeps your lawn green and helps your flowers grow. You can wash your car anytime.

When the same passage is rewritten using sentences of several different structures—a mixture of simple, compound, and complex sentences—the passage becomes easier to read. The variety of structures makes the passage not only livelier but clearer.

Revised passage with a variety of sentence structures

When I moved from California to New Jersey, I had to adjust to a different climate. California has a milder climate than New Jersey, with less contrast between the seasons. In California you may never have to cancel a picnic because of the rain. Then again, you may not have enough water to water your lawn or wash your car. In New Jersey, on the other hand, rain falls every season, so you cannot always plan on good weather, even in the summer. However, the rain does keep your lawn green and helps your flowers grow, and you can water your lawn.

EXERCISE E: Using Different Sentence Structures. Rewrite the passage below using a variety of sentence structures.

(1) Ted had never skied before. (2) He was having trouble with his skis. (3) He edged his long skis toward the chairlift. (4) The next chair would soon round the curve. (5) Standing next to him was Beth. (6) She was a good skier. (7) They waited for the chair to scoop them up. (8) Ted bit his lip to control his shaking. (9) He maneuvered his skis onto the platform. (10) Then he put his poles in his right hand. (11) He turned and reached with his left hand. (12) The chair arrived. (13) Ted took a deep breath. (14) He sat down with a slap. (15) He and Beth swung up the mountain. (16) They were high above the skiers. (17) Beth smiled at him. (18) "Good job," she said. (19) He felt safe at last. (20) Soon, however, they arrived at the top of a steep slope.

DEVELOPING WRITING SKILLS: Writing Varied Sentences. Rewrite the following composition, varying the lengths, openers, and structures of the sentences.

(1) Kangaroos are remarkable creatures. (2) They should delight even the most casual animal watcher. (3) They are sweet-faced. (4) They are furry. (5) They are a little bottom-heavy. (6) This makes them look almost comical. (7) But kangaroos are aces in sports. (8) They are remarkably coordinated. (9) They are excellent in jumping. (10) They are also good at a kangaroo version of karate.

(11) The largest male kangaroos are called boomers, and they can measure as much as seven feet in height standing erect and can weigh as much as two hundred pounds and can easily run at speeds of twelve to fifteen miles per hour for considerable distances. (12) They can reach speeds of more than thirty miles an hour for shorter distances.

(13) Kangaroos appear to be timid. (14) However, they will fight if the need arises. (15) When they are attacked, kangaroos kick powerfully with their hind feet. (16) Their hind feet have razor-sharp claws. (17) Their tails are also useful in fighting. (18) A kangaroo's tail is used for balance. (19) It gives the kangaroo leverage when it kicks. (20) Kangaroos are not as defenseless as they may at first seem.

459

20.3 Making Clear Connections

In addition to varying your sentences, you can make your writing style smoother by showing clear connections between ideas. Words and phrases that connect your ideas from sentence to sentence are called *transitions*. You can also link ideas within individual sentences, making use of either *coordination* or *subordination*.

Using Transitions

You can often improve your sentences by supplying transitions between sentences that might otherwise be misunderstood. Generally coming at or near the beginning of sentences, transitions prepare the reader for the idea that follows. They tell the reader that events happened in a particular order, that there is a contrasting idea ahead, or that another example is coming up.

Use transitions between sentences to clarify relationships between ideas.

Transitions connect ideas by establishing relationships, such as *time, contrast, result,* and *addition,* between the ideas. The following chart presents some of the transitions most commonly used to show these relationships.

TRANSITIONS GROUPED BY KINDS OF RELATIONSHIP				
Time			**Contrast**	
after	earlier	meanwhile	however	nevertheless
afterward	final	since	in contrast	on the contrary
before	first	then	indeed	on the other hand
during	later	until	instead	yet
Result			**Addition or Example**	
as a result	so		also	furthermore
because	then		and	in addition
consequently	therefore		besides	moreover
on account of	thus		for example	too

The following examples show how transitions can connect sentences. The sentences without transitions seem disjointed. The corrected versions, however, clarify the ideas by showing time, contrast, result, or addition. Notice that a transition need not always fall at the beginning of the second sentence.

UNCONNECTED: We played ten innings of softball on the field.
We piled into the tractor for a ride to the pond.

PROBLEM: When did these actions take place?

WITH A TRANSITION
SHOWING TIME: We played ten innings of softball on the field. *Later in the afternoon,* we piled into the tractor for a ride to the pond.

UNCONNECTED: The dragons in Tolkien's books are dangerous enemies of people, elves, and dwarves.
McCaffrey's dragons are loyal, obedient companions to the men and women who ride them.

PROBLEM: What is the relationship between the two descriptions of dragons?

WITH A TRANSITION
SHOWING CONTRAST: The dragons in Tolkien's books are dangerous enemies of people, elves, and dwarves. McCaffrey's dragons, *however,* are loyal, obedient companions to the men and women who ride them.

UNCONNECTED: The cable cars stopped running at midnight.
The tourists walked fifteen blocks up and down the hills to their car.

PROBLEM: A reader might guess that the tourists walked because of the cable cars' stopping but cannot be sure of the connection between the ideas.

WITH A TRANSITION
SHOWING RESULT: The cable cars stopped running at midnight. *Consequently,* the tourists walked ten blocks up and down the hills to their car.

UNCONNECTED: Many writers of science fiction use imaginary worlds to make serious comments about modern problems. *Star Trek* often focused on the problem of competition for natural resources.

PROBLEM: The reader must guess whether or not the second sentence elaborates on the first.

461

Many writers of science fiction use imaginary worlds to make serious comments about modern problems. *Star Trek, for example,* often focused on the problem of competition for natural resources.

EXERCISE A: Using Transitions. Improve each pair of sentences by adding the kind of transition shown in parentheses.

EXAMPLE: Terri finished putting the final coat of paint on the house. Her father helped her return the equipment to the garage. (Time)

Teri finished putting the final coat of paint on the house. Afterward, her father helped her return the equipment to the garage.

1. Kurt had not made a single mistake when he finished his routine on the parallel bars. He received a perfect score from the judges. (Result)
2. We waited at the train station for over two hours. Poor Marie was looking for us at the bus depot. (Time)
3. The crisp, cool air and colorful foliage make autumn my favorite season. I've always liked the warm breezes and fresh green of spring. (Contrast)
4. We may soon be eating foods that come from sea farming. Algae is a high-protein crop now being harvested. (Addition)
5. The snow continued to fall through the night. School was canceled the next day. (Result)
6. Some of the city workers travel to their jobs by car. Many workers prefer a more economical form of commuting, such as the bus. (Contrast)
7. The country's citizens protested the high unemployment and the low standard of living. Many believed the ruler had accumulated riches at their expense. (Addition)
8. Some animals left their imprints in mud long ago. The mud with the imprints hardened, forming fossils. (Time)
9. Mark stayed up half the night to cram for his biology exam. He fell asleep in the middle of the test. (Result)
10. Rattlesnakes release a deadly poison through their hollow teeth, or fangs, when they bite. Copperheads and water moccasins are poisonous. (Addition)

Using Coordination

In addition to connecting ideas in separate sentences with transitions, you will often want to join related ideas of equal importance through coordination.

Whenever you use a conjunction such as *and* or *or* to form a compound subject, verb, complement, or other sentence part, you are using coordination. You are also using coordination whenever you write a compound sentence. The use of coordination in compound sentences allows you to tell the reader that two or more equally important ideas belong together.

Use coordination to connect equally important ideas smoothly and clearly.

The following chart shows the four basic methods of forming compound sentences. In all four cases, particularly in the last, the ideas connected must be equally important and closely related.

METHODS OF COORDINATION	
With Coordinating Conjunctions	**With Correlative Conjunctions**
and　　　or but　　　so for　　　yet nor	both . . . and either . . . or neither . . . nor not only . . . but also
With Semicolons and Conjunctive Adverbs	**With a Semicolon Alone**
; consequently,　　; indeed, ; finally,　　　　; moreover, ; furthermore,　　; otherwise, ; however,　　　; therefore,	;

Notice in the following examples that coordination, like transitions, can help clarify the relationhip between your ideas. The unconnected sentences leave the reader with certain unanswered questions. The use of coordination answers these questions.

UNCONNECTED: Becky wants a dog for her apartment. She knows a dog requires room to run.

PROBLEM: The writer suggests a contradiction but does not make it clear.

WITH COORDINATION: Becky wants a dog for her apartment, *yet* she knows a dog requires room to run.

UNCONNECTED: They will drive to Vermont to see the leaves turn in the fall. They will travel to Washington, D.C., to see the cherry blossoms in the spring.

PROBLEM: Will they take both trips or only one?

WITH COORDINATION: *Either* they will drive to Vermont to see the leaves turn in the fall, *or* they will travel to Washington, D.C., to see the cherry blossoms in the spring.

UNCONNECTED: We explored the shops in town. We did not find anything interesting.

PROBLEM: The sentences do not indicate any clear relationship.

WITH COORDINATION: We explored the shops in town; *however,* we did not find anything interesting.

When you use coordination, you must also watch out for three special problems: (1) connecting unrelated ideas, (2) establishing a vague connection between ideas by using the wrong conjunction, and (3) connecting too many ideas.

Sometimes, when you are writing quickly, you may link unrelated ideas. If you have done so, separate the ideas and add any necessary words to make your ideas clear.

UNRELATED IDEAS: Left alone for hours, the puppy pulled all of the shoes out of the closets, *and* she loved to beg for food from guests.

SEPARATED: Left alone for hours, the puppy pulled all of the shoes out of the closets. *Another of the puppy's tricks* was begging for food from guests.

The careless use of the wrong conjunction can also make your ideas unclear. You can correct such connections by changing the conjunction or conjunctive adverb. Or, if the ideas are closely connected, you can use a semicolon alone.

VAGUE CONNECTION: He liked the cost of the bus, *and* he preferred the reliability of the train.

CLEAR CONNECTION: He liked the cost of the bus, *but* he preferred the reliability of the train.

A third problem results from overusing coordination. You may sometimes become carried away with *and*'s, *but*'s, and *or*'s and blur your ideas. You can clarify a sentence with too many ideas by breaking it into parts. Use coordination only when it furthers the meaning.

TOO MANY IDEAS: While racing across three lanes of traffic on her bicycle, she lost control, *and* her bicycle tipped over, *and* she scraped her knee.

CLEARER IDEAS: While racing across three lanes of traffic on her bicycle, she lost control. Her bicycle tipped over, and she scraped her knee.

EXERCISE B: Correcting Problems with Coordination. In each sentence, correct the problem indicated in parentheses.

EXAMPLE: The batter stepped up to the plate; furthermore, he stared defiantly at the pitcher. (Vague connection)

The batter stepped up to the plate; he stared defiantly at the pitcher.

1. Bionic parts are mechanical devices used to replace defective parts of the body, and many people also use pacemakers. (Vague connection)
2. The Asian flu struck last winter, and everyone in our class became ill at the same time, and the list of absentees in the school was the longest it has ever been, but the school did not close. (Too many ideas)
3. The car skidded into the ditch beside the deserted road, and Mark was hungry and tired. (Unrelated ideas)
4. Traveling abroad exposes a person to unfamiliar customs, and most people adapt quickly. (Vague connection)
5. Frank's seat was too far from the stage, and a heckler in the crowd was annoying everyone around him, and the sound system was buzzing, and the intermissions were too long, but the band played nearly all its most popular songs. (Too many ideas)

6. The advertisement claimed that the car got good mileage, and the gas tank had to be refilled frequently. (Vague connection)
7. Leslie will train to become a ballerina, and she will visit New York in the spring. (Unrelated ideas)
8. The weather forecasters had predicted heavy rains, but it was clear and sunny this morning, and there wasn't a cloud in the sky, but, nevertheless, we were still worried that the forecasters might turn out to be right. (Too many ideas)
9. Sylvia smashed the serve past Stan's elbow, yet she won the regional table tennis tournament. (Vague connection)
10. Long-distance phone calls can be expensive, and Joan has three telephones in her office. (Unrelated ideas)

Using Subordination

Subordination is the process by which you connect two unequal but related ideas to form a complex sentence. The subordinate idea limits, develops, describes, or adds meaning to the main idea. As with transitions and coordination, subordination is a means of making your writing clearer to the reader.

Use subordination to connect ideas of unequal importance and show the precise relationship between the ideas.

The following chart shows some of the most frequently used subordinating conjunctions.

SUBORDINATING CONJUNCTIONS			
after	before	so that	when
although	even though	than	whenever
as if	if	though	where
as long as	in order that	unless	wherever
because	since	until	while

When you are connecting main ideas and subordinating ideas, there are two things you should try to avoid: (1) reversing the main idea and the subordinate idea and (2) using coordination instead of subordination.

Sometimes when you are combining two sentences to make

a complex sentence, you will have to choose carefully which idea to subordinate. If you try to put the more important idea into a subordinate clause, the sentence will not make sense.

ILLOGICAL SUBORDINATION: *Because* the television camera focused on him, he wore a spectacular umbrella hat to the football game.

LOGICAL SUBORDINATION: *Because* he wore a spectacular umbrella hat to the football game, the television camera focused on him.

Another problem occurs when coordination is used to connect ideas that can more clearly be connected by subordination. In the following example, subordination shows a much clearer relationship between the ideas.

WEAK COORDINATION: The storm extinguished the lights in the dining room, *and* the waitresses and waiters ran to find the old gas lanterns.

CLEAR SUBORDINATION: *When* the storm extinguished the lights in the dining room, the waitresses and waiters ran to find the old gas lanterns.

EXERCISE C: Correcting Problems with Subordination.
Improve each sentence by correcting the problem indicated in parentheses.

EXAMPLE: Martha Jane Canary warned her suitors that they were courting calamity, and she obtained the nickname of Calamity Jane. (Weak coordination)

Because Martha Jane Canary warned her suitors that they were courting calamity, she obtained the nickname of Calamity Jane.

1. When he would not eat any foods except those in his special diet, he considered himself to be in serious training. (Illogical subordination)
2. His fever broke last night, and only his cough remained a problem. (Weak coordination)
3. Because the foreign exchange student could not pay for a place to stay, she had lost all of her traveler's checks. (Illogical subordination)

467

4. I approached the swaying bridge, and I felt my knees weaken beneath me. (Weak coordination)
5. Although the train blocked the tracks during rush hour, the fire was quickly extinguished. (Illogical subordination)
6. The Smiths wanted to buy the house, and the house needed many repairs. (Weak coordination)
7. Because she refused to call him by his nickname, she thought it was foolish. (Illogical subordination)
8. The man had been convicted of the crime, and he was sentenced to prison. (Weak coordination)
9. When Eliot won by an overwhelming majority, he ran for president of the student body. (Illogical subordination)
10. Thick fog engulfed the foundering vessel, and the new pilot began to panic. (Weak coordination)

DEVELOPING WRITING SKILLS: **Using Transitions, Coordination, and Subordination.** Improve the following composition by adding transitions and making appropriate use of coordination and subordination.

(1) When Jenny discovered the body, she screamed. (2) She cried for help. (3) Everyone came running in from different rooms. (4) The inspector gathered them all together. (5) He asked where each of them had been. (6) The murder was committed.

(7) The cook said she had been in the next room. (8) She said she had heard no strange sounds. (9) She seemed nervous. (10) She was hiding something. (11) She was afraid to tell the truth. (12) Countess Vanessa had been upstairs. (13) She had been watching television. (14) She had heard nothing. (15) Her bedroom was soundproof. (16) Lord Philip had been playing the stereo in his study. (17) He had turned up the volume. (18) He had not heard the sounds.

(19) The inspector was able to eliminate only one suspect. (20) This person had broken the law in another way. (21) He had been caught speeding. (22) The Duke was murdered. (23) The butler had been at the police station paying a traffic ticket. (24) The inspector could be certain of one thing. (25) The butler hadn't done it.

Skills Review and Writing Workshop

Sentences

Rewrite the following paragraph to improve the style of the sentences.

(1) Whenever I ate at the Blue Dolphin, I visited Hawleyville. (2) The Blue Dolphin was a small diner. (3) It was located on the wrong side of town. (4) Its paint had started peeling. (5) A row of stools stood inside. (6) On the counter, covered plates displayed day-old doughnuts and a large tureen of soup simmered on a gas stove and on one of the old grills hamburgers sizzled in their own grease. (7) A neon sign was in the window. (8) It used to say, "Open 24 hours." (9) Only the word "Open" was lit up. (10) The people of Hawleyville didn't believe in wasting words, but "Open" was enough for them.

USING COMPOSITION SKILLS IN WRITING
Writing a Job Description

One way to hold the interest of your readers is to improve the style of your sentences and vary their structures as much as possible. Suppose you could design an ideal job. Write a description of your "dream" job by following the steps below.

Prewriting: Consider a job that you would enjoy doing. Then think of all the desirable elements that job might have, such as pay, working hours, travel, opportunity for creative expression, and so on.

Writing: Being with a short explanation of the job. Then describe all its elements, beginning with the most important one.

Revising: Look over all of your sentences and change any that could be improved. After you have revised, proofread carefully.

UNIT V

Composition
Forms and Process of Writing

21

Paragraphs

Well-written sentences are not enough to make your writing clear and understandable. Sentences must be further organized into meaningful units of thought.

After sentences, the most basic unit of thought in writing is the *paragraph*. The indentation of the first sentence of a paragraph tells the reader that a new unit of thought follows.

21.1 Understanding Topic Sentences and Support

A paragraph develops one main idea, which is usually stated in a sentence called the *topic sentence*. Every other sentence, every fact, example, and detail, should *support* the topic sentence.

Topic Sentences

A good topic sentence captures the general idea of the paragraph better than any other sentence.

The topic sentence states the main idea of the paragraph.

The topic sentence is usually found at the beginning of a paragraph, where it gives a preview of and direction to the sentences that come after it, as in the following example. Notice that all of the other sentences in the paragraph support the main idea with facts.

TOPIC
SENTENCE

Supporting
information

Controlling the entry of foreign pests is the job of the United States Department of Agriculture's Animal and Plant Health Inspection Service, nicknamed APHIS. Some 700 APHIS inspectors work around the clock at 100 ports of entry. In a year's time, they inspect some sixty-four million pieces of baggage carried by air travelers from foreign countries. They also meet about 62,000 ships and inspect roughly five million pieces of seagoing baggage. On the Mexican border, they check more than forty-five million automobiles annually and about 100,000 railroad cars. They also screen some sixty million pieces of mail and examine about four million cargo shipments.—George S. Fichter

Sometimes, however, the topic sentence comes at the end of the paragraph, where it draws a conclusion or functions as a summary. In the following paragraph, the topic sentence, which is at the end, states the conclusion of the preceding ideas and adds a finishing touch.

Supporting
information

TOPIC
SENTENCE

Smoke curled from under the eaves and rose from the roof. Flames shooting from the window arched upward toward the sky. Some of the floors and interior walls thundered downward, spraying sparks and glowing cinders through lower doors and windows. *The building could not be saved.*

Less frequently, a topic sentence comes in the middle of a paragraph, especially when the paragraph is part of a longer piece of writing. In such paragraphs the beginning sentences may function as a transition between paragraphs as well as an introduction to the topic sentence. In the following example, the first sentence paves the way for the topic sentence.

Introductory
sentence

TOPIC
SENTENCE

Dancing and chanting to the rhythmic beat of the drums, Polynesian students give visitors to the Polynesian Culture Center a glimpse of Hawaii's past. *Through its exhibitions, the Polynesian Culture Center shows visitors the many elements of Hawaiian culture brought to Hawaii by its original inhabitants, the Polynesians.* For example, the Center shows the similarities between Polynesian and Hawaiian villages

Supporting
information

with life-size models. In addition, the Center drama-
tizes Hawaiian legends of ancestors journeying across
the ocean in large canoes of hollowed logs. Gardens
of banana, sweet potato, taro, and breadfruit plants
exhibit the food carried by the ocean travelers to their
new home.

Whatever its position, the topic sentence will always state
the idea that provides the logical connection among all of the
other information in the paragraph.

EXERCISE A: Locating Topic Sentences. Write down the
sentence in each of the following paragraphs that states the
main idea of the paragraph.

(1) In addition to insects there are other animals that are
harmful to man. Of these the greatest pest is the rat. It is esti-
mated that the rats in the United States do more than
$200,000,000 worth of damage each year. The rat is an animal
which is well adapted to living anywhere that man lives. It
steals man's food. Rats are attracted to the phosphorus in
matches. Rats often cause expensive and dangerous fires, since
they may light matches while dragging or chewing on them.
They cause short circuits by gnawing away electric wire insulation. Worst of all, rats carry various insects about with them.
The flea which carries typhus fever lives on rats. Another flea
which is a carrier of bubonic plague also lives on rats.—Ames,
Baker, and Leahy

(2) On the third of June it rained. Gray, soggy clouds
swathed the hills. The snow, so hard in winter that the tracks
of our heavy sleds were barely discernible, became mush.
Water trickled down the rocks. Lichens and mosses, desiccated
and brittle in winter, avidly absorbed the moisture and shim-
mered with renewed life. Within a few days, the sun came out
and at last spring was triumphantly upon us. In one short week,
all of nature's pent-up vitality seemed to burst forth in fervent
renewal, in resurrection, and in life.—Fred Bruemmer

(3) In the last ten years, the Italians have made an effort to
stop the deterioration of Venice. For years soot and smoke have
discolored and eroded the city's marble palaces and monuments. Recently, however, many factory owners have helped re-

474

duce pollution by filtering the smoggy output of smokestacks. Increasingly, citizens are heating their homes with cleaner fuels, such as natural gas. In an effort to combat the most serious threat to Venice, the sinking of land and buildings into the Adriatic, city officials have taken action to maintain the water table at its present level so that Venice will remain above sea level. By building aqueducts to import drinking water, Venetian officials expect to keep the water table at a safe level.

(4) Early almanac editors were believed to possess a gift for prophesying weather; but, in fact, mariners were casting their nets and farmers were planting their crops according to predic-, tions derived from superstition, myth, and such dubious adages as "If cats do lick their forefeet and with them wash their head, it is a sign of rain." Almanac buffs fondly tell of the time one editor accidentally left out a prediction for July 13. He told his young apprentice to fill in the forecast as best he could. The young man predicted rain, hail, and snow, and according to records, it did rain, hail, and snow on that July 13, raising the esteem of the almanac (and the young apprentice) considerably.—Adapted from Shaaron Cosner

Support

Supporting information is specific information that helps a reader understand the topic sentence. Whenever you write a paragraph, you must always be sure that there is enough supporting information to develop the topic sentence completely.

There are several different kinds of supporting information from which you can choose—examples, details, facts, reasons, and incidents.

Recognize the basic kinds of supporting information that can be used to develop a topic sentence: examples, details, facts, reasons, and incidents.

Frequently a paragraph will use a combination of these different kinds of supporting information.

Examples. Because topic sentences usually are rather general statements, they need to be supported with specific examples. An *example* is a specific instance of a general idea or principle. In some cases, a topic sentence will need only two or three examples; others may need four or more examples to be developed thoroughly.

In the following paragraph, examples are used to develop the topic sentence. Notice that each of the examples helps to explain the main idea. Also notice that the last sentence acts as a summary for the paragraph.

TOPIC SENTENCE	*The German shepherd, a breed of dog that originated in northern Europe, performs many services for people.* Once used mainly for herding sheep, German
Examples	shepherds today help police in tracking and capturing criminals. In addition, these dogs often function as guards in stores, factories, and private houses. As seeing-eye dogs, German shepherds have earned respect for their keen, careful guiding of the blind. Intel-
Concluding sentence	ligent and versatile, German shepherds remain a popular, useful breed of dog.

Details. In paragraphs that describe a place, person, or action, much of the supporting information will probably be made up of details. *Details* are pieces of information that help a reader visualize and understand what the writer is describing. In storytelling and descriptive writing, especially, details place the reader in the scene.

In the following paragraph, details are used to help the reader see what the character sees.

Introductory sentence	Curious to know what this Cutter Gap looked like, I slid out of bed and hobbled stiffly over to one of the windows. *Nothing had prepared me for what met my*
TOPIC SENTENCE	*eyes.* Mountain ranges were folded one behind the other, in the foreground snow-covered; behind that, patches of emerald green showing through; on be-
Details	yond, deeper green. Then the blues began. On the smoky blue of the far summits fluffy white clouds rested like wisps of cotton. I counted the mountain ranges, eleven of them rising up and up toward the vault of sky. The Great Smokies . . . now I understood. That peculiar smoky-blue color and the adjective "great"—so right for these towering heights.—Catherine Marshall

Facts. Some topic sentences, especially those presenting new ideas, can best be supported by facts. A *fact* is a piece of information that can be verified. It provides concrete evidence to prove a statement presented in the topic sentence.

Facts are used to develop the following paragraph. Notice that all the facts work together to present one main idea.

TOPIC SENTENCE	*Antarctica has the most hostile environment on earth for humans.* Not a tree or bush grows there. No human beings are native to the land. The only permanent in-
Facts	habitants, such as seals, penguins, and a few other birds, must feed in the sea. Approximately ninety-five percent of the world's permanent ice is in Antarctica. It has been estimated that if all this ice melted it would raise the level of the oceans by about 200 feet (60 meters), thus flooding a considerable portion of the earth's surface. Antarctica is the coldest and windiest of all the continents. The Soviet Union's Vostok Station recorded a temperature of 126.9 degrees below zero Fahrenheit on August 24, 1960, the lowest temperature ever recorded anywhere in the world.—George F. Dufek

Reasons. When a topic sentence presents an opinion that another person might challenge or question, it will generally be supported with reasons. If the writer fails to support a controversial statement with evidence or reasons, a reader may disregard the opinion.

The topic sentence of the following paragraph expresses the writer's preference for swimming in a lake. The supporting information offers three reasons to help the reader understand and perhaps convince the reader to accept the writer's point of view. Notice that the final sentence wraps up the writer's reasons.

TOPIC SENTENCE	*I prefer swimming in a mountain lake to swimming in a pool.* The crisp mountain air around a lake invig-
Reasons	orates and pleases me. I like a lake's underwater life, such as minnows and trout, and I enjoy observing the plant life around me. Most important, a lake usually has no chemicals, such as chlorine, that can smell
Concluding sentence	bad and burn my eyes. Lake water is clean, natural, and more refreshing for swimming.

Incidents. The best way to develop some topic sentences is to tell a little story or incident. An *incident* is an extended example. One well-developed incident including details and description is usually enough to illustrate a topic sentence. Frequently, paragraphs developed by an incident have a topic sentence at the end. Notice that the topic sentence in the following paragraph also summarizes the incident.

Incident   When I awoke this morning, I realized that my alarm had failed to go off, making me late for school. I jumped into my clothes, swept up my books, and dashed out the front door. Sheets of rain greeted me, full face! Turning abruptly, I ran back inside, threw on my raincoat, grabbed an umbrella, and rushed out once more. Trotting to the bus stop, I became wet and cold, and the long wait for the bus made things worse. The ride to school was quick because of light traffic at the "off hour," but I was uneasy because I dreaded my entrance into class, which was already in progress. My last hurdle, the path to the school's front door, was littered with deep puddles, but I made it—only to be greeted by one more obstacle: The door was locked. "Oh, no. It's Saturday," I muttered to myself, the reali-

TOPIC   zation hitting me like a wet towel. *Some days it doesn't*
SENTENCE   *pay to get out of bed.*

EXERCISE B: Recognizing Support for Topic Sentences. Examine the paragraphs in Exercise A. Then tell which one is developed mainly with (a) examples, (b) details, (c) reasons, and (d) an incident.

DEVELOPING WRITING SKILLS: Practicing with Topic Sentences and Support. Using a topic from the following list, write a topic sentence. Then make a list of supporting information.

Buying clothes	Ways to save time
Earning money	Health and exercise
Energy conservation	Natural catastrophes
Today's cars	Famous inventions
Exploration of space	Famous athletes
World leaders	New technologies

Understanding Unity and 21.2 Coherence

A good paragraph has *unity* because all of the information supports the topic sentence. It has *coherence* because the ideas flow naturally from one to another.

Unity

In a unified paragraph, all of the sentences stick to the main idea presented in the topic sentence.

A paragraph has unity if all of its sentences relate closely to the topic sentence.

When you write a paragraph, check to make sure that all of the sentences belong. In the following paragraph, for example, the fourth and fifth sentences do not fit.

TOPIC SENTENCE	Every student should develop a good speaking voice. A strong, clear voice indicates that a speaker is confident of his or her knowledge or ideas. A good speaking voice aids class discussions because more students become involved if they can hear each other's
Unrelated information	comments. *Mumbling can indicate shyness or unwillingness to cooperate. Or a student may speak indistinctly because of braces on his or her teeth.* Finally, speaking so that others can easily hear suggests that the speaker is interested in the topic and cares enough to contribute.

Since the sentences about mumbling and braces destroy the unity of the paragraph, the writer should remove them.

EXERCISE A: Recognizing Unity in Paragraphs. Write down the unrelated sentences in the following paragraphs.

(1) Travel agencies help their customers plan all kinds of travel arrangements. For example, they make reservations for customers on airlines and try to find the most economical rates and the most convenient flights. They book accommodations at hotels and make arrangements for rental cars. Travelers should

479

always plan to take proper clothing on vacations. Maps and booklets describing places to visit, scenic spots, and good restaurants can also be useful. In addition, the agencies can help with applications for passports and provide advice on exchanging American money for foreign money.

(2) Today, weather satellites are used to gather information about hurricane activity. Three times a day, a weather satellite sends photographs of the Caribbean and the Atlantic Ocean to the Miami Hurricane Center. Other satellites, such as *Telstar,* relay television programs and other communications between continents but do not record weather conditions. Teams of hurricane experts study pictures from weather satellites, paying close attention to the movement of cloud formations. Weather phenomena such as tornadoes would not follow the same pattern as hurricanes, nor would tornadoes develop over bodies of water. Hurricane information collected by weather satellites is then fed into computers. All information is shared with other centers, especially those that may be threatened by a hurricane.

(3) The three kinds of rocks on the earth are classified by the ways they were originally formed. Igneous rocks, such as granite, were once molten. These rocks were formed when molten material in the earth or molten material that reached the surface of the earth cooled. Sedimentary rocks, such as shale, limestone, and sandstone, were formed when rock particles settled in layers and hardened. They are probably the oldest rocks on earth. Metamorphic rocks are actually igneous or sedimentary rocks that were changed by heat and pressure to form new rocks. Many important ore deposits around the world are metamorphic rocks.

Coherence

In a coherent paragraph, supporting information is arranged in a logical order and linked with transitions, repetition of main words, and, in some paragraphs, with a concluding sentence.

Orders for Supporting Information. When supporting information is presented in a clear, logical order, the reader can sense where the paragraph is going.

The supporting information in a paragraph should be presented in a logical order.

Five orders are most frequently used to achieve a logical flow of ideas.

ORGANIZATION OF PARAGRAPHS	
Order	**Use**
Chronological (time)	Gives a sequence of events; tells what happened first, second, third, and so on
Spatial (space)	Arranges details from nearest to farthest, top to bottom, left to right, and so on
Order of Importance	Ranks information from least important to most important or vice versa
Comparison and Contrast	Presents similarities and differences between items
Developmental	Arranges information from one point in the topic sentence to another

When a topic sentence calls for the description of an action, the recounting of an incident, or the explanation of a process, the most effective order is usually *chronological order*. With chronological order, you would present supporting information in a time sequence, usually from first to last.

The following paragraph uses chronological order. Notice that the words *first, next,* and *last* highlight the order of the steps.

TOPIC SENTENCE Building home bookshelves is relatively simple. *First,* you have to buy the necessary materials. Shelving lumber, cut to any size you wish, can be purchased at most lumber yards, as can the wall brackets and runners needed to hold the shelves in place. *Next,* you need to

481

mount the runners on the wall (screws for this purpose are included with the runners) and then attach the shelf brackets to the runners. The *last* step is the simplest: Merely set the shelves in place.

When a topic sentence describes a person, place, or thing, the supporting information can be ordered by position, that is, *spatially*. A spatial order helps the reader picture the scene by presenting things from top to bottom, from the outside to the center, from far to near, and so on.

The following paragraph uses spatial order to help the reader visualize a house and follow the writer's movements. The words *outside, inside, above,* and *in front of* serve as guides, giving the reader a clearer picture of the house.

Support
organized
spatially

Outside the house there were window boxes full of flowers and rows of pink azalea bushes lining the path I took to the front door. Once *inside* the massive oak door, I stood in an oak-paneled entrance foyer larger than most people's living rooms. *Above* me, I saw an enormous crystal chandelier hanging on a chain from the ceiling, which must have been two or three stories high. Several yards *in front of* me was the most elegant staircase I have ever seen. It began from an exposed balcony and circled downward around two walls of the

TOPIC
SENTENCE

foyer. Without a doubt, I thought, this is the grandest house I had ever visited.

The support for a topic sentence that states a personal preference or belief is often presented in *order of importance*. It is usually wise to begin with the least important point and build up to the most important, most effective point. Furthermore, the last point is also the one that the reader will probably remember best.

The following paragraph uses order of importance. The expressions *one, even greater,* and *most significantly* indicate that the paragraph moves from the least important point to the most important.

TOPIC
SENTENCE

Every student should join Glenwood High's General Organization. *One* benefit of belonging to G.G.O. is free admission to all G.G.O. dances and free refresh-

482

Support
organized
by order of
importance

ments. An *even greater* advantage is that a G.G.O. member is able to obtain inexpensive guest passes to football, basketball, and baseball games. *Most significantly,* since G.G.O. runs the school's clubs, G.G.O. members plan and vote money for all of the extracurricular activities in the school.

Some paragraphs show the similarities and differences between two or more items. Showing similarities is called *comparing.* Showing differences is called *contrasting.* A paragraph may do either one or sometimes both at the same time.

Two orders are possible in comparing, contrasting, or showing both similarities and differences. In writing about the two items A and B, all of the points about A can be covered and then all of the points about B: AAA-BBB. Or, the two items can be covered point by point: AB-AB-AB. Either order is acceptable, but some paragraphs may be easier to write one way than the other.

In the following paragraph, squash and handball are compared and contrasted point by point according to court, equipment, and method of scoring. The words in italics help make the on-going comparison clearer.

TOPIC
SENTENCE

Comparison
and
contrast
organized
point by
point

Squash and handball are similar in some ways but different in others. Squash is an indoor game played on an enclosed court with four walls. Handball, *too,* can be played indoors on an enclosed court with four walls, but it also has a three-wall, indoor version and a one-wall, outdoor version. The equipment for squash includes a racket that is longer and lighter than a tennis racket and a hard, hollow, rubber ball about the size of a golf ball. In handball players use their hands *instead of* a racket, and the rubber ball is slightly bigger and bouncier than a squash ball. In *both* games players take turns hitting the ball against the front wall of the court, although the ball can bounce off any of the four walls. In handball, the ball can *also* bounce off the ceiling. In *both* games players try to place the ball so that their opponents cannot hit it before it bounces twice, but in squash the ball must be hit between lines on the walls. Players of *both* games can score only on their own serves. The first player to score fifteen points wins in squash. *However,* a player must score twenty-one points to win in handball.

It would also have been possible to arrange the material so that all three items—court, equipment, and scoring—were discussed together for squash and then all three items for handball.

A final order that is useful for paragraphs is *developmental order*. Developmental order can be used when the topic sentence divides the topic into categories, when supporting reasons or examples are equally important, or when no other order suggests itself.

The following paragraph uses developmental order to arrange supporting information. The examples in the paragraph follow the order suggested by the topic sentence: "strong hands, good peripheral vision, balance and coordination, and courage." The words in italics help the reader follow the progression of ideas.

TOPIC
SENTENCE

Support
organized
by develop-
mental order

A good quarterback should have strong hands, good peripheral vision, balance and coordination, and courage. Strong hands give a quarterback control over the football so that it can be thrown quickly and accurately. Good peripheral vision allows a quarterback to see all of the receivers going out for a pass during a play. *Together,* strong hands and good peripheral vision help reduce a quarterback's chances of throwing interceptions. A quarterback *also* needs balance and coordination so that he can pivot rapidly and throw the ball before he is hit by opposing players. *Finally,* a quarterback needs courage to keep his head and throw the ball accurately as the other team's defense is bearing down upon him.

Transitions for Paragraphs. Transitions are words and phrases that act as bridges between ideas. They connect the writer's thoughts by clarifying the kind of logical relationship that exists between the ideas.

Connect the supporting information in a paragraph with transitions.

484

The words italicized in the preceding paragraphs are transitions that help indicate the kind of order used for the supporting information. As the following chart shows, each kind of order can be reinforced by using appropriate transitions. Some of the transitions are used at the beginning of sentences; others are used later in the sentences, as you can see in the paragraphs in the last few pages.

SOME USEFUL TRANSITIONS		
Chronological		
after	first	next
at last	last	now
before	later	soon
finally	meanwhile	then
Spatial		
above	beneath	inside
ahead	beyond	near
below	in back of	next to
behind	in front of	outside
Order of Importance		
another	furthermore	next
even greater	moreover	one
finally	most important	second
first	most significantly	third
Comparison and Contrast		
again	both	like
also	however	similarly
although	in contrast	than
as in	instead of	too
Developmental		
along with	for example	in fact
also	for instance	namely
as a result	furthermore	next
consequently	in addition	therefore
finally	in conclusion	together

Notice that some of the paragraphs in the preceding section need many transitions to be clear. Others require only a few well-placed transitions. Also notice that transitions are used not only to guide the reader but also to create a smooth flow of ideas.

Repetition of Main Words. Paragraphs can also be made more coherent through the repetition of main words, which helps the reader follow the ideas more closely. Sometimes a word can be repeated exactly; other times, a synonym should be used for a main word to avoid monotony.

Link supporting information with repeated main words and synonyms.

In the following paragraph, repetitions of main words and synonyms are italicized. Notice that the repetitions and synonyms show a connection between the topic sentence and each of the reasons. One thread in the paragraph is formed by the words *sympathy, empathizes, care, feels compassion,* and *aches*. Repetitions of the words *Charlie* and *reader* form two more threads. Still another thread comes near the middle of the paragraph, formed by *loneliness, isolation,* and *alone*.

TOPIC
SENTENCE

Repetition
of main
words and
synonyms

Charlie Gordon, the main character in the novel *Flowers for Algernon,* evokes great *sympathy* from the *reader*. The *reader* naturally *empathizes* with *Charlie* as *Charlie* tells his own story of his development from a mentally retarded person to a genius. The *reader* sees and feels what *Charlie* sees and feels. *Charlie's loneliness* and *isolation* also make the *reader care* for him. The *reader feels compassion* for *Charlie* when his classmates, playmates, and later his fellow workers play tricks on him and laugh at him because he is mentally retarded. Even when *Charlie* becomes a genius through an operation, he is still *alone* because now no one understands his brilliant mind. Furthermore, *Charlie* can never have a lasting relationship with Alice, the woman he loves, because of his early retardation, his later brilliance, and his troubled future. Perhaps the greatest reason for the *reader* to *sympathize* with *Charlie* is that the operation that made *Charlie* a genius eventually destroys his mind and then kills him. Worst of all, *Charlie* knows that he is going to regress and die. The *reader aches* for him at the end of the story as Charlie awaits death.

Concluding Sentences. A concluding sentence can complete a paragraph and bring it to a satisfactory end in several ways. It may, for example, summarize the ideas of the paragraph. Or, the concluding sentence can restate the topic sentence in different words, reminding the reader of how the paragraph started and neatly tying everything together. In either case, the concluding sentence adds a final touch.

When appropriate, clarify the progression of ideas by adding a concluding sentence.

In the following paragraph, the concluding sentence captures the main idea of the paragraph and adds a finishing touch.

TOPIC
SENTENCE

Concluding
sentence

The world of Greek mythology was not a place of terror for the human spirit. It is true that the gods were disconcertingly incalculable. One could never tell where Zeus' thunderbolt would strike. Nevertheless, the whole divine company, with a very few and for the most part not important exceptions, were entrancingly beautiful with a human beauty and nothing humanly beautiful is really terrifying. The early Greek mythologists transformed a world full of fear into a world full of beauty. — Edith Hamilton

EXERCISE B: Recognizing Order in Paragraphs. Write the type of order used in each of the following paragraphs.

(1) The impressive Gateway Arch, a monument to American expansion, dominates the city of St. Louis, Missouri. Outside, its stainless steel surface reflects sunshine in an arch that stretches into the sky. Inside, a large open area at the base houses a museum commemorating western pioneers. From a station in this base, futuristic cars travel up through the steel interior of the monument. At the top an observation desk has narrow windows, which afford the visitor a view from a height of 630 feet. From this height one can view the sprawling city of St. Louis, as well as the nearby state of Illinois.

(2) Beyond stylistic similarities, Switzerland and Nepal would at first appear to have little more in common than their mountain environments. The former is the epitome of modernization, while the latter is one of the world's least developed countries. Today, Nepal is struggling to establish a simple road system, while Switzerland's cantons are linked by modern highways and an extensive electric rail network. Most of Nepal is accessible only on foot; the Swiss, in contrast, can speed over 15,000 miles of track so rapidly that passengers complain of being unable to enjoy the mountain landscape. Nepal, where the per capita income is less than $120 per year, faces a vast developmental task, while Switzerland, with its industrial and commercial empires, is home to one of the world's great concentrations of wealth. — Robert E. Rhoades

(3) When Anne Sullivan came to teach seven-year-old Helen Keller, she encountered a child who could not speak, hear, or see. At first, Helen violently rejected her new teacher, but after much patience, Anne Sullivan broke into the girl's isolated world by teaching her to communicate using touch signals. After years of effort, Helen was able to enter college, where she later graduated with honors.

(4) Examining career options while you are still in high school may help you when you graduate. First, by learning about the jobs available now, you can predict what jobs may be available later, when you are looking for work. Since you will know what is available, you can better decide the right path for you. In addition, you may find information about "intern" opportunities, which offer entry-level training for students while they are still in school. More important, if you can decide on a career goal early in life, you will have that much more time to gain the experience, educational background, and training needed by the best-qualified applicant for the job in which you are interested.

EXERCISE C: Recognizing Transitions and Main Words in a Paragraph. List the transitions found in the following paragraph. Then list two groups of main words.

(1) Some psychiatrists believe that the different positions people assume during sleep reflect their personalities. (2) For

example, some people sleep face down, stretched across the bed, as if they were in control of their sleeping area. (3) These people tend to be in control of their waking lives, too, usually through a careful structuring of their lives. (4) Confident and secure individuals seem to sleep on their backs, with their arms placed slightly away from the body. (5) On the other hand, the insecure or timid individual often assumes the fetal position, the curved position of a baby before it is born. (6) Although theories relating to sleeping positions and personality have not been proven, studies that have been done make interesting reading. (7) After all, everyone enjoys learning about themselves.

DEVELOPING WRITING SKILLS: Practicing with Different Orders. Write down the best order for a paragraph based on each of the following topic sentences. Then choose two topic sentences and write paragraphs based on each one, being sure to use appropriate transitions.

1. Crash diets are an unhealthy way to lose weight.
2. The ear is specially structured so that vibrations are transformed into sounds that the brain can "hear."
3. Although he wrote at about the same time as Nathanial Hawthorne, Edgar Allan Poe's style differed from Hawthorne's style in many ways.
4. The government has established many national and state parks so that people can enjoy the land, wildlife can be preserved, and history can be remembered.
5. The Appalachian Trail, a popular hiking path that stretches from Georgia to Maine, passes through several mountain ranges.
6. The special effects in the science fiction movie often help determine the film's popularity at the box office.
7. The town clean-up can take place only if you vote yes.
8. It took many years, as well as several different stages of growth, for the cleared land around the old mining town to become forest again.
9. Some zoos keep animals in areas similar to the animals' native habitats, while other zoos do not.
10. You can determine a person's mood by interpreting his or her body language.

21.3 Planning Your Paragraph

There are certain steps you can follow that can help you plan a paragraph.

PREWRITING: Exploring Topics

The first step in planning a paragraph is finding a topic that is the right size to be covered in a paragraph. The second step involves deciding what you want to say about this topic. The final step is the actual writing of a good topic sentence.

Generating Ideas and Choosing a Topic. You can find ideas for paragraph topics by examining your interests and experiences. You can use methods such as interviewing yourself, free writing, journal writing, reading and saving, clustering, cueing, and brainstorming to find ideas for topics. These methods for generating ideas are discussed in Section 18.1

Narrowing a Topic. You will usually have to narrow a general topic down into a paragraph topic by thinking of all the subcategories of the general topic.

Find a suitable paragraph topic by dividing a general topic into smaller topics.

For example, if you want to write about skateboards you would probably first realize that you cannot cover the entire topic in one paragraph. You would then find that there are dozens of smaller topics under the general topic of skateboards. Among the smaller topics you might think of and jot down on a piece of paper are those shown in the following chart.

DIVIDING A GENERAL TOPIC INTO SMALLER TOPICS	
General Topic	**Smaller Topics**
skateboards	skateboards as a fad dangers of skateboards upkeep of skateboards best models of skateboards riding skateboards

Focusing on a Main Idea. After you have a suitable paragraph topic, you must focus on a main idea. To do this, think about the people to whom you are writing (that is, your audience). You should also focus on your purpose in writing.

Focus on your main idea by thinking about your audience and purpose.

You should have an audience in mind for every paragraph you write. You should decide if you want to write to someone who knows something about the topic or to someone who knows nothing about it, someone who agrees with you or someone who does not. Ask yourself questions about your audience. If you write down your questions and the answers, you will then have a list of possible ideas about your topic.

The following chart shows how asking questions can lead you to main ideas. For the topic on skateboards as a fad, you might choose an audience that knows little about the fad.

QUESTIONS LEADING TO POSSIBLE MAIN IDEAS	
Paragraph Topic: Skateboards as a fad	
Questions	**Possible Main Ideas**
Why might my audience be interested in the topic?	Skateboards were a major fad last year.
What might my audience want to learn about my topic?	A number of amusing things happened because of the fad.
What is the most important thing to tell them about the topic?	The skateboard fad was lively but a waste of time.

Whatever main idea you choose to write about, you should give some thought to the purpose it suggests. For instance, the first two main ideas listed in the preceding chart suggest that your purpose would be to inform and to tell a story. The third, on the other hand, shows that you are presenting an opinion. It suggests that you would be trying to persuade the audience to accept your viewpoint.

Writing Your Topic Sentence. Once you have selected a main idea that suits both the audience and the purpose you have in mind, you should be ready for your next planning step: writing a topic sentence.

State your main idea in a topic sentence that suits your audience and purpose.

You should write your topic sentence several times to find a version that sounds right to you. Experiment with different words and different lengths.

Using the first main idea in the previous chart, you might draft the following topic sentences.

POSSIBLE COMPLETED TOPIC SENTENCES
1. By far the biggest fad at our school most of last year was skateboarding.
2. A skateboard fad swept our school last year.
3. During the fall, skateboarding was very popular at our school, but interest slackened by spring.
4. Many students at our school had skateboards last year.

When you have listed two or more versions of your topic sentence, choose the one that is the clearest, most direct statement of your main ideas.

EXERCISE A: Finding a Paragraph Topic. For *five* of the following general topics, list as many subcategories or smaller topics as you can. Then write the five subcategories or smaller topics you like best.

Vacations	Pets	Books
Clubs	Homework	Transportation
A hobby	Movies	Department stores
Sports	Diseases	Future courses
Careers	Dances	Newspapers

EXERCISE B: Creating a Topic Sentence. Using one paragraph topic you choose in Exercise A, determine the audience you want to write for. Ask yourself questions about the topic and your audience and select a main idea based on the answers to your questions. Then decide on the purpose of your paragraph and write four versions of your topic sentence. Circle the one you like best.

PREWRITING: Brainstorming for Support

After you have written a topic sentence, the next step in writing a paragraph is gathering enough supporting information to fully explain your main idea.

Brainstorm for examples, details, facts, reasons, or incidents that explain your topic sentence.

There are several ways to produce a list of supporting information. One effective way is to put yourself in the reader's place: Ask yourself questions that a reader might want answered about your main idea. Then list as many examples, details, facts, reasons, or incidents as you can that help answer the questions.

The following chart shows the process of questioning and answering to find supporting information for one of the topic sentences on skateboarding.

QUESTIONING TO FIND SUPPORT FOR A TOPIC SENTENCE
Topic Sentence: A skateboard fad swept our school last year.
Why was it a fad?
—everyone talked about it —students were left out if they didn't have one —six out of ten students had one	—after six months people were bored with them —skateboards are easy to maintain
What happened when the fad swept the school?
—skateboard competitions were held on the sidewalks —new skateboard clubs started —cheerleaders did routines	—on skateboards at games —a few students skateboarded while listening to radios

EXERCISE C: Planning Support for Your Topic Sentence.
Using the topic sentence you wrote for Exercise B, write two or three questions for which the audience would expect answers. Then answer the questions by listing as many examples, details, facts, reasons, or incidents as you can.

493

PREWRITING: Organizing Your Support

After you have written a topic sentence and listed supporting information, organize your support for the reader.

Checking for Unity. Your first organizing task is to examine the supporting information for unity. Cross any unrelated material off your list.

Eliminate unrelated supporting information.

Look at the support for the topic sentence on skateboards. Two of the items—those covering maintenance and radios—stray too far from the topic sentence and should be eliminated. The remaining items are all related directly to the topic sentence and will therefore comfortably fit into the paragraph.

EVALUATING A LIST OF SUPPORT

Topic Sentence: A skateboard fad swept our school last year.

Why was it a fad?

—everyone talked about it
—students were left out if they didn't have one
—seven out of ten students had one

—after six months people were bored with them
—skateboards are easy to maintain

What happened when the fad swept the school?

—skateboard competitions were held on the sidewalks
—new skateboard clubs started
—cheerleaders did routines

—on skateboards at games
—a few students skateboarded while listening to radios

Ordering and Outlining Your Supporting Information. You should next decide how to present the supporting information so that it will be clear to your readers.

Choose the best order for your support and outline your paragraph using that order.

Your topic sentence and support should suggest a particular order for your paragraph. For example, the topic sentence about skateboards refers to time, "last year." You might therefore choose *chronological* order as the most appropriate order.

The final step in planning a paragraph is preparing an outline. Begin by putting your topic sentence at the top of the page. Then, using the order you have chosen, set up your supporting information in a modified outline. Add a concluding sentence to the outline if you think one would be helpful.

Topic Sentence

A skateboard fad swept our school last year.

Fall

1. Skateboards suddenly appeared in the fall
2. Students felt left out if they didn't have one
3. Seven out of ten students purchased one during the fall
4. Cheerleaders used them in routines at football games

Winter

1. Clubs formed during the winter
2. Competitions were organized

Spring

1. Everyone was tired of skateboards
2. Fad died out

Concluding Sentence

Finally, like all true fads, skateboards disappeared from school life almost as quickly as they had appeared.

EXERCISE D: Preparing to Write a Well-Organized Paragraph. Using the list of support you made for Exercise C, evaluate the support for unity. Then choose the order best suited to the support and write a modified outline for a paragraph.

DEVELOPING WRITING SKILLS: Planning a Paragraph. Select one of the general topics listed below. Then follow the steps in this section to write a topic sentence, find support, and create a good outline.

A crazy clothing fad	The funniest movie you ever saw
Your favorite food	Your worst grade
A career that interests you	The first day of a new job
Taking a science course	Your finest hour

495

21.4 Drafting Your Paragraph

Once you have outlined your paragraph, the actual writing should go quickly. You simply have to follow your outline to create a first draft.

WRITING: Creating a First Draft

As you write your first draft, think about your audience. Concentrate on presenting your ideas clearly enough that your audience will easily be able to follow your thoughts.

Write a first draft, using your outline and trying to make everything as clear as possible to your audience.

The following paragraph has been written with its audience constantly in mind. It uses transitions such as *first* and *finally* to present the skateboard fad in clear chronological order. It also repeats the main words *skateboard* and *fad* from time to time so that the reader can see how closely the supporting information is related to the topic sentence. The concluding sentence adds a final touch and puts the whole paragraph in perspective for the reader.

TOPIC
SENTENCE

Supporting
information

Concluding
sentence

A skateboard fad swept our school last year. Early in the fall, skateboards first appeared and soon overran the school. Students began to feel left out if they didn't participate. In fact, an informal survey showed that seven out of ten students acquired a skateboard during the autumn months alone. In October, the cheerleaders took up the fad and did routines on skateboards at rallies and football games. By winter, the biggest enthusiasts had formed skateboard clubs. The clubs sponsored competitions, which attracted much publicity, on the sidewalks in the neighborhood and at the local skateboard park. For six months the whirl of skateboard wheels dominated our school. By spring, however, most students were bored with the new interest. Finally, like all true fads, skateboards disappeared from school life almost as quickly as they had appeared.

EXERCISE: Writing a First Draft. Following the modified outline you prepared in Exercise D on page 495, write the paragraph, concentrating on making things clear to the audience you have chosen. Underline any transitions and main words in your paragraph.

DEVELOPING WRITING SKILLS: More Work with First Drafts. Following the modified outline you created for the Developing Writing Skills activity on page 495, write another first draft. Again, focus on your audience and try to make everything as clear as possible.

Polishing Your Paragraph 21.5

To make your paragraphs something you can truly be proud of, you must learn how to revise them. Despite all of the planning that goes into a paragraph, there may still be some flaws in it when you finish the first draft. Thus, you should evaluate each paragraph carefully.

Specifically, you should check your paragraph for weaknesses in the topic sentence, in the supporting information, and in overall unity and coherence. Then you can make any necessary changes. Finally, take time to proofread your paragraph for mistakes in grammar, mechanics, and spelling.

The following suggestions should help you carry out all of these steps.

REVISING: Using a Checklist

After you have written the first draft of your paragraph, evaluate it thoroughly.

Use a checklist to evaluate the first draft of your paragraph.

The following checklist will help you discover any problems or weaknesses that need to be corrected in your paragraph. When you have thought about and answered each question in the checklist, you should have a good idea of where any weak spots may be in your paragraph.

497

CHECKLIST FOR REVISING

1. Do you have an easily recognized topic sentence?
2. Does your topic sentence contain the main idea of the paragraph?
3. Does your topic sentence suit your audience and purpose?
4. Is your topic sentence in the most effective position?
5. Have you met the reader's expectations by providing enough examples, details, facts, reasons, or incidents?
6. Does all of your supporting information contribute to the development of the topic sentence?
7. Have you arranged your supporting information in the most logical order?
8. Are there any places where you might add transitions to connect ideas more clearly?
9. Are there any places where adding a main word might make the ideas clearer?
10. Does your paragraph need a concluding sentence?

EXERCISE A: Using a Checklist to Revise. Use the checklist on this page to evaluate a paragraph you have recently written. Then write one or two sentences each evaluating your (1) topic sentence, (2) support, (3) unity, and (4) coherence.

REVISING: Improving Your Topic Sentence

Sometimes in rereading a paragraph, you will find that the topic sentence and the supporting information do not fit together logically. The topic sentence may be so broad that it does not really present the main idea of your paragraph. Or, it may be so narrow that it does not completely cover the supporting information used in the paragraph. In some cases the paragraph may even lack a real topic sentence. In all of these situations, you should revise the topic sentence.

Revise a topic sentence that is too general or too specific for the supporting information.

In the following paragraph, the topic sentence at the end is too general because it focuses on "putting on a play" while the supporting information before it focuses on only the hard jobs of actors.

Topic sentence that is overly general

Actors work very hard to memorize the many lines of their scripts. Actors must know the lines of the other characters to know when to speak. In addition, they have to learn how to move on stage and remember where to be on stage every moment. *Putting on a play is hard work.*

A more precise topic sentence for this paragraph would focus on acting: *Acting is difficult work.*

In the next paragraph, on the other hand, the topic sentence, which follows an introductory sentence, is too specific. It mentions one obstacle to keeping a journal, but the paragraph presents several obstacles.

Topic sentence that is too specific

Many famous writers have first captured their imaginative ideas in journals. *The average young person, however, must overcome one major obstacle in keeping a journal.* Thinking of good ideas to put in a journal takes energy and creativity. You don't want a journal full of bland, boring ideas. Instead, you want to remember your best ideas, your most vivid impressions, your strongest feelings, the most unusual people you have seen, and the strangest experiences you have had. Expressing ideas worth remembering also takes time. Finally, if you give energy and time to your journal, it is highly personal, not meant to be read by curious brothers and sisters or friends. You will probably have to hide your journal where it won't tempt others to discover your innermost thoughts.

A better topic sentence for this paragraph would focus on all the obstacles: *The average young person, however, must overcome at least three obstacles in keeping a journal.*

EXERCISE B: Revising Topic Sentences. Briefly describe why each underlined topic sentence does not fit its paragraph and then revise it.

499

(1) The first tales of vampires were folktales spread among the people of eastern Europe in the 18th and 19th centuries. In this century dozens of horror movies about vampires have been made, to the delight of audiences. Many have been box-office successes. In addition, hundreds, perhaps thousands, of books and stories have been written on the subject of vampires. Recently a book in which a vampire was "interviewed" became a best seller. <u>Monsters have long held a certain glamour for the general public.</u>

(2) <u>Newspapers usually provide more detailed coverage of events than television does.</u> Newspapers keep you informed of what is happening in the world, giving you pages of articles to read at your leisure. Television provides visible, up-to-the-minute coverage of local, national, and world events, from sports to politics to entertainment, but the coverage is generally in two- or three-minute segments. Radio stations often offer more news broadcasts than television does, but they also tend to give quick coverage to news.

(3) <u>Modern medical discoveries have helped people stay healthy.</u> Vitamin A, for example, helps to guard against colds and infections. A vitamin that is found in many fruits and vegetables, vitamin C guards against scurvy and tooth decay. Vitamin D also helps develop strong teeth, and it helps to guard against bone and muscle degeneration, too. Other vitamins, such as the B vitamins, help to protect against such problems as fatigue, skin disorders, and loss of hair.

(4) <u>The train was delayed because the engine failed.</u> Outside Chicago more than eight feet of snow had piled up on the tracks and had to be cleared by special plows. Then the sharp drop in temperature caused the track switches to freeze further down the line. We had to stop every few miles to get the go-ahead from the stations beyond. Then, just ten miles from Pittsburgh, the engine broke down, and we had to wait for a mechanic to fix it. We finally pulled into Pittsburgh over ten hours late!

REVISING: Improving Your Support

A paragraph that seems incomplete or unconvincing may lack appropriate supporting information.

500

Revise incomplete or unconvincing paragraphs by adding specific examples, details, facts, reasons, or incidents that support the topic sentence.

The following paragraph does not contain enough supporting information. Although the supporting facts and details are related to the topic sentence, they merely skim the surface.

Paragraph with too little support

Let's examine the appearance of the sea horse, another of nature's warm-water fish. Sea horses rarely grow to be longer than the palm of your hand, and because they are so small, they might appear to be pieces of seaweed drifting underwater.

Now read a revised version of the paragraph, with additional supporting information. The revised paragraph gives a more complete picture of the appearance of a sea horse.

Well-developed paragraph with enough support

Let's examine the appearance of the sea horse, another of nature's warm-water fish. Sea horses rarely grow to be longer than the palm of your hand, and because they are small, they might appear to be pieces of seaweed drifting underwater. The heads of sea horses look like the heads of horses, which is how sea horses got their name. Their bodies are made up of bony plates, held together by a series of tiny spines resembling horses' manes. The bodies curve at the end to form a pointed tail that helps them to move quickly through water.

Sometimes a paragraph has the wrong kind of supporting information. In the following paragraph, only generalizations and weak, unsupported opinions are used as support.

Paragraph with generalizations and unsupported opinions

For a thrilling experience, visitors to New York should travel to the top of the World Trade Center. The two towers in downtown Manhattan are incredibly tall. Quickly, special express elevators take visitors to the top of the towers. The greatest thrill is the sensation of the elevator going up. From the top of the tower, the view is terrific. Everything looks much better from up high. The most enjoyable thing to do is to look down. From that height visitors feel tremendous.

501

When the generalizations and opinions are replaced with specific facts, examples, and details, the paragraph becomes more interesting and convincing.

Well-developed paragraph with facts, examples, and details

For a thrilling experience, visitors to New York City should travel to the top of the World Trade Center. The two towers of steel and glass rise to a dizzying height of 110 stories. Special express elevators whizz visitors up 107 stories in just fifty-eight seconds. The riders' bodies seem to grow heavier, their stomachs leap, and their ears pop. On the enclosed deck, floor-to-ceiling windows give visitors the illusion of being suspended in the air. Above the 110th floor, visitors can stand on the highest outdoor observation platform in the world. With the winds from New York Bay whipping their hair, visitors can view other skyscrapers, among them the Empire State Building and the Chrysler Building. Directly below, matchbox cars and miniature people crowd the streets, and hordes of taxis scurry back and forth like yellow bugs. High above New York City's noise and bustle, visitors feel remote and almost superhuman.

EXERCISE C: Revising Supporting Information. Improve each paragraph by adding further supporting information or by replacing generalizations and weak opinions with examples, details, facts, reasons, or incidents.

(1) Prices today have gone way out of control. Almost everything costs a lot more than it used to. Newspapers once cost only ten or fifteen cents but not anymore. And that is nothing compared to other goods and services. Look what has happened to the price of gasoline.

(2) To be a good babysitter, you must have patience. All little children are sometimes bratty. They like to test a new babysitter to see how he or she will react. If you can be understanding and patient, you will show them that you care. Children are always nervous with a babysitter. Patience will help. If you are patient, the children will look forward to having you babysit another time. That is, if you weren't driven to nervous collapse after the first time!

(3) In order to be a good student and earn high grades, you must fulfill certain requirements. The most basic requirement is, of course, steady attendance. You should attend all classes—or as many as possible—in order to keep up to date with the classwork and assignments. Another requirement is that you pay attention in class: Listen, ask questions, and participate as much as you can.

(4) Shakespeare's *Romeo and Juliet* is one of the most popular of his plays. In one good scene, Romeo expresses his love for Juliet for the first time. The most exciting scene occurs when Romeo fights his famous duel with Tybalt, Juliet's cousin. People enjoy the play because its theme still has meaning today, although Shakespeare wrote the story a long time ago. Because of its popularity, *Romeo and Juliet* is often performed. It has been made into a movie several times, too.

REVISING: Checking for Unity

When you are revising a paragraph, be sure to check for unity, as well as for a good topic sentence and adequate supporting information. In a unified paragraph, all of the supporting information must relate to the main idea stated in the topic sentence.

Eliminate supporting information that is unimportant or does not relate directly to the topic sentence.

In the following paragraph, the writer switched the topic somewhat in the middle of the paragraph. As a result, there are unrelated sentences that destroy the unity of the paragraph and may confuse the reader. These unrelated sentences are shown in italics.

Paragraph with unrelated sentences   The cell, the basic structural unit of plants and animals, is composed of three main parts. The outer wall of the cell, the cell membrane, is a thin film that covers the cell. The material inside the cell, known as the cytoplasm, is a jelly-like subtance that circulates within the cell. *Cells differ in shape. A wood cell is long and thin, whereas a red blood cell is round and microscopic.*

The nucleus of the cell is found within the cytoplasm. The nucleus controls such activities of the cell as growth.

If the fourth and fifth sentences are removed, the paragraph will make more sense because the rest of the sentences describe the three main parts of the cell mentioned in the topic sentence.

EXERCISE D: Revising for Unity. Rewrite the following paragraph, removing any information unrelated to the topic sentence.

(1) The periodical cicada lives longer than any other insect. (2) Every seventeen years, this insect emerges from the ground, having grown from about six-hundredths of an inch to about one inch in length. (3) It then continues to live, as an adult cicada, for about one week. (4) Periodical cicadas were thought to be locusts by Pilgrims, who mistook their sudden appearance in large numbers for a plague of grasshoppers like those mentioned in the Bible. (5) Locusts are a type of grasshopper that feeds heavily on vegetation. (6) Scientists have not yet been able to determine why the cicada lives so long, but the study of its life cycle has already added greatly to our knowledge of insect life.

REVISING: Improving Coherence

If your paragraph is difficult to follow or your supporting information is unconnected, your paragraph lacks coherence. With some paragraphs you can make the needed connections simply by adding a few helpful transitions, repeating a few main words, or adding a concluding sentence. With other paragraphs, however, you may have to reconsider the order of your supporting information.

Reorganize supporting information, add transitions, repeat main words, and add a concluding sentence where needed to achieve coherence.

In the following paragraph, the writer has tried to use spatial order but has not used it effectively. Because the supporting information jumps around, the paragraph is confusing.

504

Paragraph with disorganized support

I will never forget my one and only experience with a "minor" earthquake, as it was later labeled by the news media. The roof beams creaked so much that I feared the roof would come crashing down. The floor beneath my feet felt suddenly unsteady, as if it were being made to vibrate by a powerful motor buried deep under the house. Small chips of plaster fell from the ceiling, landing on my hair and shoulders. Both my dog, who was hiding under the bed, and I were terrified.

If the writer were to revise the paragraph so that the description of the effects of the earthquake began with the floor and moved to the ceiling, the paragraph would make more sense. The support would then be organized spatially.

Paragraph with well-organized support

I will never forget my one and only experience with a "minor" earthquake, as it was later labeled by the news media. The floor beneath my feet felt suddenly unsteady, as if it were being made to vibrate by a powerful motor buried deep under the house. Small chips of plaster fell from the ceiling, landing on my hair and shoulders. The roof beams creaked so much that I feared the roof would come crashing down. Both my little dog, who was trembling while hiding under the bed, and I were terrified.

EXERCISE E: Revising for Coherence. Reorganize and rewrite the following paragraph. Add any transitions and repeat any main words and synonyms that you think necessary.

(1) In 1960 Steinbeck won the Nobel Prize in Literature. (2) Steinbeck was born in Salinas, California, a town of laborers and ranch workers. (3) He learned about the farm and factory workers about whom he later wrote. (4) His first popular book, *Tortilla Flat,* was rejected by nine different publishers before it was finally published. (5) He attended Stanford University in California, while occasionally working as a laborer. (6) He worked as a reporter in New York City but returned to California because of ill health. (7) Perhaps his best novel, *The Grapes of Wrath,* was published in 1940. (8) There were many ups and downs in John Steinbeck's life.

505

REVISING: Proofreading Your Paragraph

Once you have found any problems in your paragraph and corrected them, you should check your grammar, mechanics, and spelling.

Use a checklist to help proofread your final paragraph.

The following checklist points out the kinds of errors you should look for when proofreading the final copy of your paragraph.

CHECKLIST FOR PROOFREADING A PARAGRAPH

1. Does your paragraph have any sentence errors (fragments, run-ons, or problems with modifiers)?
2. Have you used verbs and pronouns correctly?
3. Have you capitalized properly?
4. Have you used periods, commas, apostrophes, and other punctuation marks where they are needed?
5. Have you checked the spelling of any words that do not look right or that you often misspell?

You may be able to correct a few minor errors you catch right on your final copy. If you find major errors or a number of errors, however, recopy the paragraph and proofread it again.

EXERCISE F: Proofreading Your Paragraph. Using the checklist on this page as a guide, proofread the paragraph you revised in Exercise E. If you find many mistakes, recopy the paragraph and proofread it again.

DEVELOPING WRITING SKILLS: Revising Your Paragraphs. Using a paragraph you have written recently, revise it by following each of the steps presented in this section. Submit both the original and revised versions of the paragraph to your teacher.

Writing Workshop: Paragraphs

ASSIGNMENT 1

Topic   Great Human Feats

Form and Purpose   A paragraph that narrates the events of an unusual and remarkable human feat

Audience   Producers of the television show *Amazing Feats*

Length   One paragraph

Focus   Choose a human feat that can be adequately covered in a single paragraph. You should convey why it was a remarkable feat and how it was accomplished.

Sources   Newspapers, a book of records, biographies

Prewriting   Write notes about your main idea and the events of the feat. Use questions like those on pages 491 and 493. Then outline the events in chronological order.

Writing   Write a draft that includes a topic sentence and that narrates the events of the feat.

Revising   Revise your paper using the checklist on page 498. Then proofread it using the checklist on page 506.

ASSIGNMENT 2

Topic   How Animals Communicate

Form and Purpose   A paragraph explaining how an animal communicates with other members of the same species

Audience   Readers of a ninth-grade science textbook

Length   One paragraph

Focus   Explain the communication methods of an animal. Include facts, details, and examples that support your explanation.

Sources   Magazine articles and books about animals, interviews with animal trainers or pet store owners

Prewriting   Your main idea should identify the animal and its primary method of communication. Make notes that support and explain your main idea. Choose a clear, logical method of organization (p. 481).

Writing   Write a paragraph that includes a topic sentence, details that explain the method of communication, and transitions that link related sentences and ideas (p. 485).

Revising   Use the checklist on page 498 to help you revise. Then write a final version. Proofread it by using the checklist on page 506.

Topics for Writing: Paragraphs

Simple Alarm Clock

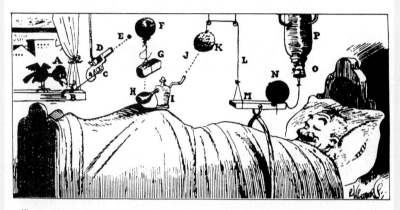

The early bird (**A**) arrives and catches worm (**B**), pulling string (**C**) and shooting off pistol (**D**). Bullet (**E**) busts balloon (**F**), dropping brick (**G**) on bulb (**H**) of atomizer (**I**) and shooting perfume (**J**) on sponge (**K**)—As sponge gains in weight, it lowers itself and pulls string (**L**), raising end of board (**M**)—Cannon ball (**N**) drops on nose of sleeping gentleman—String tied to cannon ball releases cork (**O**) of vacuum bottle (**P**) and ice water falls on sleeper's face to assist the cannon ball in its good work.

The cartoon above substitutes a very elaborate, complicated method for a simple invention—the alarm clock. Choose a topic from the list below, or let the cartoon suggest a topic. Then plan, write, and revise a paragraph about your topic.

1. The Most Important Invention
2. The Most Useless Invention
3. The Most Dangerous Invention
4. How One Invention Often Leads to Another
5. A Persuasive Ad for a Real or Imagined Invention
6. How Human Beings Can Complicate Simple Things
7. Is the Process of Invention a Creative Act or an Accident?
8. Why People Invent
9. A Description of a Common, Simple Invention (without naming it)
10. A World Without the Invention of Language

509

22

Kinds of Writing

There are four common kinds of writing, each with a different purpose. *Expository writing* explains, gives information, or instructs. *Persuasive writing* attempts to convince or urge a reader to action. *Descriptive writing* enables a reader to see or experience a person, place, or thing. *Narrative writing* tells a story by relating a sequence of events. This chapter uses paragraphs as models to discuss these basic kinds of writing because paragraphs are concise units in longer works.

22.1 Expository Writing

The purpose of expository writing is to explain. In reports for science, papers for history, analyses of stories for English, or a summary of your qualifications on an application, you will use expository writing.

Understanding Expository Writing

Expository writing has certain distinctive features. The purpose is to explain an idea,to present information, or to give instructions. The desire to communicate clearly with a particular audience is also reflected in the supporting information and the word choice.

Topic Sentences in Expository Paragraphs. The topic sentence of an expository paragraph should express the main idea clearly in words that define and limit the topic for the reader.

The topic sentence of an expository paragraph is a direct factual statement of the main idea.

The main ideas in the following topic sentences are stated clearly and directly to prepare the reader for an explanation. The first topic sentence prepares the reader for a *process* to be explained in detail in the paragraph. The others present *ideas* to be explained or compared. Notice that all of these topic sentences assume an audience with little previous knowledge of the topic.

EXPOSITORY TOPIC SENTENCES	
Topic Sentences	**Items to be Explained**
To ride a wave in an outrigger canoe, you must follow three simple steps.	The three steps of riding a wave
According to psychologist James Dobson, fighting and denying reality are two common but unhealthy ways to handle a sense of inferiority.	The two ways people handle a sense of inferiority, and why they are unhealthy
The average beach on the Atlantic Coast differs in a number of ways from the average beach on the Pacific.	The differences between the Atlantic and Pacific Coast beaches

When you write a topic sentence for an expository paragraph, you should try to avoid words that make your topic sentence controversial. Your purpose is to explain, not to persuade, so you should avoid opinionated statements that call for arguments.

Notice the difference between the statement of fact and the statement of opinion in the following two topic sentences at the top of page 512.

STATEMENT OF FACT: Doctor J. has earned distinction as a professional basketball player.

STATEMENT OF OPINION: Doctor J. is the best athlete ever to play professional basketball.

Supporting Information in Expository Paragraphs. To explain the main idea presented in the topic sentence, an expository paragraph will often rely heavily on factual evidence.

Supporting information in expository paragraphs should be factual and clear.

In the following paragraph, facts and examples are used to give the reader a clear understanding of how a leaf works.

TOPIC SENTENCE (factual statement)

Facts and examples

A leaf is a self-regulating system. Both sides of a leaf have a protective covering or "skin." This "skin" is transparent in order that light may enter the leaf. Food, water, and other materials are transported back and forth in hollow tubes called veins. The underside of a leaf contains many direct pore-like openings called stomates. It is through the stomates that leaves are able to breathe. The leaf is able to open or close the stomates in order to control the amount of material entering or leaving the leaf. For example, if there is too much water in a leaf, the excess can be eliminated through the stomates.—Ames, Baker, and Leahy

Language and Terms in Expository Paragraphs. Since expository paragraphs are generally aimed at readers unfamiliar with the topic, the writer must choose language the reader understands. Appropriate language does not confuse the reader with technical terms, nor does it talk down to the reader.

Use appropriate language and define technical terms so that your audience will understand you.

In the paragraph on the leaf, the language is clear and direct. Terms such as *veins* and *stomates* are defined.

EXERCISE A: Identifying Expository Topic Sentences. Label each of the following topic sentences as a *statement of fact* or a *statement of opinion.*

512

EXAMPLE: Coral reefs are formed by millions of tiny organisms.

    statement of fact

1. Space exploration is our most important national priority.
2. Recent developments in food research indicate that in the future some of our foods may contain cotton and algae.
3. Our school should establish a bookstore run by students.
4. The force of the flowing waters of the Colorado River carved the Grand Canyon.
5. Three economic conditions may have helped cause the depopulation of the English countryside in the 1700's.
6. Many labor strikes could be avoided through arbitration.
7. The Sears Tower in Chicago is the world's tallest building.
8. Mozart was the greatest composer of the eighteenth century.
9. The gross national product is the total value of goods and services produced in the United States.
10. The salaries of professional athletes are too high.

EXERCISE B: Examining the Language of an Expository Paragraph. The following paragraph contains a number of examples of language that is too technical for general readers. Find at least five examples and write them on your paper.

(1) The Elmo Bumpy Torus concept is one of the most complicated experimental systems ever attempted in fusion research. (2) If successful, it promises to lead to an economical toroidal reactor with good accessibility for construction and improvements and the advantages of modularity, direct-current "steadystate" operation, and lowered requirements for auxiliary heating power. (3) A toroidal magnetic confinement device, the EBT uses a rippled magnetic field to achieve MHD equilibrium, keeping the plasma from drifting into the walls of the torus through magnetic drift.—Charles B. Stevens

PREWRITING, WRITING, and REVISING: Creating Expository Paragraphs

The key to creating good expository paragraphs is to concentrate on your purpose—to explain or inform—throughout all of the planning, writing, and revising steps.

In creating an expository paragraph, concentrate on explaining something clearly to your audience.

In planning expository paragraphs, you should begin by making sure you have a topic that can be treated in a factual manner. As you work toward a good topic sentence, concentrate on what your audience might want or need to learn.

Gather supporting information by putting yourself in your reader's place. Ask yourself, "What terms or concepts must be defined? What examples, details, facts, reasons, or incidents would make the main idea clear?"

Organize the supporting information to present your explanation clearly and effectively. To explain a process or give instructions, you can use chronological or spatial order. To explain the similarities and differences of two or more items, you will want to use a comparison-and-contrast order.

Whatever order you choose, as you write expository paragraphs, use transitions to make the order clear to the reader. Transitions not only connect the items of supporting information; they also indicate the kind of order being used.

The following paragraph tells how to travel from a hotel to the San Juan airport. Notice that the directions are presented in chronological order. The transitions *first, then, shortly,* and *soon* give the reader an idea of the time involved in following each instruction. The paragraph also uses spatial order. It is organized by location as well as by time. The phrases *right, along Ashford Avenue, away from, end of the bridge,* and so on act as additional transitions.

TOPIC SENTENCE (factual statement)	To reach the international airport, you must take the following ten- or fifteen-minute ride from the hotel. Leaving the hotel driveway, you turn right and drive along Ashford Avenue. *First,* you will cross a bridge that takes you away from the Condado area. When you
Instructions in chrono- logical and spatial order	reach the end of the bridge, you *then* take the first right, following signs for Fernandez Juncos Boulevard. You will *shortly* see a sign for Route 26. Turn left and drive along Route 26 for about five miles. *Soon* you will come to a bank of traffic lights and a sign that reads "Aeropuerto." On your left will be the airport entrance.

In revising expository paragraphs, make sure that all the ingredients in the paragraph work together to present your main idea clearly. Check to see that you have enough supporting information and that it is in a logical order. See that you have linked your support with appropriate transitions. Also make sure that your language is clear and that any unfamilar words are defined.

EXERCISE C: Planning Expository Paragraphs. Choose one topic from each of the following three lists. Narrow down any topic that is too large. Write a topic sentence for each topic you choose. Gather support for each topic sentence. Then choose the best order for each of the three paragraphs and write a modified outline for each one.

Explaining a Process	Explaining Concepts or Events	Explaining Similarities or Differences
Training a pet	The two-party system	Two ways to travel
Painting a room	A holiday tradition	Two similar sports
Changing a tire	History of sports	Two schools
Tying a bow tie	The balance of trade	Two twins
Becoming physically fit	An international event	Two television stations

DEVELOPING WRITING SKILLS: Writing and Revising Expository Paragraphs: Use the three topic sentences you chose and the supporting information you gathered in Exercise C to write one expository paragraph that explains a process, one that explains a concept, and one that compares and contrasts, following these instructions.

1. As you write, concentrate on connecting your ideas by using appropriate transitions. Also, be sure to define any difficult terms or words that may be unfamiliar to your audience.
2. As you revise, think about the following questions: Have you explained the main idea clearly with enough supporting information? Have you used the best order? Have you used appropriate transitions? Have you used language the reader can understand?

22.2 Persuasive Writing

Persuasive writing takes a stand on an issue and defends it. It tries to persuade readers to agree with its position.

Understanding Persuasive Writing

Good persuasive writing has certain special features. The topic sentence in a persuasive paragraph clearly states an opinion.The supporting information should consist of the best evidence in support of the opinion. In addition, because you are seeking to change minds, you should carefully consider the effect on your audience of your choice of words.

Topic Sentences in Persuasive Paragraphs. The topic sentence of a persuasive paragraph should present an opinion clearly and directly. The opinion should be an idea with which other people may disagree. It should also be an opinion on a topic that you think is worthwhile discussing.

A topic sentence for a persuasive paragraph should be a focused opinion on a significant topic.

Notice that each of the persuasive topic sentences in the following chart is clearly controversial. A pro and con form of each sentence is included.

PERSUASIVE TOPIC SENTENCES	
Pro	**Con**
Leashing laws should be made more strict in our community.	Leashing laws should not be made more strict in our community.
F.M. radio stations in the city are better than A.M. radio stations.	A.M. radio stations in the city are better than F.M. radio stations.
The city should ban roller skating on streets and sidewalks.	The city should continue to allow roller skating on streets and sidewalks.

The topic sentence for a persuasive paragraph should not be a purely factual statement that calls only for explanation, such as *The three branches of our national government are the executive, legislative, and judicial branches.* Nor should it be an insignificant or highly personal opinion of little interest to anyone else, such as *Hotdogs are delicious* or *My sister is a pest.* Instead, topic sentences present an *opinion* of interest and importance to other people.

Supporting Information in Persuasive Paragraphs. Use the strongest possible evidence to defend your opinion.

Supporting information in a persuasive paragraph should be strong evidence.

You will probably find examples, reasons, and facts to be the most useful support for developing persuasive paragraphs. Supporting information that can be proved or documented by books or experts will often make your case more convincing. Therefore, you may want to do some careful research. Above all, avoid using support that presents only weak opinions.

In the following paragraph, notice that the call to action in the topic sentence is supported by three specific examples.

TOPIC
SENTENCE

Three
examples

If we cooperate, we can restore the attractiveness and safety of our apartment building, which is now threatened by vandalism. First of all, each of us can donate some time and a little physical labor to repair the existing damage. In addition, each tenant can give money to the Lobby Improvement Fund to help cover the cost of new lighting fixtures, bulbs, mailbox locks, and panes of glass. Most importantly, we can help prevent future vandalism by reporting to the superintendent the presence of any strangers who seem to be loitering in or around the building. If we fail to take this problem into our own hands, we will only suffer repeated damage and encourage the further decay of our building.

The Use of Reasonable Language. Whenever you are writing persuasive paragraphs, you should be careful to avoid using language that may annoy, anger, or confuse your readers.

Use reasonable language in persuasive paragraphs.

You will never persuade anyone if you offend them by calling their favorite kind of car a *piece of tin,* their political party *scheming capitalists* or *un-American radicals,* or their favorite athletic team *uncoordinated fools.* If you are not calm, objective, and reasonable in your writing, the reader will not bother to consider your ideas.

In the paragraph on page 517, notice how the writer remains calm and reasonable even though the subject is a serious one.

If you want to persuade, you should also use words that your readers can understand. Do not lose your readers by using technical terms without defining them. Any word or term that may unnecessarily confuse readers should be avoided.

EXERCISE A: Recognizing Persuasive Topic Sentences.
Label each of the following as a *persuasive topic sentence* or an *insignificant opinion.*

EXAMPLE: It's too cold in the winter in our state.

insignificant opinion

1. The best ice cream flavor in the world is strawberry mocha.
2. Our school should give credit for activities such as band.
3. Talking on the phone is the most relaxing thing on earth.
4. Bicycle riding in the city park should be made illegal.
5. Blue is a more beautiful color than green.
6. The legal drinking age in this state should be changed.
7. Word processors are often a big help to writers.
8. It's time for voters to remove Senator Smith from office.
9. More students should study abroad during the summer.
10. Looking for a summer job is a nuisance.

EXERCISE B: Examining the Language of a Persuasive Paragraph. List at least five examples of emotional language and confusing terms from the following paragraph.

(1) It's time those fools in charge of the darkroom realize that they are supposed to be giving us service, not taking it away. (2) Their latest goof has been to reduce lab working hours. (3) Even the best shutterwork will be spoiled if there is not adequate time to process film and prints. (4) In fact, we already have such poor facilities and crummy service that the

518

fixer is always contaminated and both the enlarger and the water bath have been out of order for six weeks. (5) The only solution to this problem is to fire those incompetent slobs and hire people who know how to run a business.

PREWRITING, WRITING, and REVISING: Creating Persuasive Paragraphs

The key to creating good persuasive paragraphs is to concentrate on your purpose—to persuade someone to accept your opinion—throughout all the planning, writing, and revising stages.

In creating a persuasive paragraph, concentrate on the need to convince your audience.

In planning persuasive paragraphs, always assume that your audience is opposed to your viewpoint. When you write a topic sentence, therefore, choose words that will make your position clear to the audience as well as words that you will be able to defend.

Gather the most convincing examples and reasons to back up your opinion. Try thinking of arguments on both sides of the issue. This will help you to make sure your support will cover all major points.

Organize supporting information in a manner that will help you convince your readers. Order of importance is particularly useful in persuasive paragraphs because it allows you to lead the reader along as you gradually build up to the strongest argument. No matter what order you use, remember that your arguments should be logical and easy to follow. Frequently, you may also want to add a concluding statement that offers a summary, a final warning, or a call to action.

Persuasive writing can resemble a debate, taking both sides into account. In the following paragraph, the writer mentions arguments on the other side and then counters them.

TOPIC
SENTENCE
(controversial
statement)

Until better sources of energy are found, nuclear power is the answer to our growing energy needs. Given the enormous demands by industry and private consumers for electrical power, conventional means of generating power are no longer adequate. Water power and coal have proved too costly or un-

519

clean as power sources, and in the foreseeable future, the world's supply of petroleum will be depleted. The use of solar energy and the development of synthetic fuels may prove valuable, but they are still in their infancy. Nuclear power plants are available today.

Three reasons in developmental order

Although they are expensive to construct, they are efficient and economical in the long run because breeder reactors can recycle nuclear waste. Though everyone looks forward to safer and more efficient sources of energy, nuclear energy is the best choice for today.

Concluding sentence

Notice how the writer recognizes the opposing viewpoint in the paragraph by mentioning other possible energy sources—water power, coal, petroleum, solar energy, and synthetic fuels. Also, the writer admits that nuclear power plants are expensive to build and that the search for a safer, more efficient source of energy should continue. While acknowledging these opposing arguments, the writer counters each with arguments *for* the use of nuclear power.

In revising persuasive writing, check for anything that might make a reader reject your opinion. You may need to add or replace supporting information. You may also need to put your supporting information in a more logical order or add transitions. Finally, be sure that your language is reasonable.

EXERCISE C: Planning a Persuasive Paragraph. Choose one of the following topics and narrow it down as necessary. Write a topic sentence and gather support. Then choose an appropriate order and write a modified outline.

Compulsory gym classes
Space exploration
A current sensation
A recent movie

Changing something at school
Improving a building
Reading a particular book
Passing a new law

DEVELOPING WRITING SKILLS: Writing and Revising a Persuasive Paragraph: Write a persuasive paragraph using the outline you prepared for Exercise C. Then check your paragraph for logical order, appropriate transitions, and reasonable language and correct any problems you discover.

520

Descriptive Writing 22.3

When you use words to help someone else picture a sight you have seen or imagined—for example, the clouds before a blizzard or the crowd at a homecoming game—you are using many of the skills needed to write a description.

Understanding Descriptive Writing

Descriptive writing re-creates sense impressions: sights, sounds, smells, and tastes. It uses language to capture a *dominant impression* or mood.

Topic Sentences in Descriptive Paragraphs. The topic sentence of a descriptive paragraph should present a general, or dominant, impression of whatever you have chosen to describe.

A topic sentence in a descriptive paragraph presents a dominant impression.

The topic sentence of a descriptive paragraph should focus the reader's attention on a specific person, place, object, or experience. It should not be either a statement that calls for a factual explanation or an opinion that must be backed up with reasons. Notice the differences among these three sentences.

FOR AN EXPOSITORY PARAGRAPH: Recent studies have shown that dogs try to imitate the behavior of their masters.

FOR A PERSUASIVE PARAGRAPH: Dogs should be forbidden in our town parks.

FOR A DESCRIPTIVE PARAGRAPH: The dog, howling in the alley, was a lonely outcast.

The last topic sentence presents a dominant impression that can be supported by details about the physical appearance and behavior of the "lonely outcast" dog.

Notice that each of the following topic sentences suggests a dominant impression or a mood. Readers will expect the paragraphs to present details that contribute to the dominant impression or mood and make it more vivid.

521

DESCRIPTIVE TOPIC SENTENCES	
Topic Sentences	**Dominant Impressions**
She was a woman with a broom or a dustpan or a washrag or a mixing spoon in her hand.—Ray Bradbury	Feeling of useful activity
It was a miserable place to which no one would choose to go.	Feeling of bleakness and misery
The full moon hung over North Dormer, whitening the mist that filled the hollows between the hills and floated transparently above the fields.—Edith Wharton	Feeling of strangeness and uneasiness

The location of the topic sentence should be chosen care-fully. If the topic sentence comes at the beginning of a descriptive paragraph, it can arouse a reader's curiosity to "see" the scene suggested by the topic sentence in greater detail. If the topic sentence comes at the end of the paragraph, it can summarize the dominant impression by telling the reader what the details add up to.

Supporting Information in Descriptive Paragraphs. Descriptive paragraphs may contain facts and examples, but they generally rely mainly on details to support the dominant impression. The words used usually appeal to the reader's senses and emotions as well as to the reader's understanding.

Supporting information in descriptive paragraphs should consist of specific details.

In the following paragraph, which describes a gloomy, unappealing woman, the writer focuses on physical characteristics and clothing to convey a dominant impression of harshness. The dominant impression, given by the words *dark* and *foreboding*, is developed by these details: *Heavy, black eyebrows, furrowed forehead, severe bun, tarnished hoops, brass hinges,* and *brass chain*. Notice that the descriptive words and references to metal appeal to the sense of touch and suggest coldness.

TOPIC
SENTENCE
(dominant
impression)

Details

Concluding
sentence

Miss Crabtree's appearance was dark and foreboding when she arrived at our door. Her heavy black eyebrows met above her nose because her forehead was heavily furrowed. Her hair was pulled into a severe bun, and she wore tarnished hoops in her ears. At her side she clasped a large leather bag with brass hinges and a heavy brass chain. Somehow we knew that Miss Crabtree's arrival marked an uncomfortable change in our lives.

The Language of Description. The language used in descriptive paragraphs should differ from the language used for explaining or persuading.

Descriptions should use colorful language, sensory impressions, and figures of speech.

Colorful words help make your descriptions real to the reader by conveying a picture, a feeling, or both. Most of the details used in the description of Miss Crabtree are phrased in colorful words. To engage the reader's senses, you should also make use of *sensory impressions*. These are words that describe sounds, smells, tastes, textures, and so on. Using these words will make your writing seem much more alive.

SENSORY IMPRESSIONS: the crackle and rustle of tissue paper

golden stickiness of honey

the pin-pricking sting of thawing feet

the noisy clanking of a radiator

Another way to involve a reader in your description is to use figures of speech, such as *similes* and *metaphors*. Similes and metaphors are comparisons. A simile takes two essentially unlike things and draws an imaginative comparison between them using the word *like* or *as*.

SIMILES: The seagulls hovering above the beach looked *like* a mobile suspended from the sky.

The chattering squirrels sounded as unfriendly *as* a group of angry customers.

523

In a metaphor the words *like* and *as* are omitted, and the two things become identical.

METAPHORS: His empty office was a bone picked clean.

With the lights on, the chandelier was a shimmering rainbow of color.

Some similes and metaphors that were once original have lost their vividness through overuse. These overused similes and metaphors are called clichés and dead metaphors. Phrases such as *busy as a bee, timid as a mouse, a show stopper,* and *a thorn in the flesh* have been used so often that they have a stale sound. Try to avoid these dull expressions by choosing more descriptive ones.

In the following paragraph, the writer skillfully uses different kinds of descriptive language to create a vivid impression for the reader.

TOPIC
SENTENCE
(dominant
impression)

Colorful
language,
sensory
impressions,
and figures
of speech

On a recent trip, I found myself traveling in an *airborne relic*. I sat in the first of five passenger seats arranged in single-file in the *rusty* interior of the plane, a *single-engine day-tripper*. As I tried to peer out the *scratched, filmy window,* I reluctantly inhaled the *stuffy air, heavy with a mildew smell, dust,* and *gasoline fumes*. Rising hesitantly, the plane coughed, wheezed, and shook *like an old man with failing lungs*. Although I was strapped in place by a *frayed, crusty* seatbelt, I *shuddered* with each *bump, thud,* and *cantankerous crank* of the antique aircraft. The vibrations of this *perpetual earthquake almost cut my brain loose* from my skull, and my teeth began *to ache from being clenched*. The *plane was a pterodactyl* and belonged to an earlier age.

EXERCISE A: Recognizing Descriptive Topic Sentences.
Label each of the following topic sentences as *descriptive, expository,* or *persuasive*. Then identify the dominant impression suggested by the descriptive topic sentences.

EXAMPLE: The old couple strolled through the garden of the ruined mansion, speaking softly of other times.

descriptive   feeling of gentle acceptance

524

1. A glow of colors from the rising sun spread across the sky like an artist's pastels.
2. Researchers have recently investigated how important sleep is to physical and emotional health.
3. Our student body should overcome its apathy toward musical and dramatic programs.
4. The constant throb of drums from the stereo in the apartment below vibrated in my head.
5. The snow covered the sidewalks slowly, looking like a layer of gauze.
6. The study of genealogy can be both frustrating and fascinating.
7. The school library will continue to deteriorate if its budget is not increased.
8. An excited feeling of anticipation rippled through the crowd as they watched Dunlop cast his spell on the team and the whirling ball.
9. The bearded old man was as weathered as the shack behind him.
10. Our city should provide faster, more dependable public transportation.

EXERCISE B: Using Colorful Words and Sensory Impressions. List at least three descriptive phrases or sensory impressions for each item. Try to use colorful words to describe each item as you would experience it through your senses.

EXAMPLE: traffic on a busy street at night

the whoosh of cars, screeching tires, groaning engines of trucks and buses

1. diving into a pool of cold water
2. rain on a car's roof
3. a bakery
4. running barefoot across hot pavement
5. eating a caramel apple
6. dawn in the mountains
7. arriving at a formal party
8. riding on a bus
9. walking through an empty building
10. an approaching ambulance

525

EXERCISE C: Writing Similes and Metaphors. Complete each sentence with a vivid, imaginative simile or metaphor. Label each completed sentence as a *simile* or a *metaphor.*

EXAMPLE: The hungry mosquitoes swooped toward the guests like

              The hungry mosquitoes swooped toward the guests like dive bombers.   (simile)

1. To the baby security was
2. The fly ball smashed into her glove like
3. The massive black clouds were
4. The shooting fireworks were as deafening as
5. The lemon drink tasted like
6. The earthquake made the room look like
7. As she listened to his complaints, her eyes became
8. The new house smelled like
9. At dusk, the trees bending in the wind became
10. Under his feet, the soft ground was

PREWRITING, WRITING, and REVISING: Creating Descriptive Paragraphs

To prepare good descriptive paragraphs, concentrate on giving the reader a vivid sense of whatever you are describing.

Concentrate on making your descriptive paragraphs as vivid as possible.

In planning descriptive paragraphs, you will need to decide on the dominant impression you want to present and then set forth that impression in a topic sentence. Supporting details should develop naturally from topic sentences. They can be drawn from direct observation or from your imagination, depending on whether you are writing about something real or something imaginary. Be sure to include enough details for the reader to be able to visualize clearly what you are describing.

You can also help the reader to visualize by organizing the description around a specific *point of observation*. For example, your view of a parade would differ greatly depending on whether you were standing in the crowd or riding in one of the floats. In most descriptive paragraphs, the point of observation can be made clear to the reader through the use of devices such as transitions.

The following paragraph describes an unusual doctor's office using spatial order. Notice how the transitions *around, lower, upper, over, in the ... corner,* and *within* move the reader's eyes throughout the office and help the reader picture the room. It is as if the reader were standing with the writer at a point of observation near the door. Notice also that all of the details support the dominant impression stated in the topic sentence that the study is "a very curious place."

TOPIC
SENTENCE
(dominant
impression)

Details
in spatial
order

If all stories were true, Dr. Heidegger's study must have been a very curious place. It was a dim, old-fashioned chamber, festooned with cobwebs, and besprinkled with antique dust. *Around* the walls stood several oaken bookcases, the *lower* shelves of which were filled with rows of gigantic folios and black-letter quartos, and the *upper* with little parchment-covered duodecimos. *Over* the central bookcase was a bronze bust of Hippocrates, with which, according to some authorities, Dr. Heidegger was accustomed to hold consultations in all difficult cases of his practice. *In the* obscurest *corner* of the room stood a tall and narrow oaken closet, with its door ajar, *within* which doubtfully appeared a skeleton.—N. Hawthorne

In revising descriptive paragraphs, try to make the dominant impression more vivid. You can do this by adding further details or replacing ineffective details. You can also further enrich your descriptive language, but be careful not to get carried away with figures of speech. Finally, be sure that you have used a clear point of observation.

EXERCISE D: Developing a Clear Point of Observation.
Organize the following topic sentence and list of supporting details into a descriptive paragraph using spatial order and appropriate transitions.

TOPIC SENTENCE: When Dave and Bob walked into the forest glen, they felt as if they had entered a quiet, green room.

527

1. Next to the brook, willowy reeds rustled in the breeze.
2. The brook, which ran at their left, splashed and gurgled in a miniature waterfall.
3. The two boys, reluctant to disturb the hushed stillness of the glen, held their breath as they tiptoed in.
4. To their right, hemlocks fenced off the rest of the glen.
5. Its clear water looked cool and inviting.
6. Beyond the reeds pillars of pine trees guarded the glen.
7. With each footstep, a piney smell rose from the carpet of needles.
8. All sounds were muffled except for a chattering brook.
9. The pines and hemlocks seemed to support the sky.
10. The blue dome of sky that capped the glen closed it off and made it complete.

EXERCISE E: Planning a Descriptive Paragraph. Choose one of the following subjects and narrow it down. Develop a dominant impression by observing your subject carefully and then state your dominant impression in a topic sentence. Gather support through further observation. Then organize your support.

Your school locker	Your best friend	A grocery store
A refrigerator	An unusual neighbor	An ugly building
A rug	A baby	A school gymnasium

DEVELOPING WRITING SKILLS: Writing and Revising a Descriptive Paragraph. Write the paragraph you planned in Exercise E, using colorful language, sensory impressions, and perhaps a few similes and metaphors. Be sure to connect your details with transitions. After you have written your paragraph, check its content, organization, and language and correct any problems you discover.

22.4 Narrative Writing

If you were to give a friend a detailed account of your first day as a camp counselor, you would be telling a story step by step in chronological order. You would be using the ingredients of narrative writing.

Understanding Narrative Writing

The purpose of a narrative writing is to tell a story, true or fictional, usually to entertain.

Topic Sentences in Narrative Paragraphs Many narrative paragraphs in longer works by professional writers lack topic sentences although the paragraphs themselves are still unified and coherent. This section will focus on narrative paragraphs that tell complete stories. For this kind of narrative paragraph, you should have a topic sentence. It can present a general truth, lesson, or discovery that the story illustrates or it can simply start the action of the story.

A topic sentence for a narrative paragraph should present a general truth or set the scene and prepare the reader for the events to follow.

A topic sentence can be especially effective at the beginning or the end of a narrative paragraph. At the beginning of a paragraph, the topic sentence can arouse curiosity and focus the reader's thoughts. A topic sentence at the end of a paragraph can function as a humorous or serious conclusion.

Any of the topic sentences in the following chart would be suitable for a narrative paragraph and could appear at the beginning or the end of the paragraph.

NARRATIVE TOPIC SENTENCES	
Topic Sentences	**What They Do**
First impressions of people are not always correct.	States a general truth
Never turn your back on the ocean.	States a lesson learned
Little did I know that I could not avoid him.	States a discovery made
The day the enormous cat first meowed at her doorstep she knew it was a troublemaker.	Sets the scene and prepares the reader for events to follow

529

Supporting Information in Narrative Paragraphs. All narrative paragraphs have a *point of view,* the perspective of the person who is telling the story. For example, you can put yourself in the story and relate the action as you experienced it, or you an relate the action as another person or a character experienced it. Whoever tells the story, the supporting information in the paragraph should consistently reflect the storyteller's point of view.

Supporting information must maintain a consistent point of view.

The following paragraph relates a story illustrating a general truth the writer has discovered personally: *Life with a younger brother is often one frustration after another.* The paragraph uses specific physical details as support. Notice the writer presents only those details that would be seen from a personal point of view.

Events seen from a personal point of view	This morning I couldn't find my car keys anywhere. I searched all over: in my pockets, in the dresser, in my closet, on the kitchen table, even on the window sills. Finally, I ran anxiously to the back porch to ask my family if anyone had seen my keys, and there was my younger brother trying to adjust his skates with my keys. Although I was very angry, I was so late that I simply took the keys and ran to the car, only to find the driveway cluttered with my brother's skateboard, bicycle, and basketball. Just as he was about to skate away, I caught him and made him pick up his toys so I could back the car out of the driveway. Getting into the car, I
TOPIC SENTENCE (general truth)	discovered his baseball uniform draped over the front seat. I threw it in the back seat and eased out of the garage, already twenty minutes late. Life with a younger brother is often one frustration after another.

Language in Narrative Writing. In order for a narrative to grab the reader's attention, it should appeal to the reader's senses, emotions, and imagination with the language of description: colorful words, sensory impressions, and vivid similes and metaphors. (See Section 22.3 for a more complete explanation of colorful words, sensory impressions, and similes and metaphors.) Most narrative paragraphs you write should also contain strong action verbs.

Use colorful words, sensory impressions, similes and metaphors, and strong action verbs in narrative writing.

In the preceding paragraph, the reader sees the events through the writer's eyes. The colorful words, sensory impressions (especially visual details), and strong verbs help the reader see and experience the action.

EXERCISE A: Practicing with Topic Sentences for Narrative Paragraphs. Choose five of the following topics and write a topic sentence for each.

EXAMPLE: Moving to a new town

We had expected Louisville to be a quiet place.

First babysitting job	An argument with a friend
First time at bat	An incident while traveling
Meeting a new person	A frightening moment
A shopping trip	Handling a friend's problem
A sister's biggest success	Where a nickname came from

EXERCISE B: Identifying Descriptive Language in a Narrative Paragraph. The following paragraph from Charles Dickens' *Great Expectations* contains a number of examples of colorful words, sensory impressions, and strong verbs. Find at least five examples of vivid language and write them on your paper.

(1) It was in this place, and at this moment, that a strange thing happened to my fancy. (2) I thought it a strange thing then, and I thought it a stranger thing long afterwards. (3) I turned my eyes—a little dimmed by looking up at the frosty light—towards a great wooden beam in a low nook of the building near me on my right hand, and I saw a figure hanging there by the neck. (4) A figure all in yellow white, with but one shoe to the feet; and it hung so that I could see that the faded trimmings of the dress were like earthy paper, and that the face was Miss Havisham's, with a movement going over the whole

531

countenance as if she were trying to call me. (5) In the terror of seeing the figure, and in the terror of being certain that it had not been there before, I at first ran from it, and then ran towards it. (6) And my terror was greatest of all when I found no figure there.—Charles Dickens

PREWRITING, WRITING, and REVISING: Creating Narrative Paragraphs

To prepare good narrative paragraphs, you must concentrate on making the sequence of events clear to your audience.

In writing narrative paragraphs, concentrate on presenting a clear sequence of events.

In planning narrative paragraphs, you must decide what kind of a topic sentence you want to write. You may want to present some general truth or you can use your topic sentence simply to start the action.

For supporting details, you should draw on what you have seen, heard, felt, observed, or imagined. Your own experience and knowledge will provide raw material for your story. List the real or imaginary events chronologically by continuously asking yourself, "What happened next?" Then examine your list to see if any details are unnecessary or inconsistent. Ask yourself, "Does the reader need to know this?" Then eliminate all unnecessary and inconsistent details.

In organizing and writing about the events in your narrative paragraph, remember to focus the reader's attention on the action. Try to build suspense, while using transitions to indicate the passage of time and changes in location. Remember that you want to make the reader feel he or she is witnessing the events.

In the following paragraph, the topic sentence sets the scene for the story: *December 7, 1941, began as ordinarily as any other day.* Transitions indicating the time—*before dawn, while, once inside, soon, for a moment,* and *then*—help show the order of events.

TOPIC SENTENCE   For Arnold and Anna Shields, December 7, 1941, began as ordinarily as any other day. They got up *before*

532

(to start the story)

Events presented chronologically

dawn, and drove to their bakery, parking their old Packard behind the store. Arnold unlocked the door to the bakery *while* Anna got the pies they had baked the night before out of the trunk of the car. *Once inside,* they heated the ovens and prepared to bake bread and muffins, exactly as they had done every day for five years. *Soon* Arnold unlocked the front door for the customers and turned on the sign in the window that said "Bakery." *For a moment* he watched cars moving along Santa Monica Boulevard. *Then* he walked to the back of the store to turn the radio on to the familiar soft music. News of the attack on Pearl Harbor was still an hour or more away.

In revising narrative paragraphs, be sure that the chronological order of events has been made clear by transitions. You should also check to make sure that your language is both active and colorful.

EXERCISE C: Planning a Narrative Paragraph. Choose one of the topics listed in Exercise A (one that you did not select before) and narrow it down as necessary. Write a topic sentence and gather your support. Then organize your support and prepare a modified outline.

DEVELOPING WRITING SKILLS: Writing and Revising a Narrative Paragraph. Write the paragraph you planned in Exercise C. Then check your paragraph for a consistent point of view, helpful transitions, and colorful, precise language and correct any problems you discover.

Writing Workshop: Kinds of Writing

ASSIGNMENT 1

Topic Seizing a Scene

Form and Purpose A paragraph that conveys a dominant, favorable impression of a scene to readers

Audience Readers of the newspaper's "Travel" section

Length One paragraph

Focus Choose a scene that interests you and that impresses you. In a description of the scene, cite specific sensory details that convey a dominant impression of the scene.

Sources Personal experiences, books, films

Prewriting Write the dominant impression that you want to present. Then make notes about the scene. Each note should vividly support the dominant impression.

Writing Write a draft that includes a topic sentence which conveys the dominant impression. Write vivid details of the scene and organize them spatially.

Revising Check the content, organization, and language. If necessary, add colorful sensory words and transitions between sentences. Then write a final version.

Folklore in Ayachucho

ASSIGNMENT 2

Topic A Persuasive Letter to the Editor

Form and Purpose A letter to the editor that persuasively argues your focused opinion or point of view

Audience Readers of a newspaper or news magazine

Length One paragraph

Focus Identify an important issue and state your opinion. Support your opinion with examples, facts, and reasons.

Sources Daily newspaper, weekly news magazine

Prewriting Choose a significant topic or issue. Write a focused opinion about the issue. Make notes about specific facts, examples, and reasons that support your opinion.

Writing Include a persuasive topic sentence and supporting details presented in order of importance. Conclude with a summary statement, a warning, or a call to action.

Revising Revise your paragraph for logical order, transitions, and reasonable language.

Topics for Writing: Kinds of Writing

The photo above may suggest the past, present, or future of both real and imaginary worlds. Plan, write, and revise a descriptive, persuasive, narrative, or expository paragraph about a topic related to the photo. If you prefer, write a single paragraph about one of the following topics.

1. Living Conditions on Another Planet
2. The Benefits of Space Exploration
3. Space Colonies in the Year 3000 (a description)
4. Why a Particular Science-Fiction Film or Book Was or Was Not Good
5. A Narrative Account of a Real or Imaginary Space Exploration Event
6. An Inhabitant of Another Galaxy's View of Human Beings
7. Why Humans Need to Explore the Unknown
8. The Process of Launching a Rocket
9. A Description of Landing on a Remote Planet
10. Other Intelligent Life Forms in the Universe—Yes or No?

23

Essays

In your work now and in the future, you will often be asked to write well-organized compositions to show your knowledge of different topics. If you understand what goes into an essay and how to write one, you will find these writing assignments easier and more enjoyable.

Understanding Essays   23.1

An essay is composed of a group of related paragraphs that work together to present one main point. Once you understand the basic structure of an essay, you can adapt the form to fit different topics and assignments.

The Parts of an Essay

An essay has three parts: (1) an *introduction,* which presents the main point of the essay; (2) a *body,* which consists of two or more paragraphs that support or explain the essay's main point; and (3) a *conclusion,* which summarizes the main point and brings the essay to a close.

Notice in the following diagram that the introductory paragraph includes a *thesis statement,* which states the main point of the essay. The thesis statement is the idea explained and supported in the essay. Each paragraph in the body of the essay develops one aspect of the main point. The conclusion is often, but not necessarily, a separate paragraph. It restates the main point and concludes the essay.

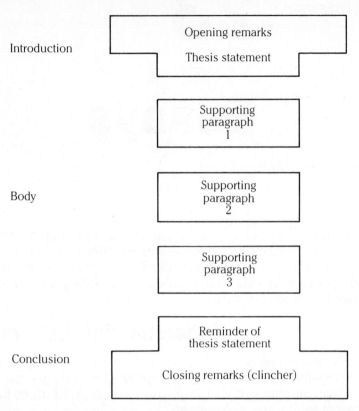

Introduction — Opening remarks / Thesis statement

Body — Supporting paragraph 1 / Supporting paragraph 2 / Supporting paragraph 3

Conclusion — Reminder of thesis statement / Closing remarks (clincher)

The Introduction. The introduction is a vital part of an essay. It indicates the purpose of the essay, telling whether the essay will be expository or persuasive. The most significant function of an introduction, however, is to present the thesis statement.

The introduction indicates the essay's purpose and presents the main point in a thesis statement.

Most introductions begin generally, with background information or an incident and then lead into the thesis statement. Notice in the following introduction how the writer prepares the reader for a persuasive essay that argues against whaling. The introduction presents general historical information, closes in on the problem, and then narrows the focus to the thesis statement, which is the writer's proposed solution.

538

Introduction   In the eighteenth and nineteenth centuries, whalers put to sea for two or three years at a time. Armed only with harpoons, lances, and daring, they brought back needed whale oil, bone, and ivory. In the twentieth century, however, high-speed boats, explosive harpoons, and gigantic floating factories have mechanized the killing process. Whales are being killed in great numbers even though synthetic materials can be used in place of whale products. The International Whaling Commission (IWC) has recently outlawed factory ships, but whales remain in danger of extinction. *Whales will survive only if the IWC declares a*

Thesis   *worldwide moratorium on hunting whales and if pi-*
statement   *rate whalers are stopped.*

In addition to presenting the main point, the thesis statement can also break down the main point into smaller points, which are called subtopics. Notice that all of the thesis statements in the following chart include subtopics, which outline the direction the body of the essay will take.

EXAMINATION OF THESIS STATEMENTS		
Thesis Statements	**Purposes**	**Stated Subtopics**
To operate a switchboard you must answer incoming calls, test for busy signals, and connect the caller with the desired extension.	to explain	(1) answer incoming calls (2) test for busy signals (3) connect the caller
Some of the stunts a person can do in hotdog or freestyle skiing are the Spread Eagle, the Iron Cross, and the Mobius Flip.	to explain	(1) Spread Eagle (2) Iron Cross (3) Mobius Flip
Children should not be encouraged to believe in Santa Claus because Santa fosters commercialism and selfishness.	to persuade	(1) commercialism (2) selfishness

539

The Body. Each paragraph in the body should support the thesis statement with examples, details, facts, reasons, or incidents. The supporting information should be organized by means of *subtopics*.

The body of an essay develops the thesis statement, treating one subtopic at a time.

The subtopics can be mentioned directly in the thesis statement, as in the examples on page 539, or they can simply be a logical outgrowth of the thesis statement. One or more paragraphs should be used to develop each subtopic. The presentation of subtopics in the body of an essay should follow a logical order.

The following chart lists common orders for arranging subtopics and suggests sample essay topics that might best be developed using each order.

ORDERS FOR SUBTOPICS IN THE BODY OF AN ESSAY	
Orders	**Sample Topics**
Chronological (subtopics arranged in a time sequence)	How to clean a tropical fish tank
	Events leading to the defeat of the Spanish Armada
Spatial (subtopics arranged by location or position)	Some places to visit in Maine
	The structure of a hydroelectric power plant
Order of Importance (subtopics arranged from least important to most important or vice versa)	The need to tighten security on large university campuses
	Reasons for establishing a work/study program at school
Developmental (subtopics of equal emphasis arranged logically)	Some of the benefits of a lower speed limit
	Three of the best rivers in the country for canoeing

Transitions should guide the reader from idea to idea within paragraphs and between paragraphs in the body of the essay.

540

The Conclusion. The conclusion is usually a short, separate paragraph at the end of the essay. It generally begins with a reminder of the thesis statement. The conclusion should leave the reader feeling that the topic has been covered thoroughly. In many cases, you may want to make the last sentence of the conclusion a *clincher*—a forceful sentence that drives home the main point.

The conclusion refers back to the thesis statement and brings the essay to a close.

The following conclusion demonstrates these functions.

Reminder of thesis statement	*Only by ending all hunting of whales can whales be preserved.* If the killing of whales continues unchecked, the noble animals described in Melville's *Moby Dick* will soon become as legendary as Moby Dick himself.
Clincher	

Putting the Parts Together. The following five-paragraph essay, written by a student, illustrates the structure of the basic essay. The writer has analyzed one of the main characters in a novel by concentrating on three subtopics. The comments to the left of the essay point out the essay's structure. Also notice the transitions in italics.

Introduction	<div align="center">Conrad</div> A teenaged boy has to deal with many problems while growing up, but fifteen-year-old Conrad in the novel *Ordinary People* faced problems that even many adults can't handle. *Before his brother's death* in a sailboat accident, Conrad was a normal, happy boy. He had friends, was a member of the swimming team, and did well in his schoolwork. *But after the*
Thesis statement	*accident* Conrad withdrew and became secretive, and *later on* was plagued with worries and insecurities that almost destroyed him.
Body paragraph 1 (develops subtopic 1—withdrawal	*After his brother's death,* the Conrad everyone had known disappeared, as the boy become more and more secretive and withdrawn and seemed to lose contact with everything around him. *The first indication* came in his schoolwork. Suddenly Conrad, a straight-A student, began to get D's and F's in his

541

classes without telling his parents. *Eventually,* he tried to kill himself and was placed in a mental hospital, where he was diagnosed as a schizophrenic and received psychiatric treatment for eight months. *But after being released* from the hospital, Conrad was still withdrawn—for example, he quit the swimming team without telling anyone. It seemed that he might never open up to the outside world again.

Body paragraph 2 (develops subtopic 2— worrying)

Besides his withdrawal from other people, Conrad also needed to overcome his compulsive worrying, especially after his return from the hospital. *On his first night home,* he thought he was losing his mind because he couldn't remember his neighbor's name. *Another time* he worried for days that he might be sent back to the hospital because he had punched another boy. *Most of all,* Conrad worried about worrying. He thought it was a sign that he was crazy. But he began to recover when he *finally* realized that all people worry, and that he should not be so afraid of his own thoughts.

Body paragraph 3 (develops subtopic 3— insecurity)

Perhaps an even harder fight was Conrad's battle against his feelings of insecurity. His insecurity was probably the biggest roadblock to his recovery. *In the hospital* Conrad had not been especially insecure because everyone had the same problems he had. *But as soon as he went home,* the feeling of not belonging surrounded him. At school Conrad was treated like a crazy man, someone of whom everyone else was afraid. Even his best friend avoided him. *Soon* Conrad was afraid to talk to anyone for fear of saying something wrong. But he forced himself to make the effort. He was like a tightrope walker, trying to balance on a wire without falling off. It was very hard on him, but Conrad was determined to make it to the other side and to fit in with the rest of the world.

Conclusion with reminder of thesis statement

Conrad went through a great deal during his adolescence. He managed to survive his brother's death, along with the long struggle against withdrawal, worry, and insecurity that followed it. He had to fight a tough battle back to a normal life, but he fought it and, *in the end,* he won.—Mary Reynolds

EXERCISE: **Understanding an Essay.** Reread the preceding essay on Conrad and answer these questions about it.

1. How does the writer get the reader's attention in the introduction?
2. What main idea is presented in the thesis statement?
3. Does the thesis statement list any subtopics? If so, what are they?
4. What is the writer's purpose? What words or phrases in the introduction suggest the purpose?
5. What is the overall order of the subtopics in the body of the essay?
6. What is the topic sentence of each body paragraph?
7. What are two kinds of support used in the body of the essay? Give examples of each.
8. What kind of order is used within each paragraph? List the transitions in each paragraph that tell you the order.
9. What sentence in the conclusion is a reminder of the thesis statement?
10. What additional, closing statement does the conclusion make to pull the whole essay together?

DEVELOPING WRITING SKILLS: Practicing with Thesis Statements. Using the chart on page 539 as a model, write one thesis statement for an essay that explains and one for an essay that persuades. Include subtopics in each, arranging them in the logical order you would use when writing the essay.

Writing an Essay 23.2

When you first sit down to write an essay, the task may seem overwhelming. You may wonder where to start. Even professional writers often have difficulty in starting an essay. They generally follow certain steps to make the process of writing an organized and productive one.

There are several steps that you can use to make writing an essay a manageable and rewarding task. This section will lead you through these planning, writing, and revising steps so that you can make all of the parts of your essay work together as a complete and unified whole.

PREWRITING: Planning Your Essay

Careful planning is crucial to writing a successful essay.

Generating Ideas and Choosing a Topic. To find ideas for an essay topic use techniques such as interiewing yourself, free writing, reading and saving, clustering, cueing, and brainstorming. You can review these methods of generating ideas by rereading Section 18.1.

Narrowing a Topic. The first topic you think of will usually be too broad for a four-to-six paragraph essay. You will need to narrow it down to a suitable essay topic.

Find a suitable essay topic by dividing a general topic into smaller, more manageable topics.

You might, for example, begin by choosing a general topic such as summer jobs. You might then divide this topic into smaller ones to produce a list similar to the one in the chart.

DIVIDING A GENERAL TOPIC TO FIND AN ESSAY TOPIC	
General Topic: Summer Jobs	
Possible Essay Topics	
Benefits of summer jobs	Finding a summer job
Volunteer work in the summer	Summer jobs available in the area
Interviewing for a summer job	Part-time summer jobs
Babysitting in the summer	Working in a factory
Filling out job applications	Counseling at a camp
Setting up a gardening service	A summer job versus summer school
Good summer jobs for high school students	Writing résumés for summer jobs
Waiting on tables	

Preparing a Thesis Statement. Once you have a suitable essay topic, you should think about what you plan to say about it in your essay. You can then phrase your main point in a thesis statement, which will direct the whole essay.

To shape an essay topic into a thesis statement, decide to whom you are speaking, what you want to say, and why.

State your main point in a thesis statement that suits your audience and purpose.

With your essay topic in mind, decide if you will be writing for beginners, experts, friends, a general audience, people who agree with you, or people who disagree with you. Once you have some idea of your audience's interests, background, and knowledge, you can ask yourself what that audience would want to know about the topic. The following chart lists some of the questions you might ask yourself if you were writing for a general audience on the topic of waiting on tables. The chart then lists the main points that the questions might suggest.

QUESTIONS LEADING TO POSSIBLE MAIN POINTS	
Essay Topic: Waiting on Tables	
Questions	**Main Points**
What should any audience know about waiting on tables?	Waiting on tables teaches valuable skills.
What is a common mistake people make in thinking about waiting on tables?	Some people think that waiting on tables is easy.
What are some of the major responsibilities involved in waiting on tables?	Responsibilities include taking correct orders, collecting orders from the kitchen, and serving customers politely and efficiently.

When you have a list of possible main points, select the one you will use in your essay, making sure that it suits the purpose you have in mind. The first two main points in the chart above are opinions with which other people might disagree. They would suit essays written to persuade. The third main point would suit an essay that explains or informs.

Next, write three or four different thesis statements to find a version that says exactly what you want to focus on in your essay. After experimenting with several thesis statements, you should have a list similar to the one in the following chart.

545

POSSIBLE THESIS STATEMENTS
Main Point: Waiting on tables teaches valuable skills.
1. Waiting on tables teaches a person valuable skills.
2. The responsibilities of waiting on tables teach valuable skills.
3. Waiting on tables is a good summer job because it teaches a person valuable skills.
4. Waiting on tables can teach a person to work efficiently and to relate well to other people.

Now, choose the thesis statement that most clearly expresses the point you are trying to make. You might choose the fourth thesis statement in the chart above because it is clear and because it breaks the main point into two useful subtopics.

Brainstorming for Supporting Information. To find support for your thesis statement, ask yourself questions a reader might want your essay to answer and explain.

Brainstorm for examples, details, facts, reasons, and incidents to support your thesis statement.

Using your thesis statement, produce a list of supporting information similar to that in the following chart.

BRAINSTORMING FOR SUPPORT FOR A THESIS STATEMENT
Thesis Statement: Waiting on tables can teach a person to work efficiently and to relate well to other people.
What does waiting on tables involve? —being in charge of a station or counter —working six-hour shifts —serving meals to as many as —trying to please customers twenty-five people at a time
How does the job "teach"? —through daily experience —learning from other workers —learning from mistakes —through constant practice

546

Why are the skills valuable?
—the skills needed by a waitress or waiter will be useful in future jobs and in school work
—a person learns to be quick, alert, organized, and calm under pressure
—a person also learns how to save time, to juggle many details at once, and to cope with difficult people

How does the job teach efficiency?
—demands that a person be responsible for serving many customers
—involves customers who are constantly arriving and leaving
—calls for serving a meal in several stages: handing out menus; pouring water; bringing bread; taking orders; serving soups and salads, main dishes, coffee, and desserts; writing up checks
—demands that a person learn to do several things at once
—requires a constant checkup on customers during their meal
—demands that a person learn how to save both energy and time
—requires that a person learn to limit trips to the kitchen
—calls for carrying many plates and glasses without dropping them

How does the job teach a person to relate well to other people?
—teaches behavior needed to make money: be polite, friendly, helpful at all times, patient, confident with strangers
—demands that a person learn to handle problems under pressure:
  —little children spilling things
  —customers in a rush
  —customers changing their orders at the last minute
  —restaurant running out of some item on the menu
—requires that a person meet and cope with all kinds of people:
  —some customers too friendly and talkative
  —some people irritable and critical
  —some people play tricks, such as putting pennies in a full, upside-down water glass, putting plastic bugs in the food
  —some people are messy and spill food on table, seats, and floor

547

Organizing the Body of Your Essay. Once you have listed as much supporting information as you can think of, you should group your support into subtopics and then outline the body of your essay.

Group your supporting information into subtopics and outline the body of your essay.

To find subtopics, look for natural divisions in your thesis statement. Then see if your supporting information fits comfortably into those divisions. Obvious subtopics for the supporting information gathered for the essay about waiting on tables are (1) working efficiently and (2) relating well to other people. Most of the information in the list can be used to develop these two subtopics.

The number of paragraphs needed in an essay depends on the amount of information you wish to include. You can usually count on having one short paragraph for the introduction and one short paragraph for the conclusion. For most essays you can also plan on one paragraph for each subtopic.

Once you have decided on the subtopics you want to develop, you must decide in what order you want to develop them. As with paragraphs, essays can be organized chronologically, spatially, in order of importance, or developmentally. The following chart shows a plan for organizing the essay about waiting on tables using order of importance for the two subtopics in the body of the essay.

POSSIBLE PLAN FOR AN ESSAY	
First paragraph	= Introduction
Second paragraph	= Subtopic 1: Working efficiently
Third paragraph	= Subtopic 2: Relating well to other people
Fourth paragraph	= Conclusion

When you have decided on an overall plan for your essay, you should make a list all of your supporting information by subtopic. Eliminate any information that does not directly develop each subtopic. Then outline the body of your essay using a modified or topic outline. Following is an outline for the body of the essay about waiting on tables.

548

Thesis Statement
Waiting on tables can teach a person the valuable skills of working efficiently and of relating well to other people.

Subtopic 1: Learning to Work Efficiently
1. Efficiency learned through handling many customers
   —handling a station of four or more tables or counter space
   —handling as many as twenty-five people at once
2. Efficiency learned through having to do three things at once
   —dealing with customers continuously arriving and leaving
   —serving a meal in several stages: handing out menus; pouring water; bringing bread; taking orders; serving soups and salads, main dishes, coffee, and desserts; writing up checks
3. Efficiency learned through having to save time and energy
   —limited number of trips to the kitchen
   —carrying many plates and glasses without dropping them
4. Possible concluding idea: With six–hour shifts and juggling many details, a person learns to be quick, alert, and organized.

Subtopic 2: Learning to Relate Well to Other People
1. Mastering certain behavior in order to please customers and make tips
   —being polite, friendly, helpful, patient, and confident with strangers
2. Meeting and coping with all kinds of people
   —some customers too friendly and talkative
   —some customers irritable and critical
   —some customers play tricks: put plastic bugs in food
3. Most important: developing skills with people in pressured situations
   —handling customers in a rush
   —handling customers when restaurant runs out of some item on the menu
   —handling customers changing their orders at the last minute
   —handling customers when a child spills food on the floor
4. Possible concluding idea: Future jobs will be easier for a person who has learned through waiting on tables to be calm under pressure and to cope with different people.

When you are writing your outline, be sure to continue evaluating your thesis statement and support. Make any adjustments and revisions that seem necessary. You should also jot down ideas for the title, introduction, and conclusion.

EXERCISE A: Planning an Essay. Choose one of the following general topics and plan an essay about it. Follow the directions below.

Travel	Wild animals	Cooking
American history	Popular dances	Camping
Zoos	Recreation	Part-time jobs

1. Find a good topic by dividing a general topic into at least three smaller topics. Choose one of these smaller topics to write about.
2. Develop possible main points by thinking about what your audience might want or need to know. Consider your purpose as well. Then choose one main point and write three or four versions of a thesis statement that expresses the main point. From these select one thesis statement to use.
3. Brainstorm for support by asking yourself questions your audience would expect to have answered. List as many facts, details, examples, reasons, and incidents as you can.
4. Organize your essay by finding subtopics and grouping your supporting information under each subtopic. Prepare a modified outline of the body of your essay and list ideas for the title, introduction, and conclusion.

WRITING: Creating a First Draft

With an outline and ideas for your title, introduction, and conclusion, you should be ready to draft your essay. As you write your first draft, concentrate on connecting your ideas with transitions.

Use your outline to write a complete first draft.

If you were writing an essay on the subject of waiting on tables, it might be similar to the following essay. The notes in the margin show how it follows the outline. The italicized transitions connect thoughts between and within paragraphs.

Introduction

A Good Summer Job

Some people would describe a good summer job as one that takes little effort and pays well. Others would say that the best place to work in the summer is Hawaii, the Rocky Mountains, or Florida. Still others would maintain that a good summer job prepares a person for a career. Among the best summer jobs, *however,* are those that offer advantages in both the present and the future by training a person to work hard and to face all kinds of people. Working as a

Thesis statement

waiter or waitress is one such job. Waiting on tables can teach a person the valuable skills of working efficiently and of relating well to other people.

Topic sentence for subtopic 1

A good waiter or waitress learns to work efficiently in order to survive a truly demanding job. A waiter or waitress may be responsible for as many as twenty-five customers at a time at four or more tables or at a long stretch of counter. To provide all of his or her customers with good service a waiter or waitress must learn to do many things at once. Each table of customers requires immediate attention. Menus and water must be given out. *Then* orders must be taken, soup and salads delivered, main dishes served, orders for dessert taken, and checks supplied. The customers must *also* be checked regularly to see if they want anything else. *Finally,* a waiter or waitress must learn efficiency in order to avoid wasting time and energy. A person waiting on tables learns to make as few trips to the kitchen as possible and to carry a large

Concluding sentence for subtopic 1

number of plates and glasses safely at once. By racing around during six-hour shifts and doing three things at once, a waiter or waitress becomes quick, alert, and organized.

Topic sentence for subtopic 2

A waiter or waitress can learn an *even more* valuable skill—the ability to relate to people—through serving all kinds of customers in all kinds of situations. A certain behavior must be mastered if a waiter or waitress is to please customers and make good tips: confidence with strangers, politeness, friendliness, helpfulness, patience, and calmness at all times. Waiting on tables *also* enables a person to learn to cope with all sorts of difficult people: the talkers, the complainers, and the tricksters. A waiter or waitress learns to respond pleasantly to the woman who will not stop talking about her daughter or her dog. When a couple complains about the prices and items on the menu, a good waiter or waitress remains calm. When a customer puts a plastic fly in his salad or green drops in his coffee and then protests that his food is inedible, a good waiter or waitress knows how to take a joke. *Most of all,* in pressured situations, a waiter or waitress must learn how to handle people and stay in control. Some customers may announce that they are in a rush and demand special service. A waiter or waitress may have to tell a grouchy man slouching behind his newspaper that the restaurant has just run out of the dinner he ordered. At the last minute, some customer may change an order from veal parmigiana to a steak sandwich. A child may dump over chocolate milk or spill pancakes and syrup for the waiter or waitress to clean up. If the waiter or waitress can learn to remain courteous when customers are insensitive and rude and when everything else goes wrong, that person will have acquired skills that will be beneficial on the job and useful throughout life.

Concluding sentence for subtopic 2

Conclusion with reminder of thesis statement

Waiting on tables is an experience a person should not miss because it teaches the efficient use of time and energy and the skill of coping with diverse people. *In addition* to these advantages, a restaurant may overlook a mountain range, a beach, or the lights of a city or may employ waiters and waitresses from other schools or even from other states. One benefit of waiting on tables is definite, however: A waiter or waitress will find chemistry, English, or another job easier after having learned to serve sixty dinners a night to demanding adults and wiggly children.

Clincher

EXERCISE B: Writing an Essay. Write the essay you planned in Exercise A. As you write your first draft, be sure to use transitions within and between paragraphs to connect your ideas.

552

REVISING: Polishing Your Essay

Revising gives you a chance to make sure that you have said what you intended to say. You should also check your essay for correctness in grammar and other technical matters. Examine your essay with an eye toward making any improvements you can.

Use a checklist to revise your first draft for sense, grammar, mechanics, and spelling.

The following checklist can be used during this last step of writing an essay. It will show you what to look for to carry out a thorough examination of your first draft.

CHECKLIST FOR REVISING

1. Do you have a good title for the essay?
2. Does the introduction lead up to the thesis statement by getting the reader's attention, providing background information, and indicating your purpose?
3. Does the thesis statement express a clearly focused main point that is appropriate for your audience and purpose?
4. Does the body of the essay thoroughly develop the main point with well-chosen supporting information?
5. Are the subtopics arranged logically and developed in an appropriate number of paragraphs?
6. Does each paragraph in the body have a clear topic sentence?
7. Are the ideas in each paragraph organized logically and connected with transitions?
8. Should any individual sentences be reworded for smoothness or clarity?
9. Does the conclusion include a reminder of the thesis statement and bring the essay to a satisfying end?
10. Are there any mistakes in grammar, mechanics, or spelling?

If your essay does not meet each of these requirements, make the necessary changes. When your essay passes your examination, make a final copy. Be sure to proofread your final copy again for typographical errors.

553

EXERCISE C: Revising an Essay. Examine the first draft you wrote for Exercise B using the checklist on page 553. Make any necessary changes and then prepare a clean copy.

DEVELOPING WRITING SKILLS: Planning, Writing, and Revising an Essay. Follow the steps presented in this section to plan, write, and revise an essay on a topic of your own choice.

23.3 Writing Different Kinds of Essays

The most frequently written kinds of essays are expository essays and persuasive essays. An *expository essay* explains a process, an event, or an idea by giving factual information; it informs the reader. A *persuasive essay* expresses an opinion; it tries to convince the reader or change his or her mind about a controversial issue.

Writing Expository Essays

In order to write a successful expository essay, you must keep the purpose of the essay in mind at all times.

Understanding Expository Essays. An expository essay instructs and informs. It uses facts to explain a process, an event, or an idea. The whole essay, from the introduction to the conclusion, works to explain something to the reader.

The purpose of an expository essay is to explain or inform.

The thesis statement found in the introduction of an expository essay states a fact, not an opinion. A factual statement can be checked or verified, whereas a statement of opinion is a personal belief that can be debated.

Notice the difference between a statement of fact and a statement of opinion in the following examples.

STATEMENT OF FACT: A football team has more players than a basketball team.

STATEMENT OF OPINION: Football is a more exciting sport than basketball.

The following chart contains examples of thesis statements for expository essays. These factual statements may or may not include stated subtopics.

SAMPLE THESIS STATEMENTS FOR EXPOSITORY ESSAYS	
Thesis Statements	**Stated Subtopics**
Aerobic exercise improves circulation and muscle tone.	(1) circulation (2) muscle tone
Racquetball is an expensive yet popular sport.	(1) expense (2) popularity
Michelangelo was a 16th century Italian painter who is best known for his painting of the ceiling of the Sistine Chapel.	none stated

The body of an expository essay uses facts and examples to explain the main idea and the subtopics that follow from it. This supporting information may be based on the writer's personal experience or may be obtained through research. The body presents enough explanations, definitions, or examples to cover the main idea thoroughly.

The conclusion of an expository essay shows the reader that the topic has been covered completely. The conclusion may do this in any of several ways: it can restate the main idea directly, mention the subtopics, or summarize the highlights of the supporting information, depending on which would best clarify the essay.

The tone of an expository essay reflects the informative purpose. Direct, objective language, factual statements, definitions, and examples help create an informative tone.

Prewriting, Writing, and Revising. When preparing an expository essay, you should follow the basic prewriting, writing, and revising steps used for any essay. However, you should adapt each of these steps to the informative purpose of the expository essay.

In preparing an expository essay, concentrate on explainng your main idea clearly and completely.

555

There are several specific suggestions you can use to adapt the writing process to an informative purpose.

In planning an expository essay, be sure to narrow your topic to an idea that can be thoroughly explained in one essay. Draft a thesis statement that has a clear explanatory purpose; carefully avoid statements of opinion. Then gather enough examples, illustrations, and definitions to explain fully your thesis statement and cover each subtopic. Prepare an outline that presents your information in the most logical, understandable order.

Based on your outline, write a first draft of your essay. The first draft should contain all the parts of an essay. Be especially careful to link together your supporting information with transitions so that your explanation will be easy for the reader to follow.

To revise your essay, look closely at the content and organization, keeping in mind the aim of informing. Look for places where you may have left out information that would help the reader to understand. Also check for and remove any irrelevant information.

The following suggestions will help you adapt the revising step to expository essays.

SUGGESTIONS FOR EVALUATING AN EXPOSITORY ESSAY

1. Evaluate the clarity of your explanation by having someone unfamiliar with your topic read the essay and try to summarize the information you present.

2. Evaluate the completenes of your explanation by having someone unfamiliar with your topic read your essay and write down any important questions about the topic that your essay fails to answer.

3. Ask a reader to identify any passages in which your tone is not factual and informative.

4. If your essay explains a process or a procedure, have someone try to follow the steps as you have presented them.

After revising the content of your essay and checking the grammar, mechanics, and spelling, make a clean final copy and proofread it for typographical errors.

556

EXERCISE A: Understanding an Expository Essay. Carefully read the following expository essay. Then answer the questions that follow the essay.

The Basics of Word Processing

More and more people are switching from typewriters to word processors for writing. Word processing is a form of computerized typing that allows the writer to record and store information and then later retrieve and revise it.

The main components of a word processor are a keyboard, a video display screen, a computer, a disk drive, and a printer. The keyboard is similar to a typewriter keyboard, but it may contain special word-processing function keys, such as keys labeled retrieve, save, move, and delete. The keyboard allows the writer to enter text into the computer's memory. As the text is entered into the computer, it is shown on a video display screen, usually located right above the keyboard. The screen is a television monitor that displays letters, numbers, and the other characters. The computer itself—or central processing unit (CPU)—contains the circuits that make it possible to manipulate or "process" the words. Disk drives connected to the computer record information from the screen and store it on plastic disks. Disk drives can also replay stored information at a later date. When a printer is connected to a word processor, the stored information can be transferred to a printed page. This printed page is the hard copy of the stored text.

Because the word processor allows the writer to record and store what has been typed, the text can be retrieved later for revision. This means that the writer can leave incomplete work and finish it some other time. But perhaps more important, a writer can retrieve a complete first draft, revising and editing it until fully satisfied. The special editing functions of a word processor make the physical task of revising material relatively simple. The stored material is "called up" and again displayed on the monitor. The writer can then move a cursor—a blinking pointer—anywhere in the material to correct errors or change words. By striking one or two keys, the writer can delete, insert, or move words, sentences, or whole paragraphs at a time. All of this can be done without retyping the material each time a change needs to be made.

Considering all the special revision features a word processor offers, it is not surprising that more and more writers are turning to word processing. By reducing the physical work involved in revising, word processors allow the writer to concentrate on the mental work.

1. Which paragraphs are the introduction, body, and conclusion?
2. Which sentence in the introduction is the thesis statement?
3. Is the thesis statement a fact that can be verified?
4. What subtopics of the main idea are presented?
5. In what order are the subtopics presented in the body?
6. What kind of supporting information is presented in each paragraph of the body?
7. What is the tone of the essay? Identify specific words and items of support that contribute to the tone.
8. What transitions are used to connect the items of support?
9. Which sentence in the conclusion refers back to the thesis statement?
10. Which subtopic or subtopics are referred to in the conclusion?

EXERCISE B: Writing an Expository Essay. Choose one of the topics below and then follow the planning, writing, and revising steps for essays given in Section 23.2. When you revise, use one of the suggestions in the chart on page 556 as well as the general revision chart in Section 23.2.

Student government	Planning a vacation
The ideal car	Soap operas
Fashion trends	How to get better grades
Today's slang	Changes in transportation
Tips for joggers	Computers in school

Writing Persuasive Essays

A persuasive essay is similar to an expository essay in basic structure, but its purpose is very different.

Understanding Persuasive Essays. While expository essays are informative and factual, persuasive essays try to change the reader's mind on a debatable issue.

558

The purpose of a persuasive essay is to convince the reader.

Before presenting the thesis statement, the introduction to a persuasive essay often gives background information to help the reader understand the issue to be debated in the paper. The thesis statement can then state the writer's opinion or position on the issue, either pro or con.

The chart contains sample persuasive thesis statements.

SAMPLE THESIS STATEMENTS FOR PERSUASIVE ESSAYS	
Pro	**Con**
The four-day work week will make America more productive.	A four-day work week will not make America more productive.
Our senior citizens should be given more free admission privileges.	Senior citizens already have sufficient free admission privileges.
Courses in chemistry and biology should be added to graduation requirements.	Additional courses in chemistry and biology should not be required.
The programming on cable TV is superior to the programming available on the commercial networks.	The programming on the commercial networks is superior to the programming on cable TV.

In order to present convincing arguments, the body of the paper must offer solid evidence in a logical, convincing order. Reasons, examples, details, and illustrations can be used to prove the thesis statement. Generally, each paragraph in the body of the paper provides additional evidence to support the thesis statement. The body paragraphs can also answer arguments that might be raised in opposition to the thesis.

The conclusion is very important in a persuasive essay because it is the part of the essay that the reader will remember best. Therefore, the conclusion should not only restate the thesis but also summarize the strongest arguments. Ideally, it should contain a clincher—an especially forceful closing comment that ties the argument together and wins the reader over.

The tone of a persuasive essay is forceful, since its aim is to convince, but it must always remain reasonable, unemotional, and clear. The main purpose of a persuasive essay is to convince the reader, but in order to reach that goal the essay must also inform—it must present clear ideas and logical support so that readers can make up their own minds.

Prewriting, Writing, and Revising. To write a persuasive essay, follow all the prewriting, writing, and revising steps presented earlier in this chapter. However, you should adapt each step to the special purpose of convincing an audience.

In preparing a persuasive essay, concentrate on convincing your audience.

You must thoroughly understand your audience if you want to be convincing. The following chart shows questions you might ask yourself to analyze your audience and begin planning your essay.

QUESTIONS FOR ANALYZING THE AUDIENCE FOR A PERSUASIVE ESSAY

1. Who are the people in my audience? What are their backgrounds—cultural, professional, educational, and so on?
2. What do they already know about the topic?
3. Is their position on this issue likely to be the opposite of mine? What arguments would they use to support their own side of the question?
4. What kinds of arguments and evidence would appeal to this audience?
5. What questions might they ask about my position on this issue?

You must also carefully consider the evidence available for and against your opinion. It is often helpful to make two lists of supporting information, one containing the arguments for your opinion and the other containing the arguments against. By comparing the two lists, you will be able to support your opinion and answer any opposition you might encounter. You may want to devote a paragraph or more of the body of your essay to answering arguments that could be raised by the other side.

In planning the organization of your essay, you will often want to place your most convincing argument last. This is the argument the reader is most likely to remember and act on. Whatever order you chose, make sure it is the most effective one for your particular arguments and evidence.

In writing your first draft, be sure to keep your language reasonable and clear. Weigh the effect of each statement on your audience.

When you revise a persuasive essay, check to see whether your arguments are sound and whether you have used the strongest evidence. The following suggetsions can help you to evaluate and revise a persuasive essay.

SUGGESTIONS FOR EVALUATING A PERSUASIVE ESSAY

1. Find someone with no strong feelings one way or the other about the topic of your essay. Ask that person to read your essay and to comment on whether or not your arguments and evidence are convincing. Have your reader point out specific strengths and weaknesses. Then make any necessary changes to strengthen your arguments.

2. Find someone who completely disagrees with your position. Ask that person to read your essay and to comment on the strength of your arguments and evidence. Have your reader point out arguments for the other side that you may have overlooked. Make any necessary improvements to strengthen your essay.

EXERCISE C: Understanding a Persuasive Essay. Read the following persuasive essay. Then answer the questions that follow the essay.

Safer Bike Riding

As Americans search for alternative methods of transportation, many people are turning to bicycling. Riding a bicycle, however, is not always safe on today's crowded roadways. Cyclists often have to compete with motorists and pedestrians for space. This problem could be remedied if cities and towns provided designated bike routes for cyclists.

Designated bike routes—paths set up and clearly labeled for

cyclists only—are needed for the safety of bicyclists, motorists, and pedestrians alike. Most roadways were not constructed with bicycle traffic in mind. Whether an open highway or a downtown street, roadways rarely have shoulders wide enough or smooth enough for safe cycling. When a roadway lacks an adequate shoulder, the cyclist often has to move into the car lane. This causes problems for the motorist who must swerve to avoid the cyclist. When moving out of a rider's way, the motorist may be forced into another lane of traffic, making an accident likely. On the other hand, if the cyclist rides on the sidewalk, there is a risk of collision with pedestrians.

Special bike routes, it might be argued, are too expensive to construct. Reducing traffic accidents and saving lives, of course, are worth any cost. Often, however, the cost would be lower than people think. Not all cities and towns will need to construct completely new bike routes. In some places, especially where pedestrian traffic is light, parts of sidewalks can become the designated routes for cycles, and at little expense. Parts of existing sidewalks can be made into bike paths by building a ramp at the corner curbs, something that has often already been done to accommodate wheelchairs. By combining ramped sidewalks with separate bike paths, a total bicycle route can be inexpensively constructed in many areas.

Designated bike routes are not a luxury for cyclists but a necessity for everyone who travels. By providing special areas where cyclists can ride, cities and towns will be making roadways safer not only for cyclists, but for motorists and pedestrians as well. Designated bike routes would benefit the whole community.

1. Which paragraphs are the introduction, body, and conclusion?
2. Which sentence in the introduction is the thesis statement?
3. What other information is presented in the introduction?
4. What major reasons are given in the body to support the position taken by the thesis statement?
5. What kinds of supporting information are given as evidence? List two items of supporting information from each paragraph of the body.
6. Are any opposing arguments addressed? If so, how are the opposing arguments countered?

7. Are any terms defined for the audience? If so, which ones?
8. What is the tone of the essay? List three examples of words and items of support that contribute to the tone.
9. Which sentence in the conclusion offers a reminder of the thesis statement?
10. Which sentence in the conclusion is the clincher?

EXERCISE D: Writing a Persuasive Essay. Choose one of the topics listed below and then follow the planning, writing, and revising steps for essays given in Section 23.2. When you revise, use one of the suggestions in the chart on page 561 as well as the general revision chart in Section 23.2.

Setting up a national drinking age

Free admission to public parks for senior citizens

Changing required courses

Abolishing athletic scholarships in colleges

Raising or lowering the national speed limit

A candidate for election

DEVELOPING WRITING SKILLS: Writing Different Kinds of Essays. Use a topic of your own as the basis for two separate essays. First prepare an expository essay and then prepare a persuasive essay on the same general topic. Then make a list of the specific ways that the two essays differ.

Writing Workshop: Essays

ASSIGNMENT 1

Topic   The Value of Sports

Form and Purpose   An essay that persuades readers to agree with your views

Audience   Readers of your school newspaper

Length   Four to six paragraphs

Focus   Narrow the topic to several significant values of a particular sport. Try to include supporting quotes or incidents from the lives of well-known athletes.

Sources   Biographies and autobiographies of athletes, magazine articles, interviews

Prewriting   Write a thesis statement stating your main idea and purpose. Brainstorm for support. Organize your support and prepare an outline.

Writing   Use your outline to write a first draft.

Revising   Use the checklists on pages 553 and 561 to help you make changes. Then write a final, corrected draft.

ASSIGNMENT 2

Topic   The Language of Appearance

Form and Purpose   An essay that informs readers how personal appearance can be a method of communication

Audience   Readers of *Teen Times* magazine

Length   Four to six paragraphs

Focus   Develop a thesis statement about the importance of personal appearance. Support the thesis by giving examples in which personal appearance communicates either a positive or a negative image.

Sources   Personal observation and experiences, magazines, interviews with friends, relatives, and other adults

Prewriting   State your main idea and purpose in a thesis statement. Brainstorm for support. Organize your support and prepare an outline.

Writing   Use your outline to write a first draft of your essay.

Revising   Use the checklists on pages 553 and 556. Make any needed changes and write a final, complete version.

Topics for Writing: Essays

One or both of the above photos may suggest an idea for an essay. Write an essay about that idea, or choose one of the following topics for an essay.

1. A Great Place to Live
2. Why Cities Exist
3. A Great Place to Visit, but Not to Live
4. City vs. Rural Life
5. How to Survive in a City (or Rural Area)
6. Only Nature Is Real
7. Isolation
8. People Make the Difference
9. Urban Renewal and City Growth
10. Why Nature Must Be Preserved

Chapter 24

Research Papers

During your years in school, you will probably prepare many research papers. This chapter will show you ways to use and acknowledge sources of information to produce well-written papers. It will also explain the structure and features of a research paper and give you steps to follow in preparing them.

Understanding Research Papers 24.1

A *research paper* contains facts and examples gathered through reading. It includes references to the sources you have used and a list of sources at the end.

Sources of Information

Research—finding information—is vital in preparing these papers. You will need to consult a variety of sources such as encyclopedias, atlases, almanacs, other books, magazines, and newspapers. You can find sources of specific information by using the library card catalog and *The Readers' Guide to Periodical Literature*. (See Sections 35.1 and 35.2 for more details on using the library to find reference materials.)

Citing Sources of Information. When you use sources of information, you need to cite, or give credit to, your sources.

A research paper gives credit to sources of information in footnotes at the bottom of the page or at the end of the paper.

567

When you are writing a paper with footnotes, you begin by placing small numbers after each item you have taken from a source. Then, at the bottom of the page or at the end of the paper, you give details about each source. The following example from a student's paper about the first walk on the moon shows how the system works.

Use of footnotes   Some ten hours after the landing, Astronaut Armstrong began EVA, extravehicular activity, backing feet first out of the hatch on his belly.[1] Astronaut Aldrin followed twenty-five minutes later.

About his first impression, Armstrong reported, "Of course the sights were simply magnificent, beyond any visual experience that I had ever been exposed to," and Aldrin described the sights as "a unique, almost mystical environment."[2]

---

[1]Flight Plan of Apollo II," Time, July 18, 1969, p. 20.

[2]Norman Mailer, Of a Fire on the Moon (Boston: Little, Brown, and Company, 1971), pp. 395–396.

The following chart shows acceptable forms for citing a number of different kinds of sources. Notice that in all of the citations the authors' names are written first name first. If a source does not have an author, list exactly the same information, beginning with the book title or article title.

FORMS FOR CITING SOURCES	
Kinds of Sources	**Footnotes**
Book	[1]Elizabeth K. Martin and C. J. Howard, Technique: Studies in Composition, 2nd ed. (New York: Harper and Row, 1977), p. 41.
Magazine Article	[2]John Newhouse, "Letter from Cairo," The New Yorker, July 30, 1984, p. 68.
Encyclopedia Article	[3]Mary Francis Gyles, "Pompeii," The World Book Encyclopedia, 1984 ed.
Newspaper Article	[4]Dorothy J. Gaiter, "Scouts Tailor Programs for Urban Youths," The New York Times, November 1, 1980, p. L29.

NOTE ABOUT THE MODERN LANGUAGE ASSOCIATION (MLA) SYSTEM FOR CITING SOURCES: The 1984 MLA Handbook endorses a system for citing sources that is becoming more and more widespread, especially in colleges and universities. Instead of placing a number in the paper and a footnote below or at the end, this system calls for adding the citation right in the paper.

The citation goes in parentheses and lists just the author's last name and the page number. Since all papers have complete lists of sources, called *bibliographies*, at the very end, this information is enough for the reader, who can check the bibliography for details. When there is no author, the title of the book or article is given with the page number. When there is no page number, as in an encyclopedia article, just the author's last name or the article is given.

The following examples show how the footnotes shown on page 568 would appear in the text, using this method.

SAMPLE CITATIONS	
Kinds of Sources	**Sample Citations**
Book with One Author	(Mailer 395–396)
Book with Two Authors	(Martin and Howard 41)
Magazine Article	(Newhouse 68)
Encyclopedia Article	(Gyles)
Newspaper Article	(Gaiter L29)
Article Without Author	("Flight Plan of Apollo II" 20)

Avoiding Plagiarism. In addition to knowing *how* to acknowledge a source of information, you should know *when* to indicate that you have borrowed information. In research papers, be careful to avoid plagiarism. *Plagiarism,* the act of presenting someone else's ideas or words as your own, is a form of cheating. Since you are supposed to show sources in these papers, it is also counterproductive.

In research papers, avoid plagiarism by citing sources for all nonoriginal words, facts, or ideas.

You should cite your source of information in each of the following instances. First, you must do so when you use the exact words of someone else, whether spoken or written. Second, you must do so when you borrow a fact or idea that is not widely known and would not be found in several different books. Third, you must do so when you paraphrase, or reword, a specific idea or a series of ideas.

In the following two passages, notice the obvious similarity between the source—an encyclopedia article—and the plagiarized passages in an unacceptable paper. Word-for-word repetitions are shown in italics.

Encyclopedia article   The creation of the United Nations was not the result of a lightning decision. This world organization followed the League of Nations, which was unable to survive the lawlessness of Nazi Germany, Fascist Italy, and Imperial Japan and the 1939 attack on Finland by the Soviet Union. A fatal weakness of the League was that the United States was not a member. Yet the League's weaknesses did not blind statesmen and many other people to the need for creating a more effective successor. As the Charter of the United Nations so poignantly says, the people of the new organization are "determined to save succeeding generations from the scourge of war which twice in our lifetime has brought untold sorrow to mankind. . . ."—<u>Lands and Peoples</u>

Unacceptable paper with plagiarism   The United Nations was formally established in 1948, but it was *not the result of a lightning decision*. The UN replaced the League of Nations, *which was unable to survive the lawlessness of Nazi Germany, Fascist Italy, and Imperial Japan and the 1939 attack on Finland by the Soviet Union*. The purpose of the United Nations was *to save succeeding generations from the scourge of war.*

Now read the following passage, which shows correct use of information from a source. Notice that uncited words and ideas are not taken directly from the source. The facts that are used at the beginning are widely known and do not require citation. The word-for-word borrowing from the source found at the end of the passage has been correctly placed in quotation marks and properly cited.

570

Acceptable paper with cited source

The United Nations was formally established in 1948 after the collapse of the League of Nations and the horrors of World War II. The United Nations stated that one of its goals would be "to save succeeding generations from the scourge of war which twice in our lifetime has brought untold sorrow to mankind. . . ."[1]

---

[1] "United Nations," Land and Peoples, 1973 ed.

Writing a Bibliography. In doing research for a paper, you will probably consult many books and magazines. While you may not need to cite all of these sources in your paper, you should present a list of all sources in a bibliography at the end of your paper.

A research paper contains a bibliography, which lists all the sources consulted.

Each item in your bibliography should include complete information about the source. The sources should be listed in alphabetical order by the authors' last names or by the titles of articles or books when an author's name is not given. Disregard the words *The, An,* or *A* at the beginning of a title.

The following chart shows the basic bibliography forms for the items in the chart on page 568.

FORMS FOR BIBLIOGRAPHY ENTRIES	
Kinds of Sources	**Bibliography Entries**
Book	Martin, Elizabeth K., and C. J. Howard. Technique: Studies in Composition, 2nd ed. New York: Harper and Row, 1977.
Magazine Article	Newhouse, John. "Letter from Cairo." The New Yorker, July 30, 1984, pp. 68–69.
Encyclopedia Article	Gyles, Mary Francis. "Pompeii." The World Book Encyclopedia, 1984 ed.
Newspaper Article	Gaiter, Dorothy J. "Scouts Tailor Programs for Urban Youths." The New York Times, November 1, 1980, p. L29.

EXERCISE A: Practicing with Footnotes and Bibliography Entries. Choose a famous person, an important event, or a place of interest to you. Go to the library and use the card catalog and *The Readers' Guide to Periodical Literature* to find at least one book and one magazine article on your topic. Write a footnote for each source. Then write a bibliography of the sources on a separate page.

Structure and Features

A research paper is similar to an essay except that it always requires citations of information. Like an essay, a research paper should be a unified piece of writing with a three-part structure—a beginning, a middle, and an end. As in an essay, all three parts should develop one main point. In addition, research papers should include references to sources of information throughout and a list of all sources used at the end.

A research paper includes an introduction with a thesis statement, a body, a conclusion, citation of sources throughout, and a bibliography.

The *introduction*, which usually consists of one paragraph, should arouse the interest of the reader, provide background information, and prepare the reader for the body of the paper. It should also include a *thesis statement*, which expresses the main point of the paper in one sentence. The thesis statement is usually placed at the end of the introduction.

The *body*, or middle section, consisting of two or more paragraphs, should support the thesis statement with facts, examples, reasons, details, or incidents. The body paragraphs should also present subpoints or subtopics of the main topic. Each paragraph should develop one idea related to the thesis statement. The subtopics presented in the body paragraphs can be arranged in chronological order, spatial order, order of importance, or developmental order. Transitions should be used to guide the reader through the paper and to connect ideas.

The *conclusion* of the paper, generally the last paragraph, should include a reminder of the thesis statement as well as general concluding remarks that leave a reader with a satisfactory understanding of the topic.

572

Research papers also include citation of sources in footnotes at the bottom of the page or at the end of the paper. At the very end of the paper, there should be a bibliography.

NOTE ABOUT SPECIAL FEATURES: A research paper should also include a title page with the title of the paper, the writer's name, the class, and the date. A sentence or topic outline of the paper may be required as well.

The following illustrates the general structure of a research paper. Notice that the supporting information in the body of the paper is presented in chronological order. Also notice that the footnotes at the end give full information for the first citation of a work and abbreviated information for later entries.

The Great (and Strange) Chicago Fire of 1871

Introduction	The Great Fire that burned down much of Chicago in 1871 became a legendary event in its time,
Thesis statement	and its fame has lasted through the years. Perhaps one reason that the Great Fire is so memorable is that it involved so many peculiarities and contradictions. It began humbly but spread spectacularly throughout the city; it destroyed a massive amount of property but miraculously took a relatively small toll of human life; it somehow left Chicago ready and able to bound back to become the largest city in the Midwest within just a few years.
Subtopic 1	The Great Fire did indeed begin, as the stories say, in the cowshed of Mrs. Patrick O'Leary, at 8:45 p.m. on Sunday, October 8, 1871.[1] The O'Learys lived on the west side of Chicago, but the winds propelled the fire northeastward toward the center of the city.[2] By midnight it had reached the south fork of the Chicago River, and observers expected the fire to be contained by the river.[3] Fireballs leaped over the river, however, and later, on Monday, October 9, they jumped the north branch of the river to devastate the north side of the city. The fire raged for over twenty-four hours and ended only when rain began to fall on Monday night.[4]
Subtopic 2	When the flames finally went out, only a handful of buildings were still standing in an area of three

and one-third square miles, which was about one-third of the city. The Great Fire completely leveled Chicago's business district and resulted in a loss of over $180,000,000 worth of goods and property. About one-third of the city's 300,000 residents were left homeless. Surprisingly, however, the fire took a relatively small number of lives. Only about three hundred people died in the Great Fire of Chicago, while a fire on the very same evening in Peshtigo, Wisconsin, took over 1,100 lives.[5]

Subtopic 3

Perhaps even more surprisingly, Chicago's growth as a city appears to have been spurred, rather than checked, by the Great Fire. Within a week, banks re-opened for business, and merchants began to sell their goods from makeshift stands and shacks. The city quickly began to rebuild what the fire had destroyed, but on a much grander and more ambitious scale.[6] By 1880, less than ten years after the fire, Chicago had passed St. Louis as the most populous city in the Midwest and had become the center of commerce for the entire region.[7]

Conclusion with reminder of thesis statement

The Great Fire, therefore, may be most fascinating for its numerous surprises and contradictions. A final note, and one that suits the peculiar nature of this fire: The house of Mr. and Mrs. Patrick O'Leary was left standing when the flames finally died.

---

[1]Herman Kogan and Robert Cromie, The Great Fire: Chicago 1871 (New York: G.P. Putnam's Sons, 1971), p. 50.

[2]Robert P. Howard, Illinois: A History of the Prairie State (Grand Rapids, Mich.: William B. Eerdmans Publishing Company, 1972), p. 348.

[3]The Great Chicago Fire: Letters by Men and Women Who Experienced Its Horrors (Chicago: The Chicago Historical Society, 1946), p. 25.

[4]Howard, Illinois, p. 531.

[5]Kogan and Cromie, The Great Fire, p. 113.

[6]Howard, Illinois, pp. 352–353.

[7]Howard, Illinois, p. 353.

BIBLIOGRAPHY

The Great Chicago Fire: Letters by Men and Women Who Experienced Its Horrors. Chicago, Illinois: The Chicago Historical Society, 1946.

Howard, Robert P. Illinois: A History of the Prairie State. Grand Rapids, Michigan: William B. Eerdmans Publishing Company, 1972.

Kogan, Herman, and Robert Cromie. The Great Fire: Chicago 1871. New York: G. P. Putnam's Sons, 1971.

Pierce, Bessie. A History of Chicago, vol. 2 and 3. Chicago, Illinois: University of Chicago Press, 1976.

EXERCISE B: Understanding Research Papers. Answer the following questions about the paper on the Chicago Fire.

1. What does the reader learn in the introduction?
2. What makes the thesis statement different from the other sentences in the introduction?
3. What subtopics are covered in the body?
4. How are the subtopics related to the thesis statement?
5. How are the subtopics arranged?
6. What transitions connect ideas between and within paragraphs?
7. What are two functions that the conclusion serves?
8. How many footnotes are given?
9. How many *different* sources are cited in the paper?
10. How does the form of the bibliography items differ from the form of the footnotes?

DEVELOPING WRITING SKILLS: Practicing with Thesis Statements for Research Papers. Choose one of the following topics. At the library, find at least three sources of information and glance through the contents of each. Then prepare rough versions of two different thesis statements.

Eighteenth-century pirates	The Bermuda Triangle
Silent movies	Nuclear power
A famous baseball player	Undersea mining
An important leader	The dangers of a certain career
An endangered species	A famous writer of mysteries

24.2 Writing a Research Paper

Writing a research paper involves many of the same basic planning, writing, and revising steps that essays do. These steps, however, must be slightly modified to meet the special demands of conducting and properly citing your research.

PREWRITING: Planning Your Paper

When you plan a research paper, you should select your topic carefully. Consider your own interests as well as the information available on the topic.

Choosing a Topic and Narrowing It Down. The first thing to do when you are beginning work on a paper is to choose a general topic that interests you. Then you should go to the library to determine how much information is available on the topic you are considering. Avoid topics about which there is little information, such as a minor, recent news item.

Select a topic that is interesting, that can be supported with enough information, and that is narrow enough for one paper.

You will often find that the sources you have consulted to find out if there is enough information will also help you find a smaller topic that is narrow enough for a research paper.

If you were to choose space exploration or child aubse as your general topic, you would be likely to find many smaller topics under the general topic. The chart gives examples.

GENERAL TOPICS WITH POSSIBLE SMALLER TOPICS		
General Topics:	**Space Exploration**	**Child Abuse**
Smaller Topics:	*Mariner* space flights	Causes of child abuse
	Mineral analysis of moon rocks	Child abuse cases
	Possibility of life on Venus	Agencies and programs that combat child abuse

576

Focusing a Topic. Before you undertake your research, jot down about five questions that you want to learn about as you read your sources. Then draft a rough version of your thesis statement.

Prepare to do research by determining questions to answer and by drafting a rough version of your thesis statement.

If your topic were agencies and programs to combat child abuse you might write questions such as these.

SAMPLE QUESTIONS

1. What are some of the agencies that combat child abuse?
2. What specific programs have been set up to help fight child abuse?
3. What does each agency and program do?
4. How effective are these agencies and programs?
5. Who else is working to eliminate child abuse?

With these questions in mind, you can jot down a rough version of your thesis statement. Although you may have to revise it several times during and after taking notes, having a rough version of your thesis statement at this point will help you focus your thoughts and direct your research.

For the topic on child abuse, you might write the following rough thesis statement.

ROUGH THESIS STATEMENT: Several agencies and programs are attempting to deal with the problem of child abuse.

Making Bibliography Cards. Before you begin taking notes on your sources, you should make bibliography cards. This will help you keep track of your sources and make it easier to cite sources and write your bibliography.

Keep complete information about each source you use for your bibliography.

The following chart gives suggestions for preparing bibliography cards.

577

GUIDELINES FOR PREPARING BIBLIOGRAPHY CARDS

1. Use one note card for each source.
2. On the top of the card write complete information as it will appear in your bibliography. See page 571 for the information needed for each kind of source.
3. If the source is a library book, include the call number. You might need to find the book again.
4. Note any illustrations, maps, or charts that you might use.

How many sources you will need will depend on your topic and your teacher's requirements. You should always try to use at least three sources. If you cannot find at least three sources of information on a topic, try another topic.

Taking Notes. Now that you have a direction for your research and a general knowledge of the sources you will consult, you should begin taking notes in an organized fashion. Remember that you will want notes that are easy to use when you begin to write your paper.

Take accurate notes to answer the questions you asked about your topic. Include page references.

Start taking notes from the source that appears to contain the most complete coverage of your topic. Skim the material first and then take notes. For each source write down only information that is directly related to your topic and that you have not already recorded from another source.

The chart suggests an orderly system for taking notes.

SUGGESTIONS FOR TAKING NOTES

1. Use a separate card for each new subject under a source.
2. Place citation information for each source in the upper left-hand corner of the card.
3. Place a subject heading in the upper right-hand corner of each card.
4. Always include a page number for each citation.
5. Clip together the note cards from a single source.

When a source contains information that you want to quote, you should record the exact words in quotation marks. At other times, paraphrasing will generally be sufficient. Whether you quote or paraphrase, you should always include page numbers to indicate where you found each piece of information. The following card illustrates these methods of taking notes.

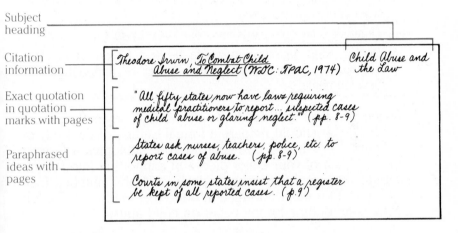

Subject heading

Citation information

Exact quotation in quotation marks with pages

Paraphrased ideas with pages

Theodore Irwin, To Combat Child Abuse and Neglect (WDC: SPAC, 1974)   Child Abuse and the Law

" All fifty states now have laws requiring medical practitioners to report... suspected cases of child abuse or glaring neglect." (pp. 8-9)

States ask nurses, teachers, police, etc. to report cases of abuse. (pp. 8-9)

Courts in some states insist that a register be kept of all reported cases. (p. 9)

Writing a Precise Thesis Statement. When you have completed your research, revise your thesis statement.

Revise your thesis statement to reflect your research.

Try to find the most precise wording for your thesis statement, drawing on the information you have in your notes. For the paper on child abuse, the following revised thesis statement might be written.

REVISED THESIS STATEMENT: The courts as well as many private and public agencies are striving to eliminate child abuse.

Preparing an Outline. With supporting information gathered from your research and a revised thesis statement, you can begin to organize your paper so that it will present your knowledge of the topic clearly and logically.

Arrange your information in a formal outline.

In order to select the information you want to include in the body of your paper, you should have your thesis statement and your notes before you. Then begin grouping your ideas and the information gathered from research following these steps.

STEPS FOR ORGANIZING A RESEARCH PAPER

1. Decide what subtopics (subpoints of the thesis statement) you want your paper to cover.
2. Organize your note cards and your ideas by subtopic.
3. Decide what organization would be best for presenting the subtopics—chronological, spatial, order of importance, or developmental.

When you have decided how you want to organize your information, you should prepare a formal outline of the body of the paper. You should give each of your subtopics a Roman numeral, each of your major pieces of supporting information a capital letter, and each smaller detail an Arabic number. (See Section 32.2 for more information on formal outlines.) The following is an outline for the paper on child abuse.

I. Government attempts to combat child abuse
   A. Action by courts and state governments
      1. Laws that apply to doctors
      2. Laws that apply to nurses, teachers, the clergy, and police
   B. Federal programs
      1. Title IV
      2. National Center on Child Abuse and Neglect
II. Private and public agency attempts to combat child abuse
   A. Programs that deal with suspected child abuse and neglect
      1. Counseling of parents
      2. Emergency day-care centers
      3. Public service announcements
   B. Parents Anonymous
      1. Chapters in America, Europe, and Asia
      2. Emergency help offered
      3. Weekly meetings held

C. Hospitals, universities, other public institutions
   1. Children's Hospital in Boston
   2. UCLA Neuropsychiatric Institute
   3. New York Foundling Hospital
   4. Foster Grandparents of Denver

When you have finished your outline, examine it to see if you have enough information to cover each subtopic. If you do not, check additional sources to find additional information or eliminate the subtopics you cannot develop adequately. You should also jot down any ideas you have for a title, introduction, and conclusion.

EXERCISE A: Choosing a Topic and Narrowing It Down. Choose one of the following topics. Check to see if enough material is available on your topic by consulting the card catalog and *The Readers' Guide to Periodical Literature* in the library. Then find four smaller topics that are aspects of your topic. Choose one to write about. Finally, think of five questions that you might ask about the topic and write a rough thesis statement.

The Alaskan gold rush	Electric cars
Scuba-diving equipment	Causes of tidal waves
The Coast Guard	The life of a famous author
Formation of volcanoes	The Grand Canyon

EXERCISE B: Carrying Out Your Research. Use the topic you chose in Exercise A and follow these instructions.

1. Prepare bibliography cards for all the sources you expect to use.
2. Take notes from the sources. Try to include some direct quotations. Be sure to include all of the necessary information on each card.

EXERCISE C: Organizing a Research Paper. Revise your rough thesis statement so that it reflects the research you did in Exercise B. Then organize your notes into subtopics and write a formal outline for the body of your paper. Finally, list ideas for your title, introduction, and conclusion.

WRITING: Creating a First Draft

When you have a complete outline and ideas for your title, introduction, and conclusion, you are ready to begin writing.

Use your outline and notes to write a first draft.

Your outline should also help you to cite your sources. Arrange your notes in the order in which the information will appear in your paper. Whenever you use a quotation or a non-original fact or idea, even a paraphrased one, cite the source. Use the footnote forms shown in Section 24.1, placing your footnotes either at the bottom of each page or at the end of the paper. At the very end of the report, include a bibliography.

Here is a draft of the paper on child abuse. The notes in the margins indicate how the organization of subtopics follows the outline. Footnotes and the bibliography come at the end.

Agencies and Programs to Combat Child Abuse

Introduction

Hospital files, police reports, and court records all attest to the horrors of child abuse. Each year, hundreds of thousands of children are hurt or neglected, and many suffer serious injuries. Babies are whipped with belts and ropes. Fragile arms are broken. Tragically, many infants and young children die of wounds caused by adults. Does anybody care enough to help? Fortunately, the answer is yes. The courts as well as many private and public agencies are striving to combat child abuse.

Thesis
statement

Subtopic 1A

The courts and state governments are certainly helping to fight child abuse. "All fifty states now have laws requiring medical practitioners to report . . . suspected cases of child abuse or glaring neglect. And virtually every state provides immunity from legal action for physicians."[1] Many states ask nurses, teachers, the clergy, and others to report child abuse. Each year, family courts separate about 150,000 children from abusing parents, and "more than twice that number are yielded to state custody voluntarily by their parents under threat of prosecution."[2]

Raised
numbers show
that the
source will
be given in
a footnote

Subtopic 1B

The federal government has also spent money and set up programs to try to protect children from harm. For example, the government has set up a program called Title IV, which is part of the Social Security Act. This program offers such services as "short-term care outside the home for endangered children, counseling to parents, and homemaker services."[3] To run this program, the federal government now spends about $200 million a year.[4] Specially trained professionals also try to help troubled families improve their home lives. In some cases, they will take children temporarily out of a home where there are serious problems. In addition, the government has set up programs to train people across the country to help stop child abuse. The government's National Center on Child Abuse and Neglect, for example, sends teams of specially trained people to those communities that need help starting programs. The Center also studies the causes, prevention, and treatment of child abuse.

Subtopic 2A   In addition to the actions of the federal and state governments, many cities have special programs of their own and support private groups that treat child abuse. One program found in many cities is called SCAN, which stands for Suspected Child Abuse and Neglect. SCAN is a private, nonprofit organization that counsels parents. Sometimes SCAN workers visit homes to help parents and children live together. Workers will try "to break the violence cycle by suggesting ways of dealing with . . . problems and easing emotional strains."[5] Many SCAN centers in different cities have emergency day-care centers. In a child abuse emergency, the day-care center will take care of the children while the SCAN men and women work with the parents. One of the purposes of SCAN is to help abusing parents control their anger or other problems that lead to their hurting children. SCAN also tries to educate the public to the problem by placing ads in magazines, newspapers, and store windows and on the radio. It also tries through other means to bring in volunteers and raise funds. SCAN/New York asks everyone to care and, if possible, to help. In The

583

<u>New York Times</u>, SCAN/New York showed a picture of a beaten child with the message, "You really should get to know the person who did this."[6]

Subtopic 2B   Another important program is called Parents Anonymous. Also a private, nonprofit organization, Parents Anonymous has about one thousand chapters in the United States and additional chapters in Europe and Asia. Although the program has been helping parents and children for only about ten years, it has reached thousands of people. Parents Anonymous offers to help any parent who wishes to control the urge to hurt his or her children and understands that few parents want to be child abusers. Volunteers and staff people believe that they can help parents control their anger and improve their treatment of their children, and they report success. Parents Anonymous offers emergency help any time of the day or night. It also has weekly meetings so that parents can work steadily to improve their family lives.

Subtopic 2C   Many public institutions, such as city hospitals and universities, provide help for abused children and disturbed parents. In Boston, for example, the Children's Hospital Medical Center operates a program called Trauma X Group. Doctors, nurses, and psychologists at this hospital help social workers prevent child abuse. Together, these people treat victims of abuse, counsel parents, and visit homes after children are released from the hospital. A similar program is run at the UCLA Neuropsychiatric Institute in Los Angeles. Like most child abuse programs, this one is "based on the premise that . . . parents are looking for someone who can help them."[7] Among New York's programs is the Department of Emergency Children's Services. This department has a hot line with a toll-free number. At the New York Foundling Hospital, doctors, nurses, and other professionals play the role of parents to adults who abuse their children in order to help them learn how to be better parents. Perhaps the most innovative programs dealing with child abuse are in Denver, Colorado. One of Denver's programs, called Foster Grandparents, uses volunteers who are

584

over sixty-five years old to help, guide, and love abused children and abusing parents.

Reminder of thesis statement Many private and public programs have been set up to reach children and parents in trouble, and many of the programs are helping. Child abuse cannot be eliminated easily. It may never be eliminated completely. But in every village, town, and city, people who care are working through federal programs, private organizations, and public agencies around the clock, seven days a week to help eliminate child abuse. Through these programs these people are helping provide protection, care, and love to children and counseling and guidance to adults.

---

[1]Theodore Irwin, To Combat Child Abuse and Neglect (Washington, D.C.: The Public Affairs Committee, 1974), pp. 8–9.

[2]"Child Abuse and Snooping," The New York Times, April 20, 1977, p. A25.

[3]Irwin, To Combat Child Abuse and Neglect, p. 11.

[4]Irwin, To Combat Child Abuse and Neglect, p. 11.

[5]Irwin, To Combat Child Abuse and Neglect, p. 18.

[6]"Fighting Child Abuse," The New York Times, June 19, 1979, p. D16.

[7]Irwin, To Combat Child Abuse and Neglect, p. 15.

BIBLIOGRAPHY

"Child Abuse and Snooping." The New York Times. April 20, 1977, p. A25.

"Fighting Child Abuse." The New York Times. June 19, 1979, p. D16.

"In Massachusetts: A Hot Line to Tragedy." Time, November 6, 1978, pp. 6, 13.

Irwin, Theodore. To Combat Child Abuse and Neglect. Washington, D.C.: The Public Affairs Committee, 1974.

EXERCISE D: Writing a First Draft. Using your outline and list of ideas from Exercise C, write a first draft. Cite your sources of nonoriginal material and prepare a bibliography.

585

REVISING: Polishing Your Paper

In revising your paper, you should look for any mistakes you might have made as well as any ways to improve your ideas or the way you have expressed them. Try to read your paper as another person would read it. Look for confusing writing as well as for errors in grammar, mechanics, and spelling.

Examine your first draft for content and structure and revise it as necessary.

The following checklist should help you evaluate your paper.

CHECKLIST FOR REVISION

1. Does the introduction arouse interest, give necessary background information, and include the thesis statement?
2. Does the thesis statement present a clear main point?
3. Does the body present subtopics that develop the thesis statement?
4. Are the body paragraphs arranged in a logical order?
5. Does each body paragraph have a topic sentence?
6. Are the ideas in each paragraph arranged logically?
7. Are transitions used with and between paragraphs?
8. Does the conclusion contain a reminder of the thesis statement that summarizes the main point of the paper without sounding repetitious?
9. Are all quotations and nonoriginal facts and ideas cited in footnotes? Are all sources listed correctly in the bibliography?
10. Does the paper follow the rules of grammar, mechanics, and spelling?

EXERCISE E: Revising Your Research Paper. Use the checklist above to revise the report you wrote in Exercise E.

DEVELOPING WRITING SKILLS: Writing a Research Paper. Plan, write, and revise a research paper on a topic of your own following the steps in this chapter.

Writing Workshop: Research Papers

ASSIGNMENT 1

Topic Unusual Careers

Form and Purpose A research paper informing readers of the tasks, skills, and training required in an unusual job

Audience Students attending a Career Day at your school

Length Four to six paragraphs

Focus Select an unusual job, such as worm farmer, jockey, salvage diver. Then research and write a paper about the demands, skills, training, and rewards of that job.

Sources Magazine and newspaper articles, books, interviews

Prewriting Choose and narrow your topic, research it, take notes, and develop a thesis statement and an outline.

Writing Use your outline to write a first draft. Include footnotes and a bibliography.

Revising Revise your paper using the checklist on page 586.

ASSIGNMENT 2

Topic The Impact of a Great Discovery

Form and Purpose A research paper explaining how a particular discovery had a great impact on people's lives

Audience Producers of a public-television series entitled *Shaping the World*

Length Four to six paragraphs

Focus Choose a single, important discovery from the past. Explain what it was and how it affected the world at that time or the course of history.

Sources Books, magazines, newspaper articles

Prewriting Research your topic, take notes, and develop a thesis statement and an outline.

Writing Write a first draft by following your outline. Use footnotes and compile a bibliography for your sources.

Revising Revise your paper using the checklist on page 586.

Benjamin Franklin's Experiment of June 1752

Topics for Writing: Research Papers

Choose a topic from the list below, or let the map below suggest a topic to you. Narrow your topic so that it is suitable for a brief research paper. Then write a paper of four to six paragraphs. Include footnotes and a bibliography.

1. The Incan Empire
2. Mexican Pyramids
3. Cortés and the Aztecs
4. The Mayan Calendar
5. Gold in the Americas
6. Macchu Picchu
7. The South American Llama
8. Music of the Andes
9. Where Did the First Americans Come From?
10. Darwin in the Galapagos Islands

PEOPLES OF THE AMERICAS BEFORE 1492

Chapter 25

Writing About Literature

After reading a work of literature in school or on your own, you may be asked to write a *book report* or a *literary analysis paper*. Although book reports and literary analysis papers are both concerned with the basic elements of a work of literature, such as theme, character, and plot, they follow different formats.

25.1 Book Reports

A book report generally presents a brief summary of and comments about something you have read. Book reports vary depending upon the type of book you are writing about and the requirements of your teacher. There are, however, several basic features that are common to almost all book reports.

Understanding Book Reports

A book report is usually written for an audience that has not read the book. Its purpose is to acquaint the reader with the work by commenting on the contents and expressing an opinion about whether the book is worth reading.

A book report informs the reader about a work of literature and makes a recommendation.

A book report follows a special format in order to present the work of literature clearly and logically. The following chart shows an example of a book report format.

PARTS OF A BOOK REPORT	
Introduction	Identifies the book by title and author and gives a brief summary of the contents
Body	Focuses on specific elements of the book, such as theme, character, or setting
Conclusion	Gives an overall evaluation of the book and makes a recommendation

A book report begins by identifying the book by title and author and then gives a brief overview of the book's contents. The report then focuses on some particular elements of the book, such as theme or character, supported by evidence from the book itself. Finally, it gives an overall evaluation of the book and makes a recommendation.

The body of the book report usually focuses on one or more of the basic elements of a work of literature, such as theme, character, or point of view. The following chart briefly defines some of the most important elements you will find in a book, particularly fiction.

ELEMENTS TO EXAMINE IN A WORK OF LITERATURE	
Elements	**Definitions**
Theme	A general truth or observation about life or people—the message the author is trying to convey. The theme is often not stated directly, but it is the main idea that ties the work together.
Character	A person in the story. Characters are revealed in several ways: by what they do, by what they say, by what other characters say about them, by how other characters react to them, and sometimes by the narrator's direct statements about them.

Conflict	A struggle between opposing forces or people. Conflict can be external—character against character, character against society, character against Fate or God. Conflict can also be internal—a character against some aspect of himself or herself: For example, a character may have to choose between what is right and what is easiest.
Plot	The sequence of events in a story. The plot usually builds to a *climax* or turning point, which resolves the conflict.
Setting	The time and place of the action. A story may take place in the past, present, or future or in any location, real or imaginary. The setting is the world of the story; it can affect the plot and characters.
Point of View	The person telling the story is called the narrator. A first-person narrator uses the pronoun "I" and participates in the story, recounting events as he or she experiences them. A third-person narrator tells a story more objectively, from the outside, using "he" and "she." An omniscient third-person narrator can see into the minds of the characters.

The report below shows the format of a book report. After a short introductory paragraph, the body of the report focuses on two elements. It concludes with a paragraph that gives an overall evaluation of the book and makes a recommendation.

Report on Twenty Thousand Leagues Under the Sea

Introduction with brief summary

Jules Verne's science fiction novel *Twenty Thousand Leagues Under the Sea* describes a fantastic ten-month submarine voyage. This voyage takes place in the 1860's, which was decades before submarines were actually navigating the seas. Traveling from the south seas to the polar cap, the ship, under the iron-fisted rule of Captain Nemo, encounters a series of unusual and often life-threatening events. The story is told by Pierre Arromax, a French scientist known for his studies of natural science. Arromax, his servant, and a friend become castaways rescued by Captain Nemo and then held captive aboard his ship, the Nautilus.

Body paragraph 1 (discusses first element)

The most intriguing character in the novel is the mysterious Captain Nemo. Little is known about his past, and even his true identity is hidden by his name—Nemo means "no man" in Latin. An air of mystery surrounds Captain Nemo from the first time he appears until the end of the book. As the voyage progresses, Arromax and the reader receive clues about Nemo's past, but these clues are never fully explained. Captain Nemo's personality is as mysterious as his past. He seems at times full of hatred for humankind and at other times full of compassion for his shipmates and captives. When a sailor dies, for example, Captain Nemo conducts an elaborate burial ceremony undersea and leads the men in prayer. Yet at another time he gives orders to ram a ship, killing all aboard without explanation.

Body paragraph 2 (discusses second element)

The book is fascinating for its setting as well as its characters. During the ten months Arromax is on board, the Nautilus sails to exotic places, from the coral reefs of the Pacific to the South Pole. It even sails under the isthmus of Suez. The captives and crew make expeditions into the beautiful undersea world. The world they see is described in vivid detail. Many types of sea plants and fish are minutely described as is the undersea terrain. When they walk around the mythical lost continent, Atlantis, the reader can see the mountains and temples. Undersea forests and sunken vessels seem real.

Conclusion with overall evaluation and recommendation

The book holds the reader's interest with its mystery, suspense, and exotic settings. By traveling with Captain Nemo, the reader is given a unique adventure and a lesson in marine biology. One does not have to be a fan of science fiction to enjoy this adventure novel.

593

EXERCISE A: Understanding a Book Report. Answer each of these questions about the preceding book report on *Twenty Thousand Leagues Under the Sea*.

1. Does the writer clearly identify the book by author and title?
2. Does the introduction adequately summarize the contents of the book?
3. What other information is presented in the introduction?
4. Which element of the novel is discussed in the first body paragraph?
5. What kind of supporting information is used in the first body paragraph? Give two examples.
6. What element of the novel is discussed in the second body paragraph?
7. What kind of supporting information is used in the second body paragraph? Give two examples.
8. What is the writer's opinion of the book as a whole?
9. Is the writer's overall evaluation based on specific elements examined in the body? If so, which ones?
10. Based on the writer's comments, would you like to read the book? Why or why not?

PREWRITING, WRITING, and REVISING: Preparing a Book Report

In writing a book report you should follow the same basic steps as in writing any composition. You will need to plan your report, prepare a first draft, and revise.

Prewriting. In preparing a book report, you must first choose the specific elements of the book you wish to discuss. You should then decide what you wish to say about each element and find appropriate evidence in the book to support your ideas.

Choose one or more elements to discuss, and then gather and organize supporting information.

The following list was prepared for a book report on the novel *The Good Earth*. The writer decided to discuss the theme of the book and one of the major characters, named O-lan, and then went through the story, gathering support.

594

LIST OF SUPPORTING INFORMATION FOR A BOOK REPORT	
Book: <u>The Good Earth</u> by Pearl S. Buck	

Theme: The land

—title of books suggests that the land is the main theme

—story of Chinese peasants in the early 1900's

—farmers living close to land

—Wang Lung and his family working hard to raise crops

—family lives through drought and famine

—humble family presented in heroic way

—Wang Lung's beliefs about the goodness of the land

—Wang Lung becomes a rich landlord

—moves to town and neglects the land

—thinks about the land when he is in the city

—returns to the land when problems arise

—people change but land remains the same

—land gives comfort and hope

Character: O-lan

—former slave, Wang Lung's wife

—has large, unbound feet

—respects land and husband

—suffers the pain of childbirth alone

—proud of new baby son

—dresses son in red to visit former mistress

—cares for family

—helps family survive famine

—ignores concubine

—feels her main accomplishment is having sons

—a model of wife's role in a Chinese marriage of that time

—finally accepts death as she accepts life

With a list of supporting information, you are ready to organize your material. Now you should decide what to say in your introduction and what kind of general evaluation you want to give in your conclusion. You must also consider the order of the body paragraphs.

It may be helpful for you to construct an outline with material drawn from your list of support. The following outline was made for the book report on *The Good Earth*, based on the list of supporting information shown above.

595

I. Introduction
   A. Title—The Good Earth
   B. Author—Pearl S. Buck
   C. Summary—Story of Wang family in China
      1. Peasant farmer, rich landlord
      2. Drought, famine, floods, and prosperity
II. First element—Theme: The land
   A. The land remains constant
   B. The land can be cruel
   C. The land rewards hard work
III. Second element—Character: O-lan
   A. Quiet
   B. Hard worker
   C. Respectful of land and husband
   D. Proud of sons
IV. Conclusion
   A. Tale of one family's survival
   B. Well worth reading

Writing. When writing a book report, always prepare a first draft. The first draft should follow your outline.

Use your outline and list of support to write a first draft.

As you are writing, refer to your list of supporting information. Concentrate on connecting your ideas with transitions. Be sure to place any direct quotations in quotation marks and give the page number in parentheses.

Remember that this is a first draft, and you will have a chance to revise it later. Therefore, you do not have to worry about getting everything exactly right the first time. The main purpose of the first draft is to shape all your ideas and information into a whole. The following is a first draft of a book report on *The Good Earth*.

Report on The Good Earth

Introduction with brief summary
     The Good Earth by Pearl S. Buck is the story of a Chinese peasant, Wang Lung, who rises from a poor farmer to a rich landlord during the early 1900's. The book tells of the joys and disappointments of Wang

596

Lung and his family as they journey through life facing drought, famine, floods, and war as well as prosperity. It is the story of Wang Lung's determination and his commitment to the land.

Body paragraph 1 (discusses first element— theme)

The title of the book reflects its theme—<u>The Good Earth</u>. The earth is the unifying thread that runs through Wang Lung's life. The earth, he believes, is good to a person who works hard and is good to it. In the beginning Wang Lung works the land so that he can buy a wife and have sons. He lives in an earthen hut and makes sacrifices to earth gods. Even when his family is facing starvation because of a severe drought and they must leave the farm, Wang Lung will not sell the land. When they return to the farm after the drought, the narrator states that Wang Lung wished to see no one but wanted to "be alone on his land" (page 123). The land provides comfort and hope. When Wang Lung becomes prosperous, he neglects his land for a while, leaving it in the capable hands of his overseer. But he returns to his hoe when problems arise. Even as he approaches death in his rich house in town, Wang Lung's thoughts are with his land. He tells his sons to keep the land, and he goes back to the earth hut he lived in as a young man.

Body paragraph 2 (discusses second element— character)

O-lan, Wang Lung's wife, also has great respect for the land. Although O-lan had worked as a slave in a house in town, she goes into the fields to help her husband as soon as she is married. Unlike the wealthy Chinese, O-lan did not have her feet bound as a girl; therefore, her feet are large and strong, permitting her to work long hours in the field. O-lan is the model Chinese wife of the time—humble, quiet, and obedient. She never complains—not when she bears children alone, not when the family faces starvation, and not when her husband purchases a concubine. O-lan believes that her greatest accomplishment in life is having sons, and she is extremely proud of them. When her first son is born, she dresses him in finery and takes him to show her former mistress. O-lan accepts death as she accepts life. When she knows that

	she is dying, she is content because she has left sons who will one day have children of their own to carry on the family tradition.
Conclusion with overall evaluation and recommendation	The Good Earth is a heroic tale of one family struggling to survive in a harsh world. It gives a sympathetic portrait of a way of life few of us could ever see at first hand. Pearl S. Buck's careful depiction of Wang Lung and his family gives the reader insight into people who never give up. It is well worth reading.

Revising. You should carefully revise your book report after you have completed your first draft. During revision you can add new information, delete material, and reorder what you have written. You can also rewrite sentences and change the wording, grammar, mechanics, and spelling.

Use a checklist to revise your book report.

The following checklist suggests questions that you might ask yourself during revision.

CHECKLIST FOR REVISING A BOOK REPORT

1. Does your introduction clearly and completely identify the book and its author?
1. Do the elements you discuss in the body represent the book accurately?
3. Is there additional or different supporting information that would make your ideas clearer?
4. Is there unnecessary information that you could take out?
5. If you used direct quotations, are they accurate? Are page numbers included?
6. Are your ideas organized logically from the beginning to the end of the report?
7. Could any transitions be added to make the report read more smoothly?
8. Does your conclusion make a clear recommendation?
9. Should you rewrite any sentences for clarity?
10. Does your report contain any mistakes in grammar, mechanics, or spelling?

After you have made all of your revision changes, carefully recopy your paper in final form. When your final copy is ready, proofread it at least once for typographical errors.

EXERCISE B: Planning a Book Report. Choose a book that you have read recently and decide on at least two elements of the book to discuss. Next, make a list of supporting information and organize your material into an outline.

EXERCISE C: Writing a Book Report. Write a first draft of your book report, using the outline and list of supporting information you prepared in Exercise B.

EXERCISE D: Revising a Book Report. Using the checklist on page 598, examine the book report you wrote in Exercise C. Then revise it to correct any problems that you discover. Finally, make a clean copy and carefully proofread it for typographical errors before submitting it to your teacher.

DEVELOPING WRITING SKILLS: Planning, Writing, and Revising a Book Report. Follow these instructions to prepare a second book report.

1. Choose a work of literature to write a book report about. Follow all the steps presented in this chapter to plan your report and write a first draft.
2. When you have a first draft, exchange reports with another student.
3. Using the revision checklist on page 598, answer each question about the other student's paper. Also write a few sentences as a brief critique of the report as a whole. Make specific suggestions for improvements on the paper itself in a contrasting color of ink. Return the paper with your comments to the other student.
4. When you receive your own paper back, revise it, taking into account the other student's critique and comments. Make a clean copy of the revised paper.
5. Hand in the clean copy together with the marked first draft and the other student's comments.

25.2 Papers Analyzing Literature

A literary analysis paper is a written interpretation of a work of literature—a short story, a novel, a poem, a play, or a work of nonfiction, such as a biography.

Understanding Literary Analysis Papers

Like book reports, literary analysis papers discuss works of literature. But there are important differences between them. Since the audience for a book report generally has not read the book, a book report begins with an overview and ends with a recommendation. Literary analysis papers, however, are usually written for an audience familiar with the work being discussed. Therefore, a literary analysis paper does not include an overview; nor does it necessarily include a recommendation. Instead, it interprets and analyzes the work.

A literary analysis paper helps interpret a work for the reader.

Like an essay, a literary analysis paper states a main point, which is supported by evidence from the work itself.

Literary analysis papers generally follow a format similar to the one shown in the following chart.

PARTS OF A LITERARY ANALYSIS PAPER
Title
May simply name the work being analyzed but can also indicate the main point and approach of the paper
Introduction
Identifies the work and author; if necessary, gives further information, such as when and where the author lived
Specifies the kind of work, such as sonnet or historical novel
Gives some idea of the author's purpose in writing the book if such information is useful
States the main point that will be made in the paper

600

Body
Presents subtopics of the main point, usually one subtopic per paragraph
Uses a logical order, such as chronological, spatial, order of importance, comparison and contrast, or developmental
Supports the main point with quotations, examples, details or incidents drawn from the work
Provides enough information to make the reader feel that the main point has been fully explained

Conclusion
Recalls the main point made in the introduction
Shows how the main point helps explain the work as a whole
Makes closing remarks that pull the whole paper together

Like the title of an essay, the title of a literary analysis paper can be used to capture the writer's main point. A literary analysis paper begins with an introduction that identifies the work and states a main point about the element or elements that will be investigated. The body of the paper presents subtopics of this main point. The body also includes supporting information—examples, details, incidents, and perhaps direct quotations—taken from the work. The paper ends with a reminder of the main point and a comment on how it helps explain the work of literature as a whole.

The following literary analysis paper on Ernest Hemingway's *The Old Man and the Sea* shows this basic format.

The Triumph of Santiago

Introduction with statement of main point	Santiago, the major character in Ernest Hemingway's novella <u>The Old Man and the Sea</u>, is a man who lives by his own code of what is success or failure. Because he is resolute and courageous in following his code, he finally triumphs.
Body paragraph 1 (discusses first subtopic)	Santiago's resoluteness, his will to succeed, is introduced early in the novel and remains throughout. Although he has not caught a fish in eighty-four days, Santiago still keeps going out every day, believing that

he will soon catch a great fish. The old man's determination is also shown in the narrator's physical description of him: "Everything about him was old except his eyes and they were the same color as the sea and were cheerful and undefeated" (page 10). There is something within him that keeps him going, that will not admit defeat—defeat by age or by the sea—and this shows in his eyes.

Body paragraph 2 (discusses second subtopic)

The Old Man's courage is displayed in several ways throughout the novel. He is courageous in spirit as well as in actions. At the beginning of the novel, Santiago accepts possible defeat; he does not give in to it, but he accepts it. When he has not caught a fish in eighty-four days, he does not complain nor does he put the blame on anyone or anything else. He also accepts his isolation in the community without complaint. As the narrator tells us, "many of the fishermen made fun of the old man and he was not angry" (page 11).

Body paragraph 3 (discusses third subtopic)

Santiago's courage is also evident in his actions. When he finally catches the great fish, he endures three days of painful battle without giving up. Knowing he faces possible death, he continues his fight against great odds. He also has the courage to face great loss and does so when the sharks attack and devour his catch. Santiago accepts this without question: "And what beat you, he thought. 'Nothing,' he said aloud, 'I went out too far'" (page 120). He calmly and courageously accepts the responsibility for his loss.

Conclusion with reminder of main point and closing remarks

In the end, however, Santiago triumphs. He has shown the other fishermen, but more importantly himself, that he is in control of his own spiritual destiny. He can face death and win. His victory is not a materialistic one, but one of the spirit. He is victorious because he knows he fought honorably and well, according to his own beliefs. Santiago faces old age, he faces nature, and he faces death. Because he faces all of these difficult challenges on his own terms, resolutely and with courage, he is triumphant.

EXERCISE A: Understanding a Literary Analysis Paper.
Carefully reread the paper on *The Old Man and the Sea* and then answer the following questions.

1. What is the main point stated in the introduction?
2. How does the title help prepare for the main point?
3. What other information is presented in the introduction?
4. What subtopics are discussed in the three body paragraphs?
5. How are the subtopics related to the main idea?
6. Give two examples of the supporting information presented under each subtopic.
7. In what order are the subtopics presented?
8. Which sentences in the conclusion refer back to the main point stated in the introduction?
9. Does the conclusion add to your understanding of the main point? If so, what does it add?
10. Does the conclusion help you understand the work as a whole? If so, in what way?

PREWRITING, WRITING, and REVISING: Preparing a Literary Analysis Paper

Writing a literary analysis paper is similar to writing an essay. However, in the planning stage you will reverse a few steps since you must first analyze the work before you can decide on a main point.

Prewriting. When you have selected a work of literature to write about, begin planning your main point by analyzing one or more elements in the work. These elements are listed in the chart on pages 591 and 592.

Analyze one or more elements to reach a main point, and then organize your support under subtopics of the main point.

The questions in the following chart will help you think more carefully about each element and decide which element or elements you would like to explore in more detail and how you will interpret them.

QUESTIONS FOR ANALYZING A WORK OF LITERATURE

Theme

1. Why do you think the author wrote this work?
2. Did the work make you see something in a new way?
3. What general idea ties the whole work together?

Character

1. Which character do you like most or least? Why?
2. Which character do you come to know best? How?
3. How do the characters change?

Conflict

1. What force or person did the main character seem to be struggling against?
2. What incident is a good example of this conflict?
3. Is this conflict resolved in the book? If so, how?

Plot

1. What is the turning point of the story? What makes this incident stand out from the rest of the work?
2. How does the author maintain your interest in the development of the story throughout the book?
3. Does the ending seem to grow logically and naturally out of the story? Why or why not?

Setting

1. How is the setting different from your own time and place?
2. Is the setting convincing?
3. How does the setting affect the plot and the characters?

Point of View

1. Who is telling the story?
2. How does the point of view affect the way you understand the story?
3. How would the story be different if told from a different point of view?

After you have used these questions to analyze the work, make a rough list of supporting information. The following list of ideas and supporting information was prepared for a paper about the theme of the short story "One Ordinary Day, with Peanuts."

**SUPPORTING INFORMATION FOR A
LITERARY ANALYSIS PAPER**

Short story: "One Ordinary Day, with Peanuts" by Shirley Jackson

Element to examine: Theme

Why do you think that the author wrote this story?

—author seems to want to examine the idea of good and evil

  —Mr. Johnson does many things that make him appear good
    —kind to children and animals
    —gives out candy, peanuts, and money
    —helps two young people enjoy a pleasant day
  —later on, he turns out to be evil
    —wife does bad deeds at the same time he does good deeds
    —they reverse roles each day; one does good deeds while the other does bad deeds

---

Did the story make it possible to see something in a new way?

—makes the reader think that good and evil are not two separate things
—they could be like Mr. and Mrs. Johnson, two sides of a coin
—story surprises the reader into seeing things differently: at first the reader thinks Mr. Johnson is a good man, but the surprise ending changes the way the reader sees him
—story might change the way the reader sees real people who seem to be doing good deeds but are not totally convincing about it

---

What general idea seems to hold the whole story together?

—the way Mr. and Mrs. Johnson reverse roles seems to tie everything in the story together
—it explains Mr. Johnson's behavior
—could also explain why other characters are often suspicious of him, as if they sense what he really is
—reversal implies that the ideas of pure good and pure evil are so close that one can be disguised as the other

---

605

After you have made a rough list of support, examine it and decide what your main point will be. Try to state your main point in a single sentence. Then decide on the subtopics of the main point that you will examine in the body of the paper.

When you have a statement of your main point and a group of subtopics, you can begin organizing your paper. Prepare a general plan of your paper, such as the one below, showing the order of subtopics.

PLAN FOR A LITERARY ANALYSIS PAPER	
First paragraph	= Introduction Main point to discuss: Evil can be disguised as good.
Second paragraph	= Subtopic 1: Mr. Johnson's good deeds
Third paragraph	= Subtopic 2: Author's purpose in presenting Mr. Johnson in this way
Fourth paragraph	= Subtopic 3: Reversal of good and evil in surprise ending
Fifth paragraph	= Conclusion

Now you are ready to make a complete outline. The outline should help you arrange your information into an introduction, body, and conclusion. It should be organized according to your general plan and include all of the supporting information you plan to use in the paper.

The following outline was prepared from the plan and the list of supporting information for "One Ordinary Day, with Peanuts."

    I. Introduction
       A. Type of work—Short story
       B. Title—"One Ordinary Day, with Peanuts"
       C. Author—Shirley Jackson
       D. Element to examine—Theme
       E. Main point of paper—Evil can be disguised as good
   II. Body
       A. Mr. Johnson's good deeds
          1. Kind to various people and animals
          2. Helps two commuters spend pleasant day
          3. Gives out flower, candy, and peanuts

      B. Author's purpose in presenting Mr. Johnson this way
        1. Makes readers lower their guard
        2. Author deceives readers
        3. Sets up a surprise ending
      C. Surprise ending
        1. Mrs. Johnson's bad deeds
        2. Unexpected connection between good and evil
        3. Ironic twist when they exchange roles next day
   III. Conclusion
      A. Reminder of main point from introduction
      B. Closing remarks: Theme of good and evil ties whole story together

Writing. A well-organized outline will guide you in writing a first draft of your paper. In drafting your paper, concentrate on connecting the items in your outline with transitions.

Use your outline to write a first draft.

The following paper was written based on the outline and list of supporting information prepared for "One Ordinary Day, with Peanuts." Your own first draft may not be as polished as this. Do not worry; you will have time to polish your first draft during revision.

Good and Evil in "One Ordinary Day, with Peanuts"

Introduction with statement of main point

    "One Ordinary Day, with Peanuts," by Shirley Jackson, explores the difference between appearance and reality. Throughout this seemingly simple story, the main character, Mr. Johnson, goes out of his way to perform good deeds. It is not until the surprise ending that the reader realizes the story's serious theme: Evil can often be disguised as good.

Subtopic 1: good deeds

    Mr. Johnson is portrayed throughout the story as an innocent, uncomplicated, kind man. He begins his day in a cheery mood and remains this way until the end. He greets everyone he meets with a smile, and he offers help to complete strangers. One time, for example, he stops two harried commuters and pays them to take the day off to enjoy each other's company. When Mr. Johnson offers them money, they are suspicious at first, but, as the narrator points out, the offer "could not be, coming from Mr. Johnson, anything but the statement of a responsible and truthful and respectable man" (page 221).

Subtopic 2: author's purpose

This is the same impression that the reader has of Mr. Johnson. He is kind, considerate, and unbelievably generous to everyone he meets. If he is not offering strangers money, he is giving them flowers or candy or peanuts. He even stops to give a peanut to a stray dog. By portraying Mr. Johnson in such an honest, simple, and straightforward manner, Jackson does not prepare the reader for the ending, which creates an ironic twist and gives new meaning to the story.

Subtopic 3: surprise ending

When Mr. Johnson returns home at the end of the story and asks his wife how her day went, she begins to describe her day's bad deeds as simply and straightforwardly as her husband's good deeds. Mr. Johnson accepts her story and listens sympathetically as she explains that she had a fine day, "accused the woman next to me of shoplifting and had the store detective pick her up. Sent three dogs to the pound— you know, the usual" (page 227). Mr. Johnson's calm acceptance of his wife's behavior and the role reversal at the end of the story catch the reader off guard.

Conclusion with reminder of main point and closing remarks

By the end of the story, the word "ordinary" in the title itself has become ironic. Mr. Johnson's good deeds become tainted as the reader realizes that an "ordinary" day to the Johnsons means taking turns at playing good and evil. It is even more disturbing to realize that they do so without any feelings of conscience or guilt. After reading the story's surprise ending, the reader is forced to reconsider Mr. Johnson and his good deeds. Jackson makes the reader realize that good may often be a thin cover for evil.

Revising. After you have written a first draft, you still have another chance to improve your literary analysis paper. During revision you can change part or all of your paper. You can insert new ideas, delete old ones, and change the order of the content. You should also look for errors in sentence structure, grammar, mechanics, and spelling.

608

Use a checklist to revise your paper.

The following checklist will help you in revising your paper. Try to answer each question, and then change your paper to correct any problem you discover.

CHECKLIST FOR REVISING A LITERARY ANALYSIS PAPER

1. Does the title give a general indication of the main point to be presented?
2. Is the main point clearly stated in the introduction?
3. Does the body of the paper supply enough evidence to support the main point?
4. Is there irrelevant information that should be eliminated?
5. Are direct quotations given accurately and accompanied by page numbers?
6. Can the reader follow the development of the main point from the introduction through to the conclusion?
7. Is the conclusion consistent with the evidence presented in the body?
8. Does the conclusion reinforce the main point?
9. Should any sentences be rewritten for clarity?
10. Are there any mistakes in grammar, mechanics, or spelling?

After you have revised the paper, prepare a clean final copy and proofread it.

EXERCISE B: Planning a Literary Analysis Paper. Select a work of literature, perhaps from those you have read recently for class. Choose one or more elements that you want to examine in a paper and gather information from the work. Then decide on your main point and develop subtopics. Prepare an outline based on your plan and the material you have collected.

EXERCISE C: Writing a Literary Analysis Paper. Write a first draft based on the outline you prepared in Exercise B. Concentrate on connecting your ideas with transitions.

609

EXERCISE D: Revising a Literary Analysis Paper. After some time has elapsed, reread the draft you wrote in Exercise C using the checklist on page 609 as a guide. Make any necessary changes and then prepare a clean final copy. Remember to proofread the final copy before submitting it to your teacher.

DEVELOPING WRITING SKILLS: Planning, Writing, and Revising a Literary Analysis Paper. Follow these instructions to plan, write, and revise a second literary analysis paper.

1. Choose a work of literature to write about. Follow all the steps presented in this section to plan your paper and write a first draft.
2. When you have a first draft, exchange papers with another student.
3. Using the revision checklist on page 609, answer each question on the checklist about the other student's paper. Also write a brief critique of the paper. Mark specific recommendations for improvements on the paper in a contrasting color of ink.
4. When you receive your own paper back, revise it, taking the other student's comments into account. Make a clean final copy.
5. Hand in the clean copy together with the marked first draft and the critique of your paper.

Writing Workshop: Writing About Literature

ASSIGNMENT

Topic   The Same Theme in Two Different Stories or Novels

Form and Purpose   A literary analysis paper explaining how a similar theme is developed in two different novels

Audience   Readers of a Book Review column in a newspaper or weekly magazine

Length   Five to six paragraphs

Focus   State a theme and identify two different novels in which it is developed. Then tell how each writer develops the theme.

Sources   Literature textbook, novels

Prewriting   Use the questions on page 604 to write notes about the two different novels. Then decide on three or four main points of comparison between the two writers' theme development. Write an outline for your paper.

Writing   Write a first draft using your outline.

Revising   Revise your paper using the checklist on page 609.

Marc Chagall, *Mandolin Player*

Antiveduto Della Grammatica,
Un Suonatore

611

Chapter 26

Personal Writing

Personal writing is writing about your own life. You can write about your life in a number of different ways. You can, for example, keep a *journal*, making a day to day record of events and thoughts. Or you can prepare an *autobiography*, telling part or all of the story of your life.

26.1 Journals

A journal records the details of someone's life. Some journals are private, meant for the writer's eyes alone. In this chapter, however, you will learn about journals that are written to be shared with others.

Understanding Journals

Although journals will vary greatly from person to person, all journals serve the basic purpose of allowing people to save important information about their lives.

A journal is an ongoing record of important events and personal observations.

Kinds of Journals. Some people keep journals to record each day's events and, perhaps, their feelings about these events. Other people write in their journals only to fulfill a special purpose, such as keeping a record of a trip.

The following chart lists different kinds of journals according to the specific purposes they fill. Notice that the writing time varies depending on the purpose.

KINDS OF JOURNALS	
Purposes of Journals	**Probable Writing Time**
To summarize everyday experiences	Daily
To express personal feelings and insights	Daily or several times a week
To record special experiences	As each occasion arises

Journal Entries. Just as people keep journals for different specific purposes, they also write their journal entries in different forms. Some use long, occasional entries that are similar to short stories or essays. Others write shorter entries recording bits of information, fragments of conversation, or comments on, for example, books read or movies seen. Depending on the writer's purpose, the journal entry can be almost any length.

Regardless of its length, a journal entry generally includes details about people, places, and events, as well as personal impressions and feelings. It records the kinds of vivid details and immediate personal reactions that would otherwise eventually be forgotten and lost.

The following journal entry records events from a single day in the writer's life, a day she began a perilous journey. Notice the details about the time, place, and events. The entry also includes the writer's personal impressions about people as she began the journey.

Descriptive details	The twenty–seventh of July, 1931, was clear and hot. The heat of a whole summer was condensed dripping into that afternoon. A small crowd of people
Setting	pressed tightly against the gates of the long ramp at College Point, Long Island. As we drove in I saw
People	many familiar faces. We had all spent sweltering days together on that wooden ramp, watching trial flights.

	Now the preparation was over, we were ready to go.
Personal	I supposed they were as relieved as we. Friends came
observations	up to say goodbye. "We all hope you are going to get
	through it all right," with voices and expressions that
Dialogue	said, "But we don't think you've got much chance."
	Picking up our baggage, we hurried into the shade
Events	of the factory office. A dark heavy heat hung over
	everything. Men in shirt sleeves ran in and out. . . .

—Anne Morrow Lindbergh

EXERCISE A: Understanding a Journal. Reread the preceding excerpt from a journal. Then answer these questions.

1. Why do you think the author wrote this entry?
2. How frequently do you think the author made her entries?
3. What events is the author writing about in the entry? Where do these events take place?
4. What are three descriptive details in the passage?
5. What personal observations does the author relate?

EXERCISE B: Looking at Journal Entries. Locate two or three published journals. Read several entries from each and find one entry that interests you. Answer the questions in Exercise A for that entry.

Keeping a Journal

You can think of your journal as a place to collect experiences and thoughts worth saving. Your journal will probably include events that happen in your life. However, you can also include your personal feelings about people and things.

Record events and ideas in chronological order and include vivid, significant details.

A journal is an informal kind of writing. Nonetheless, you will generally write a better and more rewarding journal if you follow some basic planning and writing steps.

Planning a Journal. Planning your journal in advance will help make the actual writing of your journal easier and more enjoyable. Use the planning suggestions in the following chart.

614

PLANNING A JOURNAL

1. Decide on the purpose of your journal. Decide whether you want to record daily events, set down important ideas and feelings, record important events, or keep a record of special experiences.
2. Decide how often you will write entries. Your purpose will help you make this decision, but also consider your own habits: How serious a commitment of your time do you want to make to a journal?
3. Take notes about the things that happen to you. Try to answer questions such as Who? What? When? Where? and Why? Jot down answers to as many of these questions as you can.
4. Brainstorm for details. Probe your mind for descriptive details about the people, places, and things in your notes. Add these details to your notes.

With a clear idea of why you are writing your journal and what should go into it, you will be ready to prepare the individual entries. Use the overall purpose of the journal as a guide to preparing the individual items. For instance, if you are keeping a daily journal of your activities, you probably will want to take notes on all major events in a day. However, if you are keeping a specialized journal such as a travel journal, you will probably record only the people you meet and the places you see when you travel.

The following chart shows how someone could plan an entry in a travel journal. The notes for the entry are based on four questions that are key to a travel entry.

PREPARING TO WRITE A JOURNAL ENTRY	
When?	Second day of our car trip to Texas
Who?	Dad, Mom, and me
Where?	Flatlands along the Louisiana coast
What?	Features of the countryside —very different from home —flatter land —oaks with Spanish moss —old mansions

Writing a Journal Entry. As you write your entry, relate events in chronological order and link them with transitions. You may also want to add further descriptive details or add your personal observations and remarks about events you record.

Here is a selection from a student's travel journal. Notice that the writer treats the items from the notes above in chronological order and uses transitions such as *occasionally* and *finally* to help clarify the time sequence. Notice also that the writer has included many descriptive details as well as a personal observation at the end.

<u>Louisiana, July 28</u>

Time and place	This was our second day on the road; we covered nearly 400 miles. We drove through some beautiful countryside with rolling hills of red earth and jack
Descriptive details	pines with cabins scattered among them. It was certainly different from the mountains and trees at home. The land gradually became flatter and instead of pines
Chronological order	there were oaks with Spanish moss hanging from them, which looked eerie in the late afternoon sunlight. Occasionally, I caught a glimpse of an old Southern mansion sitting back among them like a movie set from <u>Gone with the Wind</u>. We stopped driving, finally,
Personal observation	at 5:00 p.m. Dad was tired, Mom was hungry, and I was bored.

EXERCISE C. Planning Your Journal. Think about what kind of journal you would enjoy writing. Decide on the purpose of your journal and how frequently you will write entries in your journal. Then take notes for your first journal entry.

EXERCISE D: Writing a Journal Entry. Use the notes you prepared in Exercise C to write your first entry. Try to make your ideas come alive with vivid details.

DEVELOPING WRITING SKILLS: Keeping a Journal. Continue making entries in the journal you began in Exercise D. Do not worry if you miss a day on which you were supposed to add an entry. Make one the next day instead.

Autobiographies 26.2

An *autobiography* is the story of a person's own life. In book-length autobiographies, people usually tell the full stories of their whole lives. In shorter autobiographies, sometimes the length of essays, people cover only brief episodes or portions of their lives.

Understanding Autobiographies

An autobiography is always written from a first-person point of view, using the pronouns "I" and "me." This is because it reflects a person's own true recollections.

An autobiography is a true story that a person tells about his or her own life.

Whether long or short, an autobiography contains many features found in a short story. It will have a beginning and an ending. It will also have a setting, one or more related incidents that may resemble the conflict in a short story, and at least one character.

The following chart shows how to adapt the general features of a short story to the special needs of writing an autobiography.

FEATURES OF AN AUTOBIOGRAPHY	
Features	**Use in an Autobiography**
Point of View	The writer tells his or her own story using *I, me, we,* and *us.*
Setting	In a brief autobiography, the writer often focuses on his or her arrival at a new place. In longer biographies, the setting often shifts as the person's life moves on.
Incidents	A brief autobiography will focus on one or more related incidents taking place during a specific period in the writer's life. As in a story, events follow chronological order until they reach a satisfying conclusion.

Characters	Presenting vivid characters can help the writer avoid the monotony of focusing exclusively on personal thoughts and feelings.
Dialogue	Dialogue can reveal the feelings of the other characters and how the writer relates to them.
Descriptive Details	Details about setting and characters help readers to visualize the writer's world.

Following is an excerpt from an autobiography by a famous person. Notice that it focuses on a specific time in the writer's life: his family's trips during his childhood to the mountains in Colorado. Notice also that it includes not only the features of a short story but also a number of personal reactions and observations.

Setting

I loved those trips to Colorado. We would always set out in the morning before the sun came up, to avoid the heat—this was years before air conditioning—and the thrill of dressing and having breakfast in the dark, then piling into our 1938 De Soto and turning the headlights west—it was all I could do to get my breath. When you get to the foothills of the Rockies and then abruptly enter Big Thompson Canyon, it's awesome even for an adult. For me, the first time, as a kid of four, it was terrifying. I became hysterical, because I thought the sheer cliffs on both sides were going to fall down on us. I don't know whether my parents wrapped me in a wet sheet or what, but when they finally calmed me down I wanted to get back to the plains immediately.

Minor incidents and descriptive details

Characters

Personal reaction

Once I got over the initial shock, I came to love the mountains, although they could, and still can, scare me some. Once we were visiting in the cabin of an old character who had been in the Buffalo Bill show, and I suddenly noticed that all the adults were acting strange and had gone quite pale. Someone said, "Cover up the bacon on the stove," and Elmer, the character, loaded a rifle. A grizzly had roared outside, and there were stories that a few days earlier a hungry

Major incident

Characters

618

Personal
observations — bear had torn open a cabin, and one of its occupants, in the next canyon. It's shocking for a kid to see the adults frightened. In this case, however, the grizzly went away. Somewhere there's a snapshot of all of us, out in front of the cabin, labeled "After the Grizzly." When it was over, I felt I had endured a real western adventure, and used to embellish the story with sounds of clawing on the shutters and still other

Personal
observations — details to make me wondrous in the eyes of my audience.—Dick Cavett

EXERCISE A: Understanding an Autobiography. Reread the selection from Dick Cavett's autobiography and answer the following questions.

1. What specific period of the author's life is covered?
2. What events mark the beginning and end of the selection?
3. Who else besides the author is part of the story?
4. What does the use of dialogue accomplish in the selection?
5. List three descriptive details in the selection.

EXERCISE B: Examining Autobiographies. Locate and examine two or three autobiographies. Read some part of each. Find one selection that interests you, and then answer the questions in Exercise A for that selection.

PREWRITING, WRITING, and REVISING: Creating an Autobiography

To write an autobiography, you need to follow certain planning, writing, and revising steps. Throughout these steps, focus on offering readers interesting insights into your life.

Prewriting. The first step in creating an autobiography is to choose a specific time span and setting to write about. Then you should make notes about other key elements.

Choose the time span, setting, incidents, and characters for your brief autobiography.

As you choose a specific span of time and setting to write about, think about the length of your autobiography. For instance, a two- or three-page autobiography will probably cover a brief time span—a day or a week, perhaps.

Also think of the minor and major incidents that happened during that period. In addition, search your memory for details about the people, places, and events you will describe.

Following is an example of how to plan an autobiography by focusing on a specific period in your life.

PLAN FOR AN AUTOBIOGRAPHY	
Time Span and Setting	**First Week in Heron Bay**
Incidents	Moving into a new house
	Walks through the village
	Saying hello to new neighbors
	Meeting my future best friend
Characters	New neighbors —Mr. and Mrs. Miller —"Granny" Jones
	Storekeepers in town
	My new friend

Writing. Out of your plan, a clear series of events should emerge. Write about the events in chronological order using complete sentences. Add further descriptive details or observations as they occur to you. Use transitions and other linking devices to help your reader follow the sequence of events.

Use your plan to write a first draft.

The following selection shows the opening of an autobiography. Notice that it immediately focuses on a certain period in the writer's life. This particular autobiography begins by describing the setting and the first of a series of events.

Setting

Personal observations

Opening incident

The peacefulness of Heron Bay gave me no hint of the great activities—and friendship—that would soon fill this memorable time of my life. The noise that we and our movers created as we moved into the new house seemed to be a terrible imposition upon the tranquility of this little community by the sea. In fact, as soon as I stepped out of the front door, closing it

Dialogue

against the commotion within, I felt tantalized by a new world of crisp, salty softness.

"You must be new here!" These were the first words spoken to me in Heron Bay. I had walked only a few hundred feet from our new house. . . .

Revising. When you have created a first draft of your autobiography, reread it and look for ways to make improvements. Use the following checklist for guidance.

CHECKLIST FOR REVISING AN AUTOBIOGRAPHY

1. Have you used the first-person point of view consistently?
2. Are the time span and setting made clear to the reader?
3. Do you present key events in clear chronological order?
4. Have you included vivid descriptive details?
5. Have you included interesting personal observations?

EXERCISE C: Planning an Autobiography. Choose a period of your life to write about. Identify the time span, setting, incidents, and characters you will write about. Use the chart on page 620 as a guide to gathering and organizing information.

EXERCISE D: Writing and Revising an Autobiography. Write a first draft of your autobiography based on the material you prepared in Exercise C. Then use the checklist above to revise your draft. Make a clean, final copy and proofread it.

DEVELOPING WRITING SKILLS: Writing Autobiographically. Practice writing autobiographically by writing about a different part of your life or by pretending you are someone or something else. Choose an idea from the following list. Then follow the planning, writing, and revising steps in this section.

A trip that you took to a different region
Your experience with a visitor to your home, town, or country
A time when you learned valuable lessons
Your life as a housecat, dog, or canary
Your experiences as a famous entertainer or athlete

Writing Workshop: Personal Writing

ASSIGNMENT 1

Topic The Process of Communicating

Form and Purpose A summary of journal entries that describe methods of communication

Audience Yourself, possibly classmates

Length At least five journal entries, one each day over a one-week period; a two- or three-paragraph summary

Focus Write daily observations about how you and other people communicate. Then develop and support a thesis statement about communication.

Sources Personal experiences and observations

Prewriting Write a list of communication methods. Record daily journal entries about communication experiences and observations. At the end of a week, review your journal.

Writing After reviewing your notes, write a thesis statement about human communication. Develop the thesis with several examples or incidents from your journal entries.

Revising Review your writing with this question in mind: Does it say exactly what I want to say?

ASSIGNMENT 2

Topic An Autobiographical Sketch Regarding an Emotion

Form and Purpose A brief autobiographical sketch that conveys an experience related to a single emotion

Audience A friend

Length Three to five paragraphs

Focus In describing the events of the experience, use dialogue if other people were involved. Use details in the setting to convey a suitable mood.

Sources Personal experiences

Prewriting Select an emotion that interests you. Think of a personal experience that relates to that emotion. Write a plan like the one on page 620.

Writing Use your plan to write a first draft. If possible, include dialogue when narrating the incidents.

Revising Revise your paper using the checklist on page 621.

Vincent van Gogh, *Self-Portrait*

623

Topics for Writing: Personal Writing

We all have many personal experiences worth recording. If the cartoon above suggests an experience to you, write about it, or select one of the topics below. Each day in a journal, record your thoughts, feelings, and observations related to the topic. Write in your journal for at least two weeks.

1. How I Felt About a Major News Event of the Day
2. Places I Have Never Been
3. Silence—What It Means
4. Why I Wish I Were an Adult
5. Why I'm Glad I'm Not an Adult
6. How the Weather Affects Me
7. What Can I Do to Help?
8. What Is Really Valuable?
9. What I Try to Avoid
10. Where Am I Going?

Chapter 27

Short Stories

A story is a sequence of events told from a particular point of view. To write a short story, you will need many of the skills necessary for other forms of writing. But you will also need to develop new skills to meet the special demands of telling a story.

Understanding Short Stories 27.1

A *short story* is a fictional narrative. In its simplest terms, it is a series of imaginary events involving a person or a group of persons. You can begin to understand better what a short story is by focusing on the people in a story and the things that they do.

Character and Plot

The people in a story are called the *characters*. The events that happen to them or that they cause to happen are called the *plot*.

Character. Since short stories are brief, there is not usually enough time to slowly build up a character, bit by bit, as in a long novel. Instead, each character is usually established quickly and economically. To accomplish this, short story writers generally concentrate on giving one *dominant impression* of a character immediately.

In a short story, each character creates a single, dominant impression.

What the character does, says, and thinks, how he or she looks or dresses, should add up to convincing person. Creating a single impression with a character in a short story is similar to writing a good descriptive paragraph, as discussed in Section 22.3. But in addition, characters in stories are often established by *dialogue*. Notice in the following example how dialogue reinforces the dominant impression created by the descriptive details.

Characterization with action, dialogue, and descriptive details	On the day before the opening game, Rolf was suddenly cut from the varsity baseball team. Shuffling into the locker room, he created little dust clouds with every step. A crumpled baseball cap dangled from one hand. A rip in his threadbare jeans exposed a raw, pebbly knee, and his shirt hung out of his pants, loose and mud-spattered. His face was red and stretched, his eyes glazed.
	"I've had it," he said, to no one in particular.
	"I'm never going to try out for another team as long as I live."

The amount of time spent detailing a character helps the reader to know which are the major characters in a story and which are the minor ones. But perhaps more important, it is the plot that will make particular characters stand out as the major figures.

Plot. A plot is a sequence of events. In order for the plot to develop, the main character must come into *conflict* with someone or something and act to resolve the conflict.

A plot is a series of events involving a conflict.

A conflict may be either external or internal. An external conflict is between the main character and some other person or outside force, such as nature or society. An internal conflict is within the character's own mind.

The plot of a short story works out the conflict in a swift, economical way. While a novel can include many related events and simultaneously develop two or three separate plots, a short story is more compact. Its plot generally leads up to a single important event.

Usually the plot develops through several stages, as shown in the following chart.

626

THE PLOT OF A SHORT STORY

Stages	What Happens
Exposition	Introduces the setting and major characters
	Establishes the narrator's point of view
	Gives necessary background information
Opening incident	Introduces the conflict
	Sets the plot in motion
Rising action	Presents further incidents to develop plot and characters
	Intensifies the conflict
Climax	Brings the conflict to a high point
	Presents a decisive event that changes the course of events
Falling action (not always included)	Can briefly show the effects of the climax in order to prepare the reader for the conclusion
Conclusion	Resolves the conflict
	Brings the story to a close

EXERCISE A: Understanding Characters. Review a short story you have read recently and answer the following questions. Identify the story by title and author on your paper.

1. Who is the main character? Why is this character, rather than some other character, at the center of the story?
2. What is the dominant impression created by the character? What factors contribute to this impression?
3. Who are the secondary characters in the story? How do they relate to the main character?
4. Is dialogue used to present the characters? If so, how do their speeches reveal their personalities?
5. Is the main character involved with an exterior or an interior conflict? Are other characters involved in the conflict? If so, how?

EXERCISE B: Understanding Plot. Using the same story you examined in Exercise A, answer the following questions.

1. What information is presented in the exposition?
2. What incident begins the movement of the plot?
3. What incidents make up the rising action of the story?
4. What is the climax of the story? How does this turning point change the course of events?
5. How is the conflict resolved at the end of the story?

Point of View

Point of view is the way in which the story is narrated. It is the method, the vantage point, that the writer uses to tell the story.

A story is narrated from a single, consistent point of view.

There are three basic points of view for the writer to choose from: first person, limited third person, and omniscient third person. The following chart explains these three basic points of view, also called *narrators*.

KINDS OF NARRATORS	
Narrators	**Functions**
First person	The narrator, using the word "I," tells the story and participates in the action, giving details as he or she sees them. The "I" may be either the author or a character created by the author.
Limited third person	The narrator, who is not in the story, tells the story through the use of "she" or "he." The narrator cannot see into the minds of the characters.
Omniscient third person	The narrator, who is not in the story, tells the story through the use of "she" or "he." The narrator can see into the minds of the characters and tell their thoughts.

Following are three versions of the same story told by three different narrators. Notice the difference between what the reader sees with each narrator.

In the first version, the narrator tells her own story.

First-person narrator I turned back to my bucket and sponge, and I could feel the tears burning in my eyes. I wanted so much to go to the ball, but my stepsisters would not hear of it. When they left the chamber, slamming the door as they went, I knew there was no point in crying anymore. I could only go back to scrubbing the floor.

In the second version, the narrator, limited third person, tells the story very simply, as an invisible bystander.

Limited third-person narrator Tears in her eyes, Cinderella turned back to her bucket and sponge. She jumped when the door to the chamber slammed behind her as her stepsisters, laughing, left for the ball. Cinderella straightened her back and resumed scrubbing.

In the last version, the narrator is omniscient third person. Notice that the narrator relates Cinderella's thoughts and feelings as well as her actions.

Omniscient third-person narrator Hurt and disappointed, Cinderella turned back to her bucket and sponge. The thought of missing the ball brought tears to her eyes. Cinderella jumped when the door slammed behind her. Then she straightened her back and resumed scrubbing, knowing that her stepsisters were on their way to the ball.

EXERCISE C: Understanding Point of View. Using the story you examined in Exercises A and B, answer the following questions.

1. Who is telling the story?
2. Which of the three points of view discussed in this section is used to narrate the story?
3. What evidence is there in the story that it is being told from this particular point of view?
4. How would the story be changed if it were told from another point of view?

629

5. Why do you think the author chose this point of view?

DEVELOPING WRITING SKILLS: Rewriting a Short Story.
Reread the beginning and the end of the story you examined in Exercises A through C or some other short story that you have read recently, and follow these instructions.

1. Rewrite the opening paragraphs of the story from a different point of view. For example, if the story was originally written from an omniscient third-person point of view, rewrite it as a first-person narrative.
2. Select a passage in the story that presents the main character. Rewrite the passage to create a different dominant impression. For example, if the character is presented as essentially good, rewrite the passage to make the character evil.
3. Rewrite the closing paragraphs of the story so that the plot ends in a way opposite from the original ending. For example, if the main character fails to achieve a goal in the original story, rewrite the ending so that the main character succeeds.

27.2 **Writing a Short Story**

The process of writing a short story follows many of the same basic steps as other kinds of writing. This section will offer suggestions that will help you to plan, write, and revise your own short story.

PREWRITING: Planning Your Short Story

There are a number of ways to begin planning a short story. You may start with a conflict you want to explore, with a plot you wish to develop, or with one or more characters you want to describe, or even with a setting.

Plan a short story by assembling details about characters, conflict, and setting and making them work within a general plot outline.

You may find it easiest to begin with a character that interests you. Brainstorm for ideas by asking yourself a series of questions about your character. The following list of questions may help you to focus your ideas.

QUESTIONS FOR DEVELOPING A CHARACTER

1. What is the identity of the character (name, age, sex, nationality, era, and so on)?
2. What does the character look like? How does the character talk and move?
3. What are the character's outstanding personality traits? What are his or her strengths and weaknesses?
4. What are the character's family and friends like? Should they be brought in to clarify the main character?
5. What dominant impression should the character create?

Once you decide on a main character, you can begin to develop a conflict in which your character is involved. The following questions might help you think out the conflict in your story.

QUESTIONS FOR DEVELOPING CONFLICT

1. What kind of conflict is the main character involved in? Is the conflict in the story external or internal?
2. If the conflict is external, who or what is in opposition to the main character? Is it another character, society, nature, or some other force?
3. If the conflict is internal, what elements within the main character are opposed to each other? Does the character have divided loyalties? Is the conflict emotional, moral, intellectual? Does the character have to make an important decision?
4. What event or series of events would best show the conflict?
5. If the conflict is between two characters, should the reader have a clear sense of who is right and who is wrong?

After answering these questions, try to state the conflict in a sentence or two.

631

When you have decided on your main character and conflict, you can then sketch a plot that develops around them. Remember that the plot for a short story should focus on one main event, the climax. Make a list of all the smaller incidents in your short story, too, so that you will be able to work out a complete plot. Also jot down information about minor characters and ideas for any dialogue you want to include. Finally, write down some details of the setting; locating your story in time and space will give you a way to start telling the story.

Organizing all of your information into a plot outline will help you plan the story's action from beginning to end. You may find it helpful to use the basic plot structure shown in the chart on page 627, filling in each section with the information you will use. Of course, you may want to vary the structure somewhat to fit the specific plot you have in mind.

Once you have your story outlined, you will be in a good position to decide what point of view to use. To choose an appropriate point of view, think about the dominant impression you want your main character to create as well as the kind of conflict in your story. It might be most effective, for example, to present an internal conflict from a first-person point of view. But there might also be advantages to showing this kind of conflict from an omniscient third-person point of view, in which the conflicting inner feelings of several different characters could be presented and compared.

With a detailed plot outline prepared and a decision made about the narrator, you are ready to draft your story.

EXERCISE A: Planning a Short Story. Decide on a character that interests you and use the questions in the chart on page 631 to develop the character. Then use the other chart on page 631 to create a conflict in which the character is involved. Finally, write a plot outline based on the character and conflict and decide on a point of view.

Writing: Creating a First Draft

When you have gathered information on character and conflict, prepared a plot outline, and decided on a narrator you are ready for the next step: creating your first draft.

Follow your plot outline to write a first draft of your story using a consistent point of view.

As you follow your outline, concentrate on connecting the ideas and events into one continuous flow using transitions and other linking devices, such as repeated main words. Be sure not to leave out information that the reader will need to follow the plot. Also be careful to avoid words and statements that are inappropriate to your narrator. Finally, you will need to give your story a title.

The following story was written by a student. The notes in the margin show how it follows the basic plot structure shown in the chart on page 627. They also point out other important details that make the development of the story coherent.

The Storm

EXPOSITION

He stood at the open front door of the farmhouse, his hands in his pockets, and squinted at the sky. From the kitchen where Esther was preparing supper the smell of pot roast drifted out to him on the heavy, humid air. Judy, their three-year-old, probably was hovering anxiously around the edges of his wife's skirt, hoping to help, but no doubt only getting in the way. Mike, the baby, would be asleep.

The man pushed the screen door now and walking to the edge of the porch, looked at the western sky.

OPENING
INCIDENT

The days were still long; the sun was still high now, at 5:30. A low bank of gray clouds marred the shimmery smoothness of the hot atmosphere. Esther had told him about the radio's storm warnings when he came in from the field—severe thunderstorms with the possibility of a tornado.

The weather was right for bad storms; it had been hot, sticky hot, all day, and even now the air remained thick and oppressive.

Dialogue

"Bill, will you come see if the roast is done while I get Mike's formula ready?"

He heard Esther's call and looked once more at the clouds in the west before going into the house.

"Roast?" he asked absently.

"It should be about done. Bring it to the table?"

633

He called, "Come on, Judy, time to eat," and watched her coming in her half-walk, half-run way. Catching her beneath the arms, he set her in the high-chair and swung the tray down over her head. Bringing in the roast, he sat down and started filling their plates.

"You came home kind of early tonight. Tired?" Esther asked. She held the baby in her lap and tested the formula on her wrist.

"Oh, not really."

He didn't want to talk; he was thinking about the clouds he had seen gathering all afternoon.

"I finished weeding the vegetable patch today," Esther said.

He nodded but remained silent. They ate quietly.

"We really might get a storm," he finally said, his mouth full. "It's black in the west. The humidity was bad today."

"I know," Esther answered. "Everything's been damp. The laundry still isn't dry. It's terrible. I wish it would just rain and get it over with."

Later, as they finished washing the dishes, he watched the sky through the kitchen window and wondered how much further the clouds would move up from the west. It was getting dark, too dark, for only 6:30. It had gotten so dark that Judy had gone to bed without complaining, thinking it was late. Hurriedly he dried the last pieces of silverware and dropped them into their divided drawer.

"Esther, you don't know what tonight's paper said about the weather, do you?"

"Just more of the same."

"Let's go outside. I want to see how it looks; anyway, it's still too hot in here."

She nodded and they went onto the porch, she to sit in the chair and he to squat by the steps and lean against the wooden railing.

He unfolded the newspaper and slipped a section from it and handed it to her. Then he raised his head to sight the turbulent clouds against the edge of the roof. They had moved slowly eastward, almost to the

634

horizon. Nearer at hand, the sky turned to an angry mass of gray. He knew the storm was coming now.

Character's thoughts

Esther still read the newspaper as if nothing were happening.

He glanced at his watch, sitting quietly and waiting. Over the far field the sky grew leaden. Occasionally and then more frequently, it flashed white with sheet lightning high up in the clouds. The lightning flashed again like distant artillery fire. In a few moments the low rumble came.

"I'm going in, honey. It's too dark to read out here any more."

She stood for a moment inside the screen door. "Looks like rain for sure, doesn't it? Maybe you should bring the kids' toys in off the porch and put the playpen up against the house."

Description

"Yeah, in a minute." The lightning was coming in streaks now, not just the far-away sheets. He stepped up onto the porch and folded down the sides of the playpen and lifted it up next to the house. He stood quietly watching the clouds travel. The rain had not come yet, nor the wind, only thunder and lightning. Jagged spikes of lightning silhouetted the trees at the edge of the field. Fascinated, he watched; then, hearing the radio, he walked back to the screen door.

"Did they say anything about the storm?"

"Nothing yet," she answered. "Come in and read the paper."

He picked up Judy's toy box and carried it into the front room. Esther sat on the couch and was busy writing a letter.

CLIMAX

A white-hot flash of lighting, followed almost instantly by thunder, deep and near, quickly brought him back outside. The thunder rolled heavily over the fields and seemed to take forever to die away. The first slight wind came, high in the branches of the trees. Wind was moving among the trees, working and limbering the heavy, thick branches. As it moved down from the tree tops, the storm struck.

The heavy trees in the front yard slowly bent further than he had ever seen them bend. But the rain still did not come. The high branches twitched crazily and the lower, stouter limbs bent and swayed under the weight of the wind. The driven air hissed through the leaves, tearing them from the branches. He stood on the porch and watched, and now even Esther stood at the screen door. She watched and when she had seen, she came to stand beside him.

"It's really going to be bad, isn't it?"

He looked strangely unworried. "Better close up the shutters."

The rain was coming now. The wind hung sheets of rain from the arched branches, from the eaves of the house, from the swaying power line. As the strain increased, he watched the branches split, the gutters of the house sag, spilling water over their edges.

The power line snapped—above his head the porch light flashed, then glowed red-orange, and faded. Soon the phone lines would be gone too. He lit the hurricane lamp kept on the porch for emergencies. Esther was shuttering the windows and he heard Judy start to cry. Wet leaves blew into the porch.

The wind came in billowing waves now, driving the rain before it. Even the thick trunks of the trees bent and moved. Never had he seen the tree trunks move.

Esther came to the door with Mike over one arm. "Bill, we'd better get the kids down to the basement. Do you think it's a tornado, after all?"

"Go on, I'll be down in a minute."

CONCLUSION   He watched them disappear into the dark house, then leaned over the porch rail and looked west. Driving rain now obscured the outline of even the nearest trees. He could see nothing beyond the light of the storm lantern. Yet he stood there for hours, looking out into the storm.—Richard D. James

EXERCISE B: Drafting a Short Story. Following the plot outline you prepared in Exercise A, write a first draft of your story using a specific point of view. Be careful to connect the items on the outline with transitions and other linking devices. When you have finished drafting the story, add a title.

636

REVISING: Polishing Your Short Story

During revision you can delete or add ideas, change the order of events, or experiment with different beginnings and endings, rewriting until you are satisfied. You should also review your individual sentences for correctness and for style.

Use a checklist to revise your short story.

The following checklist will help you revise your story.

CHECKLIST FOR REVISING A SHORT STORY
1. Does the main character create a dominant impression?
2. Is the kind of conflict involved, internal or external, made clear to the reader?
3. Is the plot developed logically and fully?
4. Are the events recounted from a consistent point of view?
5. Are there paragraphs and individual sentences that should be rewritten for style and correctness?

EXERCISE C: **Revising a Short Story.** Use the checklist on this page to examine and revise the first draft you wrote in Exercise B. If necessary, make a clean copy of your revised story. Be sure to proofread your final copy.

DEVELOPING WRITING SKILLS: **Rewriting a Short Story.** Using the short story you wrote in Exercises A through C, follow these instructions.

1. Select a minor character in your original story or create a new character, and using the chart on page 631, develop enough new ideas to make him or her into the main character in the story.
2. Rethink the conflict in your story so that it centers on your new main character.
3. Write the new version of your story and then revise it, trying to make it as good as or even better than the first story. Submit both versions to your teacher.

Writing Workshop: Short Stories

King Kong

ASSIGNMENT 1

Topic   Extending a Story That Interests You

Form and Purpose   To entertain readers with an extended version of a story

Audience   Ninth-grade readers of a school literary magazine

Length   Three to five pages

Focus   Use the characters from a story that interests you in a story of your own. Your plot should develop a conflict in a new setting and should include dialogue.

Sources   Literature textbook, short story collections, short story magazines, television shows

Prewriting   Read the original story and make notes about each main character's appearance, personality, and dominant impression. Plan a new story with the same characters. As a planning aid, use the conflict checklist on page 631. Decide on a point of view for telling the story.

Writing   Use your notes and story plan to write a first draft.

Revising   Revise your story using the checklist on page 637.

ASSIGNMENT 2

Topic   Lost in the Past

Form and Purpose   An entertaining short story about a person from the present who is caught in the past

Audience   A science fiction film director

Length   Three to five pages

Focus   As the main character, narrate the story from a first-person point of view. Your story should be clearly set in the past and should develop a conflict.

Sources   Historical books, magazine articles about the past, illustrations and photos about the past

Prewriting   Choose your setting. Write notes about the conflict by using questions like those on page 631.

Writing   Use your notes when writing a first draft.

Revising   Revise your story using the checklist on page 637.

Topics for Writing: Short Stories

Charles Adams, © 1969, The New Yorker Magazine, Inc.

"Now maybe they'll be moved to do something about water pollution!"

If the situation in the above cartoon stimulates a story idea, write a short story about it. If you prefer, use one of the titles below as a starting point for a short story.

1. Life on Earth, 2099 A.D.
2. An Urban Love Story
3. Revenge of the Water Monsters
4. The Scientist's Discovery
5. 20,000 Leagues Under the River
6. Discovery of Planet X
7. A New Kind of Pollution
8. Earth Was a Nice Planet, While It Lasted
9. The Factory Owner and the Conservationist
10. The Animals Had the Last Word

Chapter 28

Letters

Whether you are sharing experiences with friends, making invitations, requesting information, or registering complaints, you will often need the skills involved in writing letters.

Looking at Letters 28.1

The type of letter you write will depend on the purpose of the letter. Letters can generally be divided into three major groups: *friendly letters, social notes,* and *business letters.*

Friendly Letters and Social Notes

Friendly letters are generally casual. Social notes, although more formal, are still a highly personal form of communication. Nevertheless, certain rules should be followed for both.

The Parts of the Friendly Letter and Social Note. Both of these types of letters contain five basic parts.

Friendly letters and social notes contain a heading, a salutation, a body, a closing, and a signature.

The *heading* is usually placed in the upper right-hand section of the letter. It contains your own street address in the first line and your town or city, state, and ZIP code in the second. (The country is also included if you are writing to someone in another nation.) Also included, in the third line of the heading, is the date that the letter was written.

641

The *salutation*, or greeting, is placed below the heading on the left-hand side of the page. The salutation of a friendly letter usually begins with the word "Dear," followed by the name of the person to whom you are writing. A comma follows the salutation.

EXAMPLES: Dear Pat,   Dear Miss Miller,

Dear Aunt Dolly,   Dear Mr. Lowy,

Dear Dr. Kelton,   Dear Ms. Arn,

More casual salutations may be used with close friends.

EXAMPLES: Hi, Jeff,   Hello, Buddy,

Hi, old Friend,   Greetings,

The *body* of a friendly letter is placed under the salutation. It can be of any length and can contain any information you want to send.

The *closing* is placed in the lower right-hand section of the letter, beneath the body. The first word of a closing is always capitalized, but the other words in the closing are usually *not* capitalized. A comma is placed at the end. A closing may be slightly formal, casual, or affectionate. The closing you choose will depend upon your relationship with the person to whom you are writing.

EXAMPLES: Sincerely yours,   Best wishes,

Yours truly,   Love,

The *signature*, the last part of a friendly letter, is placed beneath the closing. Again depending upon your relationship with the recipient of the letter, you may choose to sign your full name, your first name only, or a nickname. Your signature should be written in ink, even if you have typed the rest of the letter.

When you write invitations, perhaps the most common kind of social notes, you should also include an *R.S.V.P.* This abbreviation requests an immediate answer and is placed conspicuously in the lower left-hand corner of the invitation. Often, the sender of an invitation needs an exact count of people planning to attend. If you are the receiver of an invitation requesting you to reply, your answer should be written unless a phone call is mentioned or appropriate.

642

Different Styles for Friendly Letters and Social Notes. When organizing the parts of a friendly letter or social note, you may choose between two styles.

Use either indented or semiblock style in writing friendly letters or social notes.

Following are illustrations of these two styles. Notice that in the *indented style* the heading, closing, and signature are not placed in a straight line. In the *semiblock style*, however, the heading, closing, and signature are lined up.

Indented Style   **Semiblock Style**

The style of the return address on the envelope, in the upper left-hand corner, and the address of the person to whom you are sending the letter should follow the indentation used in the letter itself.

Indented Style   **Semiblock Style**

A few additional guidelines for addressing envelopes are presented in the following chart.

GUIDELINES FOR ADDRESSING ENVELOPES

1. If you typed the letter, type the addresses on the envelope. If you handwrote the letter, write the addresses also.
2. Avoid using titles such as *Mr., Miss,* and *Ms.* in writing your own name in the return address.
3. Avoid abbreviations that will not be immediately clear in either the return address or the main address.
4. Be sure to include ZIP codes in both addresses.
5. With small envelopes write the return address on the back. Check that small envelopes meet postal regulations.

Some social stationery folds in half to fit easily into the matching envelope. Larger sheets of paper, however, should be folded in thirds, as shown in the following illustration.

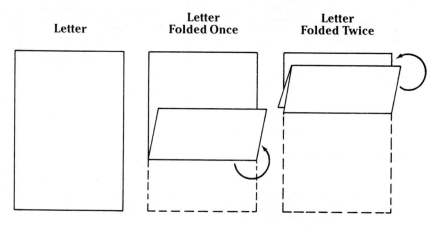

| Letter | Letter Folded Once | Letter Folded Twice |

Your letter should be handwritten or typed, but not both. (The only exception to this is the signature, which must be handwritten even if you type the letter.) If the letter is hand-written, be sure that the letter and envelope are legible. Blue or black ink on white paper is usually the easiest to read. Legibility can also be improved by generous margins.

EXERCISE A: Practicing with the Different Parts of Friendly Letters and Social Notes. Write two examples of a heading, a salutation, a closing, and a signature.

EXERCISE B: Practicing Different Styles. Prepare two skeleton letters (using lines rather than words in the body), one in indented style and one in semiblock style, using your own address for the heading. Make sure that all five parts of a letter are in place. Then prepare envelopes for both letters.

Business Letters

The business letter resembles the friendly letter but it is more formal, structured, direct, and concise.

The Parts of the Business Letter. Business letters should contain six specific parts.

Business letters should contain a heading, an inside address, a salutation, a body, a closing, and a signature.

The *heading* appears at least one inch below the top of the page. It should contain your complete address and the date on which you are writing. This heading is similar to that of a friendly letter.

The *inside address* appears two to four lines beneath the heading on the left-hand side. It includes the name (and business title, if applicable) of the person or business to which you are writing, followed by the full address.

EXAMPLES:

Dr. Richard B. Sheperd	Complaint Department
Dean of Admissions	Taylor and Smith
School of Agriculture	1000 Main Street
Moorhead, Minnesota 56560	Austin, Texas 78712

The *salutation*, or greeting, appears two lines beneath the inside address. Proper salutations when you are not addressing a specific person include *Dear Sir, Dear Madam,* or *Dear Sir or Madam,* followed by a colon. If you are writing to a specific person, use the person's name: *Dear Mrs. Stuart, Dear Dr. Sheperd.* The name should be followed by a colon.

The *body* of a business letter begins two lines beneath the salutation. It may be any length, but it should be typed, like the rest of the letter, and single-spaced. If the body of the letter is very short, however, you may double-space it.

The *closing* appears two or three lines beneath the body. It begins with a capital letter and ends with a comma. A closing in a business letter should always be formal.

EXAMPLES: Sincerely,   Very truly yours,

Your *signature* should be written in ink beneath the closing. If you have typed the rest of the letter, you should type your full name beneath the signature. A woman may indicate in parentheses to the left of the typed name how she wishes to be addressed (*Mrs., Ms., Miss*).

Different Styles for Business Letters. As with friendly letters, you must select a style for your business letters.

Use block, modified block, or semiblock style in writing business letters.

In *block styles*, all parts of the letter are placed along the left margin, as in the following example.

Block Style

Heading	
Inside address	
Salutation	
Body	
Closing	
Signature	
Name	

Notice that in the block style the first line of each paragraph is not indented. Instead, it begins at the left margin. Notice also that a space is left between paragraphs in the body to show where one paragraph ends and the next one begins. Because it is easy to set up, block style is widely used today.

In the *modified block style* and the *semiblock style*, the heading of the letter is placed in the upper right-hand section of the page, not along the left margin. The closing and signature are placed in the lower right-hand section lining up with the heading. The other parts of the letter—the inside address, the salutation, and the body—are placed along the left margin. The only difference between the two styles is in the setup of the paragraphs. In the modified block style, the paragraphs are not indented; in the semiblock style, they are indented.

Modified Block Style   **Semiblock Style**

Heading
Inside
address
Salutation

Body

Closing
Signature
Name

Occasionally a business letter requires a second page. Whether you are using block, modified block, or semiblock style, you should place the following information at the top of the second page: the name of the person to whom you are writing, the page number (*Page 2*), and the date.

In addressing the envelope, you should not mix handwriting and typewriting. All parts of the envelope should, like the letter itself, be typed. The example on the next page shows the proper form.

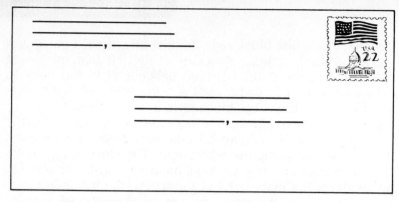

If you are using standard-sized, white paper for your letter, you should also use a standard-sized, white envelope, measuring 9½ × 4 inches.

The following guidelines may be of help in addressing the envelope.

GUIDELINES FOR ADDRESSING BUSINESS ENVELOPES

1. Use block style for both the main address and your return address. Do not indent any of the lines in the address.

2. Avoid using titles such as *Mr., Miss,* or *Ms.* in your own name. Avoid using abbreviations that will not be immediately clear.

3. Be sure to include ZIP codes in both addresses.

4. If you use stationery with your return address already printed in the front or back of the envelope, do not repeat this information.

With standard-sized paper and envelopes, fold the letter into thirds to fit the envelope. The process is the same as the one given for the friendly letter on page 644.

Your business letters should always be neat, clean, and legible. The use of unruled, standard-sized, white paper with matching envelopes should help. The use of a typewriter, with extra spacing between parts and paragraphs, will also help. In addition, you should center your letter on the page with at least one-inch margins and check carefully for correct grammar, mechanics, and spelling.

Before you send a business letter, you should always make a copy for your records. It will be helpful if some misunderstanding arises or if your letter is somehow lost.

EXERCISE C: Practicing with the Different Parts of Business Letters. Write two examples of each of these parts of a business letter: heading, inside address, salutation, closing, and signature.

EXERCISE D: Practicing Different Styles. Prepare three skeleton letters (using lines rather than words in the body): one in block style, one in modified block style, and one in semiblock style. Prepare one envelope for all three letters.

DEVELOPING WRITING SKILLS: Identifying Kinds of Letters. Identify the types of letters (*friendly letters, social notes,* or *business letters*) described by each question. Note that some questions have more than one answer.

EXAMPLE: Which letters should be written on standard paper?

business letters

1. Which letters would most likely be typed?
2. Which letters might include an *R.S.V.P.*?
3. Which letters always use a comma in the salutation?
4. Which letters always use a colon in the salutation?
5. Which letters are written to offer an invitation?
6. Which letters use a comma in the closing?
7. Which letters can be written using indented style?
8. Which letters can be written using a strict block style?
9. Which letters always show at least two different ZIP codes?
10. Which letters have only one style for envelopes?

Writing Letters 28.2

Once you understand the basic parts and styles of letters, you can concentrate on the writing itself.

Writing Friendly Letters and Social Notes

Friendly letters are generally intended merely to help friends keep in touch. Social notes usually have a more specific, limited purpose, often tied to a particular event. These notes are usually shorter and often more formal than friendly letters.

Friendly Letters. In friendly letters you have more choice of content than you do in more formal types of writing. Even so, good organization helps.

Friendly letters should express your ideas in vivid language and should be clearly organized for the reader.

To make your letter vivid, use sensory impressions—descriptions that appeal to sight, hearing, smell, and so on. Strong verbs and colorful words are also useful. Relate incidents as you would tell a story.

Try not to apologize repeatedly for such things as having delayed in writing or for running out of ideas. Finally, try to end your letter on a positive note, one that will encourage the reader to reply. Avoid weak closing statements such as "It's late so I'll end this letter."

With these general suggestions in mind, consider the more specific items in the following chart.

STEPS IN WRITING A FRIENDLY LETTER

1. Reread recent letters from the person to whom you are writing. Make a note of any questions the person may have asked.

2. Jot down ideas, impressions, and events you want to include in your letter. Include answers to the person's questions and items that are likely to be of special interest to the person.

3. Choose the letter style you want to use, indented or semi-block, and stick to it as you write.

4. In writing the letter, strive to be clear, specific, interesting, and neat.

5. Proofread your letter by reading it aloud.

6. Correct any errors in grammar, mechanics, or spelling.

With care you can probably write a letter as good as or better than the following example. Note that the letter is casual and friendly and includes details about people and events that the writer knows will interest the reader.

1401 South M Street
Lincoln, Nebraska 68502
March 13, 1986

Hi Al,

It seems like years since you moved to Virginia Beach, but it has only been three weeks. Time has certainly dragged during these three weeks, and everybody talks about you as if you were just around the corner.

School just isn't the same without you to liven things up. Susan, Tim, and I miss your funny comments and cartoons in algebra. The other day Jack was writing an equation on the board. Everyone noticed that he was trying to imitate your printing and draw one of your cartoons. Ms Osserman asked him what he was doing. He explained he was just calculating. She told him to sit down and not to try to be "the new Al." See, I think she misses your joking, too.

I've been having a few problems of my own lately. Friday I was in a rush and tried to leave gym class without taking a shower. Of course Coach Badalucco stopped me in the hall and sent me back. As a result I was late for history, didn't have time to finish the test, and had to stay after school to make up the tardy. What a rotten day!

All of us at South Lincoln High miss you very much. Why don't you move? Seriously, can you arrange a visit during vacation? In any event I hope you can write back soon. We want to hear all about your new school.

Your friend,
B. B.

Social Notes. Social notes are different from friendly letters in that they generally serve a specific purpose.

A social note should focus on a single purpose.

651

Social notes relay information between people. Social notes are also sometimes necessary to show appreciation and good manners or to relay feelings. The following are six kinds of social notes with different purposes.

An *invitation* should specify the social occasion, date, time, and place, as well as information about what to bring or wear. The invitation should also request a response. The abbreviation *R.S.V.P.*, placed in the lower left-hand corner of an invitation, asks the receiver to respond. This abbreviation can be found in the appropriate place in the following example.

127 27th Street
Manhattan Beach, California 90266
March 1, 1986

Dear Allison,

    You are cordially invited to attend a celebration dinner that I am preparing for all members of our lacrosse team. Having enjoyed our most successful season in several years — seven wins and only one loss — we have much to be proud of.

    The celebration dinner will be held at my home at 6:00 p.m. on Saturday, March 31. Dress is casual.

    I'm looking forward to having you there.

               Sincerely,
               Mary Larson

R.S.V.P.

A *letter of acceptance* can be brief, but you should repeat the date, time, and place to show that you understand them. You should also express your appreciation for having been invited.

652

You should promptly send a *letter of regret* if you are unable to accept an invitation, offering a definite reason for being unable to attend. Express your regret in a personal way.

A *thank-you note or letter* can express your gratitude for another person's thoughtfulness in sending you a gift or in acting as your host. A thank-you letter should be written promptly, mentioning the gift or occasion by name.

A *letter of congratulation* lets you share another's happiness and shows others that their achievements have not gone unnoticed. A letter of congratulation should be handwritten.

A *letter of condolence*, expressing sympathy for an injury, illness, or loss of some kind, should be written with great tact. A letter of condolence should generally be brief. It should always be handwritten.

EXERCISE A: Writing a Friendly Letter. Write a friendly letter to a real or imagined friend or relative who lives far away. Be sure to include all five parts of a friendly letter. In the body of the letter, include at least one paragraph describing a person or recounting an event that you think will interest your reader.

EXERCISE B: Writing Social Notes. Write an invitation to a social event. Exchange invitations with another student and then write a letter of acceptance or regret.

Writing Business Letters

Business letters have a wide variety of purposes. All, however, have a basic purpose of conveying information clearly and directly in as few words as possible.

Business letters should state their purpose as clearly and directly as possible.

In the following pages, you will find ideas for writing five different types of business letters.

When you ask for information, you are writing a *letter of request*. Such a letter asks someone, usually a business person, to send information or material that you need. Letters of request should always be polite, especially since they often ask someone to go out of his or her way. They should also be brief. Make your specific request in the first or second sentence. Generally, you will also want to mention the reason for your request at this point. In a later sentence, remember to thank the person for taking time to help you.

Notice how quickly the writer of the following letter of request conveys all the essential information.

666 Columbus Avenue
Dayton, Ohio 45411
March 13, 1986

Chamber of Commerce
Mexico City, Mexico

Dear Sir or Madam:

I am writing a research paper for my Spanish class, and my topic is "Places of Interest in Mexico." I would appreciate any information that you could send dealing with historical sites in Mexico City.

Thank you for your assistance.

Sincerely,

Robert Tobias

Robert Tobias

An *order letter* is usually written in response to an advertisement. Include all necessary information about the item you want: its name, the quantity you want, the price, the size, and so on. Also give the total dollar amount of your order and specify the method of payment: check, money order, or C.O.D. In addition, give the date and number, if applicable, of the catalog from which you are ordering. Finally, indicate if you need the item by a particular date.

In making a request for a job you may need to write a *letter of application*. In this type of letter, quickly identify the position you are applying for and how you heard about it. If your letter accompanies a résumé, you may also want to summarize the main points of your résumé, especially your experience. If the letter takes the place of a résumé, you must offer detailed information about your job objectives, schooling, and experience. In addition, give your phone number and mention dates when you will be available for an interview.

A *letter of complaint* is generally written to ask a company to adjust an order or to correct a mistake in some business transaction. It should include any information that might help the company solve the problem. It should also be polite, for mistakes often happen unintentionally.

The *letter of opinion* is a somewhat different kind of business letter. You might wish to write to a company to praise or criticize its method of doing business. You might write to a newspaper, magazine, or television station to express your views on public issues. In this type of letter, state your opinions clearly and provide reasons to support them.

EXERCISE C: Writing an Order Letter. Find an advertisement in a magazine, newspaper, or catalogue for an item that you can order by mail. Write an order letter and an envelope for the letter.

DEVELOPING WRITING SKILLS: Writing Letters. Identify a purpose you have for writing a friendly letter, a social note, or a business letter. Review the characteristics of the specific kind of letter you have chosen as presented in this chapter. Then write the letter, proofread it, and prepare an envelope for it.

Writing Workshop: Letters

ASSIGNMENT 1

Topic   Exchanges from the Past and Present

Form and Purpose   An exchange of friendly letters between a famous person from the past and someone from the present; you choose the purpose.

Audience   The two people sending and receiving the letters

Length   Two letters of one to three paragraphs each

Focus   Compose the two letters so that they reflect the distinct personalities of the writers in an interesting exchange of ideas, issues, or feelings.

Sources   Biographies, history books, magazines

Prewriting   Select a famous person from the past and one from the present. Research and write notes about their lives and personalities. Decide on a topic that might interest the two people, and determine the purpose of the letters.

Writing   Use your notes and the checklist of steps on page 650 to write first drafts of each letter.

Revising   Proofread and correct any errors in each letter. Then prepare final copies.

ASSIGNMENT 2

Topic   Complaining with a Touch of Class

Form and Purpose   A business letter that analyzes the food and service in a restaurant and offers compliments, complaints, opinions, and/or suggestions for change

Audience   The manager or owner of the restaurant

Length   One to three paragraphs

Focus   Cite your opinion of the food and service. Then offer constructive criticism and suggestions for change.

Sources   Personal experience of eating in a restaurant

Prewriting   Make notes about the restaurant's food and service. Decide on your purpose.

Writing   Write a first draft of your business letter in a polite, formal tone and style.

Revising   Correct any errors in grammar, mechanics, spelling, and business letter conventions. Then write a final version of the letter.

Topics for Writing: Letters

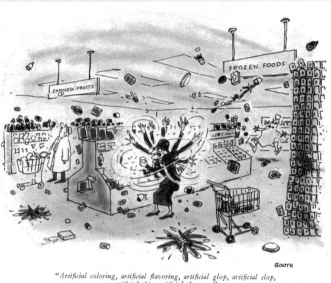

Booth, © 1972, The New Yorker Magazine, Inc.

BOOTH

"Artificial coloring, artificial flavoring, artificial glop, artificial slop, artificial this, artificial that . . ."

The cartoon above may suggest a purpose, audience, and content for a personal or business letter. Either write that letter, or choose one of the purposes below for a letter. Decide on your audience and the form of the letter.

1. An Order for Natural Foods Products
2. A Request for Advice on Nutrition
3. An Invitation to a Dinner Party
4. A Thank-You Note for a Home-Made Birthday Cake
5. An Application for a Job at a Supermarket
6. A Letter Describing an Interesting Event You Witnessed
7. A Letter to the Editor of a Newspaper About a Consumer Issue
8. A Letter of Complaint About a Product
9. A Letter to Return Defective Merchandise You Bought
10. A Letter About Something Important That Happened to You

Chapter 29

Essay Exams

Answering an essay examination question is similar to writing a paragraph or essay. You must be careful, however, to take into account the added pressure of time.

Preparing Answers to Essay Exams 29.1

Planning how to use your time is the first step in preparing answers to essay examinations.

Budgeting Your Time

Spend a few minutes at the beginning of a test previewing the instructions and questions.

Plan your time before you begin an essay exam and check to make sure you remain on schedule.

Estimate which questions will take the most time and then budget your time for the entire test. You should spend about half your time planning your answers and half your time writing them. Be sure to save a little time for proofreading.

EXERCISE A: Planning Ahead. Explain how you would divide your time in each of the following situations.

EXAMPLE: Thirty minutes for two essay questions

two minutes for previewing and fourteen minutes for planning, writing, and proofreading each essay

1. Forty minutes for three equally difficult essays
2. Forty-five minutes for ten true/false items and two essays
3. Forty-five minutes for ten true/false items and one essay
4. One hour for twenty multiple-choice items and two essays
5. Thirty minutes for one essay
6. Forty-five minutes for one very difficult essay and one easier essay
7. Thirty-five minutes for ten one-sentence answers and one essay
8. Forty-five minutes for one difficult essay and two easier essays
9. Twenty minutes for one essay
10. Thirty minutes for five true/false items and one essay

Interpreting the Question

In order to write an appropriate answer, you must understand precisely what the questions asks of you.

Read the question several times to determine exactly what information is expected.

The following chart lists the key words to look for.

KEY WORDS IN ESSAY EXAM QUESTIONS		
Kinds of Questions	**Key Words**	**What You Should Do**
Comparison	*compare, similarities, resemblances*	Look for and stress similarities.
Contrast	*contrast, differ, differences*	Look for and stress differences.
Definition	*define, explain*	Explain what something is or means. Give examples.
Description	*describe*	Give the main features with specific examples.
Diagram	*diagram, draw, chart*	Give a drawing or chart; label and explain it.

Discussion	*discuss, explain*	Support a general statement with facts and examples.
Explanation	*explain, why, what, how*	Give information that tells why, what, or how.
Illustration	*illustrate, show*	Give concrete examples and explain them.
Opinion	*in your opinion, what do you think*	Take a stand and support it with examples and reasons.
Prediction	*If . . . then What . . . if*	Show what would happen if the *if* statement were true.

EXERCISE B: Interpreting Essay Exam Questions. Identify key words and explain what to do to answer each question.

EXAMPLE: Describe the setting of *Wuthering Heights.*

describe   Give the main features with examples.

1. How did the Monroe Doctrine change foreign policy?
2. Why did many nineteenth-century Americans go west?
3. Show how two stories reflect different attitudes to war.
4. How do white blood cells defend against infection?
5. In your opinion, is *Catch 22* a comedy or a tragedy?
6. If you were standing on the moon, what would you weigh?
7. Give your own explanation of the ending of "Charles."
8. How did the French Revolution change French society?
9. Describe the structure of the carbon molecule.
10. Define the term *quotient.*

Planning Your Answer

After you are sure of the question, you can plan your answer.

Plan your answer by listing your ideas and organizing them in a modified outline.

List any ideas that seem to answer the question. Then write a single statement that sums up your ideas and prepare a modified outline. Add a concluding idea to show completeness.

661

Following are two modified outlines. The first develops a paragraph-length answer to the question "What factors caused the United States to enter World War I?" The second outlines an essay-length answer to the same question. Your test instructions will tell you which length answer to write.

ORGANIZED ANSWERS

Paragraph Length

Topic Sentence: America entered World War I because of three threats to its security.
1) Threat to Mexico
2) Aggressive dictatorships
3) Attacks on Americans at sea
Concluding Idea: America needed to protect itself and other democratic nations.

Essay Length

Thesis Statement: Three threats finally forced America to enter World War I: threats to American security, threats to democracy throughout the world, and threats to freedom of the seas.
Threat to domestic security
—Zimmerman telegram
—Germany's plans for Mexico
Threat to other countries
—Democracies in Europe
—Conflict with dictatorships
Threats to freedom of the seas
—Loss of American lives
—Sinking of American ships
Concluding Ideas:
—U.S. entry into the war
—America's need to protect itself and other democracies

EXERCISE C: Outlining Answers. Use a question from Exercise B or a question of your own and list the facts and other ideas that you would use in your answer. Then arrange the information in a modified outline for a paragraph-length answer.

Writing Your Answer

In writing your answer, stick to your modified outline.

Write a paragraph-length or essay-length answer based on your outline.

Following is a sample paragraph-length answer written from the preceding modified outline.

662

TOPIC SENTENCE	America entered World War I because of three threats to its security. The Zimmerman telegram caused Americans to believe that Germany hoped to
Supporting information	involve the United States in a war with Mexico. Many Americans also believed that the European conflict threatened democracies around the world. Germany and Austria-Hungary were dictatorships with little regard for the rights of other countries. More immediate was the German threat to American lives at sea. German submarines sank American merchant ships visiting European ports. When the United States finally entered the war on April 6, 1917, many Americans
Concluding idea	believed that they had to enter to protect their own country as well as other democratic countries.

EXERCISE D: Writing Your Answer. Use your outline from Exercise C to write a paragraph-length essay answer.

Checking Your Answer

Check your answer carefully before you hand in your exam.

Proofread for clarity and correctness.

The checklist shows the major points you should check.

CHECKING YOUR ANSWER
1. Does the answer directly respond to the question that was asked and stick to the topic?
2. Is there a clear topic sentence or thesis statement with enough supporting information?
3. Are there any mistakes in grammar, mechanics, or spelling?

EXERCISE E: Proofreading Your Answer. Reexamine the paragraph you wrote in Exercise D using the checklist above.

DEVELOPING WRITING SKILLS: Preparing Answers to Essay Exams. Gather a number of essay questions from different classes. Select one of them and write an essay-length answer, following the steps presented in this chapter.

Writing Workshop: Essay Exams

ASSIGNMENT

Topic   Essay Exam in the Area of Science or Social Studies

Form and Purpose   An answer to an essay-exam question that requires a thorough discussion or explanation

Audience   A classmate

Length   One to three paragraphs

Focus   Ask a classmate from a science or social studies class to write an essay-exam question requiring a discussion or explanation. Write an answer in which you support a main idea with specific facts and examples.

Sources   Personal knowledge, textbooks

Prewriting   Identify the key words in the question. Write either a topic sentence or a thesis statement. Then outline supporting facts and details.

Writing   Use your notes and outline to write a first draft.

Revising   Revise your answer using the checklist on page 663 and submit a final copy to your classmate for evaluation.

UNIT **VI**

Vocabulary and Spelling

Chapter 30

Vocabulary Building

A large vocabulary will help you in both your reading and your writing. It can improve your understanding of the material you read as well as increase your ability to express your own ideas. In order to increase your vocabulary, you must know what to do when you come across a word you do not know. This chapter will show you ways to learn and remember many of the new words you are likely to meet every day.

30.1 Increasing Your Vocabulary

There is no easy way to increase your vocabulary. A good vocabulary requires time and effort on your part. This section discusses a number of ways to build your vocabulary, but it is important to remember that the surest route to a strong vocabulary is making an effort every day to remember and to use the new words you encounter.

Using a Dictionary and Thesaurus

Two very useful books that can help you increase your vocabulary are the dictionary and the thesaurus. You will learn more about the dictionary in Chapter 35. For now, you should be aware that the dictionary is an authority on the meaning, spelling, and pronunciation of words.

Use a dictionary to find the meaning, spelling, and proper pronunciation of words.

One of the best ways to build your vocabulary is to get into the habit of consulting a dictionary any time you come across an unfamiliar word. In order to make the best use of a dictionary, there are several guidelines you should keep in mind.

First, you will often have to remove an ending before you look a word up. For example, if you want to find *exhilarated,* you will have to look up *exhilarate.*

Second, study the pronunciation of the word you look up, which is usually given in parentheses right after the word. If you know how to pronounce a word, you are more likely to remember it and make it a part of your working vocabulary.

Third, study the information about the origin of the word, generally supplied in brackets. Knowing where a word came from can help you remember the meaning of the word.

Fourth, you should pay attention to the different meanings that a single word can have. Many words in English have a number of meanings, depending on how they are used.

Finally, you should notice the abbreviations that are used in the definitions to indicate what part of speech the word is. Many words can serve as different parts of speech. Thus, for a simple word like *next,* you will find definitions for its use as an adjective (*adj.*), an adverb (*adv.*), a preposition (*prep.*), and a noun (*n.*).

A thesaurus can also help you increase your vocabulary. It will provide lists of words that are similar in meaning to the ones you look up. It may also provide detailed explanations about the slight differences in meanings between similar words. (See Section 35.2 for further information about the thesaurus.)

Use a thesaurus to find information about words that are similar in meaning.

A thesaurus is often valuable when you are writing. You may find yourself using the same word over and over again. With a thesaurus, you can find more vivid words and at the same time increase your vocabulary.

Do not, however, simply pick a new word that sounds interesting. If the thesaurus does not give enough information about the word you want to use, look it up in a dictionary.

667

Make sure you know just how it should be used before you actually use it.

A dictionary and thesaurus can both be very helpful. Remember, however, that words are for communication. While you use the two reference books for basic information, you should also watch the way words are used in your reading. One of the best ways to make a new word part of your permanent vocabulary is to study how the word is used each time you come across it. After you have read the word several times, it will start to become a natural part of your vocabulary.

EXERCISE A: Using the Dictionary to Increase Your Vocabulary. Look up each word in your dictionary and write the definition for the part of speech indicated in parentheses.

EXAMPLE: exonerate (verb)

to prove to be not guilty

1. jeopardize (verb)
2. taut (adjective)
3. ostentatious (adjective)
4. coerce (verb)
5. deflect (verb)
6. mundane (adjective)
7. knell (verb)
8. monotonous (adjective)
9. gossamer (adjective)
10. obloquy (noun)

EXERCISE B: Using the Thesaurus to Increase Your Vocabulary. Find a word similar in meaning to each one below.

EXAMPLE: beginner

novice

1. adequate
2. scold
3. coward
4. earnest
5. flexible
6. loyalty
7. confusion
8. efficient
9. ghost
10. happy

Recognizing Related Words

Knowing how words are related to each other can help you increase your vocabulary. Three kinds of words especially useful to know are *synonyms, antonyms,* and *homonyms.*

One of the most common ways to remember new vocabulary words is to make use of synonyms.

Synonyms are words that are similar in meaning.

As you have already learned, the basic purpose of a thesaurus is to provide lists of synonyms for the words you look up. Dictionaries, too, sometimes provide lists of synonyms after definitions. It is sometimes easier to remember the meaning of a word if you associate it with a word you already know. The meaning of *benevolence*, for example, is easier to remember if you associate it with the synonym *kindliness*.

Antonyms can help you remember the meaning of words.

Antonyms are words that are opposite in meaning.

If, for example, you wanted to remember that *recalcitrant* means "refusing to obey authority or follow orders," you could remember that the word is an antonym of *obedient*.

It is also useful to know about homonyms so that you can make important distinctions between some words.

Homonyms are words that sound alike but have different meanings and spellings.

You would, for example, want to make sure that you know the difference between *holy* (meaning "sacred") and *wholly* (meaning "entirely"). Though these two words are usually pronounced the same, they have different spellings and meanings.

EXERCISE C: Recognizing Synonyms, Antonyms, and Homonyms. Identify each pair of words as *synonyms, antonyms,* or *homonyms.*

EXAMPLE: neat/tidy

           synonyms

1. negative/positive
2. there/their
3. oppose/defend
4. achieve/attain
5. knight/night
6. careful/negligent
7. our/hour
8. arrogant/humble
9. expel/oust
10. main/mane

Remembering Vocabulary Words

Even if you use a dictionary and thesaurus regularly, there will still be some words that are harder for you to remember than others—especially those words that you do not encounter very often. Following are a number of suggestions on how to reinforce your memory of the vocabulary words once you have determined their meanings.

Use a variety of methods for studying and reviewing new words.

Using a Vocabulary Notebook. In each of your subjects, you are likely to come across words that you will need to know for tests. Knowing these words can also help you increase your general knowledge of words and your ability to express your thoughts. Because words are so important in so many different activities, you may find it worthwhile to set up a separate vocabulary section for each of your subjects in your notebook.

One of the best ways to set up a notebook page for vocabulary words is shown in the following illustration.

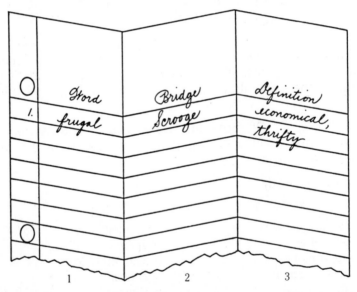

Using this three-column format, place the words you want to learn in the first column and the definitions of the words in the third column. The middle column offers a space for *bridge words*—clues or hints that can help you remember each definition. If, as in the example, you want to remember that the word *frugal* means "thrifty," you might use the bridge word

Scrooge, the name of Charles Dickens' famous miser. When studying, you can either cover the third column with another piece of paper or fold the paper back to hide the definitions.

Using Flashcards. Flashcards can also be very helpful when you are learning new words. On the front of an index card, write the word you want to learn. If it is difficult to pronounce, copy the phonetic spelling of the word from the dictionary, as in the following example. In the lower right corner of the card, write a bridge word in pencil. When you no longer need this hint to remember the definition of the word, you can erase it. On the back of the card, write the definition of the word. You may also find it helpful to use different colors of cards for nouns, verbs, adjectives, and adverbs. The color will provide an additional clue to the meaning of the word.

frugal *(froo′g′l)* *Scrooge*	*economical, thrifty*

When you have a stack of ten or more flashcards, use the following steps to drill yourself.

USING FLASHCARDS

1. Flip through the cards quickly, trying to associate the words with the definitions.

2. Then look at just the fronts of the cards, defining each word and using it in a sentence.

3. Place cards with words you cannot define in a review pile.

4. Repeat the first three steps until there are no cards in the review pile.

5. Look at just the backs of the cards, giving the word that goes with each definition and using the word in a sentence.

6. Place cards with words you do not know in the review pile.

7. Repeat these last two steps until there are no more cards in the pile.

Using a Tape Recorder. When reviewing your new words at home, you may find a tape recorder very helpful. Speaking, repeating, and hearing your new words spoken aloud can often make it easier to learn them. The following steps can be used when you study with a tape recorder.

USING A TAPE RECORDER

1. Read a vocabulary word into the tape.
2. Leave approximately five seconds of blank space on the tape and then give a definition.
3. Follow the definition with a sentence using the word in context or with a short story or interesting incident that will help you remember the word and its meaning.
4. Leave another blank space of approximately five seconds on the tape.
5. Continue with the remainder of the vocabulary words in the same fashion.
6. Study the words by replaying the entire tape, filling in the first blank space with a definition spoken aloud and the second blank space with the vocabulary word spoken aloud.
7. Rerun the tape until you are able to give all of the definitions and words without hesitation.

Listening to your tape several times a week can help you make new words a permanent part of your vocabulary.

Working with a Partner. Reviewing vocabulary words with a partner provides a chance for oral drill as well as often-needed encouragement.

Begin by deciding who will read the words and who will define the words in the first round. The person reading the words should do so rapidly. If the person defining the words is slow to respond, the reader should provide a bridge word. The reader should continue reading the words until the definer can correctly define them all. Then the reader should read the definitions, and the definer should supply the word that matches each. Again, the reader should continue until the definer has successfully identified each word. During the second round, the partners should change roles.

EXERCISE D: Using Different Study Methods. After reviewing vocabulary words using the three-column notebook format and at least two of the other three methods explained here, decide which method works best for you. Then choose a second method that you can use occasionally to add variety to your study. Explain the reasons for both choices.

DEVELOPING WRITING SKILLS: Using Vocabulary Words in Writing. Choose the ten most difficult words you currently need to learn at school. Make each of these part of your working vocabulary by using each word in a sentence that clearly shows the meaning of the word.

Using Context 30.2

Sometimes you can determine the meaning of a new word from the sentence or passage in which it is used. The sentence, the surrounding words, or the situation in which a word is used is the word's *context*.

Recognizing Context Clues

By examining the meaning of a sentence, you can often make a reasonable guess about the meaning of a word.

Use context clues to guess the meanings of new words.

Study the following example to see how the context aids the reader in understanding the word *intimidated*.

EXAMPLE: The winning record of our team *intimidated* the other team so much that they didn't want to play us.

CLUES: In this sentence the words "winning record" suggest strength and power. The words "didn't want to play us" suggest fear and worry.

GUESS: *Intimidate* must mean "frighten."

Indeed, *intimidate* does mean "to make timid; make afraid; overawe." The steps in the chart on the next page will help you use the context of a word to find clues to its meaning.

673

USING CONTEXT CLUES

1. Read the sentence, leaving out the unfamiliar word.
2. Find clues in the sentence and guess the word's meaning.
3. Read the sentence again, substituting your guess for the unfamiliar word.
4. Check your guess by looking up the unfamiliar word in the dictionary. Write the word and its definition in the vocabulary section of your notebook.

Notice how these four steps can be useful in guessing the meaning of *contraband* in the following sentence.

EXAMPLE: The police recovered the *contraband* being smuggled in from India.

Step 1: The police recovered the _____ being smuggled in from India.

Step 2: *Clues:* "police recovered," "smuggled"
Guess: contraband means "illegal goods"

Step 3: The police recovered the *illegal goods* being smuggled in from India.

Step 4: In the dictionary, *contraband* means "goods forbidden by law to be imported or exported; smuggled merchandise."

EXERCISE A: Recognizing Context Clues. Using the example above as a model, make a guess about the meaning of the underlined word in each sentence. Then check a dictionary to see how close your guess is to the meaning of the word.

1. After examining the evidence, Sherlock Holmes <u>surmised</u> that the criminal had escaped through the back door.
2. Because of his hesitation, I was <u>skeptical</u> that he really wanted to join our group.
3. My father remained <u>intransigent</u> and would not change his mind about buying me a new bicycle.
4. After a few minutes in the pool, we became <u>inured</u> to the cold water.
5. His <u>mendacity</u> was so well known in the town that no one believed him when he said he would never tell a lie again.

674

6. When she actually gave up her vacation to help save the hospital, I knew her sense of <u>altruism</u> went beyond words.
7. The shocking results of their last argument were apparent when the lawyer read the <u>codicil</u> to her will.
8. As the organist played the <u>dirge</u>, the mourners filed out.
9. After much effort, she <u>extricated</u> herself from the net.
10. The <u>gaudy</u> decorations, combining all the colors of the rainbow, made the very proper Mrs. May quite ill-at-ease.

Using Context Clues in Daily Reading

Much of your daily reading is probably devoted to such material as newspapers and magazines. To increase your general vocabulary, it is important to make an effort to determine the meaning of unfamiliar words in your daily reading.

Use context clues to determine the meaning of unfamiliar words in your daily reading.

The following paragraph was taken from the kind of article you might find in the sports section of a news magazine. Read it through and try to determine the meaning of each underlined word from its context in the sentence. Write down what you think each word means.

EXAMPLE: Julius Erving, known as "Dr. J.," is a basketball player with a dazzling <u>repertoire</u> of moves. Opponents are often <u>confounded</u> by Dr. J.'s bewildering series of leaps, twists, and swoops. One of his most <u>distinctive</u> and popular moves is the "stuff shot." As fans shout in a <u>frenzy</u>, Dr. J. races down the court, soars up, and slams the ball down through the basket. <u>Bedlam</u> breaks out! Surprisingly, Dr. J. was a <u>mediocre</u> basketball player in high school, and for two years he was only a second-string forward. But in his last year of high school things began to <u>jell</u> for him. Whenever his team was threatened and plays began to <u>fizzle</u>, Julius Erving was summoned by his coach to rescue the team from its very <u>precarious</u> situation. That's when teammates <u>bestowed</u> on him the title of "Doctor," and he's been called "Dr. J." ever since.

675

Using Context Clues in Daily Reading. For each word, choose the meaning that most closely matches the meaning of the word as it was used in the paragraph you just read.

EXAMPLE: player   (a) recorder; (b) athlete;
                    (c) expert; (d) winner

          athlete

1. repertoire   (a) list of songs; (b) surplus;
                 (c) repetition; (d) collection
2. confounded   (a) confused; (b) frightened;
                 (c) discovered; (d) dazzled
3. distinctive   (a) celebrated; (b) characteristic;
                 (c) unusual; (d) difficult
4. frenzy   (a) shout; (b) heavy club;
                 (c) frantic outburst; (d) cheer
5. bedlam   (a) bad times; (b) prolonged noise;
                 (c) trouble; (d) nightmare
6. mediocre   (a) unusual; (b) fine;
                 (c) horrible; (d) ordinary
7. jell   (a) take shape; (b) look strange;
                 (c) fall apart; (d) improve
8. fizzle   (a) flare up; (b) dampen;
                 (c) fall apart; (d) forget
9. precarious   (a) unlikely; (b) protected;
                 (c) gloomy; (d) risky
10. bestowed   (a) honored; (b) loaded;
                 (c) gave; (d) offered

Using Context Clues in Textbook Reading

The material presented in textbooks often includes technical words or ordinary words used with a special meaning.

Use context clues to determine the meaning of unfamiliar words in your textbook reading.

The following paragraph is similar to material you might read in your social studies textbook. After you read through it, try to determine the meaning of each underlined word by its context. Write down what you think each word means.

676

EXAMPLE: Soon after the German army invaded France during World War II, armed resistance in that country was crushed. Most French soldiers had no <u>alternative</u> but to surrender. Among those taken prisoner was General Henri Giraud, a man well known to the Germans for his achievements in World War I. In that war Giraud had been wounded and captured by the Germans; yet despite <u>adverse</u> conditions, he had <u>contrived</u> a way to escape. This time the Germans were taking no chances with Giraud, and he was placed in a special prison in Germany—a fortress that stood on a high cliff. Giraud was no longer a young man, but he was <u>resourceful</u> and <u>methodical</u>, and he felt equal to the challenge of escaping. Using the <u>pretense</u> that he was interested in learning languages, he conversed daily with his guards in German and, in time, he became <u>proficient</u> in that language. Being able to speak German was a <u>crucial</u> element in his escape. Then he had friends send him packages of food that were tied with twine. Inside the food his friends had hidden wire and a civilian hat. With the twine and wire, Giraud succeeded in making a 150-foot rope. One night he climbed down the rope and, <u>attired</u> in a raincoat and civilian hat, he headed for the railroad station and, <u>ultimately</u>, to freedom.

EXERCISE C: Using Context Clues in Textbook Reading.

For each word, choose the meaning that most closely matches the meaning of the word as it was used in the paragraph you just read.

1. alternative   (a) means; (b) choice;
                    (c) action; (d) reason
2. adverse   (a) sad; (b) wrong;
                    (c) unfavorable; (d) unlikely
3. contrived   (a) thought up; (b) built;
                    (c) hoped for; (d) uncovered
4. resourceful   (a) strong; (b) inventive;
                    (c) reluctant; (d) daring
5. methodical   (a) creative; (b) imaginative;
                    (c) orderly; (d) clever

6. pretense   (a) good reason; (b) understanding;
                      (c) false claim; (d) example
7. proficient   (a) skilled; (b) proud;
                      (c) hopeless; (d) sneaky
8. crucial   (a) criticized; (b) essential;
                      (c) crushed; (d) extra
9. attired   (a) carrying; (b) dressed;
                      (c) hidden; (d) covered
10. ultimately   (a) then; (b) next;
                      (c) hopefully; (d) finally

Using Context Clues in Pleasure Reading

Most people find reading stories to be easier than other kinds of reading. The reason for this may be that most stories have a general rather than a technical vocabulary. Even so, you may find some unfamiliar words. You should try to determine the meaning of these unfamiliar words by examining their context. The more words you understand, the more enjoyable reading can be.

Use context clues to determine the meaning of unfamiliar words in your pleasure reading.

After you read the following paragraph, look back at the underlined words in the paragraph and try to determine their meaning from their context. Write down what you think each word means.

EXAMPLE: In 1955, when Jill Kinmont was seventeen, she was America's top junior woman skier. In that year Jill had a serious skiing accident that left her almost completely paralyzed from the shoulders down. In the aftermath of the accident she underwent a personality change. She became very quiet and pensive. In time, she began to weigh what she would do with her life. She did not want to burden her family with the care of a helpless daughter. Besides, her self-esteem would not allow her to remain dependent on other people, even family members. Jill had the use of only a few muscles in her hands and arms. In the beginning, it was torture for her to move her wheelchair by herself. Just to move the wheelchair twenty-five feet took Jill at least an hour. But the difficulties of moving about did not <u>quench</u> her unconquerable spirit. She <u>adhered</u> to a <u>rigorous</u> schedule of physical exercise, and she <u>channeled</u> her energies toward doing many things for herself. A friend <u>improvised</u> a metal brace for her hand; with the brace she learned to hold a pen and write. Jill later went to college and eventually became a teacher. Two movies have been made about her life: *The Other Side of the Mountain* and *The Other Side of the Mountain, Part II.* The story of Jill Kinmont's life and her struggles to overcome her limitations has been an <u>incentive</u>, as well as an inspiration, to many other handicapped people.

EXERCISE D: Using Context Clues in Pleasure Reading.
For each word, choose the meaning that most closely matches the meaning of the word as it was used in the paragraph you just read.

1. aftermath   (a) side effect; (b) confusion;
                       (c) time following; (d) wreckage
2. pensive   (a) personal; (b) thoughtful;
                       (c) petty; (d) silly
3. weigh   (a) measure; (b) look closely at;
                       (c) direct; (d) carefully consider
4. self-esteem   (a) self-respect; (b) self-pity;
                       (c) sufficiency; (d) self-support
5. quench   (a) quiet; (b) harden;
                       (c) lighten; (d) overcome
6. adhered   (a) became addicted to; (b) obtained;
                       (c) followed closely; (d) adjusted
7. rigorous   (a) daily; (b) strict;
                       (c) righteous; (d) straight
8. channeled   (a) forced; (b) challenged;
                       (c) brought; (d) directed
9. improvised   (a) imaginatively created; (b) bought;
                       (c) improved upon; (d) hammered out
10. incentive   (a) benefit; (b) help;
                       (c) encouragement; (d) valuable

679

DEVELOPING WRITING SKILLS: Using Context Clues to Complete Sentences. Choose the word from the following list that best completes each sentence. Write each word on your paper.

alternative	improvised	resourceful
bedlam	incentive	rigorous
confounded	mediocre	
contrived	methodical	

1. She is a _____ tennis player but an excellent swimmer.
2. When the rock star arrived, the school auditorium was in a state of _____ .
3. The doctors were _____ when the third treatment failed to work.
4. Only a _____ hiker could have survived the night on the mountain.
5. Finally, the robbers _____ a new means of entering.
6. With the road flooded, we had no _____ but to find another route.
7. Try to organize your thoughts in a _____ manner.
8. The manager promised the employees extra pay as an _____ to complete their work on time.
9. After the cyclone many people were homeless and had to live in _____ shelters made from scrap boards and pieces of tin.
10. The soldiers underwent _____ training in preparation for the attack.

30.3 Using Structure

Many words can be broken into two or three different parts that contribute to the general meaning of the word. The word *inspection*, for example, is made up of three different parts: a *prefix*, a *root*, and a *suffix*. Each of these parts can help you determine the meaning of the word.

A prefix is one or more syllables placed before a root. The prefix in *inspection* is *in-*, which means "into." A root is the base of the word. The root in *inspection* is *-spec-*, which means "see." A suffix is one or more syllables added at the end of a root. The suffix in *inspection* is *-tion*, which means "the act of."

If you combine the meanings of all three parts, you find that the meaning of *inspection* is "the act of seeing or looking into."

Some words consist of roots alone (as in the word *place*). Other words have prefixes and roots (as in the word *misplace*). Still other words have roots and suffixes (as in the word *placement*). Finally, as you have seen in the word *inspection*, some words can be made up of all three parts.

Using Prefixes

One of the easiest ways to build your vocabulary is to learn how prefixes change the meanings of many words you already know. You may thus find it useful to memorize the prefixes in the following chart. Most come from Latin; *mis-* and *un-* are native English prefixes.

Use the meanings of prefixes to determine the meaning of unfamiliar words.

When you study the prefixes in the following chart, try combining them with root words you already know. You can probably come up with a long list of words using just these fifteen prefixes.

FIFTEEN COMMON PREFIXES		
Prefixes	**Meanings**	**Examples**
ad-	to, toward	ad- + -minister = to administer or to be of service to
circum-	around, about	circum- + -navigate = to circumnavigate or to sail around
com-	with, together	com- + -press = to compress or to press together
de-	away from, off	de- + -control = to decontrol or to take the controls away

dis-	away, apart	dis- + -arm = to disarm or to take the arms away
ex-	from, out	ex- + -change = to exchange or to change from
in-	not	in- + -human = inhuman or not human
in-	in, into	in- + -dent = to indent or to bite into
inter-	between	inter- + -national = international or between nations
mis-	wrong	mis- + -understand = to misunderstand or to understand incorrectly
post-	after	post- + -graduate = postgraduate or a person after graduation
re-	back, again	re- + -new = to renew or to make new again
sub-	beneath, under	sub- + -marine = submarine or beneath the sea
trans-	across	trans- + -mit = to transmit or to send across
un-	not	un- + -happy = unhappy or not happy

As you learn the prefixes in the chart, you should recognize that some of them change their last letters when they are connected to certain words. The reason for the change is to make the words easier to pronounce.

EXAMPLES: ad- becomes   ac- in acknowledge
                                 ap- in appoint
                                 as- in assure

682

in- becomes	il- in illegal
	im- in impossible
	ir- in irregular
com- becomes	co- in cooperate
	con- in conjunction
	cor- in correspond
sub- becomes	suc- in success
	suf- in suffer
	sup- in suppress

EXERCISE A: Working with Prefixes. Use your knowledge of prefixes to guess the meaning of each word. Then look up each word in the dictionary and write a brief definition of the word.

EXAMPLE   intercollegiate

between or among colleges

1. inescapable
2. rekindle
3. inflame
4. subnormal
5. ascertain
6. contemporary
7. untoward
8. circumstance
9. transatlantic
10. derail
11. postdate
12. disassociate
13. misinterpret
14. exclude
15. intercontinental
16. submerge
17. transplant
18. unlearned
19. expire
20. mistake

Using Roots

The root carries the basic meaning of a word and, therefore, plays a very important part in forming new words.

Use roots to determine the meanings of unfamiliar words.

The chart on the next page lists fifteen of the many roots used in English words. Even with these few, you can add other word parts to form a wide variety of English words. Most of the entries are from Latin; *-graph-* is from Greek. Additional spellings are shown in parentheses.

FIFTEEN COMMON ROOTS		
Roots	**Meanings**	**Examples**
-cap- (-capt-)	to take or seize	in- + -cap- + -able = incapable or not able to take
-dic- (-dict-)	to say or point out	dict- + -ation = dictation or the act of saying
-duc- (-duct-)	to lead	con- + -duct = to conduct or or to lead together
-fac- (-fact-)	to do or make	fact- + -ual = factual or being truly done or made
-graph-	to write	graph- + -ic = graphic or characteristic of writing
-mit- (-mis-)	to send	trans- + -mit = to transmit or to send across
-mov- (-mot-)	to move	mot- + -ion = motion or the act of moving
-pon- (-pos-)	to put or place	com- + -pon- + -ent = component or something put with something else
-puls- (-pel-)	to drive	re- + -pulse = to repulse or to drive back
-scrib- (-script-)	to write	in- + -scribe = to inscribe or to write into
-spec- (-spect-)	to see	in- + -spect = to inspect or to see into
-ten- (-tain-)	to hold	con- + -tain = to contain or to hold together
-ven-(-vent-)	to come	in- + -vent = to invent or to come into
-vert- (-vers-)	to turn	re- + -verse = to reverse or to turn back
-vid- (-vis-)	to see	vis- + -ion = vision or the act of seeing

EXERCISE B: Using Roots to Define Words. For each word in the first column, write the letter of the meaning in the second column.

1. visionary		a.	to place a burden on
2. repel		b.	a manner of speaking
3. revert		c.	a group meeting
4. retentive		d.	someone who sees afar
5. convention		e.	a figure written below another
6. impose		f.	to turn back
7. subscript		g.	able to hold on to
8. captivate		h.	to drive back
9. graphology		i.	distant in space or time
10. indication		j.	to undermine or overthrow
11. induce		k.	the study of handwriting
12. factotum		l.	to lead someone to some action
13. circumspect		m.	looking at something carefully
14. remote		n.	lessening of symptoms
15. submission		o.	to gain the interest of
16. diction		p.	someone who can do many things
17. subvert		q.	to drive someone to some action
18. remission		r.	something sent under special cover
19. convene		s.	to come together
20. compel		t.	something that points in a certain direction

Using Suffixes

Some word endings are used to form the plurals of nouns, such as the -s in *dogs* or the -es in *foxes*. Other word endings are used to show the tenses of verbs, such as the -s in *wants,* the -ed in *wanted,* or the -ing in *wanting.* The word endings in the chart on the next page, however, are those that are used to form new words. By learning these suffixes, you will be able not only to form many new words but also to guess at the meanings of other new words.

Use suffixes to determine the meanings of unfamiliar words.

Most of the suffixes in the chart are Latin; *-ful, -less, -ly,* and *-ness* come from native English. Additional spellings are again shown in parentheses.

685

TEN COMMON SUFFIXES

Suffixes	Meanings	Examples
-able (-ible)	capable of being	sustain- + -able = sustainable or capable of being sustained
-ance (-ence)	the act of	clear- + -ance = clearance or the act of being cleared
-ate	make or apply	activ- + -ate = activate or make active
-ful	full of	scorn- + -ful = scornful or full of scorn
-ity	the state of being	intens- + -ity = intensity or the state of being intense
-less	without	hope- + -less = hopeless or without hope
-ly	in a certain way	careless- + -ly = carelessly or done in a careless way
-ment	the result of being	improve- + -ment = improvement or the result of being improved
-ness	the state of being	hopeless- + -ness = hopelessness or the state of being hopeless
-tion (-ion, -sion)	the act or state of being	admis- + -sion = admission or the act of being admitted

Suffixes can also tell the part of speech of a word. The following show the parts of speech indicated by the suffixes. Notice that *-ful* and *-ly* can both form two parts of speech.

NOUNS: -ance   VERB: -ate   ADJECTIVES: -able   ADVERB: -ly
       -ful   -ful
       -ity   -less
       -ment   -ly
       -ness
       -tion

EXERCISE C: Determining Parts of Speech and Meaning from Suffixes. Use your knowledge of suffixes to determine the part of speech and meaning of each word. Then look up each word in the dictionary and write the part of speech and a brief definition.

EXAMPLE: scarcity

noun   the state of being scarce or limited

1. containment
2. divisible
3. bountiful
4. inference
5. motivate

6. goodness
7. community
8. witless
9. adaptation
10. northerly

DEVELOPING WRITING SKILLS: Using Structure Clues to Complete Sentences. Choose the word from the following list that best completes each sentence. Write each word on your paper.

avidly   inscription   repulsive
compelled   irregular   tenacity
cooperate   intervened
indicative   refreeze

1. We will finish the job sooner if we _____.
2. You should never _____ food that has begun to thaw.
3. The printed paper looked messy because the margins were so _____.
4. The teacher _____ to settle the argument.
5. Although the food was _____ to her, Kim ate it in order to be polite.
6. The _____ on the old gravestone was impossible for us to read.
7. The passenger's illness _____ the pilot to make an un-scheduled landing.
8. Only her _____ enabled her to make it to the finish line of the grueling race.
9. Their efforts to improve the neighborhood were _____ of their desire to help.
10. Laurie disliked biographies, but she spent a lot of time reading mysteries _____.

687

30.4 Exploring Etymologies

The origin and history of a word is called its *etymology*. As mentioned in Section 35.3, some dictionaries give information about a word's etymology in brackets before or after the definition. The information is usually given in a very abbreviated form, using both symbols and abbreviations. To make the fullest use of this information, you should become familiar with these symbols and abbreviations by studying the explanations found at the front or back of your dictionary.

Knowing the etymology of a word can often help you remember its meaning. In this section, you will learn about words that have been borrowed from other languages, words that have changed their meanings over the years, and words that have been created for a variety of reasons.

Borrowed Words

For centuries speakers of English have been borrowing words from other languages. Some of these words were borrowed so long ago that it probably never occurs to you that they came from another language. These words are called *loanwords*.

Loanwords are words in the English language that have been borrowed from other languages.

Most of the loanwords in the English language have come from Latin and French. Many of the words borrowed from Latin are for abstract ideas. For example, *honesty, doctrine,* and *religion* can all be traced back to Latin. Many of the words borrowed from French are also for abstract ideas, but other French loanwords are for common items. Both *column* and *college,* for example, were borrowed from the French language.

There are few languages from which English has not borrowed at least a few words. The old Scandinavian languages have provided many of the words used every day. *Egg, ski, skirt, skin,* and even such pronouns as *they* and *their* were borrowed from the Scandinavian languages during the time of the Viking invasions of England around 1000 A.D.

Many examples of loanwords from other European languages can also be found. From the Italian language, English has borrowed such words as *gondola, soprano,* and *piano.* From Spanish, English has borrowed the words *iguana, rodeo, alligator,* and many others.

Some words have been borrowed from Native American languages also. This is particularly true of place names in the United States. The word *Connecticut,* for example, comes from the Algonquian word meaning "place of the long river." *Susquehanna* comes from the Iroquoian language. *Idaho* comes from the language of the Shoshone.

EXERCISE A: Discovering the Sources of Loanwords. In a dictionary that provides etymologies, look up each word below and write the language of origin. When more than one origin is given for a word, use the first.

EXAMPLE: envy

French

1. expect	11. igloo
2. piccolo	12. faith
3. habit	13. harmony
4. desert	14. exit
5. liberty	15. physics
6. royal	16. demon
7. democracy	17. museum
8. myth	18. rack
9. spectrum	19. tea
10. thermos	20. quilt

EXERCISE B: Finding Loanwords in the Dictionary. In a dictionary that provides etymologies, find at least one word from each of the following languages.

EXAMPLE: Greek

tantalize

1. Latin	6. Chinese
2. French	7. Dutch
3. Spanish	8. Native American
4. German	9. Arabic
5. Italian	10. Russian

Words with New Meanings

In addition to the expansion of the English language caused by borrowing words from other languages, English is constantly growing because English speakers give new meanings to old words.

The English language grows by giving new meanings to old words.

Only two centuries ago, for example, the word *fond* meant "foolish." In Shakespeare's time, four centuries ago, the word *issue* regularly meant "offspring or children."

It is also common for a word simply to gain additional meanings. The word *fast,* for example, can still mean "firm or fixed" when used as an adjective, but it is more commonly used now to mean "quick." The word *sanguine* can still mean "of the color of blood," but now it more commonly means "cheerful and optimistic."

Many new words are added to the language when two existing words are joined together to form a third word with a new meaning. Consider such words as *doghouse, archway, caretaker,* and *paperweight.*

EXERCISE C: Combining Words to Create New Words.
Match each word in the first column with the appropriate word in the second column and write the words you have formed on your paper.

EXAMPLE: green   house

greenhouse

1. land	a. gate
2. slap	b. come
3. net	c. booth
4. over	d. stick
5. sand	e. fill
6. match	f. giving
7. tail	g. paper
8. take	h. work
9. thanks	i. book
10. toll	j. over

Coined Words

Throughout the history of the language, English speakers have been very inventive about creating new words. Some new words are created because the expanding knowledge in science and technology requires them. Others are created because of general changes in society. In either case, newly created words are known as *coinages*.

The English language grows through the addition of newly coined words.

There are several different methods by which new words are coined.

Acronyms. An acronym is a coined word that is formed from the first (or first few) letters of a series of words. The word *sonar*, for example, is formed from the first letters of "*s*ound *n*avigation *a*nd *r*anging." The telephone service known as *WATS* is an acronym for "*w*ide *a*rea *t*elecommunications *s*ervice." Many acronyms are formed from the first letters of the names of organizations. Thus, *NATO* is used to refer to North Atlantic Treaty Organization. *UNESCO* refers to the United Nations Educational, Scientific, and Cultural Organization.

"People" Words. Many words that are now taken for granted are named after people. The electrical term *watt*, for example, is named after the inventor James Watt. The word *pasteurization* is named after Louis Pasteur, who developed the process for treating milk.

Clipped Words. Some very common words are shortened versions of longer words that are now rarely used. The word *radio*, for example, is short for *radiotelegraph*. The word *bus* is a shortened form of *omnibus*.

Blends. Sometimes new words are coined by combining parts of other words. The word *skyjack* was first coined when airplanes began to be hijacked.

Brand Names. Some words start out as brand names used by particular companies for their products or services. Sometimes people begin using the brand names for the products or services even if they are supplied by other companies. Thus, people often use the word *Xerox*, which is a registered trademark, to refer to photocopying even if it is not the same method originally developed by the Xerox Corporation.

691

EXERCISE D: Finding the Origins of Acronyms and "People" Words. In a dictionary that provides etymologies, look up each of the following words and write a definition that includes the origin of the word.

EXAMPLE: ohm

        an electrical unit named after physicist G. S. Ohm

1. bloomer	6. quixotic
2. gerrymander	7. jeremiad
3. laser	8. NASA
4. jeep	9. quasar
5. Morse code	10. Rorschach test

EXERCISE E: Finding the Origins of Clipped Words, Blends, and Brand Names. In a dictionary that provides etymologies, look up each of the following words and write a definition that includes the origin of the word.

EXAMPLE: memo

        a brief note originally called a memorandum

1. co-op	6. steno
2. Dacron	7. phone
3. chortle	8. Ping Pong
4. smash	9. gym
5. exam	10. lab

DEVELOPING WRITING SKILLS: Determining Origins of Words. In a dictionary that provides etymologies, look up each of the following words and write a sentence explaining the meaning and etymology of the word.

EXAMPLE: haughty

        Haughty, which means "very proud," comes from a
        Latin word meaning "high."

1. khaki	6. nausea
2. siesta	7. sleuth
3. slogan	8. caterpillar
4. affiliate	9. canter
5. generous	10. Ferris wheel

Skills Review and Writing Workshop

Vocabulary Building

CHECKING YOUR SKILLS

Use context clues to write a definition for each underlined word in the following paragraph.

(1) Every year, the forces of erosion <u>inevitably</u> remove millions of tons of topsoil from our farmlands. (2) Wind and water erosion are the prime <u>culprits</u>, causing tremendous damage to numerous farms. (3) However, farmers have now <u>initiated</u> a number of methods to reduce erosion. (4) Shelter belts, rows of tall trees, have been planted to <u>safeguard</u> fields from strong winds. (5) As another <u>option</u>, farmers build platforms along a hillside and plant their crops on top of them. (6) These platforms catch rainwater and <u>substantially</u> reduce water erosion. (7) A third method used by farmers is to plant crops in <u>alternating</u> strips, such as corn and grass. (8) This has also cut down erosion and helped <u>preserve</u> our farmlands. (9) Although progress has been made, farmers must remain ever <u>vigilant</u> in the battle against erosion. (10) We must <u>nurture</u> the land that feeds us.

USING VOCABULARY SKILLS IN WRITING
Writing a Travelogue

A large working vocabulary is an essential tool in writing. Recall a trip that you have taken by train or automobile and write a description of your experiences along the way. Follow these steps to write your travelogue.

Prewriting: Write notes about any unusual things that you saw, people you met, or events that occurred during your trip.

Writing: Describe the most interesting events of the trip in chronological order.

Revising: Look over your words and change any that could be more descriptive or more accurate. After you have revised, proofread carefully.

693

Chapter 31

Spelling Improvement

Spelling is a valuable skill for two reasons. First, it is difficult to read material that contains a number of incorrect spellings. Second, there are cases in which the meaning of a sentence can actually be changed by an incorrect spelling. Suppose, for example, you wrote to a friend, "The bride did not wear a veil, but the flour in her hair was lovely." Your friend would probably immediately picture a bride who had white powder in her hair.

The suggestions and rules in this chapter can help you solve your own spelling problems. The chapter will help you learn to spell words you will use again and again. The first section offers some practical suggestions about how you can improve your spelling skills in general. The second section contains specific rules that can help you master some common spelling problems.

31.1 Improving Your Spelling

Many of the methods described in the first chapter of this unit for improving your vocabulary can also be useful for improving your spelling. Identifying words to learn, keeping words in a notebook, and developing strategies for learning and reviewing can help you improve your skills in both areas. When you are dealing with spelling, there are also a number of memory aids you can use.

694

Proofreading Carefully

One good strategy to use in order to improve your spelling skills is to start proofreading everything you write. By looking closely at the way you have spelled each word, you will become more conscious of the way words are supposed to look on the page.

Proofread everything you write.

If you get into the habit of proofreading your written work, you will find that it becomes automatic to look closely at each word you have chosen. As you are proofreading, you should have a dictionary close by. When you come to a word that you suspect may be spelled incorrectly, look it up.

With time and practice, you should have to consult the dictionary less often. The more times you check the spelling of a word in a dictionary, the more likely you are to remember the correct spelling the next time you use the word.

You should make a special effort to check the spelling of proper names that you use in your writing. Since you are not as likely to use proper names as frequently as you use ordinary words, you may easily forget the spelling of some proper names.

EXERCISE A: Proofreading Carefully. Each sentence below contains one incorrectly spelled word. Write the correct spelling of each misspelled word, using a dictionary when necessary.

EXAMPLE: Her salery is very high for someone so young.

            salary

1. The children are being unusually queit this afternoon.
2. We had a very pleasent picnic in the park.
3. I will be moving to Phoenix in Feburary.
4. The doctor advised her to get more exersise.
5. The beautaful tapestry had already been sold.
6. The prisonor denied that he had taken part in the crime.
7. All of the good silverwear is in the cabinet.
8. The actor's performance was applauded by the critics.
9. The nurse siad that he would accept the responsibility.
10. The host indicated that we were all wellcome at the party.

More Work with Proofreading. Each sentence in the following paragraph contains at least one misspelled word. Write the correct spelling for each one.

(1) One of Italy's most intresting tourist attractions is the anceint Roman city of Pompeii. (2) Pompeii was a thriving city during the time of the Romon Empire. (3) In 79 A.D., however, Mount Vesuvius, a volcanno less than a mile from the city, erupted with great force. (4) The city was covered with lava, ash, and cindars. (5) Many of the people living their managed to excape. (6) Others were not as fortunete. (7) What was not known for many centureis is that beneath the debris left by the erruption the principal structures of the city were perserved. (8) When the ruins were discovered, archeologests and others excavated much of the city. (9) Today, tourists can go to Italy and still see Pompeii much as it looked to its original inhabitents almost two thousand years ago. (10) Visiting Pompeii is truley a venture into the past.

Studying Spelling Demons

Some words in the English language are particularly troublesome. Sometimes the trouble arises because two words are very similar but not identical in their spelling. At other times the trouble arises because two words are pronounced the same way but have different spellings and meanings. Words can also be troublesome simply because their spelling is not closely related to the way they are presently pronounced.

Words that cause frequent spelling problems are called spelling demons. Often it is best simply to memorize them.

Recognize common words that you have problems with and take care to spell them correctly in your work.

The chart on the next page provides a list of 150 spelling demons. Read through the list and take note of the ones that you think are likely to cause you the most problems.

Be sure that you understand the distinction between those words that have very similar spellings and meanings. For example, if you know the difference between *capital* and *capitol,* you are more likely to use the correct spelling.

150 COMMON SPELLING DEMONS

abbreviate	coolly	laboratory	recede
absence	correspondence	lawyer	receipt
accidentally	counterfeit	library	recommend
achieve	courageous	lightning	rehearse
acquaintance	courtesy	loneliness	repetition
admittance	criticism	maintenance	restaurant
aisle	criticize	mathematics	rhythm
amateur	curiosity	meanness	scissors
analysis	curious	mileage	secretary
analyze	deceive	millionaire	separate
anecdote	defendant	misspell	sergeant
anniversary	desert	naturally	similar
anonymous	despair	necessary	sincerely
anxiety	desperate	neighbor	sophomore
appearance	dessert	nuisance	souvenir
argument	dining	occasion	spaghetti
athletic	disappear	occasionally	straight
attendance	disappoint	occur	substitute
awkward	dissatisfied	occurred	succeed
barrel	eighth	omitted	superintendent
behavior	embarrass	opinion	supersede
believe	emergency	parallel	suspicious
benefit	envelope	paralyze	syllable
bureau	environment	particularly	technique
calendar	exceed	permanent	temporary
capital	exercise	personally	thorough
capitol	existence	perspiration	tomorrow
captain	explanation	physician	truly
cemetery	extraordinary	possess	unnecessary
clothes	familiar	possession	vacuum
colonel	foreign	prairie	villain
column	grammar	precede	weird
committee	guarantee	preferable	whether
concede	handkerchief	preparation	
condemn	hygiene	privilege	
conscience	independence	probably	
conscious	inflammable	proceed	
continuous	interfere	pronunciation	
convenience	knowledge	psychology	

EXERCISE C: Working with Spelling Demons. Write the following spelling demons on your paper, filling in the missing letters.

EXAMPLE: commi __ __ ee

committee

1. amat __ __ r
2. ath __ __ tic
3. behav __ __ r
4. cemet __ ry
5. colu __ n
6. conven __ __ nce
7. counterf __ __ t
8. criti __ ism
9. dec __ __ ve

10. defend __ nt
11. d __ spair
12. hyg __ __ ne
13. lib __ __ ry
14. mil __ __ ge
15. n __ __ ghbor
16. n __ __ sance
17. pr __ __ rie
18. rec __ __ pt

19. reh __ __ rse
20. rest __ __ rant
21. sci __ __ ors
22. sim __ lar
23. soph __ more
24. tempor __ __ y
25. vac __ __ m

EXERCISE D: More Work with Spelling Demons. Each sentence below contains an incorrect spelling of one of the spelling demons from the chart on page 697. Write the correct spelling for each misspelled word.

EXAMPLE: Fran was embarassed when she didn't know the answer.

embarrassed

1. Rita occassionally stops by to visit her aunt.
2. We were very glad to see his familar face.
3. She said it would not be nesessary to leave the keys.
4. The existance of some species is endangered.
5. My brother is majoring in mathmatics in college.
6. The unusual incident occured just after midnight.
7. Charles is not very concious of his spelling problems.
8. We will have to take seperate cars to the concert.
9. Only by hard work can we acheive our goals.
10. The secretery was told that the report had to be typed.

Keeping a Spelling Notebook

In addition to recognizing common spelling demons, you should make it a practice to keep a list of all of the words that you regularly have trouble spelling. To start, you might gather together some of the papers and tests you have written during the last few months. Some of your work may have been corrected for spelling by teachers. For additional words, you might work with a partner and check each other's work for spelling errors. Once you know where the problems are, you can start your own personal spelling list.

Make a personal spelling list of misspelled words, enter it in your notebook, and keep it up to date.

Your personal spelling list should go in a special section of your notebook. Begin by making four columns across a page. The first column, labeled "Misspelled Words," should have a large X across it. In this column copy any misspelled words you have found in your papers exactly as you wrote them. Knowing just how you misspelled a word is helpful, since after you look up the correct spelling, you can analyze your error. Number each of the words you write in this column, using only every fourth line so that you can add information later, if necessary, in the fourth column.

	Personal Spelling List			
○	Misspelled Words	Correct Spelling	Practice Sessions	Hints for Remembering Difficult Words
	1. ~~loose~~	lose	✓	loose tooth
				What I lose is lost

At the top of the second column, write the heading "Correct Spelling." You should fill this column in only after you have found the correct spelling in the dictionary.

Label the third column "Practice Sessions." On pages 700–701 you will find some helpful ideas for conducting practice sessions. You can use this column to mark your progress.

Label the fourth column "Hints for Remembering Difficult Words." Ideas for developing these kinds of aids are found on pages 701–702.

EXERCISE E: Selecting Words for a Personal Spelling List. Look over all the writing you have done in the last month, including personal writing and school assignments. Following the illustration and explanation on page 699, record any misspelled words in a personal spelling list.

Practicing with Problem Words

Just reviewing your list of words from time to time may help you learn to spell some problem words. For others, however, you should develop a more organized study strategy.

Use the following steps when studying the problem words you have listed in your notebook.

The steps in the chart below will help you analyze words that you are having problems with. They will also give you a method of recording your success in your notebook.

STEPS FOR PRACTICING WITH PROBLEM WORDS

1. *Look* at each word carefully. Observe the arrangement of the letters in the word. Consider, for example, the word *accidentally*. Notice that there are two *c*'s and two *l*'s in the word. Then close your eyes and try to *see* the word.

2. *Pronounce* the word carefully. Divide the word into syllables, and sound the word out. Dividing a word into syllables can help you pronounce and spell it correctly. For example, pronounce *February*. Notice that there is an *r* after the *b*.

3. *Write* the word on a separate sheet of paper. As you are writing the word, pronounce it aloud.

4. *Check* to make sure that you have spelled the word correctly. If you have, place a check in the third column of your notebook. If you have not, notice the mistake you have made and then start over with the first step.

You cannot assume that you know how to spell a word if you have spelled it correctly only once. A word is mastered only when you have spelled it correctly during at least three separate practice sessions. Once you have reached this goal with the words in your notebook and have entered three separate checks in the third column, you should draw a circle around the word. Though you should review the word from time to time, you should spend most of your time studying other problem words.

EXERCISE F: Working with Problem Words. In each item, choose the word you think is correctly spelled. Then look up your answers in a dictionary. Finally, enter all words you misspelled in your spelling notebook and conduct an initial practice session.

EXAMPLE: Tod's (memery, memory) is excellent.

memory

1. It is (necessary, necesary) to proofread your work.
2. (Aparently, Apparently) they misunderstood the message.
3. The two designs were very (similiar, similar).
4. The (colonel, kernel) was in full uniform.
5. We skated to the (rhythm, rythm) of the music.
6. The group was studying the (envionment, environment).
7. Voting in an election is a (privilege, priviledge).
8. (Grammar, Grammer) is my favorite subject.
9. Don't forget to mark the date on your (calender, calendar).
10. I think a birthday is a very special (occasion, occassion).
11. They have always been the best of (friends, freinds).
12. After the hike, we were very (hungary, hungry).
13. The lecture was about modern literary (heros, heroes).
14. The nails that are on sale are in the (barrel, barral).
15. We felt a keen sense of (loneliness, lonliness).
16. The speech last night was very (memorable, memerable).
17. Each word in that poem has only one (sylable, syllable).
18. I (mispelled, misspelled) three words on the test.
19. We must (complete, compleat) the assignment by Monday.
20. Ann will be leaving on the (eighth, eigth) of this month.

Using Memory Aids

Most words can be easily learned through well-organized practice sessions and the use of rules such as those listed in the following section. For some words, however, you may find that spelling success can best be achieved through the development and use of special memory aids or hints.

Use memory aids to remember the spelling of words that you find especially difficult to spell.

Some problem words lend themselves to the development of memory aids. With some words, for example, you can find a short, easy-to-spell word hidden within the more difficult word. With other words you can associate one or more letters within the difficult word with the letters in some related word or words.

EXAMPLES:

believe	Never be*lie*ve a *lie*.
capitol	A capit*o*l building usually has a d*o*me.
conscience	Con*science* includes the word *science*.
necessary	The word ne*cess*ary *causes* problems.
prairie	There is lots of *air* on a pr*air*ie.
principle	A princip*le* is a ru*le*.
stationery	Let*ter* pap*er* is found in a station*er*y store.

Perhaps the best memory aids are the ones you develop yourself. Once you have decided that you need a memory aid to remember a certain word, develop one and enter it in the fourth column of your spelling notebook.

EXERCISE G: Developing Memory Aids. Choose five of the words in your spelling notebook and find some memory aid for each. Enter the hints in the fourth column of your spelling notebook.

EXAMPLE: calendar

A calen<u>da</u>r shows the <u>da</u>ys of the week.

DEVELOPING WRITING SKILLS: Using Problem Words in Sentences. Choose five words from the list of spelling demons on page 697 and five *other* words from your own personal spelling list. Use each of the words in a sentence of your own. Check your spelling of all words carefully.

EXAMPLE: dessert

Our host served apple pie for dessert.

Following Spelling Rules 31.2

Although some words present spelling problems, the vast majority of English words follow some regular and predictable pattern. There are, for example, rules that can be learned about writing plural forms, about writing words with prefixes and suffixes, and about the choice between *ie* and *ei*.

Plurals

The plural form of a noun is the form that means "more than one." The plural forms can be either *regular* or *irregular*.

Regular Plurals. All but a handful of nouns in English have regular plural forms ending in *-s* or *-es*.

The plural form of most nouns is formed by adding -s or -es to the singular.

As a general rule, you can just add *-s* when you are forming a regular plural.

EXAMPLES: friend, friends   holiday, holidays

magazine, magazines   restaurant, restaurants

With certain endings, however, you may have to make a choice about whether to add *-s* or *-es*. Occasionally, you may also have to change a letter or two in the word. The following chart gives rules for these special cases.

SPECIAL RULES FOR REGULAR PLURALS			
Word Endings	**Examples**	**Rules**	**Plural Forms**
-s, -ss, *-x, -z,* *-sh, -ch*	circus, dress, box, waltz, dish, church	add *-es*	circuses, dresses, boxes, waltzes, dishes, churches
-o preceded by a consonant	echo, tomato AND	add *-es*	echoes, tomatoes
	piano, solo, and other musical terms	add *-s*	pianos, solos

-o preceded by a vowel	rodeo, patio	add -s	rodeos, patios
-y preceded by a consonant	city, enemy	change y to i and add -es	cities, enemies
-y preceded by a vowel	journey, holiday	add -s	journeys, holidays
-f, -ff	chief, cliff AND leaf, loaf	add -s change f to v and add -es	chiefs, cliffs leaves, loaves
-fe	wife, life	change f to v and add -s	wives, lives

As you can see in the chart, there are only two places where you have choices. With words ending with a consonant and an -o, you should add -es unless the word is related to music. With words ending in -f and -ff, the solution is not quite so simple. For these words you can check a dictionary. If no special spelling is given, just add -s.

Irregular Plurals. Irregular plurals are not formed according to the rules above. You can, however, find them in a dictionary, listed right after the pronunciation of the word.

Consult a dictionary for irregular plurals.

The following chart lists some of these irregular plurals.

IRREGULAR PLURALS		
Singular Forms	**Ways of Forming Plurals**	**Plural Forms**
ox	add -en	oxen
child	add -ren	children
tooth, mouse, woman	change one or more letters	teeth, mice, women

radius, focus, alumnus	change -us to -i	radii, foci, alumni
alumna	change -a to -ae	alumnae
crisis, emphasis	change -is to -es	crises, emphases
Medium, datum, curriculum	change um to -a	media, data, curricula
phenomenon, criterion	change -on to -a	phenomena, criteria
deer, sheep	use singular form as plural	deer, sheep
	plural form only	scissors, slacks

Some dictionaries give a detailed explanation of the way plurals are formed and a list of irregular plurals. Check under the entry *plural*.

NOTE ABOUT PLURALS OF COMPOUND WORDS: Compound words written as single words follow the general rules for forming plurals (*cookbooks, footballs,* and *Englishmen*). To form the plural of compound words written with hyphens or as separate words, make the modified word plural (*passers-by, all-stars, suits of armor,* and *field mice*).

NOTE ABOUT SPECIAL PLURALS: In Section 17.9 you will find a discussion of the plurals of letters, numbers, symbols, and words used to refer to the words themselves.

EXERCISE A: Spelling Plurals. Write the plural for each word. Consult a dictionary when necessary.

EXAMPLE: opportunity
          opportunities

1. echo	6. ash	11. proof	16. sheep	21. goose
2. bench	7. loss	12. alley	17. peach	22. runner-up
3. fox	8. veto	13. bush	18. scarf	23. tragedy
4. mystery	9. tattoo	14. tomato	19. alto	24. mosquito
5. chorus	10. turkey	15. solo	20. calf	25. knife

Prefixes

A prefix is one or more syllables added at the beginning of a word to form a new word. The addition of a prefix does not affect the spelling of the original word.

When a prefix is added to a word, the spelling of the original word remains the same.

EXAMPLES: dis- + -appear = disappear

in- + -sincere = insincere

mis- + -inform = misinform

The rule for adding prefixes is most helpful for spelling words such as *dissatisfaction, innumerable,* and *misspell.* Notice how, in each case, the prefix is simply added to the original word and causes no change in spelling.

EXAMPLES: dis- + -satisfaction = dissatisfaction

in- + -numerable = innumerable

mis- + -spell = misspell

EXERCISE B: Spelling Words with Prefixes. Add one of the five prefixes below to each of the following words. Check a dictionary to make sure each of the words you form is a real word.

in-   mis-   un-   dis-   com-

1. spell	6. mend	11. take	16. fort
2. satisfied	7. necessary	12. organic	17. mission
3. understand	8. form	13. guide	18. known
4. possess	9. pose	14. charge	19. cast
5. ability	10. dependent	15. lodge	20. like

Suffixes

A suffix is one or more syllables added at the end of a word. The addition of a suffix, unlike the addition of a prefix, often involves a spelling change in the original word.

Be aware of spelling changes needed in some words when you are adding suffixes.

The three charts that follow summarize the major kinds of spelling changes that can take place when a suffix is added. The first chart deals with words ending in *-y*.

SPELLING CHANGES IN WORDS ENDING IN *-Y*			
Word Endings	**Suffixes Added**	**Rules**	**Exceptions**
consonant +*y* (defy, happy)	most suffixes (-ance, -ness)	change *y* to *i* (defiance, happiness)	most suffixes beginning with *i: defy* becomes *defying; cry* becomes *crying*
vowel +*y* (employ, enjoy)	most suffixes (-er, -ment)	make no change (employer, enjoyment)	a few short words: *day* becomes *daily; gay* becomes *gaily*

The next chart summarizes changes that may or may not take place in words ending in *-e.*

SPELLING CHANGES IN WORDS ENDING IN *-E*			
Word Endings	**Suffixes Added**	**Rules**	**Exceptions**
any word ending in *-e* (believe, recognize)	suffix beginning with a vowel (-able)	drop the final *e* (believable, recognizable)	1. words ending in *-ce* or *-ge* with suffixes beginning in *a* or *o: trace* becomes *traceable; outrage* becomes *outrageous* 2. words ending in *-ee: see* becomes *seeing; agree* becomes *agreeable*
any word ending in *-e* (price, nice)	suffix beginning with a consonant (-less, -ly)	make no change (priceless, nicely)	a few special words: *true* becomes *truly; argue* becomes *argument; judge* becomes *judgment*

The final chart summarizes cases in which a final consonant may or may not be changed.

DOUBLING THE FINAL CONSONANT BEFORE SUFFIXES

Word Endings	Suffixes Added	Rules	Exceptions
consonant +vowel+ consonant in a stressed syllable (rob', admit')	suffix beginning with a vowel (-er, -ed)	double the final consonant (rob'ber, admit'ted)	1. words ending in *x* or *w: bow* becomes *bowing; wax* becomes *waxing* 2. words in which the stress changes after the suffix is added: *prefer'* becomes *pref'erence*
consonant +vowel+ consonant in an unstressed syllable (an'gel, fi'nal)	suffix beginning with a vowel (-ic, ize)	make no change (angel'ic, fi'nalize)	no major exceptions

EXERCISE C: Spelling Words with Suffixes. Write the new word formed by combining each of the following words and suffixes.

EXAMPLE: safe- + -ly

safely

1. accidental- + -ly
2. occur- + -ence
3. favor- + -able
4. imply- + -ing
5. survey- + -or
6. silly- + -ness
7. imagine- + -able
8. healthy- + -ness
9. value- + -able
10. commit- + -ed
11. justify- + -able
12. encourage- + -ment
13. amplify- + -er
14. rebel- + -ion
15. continue- + -ous
16. patron- + -ize
17. vex- + -ing
18. grace- + -ful
19. love- + -ly
20. destroy- + -er

708

ie and *ei* Words

For words containing an *ie* or *ei,* spellers have traditionally relied on the following rule: "*i* before *e,* except after *c,* or when sounded like *a,* as in *neighbor* or *weigh.*" The rule can help spellers with a number of common words such as *achieve* and *receive.* Like many rules, however, this one has exceptions.

Use the traditional rule for *ie* and *ei* words after memorizing the exceptions.

Fortunately, there are not many exceptions to the traditional rule. Also, some are easy to remember because they travel in pairs (*ei*ther and n*ei*ther). Others you can associate with a related word (*their* starts off like *they*).

The following chart lists some of the common exceptions to the traditional rule. The words in the first three columns are all spelled with *ei* even though they do not immediately follow a *c* or have a long *a* sound. The words in the last column are exceptions to the rule because they are spelled with *ie* even though the *ie* follows *c.*

EXCEPTIONS TO THE RULE			
ei Exceptions			*ie* Exceptions
counterfeit	heir	sheik	ancient
either	leisure	sleight	conscience
foreign	neither	sovereign	efficient
forfeit	seismology	their	financier
heifer	seize	weird	sufficient
height	seizure		

Once you master the traditional rule and memorize the exceptions to it, you should have no trouble with *ie* and *ei* words.

EXERCISE D: Spelling *ie* and *ei* Words. Write the incomplete word from each sentence, filling in either *ie* or *ei.*

EXAMPLE: We were not sure we had suffic __ __ nt money.

           sufficient

1. Her ach _ _ vements in the field of modern art are great.
2. He was warned to stay out of misch _ _ f.
3. She felt a moment of anx _ _ ty as she entered the room.
4. The fr _ _ ght train derailed.
5. They bel _ _ ve in freedom of action.
6. Dave tried to dec _ _ ve me with false evidence.
7. The soldiers began a s _ _ ge of the fort.
8. She asked the store clerk for a rec _ _ pt.
9. When you rec _ _ ve the note, I will be on my way home.
10. In what century did Queen Elizabeth I r _ _ gn?

Words Ending in -*cede*, -*ceed*, and -*sede*

One small group of words with the endings -*cede*, -*ceed*, and -*sede* often proves troublesome to spellers. The best way to handle those words that end with these suffixes is to memorize the correct spellings.

Memorize the words that end in -*cede*, -*ceed*, and -*sede*.

The chart below lists the words with these endings that you are most likely to use in your writing.

Words Ending in -*cede*	Words Ending in -*ceed*	Words Ending in -*sede*
concede	exceed	supersede
intercede	proceed	
precede	succeed	
recede		
secede		

EXERCISE E: Spelling Words Ending in -*cede*, -*ceed*, and *sede*. Write the incomplete word for each sentence, filling in the blanks with -*cede*, -*ceed*, or -*sede*.

EXAMPLE: With much practice we knew we would
suc _ _ _ _.

succeed

1. The profits this year are expected to ex _ _ _ _ those of last year.
2. Despite the setback, we must pro _ _ _ _ according to our plan.
3. As we drove away, we watched the town re _ _ _ _ into the distance.
4. The candidate is expected to con _ _ _ _ the election in the morning.
5. Only if his friends inter _ _ _ _ with the authorities will he be safe.
6. It is unlikely that he will suc _ _ _ _ in his efforts.
7. The group discussion will pre _ _ _ _ the serving of refreshments.
8. That country might se _ _ _ _ from the organization.
9. Clare will super _ _ _ _ Chuck as vice president.
10. I will gladly con _ _ _ _ that I was wrong.

DEVELOPING WRITING SKILLS: **Using Spelling Rules.**

Write a sentence of your own using each of the following items. In addition, include at least one plural form of a noun in each sentence. (The blanks below stand for *ie* and *ei*.)

EXAMPLE: un- + -rely- + -able

> Those who are unreliable test the patience of their friends.

1. re- + -appear- + -ance
2. un- + -necessary- + -ly
3. un- + -notice- + -able
4. ach _ ve- + -ment
5. un- + -bel _ ve- + -able
6. un- + -certain- + -ty
7. ir- + -reverse- + -ible
8. un- + -remark- + -able
9. un- + -like- + -ly
10. ir- + -retr _ ve- + -able
11. s _ ze- + -ure
12. un- + -hyg _ ne- + -ic
13. in- + -conven _ nce
14. dis- + -serve- + -ice
15. re- + -occur- + -ence
16. in- + -consider- + -able
17. un- + -change- + -able
18. un- + -debate- + -able
19. in- + -describe- + -ably
20. dis- + -place- + -ment

Skills Review and Writing Workshop

Spelling Improvement

CHECKING YOUR SKILLS

Find all the misspelled words in the following paragraph and write them correctly.

(1) The preciding year has been one of the best in the history of our school. (2) Every atheletic team had a winning season. (3) This was the first time the teams had been so successful, according to our principle Mrs. Hawley. (4) Attendence at all the athletic events has also been extremely high. (5) We achieved the highest overall average in mathamatics in the state. (6) As a result, the superentendant gave us a special award. (7) Two juniors performed with the city's synphony orchestra. (8) Both played piano soloes on separate occasions. (9) We also took inumerable prizes at the county science fair. (10) It's hard to beleive we did so well, but it gives us a record to beat for next year.

USING SPELLING SKILLS IN WRITING
Writing A Dialogue

Misspelled words in your writing can distract and confuse your readers. Write an imaginary dialogue between yourself and your favorite TV or movie star. Follow the steps below to write the dialogue, and watch out for spelling errors.

Prewriting: Think of some topics that you'd like to discuss with the star and try to imagine how he or she might respond.

Writing: Begin with the most important topic to capture the attention of your readers; then follow up with the other topics.

Revising: Check your sentences for varied openings and structures. Change any words which could be clearer or more descriptive. After you have revised, proofread carefully for spelling and other errors.

UNIT **VII**

Study and Research Skills

Chapter 32

Basic Study Skills

As you progress through school, you will probably find that your course work becomes increasingly challenging, requiring more study time. You may sometimes find it difficult to juggle your schoolwork and your other activities and responsibilities. In this chapter you will practice study skills that can help you make the most of the time you have available for studying.

32.1 Good Study Habits

Good study habits require time, organization, and practice. You need to choose a study area, schedule your study time, keep track of your assignments, and establish appropriate goals.

Choosing a Study Setting

To improve your study habits, you need a space in which to work and the appropriate equipment.

Establish a study area that works well for you.

First, set up a study area where there are no distractions. Associate your study area with studying only so that when you sit down there, you will be ready to work. Your desk or table should be well lighted and equipped with materials such as paper, pencils, pens, a ruler, a dictionary, and a clock.

EXERCISE A: **Evaluating Your Study Setting.** Write a paragraph describing your study setting and materials. Then, using the features of a good study setting listed on the previous page, write another paragraph explaining how your study setting could be improved.

Developing a Study Schedule

If you carefully plan the use of your time, you should have enough time for studying, extracurricular activities, chores, and relaxation. You should also be able to complete assignments on time without rushing.

Schedule regular periods for studying.

To help yourself make the best use of your time, make a study schedule that fits your own personal needs. First, block out areas of time in which you already have activities: the regular school day, sports practice, music lessons, dinner, and so on. Second, block out at least two hours a day for studying. Then, fill in the remaining time with leisure activities.

SAMPLE SCHEDULE	
Time	**Activity**
8:00–3:00	school
3:00–5:00	after-school activity
5:00–5:30	study period
5:30–6:30	dinner and relaxation
6:30–7:15	study period
7:15–7:30	break for relaxation
7:30–8:00	study period
8:00–9:00	TV viewing
9:00–9:45	study period
9:45–10:30	pleasure reading
10:30	end of evening

Once you have established a schedule that works for you, it is important that you stick to it. A good way to maintain your schedule is to evaluate it each week and make any changes that will make it work better. Then follow the revised schedule.

EXERCISE B: Planning Your Study Schedule. Create your own study schedule, using the model on the previous page. Follow the schedule for a week. At the end of the week, evaluate your schedule and make needed changes. Keep a copy in your notebook.

Keeping an Assignment Book

Instead of trusting your memory to recall the homework assignments from each class, write down assignments and projects in an assignment book. You can use the book to list both long- and short-term assignments.

Use an assignment book to record homework assignments and due dates.

One simple way to set up your assignment book is to make four columns on each page. Use one column for subjects, one for detailed descriptions of assignments, one for dates the assignments are due, and one for checks when the assignments are completed. Notice in the sample page from an assignment book below how a long-term science project has been divided into short-term goals that the student must meet in order to complete the project.

	Subject	Description	Date due	Completed
	Science	Science Fair Satellite Model	1/20	
		1. Do library research	10/2	✓
		2. Buy materials	10/10	✓
		3. Draw up plan with Joe	10/30	✓
		4. Submit plan to Mrs. J.	11/14	
		5. Meeting with Mrs. J.	11/17	

Assignments – September 19, 1986

EXERCISE C: Setting Up an Assignment Book. Set aside a special section in your binder or buy a notebook to use as an assignment book. Date each page and record assignments using the sample above as a model.

Setting Goals

Besides setting long- and short-term goals for specific assignments, you may also find it useful to set goals to improve your general study habits.

Set long- and short-term goals to improve your general study habits.

The chart below shows a plan that might be drawn up by a student who wants to improve his or her study schedule.

SETTING LONG- AND SHORT-TERM GOALS		
Long-term Goal: To improve my study schedule		
Short-term Goals	**Timetable**	**Comments**
Reduce time spent watching TV	1 week (by Oct. 7th)	Successfully completed
Practice completing all chores by 5 P.M.	2 weeks (by Oct. 14th)	Successfully completed
Increase study time to blocks of 40 minutes minutes before break	1 month (by Nov. 1st)	More practice needed; work on concentration

When you have set your long- and short-term goals, you should strive to reach each short-term goal by the date you have established for yourself. On that date, evaluate your work to see if you have mastered the skill and met your goal.

EXERCISE D: Setting Goals for Study Skills. Select one general study skill that you want to master. Divide that long-term goal into short-term goals. Then make a chart, using the one above as a model.

DEVELOPING WRITING SKILLS: Evaluating Your Study Habits. Write a paragraph about the quality of your study schedule, the usefulness of your assignment book, and the appropriateness of any long-term goals you have set. Identify the areas you need to work on and list one way you can improve in each area.

32.2 Methods of Taking Notes

Taking notes involves writing down the important ideas you hear or read so that you will remember them. This section will help you to take notes more effectively and more efficiently.

Keeping an Organized Notebook

A good notebook provides a daily record of what has been covered in class. It may also contain notes of what you have studied at home and highlights of material from your textbook.

Keep a notebook that is organized, complete, and neatly written.

The chart below lists ways to organize a binder notebook.

ORGANIZING YOUR NOTEBOOK
1. Use three-ring, loose-leaf paper for taking notes so that you can remove and rearrange pages in your notebook.
2. Use a set of three-ring dividers to separate each subject. Arrange the dividers in the order of your class schedule.
3. Keep all papers related to each subject within that subject's divider.
4. Place a copy of your class and study schedules on the inside front cover of your notebook.

EXERCISE A: Evaluating Your Notebook. Using the four points listed above, rate your notebook. If you are not following one or more of the suggestions, reorganize your notebook so that it can be a tool to help you study more efficiently.

Making Outlines

An *outline* is a method for taking notes that shows the relationship between main ideas and other ideas that support the main ideas. There are two kinds of outlines that can be useful in taking notes: *modified* outlines and *formal* outlines.

Modified Outlines. A modified outline consists of one or more headings or titles that present main ideas, each followed by a list of supporting information. The information under each heading may be shown by numbering, lettering, indenting, or using dashes. A modified outline is useful for rapid note-taking when you are listening in class or when you are reading.

Use a modified outline to take notes while listening or reading.

Notice how the modified outline after the following passage about the discovery of oxygen underlines the main idea and numbers the major details found in the passage.

PASSAGE: Joseph Priestly discovered oxygen in 1774 while heating a chemical—red oxide of mercury—that contained oxygen. As he heated the chemical, the oxygen escaped. To test if oxygen was escaping, he put a mouse in the jar with the gas. The mouse became more active. Then he put a burning candle in a jar with the gas and found that it burned more brightly. Finally Priestly even breathed the gas himself, and he began to feel very energetic.

MODIFIED OUTLINE: The Discovery of Oxygen ◄————Main idea
1. By Priestly in 1774
2. In red oxide of mercury
3. Mouse experiment
4. Candle experiment
5. Made everything come alive } Major details

A modified outline can also be used to organize an answer to an essay exam question or to list your ideas before writing a composition.

Formal Outlines. A formal outline goes beyond a modified outline by showing not only the major details under the main ideas but also the minor details under the major details. This much detail can sometimes be useful in the notes you take when you are listening or reading. It may be even more valuable when you prepare to give a speech, answer essay questions, or write a composition.

Use a formal outline to arrange ideas when preparing major written and oral assignments.

The chart below lists a few important rules that should be followed when making a formal outline.

RULES TO REMEMBER ABOUT FORMAL OUTLINES
1. Use Roman numerals to indicate main ideas. Use capital letters to indicate major details. Use arabic numerals to indicate minor details.
2. Place a period after each numeral or letter.
3. Capitalize the first word in each line.
4. Use indentation to indicate importance. Main ideas begin at the left. Items begin farther to the right as they become less important.
5. Include at least two major details under each main idea. Include either two or more minor details or no minor details under each major detail.

There are two kinds of formal outlines: *topic outlines* and *sentence outlines*. A topic outline lists information in words or phrases; a sentence outline uses complete sentences. Notice that the following topic outline is brief, but it clearly shows the relationship between ideas.

TOPIC OUTLINE:

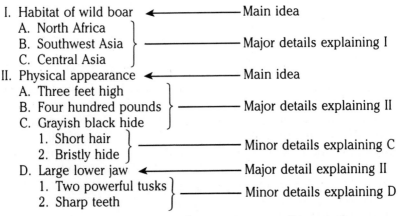

I. Habitat of wild boar ⟵——————— Main idea
   A. North Africa ⎫
   B. Southwest Asia ⎬ ——————— Major details explaining I
   C. Central Asia ⎭
II. Physical appearance ⟵——————— Main idea
   A. Three feet high ⎫
   B. Four hundred pounds ⎬ ——————— Major details explaining II
   C. Grayish black hide ⎭
      1. Short hair ⎫ ——————— Minor details explaining C
      2. Bristly hide ⎭
   D. Large lower jaw ⟵——————— Major detail explaining II
      1. Two powerful tusks ⎫ ——————— Minor details explaining D
      2. Sharp teeth ⎭

On the next page is part of a sentence outline on the same subject. Note that information is listed in complete sentences. The sentence outline is the most specific kind of outline. A

720

sentence outline can be used when you are organizing your thoughts for a speech or a composition.

SENTENCE OUTLINE:

I. The wild boar inhabits several continents.
  A. The wild boar lives in North Africa.
  B. It can also be found in Southwest Asia.
  C. It also lives in Central Asia.

EXERCISE B: Making a Modified Outline. Take notes in a modified outline form on a section from one of your textbooks.

EXERCISE C: Making a Formal Topic Outline. Using the same textbook section that you used for Exercise B, make a formal topic outline of the material.

EXERCISE D: Making a Formal Sentence Outline. Outline a composition you might write on how to do something, such as how to train a dog or how to set up a tent.

Writing Summaries

In some situations you may not have time or space to write more than a few sentences. For this kind of note-taking, a *summary* is useful. To *summarize* means to write the main ideas in a few sentences of your own.

Use a summary to take notes when you need to remember only the main ideas.

Notice that the summary of the following passage is a general restatement in two sentences of the most important information in the passage.

PASSAGE: The harp seal, *Pagophilis groenlandicus*, "the ice-lover from Greeland," wanders in summer over much of the Arctic. It ranges north of Svalbard, Franz Joseph Land, and Novaya Zemlya to within 500 miles of the Pole. It hunts the waters around all of Greenland except the northern tip. It roams westward past

721

Baffin Island and into Hudson Bay, eastward past Severnaya Zemlya to the Taymyr Peninsula in the Soviet Union. In October and November, when the northern seas begin to freeze, the seals turn south. The pack ice marches after them, and the seals retreat before it, hundreds of thousands of them. In February and March when the sea ice to the south is thickest—safest for rearing pups—the females haul out. They give birth on the frozen ocean off the Magdalen Islands in the Gulf of St. Lawrence, off Labrador, off eastern Greeland, and in the White Sea off the Soviet Union.—Kenneth Brower

SUMMARY: In the summer, harp seals inhabit the northern seas from the Pole west to Hudson Bay and east to the Soviet Union. As the northern seas freeze in the fall, the seals move south to the Gulf of St. Lawrence and the White Sea, where they have their young on the ice in the late winter.

EXERCISE E: Writing Summaries. Read a newspaper article of three to five paragraphs and summarize it. Exchange your article and summary for those of another student. Evaluate the other student's summary for accuracy and thoroughness. Then make any useful changes in your own summary.

DEVELOPING WRITING SKILLS: Evaluating Your Note-Taking Skills. Write a paragraph about the notes you took in outline form for Exercises B, C, and D, making sure to include in your evaluation the answers to the questions below.

1. Does your modified outline list supporting ideas under the main ideas?
2. Does your formal topic outline provide more detail than your modified outline on the same material?
3. Do your topic and sentence outlines have at least two subpoints or no subpoints for each major detail?
4. Is there a period after each number or letter in your topic and sentence outlines?
5. Is the first word of each line in your topic and sentence outlines capitalized?

Skills Review and Writing Workshop

Basic Study Skills

CHECKING YOUR SKILLS

Make a topic outline of the following paragraph.

Not every American President has won the popular vote. In 1876, for example, Rutherford B. Hayes received fewer votes than his opponent Samuel J. Tilden. However, Hayes came in one vote ahead of Tilden in the Electoral College vote, taken state by state, not voter by voter. The election in that year was a slow one, with late and disputed results coming in from four states. Twelve years later, in 1888, Benjamin Harrison lost the popular vote to Grover Cleveland but, like Hayes, won the Electoral College vote. Cleveland, who had been elected in 1884, stepped down from the Presidency. Four years later, however, in 1892, he beat Harrison both in popular vote and in the Electoral College and became the only President to fill two terms that were not consecutive.

USING STUDY SKILLS IN WRITING
Writing a Summary of a Poem

Summaries can help you see what is important in a reading assignment or even in a story or a poem. Follow the steps below to write a summary of a poem.

Prewriting: Carefully read a poem of ten to twenty lines over twice. Why was this poem written? What is the author trying to communicate? Take notes to help answer these questions.

Writing: In one or two sentences, state what you believe is the main idea behind the poem.

Revising: Read your summary over as if you had never read the poem. Rewrite to make the summary a better reflection of the poem. After you have revised, proofread carefully.

Chapter 33

Critical-Thinking Skills

Critical thinking is the process of analyzing, applying, and evaluating information. You may receive this information from observation, reading, or listening. In this chapter you will practice skills that help you think clearly and effectively when you read, write, speak, and listen.

33.1 Forms of Reasoning

One important aspect of critical thinking is analyzing information so you can decide whether it is *reliable*. A second important aspect of critical thinking is distinguishing between *valid* and *invalid* forms of reasoning so you can decide whether the author's position or argument holds up when you analyze it.

Using Fact and Opinion

Your first step in thinking critically is to analyze the material you are working with to find out if it is *reliable*. Unless the material is reliable, you will not be able to think clearly and effectively about it.

Analyze material first to decide if it is reliable.

In order to decide whether the material is reliable, you must be able to distinguish between fact and opinion.

724

Fact. A statement of *fact* is one that can be *verified,* or proved true. A fact is objective and can be verified by written or human authority, personal observation, or experimentation.

FACT: Some caves are vast networks of passages and chambers and contain underground lakes or waterfalls.

FACT: The expedition entered the cave at 12:15 P.M. AT 3 P.M. the storm broke.

The first example above is a fact that can be verified by checking a written authority such as an encyclopedia. The second example can be verified by checking with a reliable person who observed the events.

Opinion. A statement of *opinion* is one that cannot be verified. An opinion is subjective and must be supported with related facts before it can be accepted as *valid*. An opinion may express a person's feelings about something. It may express a judgment or make a prediction based on facts.

PERSONAL FEELING: No one ought to risk going into a cave.

JUDGMENT: Cave exploration during a storm is risky because of the danger of flooding.

PREDICTION: The members of the expedition will all get to a point of safety above the floodline in the cave.

The first example above is a purely personal statement, unsupported by facts, and cannot be considered a valid opinion. The second opinion expresses a judgment based on facts and is a valid opinion. The third opinion is a prediction and can be proved true only after the event has actually happened. This prediction is an invalid opinion since it is not supported by facts.

When you think critically, you ask yourself questions to help you analyze material. The following chart lists questions to ask yourself when distinguishing between fact and opinion statements.

FACT/OPINION STATEMENTS

1. Can the statement be checked to *verify,* or prove, that it is true? How? (dictionary, reference book, human authority, personal observation, or experimentation)

2. If the statement is opinion, do related facts support it to make the opinion valid?

EXERCISE A: Analyzing Fact and Opinion Statements.
First, identify each of the following statements as *fact* or *opinion*. Then analyze whether each fact statement is *true* or *false,* and whether each opinion statement is *valid* or *invalid.*

1. *Raiders of the Lost Ark* is the best movie ever made.
2. Jan must be a great swimmer; she has won six swim meets.
3. William Shakespeare wrote *A Midsummer Night's Dream.*
4. The World Trade Center is the world's tallest building.
5. Pete Rose broke Ty Cobb's record for total career hits.
6. The largest state in the United States is Alaska.
7. Yellowstone National Park was the first national park.
8. This winter will be a warm one.
9. With practice, students can double their reading speed.
10. Green plants use carbon dioxide and oxygen to make food.

EXERCISE B: Analyzing Fact and Opinion in Writing.
Read the following *New York Times* editorial and list the fact and opinion statements it contains. Determine whether each fact statement is true or false and whether each opinion is valid or invalid.

Taxonomists have argued for years about how to classify the giant and lesser pandas. Some say pandas are cousins to bears, others affirm their kinship to raccoons. Now, alas, the argument has been settled. The giant panda is more like a bear, the lesser panda is a close cousin to the raccoon.

How was the genealogy resolved? Having examined the pattern of evolution recorded in the molecules of pandas, bears, and raccoons, scientists from the National Cancer Institute and the Smithsonian report the following in the magazine *Nature.*

Once upon a time there was a furry quadruped that was neither bear nor raccoon. About 40 million years ago it evolved into two distinct species, bears and raccoons. Then, the raccoon line diverged into raccoons proper and the lesser panda.

Bears ambled on until 20 million years ago when the giant panda branched off as a separate species. The bear line radiated into the spectacled bear and the brown, black, and sun bears.

Bears roar, the giant panda bleats. Bears hibernate and eat meat; the giant panda doesn't hibernate and eats bamboo. It even looks like the lesser panda and its raccoon cousins. But forget all that: the giant panda is a mere bear.

726

Using Valid Reasoning

A second important step in thinking critically is to think logically, or reasonably, about the material that you have. When you think logically, you are able to draw valid conclusions.

Think logically to draw valid conclusions.

Following are discussions of four forms of reasoning: *inference, generalization, analogy,* and *cause and effect*. Each of these forms of reasoning can be used to reach valid conclusions or can be misused to reach invalid conclusions.

Inference. Sometimes the main idea of what you read or hear is *implied,* or stated indirectly. You must observe the details and make inferences about what you think is the main idea. Your conclusion must be based on the information that you have. Inference can also be used to predict reasonably or logically what will happen.

A *valid inference* is a reasonable interpretation of the information that is given. An *invalid inference* is an interpretation that is not consistent with the information that is given.

VALID INFERENCE: The two boys look exactly alike. Therefore, they are twins.

INVALID INFERENCE: The two boys are with Mr. Ruiz. Therefore, they are his sons.

The first inference is valid because it is logical to conclude that two people who look exactly alike are twins. The second example above is an invalid inference because there is no information given to suggest that the boys are his sons.

The chart below lists questions you should ask yourself when you analyze inferences.

VALID/INVALID INFERENCES

1. What details do you observe as clues to the main idea?
2. What main ideas do you conclude from these details?
3. Does your conclusion follow logically from the inferences you have made?
4. Are there any other interpretations of the details that lead to a different conclusion?

727

Generalization. A generalization is a statement that is made on the basis of a number of particular facts or cases. A *valid* generalization is a statement that holds true in a large number of cases or is supported by evidence. A *hasty* generalization is a statement that is made about a large number of cases or a whole group on the basis of a few examples and without taking into account exceptions or qualifying factors.

VALID: There are 74 girls and 66 boys in my ninth-grade class. Therefore, most of the students in my class are girls.

HASTY: My ninth-grade class has more girls than boys. Therefore, all ninth grades have more girls than boys.

The second example above is a hasty generalization because a statement is made about a whole group (all ninth-grade classes) based on only one example (my ninth-grade class).

The following chart lists questions to ask yourself to help you distinguish between valid and hasty generalization.

VALID/HASTY GENERALIZATIONS
1. What facts or cases are being presented as evidence to support the general statement?
2. Are there any exceptions to the statement?
3. Are enough cases or examples being presented?

Analogy. An analogy is a comparison between two things that are similar in some ways but are essentially unlike. A *complete* analogy is one that compares two different objects or events that are similar in some important way. The two things are compared to show the truth of one of them by showing its similarity to something more familiar. An *incomplete* analogy is one that overlooks essential dissimilarities between the two things being compared.

COMPLETE: Like the human brain, a computer stores and processes information.

INCOMPLETE: A computer is like the human brain.

The first analogy is complete because it explains the functions of a computer by comparing them to the more familiar functions of the human brain. The second analogy is incomplete because a computer and the human brain are essentially dissimilar in structure and origin. The following chart offers suggested questions you can ask yourself when analyzing analogies.

COMPLETE/INCOMPLETE ANALOGIES
1. How are the two things being compared essentially different?
2. How are the two things alike? Is the comparison logical?
3. What is the truth that the comparison tries to show?

Cause and Effect. Sometimes people conclude that one event has caused a second event because the first event happened immediately before the second. A *cause-and-effect sequence* is one in which something is caused by one or more events that occurred before it. An *unrelated sequence* is one in which the first event did not cause the second event. A sequence of events does not mean that the first event caused the later event.

CAUSE AND EFFECT: Thunder occurs after lightning because the lightning causes the air to heat and expand explosively.

UNRELATED: The telephone rang immediately after the lightning flashed.

Sometimes an event that has many causes is described as having a single cause. This oversimplification is another type of invalid cause-and-effect reasoning.

EXAMPLE: Taxation without representation caused the American Revolution.

The above example ignores the many other factors that were major causes of the American Revolution.

The following chart lists questions to ask yourself when you analyze cause-and-effect relationships.

CAUSE/EFFECT RELATIONSHIPS
1. What evidence is there that the first event or situation could have caused the second?
2. What other events may have caused the second event?
3. Could the second event have occurred without the first?

729

EXERCISE C: Analyzing Forms of Reasoning. First, identify the form of reasoning (*inference*, *generalization*, *analogy*, *cause and effect*) found in each of the following statements. Then explain whether each conclusion is *valid* or *invalid*.

1. Meat prices will go up since the cost of raising cattle has risen sharply this year.
2. Glass reflects light like a block of ice.
3. Lowering the voting age means our country will get a President who has no experience.
4. Since plants need light to grow, water your plants daily.
5. The high cost of college limits education to the rich.
6. Sarah placed second in the tennis tournament, so she must be a good player.
7. Wearing this shirt to the exam will help me get an "A."
8. Case studies show that people who smoke cigarettes increase their chances of getting lung cancer.
9. Watching television causes students to get poor grades.
10. The nervous system is like a mission control center.

EXERCISE D: Correcting Invalid Reasoning. Rewrite each sentence in Exercise C above that contains invalid reasoning. Rewrite using clear, logical thinking.

DEVELOPING WRITING SKILLS: Analyzing Writing. Carefully read the following passage. Analyze each statement and decide whether the information is *reliable* and the author's reasoning is *valid*. List your sources.

The American Civil War began after South Carolina seceded from the Union. The cause of the Civil War was the disagreement over slavery. Everyone in the North felt slavery was wrong, but everyone in the South supported it. When the war first began, the South believed that other countries would be behind it. The South believed that England and France would use their modern navies to crush the northern fleet that blockaded the southern ports. However, the Union blockade, like a cobra, circled the southern ports. With its ports blockaded, the South was unable to import goods it needed and to export cotton to England and France. England had once experienced a civil war, so many people in England wanted to recognize the South as a separate state. If England had done so, the outcome of the war might have been different. President Lincoln proved to be a great leader. He issued the Emancipation Proclamation that set all slaves free. After that, many blacks enlisted in the Union Army. This rise in enlistment caused the North to win the war.

Language and Thinking 33.2

Human beings think largely by means of language. Language is the tool that we use to make sense out of the world. Until we can express a thought in words, we usually do not understand the thought and cannot explain it to someone else. In addition to thoughts, we also express feelings by means of words. One important aspect of critical thinking is analyzing the ways a writer or speaker uses language to express thoughts and feelings. Another important aspect of critical thinking is to evaluate an author's purpose for using language.

Uses of Language

Language can be used in various ways. It is important to learn how to recognize when language is being used to communicate honestly and when it is being used to distort information and manipulate people.

Learn to identify different uses of language.

Following are some of the ways language can be used to change the meaning of a fact or an event.

Word Meanings. The *denotation* of a word is its literal or exact meaning and has a neutral tone. The *connotation* of a word is its suggested or implied meaning and has a positive or negative tone. Words get connotative meanings from the way they have been used by people over the years. Certain connotations are emotionally loaded and change meaning. The following statements are similar, and yet each would have quite a different effect on someone who had just given the speech.

DENOTATION: You delivered your speech in an even voice.

CONNOTATIONS: You delivered your speech in a firm voice.

You delivered your speech in a monotone.

731

In the first statement, the word "even" has a neutral tone. In the second statement, the word "firm" has a positive tone and suggests authority and reliability. In the third statement, the word "monotone" has a negative tone, suggesting that the speaker's voice was flat and boring.

Self-Important Language. Self-important or inflated language consists of scholarly, technical, or scientific words and overly long phrases. Self-important language is sometimes used to impress the listener or reader. Sometimes it is used to conceal rather than reveal the meaning behind the words. *Jargon* is the specialized vocabulary used by people in a profession or hobby. Jargon appears to be scientific or technical but actually may obscure ideas you could readily understand if they were stated more clearly and simply.

SELF-IMPORTANT LANGUAGE:	It is imperative that we pursue all viable options to seek out financial resources for this endeavor.
DIRECT LANGUAGE:	We need to find as many ways as we can to raise money for this project.
JARGON:	The military personnel pacified the area.
DIRECT LANGUAGE:	The soldiers killed enemy troops.

Slanting. All writers and speakers select and arrange words to communicate the meaning they want to convey. Even when a person describes something fairly and objectively, that person slants or describes the object from the way he or she sees it. However, slanting can be used dishonestly. Dishonest slanting can occur when a writer uses words with positive or negative connotations to distort the truth in order to support an opinion. Dishonest slanting can also occur when the writer presents only the facts that support the writer's point of view and leaves out other significant facts.

STATEMENT:	Crime in the United States' cities is increasing. Between the beginning of January and the end of June, crime increased 6.3 percent in urban areas.
FACT LEFT OUT:	During the first six months of the year, crime decreased five percent in seven cities.

The first statement is a dishonest use of slanting because the fact is omitted that crime *decreased* in several cities.

EXERCISE A: **Analyzing Uses of Language.** Analyze each pair of sentences for denotation/connotation, self-important/direct language, and honest/dishonest slanting.

1. Carmine offered a lame excuse for being late.
   Carmine explained her reason for being late.
2. The military effected a transfer of the agrarian population.
   The soldiers took the people away from their farms.
3. We must devise a plan that will incentivize the sales force to perform at higher levels.
   We must find a way to get our salespeople to sell more.
4. The flowers are growing in the garden.
   The fragrant roses are blooming in the garden.
5. The pilot had difficulty stopping the plane before it went off the end of the runway.
   The pilot had difficulty stopping the plane before it reached the end of the runway since the brakes had failed.

EXERCISE B: **Analyzing and Evaluating Uses of Language.** Carefully read the following passage. Analyze all the uses of connotation, inflated language, and slanting. Then, evaluate whether the author's purpose is to communicate ideas clearly and honestly. If not, explain the purpose.

Decline in students' educational performance is the result of disturbing inadequacies in the way the educational process itself is constructed. It is not our new school buildings or fancy enrichment programs that will restore the good old values of hard work and the three R's to our halls of learning. "Back to Basics" must be the watchword of every school's educational policy. In fact, looking at the lamentable past, it is the only feasible route for our educators to tread in revitalizing our educational institutions. If we pursue our goal with singleminded purpose, we can dispel the mists that cloud our vision like a wet blanket and concentrate on graduating students with a sound knowledge of basic educational skills.

DEVELOPING WRITING SKILLS: **Using Critical Thinking in Writing.** Using the critical thinking skills you have learned in this chapter, rewrite the passage in Exercise B above so that it communicates in a clear, logical, honest way.

Skills Review and Writing Workshop

Critical-Thinking Skills

CHECKING YOUR SKILLS

Rewrite the paragraph, correcting all examples of unreliable information, invalid reasoning, and misuses of language.

Television is the most important influence on people in the world today. Everyone watches it. Television has produced an oral culture so that people no longer read. Students get all of their information from television. In fact, television characters are like a family to those who watch the programs. People learn to behave like their favorite characters. Unfortunately, teenagers who watch violent programs go out and commit violent crimes. Since young children cannot tell the difference between programs and advertisements, advertisers gain a hold over viewers. We ought not to watch it as much as we do.

USING CRITICAL-THINKING SKILLS IN WRITING
Writing a Persuasive Article

Serious thinkers know the importance of honest thinking and valid reasoning in persuading readers to accept their points of view. Follow the steps below to write a persuasive article.

Prewriting: Choose an issue about which you feel strongly. First, make a list of the facts of the issue. Then, list your opinions, taking notes on how the facts support them. Then, list the opposing opinions with notes on how the facts support them.

Writing: Begin with a paragraph that tells the main facts concerning the issue and states your thesis. Then, present your arguments for your point of view, together with an honest evaluation of the opposing point of view. Write a concluding statement that sums up your reasons for your view.

Revising: Read your article to make sure that your reasoning is valid and that you have not used slanting to present opinion as fact or present only facts that support your point of view. After you have revised, proofread carefully.

34

Reading and Test-Taking Skills

Your teachers in earlier years stressed learning to read; now the stress is on reading to learn. In this chapter you will learn ways to improve your skills in reading books related to your schoolwork. You will also learn various reading styles that are appropriate for different kinds of reading material.

In school you are often tested on the material you have studied to see how well you have learned it. Few people like taking tests, but the fear of taking tests can be greatly reduced. In the final section of this chapter you will learn ways to develop your test-taking skills and build your self-confidence.

34.1
Reading Skills

You cannot read a textbook in the same way that you read a novel. Rather than reading a textbook from beginning to end, you can use reading skills that will save you time and effort.

Reading Textbooks

Most of the reading you do in school involves textbooks, specifically English, social studies, and science textbooks.

A good way to start improving your textbook reading skills is to become familiar with the parts of your textbooks. Most textbooks include a number of helpful sections at the front and back. These sections can help you become familiar with the contents of the book. You can also use some of these sections as guides when you are studying.

Identify and make use of the special sections at the front and the back of your textbooks.

Not all of your textbooks will have all of the sections mentioned here, nor will you need to use all of them regularly.

One of the best ways to become familiar with a textbook is to look first at the *table of contents*, which is found in the front of the textbook. It will show you how the book is organized by giving a list of the units and chapters in the book and indicating the pages where topics can be found. The list of chapters and their contents also provides a good overview of the material covered in the text.

USES OF THE TABLE OF CONTENTS

1. To locate general information.
2. To get an overview of the book while previewing.
3. To test your recall of information in each of the chapters while reviewing for a unit test or final exam.

The *preface* or *introduction* to a textbook, generally located just after or just before the table of contents, states the author's purpose in writing the book. It may also explain how to use the special features of the book. You should read this information and then take advantage of it as you read the book.

The *index* is found in the back of the textbook. It lists alphabetically all of the topics covered in the textbook and the pages on which they can be found. You should use this section to locate specific information. By consulting the index, you can turn directly to the information that you need.

The *glossary*, located near the index in the back of many textbooks, provides a list of terms with definitions. Generally, it will include only specialized words and related definitions taken directly from the textbook. The glossary will thus give

736

you the meanings of the terms you must know in order to understand the textbook.

The *appendix*, if the book has one, is also found in the back of the textbook. It contains a variety of information that the author considers useful to a student studying the subject of the book. This information may include charts, lists, documents, essays, or almost any other kind of material. Using the appendix can often free you from having to go to other books to locate relevant information.

If you do want to consult outside sources on your subject, the *bibliography* can be a valuable tool. The bibliography includes books and articles that the author has referred to in writing the textbook as well as other books and articles you might want to read in connection with a particular subject.

EXERCISE A: Examining Your Textbooks. Examine two of your textbooks to become acquainted with their special sections. Answer the following questions for each book.

1. According to the table of contents, how many units and chapters does the text have? Are chapters divided into smaller sections in the table of contents? What additional facts can you learn from the table of contents?
2. If there is a preface, what does it contain?
3. What are two specific pieces of information you can learn from the index?
4. Does the text have a glossary? If so, what are two pieces of information you can learn from it?
5. Does the text have an appendix? If so, what kind of information does it contain?

Using the SQ4R Method

You can also use the organization of a textbook in studying individual assignments. All you need to do is master the following six skills: *S*urvey, *Q*uestion, *R*ead, *R*ecord, *R*ecite, and *R*eview. The SQ4R method will guide you as you read, and it will later help you recall information.

Use the SQ4R method to gain a better understanding of textbook material.

The SQ4R method can help you spend your time more efficiently as you increase your comprehension skills.

SQ4R: STEPS IN READING TEXTBOOKS	
Preparing for reading:	*Survey* for an overview of the material
Focusing your reading:	*Question* before you read each section
	Read to answer the questions
	Record by taking notes on the main ideas and major details
Remembering what you read:	*Recite* by reading your notes aloud
	Review on a regular basis

The first step, *surveying*, allows you to become acquainted with what you will be reading. When you survey textbook material, you should notice these features: titles, headings, and subheadings; words in italics or bold print; introductions and summaries; pictures and captions; and questions at the end of a section or chapter. The survey should take no more than a few minutes.

The second step, *questioning*, is a good way to force yourself to think about the material before you read it. As you come to each heading and subheading, ask yourself what might be covered under the heading or subheading. Turn headings and subheadings into questions by asking *who, what, when, where, why,* and *how* about the headings. Your ability to ask yourself questions can help you focus on the main ideas and major details as you read.

The third step, *reading*, is the time to develop maximum comprehension. As you read, try to find the answers to the questions you posed in the previous step. In addition, try to determine the main ideas and major details of the material. Having prepared for your careful reading with a preview and questions, you should be able to achieve at least 70 or 80 percent comprehension.

The fourth step, *recording*, involves taking notes on the main ideas and major details. Recording information is one of the best ways of remembering what you have read. When you organize the ideas in your mind as you read and then write the

738

ideas down in outline form, you are improving your chances of remembering the material.

The fifth step, *reciting*, reinforces what you have already learned. It is particularly valuable if you seem to learn best through listening. There are a number of ways to carry out this step of the SQ4R method.

METHODS OF RECITATION

1. Recite the information you want to master aloud. This information may come from the textbook or from your notes.

2. Mentally recite information that you want to remember. Go through the information in your mind the same way you would if you said it aloud.

3. Read summaries, outlines, or other notes into a tape recorder. Then play back the tape several times.

4. Pair up with a classmate for a question-and-answer session. Change roles so that you are able to ask as well as answer questions. Both asking and answering will help you study.

The last step, *reviewing*, will help ensure that your time has been well spent. When you review, you should repeat some of the previous steps. For example, you might want to reread your notes and look again at the headings and subheadings of your textbook. When you review is almost as important as how you review. You should never allow so much time to elapse that the material seems unfamiliar to you. In order to master material thoroughly, you will need to review it a number of times before taking a test on it.

EXERCISE B: Surveying and Questioning. Choose a chapter from one of your textbooks. Read all the chapter headings and subheadings for this chapter. Then go back and turn each heading and subheading into a question.

EXERCISE C: Reading and Recording. Using the same textbook chapter you used for Exercise B, read and take notes on the chapter. Write the main ideas and major details in outline form.

EXERCISE D: Reciting and Reviewing. Using the outline you made for the textbook chapter in Exercise C, ask yourself and answer questions about material in that chapter. Or work with another student to ask and answer questions about the outlined material. Then review the material by asking yourself and answering questions about the chapter headings and sub-headings. Answer any review questions at the end of that chapter. If you cannot answer a question reread the passage that answers it.

Using Different Reading Styles

You can also improve your reading skills through knowledge of different reading styles. The three types of reading styles you need to know about and use are *phrase reading*, *skimming*, and *scanning*. Each of these three styles of reading has a different speed and a different purpose.

Learn to choose the style of reading suitable to your purpose and material.

In phrase reading (or careful reading) you should try to read as fast as you can with good understanding. Your goal should be to see words in groups. Your eyes and mind should work together to look for ideas.

In skimming, you should triple your normal rate of reading by skipping words so that you take in just enough information to get a general idea of the material.

In scanning, you should skip even more material than in skimming by moving your eyes very rapidly over lines and pages with the single purpose of finding a specific piece of information.

As a student, you will often need to use all three styles of reading. The chart on the next page further explains the styles of reading, when to use them, and what levels of comprehension to expect from each. Notice that comprehension should be high for phrase reading (at least 70 percent) and that it drops to 40 or 50 percent for skimming because you do not need to recall ideas thoroughly when you are skimming. Notice that the level of comprehension for scanning is 100 percent because you presumably find only the piece of information for which you are reading.

THREE STYLES OF READING

Style	Definition	Use	Comprehension
Phrase Reading	Reading groups of words without eliminating words to understand all of the material	For studying, solving problems, following directions	Lowest acceptable rate: 70–80%
Skimming	Skipping words in order to read rapidly and get a quick overview	For previewing, reviewing, and locating information	Lowest acceptable rate: 40–50%
Scanning	Reading in order to locate a particular piece of information	For research, reviewing, and finding information	Lowest acceptable rate: 100%

In most cases you will be using at least two out of three of the styles of reading each time you read. You should practice varying both your style and reading rate according to your purpose and the material you are reading. The chart below shows some possible ways of adjusting your reading style and rate.

VARYING YOUR READING STYLE AND READING RATE

Purpose: Reading to answer a specific question
Material: Reference book

1. Scan the index for the topic and page.
2. Locate the page and scan to locate the topic.
3. Skim to locate specific information on the topic.
4. Phrase read when the information is found.

Purpose: Studying for a test
Material: Notes

1. Skim your notes for a preview.
2. Phrase read the notes while writing summaries.
3. Skim the headings in your notes as a final review.

741

As you become familiar with the three styles of reading and their different speeds, you will learn to adjust your mind and eyes to the appropriate rate for the material you are reading.

EXERCISE E: Determining Which Style of Reading to Use. Decide which style or styles of reading you would use for each of the following purposes. Be prepared to explain your choices.

EXAMPLE: Finding an article in a magazine

scanning

1. Seeing if a book will be suitable for pleasure reading
2. Surveying the questions at the end of a chapter
3. Finding a word in a glossary of a textbook
4. Locating a particular place on a map
5. Reading and taking notes for a chapter test
6. Checking the contents of a book by using the index
7. Locating the time a bus should arrive using a bus schedule
8. Previewing a chapter
9. Reading a short story for an assignment in English class
10. Finding statistics about the population in a book of facts

Reading Critically

When you read, the first step is to read for comprehension so that you understand main ideas and major details. The second step is to read critically so that you understand more fully what you read. When you read critically, you ask questions to help you understand and analyze the ideas that an author presents. Then you evaluate how well the ideas are presented.

Read critically in order to question, analyze, and evaluate what you read.

In order to read critically, you first put together the earlier-learned reading-for-comprehension skills so that you can ask relevant questions about what you read. You must also read with an open mind and use critical-thinking skills to determine whether there is a difference between what is really being said and what you think is being said. The following chart lists the skills you need to become a critical reader. A full discussion of critical thinking is found in Chapter 33.

CRITICAL-READING SKILLS

1. The ability to differentiate between *fact* and *opinion*
2. The ability to recognize the author's *purpose* in writing
3. The ability to make *inferences* about purpose and characters
4. The ability to recognize the author's *tone* in writing
5. The ability to recognize *persuasive techniques* in writing

Fact and Opinion. If you do not distinguish between fact and opinion statements, you may be misled by what you read. When you read critically, you must analyze what you read to recognize the basis on which a statement is made. A statement of fact can be *verified,* or proved true by experimentation, records, or personal observation. A statement of opinion cannot be proved true. It must be *validated,* or supported, with valid authority or facts before it can be accepted. The following chart lists examples of fact and opinion statements and the sources to verify or validate them.

FACT AND OPINION STATEMENTS	
Fact Statements	**Sources to Verify**
The United States government has three branches. (True)	Encyclopedia, almanac, social studies text
Helium is lighter than oxygen. (True)	Experimentation, science textbook, encyclopedia
"The Raven" was written by Shirley Jackson. (False)	library, biographical dictionary
Opinion Statements	**Sources to Validate**
Scientists at Cornell feel that life was less stressful in past centuries since fewer people died of heart attacks, a stress-related disease. (Valid opinion)	Opinion is valid since it gives supporting fact and authority.
Life was easier a century ago because people did not have cars. (Invalid opinion)	Facts or authority must support this opinion before it is valid.

Author's Purpose. The next thing you do when you read critically is to determine why the author is writing. Is the author's purpose to inform you about something, to entertain you, or to convince you to buy something? The chart below lists commonly found purposes and clues to identifying them.

IDENTIFYING AUTHOR'S PURPOSE IN WRITING	
Purpose	**Informational Clues**
To inform	Series of factual statements that are verified by *experimentation, records,* or *personal observation*
To instruct	Sequential development of an idea or a process
To offer an opinion	Presentation of an issue with a predominant point of view backed up by valid authority
To sell	Persuasive techniques including facts and propaganda designed to sell an idea or a product
To entertain	Narration of an event in a humorous manner; often used to lighten a serious topic

Inference. Sometimes an author states his or her purpose in writing directly. More often, however, the purpose is *implied,* or stated indirectly. As you read, you must make *inferences,* or conclusions, about the author's purpose from clues you find in the reading. An inference is *valid* if your interpretation of the clues follows from the information the author gives.

VALID INFERENCE: Justin has won six major art awards, so he must be a talented artist.

INVALID INFERENCE: Justin is a talented artist, so he should be editor of the art magazine.

To infer that Justin is interested in or capable of being editor of the art magazine does not follow from the information given. The information given is that he is a *talented artist*.

744

Tone. Closely allied with the author's purpose is the tone of his or her writing. Tone is the attitude that the author has toward the topic. The author's attitude toward the topic affects the way you are expected to respond to that topic. Read the following two statements on the same topic and explain how you respond to each.

STATEMENT ONE: The extensive highway project has continued for several years at an annually increasing expense of one million dollars.

STATEMENT TWO: The ill-planned highway project has draggged on for six years at an ever-escalating annual expense of more than one million dollars.

The first statement presents the author's neutral attitude toward the topic. Most of the words are used in their *denotative,* or literal meaning to state information. The second statement presents the author's negative attitude toward the topic. Words such as "ill-planned," "dragged on," and "ever-escalating" have a *connotative,* or implied meaning that set the tone.

Persuasive Techniques. Writers can use the *connotation* of words to make you think or feel a certain way about the idea or product they are trying to sell you. Since writers can bend the truth to fit their purpose, you need to read critically to be aware of their persuasive techniques. The following are some commonly used persuasive techniques.

Jargon is language that appears to be scientific or technical but is vague and often meaningless. An author uses it to confuse or deceive about the real meaning behind the words.

JARGON: Due to business reversals the company is forced to eliminate your position.

DIRECT LANGUAGE: Because the company has lost money, you will lose your job.

Slanting is the use of loaded or prejudiced words that have a strong connotation to present only those facts that support the author's viewpoint. An author uses it to force the reader to make conclusions based on emotion rather than reason.

SLANTING: The President lurched hurriedly through the crowd.

OBJECTIVE LANGUAGE: The President moved quickly through the crowd.

745

EXERCISE F: Applying Critical-Reading Skills. Read the following passage and analyze how each of the following is used: *fact and opinion, author's purpose, tone,* and *persuasive techniques*. Refer to the skills you have studied in this section to develop your answers. Then evaluate how well the author has presented the material.

The computer is affecting the very fabric of society, causing both wonder and widespread apprehension. Is the computer a friend or enemy of man? Will it cause hopeless unemployment by speeding automation, that disquieting term that it has brought into the langauge? Will it devalue the human brain, or happily free it from drudgery? The answers are not all in yet, but one thing is already clear: swept forward by a great wave of technology, of which the computer is the ultimate expression, human society is surely headed for some deep-reaching changes that will prevent man from returning to an earlier, simpler way of life.

DEVELOPING WRITING SKILLS: Evaluating Your Reading Skills. After a week of practice, write a paragraph about your reading skills. Include the answers to the following.

1. Have you been using the special sections of your textbooks? Which ones are most useful?
2. Which steps of the SQ4R method have you found helpful?
3. Is your comprehension for phrase reading at least 70 percent?
4. When have you found scanning particularly useful?
5. What materials have you read recently where critical reading was necessary? Were you able to ask critical-reading questions to analyze and evaluate the material?
6. What do you need to concentrate on in the future in order to improve your reading skills?

34.2 Test-Taking Skills

Your performance on a test can be greatly improved if you prepare properly for the test, budget your time while you are taking the test, and master the various kinds of questions that are often found in tests. This section provides suggestions on how to improve all of these test-taking skills.

Taking Objective Tests

The actual taking of a test is a three-step process. First you must preview the test, then you must answer the questions, and finally you must proofread your answers to make sure you have not made any careless mistakes. You should make wise use of the test period by allowing yourself enough time to do each of these steps.

Budget your time between previewing the test, answering the questions, and proofreading.

You should always come to a test on time with the necessary equipment, such as pens, pencils, erasers, or any books you have been told to bring. When the test has been handed out and you have been told to begin, you should start your preview. Allow up to 15 percent of your time for previewing. The following chart lists some steps you might follow when you are previewing a test.

PREVIEWING THE TEST
1. Put your name on each sheet of paper you will hand in.
2. Skim through the entire test to get an overview of the format of the test and the types of questions that you will have to answer.
3. Decide on the time you plan to spend on the various sections of the test. Plan to devote the greatest amount of time to the questions that carry the most points or are the most difficult.

Once you have examined the test and decided on your approach, you are ready to answer the questions themselves. The following chart offers some suggestions on how to answer the questions.

ANSWERING THE QUESTIONS
1. If you are allowed to use clean scratch paper, jot down the information you do not want to forget.
2. Answer the easy questions in each section first.
3. Put a check beside difficult questions that you will want to come back to later.

747

Proofreading is the final step in taking a test. This step should take no more than 10 percent of your total time. The following chart explains what you should look for and check as you proofread a test.

PROOFREADING YOUR ANSWERS

---

1. Check to see that your name is on each sheet of paper used.
2. Check to see that you have followed directions completely.
3. Reread test questions and answers. Make sure you have answered all of the questions.

EXERCISE A: Improving Your Test-Taking Skills. Answer the following questions about your performance on a test you have taken recently.

1. Would your performance have been better if you had previewed the test more thoroughly?
2. Did you budget enough time for the hardest questions?
3. Did you put a check beside questions that you should have come back to later?
4. Did you miss any questions because you failed to proofread the test or proofread it poorly?
5. What could you have done to improve your performance?

Mastering Different Kinds of Objective Questions

If you are familiar with the different kinds of objective questions that are frequently asked on tests, you may improve your performance on the tests. It is also important to know various strategies for answering the different kinds of objective questions.

Use your knowledge of the kinds of questions that may be asked along with certain helpful procedures to achieve higher scores on objective tests.

The format of each objective test varies. However, there are some common guidelines that apply to all objective tests as shown in the chart on the following page.

GENERAL STRATEGIES FOR ANSWERING
OBJECTIVE QUESTIONS

1. Read each question at least *twice* before deciding on an answer.

2. Give only one answer to a question unless the instructions say otherwise. Your choices usually include a single *best* answer.

3. Answer all questions on the test. If you are not certain of an answer, make an educated guess *unless you have been told not to guess*.

4. Do not change your first answer unless you have a good reason to do so.

Besides these general suggestions for taking objective tests, you should recognize the nature of the different types of questions and the particular procedures that can make answering these questions easier.

Multiple Choice Questions. In most of your classes, you will frequently find multiple choice questions on objective tests. These questions usually include four or five possible answers. Out of the four or five answers, one or two are often obviously incorrect, one is often fairly close to the real answer, and the final incorrect answer is often very close to the real answer. You must know the material well in order to distinguish between this last incorrect answer and the correct answer. You should thus spend most of your time making your choice between these two answers. The following chart provides some hints for answering multiple choice questions.

ANSWERING MULTIPLE CHOICE QUESTIONS

1. Try to answer the question before looking at the possible answers. If your "instant response" is one of the possible answers, you can be almost certain that you have selected the correct answer.

2. If you are allowed to write on the test paper, eliminate obviously incorrect answers by crossing them out.

3. Change a question into a statement by inserting your answer. See if the statement makes sense.

749

The following question from a grammar test is an example of a multiple choice question. Try answering it before you look at the possible answers.

EXAMPLE: In the following sentence, which words function as adverbs?

    1. Quite unmistakably, the small dark figure winked back.

        a. quite, small, dark
        b. unmistakably, back
        c. small, winked, back
        d. quite, unmistakably, back
        e. quite, dark, figure, back

    Answer: d. quite, unmistakably, back

Matching Questions. Matching questions require that you connect items in one column with the items in a second column. Sometimes the two columns have an equal number of items, and sometimes the columns are unequal. The chart below offers some hints for answering matching questions.

ANSWERING MATCHING QUESTIONS

1. Determine immediately if there are an equal number of items in each column. Check the directions to see whether the items in the second column can be used more than once.

2. Read all the items in both columns before you try to match.

3. Work down the column matching the items you know first.

4. If you can write on the test paper, eliminate terms and words already used by lightly crossing them out.

5. When you come to a difficult item, attempt to recall all of the information you know concerning that item. This association process might provide a clue to the answer.

The following matching questions are from a vocabulary test. Cover the answers and try using the first, second, and fourth suggestions in the chart.

EXAMPLE: Match the words on the left with the definition on the right by writing the letter of the definition in the blank before the word.

750

—— 1. philanthropist   a. to beg; plead
—— 2. antipathy   b. to scold
—— 3. exasperate   c. face; appearance
—— 4. chide   d. strong dislike
—— 5. implore   e. one who loves people
                           f. to anger or irritate
                           g. muddy; cloudy

Answers: 1. e;   2. d;   3. f;   4. b;   5. a

True/False Questions. True/false questions usually look easy but can be very difficult. One word can make the difference between a true or false statement. The chart below lists suggestions for answering true/false questions.

ANSWERING TRUE/FALSE QUESTIONS

1. If you think a statement is true, make certain the entire statement is true. A statement that is only partially true is false.

2. Pay special attention to the word *not*. It can change the meaning of the statement.

3. Also, pay special attention to these words: *all, always, never, no, none, only*. Often, by limiting an idea too much, they make a statement false.

4. Finally, notice these words: *generally, little, most, much, often, some, sometimes, usually*. They often make a statement true.

Think about these ideas as you study the following questions.

EXAMPLE: Identify the following statements as true or false by writing *T* or *F* in the blank before each statement.

—— 1. You should review class notes on a regular basis.
—— 2. A study schedule is only necessary when you have a lot of homework.
—— 3. You should generally take study breaks every forty-five minutes or so.
—— 4. You never need to write down your study goals.

Answers: 1. T;   2. F;   3. T;   4. F

Fill-In Questions. Fill-in questions, also called short answer questions, require you to supply answers in your own words. The answers may be single words, short phrases, or short sentences. The only helpful clue to answering fill-in questions is to read the questions carefully to see if your answers make sense. Since there are few useful hints for answering fill-in questions, you should study the material especially thoroughly if you know a test will include this kind of question.

EXAMPLE: Answer the following question with words or phrases.

1. List two sound effects that Shakespeare's theater used.

a. _____

b. _____

Answers: a. trumpets and horns for battles
b. drums for thunder

EXERCISE B: Examining Questions for Objective Tests.
Using a subject you are studying in class—grammar, literature, spelling, or speech, for instance—prepare a short objective test on the material. Write five multiple choice questions, five matching questions, five true/false questions, and five fill-in questions. Exchange papers with another student and take the other student's test, writing your answers on a separate piece of paper. Exchange again and submit your own test and the other student's answers to your teacher.

DEVELOPING WRITING SKILLS: Evaluating Your Test-Taking Skills. Write a paragraph about your test-taking skills. Include the answers to the following questions.

1. Do you prepare thoroughly for your tests?
2. Do you come to tests equipped with pencil, paper, and other necessary material?
3. Do you read each question on a test at least twice before deciding on an answer?
4. Do you proofread all of your tests?
5. Which test-taking skills do you still need to work on?

Skills Review and Writing Workshop

Reading and Test-Taking Skills

CHECKING YOUR SKILLS

Read the following paragraph. Then match the words on the left with the definitions on the right by writing the number of the definition in the blank before the word.

Scientific research now indicates acid rain is developing into a national problem. Although *emissions* of sulfur dioxide, a major *precursor* of acid rain, have apparently *peaked* in the Northeast, they are increasing in the Southeast. Two general conclusions about acid rain can be made. First, acid rain is a man-made *phenomenon.* Second, crops are probably not affected significantly by acid rain. If they are, the effects can be *mitigated* so that crops grow normally.

_____ emission
_____ precursor
_____ phenomenon
_____ mitigated
_____ peaked

1. a person or thing that goes before
2. something discharged
3. reached the highest point
4. made milder, less severe
5. fact that is apparent to the senses and can be scientifically described

USING STUDY SKILLS IN WRITING:
Evaluating an Introduction

Select an introduction from one of your textbooks. Follow the steps below to write an evaluation of that introduction.

Prewriting: Did the introduction help you understand the purpose of the book? Did it point out the book's special features or special approach? If promises were made, did the book live up to them?

Writing: Your evaluation may be mixed. That is, you may praise some parts of the introduction and criticize others. Always substantiate your opinion with specifics.

Revising: Edit your evaluation to make it organized point by point. After you have revised, proofread carefully.

Chapter 35

Library and Reference Skills

One of the benefits of growing older is that you become able to obtain more information on your own. If you are curious about something, you can look it up.

The first section in this chapter explains how to find books and other materials in a library. The second section explains how to use certain reference books found in most libraries. The third section concentrates on how to use dictionaries.

35.1 Using the Library

What is a library? Is it simply a warehouse for books? Although a library does house books, its purpose is to make books and other resources readily available. Library materials are carefully organized so that they can be easily located.

The two libraries you probably know best are your school library and your public library. Both libraries contain many resources: fiction and nonfiction books, reference books, periodicals, records, tapes, and microfilms. While your school library has materials needed for school projects, as well as many books for leisure reading, your community library probably provides even more resources and services.

Both libraries are there to serve you. All they ask in return is careful treatment of library material and a relatively low noise level.

Using the Card Catalog

How can you find which books a library has without wandering through the stacks of shelves and skimming the titles? The library's central source of information for this is the *card catalog*. It gives a systematic listing of the library's materials and provides a way of finding those materials.

Use the card catalog to find information about a library's books and other materials.

The card catalog consists of small drawers that contain cards listing books alphabetically. The drawers have labels that tell you which section of the alphabet is covered by the cards in the drawer. For instance, a drawer labeled FRAS-FRI contains cards beginning with the letters *fras* through *fri*. Inside the drawers are other labels, usually on tabs above the cards, that list major names and subjects.

Four Kinds of Cards. There are four kinds of cards: author cards, title cards, subject cards, and cross-reference cards. Author cards, title cards, and subject cards are the most common. The information on the top line of the card tells you what kind of card it is.

The card below is an example of an *author card* you might find in the card catalog.

AUTHOR CARD:

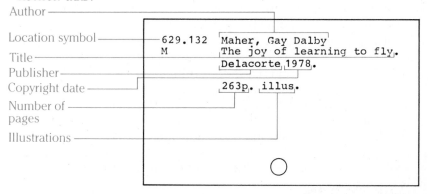

755

A typical *title card* may look like the following one. Notice that when *the* (or *a* or *an*) is the first word in a title it is overlooked in alphabetizing.

TITLE
CARD:

```
629.132   Joy of Learning to Fly
M         Maher, Gay Dalby

          The joy of learning to fly.
          Delacorte 1978.

          263p. illus.


                        ◯
```

Among the *subject cards*, you might find one like the following. The top line on a subject card is printed in capital letters.

SUBJECT
CARD:

```
629.132   AIRPLANES--PILOTING
M
          Maher, Gay Dalby
          The joy of learning to fly.
          Delacorte 1978.

          263p. illus.


                        ◯
```

As you can see, all three of the cards give the same information. In addition to the author and title of the book, the cards tell you the publisher, the copyright date, the number of pages, and whether or not the book is illustrated. They also give a location symbol, which is a group of numbers or letters that will help you find the book on the shelves.

Some catalog cards will give you even more information about books, such as a book's subtitle, a description of the contents of the book, called an *annotation*, and other subject headings under which the book is listed.

You can see from the author card at the top of the next page that some catalog cards provide a wealth of information about a book.

756

AUTHOR
CARD:

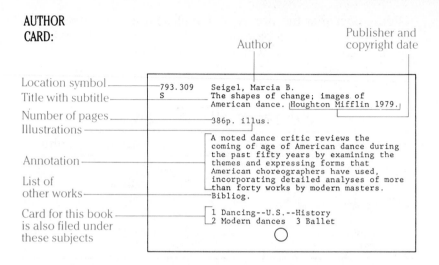

Author

Publisher and
copyright date

Location symbol ⎯⎯⎯⎯⎯
Title with subtitle ⎯⎯⎯⎯

Number of pages ⎯⎯⎯⎯
Illustrations ⎯⎯⎯⎯⎯⎯

Annotation ⎯⎯⎯⎯⎯⎯

List of
other works ⎯⎯⎯⎯⎯⎯

Card for this book ⎯⎯⎯⎯
is also filed under
these subjects

793.309
S

Seigel, Marcia B.
The shapes of change; images of
American dance. ⌈Houghton Mifflin 1979.⌉

386p. illus.

A noted dance critic reviews the
coming of age of American dance during
the past fifty years by examining the
themes and expressing forms that
American choreographers have used,
incorporating detailed analyses of more
than forty works by modern masters.
Bibliog.

1 Dancing--U.S.--History
2 Modern dances   3 Ballet

A *cross-reference card*, may be a *see* card or a *see also* card. A *see* card refers you to a different subject heading. A *see also* card refers you to additional subject headings.

CROSS-REFERENCE CARDS:

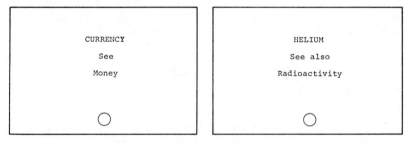

CURRENCY

See

Money

HELIUM

See also

Radioactivity

Headings used by libraries will vary. From the *see* card on the left, you can tell that the subject heading *Currency* is not used in this library. The card refers you to the subject heading *MONEY*, where books on this subject are listed. From the *see also* card on the right, you can tell that the subject heading *HELIUM* is used by the library. The card refers you to an additional heading where other books on the subject are listed. A *see also* card comes after all the other cards on a subject.

Arrangement of Cards. Some libraries group author, title, and subject cards together. Other libraries group author and title cards together and put subject cards in separate drawers.

757

Remember that the library alphabetizes by word, not by letter. Suppose you are looking for books under the subject heading *New Zealand*. You would find *New Zealand* before *Newfoundland* because all the *New* items come before the longer words that begin with *new*.

TWO METHODS OF ALPHABETIZING	
Library's Method: By Word	**Other Method: By Letter**
New Orleans	Newark
New York	Newfoundland
New Zealand	New Orleans
Newark	Newport
Newfoundland	New York
Newport	New Zealand

A few additional hints should help you when you are looking up cards in the card catalog. Authors' last names are given first and alphabetical arrangement of titles begins with the word after *a, an,* or *the*. Abbreviations are listed alphabetically as if they were spelled out. For *St.* look under *Saint*, for *Mt.* look under *Mount*, for *Mr.* look under *Mister*. All *Mc's* and *Mac's* are filed under *Mac*, and *U.S.* is filed under *United States*.

EXERCISE A: Writing Catalog Cards. Write an author, title, and subject card, using the information below.

> *The Story of Philosophy* by Will Durant, published by Simon and Schuster in 1926, with 589 pages and illustrations. The location symbol for the book is 100 over the letter D.

EXERCISE B: Alphabetizing Catalog Cards. Arrange the following subjects in the order in which they would be found in a card catalog.

1. PORTER, WILLIAM SIDNEY
2. PORTUGUESE LITERATURE
3. PORT ELIZABETH
4. PORTLAND (OREGON)
5. PORTER, KATHERINE ANNE
6. PORTER, COLE
7. PORT ARTHUR (TEXAS)
8. PORTLAND (MAINE)
9. PORTUGAL
10. PORT ROYAL

758

EXERCISE C: More Work with Alphabetizing Catalog Cards. Give the first three letters of the word you would look for to find each of the items below in the card catalog.

EXAMPLE: Edna Ferber

  fer

1. *The Armies of the Night*
2. *A Landmark History*
3. *An American Tragedy*
4. *Mr. and Mrs. Bo Jo Jones*
5. Mt. Everest

6. St. Lawrence River
7. U.S. Government
8. Edward McMurray
9. *The Enduring Hemingway*
10. Douglas MacArthur

Finding Books on the Shelves

Knowing the organization of the library will help you to find the book you want. The library distinguishes between two kinds of books: *fiction* (made-up stories) and *nonfiction* (factual material). Nonfiction includes two smaller groups that are often shelved separately: biographies and reference books.

Locating Fiction. Fiction is a term for stories created by an author. The location symbol in the upper left-hand corner of a catalog card for fiction will generally be the letter *F* for fiction. The first or first few letters of the author's last name may also be given. Books of fiction will be arranged alphabetically on the shelf according to the author's last name.

Find fiction arranged in alphabetical order by the author's last name.

To help you further, a library may label the book's spine with the letter *F* for fiction, as well as with a few letters of the author's last name. The following chart shows the order you would find four books of fiction on the shelf.

FICTION ARRANGED ALPHABETICALLY ON THE SHELF			
Steinbeck's	Steinbeck's	Stewart's	Stewart's
Cannery Row	*The Grapes of Wrath*	*The Crystal Cave*	*Nine Coaches Waiting*
F	F	F	F
Ste	Ste	Ste	Ste

Locating Nonfiction. Nonfiction includes factual material on all subjects. Most high school and public libraries organize nonfiction books by the Dewey Decimal System. First proposed by Melvil Dewey in 1876, this system of arranging books assigns numbers and letters to subjects. The location symbol in the card catalog gives you the book's Dewey Decimal number. This number is called a *call number*.

Find nonfiction on the shelves by using call numbers.

The call number consists of the Dewey Decimal classification number and the first letter or letters of the author's last name. For example, *The History of American Sailing Ships* by H. I. Chapelle has the following call number.

CALL NUMBER: 623.8 Dewey Decimal Classification Number
C Author Letter

Nonfiction books with the same classification numbers are arranged alphabetically according to the authors' last names. The following chart shows you how books with the same call number would be organized on the shelf.

ORGANIZATION ON THE SHELF BY CALL NUMBER				
551.5	551.5	551.5	551.5	551.5
S	T	V	W	Y

A library will usually help you by labeling the rows of books so that you can go directly to the row you want. If the label on a row is 300–450, you know that books with call numbers that fall between 300 and 450 are in that row.

NOTE ABOUT CALL NUMBERS: Sometimes two books will have exactly the same call number, as in the following example.

EXAMPLE: 551.5 *The Ocean of Air*
B David I. Blumenstack

551.5 *From Raindrops to Volcanoes*
B D. C. Blanehard

Because books may share a call number, you should always check to make sure you have the book you truly want.

If you know the Dewey Decimal System, you can determine the subject of a book from its number. The Dewey Decimal System divides all knowledge into ten main classes numbered from 000 to 999. The first digit on the left tells you the general subject of the book. The chart below shows the range of numbers assigned to each general subject.

MAIN CLASSES OF THE DEWEY DECIMAL SYSTEM	
Number	**Subject**
000–099	General Works (encyclopedias, periodicals, etc.)
100–199	Philosophy
200–299	Religion
300–399	Social Sciences
400–499	Languages
500–599	Science
600–699	Technology (applied science)
700–799	Arts and Leisure
800–899	Literature
900–999	History

If a book's number is in the 200 range, then you know that its general subject is religion. If a book's number is in the 400 range, then its general subject is languages.

Each digit to the right of the first digit indicates a further breakdown of the subject into *divisions*.

SAMPLE DIVISIONS OF THE DEWEY DECIMAL SYSTEM	
Main Class: Technology: 600–699	
600–609	Books on the whole subject
610–619	Medicine
620–629	Engineering
630–639	Farming
640–649	Homemaking
650–659	Business
660–669	Chemical industries
670–679	Manufactured goods
680–689	Mechanical trades
690–699	Building trades

The Dewey Decimal System can give you even more specific information about a book's content. Each division also has subdivisions. The following chart shows a Dewey Decimal number with all three parts explained.

INFORMATION IN A DEWEY DECIMAL NUMBER
822

Literature
(Main Class)

English Literature
(Division)

English Drama
(Subdivision)

Most call numbers also have decimal numbers that indicate that the subdivision has been divided into even smaller parts. In the number 822.33, for example, the first digit to the right of the decimal point indicates a subclass of English drama: the Elizabethan Period, 1558–1625. The second digit indicates William Shakespeare, the great Elizabethan dramatist.

You do not need to memorize all of the categories and subcategories of the Dewey Decimal System. However, knowing the main classes and knowing how the system works will help you to use the library more efficiently.

Note About Another Classification System: Some large libraries, such as those at colleges and universities, use the Library of Congress classification system instead of the Dewey Decimal System. The Library of Congress classification system divides books into lettered classes from A to Z. These large subject divisions are further broken down by smaller lettered and numbered divisions.

Locating Biographies and Special Materials. A biography is the factual account of a person's life. Most libraries have a separate section for individual biographies and autobiographies, in which the author and subject are the same person. The location symbol in the card catalog may include B (for biography) and the first few letters or the entire last name of the person whose life is described. The location symbol may instead include the number 92 (from the Dewey Decimal number 920 for history) and the first letters of the subject's last name. In either case, the location symbol directs you to the biography section, where you can then use alphabetical order to find the name of the person the book is about.

Find biographies in the biography section arranged in alphabetical order by the subject's last name.

Reference materials may also be shelved in their own special section of a library. Frequently the letters R or Ref will appear above the call number to indicate that the material is in a special section.

Applying your knowledge of the card catalog, the organization of the library, the Dewey Decimal System, and alphabetical grouping, you should be able to find your way around the library and make good use of its resources.

EXERCISE D: Finding Fiction. Arrange the following works of fiction in the order in which you would find them on the library shelves.

1. *Child of the Owl* by Laurence Yep
2. *Moby Dick* by Herman Melville
3. *Zorba the Greek* by Nikos Kazantzakis
4. *Roll of Thunder, Hear My Cry* by Mildred Taylor
5. *White Fang* by Jack London
6. *The House of Mirth* by Edith Wharton
7. *The Conformist* by Alberto Moravia
8. *The Left Hand of Darkness* by Ursula K. LeGuin
9. *The Heart Is a Lonely Hunter* by Carson McCullers
10. *Pedro Paramo* by Juan Rulfo

EXERCISE E: Finding Nonfiction. Arrange the following call numbers in the order in which you would find them on the library shelves.

1. 598.2 P	3. 598.3 A	5. 598.1 L	7. 598.1 Gh	9. 598.3 Z
2. 598.2 Ma	4. 598.1 Go	6. 598.2 Me	8. 598.3 Ba	10. 598.2 L

763

EXERCISE F: Finding Biographies. List the letter under which you would find each of the following biographies and autobiographies in the biography section of the library.

EXAMPLE: *Virginia Woolf: A Biography* by Quentin Bell

W

1. *The Life and Times of Rembrandt* by Hendrik Van Loon
2. *Juarez: Man of Law* by Elizabeth Borton Trevino
3. *Amelia Earhart* by Helen Acker
4. *The Biography of Humphrey Bogart* by Joe Hyams
5. *Margaret Fuller: Bluestocking, Romantic, Revolutionary* by Ellen Wilson
6. *The Life of Samuel Johnson* by James Boswell
7. *My Life with Martin Luther King, Jr.* by Coretta King
8. *Joe Namath: A Football Legend* by David Lipmann
9. *I Always Wanted to Be Somebody* by Althea Gibson
10. *Gandhi, Fighter Without a Sword* by Jeanette Eaton

DEVELOPING WRITING SKILLS: Using Your Library Skills. In your school or public library, use your knowledge of the card catalog and the organization of a library to find the following. Then write a paragraph about your library skills, indicating which library skills you most need to work on.

1. Find a catalog card that has an annotation. Copy all of the information from the catalog card onto your paper.
2. Find a card that lists two or more additional subject headings under which the card is filed. Copy all of the information from the card onto your paper.
3. Find an example of a cross-reference card that says *see*. Copy all of the information from the card onto your paper.
4. Find an example of a *see also* card. Copy all of the information from the card onto your paper.
5. List the author, title, subject, and call number of a nonfiction book you would like to read.
6. Explain in two to three sentences what the call number of the book you listed in Question 5 tells you.
7. Find the book you listed in Question 5 on the shelf. List the authors, titles, and call numbers for the books on either side of your book on the shelf. (If your book has been checked out, choose another one.)

8. Choose an author of fiction and list the titles of the books of fiction by your author that your library has.
9. List the author, title, and location in your library of a biography that you would like to read.
10. List the authors, titles, and location symbols of the books on either side of your biography on the shelf. (If your book has been checked out, choose another one.)

Using Reference Books 35.2

The reference section of your library is a hidden treasure of information as old as time and as new as today's headlines. The materials in this section are called reference materials because you refer to them for information rather than read them from cover to cover. On catalog cards the letters R or Ref above a call number, such as 031 or 912, tell you that the book is located in the reference section. Most reference books are meant to be consulted and cannot therefore be checked out of the library.

General Reference Books

General reference books include encyclopedias, almanacs, and atlases. The following pages focus on general reference books, what they contain, and how to use them.

Encyclopedias. Encyclopedias are alphabetically arranged sets of books that contain basic information on a great many subjects. While no encyclopedia contains all of the facts on every subject, you can expect to find basic information on a great many fields of knowledge.

Use general encyclopedias to get a brief overview of a subject.

Encyclopedias are relatively easy to use because they present subjects in alphabetical order and provide indexes as well as cross-references. In addition, guide words at the top of the pages tell you whether the subject you are looking for is on that page. To find more information on a subject, you can either consult the index or a list of cross-references at the end of an article. For example, at the end of the article on England in *The World Book Encyclopedia*, there is a list of over one hundred related articles that appear in the encyclopedia.

As for current information, publishers continuously revise encyclopedias. They also provide yearbooks that supply information on important events of the preceding year and summarize major developments in various fields of knowledge.

The following is a list of commonly used encyclopedias.

POPULAR ENCYCLOPEDIAS

Collier's Encyclopedia, in 24 volumes.
Compton's Pictured Encyclopedia, in 15 volumes
Encyclopedia Britannica, in 29 volumes
Encyclopedia Americana, in 30 volumes
Encyclopedia International, in 20 volumes
The World Book Encyclopedia, in 22 volumes

Almanacs. Almanacs provide both up-to-date and historical information on such topics as government, history, geography, astronomy, and weather, as well as statistics on industry, agriculture, population, entertainment, and sports. Two of the most widely used almanacs are the *Information Please Almanac* and *The World Almanac and Book of Facts*.

Use almanacs to find current facts and historical statistics on a wide range of subjects.

To find a subject in an almanac, refer to the almanac's index, which lists subjects alphabetically. Suppose you want to find out who the all-time home-run hitters in baseball are. Turning to the index in *The World Almanac*, for example, you would look under the subject *Baseball* and turn to the appropriate page, where you would find the following information.

All-Time Home Run Leaders

Player	HR	Player	HR	Player	HR	Player	HR	Player	HR
Hank Aaron	755	Mel Ott	511	Rocky Colavito	374	Joe Adcock	336	Robert Johnson	288
Babe Ruth	714	Lou Gehrig	493	Gil Hodges	370	Johnny Bench	332	Hank Sauer	288
Willie Mays	660	Stan Musial	475	Ralph Kiner	369	Hank Greenberg	331	Del Ennis	288
Frank Robinson	586	Willie Stargell	461	Reggie Jackson	369	Willie Horton	325	Frank Thomas	286
Harmon Killebrew	573	Billy Williams	426	Joe DiMaggio	361	Tony Perez	323	Ken Boyer	282
Mickey Mantle	536	Duke Snyder	407	John Mize	359	Bobby Bonds	321	Reggie Smith	280
Jimmy Foxx	534	Carl Yastrzemski	404	Yogi Berra	358	Roy Sievers	318	Ted Kluszewski	279
Ted Williams	521	Al Kaline	399	Dick Allen	351	Al Simmons	307	Rudy York	277
Willie McCovey	520	Frank Howard	382	Lee May	344	Rogers Hornsby	302	Roger Maris	275
Ed Mathews	512	Orlando Cepeda	379	Ron Santo	342	Chuck Klein	300	Brooks Robinson	268
Ernie Banks	512	Norm Cash	377	John (Boog) Powell	339	Jim Wynn	291	Vic Wertz	266

Atlases. Atlases are general reference books that contain geographical information based on maps. The maps show the locations of countries and continents and indicate population distribution, temperature, rainfall, agricultural and industrial production, natural resources, and time zones.

Use atlases to find information from maps.

Atlases have indexes in their back pages that list places in the world alphabetically and indicate where to find the maps that show these places. Suppose you want to learn about Jamaica. If you look in the index of *Rand McNally Cosmopolitan Atlas*, you will find the following information.

EXAMPLE:
Jamaica, Guthrie, Iowa C3   92
Jamaica, Queens, N.Y. (part of
    New York City) .... k13   108 ———— Location on map grid
Jamaica, Windham, Vt. E3   120
Jamaica, country, N.A. .... E13   65 ———— Page number
Jamaica, bay, N.Y. k13   108
Jamaica, chan., W.I. F6   64

Turning to page 65 of the atlas, you will find this map.

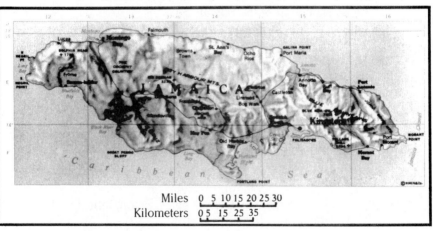

This map shows you the location of major cities such as Kingston and Montego Bay. It also shows bodies of water and mountains and includes a scale of miles and kilometers.

In addition to showing places in the world as they are today, some atlases have maps showing countries and empires at different periods in their histories. For projects in social studies, you may find the historical atlases listed in the chart on the next page helpful.

POPULAR HISTORICAL ATLASES	
Atlas of American History	*Atlas of Early American History*
Atlas of the Bible Lands	*Shepherd's Historical Atlas*
The Rand McNally Concise	*The Times Atlas of World*
Atlas of the Universe	*History*

EXERCISE A: Selecting General Reference Books. Tell what kind of general reference book you would check first to find each of the following.

EXAMPLE: Recent winners of Academy Awards

almanac

1. The fastest train in the world
2. A brief history of the life of Malcolm X
3. The population distribution and density of Australia
4. The number of elementary schools in your state
5. The reproduction of the human cell
6. The main rivers in England
7. The development of the fur trade in America
8. The election results of the 1980 Presidential election
9. The distance between Tampa, Florida, and Peoria, Illinois
10. The highest point in your state

EXERCISE B: Finding Information in General Reference Books. Use the reference books in your school or public library to find the answers to the following questions. Write both the answer and the title of the book you used.

EXAMPLE: Who won the women's singles championship at Wimbledon in 1983?

Martina Navratilova *The World Almanac*

1. What is the second most populous city in the United States?
2. Where is President Theodore Roosevelt buried?
3. When did Jane Austen die?
4. Who commissioned Michelangelo to paint the Sistine Chapel?
5. What are the names of the two longest rivers in the world?

6. Who won the Pulitzer Prize for nonfiction in 1983?
7. At what time of year does the Perseid meteor shower occur?
8. What was the northernmost point of the Roman Empire during the reign of Trajan?
9. What is the name of the first American woman astronaut to walk in space?
10. What point on the earth gets the most rain?

Specialized Reference Books

To find very detailed information on one particular subject, you can consult a specialized reference book, such as a specialized dictionary. Specialized reference books are generally shelved in the reference section according to subject divisions of the Dewey Decimal System.

Specialized Dictionaries. Because no one dictionary contains all the information you may need about words, specialized dictionaries are published.

Use specialized dictionaries to find detailed information about words.

A *thesaurus* is a specialized dictionary that gives detailed information on words with similar meanings. *Webster's Collegiate Thesaurus, Roget's International Thesaurus,* and the condensed, paperbound *Roget's Pocket Thesaurus* are commonly available specialized dictionaries of this type.

A thesaurus helps you find a better word than the one you have been using. Suppose you are writing a report and you have already used the word *exciting*. You would like now to use another word that has a similar meaning. If you turn to the index in the back of most editions of *Roget's International Thesaurus*, you will find the following information.

INDEX ENTRY: *exciting*

desirable	634.30	provocative	648.27
eloquent	600.13	thrilling	857.28
interesting	530.19	alluring	650.7

The words listed with *exciting* are called *subentries*. The number following each subentry gives the category and the paragraph where the subentry is located. Choose the subentry that comes closest to the meaning you want to express. If you were to chose *thrilling*, you would turn to category 857, paragraph 28. Using the guide numbers at the top of the page, you would find a complete text entry.

GUIDE NUMBER: 857.22–858.7

TEXT ENTRY: **.28 exciting, thrilling,** thrilly [informal], **stirring, moving, breathtaking,** excito–; agitating, perturbing, disturbing, upsetting, troubling, disquieting, unsettling, distracting, jolting, jarring; heart-stirring, heart-thrilling, heart-swelling, heart-expanding, soul-stirring, spirit-stirring, deep-thrilling, mind-blowing [slang]; impressive, striking, telling; **provocative** 648.27, provoking, piquant, tantalizing 650.7; **inflammatory** 648.28; **stimulating,** stimulative; exhilarating, heady, intoxicating, maddening, ravishing; **electric,** galvanic, charged; **overwhelming,** overpowering, overcoming, overmastering, more than flesh and blood can bear; suspensive, **suspenseful,** cliff-hanging [informal].

From the list of words closely related in meaning, you could then select the word that best fits your paper.

There are a number of other specialized dictionaries you may find useful. They include foreign language dictionaries, rhyming dictionaries, slang dictionaries, and dictionaries for a particular field, such as computer science.

Specialized Encyclopedias. For in-depth coverage of a special topic, you can use an encyclopedia specializing in a particular field.

Consult specialized encyclopedias for detailed information on a topic.

Specialized encyclopedias exist for a variety of fields. Among the major science encyclopedias are *Van Nostrand's Scientific Encyclopedia, The Cambridge Encyclopedia of Astronomy,* and *The Encyclopedia of Oceanography.* Other specialized encyclopedias are *The Book of Health, The Baseball Encyclopedia, The Encyclopedia of Sports, The Encyclopedia of Television,* and *Lillian Roxan's Rock Encyclopedia,* which contains biographical sketches of rock groups and musicians.

770

The World Encyclopedia of Comics includes biographies of comic artists and writers and the history of comics and cartoons from around the world.

Biographical Reference Books. Biographical reference books provide information on the lives of people. Since these specialized reference books contain information about people only, they are excellent sources for reports on famous people.

Use biographical reference books for information about famous people.

One particularly useful biographical reference book is *Current Biography*. As the title suggests, it contains biographies of prominent people from all over the world living at the time of publication. Included are biographies of sports figures, entertainers, political leaders, scientists, writers, and artists. *Current Biography* is published every month except December. At the end of the year, monthly issues are combined in a single volume. The first volume of *Current Biography* was published in 1940.

To use any volume of *Current Biography*, first go to the index, located at the end of the book. The following is an excerpt from the 1983 index. It lists all of the articles in the volume for 1983 as well as those from a few years before.

Subjects of articles — Mandrell, Barbara Aug 82 — Issues of
Marsalis, Wynton Oct 84 — *Current Biography*
Marshall, (Sarah) Catherine
(Wood) obit May 83

To find the article about the astronaut Sally Ride, for example, you would look in the 1983 volume.

Current Biography also has indexes for each ten-year period as well as a cumulative index covering the years since 1940. Therefore, if you are seeking information about someone who has been in the news for many years, begin with the cumulative index or the ten-year index in the 1980 volume. If the person is not listed there, look in the indexes of recent volumes.

When you find an article on the person you are researching, it will resemble the one on the next page. Notice that the article is written in a style similar to that of newspapers and magazines. The excerpt here is from the beginning of a lengthy article about Wynton Marsalis found in the 1984 volume.

Marsalis, Wynton

(mär sel´ is)

*Oct. 18, 1961– Musician. Address: b. c/o ICM
Artists, Ltd., 40 W. 57th St., New York City, N.Y.
10019*

Extolled by the renowned French trumpeter Maurice André as "potentially the greatest horn player of all time," the twenty-three-year-old trumpet virtuoso Wynton Marsalis has quickly established himself as not only a first-rate jazz artist but also as an equally talented classical musician. Since the age of seventeen, when he won an award at the prestigious Berkshire Music Center, the gifted Marsalis has continued to garner prizes, including Grammy Awards in 1984 for his classical and jazz albums, making him the first artist ever to win in both categories in one year. Even more impressive is the belief of most critics that Marsalis has yet to reach the peak of his abilities.

Wynton Marsalis, the second of the six sons of Dolores and Ellis Marsalis, was born on October 18, 1961, in New Orleans, Louisiana and raised in

Another common reference work is *Who's Who in America*, which contains biographical information on thousands of prominent Americans. It is published in two volumes every other year and includes only people living at the time of publication. *Who's Who* provides such facts as dates of birth, education, marriages, children, positions held, and addresses. Notice in the selection below that abbreviations are used to save space: *b.*, for example, means "born" and *m.* means "married to." A complete list of abbreviations is provided in the beginning of the first volume.

*WHO'S WHO
ENTRY:*

SILLS, BEVERLY (MRS. PETER B. GREENOUGH), coloratura soprano; b. Bklyn., 1929; grad. pub. schs.; student voice Estelle Leibling, piano Paolo Gallico, stagecraft Desire Defrere; hon. doctorates Harvard U., N.Y. U., New Eng. Conservatory, Temple U.; m. Peter B. Greenough, 1956; stepchildren—Lindley, Nancy, Diana; children—Meredith, Peter B. Radio debut as Bubbles Silverman on Uncle Bob's Rainbow House, 1932; appeared on Major Bowes Capitol Family Hour, 1934-41, on Our Gal Sunday; toured with Shubert Tours, Charles Wagner Opera Co., 1950, 51; debut with N.Y.C. Opera Co., as Rosalinda in Die Fledermaus, 1955; debut San Francisco Opera, 1953, La Scala, Milan, 1969, Royal Opera, Covent Garden, London, 1971, Met. Opera, N.Y.C., 1975; recital debut, Paris, 1971; appeared throughout U.S., Europe, S. Am., including Vienna State Opera, Teatro Fenice, Venice, Teatro Colon, Buenos Aires, N.Y. State Theatre, 1966, Boston Symphony, Tanglewood Festival, 1968, 69, Robin Hood Dell, Phila., 1969; star roles in Handel's Julius Caesar, Manon, La Traviata, Tales of Hoffman, Lucia di Lammermoor, Roberto Devereux, Anna Bolena, Maria Stuarda, Siege of Corinth, Thäis; gen. dir. N.Y.C. Opera, 1979—. Address: care Mgmt Ludwig Lustig 111 W 57th St New York NY 10019

A number of other *Who's Who* books contain biographical facts about people living in other parts of the world and working in fields such as religion, science, art, and government. There are also a number of *Who Was Who* books about people who are no longer living.

Another popular biographical reference book is *Webster's Biographical Dictionary*. This single-volume work contains more than 40,000 very brief biographies of men and women of all nationalities, most of whom are no longer living.

WEBSTER'S
BIOGRAPHICAL
DICTIONARY
ENTRY:

Ad'dams (ăd'ămz), **Jane.** 1860–1935. American social settlement worker and peace advocate, b. Cedarville, Ill. Grad. Rockford Coll. (1881). With Ellen Gates Starr, opened social settlement of Hull-House, Chicago (1889); its resident head (1889–1935). Became acknowledged leader of social settlement work in U.S. President, International Congress of Women (1919); presided at conventions at The Hague (1915, 1922), Zurich (1919), Vienna (1921), Washington (1924). Shared Nobel peace prize with Nicholas Murray Butler (1931). Author of *Democracy and Social Ethics* (1902), *Twenty Years at Hull House* (1910), *A New Conscience and an Ancient Evil* (1911), *The Second Twenty Years at Hull House* (1930), etc. Elected to American Hall of Fame (1965).

The biographical reference books already mentioned and others you might use are listed in the following chart.

BIOGRAPHICAL REFERENCE BOOKS	
American Authors 1600–1900	*Dictionary of Scientific*
Composers Since 1900	*Biography*
Congressional Directory	*Modern Men of Science*
Contemporary Authors	*Notable American Women*
Current Biography	*Webster's Biographical*
Dictionary of American	*Dictionary*
Biography	*Who's Who in America*
	Who Was Who in America

Literary Reference Books. For your English class, you may need to use literary reference books. There are reference books available for every form of literature.

Use literary reference books to find quotations, stories, plays, and literary facts.

773

One type of literary reference book, books of quotations, may be useful when you are looking for a quotation from a poem or speech to help you illustrate a point. You might check one of the following collections.

BOOKS OF QUOTATIONS
Familiar Quotations, edited by John Bartlett
Home Book of Quotations, edited by Burton Stevenson
The Oxford Dictionary of Quotations

How do you find the quotation you need? Most collections of quotations are arranged alphabetically by subject either in the text or in the index. Suppose you are writing a paper on the subject of *honor*. To find a quotation concerning honor, you should look under *honor* in the book of quotations.

Your library is also likely to have indexes for many forms of literature. The indexes can help you find a particular poem, play, or short story. If you do not know the title or author of a story, poem, or play, many indexes will help you by listing works by subject as well as by author and title. Some poetry indexes also include a listing of the first lines of poems. Among the common indexes are *Granger's Index to Poetry*, *Play Index*, and *Short Story Index*.

Another kind of literary reference book is the handbook. A handbook is a book of facts centered on one subject area. Literary handbooks, sometimes called *companions*, contain facts about events, places, and characters in books. *The Oxford Companion to American Literature*, for example, gives summaries of literary works and biographical sketches. *The Reader's Encyclopedia* contains lists of outstanding literary works, brief plot summaries, sketches of principal characters, and biographical information about authors.

Other Specialized Reference Books. Many libraries also have other kinds of reference books on a wide variety of topics.

Check the reference section of the library for books of information on your hobbies and interests.

The chart on the next page lists some of the guides and books on hobbies commonly available in libraries.

774

OTHER SPECIALIZED REFERENCE BOOKS	
A Field Guide to the Birds	Illustrated Encyclopedia of
A Field Guide to the Shells of	World Coins
the Atlantic and Gulf Coasts	Instruments and Devises
A Field Guide to the Stars and	The Photography Catalog
Planets	The Pictorial Encyclopedia
The Illustrated Encyclopedia	of Fishes
of Woodworking Handtools	Simple Auto Repair

EXERCISE C: Selecting Specialized Reference Books.
Give the title of the book you would use to find each of the
following.

EXAMPLE: Information about early basketball teams

The Encyclopedia of Sports

1. Information about The Who, a rock music group
2. A quotation dealing with *justice*
3. Details about early situation comedies on television
4. Five words that have a meaning similar to *confuse*
5. Details about the treatment for eye cataracts
6. Information about a strange coin you have found
7. A short biography of Dolly Madison
8. A short biography of sports star Arthur Ashe
9. A poem about the Crusades
10. Details about a constellation of stars

EXERCISE D: Using Specialized Reference Books. Use
specialized reference books to find answers to the following questions. Write both the answer and the title of the book you used.

EXAMPLE: Who wrote *The Mill on the Floss*?

George Eliot *The Reader's Encyclopedia*

1. Who said, "Politics are almost as exciting as war and quite
   as dangerous. In war you can only be killed once, but in
   politics many times"?
2. What are three novels by the Muriel Spark?
3. What are Magellanic clouds?
4. Who was Salmon P. Chase?
5. What are five synonyms for *red*?

775

6. What are three novels by the American writer Sinclair Lewis?
7. Who is Joan Aiken?
8. What is the source of the quotation: "To everything there is a season, and a time to every purpose under heaven"?
9. When was Sandra Day O'Connor born?
10. What is the rest of the verse that begins "Monday's child is fair of face"?

Periodicals and Pamphlets

Periodicals are newspapers, magazines, and journals that are issued regularly. The term *periodical* once meant all regularly issued publications except newspapers, but the term now applies to newspapers also. Though the terms *magazine* and *journal* are sometimes used interchangeably, there is a difference. A magazine is of more general interest than a journal, which contains current information in a specialized field.

The Readers' Guide to Periodical Literature. One of the most important reference aids in the library is *The Readers' Guide to Periodical Literature*, a directory that indexes articles from about 180 magazines and journals.

Use *The Readers' Guide to Periodical Literature* to find information in magazines and journals.

The Readers' Guide, as it is generally called, is published twice a month, except in February, July, and August, when it is issued only once a month. At the end of each year, the issues are combined in one hardbound volume. A complete list of the magazines that are indexed is found near the front of each volume of *The Readers' Guide.*

The Readers' Guide lists articles alphabetically by author, title, and subject. Suppose you are looking for information about rare birds. First look under the letter *r* for rare. There you would find the subject heading *Rare birds* followed by a number of other headings under which you might check. After these, the articles themselves begin appearing. The excerpt on the next page shows how they are listed. The listings may contain a number of abbreviations—for magazine names and for dates. In the beginning of each issue you will find a complete list of abbreviations.

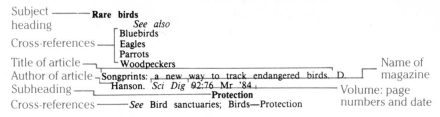

Subject heading — **Rare birds**
Cross-references — See also / Bluebirds / Eagles / Parrots
Title of article — Woodpeckers
Author of article — Songprints: a new way to track endangered birds. D. Hanson. *Sci Dig* 92:76 Mr '84.
Subheading — Protection
Cross-references — *See* Bird sanctuaries; Birds—Protection
Name of magazine
Volume: page numbers and date

In looking up a subject, you should usually begin with the most recent issue of *The Reader's Guide* and work back into earlier issues because you will generally want the latest information on a subject. Not all of the magazines you find in *The Readers' Guide* will be in your library, but most libraries have the more popular magazines.

Newspapers and Pamphlets. Newspapers and pamphlets can also be useful sources of information. There is no general index to newspapers, but many major newspapers have their own indexes. Among the newspapers that have indexes are *The New York Times, The Christian Science Monitor, The Wall Street Journal,* and *The National Observer.*

Use indexes for individual newspapers to find information in newspapers.

The newspaper index most often found in libraries is *The New York Times Index*, which indexes articles that appeared in *The New York Times* from 1851 to the present. The articles in the annual indexes are arranged alphabetically by subject, and each article is summarized. These summaries are called *abstracts*. Abstracts are very useful because they can tell you whether or not the article has the information you are looking for. Following the abstract, the date, section, page, and column in which the article can be found are listed.

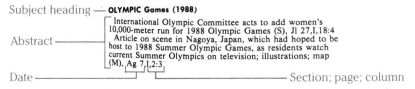

Subject heading — **OLYMPIC Games (1988)**
Abstract — International Olympic Committee acts to add women's 10,000-meter run for 1988 Olympic Games (S), Jl 27,I,18:4
Article on scene in Nagoya, Japan, which had hoped to be host to 1988 Summer Olympic Games, as residents watch current Summer Olympics on television; illustrations; map (M), Ag 7,I,2:3
Date — Section; page; column

Many newspapers, including *The New York Times*, have a microform edition for library use. A microform is a reduced photographic reproduction of printed matter on film. These films may be on rolls (microfilm) or on sheets (microfiche).

The microforms for each periodical are usually kept in special cabinets and arranged chronologically in the cabinet drawers. To view the microforms, a projector, called a *reader*, is used. A recent development in the field of microcopying is the reader-printer; with the press of a button on the reader, you can make a paper copy from the microform.

Pamphlets are booklets made with paper bindings and covering a single subject. They are often alphabetically arranged by subject in a file cabinet, usually called a *vertical file*.

Use the vertical file to find information in pamphlets.

Although you are now familiar with many of the reference materials in the library, your library can probably surprise you with other useful reference books. You should learn to find answers to your research questions, but you should also be willing to ask the librarians for help. Consider their expertise a further aid and reference tool.

EXERCISE E: Interpreting Abbreviations in *The Readers' Guide to Periodical Literature.* List the following for *The Readers' Guide* excerpt below: the title of the article, the author, the magazine, the volume, the pages, and the date. Consult the list of abbreviations in the front of the volume if you need help.

> Lost words of colonial America: a glossary. R. M. Lederer, Jr. il *Am Herit* 35:40-1 Ag/S '84

EXERCISE F: Using *The Readers' Guide to Periodical Literature.* Find the information below in a recent issue of *The Readers' Guide*.

1. Select a subject you are studying in science or social studies. Look under the subject in *The Readers' Guide*, and list all of the information given for the first three articles on the subject.
2. Now, find an article about someone you admire in sports, entertainment, government, or some other field. List all of the information given about the article, check out the article, and read it. Then write a summary of the article.

EXERCISE G: Using a Newspaper Index. Use a newspaper index in your school or public library to find three stories published on the day you were born. Give details about each story.

EXERCISE H: Using *The New York Times Index*. Find the information below in the latest volume of *The New York Times Index*.

1. Locate an entry about a recent earthquake. List the date of the article, the section (if given), the page of the article, and the column.
2. Select an article about a sports or cultural event. Write down the date of the article, the section (if given), the page, and the column. Find the newspaper in the library and locate the article. Then write down the exact headline and the name of the author (if given).

DEVELOPING WRITING SKILLS: Applying Your Knowledge of Reference Materials. Choose a subject that interests you and write a short informal report, using information from at least three of the following sources. Include a list of the reference materials you used to find your information.

1. A general encyclopedia
2. A biographical reference book
3. A magazine
4. A newspaper
5. A pamphlet

Using the Dictionary 35.3

You probably use the dictionary more often than any other reference book, but perhaps you could be making even better use of this valuable resource. A good dictionary gives you more than the meanings of words. It provides pronunciations and a key to help you pronounce words; it tells you how words are used in a sentence; it contains the history of words and often lists of words with similar meanings. Many dictionaries also give rules for spelling and grammar, information about famous people and places, and the meanings of commonly used abbreviations. Most good dictionaries have introductory notes that tell what the book contains and how it is used.

Choosing the Right Dictionary

Many people think that all dictionaries are the same. They are not. Some dictionaries are for scholars; others are for general readers. Still others are especially for students in college, high school, or elementary school.

Use the dictionary that best suits your needs.

You will want to use a dictionary that is neither too easy nor too difficult for you. It should contain all the words you are likely to encounter in your studies and should explain those words in language you can understand easily. Your needs will probably be met by a good high school or college dictionary.

DICTIONARIES RECOMMENDED FOR STUDENTS	
High School Dictionaries	**College Dictionaries**
Webster's New World Dictionary, Student Edition	*Webster's New World Dictionary, Second College Edition*
The Macmillan Dictionary	*The American Heritage Dictionary*
The Scott, Foresman Advanced Dictionary	*The Random House College Dictionary*
Webster's High School Dictionary	*Webster's New Collegiate Dictionary*

All dictionaries in the chart above are called *abridged* dictionaries. *Abridged* means shortened or condensed. Abridged dictionaries generally contain between 55,000 and 160,000 words. Abridged dictionaries usually give enough information about a word to fill most ordinary needs.

Unabridged dictionaries are useful when you need further information about a word or when you need to know the meaning of words that are not in an abridged dictionary. *Unabridged* dictionaries contain 250,000 words or more. They attempt to include all words in the language, including words no longer used. They give detailed information about how the meanings of words have changed. Two well-known unabridged dictionaries are *Webster's New International Dictionary of the English Language* and *The Oxford English Dictionary* (the OED). The first of the following definitions is from an abridged dictionary, the second from an unabridged.

780

ABRIDGED: **ray**² (rā) *n.* [< MFr. < L. *raia*] any of several fishes, as the stingray, electric ray, skate, etc., having a broad, flat body with both eyes on top, wide fins at each side, and a slender or whip-like tail

UNABRIDGED: ¹**ray** \'rā\ *n* -s [ME *raye*, fr. MF *raie*, fr. L *raia*] **:** any of numerous elasmobranch fishes of the order Hypotremata and esp. of the suborder Batoidea having the body dorsoventrally flattened often to an extreme degree with the mouth and gill clefts on the lower and the eyes on the upper surface, the pectoral fins usu. enormously developed and continuous along the margin of the head and body, the pelvic fins of moderate size, the anal fin absent, and typically a slender whiplike caudal process often with venomous spines, being adapted for life on the sea bottom, and feeding chiefly on mollusks which they crush with blunt flattened pavement teeth; *sometimes* **:** any of the typical rays as distinguished from the skates and the more sharklike members of the order — see ELECTRIC RAY, GUITARFISH, STINGRAY; compare SAWFISH

ray

When you need especially detailed information about words, you should consult an unabridged dictionary. On most occasions, however, an abridged dictionary will provide all you need.

EXERCISE A: Choosing a Dictionary That Suits Your Needs. Examine the dictionary that you usually use. Answer the following questions.

1. What is the complete title of the dictionary?
2. For what kind of audience was it written? Scholars? General readers? College students? High school students?
3. Does the dictionary have an introduction that explains how to use the book? If so, how long is this section?
4. List three technical terms that you have encountered in science, history, English, or some other class. Does your dictionary define them?
5. In your judgment is the dictionary you use suited to your present needs as a student?

Finding the Words

Using the dictionary can be frustrating if you do not know how to find words quickly. You must know at least the first several letters of a word in order to begin looking it up.

Students often ask, "How can I find the word if I don't know how to spell it?" Because there are often several spellings for the same sound, a knowledge of spelling patterns can help.

Become familiar with the spelling patterns used for different sounds in English words.

Always begin by making an educated guess. The more spelling patterns you know for a sound, the better your chances of finding a word. Some dictionaries provide a chart or list in the front of the book that shows the different spellings a sound may have in English. The chart excerpt below is from *Webster's New World Dictionary*, Student Edition.

WORD FINDER CHART		
If the sound is like the . . .	try also the spelling . . .	as in the words . . .
a in fat	ai, au	pl*ai*d, dr*au*ght
a in lane	ai, ao, au, ay, ea, ei, eigh, et, ey	r*ai*n, g*oa*l, g*au*ge, r*ay*, br*ea*k, r*ei*n, w*ei*gh, sach*et*, th*ey*
a in care	ai, ay, e, ea, ei	*ai*r, pr*ay*er, th*e*re, w*ea*r, th*ei*r
a in father	au, e, ea	g*au*nt, s*e*rgeant, h*ea*rth
a in ago	e, i, o, u	*a*gent, san*i*ty, c*o*mply, foc*u*s

Most of the time you will know the correct spelling of an unfamiliar word because you will have just encountered it in your reading. If you know the spelling, all you need to know is how to find the word quickly.

Learn to use alphabetical order to find words quickly.

All words in a dictionary are arranged in alphabetical order—letter by letter. Here are three steps to follow to find words in the dictionary quickly.

STEPS FOR FINDING WORDS QUICKLY

1. Use the four-section approach, explained on the next page.
2. Next, use the guide words at the top of the page.
3. Then, follow strict letter-by-letter alphabetical order.

To find a word quickly, first mentally divide the dictionary into the following four sections.

FOUR SECTIONS: ABCD   EFGHIJKL   MNOPQR   STUVWXYZ

The reason for the unequal division is that English words are not evenly distributed among the letters of the alphabet. Compare, for example, the number of pages your dictionary devotes to the letter *z* and the number it devotes to *c*.

The four-section approach works as follows. If you are looking up the word *cataclysm*, you know it will be in the first quarter of the book. *Montage* will be somewhere near the middle, at the beginning of the third quarter. *Xylophone* will be near the end of the book, in the fourth quarter.

Next, use the *guide words* which are printed in large type at the top of each page. The guide word at the left tells you the first word on that page; the guide word on the right tells you the last word on that page.

After you have narrowed your search down to a single page, the last step is to find your word among the several dozen on that page. Unlike cards in a library card catalog, which are alphabetized word by word (*New Zealand* before *Newfoundland*), the words in all dictionaries follow *strict alphabetical order*. That is, the words are alphabetized letter by letter (*Newfoundland* before *New Zealand*). This strict alphabetical order is observed right to the end of a word.

EXAMPLES: *neutron* before *Nevada*

Newark before *New Bedford*

Newcastle before *newcomer*

EXERCISE B: Finding Words in the Dictionary. Write the section in which each of the following words appears. Then give the guide words on each page.

EXAMPLE: pinch

third section   pinafore   pinhead

1. steeple
2. dolphin
3. Vancouver
4. length
5. mushroom
6. beforehand
7. Shakespearean
8. New York
9. knife
10. prehensile

EXERCISE C: Alphabetizing. Put the following words in alphabetical order as you would find them in a dictionary.

1. Easter Island
2. earth
3. easy
4. early
5. Eastern Roman Empire
6. earring
7. east
8. east-northeast
9. earwig
10. earn

Understanding Main Entries

In a dictionary a word and all of the information about it are called a *main entry*. The word itself is called the *entry word*. An entry word may be a single word, a compound word (two or more words acting as a single word), an abbreviation, a prefix or suffix, or the name of a person or place. Some dictionaries omit names or place them at the back of the book.

Learn to recognize and use the different kinds of information contained in a main entry.

The following are examples of the different kinds of entry words that may be found in a dictionary.

ir·ri·tant (ir′ə tənt) *adj.* causing irritation —*n.* something causing irritation —**ir′ri·tan·cy n.**

Islets (or **islands**) **of Lang·er·hans** (läŋ′ər häns′) [after P. *Langerhans* (1847–88), G. histologist] irregular groups of endocrine cells in the pancreas: they produce insulin

IRS, I.R.S. Internal Revenue Service

in- [< OFr. & ML. < L. *in-*] *a prefix meaning* no, not, without, non- *[inhumane]*: changed to *il-* before *l [illegal]*, *ir-* before *r [irregular]*, and *im-* before *m, p,* and *b [immaterial, impossible, imbecile]*

-i·na (ē′nə) [L.] *a suffix used to form* feminine names, titles, etc. *[Christina, czarina]*

Is·a·bel·la (iz′ə bel′ə) [It.] **1.** a feminine name **2. Isabella I** 1451–1504; wife of Ferdinand V & queen of Castile (1474–1504): gave help to Columbus in his expedition

Is·tri·a (is′trē ə) peninsula in NW Yugoslavia, reaching into the N Adriatic: also **Is′tri·an Peninsula**

Spelling. Although most English words have only one correct spelling, some words can be spelled in more than one way. The most commonly used is called the *preferred spelling*. Less commonly used spellings are called *variant spellings*. If the form you look up is a variant spelling, the entry will refer you to the main entry with the preferred spelling.

VARIANT
SPELLING:

Jen·ghiz Khan (jeŋ′gis) *same as* GENGHIS KHAN

PREFERRED
SPELLING:

Gen·ghis Khan (geŋ′gis kän′, jeŋ′-) (born *Temuchin*) 1162?–1227; Mongol conqueror of central Asia

If a main entry includes two entry words, the form listed first is usually the more commonly used and the preferred spelling. Sometimes a rare variant spelling is listed at the end of a main entry. Following are examples of main entries for words with more than one spelling.

COMMON
VARIANT
SPELLING:

gel·a·tin, gel·a·tine (jel′ət ’n) *n.* [< Fr. < It. < *gelata*, a jelly < pp. of L. *gelare*, to freeze: for IE. base see COOL] **1.** the taste-less, odorless, brittle substance obtained by boiling bones, hoofs, etc.; also, a similar vegetable substance: gelatin dissolves in hot water, forming a jellylike substance when cool, and is used in various foods, photographic film, etc. **2.** something, as a jelly, made with gelatin

RARE
VARIANT
SPELLING:

Par·chee·si (pär chē′zē) *a trademark for* a game like pachisi, in which dice are thrown —*n.* [p-] this game or the game of pa-chisi: also sp. par·che′si, par·chi′si

Syllabification. Dots, spaces, or slashes in an entry word indicate where that word may be divided. In the example above, notice that *Parcheesi* has three syllables; dots are used to indicate where the word may be divided. If you are in doubt about where a word may be divided, look it up in a dictionary.

When breaking words at the end of a line, remember that you cannot leave a syllable of just one letter on a line by itself. For example, the word *itinerary* is divided into syllables this way: i tin er ar y. However, you would not put the *i-* at the end of a line of writing, even though it is a syllable; nor would you write *itinerar-* at the end of a line, leaving the *-y* to stand alone on the next line. Words of one syllable are never divided.

Pronunciation. Pronunciations appear after most entry words. The dictionary indicates how to pronounce words by respelling them in a *phonetic alphabet*. This is a set of special symbols with each symbol assigned one sound. A *pronuncia-*

785

tion key at the front or back of your dictionary explains all of the symbols used in that dictionary. The syllable that gets the most emphasis has a *primary stress*, usually shown by a heavy mark after the syllable ('). Words of more than one syllable may also have a *secondary stress*, usually shown by a shorter, lighter mark (') after the syllable.

PRIMARY STRESS ONLY:

im·pu·ni·ty (im pyōō′hə tē) *n.* [< Fr. < L. < *impunis* < *in-*, without + *poena*, punishment] freedom from the danger of being punished or harmed

PRIMARY AND SECONDARY STRESSES:

jer·ry-built (jer′ē bilt′) *adj.* [prob. < name *Jerry*, infl. by JURY²] built poorly, of cheap materials

Part-of-Speech Labels. The dictionary also tells you how a word can be used in a sentence—whether it functions as a noun, verb, or some other part of speech. This information is abbreviated usually after the pronunciation, but sometimes at the end of the entry.

Some words function as more than one part of speech.

Adjective — **rough** (ruf) *adj.* [OE. *ruh:* for IE. base see RUPTURE] **1.** *a)* not smooth or level; uneven [a *rough* surface] *b)* not easily traveled; overgrown, wild, etc. [*rough* country] **2.** shaggy [an animal with a *rough* coat] **3.** moving violently; agitated; specif., *a)* stormy; tempestuous [*rough* weather] *b)* noisy or disorderly [*rough* play] **4.** harsh, rude, brutal, etc. [a *rough* temper] **5.** sounding, feeling, or tasting harsh **6.** lacking comforts and conveniences [the *rough* life of pioneers] **7.** not refined or polished [a *rough* diamond] **8.** not finished, perfected, etc. [a *rough* sketch, a *rough* estimate] **9.** needing strength rather than skill or intelligence [*rough* labor] **10.** [Colloq.] difficult, unpleasant, etc. [a *rough* time] **11.** *Phonet.* pronounced with an aspirate; having the sound of *h* —*n.* **1.** rough ground **2.** rough material or condition ☆**3.** a rough sketch or draft **4.** [Chiefly Brit.] a rough person; rowdy **5.** *Golf* any part of the course where grass, weeds, etc. grow uncut —*adv.* in a rough manner —*vt.* **1.** to make rough; roughen [to *rough* up metal with a file] **2.** to treat roughly (often with *up*) [the street gang *roughed* up their victim] **3.** to make or shape roughly (usually with *in* or *out*) [*rough* out a scheme] —*vi.* to behave roughly —**in the rough** in a rough or crude state —**rough it** to live without comforts and conveniences —**rough′ish** *adj.* —**rough′ly** *adv.* —**rough′ness** *n.*

Transitive verb

Noun

Adverb

Intransitive verb

When necessary, the dictionary shows additional information along with the part-of-speech label, such as the plural forms of nouns, the different forms of adjectives and adverbs, and the parts of verbs.

PLURAL FORM OF NOUN:

sheaf (shēf) *n., pl.* **sheaves** [OE. *sceaf*] **1.** a bunch of cut stalks of grain, etc. bound together **2.** a collection, as of papers, bound in a bundle —*vt. same as* SHEAVE²

786

FORMS OF
ADJECTIVE:

luck·y (luk′ē) *adj.* **luck′i·er, luck′i·est** **1.** having good luck; fortunate **2.** having a good result by chance *[a lucky accident led to the discovery]* **3.** believed to bring good luck *[a lucky rabbit's foot]* —**luck′i·ly** *adv.* —**luck′i·ness** *n.*

PARTS OF
VERB:

for·get (fər get′, fôr-) *vt.* **-got′** or archaic **-gat′** (-gat′), **-got′ten** or **-got′, -get′ting** [OE. *forgietan:* see FOR- & GET] **1.** to lose (facts, etc.) from the mind; be unable to remember **2.** to fail to do, bring, etc. without meaning to; neglect *[to forget to lock the door; to forget one's keys]* **3.** to overlook or ignore *[let's forget our differences]* —*vi.* to forget things —**forget it** don't trouble to think about it —**forget oneself** **1.** to think only of others **2.** to behave in an improper or unseemly manner —**for·get′ta·ble** *adj.* —**for·get′ter** *n.*

Etymologies. The origin and history of a word is called its *etymology*. In many dictionaries the etymology appears in brackets after the pronunciation or part-of-speech label. In others the etymology comes at the end of a main entry.

The information in an etymology is listed from most recent to least recent in a code made up of symbols and abbreviations. As with pronunciation symbols, the codes for etymologies vary from one dictionary to another. Knowing a word's history can sometimes help you remember the present meaning of the word. In the following example, see how the etymology can help you remember what a peninsula is. The symbol means "comes from" and L. is an abbreviation for "Latin."

EXAMPLE:

pen·in·su·la (pə nin′sə lə, -syoo-) *n.* [< L. < *paene*, almost + *insula*, island] **1.** a piece of land almost entirely surrounded by water, connected with the mainland by an isthmus **2.** any piece of land sticking out into the water —**pen·in′su·lar** *adj.*

This etymology tells you that the word *peninsula* comes from a Latin word that came from two other Latin words, *paene* meaning "almost" and *insula* meaning "island."

Definitions. Many words have multiple meanings or definitions. Meanings for the same part of speech are grouped together. Different meanings are often illustrated with a phrase or sentence showing the word in use. The entry for the word *variable* lists seven different meanings and gives two examples.

EXAMPLE:

var·i·a·ble (ver′ē ə b'l, var′-) *adj.* **1.** likely to change or vary; changeable, fickle, etc. *[in a variable mood]* **2.** that can be changed or varied *[a variable price]* **3.** *Biol.* tending to differ in some way from the type **4.** *Math.* having no fixed value —*n.* **1.** anything changeable; thing that varies **2.** *Math. a)* a quantity that may have a number of different values *b)* a symbol for such a quantity **3.** *Naut.* a shifting wind —**var′i·a·bil′i·ty, var′i·a·ble·ness** *n.* —**var′i·a·bly** *adv.*

787

Usage Labels. The way that people use a word or phrase is known as usage. Words and their meanings can have various usages depending on the particular situation or the people using them. Words or phrases used the way most people in the United States use them are considered standard English and have no special labels. Words or phrases used in an uncommon way will usually be accompanied by a *usage label*. Dictionaries indicate words or phrases used in an uncommon way with usage labels such as *Nonstandard, Archaic* (old-fashioned), *Obsolete, Rare, Poetic, Dialect, Informal* (or *Colloquial*), *Slang*, and *British*. A usage label usually appears before the definition to which it applies.

EXAMPLE: **lor·ry** (lôr′ē, lär′-) *n., pl.* **-ries** [prob. < dial. *lurry, lorry,* to tug] **1.** a low, flat wagon without sides **2.** [Brit.] a motor truck

Field Labels. Words or meanings that are used in special ways by people in a particular occupation, activity, or branch of knowledge are shown by *field labels*. Such labels usually appear before the definition.

EXAMPLE: **neg·a·tive** (neg′ə tiv) *adj.* [see prec.] **1.** expressing denial or refusal; saying "no" **2.** opposite to or lacking what is positive, as, lacking confidence, agreement, optimism, cooperation, etc. [a *negative* personality; a *negative* approach]; specif., *a*) *Biol.* directed away from the source of a stimulus [*negative* tropism] *b*) *Math.* designating a quantity less than zero, or one to be subtracted; minus *c*) *Med.* not indicating the presence of a specific disease, condition, etc. *d*) *Photog.* with the relation of light and shade the opposite of that in the thing photographed ☆**3.** *Elec.* *a*) of, generating, or charged with NEGATIVE ELECTRICITY *b*) having an excess of electrons —*adv.* no; not so: so used in radio communication —*n.* **1.** a word, phrase, statement, etc. expressing denial, rejection, or refusal ["no" and "not" are *negatives*] **2.** the side that is opposed to the proposition being debated (with *the*) **3.** an impression of a sculpture, etc. that shows it in reverse **4.** the plate in a voltaic battery where the lower potential is **5.** *Math.* a negative quantity **6.** *Photog.* an exposed and developed negative film or plate, from which positive prints are made —*vt.* **-tived, -tiv·ing 1.** *a*) to refuse; reject ☆*b*) to veto **2.** to deny; contradict **3.** to disprove **4.** to neutralize —**in the negative 1.** in refusal or denial of a plan, etc. **2.** with a negative answer —**neg′a·tive·ly** *adv.* —**neg′a·tive·ness, neg′a·tiv′i·ty** *n.*

Idioms. Expressions that have special meanings peculiar to a language are called *idioms*. Their use and meanings depend on imagination, not literal truth. "Make a big deal out of," "on the double," and "down and out" are idioms. The example at the top of the next page shows in bold print the many idioms that one dictionary lists under the word *heel*.

788

EXAMPLE: **heel**[1] (hēl) *n.* [OE. *hela*] **1.** the back part of the human foot, under the ankle **2.** the corresponding part of the hind foot of an animal **3.** that part of a stocking, sock, etc. which covers the heel **4.** the built-up part of a shoe, supporting the heel **5.** anything like the human heel in location, shape, or function, as the end of a loaf of bread, the part of the palm of the hand nearest the wrist, the lower end of a ship's mast, etc. ☆**6.** [Colloq.] a person who behaves in a mean, dishonorable way —**vt.** **1.** to furnish with a heel [to *heel* shoes] **2.** to touch or drive forward as with the heel ☆**3.** [Colloq.] to provide (a person) with money —**vi.** to follow along at the heels of someone [to teach a dog to *heel*] —**at heel** just behind —**cool one's heels** [Colloq.] to be kept waiting for some time —**down at the heel(s)** **1.** with the heels of one's shoes worn down **2.** shabby; seedy —**kick up one's heels** to be lively or merry —**on** (or **upon**) **the heels of** close behind —**out at the heel (s)** **1.** having holes in the heels of one's shoes or socks **2.** shabby; seedy —**take to one's heels** to run away: also **show one's heels** —**to heel** **1.** just behind **2.** under control [the rebels must be brought *to heel*] —**turn on one's heel** to turn around abruptly —**heel′less** *adj.*

Derived Words.

Words formed by the addition of a common suffix, such as *-ly* or *-ness*, to an entry word are called *derived words*. Derived words are found at the end of the main entry and are not defined. They often appear only with their part-of-speech labels.

EXAMPLE: **glad**[1] (glad) *adj.* **glad′der, glad′dest** [OE. *glæd*: for IE. base see GOLD] **1.** happy; pleased [I'm *glad* I wasn't there] **2.** causing pleasure or joy; making happy [*glad* tidings] **3.** very willing [I'm *glad* to help] **4.** bright or beautiful [a *glad* summer day] —**vt., vi. glad′ded, glad′ding** [Archaic] to gladden —see SYN. at HAPPY —**glad′ly** *adv.* —**glad′ness** *n.*

Synonyms and Antonyms.

A *synonym* is a word closely related but not identical in meaning to another word. An *antonym* is a word opposite in meaning. In some dictionaries you will see below the entry a block of words beginning with *SYN*. Here the differences in meaning among synonyms are explained. Antonyms are sometimes here, too, preceded by ANT.

EXAMPLE: **con·firm** (kən furm′) *vt.* [< OFr. < L. *confirmare* < *com-*, very much + *firmare*, to strengthen < *firmus*, firm] **1.** to make firm; strengthen; establish [the propaganda he read *confirmed* him in his prejudices] **2.** to make valid by formal approval; ratify [to *confirm* a treaty] **3.** to prove the truth or validity of; verify **4.** to cause to undergo religious confirmation —**con·firm′a·ble** *adj.*
SYN. —to **confirm** is to establish the truth of something that was doubtful or uncertain [to *confirm* a rumor]; **substantiate** suggests the producing of evidence that proves an earlier statement [census figures *substantiate* his claim]; **corroborate** suggests the strengthening of one statement by another [two other witnesses *corroborated* her testimony]; to **verify** is to prove the truth or accuracy of something by investigation or by comparison with a standard or the facts [to *verify* an account]; **authenticate** implies proof of genuineness by an expert [to *authenticate* a painting]; **validate** implies the confirming of something officially to be valid [to *validate* a will] —**ANT.** contradict, disprove

789

EXERCISE D: Finding Preferred Spelling and Syllabification. Use your dictionary to find the preferred spelling of each word. Then, use slashes to show the way the word is divided into syllables.

EXAMPLE: theatre–theater

the/a/ter

1. lollypop—lollipop
2. encyclopedia—encyclopaedia
3. gasolene—gasoline
4. blamable—blameable
5. catalog—catalogue
6. bandanna—bandana
7. judgement—judgment
8. calibre—caliber
9. install—instal
10. advisor—adviser

EXERCISE E: Understanding Primary and Secondary Stresses. The words below have been divided into syllables. Find the words in your dictionary. Then circle each syllable that has a primary stress, and underline any syllable that has a secondary stress.

EXAMPLE: man i cure

(man)i cure

1. su per mar ket
2. rag a muf fin
3. dy na mite
4. cen tral ize
5. plu ral i ty
6. ex ca va tion
7. u ni form
8. ex trav a gance
9. mel o dy
10. de pre ci a tion

EXERCISE F: Showing How Words Can Work. Find the following words in your dictionary and write the part-of-speech labels for each.

EXAMPLE: gear

n. adj. vt. vi.

1. hit
2. own
3. back
4. direct
5. gleam
6. lift
7. before
8. sound
9. rope
10. ground

790

EXERCISE G: Finding the Etymology. Look up the following words in your dictionary and describe the etymology of each.

EXAMPLE: algebra

Algebra comes from an Arabic word that means "the reunion of broken parts."

1. Pullman
2. cantaloupe
3. diesel
4. janitor
5. denim
6. kindergarten
7. typhoon
8. guitar
9. sherbet
10. robot

EXERCISE H: Word Meanings. Look up *snap* and *set* in your dictionary and write the definition that applies in each sentence.

EXAMPLE: The rope will *snap* if we pull any harder.

to break or part suddenly

1. There were three *snaps* on the baby's suit.
2. The dog *snapped* at the piece of meat.
3. The captain *snapped* out an order.
4. The animal trainer *snapped* a whip.
5. Kim *snapped* her fingers in rhythm to the music.
6. They were sure someone had *set* the house on fire.
7. The doctor *set* the fractured bone.
8. She got a job working on stage *sets*.
9. They bought a new *set* of dishes.
10. Mac *set* the alarm for six o'clock.

EXERCISE I: Finding Usage Labels. Use your dictionary to answer the following questions about usage labels.

EXAMPLE: What is a *Slang* meaning of *split*?

to leave a place

1. What is the British usage of the word *bonnet*?
2. What is an informal (or *Colloquial*) meaning of *huddle*?
3. What usage label accompanies the definition for *verily*?
4. What is a slang meaning of *bounce*?

5. What is the informal (or *Colloquial*) meaning of *bulldoze*?
6. What is the archaic meaning of *man*?
7. What is the slang meaning of *dump*?
8. What is the informal (or colloquial) meaning of *jibe*?
9. What is the archaic meaning of the word *gracious*?
10. What is the obsolete meaning of the word *imply*?

EXERCISE J: Finding Field Labels. Look up the words *line* and *plate* in your dictionary. Then, write the definition that follows each of the following field labels.

EXAMPLE: Geography—line

an imaginary circle of the earth, as the equator

1. Music—line	6. Dentistry—plate
2. Football—line	7. Photograph—plate
3. Mathematics—line	8. Baseball—plate
4. Baseball—line	9. Printing—plate
5. Miliary—line	10. Architecture—plate

EXERCISE K: Finding the Meaning of Idioms. Find the meaning of each idiom by looking up the underlined words.

EXAMPLE: <u>dig</u> into

to work hard at

1. <u>high</u> and dry	6. <u>fit</u> to be tied
2. on the <u>loose</u>	7. from the <u>horse's</u> mouth
3. in <u>kind</u>	8. on the <u>sly</u>
4. go to the <u>wall</u>	9. to make no <u>bones</u> about
5. in the long <u>run</u>	10. on the <u>lam</u>

EXERCISE L: Finding Derived Words. Write the words your dictionary lists as derived words for each word below.

EXAMPLE: splendid

splendidly   splendidness

1. friend	4. socialize	7. ask
2. search	5. indolent	8. scramble
3. glow	6. coat	9. frivolous
		10. feverish

DEVELOPING WRITING SKILLS: Using the Dictionary Efficiently. Use your dictionary to answer the questions below. Then write a paragraph about your skills in using the dictionary.

1. What was Mark Twain's real name?
2. Which is the preferred spelling, *medieval* or *mediaeval*?
3. How many syllables are in the word *bouillabaisse*?
4. What are the idioms listed under *word*?
5. What are the derived words under *quench*?
6. What usage label, if any, is listed for *yon*?
7. What field labels do you find under the word *strike*?
8. What are some synonyms of *rural*?
9. What usage label accompanies the word *ain't*?
10. According to its etymology, what color is associated with the original meaning of *candidate*?

Skills Review and Writing Workshop

Library and Reference Skills

CHECKING YOUR SKILLS

Take notes on the following entry from an encyclopedia.

(1) Jupiter, Saturn, Uranus, and Neptune are called *gaseous* planets. (2) Of these, Jupiter is the *largest*, with a diameter of 88,000 miles. (3) Saturn is probably *colder* than Jupiter since it is farther from the sun. (4) The *least dense* planet, Saturn would float in an ocean if there were one large enough to hold it. (5) Uranus and Neptune are *more distant* from the sun than Jupiter and Saturn. (6) They are *best* seen with a small telescope. (7) Scientists assume they are colder and *darker* than the other gaseous planets. (8) All four of the gaseous planets turn *rapidly* on their axes. (9) Thus, they have *short* days. (10) However, they revolve *more slowly* around the sun, giving them long years.

USING STUDY SKILLS IN WRITING
Preparing a Bibliography

Before you write a research report, find out what, if any, information is available in your library. The list of sources you prepare is your first bibliography. Some of those sources will be helpful. Others will not. The sources you use in writing your paper will be listed in your final bibliography.

Imagine you are writing a paper about a rock group. Follow the steps below to write a first bibliography.

Prewriting: Choose a group to research. Go to general reference books and/or specialized encyclopedias about music. Check *The Readers' Guide to Periodical Literature* and *The New York Times Index*. Find the appropriate books in the card catalog, and check the bibliographies in those books.

Writing: Arrange the list of books and articles in alphabetical order by author's name.

Revising: Be sure you have included the author's name, the title, the date of publication, the place of publication (for books), and page numbers for articles.

36

Speaking and Listening Skills

Speaking and listening are both part of one process. When someone speaks, someone also listens. Good speaking skills allow you to express your ideas more clearly. Good listening skills help you to retain more of what you hear. In this chapter you will learn to improve your speaking skills both in informal and formal situations. You will also develop your listening skills to get more out of what you hear.

36.1 Informal Speaking Skills

There are many circumstances when you will be asked to speak to groups of people. Most of the time you will speak to others in informal situations, such as speaking in class discussions or giving directions or making introductions.

Speaking in Class Discussions

Knowing how to take part in class discussions is a very useful way to improve your overall study skills. Many students are reluctant to participate in classroom discussions. The best way to overcome anxiety about talking in class is through preparation and practice.

Develop confidence about participating in class through preparation and practice.

When you take part in classroom discussions, you become an active learner. You have an opportunity to test out your ideas on others and get a reaction from them. Furthermore, you become an important part of the group learning process.

The chart below offers some suggestions to help you become more actively involved in classroom discussions.

SUGGESTIONS FOR TAKING PART IN CLASSROOM DISCUSSIONS

1. Set goals for your participation; for example, you might decide to contribute at least once to each discussion.
2. Do extra reading on the topic you are studying so that you will have something of special interest to say.
3. If possible, plan what you might say before the discussion begins.
4. Do not wait for the teacher to call on you. Raise your hand and volunteer to contribute your thoughts.
5. Follow the discussion carefully so that your response will be to the point.
6. Observe methods used by other students who make good contributions.

By using these suggestions regularly, you can build your self-confidence. If you believe that what you have to say is valuable, you will probably say it well. In turn, if you can express your ideas well, you will probably become a regular contributor to classroom discussions.

EXERCISE A: Developing Your Participation in Classroom Discussions. For each of your major subjects, set up a chart similar to the one on the next page. Include columns for the date, the topic of discussion, a tally of your comments, and an evaluation of your comments. Then, over the next month, keep a record of your contributions to every class discussion. Try both to increase the number of times you partcipate and to improve the quality of your comments.

CLASSROOM DISCUSSION CHART: ENGLISH			
Date	Topic	Number of Contributions	Evaluation
Oct. 23	O. Henry's *The Gift of the Magi*	2	Made contributions but should have taken time to review the story
Oct. 27	topic for research paper	3	Getting my topic made discussion valuable. Need to narrow topic more

Giving Directions

There will be many times in your life when you will be asked to give directions. You may, for example, be asked how to find a particular location or how to perform a certain task. Regardless of the nature of the directions, you need to make your directions as clear and accurate as you can. Do not confuse your listeners by using vague, overly general statements.

When giving directions, be as clear and accurate in your language as possible.

Notice the difference between the two sets of directions below. In the first set, the sentence is very long and the details are so vague that the listener may not easily find the location being described. In the second set, the short sentences and the specific details make the directions easy to follow.

VAGUE DIRECTIONS: Go down this street for a few blocks and then turn at the bus stop and you'll see the post office on the other side of the street.

SPECIFIC DIRECTIONS: Go west on this street for three blocks until you come to the bus stop. Turn left and go two more blocks. The post office will be the two-story red brick building on your right.

The chart below provides some suggestions for giving directions that can be easily followed.

SUGGESTIONS FOR GIVING DIRECTIONS
1. Take a moment to think through the directions before giving them.
2. Speak slowly so that your listeners can follow your directions without difficulty.
3. Choose your words carefully, being as specific as possible. Give only one step of the directions in each sentence.
4. Avoid sidetracking your listeners with unnecessary information.

EXERCISE B: Giving Directions. Work with another student on this exercise. First, think of some nearby place that your partner will know, such as the school library or cafeteria. Then, give your partner clear directions to that place without saying what the place is. See if your partner can guess what place you have given directions to. Then, switch roles and do the exercise again. Finally, write a short account of the results of your work.

Making Introductions

Suppose that you are the head of the New Students Group at your school. Your job is to meet and then introduce each new student to his or her teachers and classes. When you meet each new student, you should begin by finding out detailed information about the person such as name, school last attended, home address, school or community achievements, and special interests.

Before introducing a person find out all pertinent information about that person.

In order not to forget any important information, write down the information during your first meeting. Then memorize the information before introducing the person. When introducing the person, maintain a comfortable tone so that the person feels at ease.

799

EXERCISE C: Making Introductions. Write an introduction presenting a famous person to your class. Do not reveal the person's name and see if the class can identify the person from the details you supply.

Making Announcements

The purpose of an announcement is to give factual information that answers six questions: who, what, where, when, why, and how. You should give this information clearly and concisely so that the listeners can remember all the details.

When making an announcement, supply answers to the questions who, what, where, when, why, and how.

An announcement given over your school's public address system might answer the six questions in the following way.

ANNOUNCEMENT: This is an announcement about the Explorers Club field trip to Rambling Ravine. The trip, scheduled for this Thursday, October 16, has been cancelled because of ravine flooding. Explorers' leader, Mr. Rawlings, will announce the rescheduled date tomorrow.

Not every announcement will need to answer every question. You should, however, use the questions as a checklist to make sure you have included all necessary details.

EXERCISE D: Making Announcements. Write an announcement about a real or imaginary event that could apply to the students in your class. Make the announcement to the class and then ask one student to recall the important details.

DEVELOPING WRITING SKILLS: Evaluating Your Class Participation. Write a paragraph that includes answers to the following questions.

1. What goals have you set for participating in class?
2. Have you scheduled time to prepare for class discussions?
3. Have you raised your hand to contribute ideas to class discussions?

Formal Speaking Skills 36.2

Formal speaking requires more preparation than informal speaking. In order to be an effective speaker, you must be well prepared and you must deliver your speech smoothly and with confidence.

Recognizing Different Kinds of Speeches

The kind of speech you give will depend upon your purpose. You may decide to give an *expository* speech, a *persuasive* speech, or an *entertaining* speech. The kind of speech you give will also be based in part on the age and background of your audience.

Choose the kind of speech you will give by considering both the purpose of the speech and your audience.

An *expository* speech is given to explain an idea, a process, or an object. You might write an expository speech to explain the idea of democracy in America or to explain the process of building a tree house or to explain an object such as a baseball.

A *persuasive* speech is given to try to get the listener to agree with the speaker's position or to take some action. A persuasive speech takes a stand on a particular issue and then defends that position in a logical, orderly way. For example, you might write a persuasive speech to encourage people to take action to solve the problem of people writing graffiti on school walls.

An *entertaining* speech is given to offer the listeners something to enjoy. Entertaining can also be a secondary purpose of an expository or persuasive speech. For example, an expository speech may use something entertaining to illustrate a point.

EXERCISE A: Identifying Purpose and Audience. Label each of the following speech topics as *expository, persuasive,* or *entertaining.* Then identify who might be the audience for each kind of speech.

EXAMPLE: The need for a new gymnasium

            persuasive   local taxpayers

1. How to make a pizza
2. Why the voting age should be raised
3. Why leaves change color in the fall
4. Planting a garden
5. Ten ways to avoid cleaning your room
6. The need for more traffic lights
7. Why all kids hate broccoli
8. How to assemble a bicycle
9. The best movie of the year
10. The differences between a marionette and a puppet

Planning Your Speech

If you are asked to deliver a speech before a group of people, you should begin by thinking about your topic. Sometimes you will have an assigned topic, but more often you will get to make your own choice. Choose a topic that you like or know well. If you sound like an enthusiastic authority on the subject, your listeners will be more attentive.

Choose a subject that you know or like in order to interest your audience.

After choosing a topic, gather all the necessary information and organize it in outline form. The outline below is for a classroom speech about the steps to take in order to find a summer job. Notice that the outline contains only main ideas and their supporting details.

SAMPLE OUTLINE:

  I. Deciding on the kind of job
    A. Child-care
    B. Lawn maintenance
    C. Camp counsellor
    D. Local supermarket
 II. Finding the right job
    A. Read newspaper want-ads
    B. Read notices on store bulletin boards
    C. Post a notice on store bulletin boards
    D. Talk to school guidance counsellor

III. Landing the job
    A. Make a good impression
        1. Explain qualifications
        2. Bring references
        3. Be polite
    B. Avoid a bad impression
        1. Don't criticize one's self
        2. Don't criticize others
    C. Ask the right questions
        1. Duties of job
        2. Working hours
        3. Salary

Once you have an outline that provides sufficient information and is logically organized, you should prepare note cards that you can use when you deliver your speech. Your note cards should follow the same order as your outline. You may, however, want to abbreviate some of the information on your note cards so that it can be picked up easily by the eye. Note cards are a good way to keep key information right at your finger tips in case you cannot remember the next step or an important detail.

The chart below provides some suggestions for preparing your note cards.

PREPARING NOTE CARDS FOR A SPEECH

1. Use only a few small index cards.
2. Print all information neatly.
3. Write out quotations or facts that you want to remember exactly.
4. Write out beginning and ending statements if you think they will be useful.
5. Rely mainly on key words and phrases or clear abbreviations to jog your memory.
6. Use a clear outline form and indent all of the details under the ideas they support.
7. Use underlining and capital letters to make important information stand out.
8. Number your cards to help keep them in order.

803

The following sample note cards are based on the outline for finding a job. Notice that most of the information is not as fully stated on the note cards as it is in the outline. Remember that note cards should be used mainly as an aid for your memory. Write only the key words and phrases that you will need for your speech.

Finding Summer Job ①
I. _KIND_
  A. Child - care
  B. Lawn maintenance
  C. Counselor
  D. Supermarket

II. _FINDING_ ②
  A. Newspaper ads
  B. Read notices bulletin boards
  C. Post notices
  D. Guidance counselor

III. _LANDING_ ③
  A. Good impression - qualifications, refs, polite.
  B. Bad impression - no criticism.
  C. Right questions - duties, hours, salary.

EXERCISE B: Planning Your Speech. Prepare a three- to five-minute demonstration speech, choosing a topic from the list below or one of your own. Use outline form to organize your speech. Then write out a set of note cards following the outline.

Making a book jacket
Tying shoelaces
Hitting a baseball
Swinging a golf club
Learning to swim

Starting a campfire
Asking someone to dance
Braiding hair
Baking bread
Organizing a raffle

Delivering Your Speech

Once you have prepared your note cards, practice giving the speech at home several times until you feel comfortable using the cards. Practice in front of a mirror and, as your final practice before giving the speech in school, give your speech in front of your family. The more practice you get, the more confident you will feel in front of a group of people.

As you practice your speech, think about both the *verbal* and *nonverbal* forms of the language you use. Together, both forms make the total effect of your speech on your audience.

Be aware of both the verbal and nonverbal forms of language as you practice your speech.

Verbal language is language spoken aloud. As you practice your speech, project your voice so that it can be heard throughout the room. Vary the pitch of your voice so that it sounds like normal speech, not like a speech that has been memorized. Vary the rate of your words so that they are neither too hurried nor too slow. Clearly and correctly pronounce all of the words in your speech.

Nonverbal language is what you say without using words. The way you move, your posture, facial expressions, gestures, and appearance are all language that has meaning just as words do.

Some nonverbal language reinforces verbal language. For example, a speaker may shake his or her head while saying, "No, I do not believe that." Some nonverbal language contradicts verbal language. For example, a speaker may frown and avoid looking at the audience while saying, "I'm so happy to be here speaking with you today."

As you practice your speech in front of a mirror, look for any nonverbal language that might contradict your words. Remember that your speech actually begins before you say the first word.

EXERCISE C: Delivering Your Speech. Practice your speech at home several times over a period of three or four days. Practice improving both the verbal and nonverbal aspects of language. Then deliver your speech to your class. Look at your note cards as seldom as possible.

805

Evaluating a Speech

When you evaluate another person's speech, you are doing two things. First, you are giving constructive criticism that the speaker can use to improve his or her speaking skills. Second, you are deciding which effective speaking skills you can apply to your own speeches.

Evaluate a speech in a way that offers benefits both to the speaker and to yourself.

When evaluating a speech, note the positive features of the speech first. Then, constructively criticize the speech. Never criticize a speech without also giving a positive suggestion.

The checklist below provides some suggestions to follow when evaluating a person's speech.

CHECKLIST FOR EVALUATING A SPEECH
What Was Said?
1. What type of speech was given—expository, persuasive, or entertaining?
2. Did the speaker introduce the topic clearly, develop it well, and end in a conclusive fashion?
3. Did the speaker support main ideas with appropriate details?
How Was It Said?
1. Did the speaker approach the platform confidently and establish eye contact with the audience?
2. Did the speaker's gestures and movements confirm or contradict his or her words? Where? How?
3. Did the speaker project his or her voice loudly enough?
4. Did the speaker vary the pitch of his or her voice?
5. Did the speaker vary the rate of his or her speaking?
6. Did the speaker pronounce words clearly and correctly?

EXERCISE D: Evaluating a Speech. Using the checklist above, make a detailed evaluation of a speech given in class. Then, find two or more skills that the speaker used effectively and practice using them in a speech you will give.

DEVELOPING WRITING SKILLS: **Writing a Speech Evaluation.** Write two paragraphs evaluating a speech you have given. In the first paragraph, discuss "what was said." In the second paragraph, discuss "how it was said."

Listening Skills 36.3

Did you know there is a difference between hearing and listening? Hearing is passive; listening is active. Hearing happens naturally as sound reaches your ears. Listening requires your understanding and interpreting the sounds. Developing good listening habits requires preparation and active involvement.

Preparing to Listen

Get your body ready to listen by sitting in a position that enables you to be comfortable but alert. Get your mind ready to listen by letting go of distracting thoughts. Think about the situation—a lecture, review of homework, discussion of a story, directions you must follow—that is about to start.

Prepare to listen by giving the situation your full attention.

Focus on the speaker immediately. Try not to be distracted by the speaker's appearance or mannerisms.

EXERCISE A: **Preparing to Listen.** For one day, practice two techniques for preparing to listen. First, get rid of all distracting thoughts in each listening situation. Second, give the speaker your undivided attention immediately. At the end of the day, evaluate whether your preparing to listen helped.

Listening for Main Ideas and Major Details

A good way to improve your listening skills is to pay close attention to the main ideas and major details. As you listen, try to identify and to remember all of these ideas and details.

807

Learn to take mental notes of main ideas and major details as you listen.

When you are listening, you must be selective about what you will try to remember. As you listen, ask yourself the questions in the chart below.

QUESTIONS TO HELP YOU LISTEN
1. What is the general topic?
2. What important points are being made about the topic?
3. What needs to be remembered about each point?
4. What examples or facts relate to each point?

The answers to questions 2, 3 and 4 will be the main ideas and major details. Answering the questions as you listen will help you become an active and selective listener. With practice, you will be able to remember the information that you heard and that you may need later.

Imagine that the following announcement is made in one of your classes. Try to determine what you need to remember.

ANNOUNCEMENT: A special benefit performance of *The Nutcracker* ballet will be given at Hunter Auditorium next Friday evening at 7:00 P.M. Student tickets will be available tomorrow only in Room 333 for a price of $5.00. No student tickets will be available at the auditorium itself on the night of the performance.

By asking yourself the questions in the chart above, you should be able to remember the following information.

MAIN IDEA: A performance of *The Nutcracker* ballet

MAJOR DETAILS: Hunter Auditorium on Friday at 7 P.M.
$5.00 tickets available tomorrow only
In Room 333

EXERCISE B: Listening for Main Ideas and Major Details. Work with another student on this exercise. While one person reads aloud the first passage on the following page, the other person should listen for the main idea and major details, putting them in writing after the reading is completed. Then, reverse roles and repeat the steps with the second passage.

(1) Margaret Mead will long be remembered for her research in the field of anthropology. Born in Philadelphia in 1901, Mead studied at Barnard College and later at Columbia University, where she received her doctorate. In 1925 and 1926 she lived among the people of Samoa and studied their culture. She was especially interested in the role of culture in determining personality. Her book *Coming of Age in Samoa*, published in 1928, describes the life of young people in Samoa and compares their upbringing with that of young people in Western cultures, such as the United States. Mead's book brought her fame early in life, and she remained an influential figure in anthropology until her death in 1978.

(2) In 1803, the United States acquired a very large tract of land in a famous negotiation known as the Louisiana Purchase. The land, largely unexplored territory west of the Mississippi River, was owned by France. Under the administration of Thomas Jefferson, the United States government had proposed a much more limited purchase, mainly hoping to secure shipping channels down the Mississippi River to the port of New Orleans on the Gulf of Mexico. France, however, offered to sell the entire Louisiana Territory, ranging from New Orleans to Canada and extending as far west as the Rocky Mountains, for a bargain price of fifteen million dollars (about three cents per acre). Once the sale was official, Jefferson authorized Meriwether Lewis and William Clark to begin their famous expedition to explore the huge region out of which all or part of fifteen states would later be carved.

Following Directions

Good listening skills are especially important in the many circumstances when you are required to follow spoken directions. Fortunately, there are certain steps you can take to improve your ability to follow directions.

Learn to listen to directions by performing certain mental steps.

Use the steps in the chart below to help you understand and follow spoken directions.

STEPS TO HELP YOU UNDERSTAND DIRECTIONS
1. Prepare to concentrate.
2. Visualize each step as it is given.
3. Link each step in the directions using one or more key words from each step.
4. After hearing the directions, repeat them mentally.

Imagine, for example, that you are given these directions at the beginning of an important test. Use the steps in the chart above to help you follow the directions.

DIRECTIONS: Clear your desk of everything except the test booklet, the answer sheet, and a pencil. Write your name and the date at the top of the answer sheet. Mark all answers firmly on the answer sheet. Since there is no penalty for guessing, make sure you answer all questions. You have one hour to complete the test.

You should envision yourself (1) clearing your desk of everything except the test paper, answer sheet, and a *pencil*, (2) taking the *pencil* in hand to write your name and the date, (3) using the *pencil* to mark the answers firmly, and (4) checking the clock occasionally and using the *pencil* to complete all the questions.

In addition to running through directions mentally, there is one other thing to keep in mind. Whether you are being given directions for a test, to get somewhere, or for a homework assignment, you should make sure that you understand exactly what you need to do. If you do not understand the directions the first time, ask to have the directions repeated.

EXERCISE C: Listening to Directions. Work with another student on this exercise. First, write down clear, simple directions telling how to get from the school to where you live. Then, slowly read the directions aloud. While you read, your partner should take mental notes using the steps in the chart above. After you have read the directions, your partner should write down the directions and read them back to you. Then, switch roles and do the exercise once more.

DEVELOPING WRITING SKILLS: Evaluating Your Listening Skills. After a week of practice, write a paragraph about your listening skills. Include the answers to the following questions.

1. How often do you use the questions in the chart on page 808 to help listen for important information?
2. In the last week, have you noticed an improvement in your ability to remember the information you hear?
3. How often have you followed the steps outlined in the chart on page 810 for following directions?
4. What rating (poor, fair, good, excellent) would you give your listening skills?
5. What do you plan to work on in the future to improve your listening skills even more?

Skills Review and Writing Workshop

Speaking and Listening Skills

CHECKING YOUR SKILLS

Imagine that you are listening to the following speech. Read it and write down the main ideas and major details.

Writing is difficult. First, it is hard to get started because you can always think of something else you would rather do. Then, even when you do want to start, you have a problem thinking of a subject to write about. Finally, even when you have a subject, it is hard to organize the material. I usually know what my subject will be but I have great difficulty deciding what my starting point will be and how to develop ideas from my starting point. No wonder many writers suffer from a serious disease called writer's block. Is there a cure? There are probably as many cures as there are writers. For me, the best thing to do is try to relax and not scare myself into thinking no word will ever be put on paper. When I relax, I find that ideas come to me without consciously thinking about them. I jot down all the ideas on paper, then I sit down and try to organize them.

USING STUDY SKILLS IN WRITING
Writing an Entertaining Speech

A good speech requires careful planning, sufficient preparation, and effective delivery. Follow these steps to write an entertaining speech about your most embarrassing moment.

Prewriting: Jot down all the information you can remember about this embarrassing moment in your life.

Writing: Outline your speech and prepare note cards. Make sure that your introduction will capture your audience's attention, that the ideas in the body follow logically, and that the conclusion ends the speech in a humorous way.

Revising: Practice your speech in front of another person. Rewrite any parts that do not have the effect on your audience that you want.

Manuscript Preparation

The following pages give suggestions for basic manuscript preparation, for dealing with a number of technical aspects of writing, for giving credit to your sources, and for understanding and using correction symbols.

Basic Preparation

Whether handwritten or typed, your manuscript should follow certain basic rules. The following chart shows the suggested procedures for each style.

PREPARING A MANUSCRIPT	
Handwritten	**Typed**
1. Use white 8½ × 11 inch lined paper, but never pages ripped from a spiral binder.	1. Use white 8½ × 11 inch paper.
2. Use black or blue ink only.	2. Use a clear black ribbon.
3. Leave a margin of 1 inch on the right, using the paper's own rules as your margin on other sides.	3. Leave a margin of at least 1 inch on all sides.
4. Indent each paragraph.	4. Double-space all lines and indent each paragraph.
5. Use only one side of each paper.	5. Use only one side of each paper.
6. Recopy if necessary to make your final copy neat.	6. Retype if necessary to make your final copy neat.

You must also identify your manuscript. For long and important papers, such as reports, you will probably want an elaborate title page, as shown on page 814. The next page and all the other pages should carry only your name and the page number, beginning with page one.

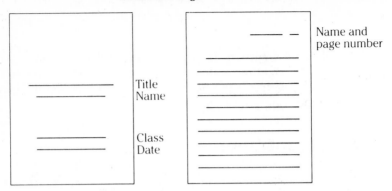

For shorter papers, use a simpler style. Basic identification appears on the first page. The second page carries your name and the page number, beginning with page two.

Without Title Page

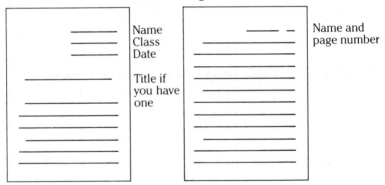

Checking Technical Matters

When preparing any manuscript, you must always check each sentence for correctness. Look for sentence errors—fragments, run-ons, and problem modifiers. Review Chapter 9, pages 176–196, if necessary. Also check the agreement of subjects and verbs. In addition, you may find it helpful to refer to the list of fifty common usage problems on pages 285–294.

Once you have checked your sentences, look for mechanical errors such as incorrect punctuation. The following chart offers basic guidelines for using punctuation marks and other mechanical items that seem to cause most manuscript problems.

CHECKING TECHNICAL MATTERS		
Item	**Basic Guidelines**	**References**
Capitalization	Capitalize proper nouns, proper adjectives, and first words.	Section 16.1, pages 302–320
Abbreviations	Avoid most abbreviations in formal writing. Feel free, however, to use abbreviations such as Mr. and Mrs., a.m. and p.m., and well-known abbreviations for organizations such as NATO.	Section 16.2, pages 321–333
Commas	Take care not to overuse commas. Check to make sure you are not dividing compound verbs with commas.	Sections 17.2 and 17.3, pages 340–356
Hyphens	Check compound words in the dictionary. Hyphenate at the end of the line only when absolutely necessary and only at a syllable break.	Section 17.8, pages 394–400
Apostrophes	Avoid using apostrophes incorrectly in personal pronouns such as *its* and *theirs*.	Section 17.9, pages 400–411
Numbers	Spell out most one- and two-word numbers and all numbers that begin sentences. Use numerals for lengthy numbers, dates, and addresses.	Section 16.2, pages 327–330
Spelling	Use a dictionary when in doubt	Section 31.2, pages 703–711

Giving Credit to Sources

Whenever you are quoting the words or using the ideas of another writer, make sure you have given credit to that person. The charts in Section 24.1 on pages 568–569 show the different forms for these kinds of citations.

Using Correction Symbols

You may find the following symbols very useful when you are proofreading your own manuscript. Your teacher may also choose to use these or similar marks when grading your papers.

	USING CORRECTION SYMBOLS	
Symbols	**Meaning**	**Examples**
ℑ	delete	The colors is red.
⌒	close up	The color is r ed.
∧	insert	The color is red.
#	add space	The coloris red.
∩	transpose	The colro is red.
ℙ	new paragraph	ℙ The color is red.
no ℙ	no paragraph	no ℙ The color is red.
cap	capitalize	the color is red
lc	use small letter	The Color is red
sp	spelling	The colar is red.
us	usage	The colors is red.
frag	fragment	The red color and the blue.
RO	run-on	The color is red the house is blue.
mod	problem modifier	Newly painted, I saw the house.
awk	awkward	The color is, I think, kind of red.

Index

Bold numbers show pages on which basic definitions and rules can be found.

817

818

819

824

825

826

827

Acknowledgments

The authors and editors have made every effort to trace the ownership of all copyrighted selections found in this book and to make full acknowledgment of their use.

The dictionary of record for this book is *Webster's New World Dictionary,* Second College Edition, Revised School Printing, copyright © 1983 by Simon & Schuster, Inc. The basis for the selection of vocabulary words appropriate for this grade level is *Living Word Vocabulary: A 43,000 Word Vocabulary Inventory* by Edgar Dale and Joseph O'Rourke, copyright © 1979.

Citations follow, arranged by unit and page for easy reference.

Grammar. **Pages 77-78** Stephen Crane, *The Red Badge of Courage* (New York: Washington Square Press, 1925).

Composition: Forms and Process of Writing. **Pages 473** George S. Fichter, "Slamming the Door on Foreign Pests," *National Wildlife* Vol. 17, No. 4 (June/July 1979), p. 130. **474** (first item) Ames, Baker, and Leahy, *Science for Your Needs* (Englewood Cliffs, NJ: Prentice-Hall, Inc. 1961), p. 101. **474** (second item) Fred Bruemmer, "Born Again: An Arctic Spring," *International Wildlife,* Vol. 9, No. 2 (March/April 1979), p. 4. **475** Adapted from Shaaron Cosner, "Almanacs: Best Sellers Based on Prophecies," *Americana,* Vol. 3, No. 1 (March 1975), p. 13. Copyright Americana Magazine, Inc. **476** From *Christy* by Catherine Marshall (New York: McGraw-Hill, Inc.). **477** George F. Dufek, "Antarctica," From *Lands and Peoples, The World Facts and Figures Index,* Vol. 7, (New York: Grolier, Inc. 1973), p. 103. **487** Edith Hamilton, *Mythology* (Boston: Little, Brown & Co., 1942). Robert E. Rhoades, "Cultural Echoes Across the Mountains." With permission from *Natural History* (January 1979). Copyright The American Museum of Natural History, 1979. **512** Ames, Baker, and Leahy, *Science for Your Needs* (Englewood Cliffs, NJ: Prentice-Hall, Inc. 1961), p. 77. **513** Charles B. Stevens, "Elmo Bumpy Torus Gets DOE Go-Ahead," *Fusion: Magazine of the Fusion Energy Foundation,* Vol. 2, No. 6 (March/April 1979), p. 9. **527** Nathaniel Hawthorne, "Dr. Heidegger's Experiment," *The Complete Short Stories of Nathaniel Hawthorne* (Garden City, NY: Doubleday, 1959). **570** From *Lands and Peoples, The World Facts and Figures Index,* Vol. 7 (New York: Grolier, Inc., 1973), p. 87. **618-619** Dick Cavett and Christopher Porterfield, *Cavett.* Copyright © 1974 by Richard A. Cavett and Christopher Porterfield. Published by Harcourt Brace Jovanovich, Inc.

Study and Research Skills. **Pages 721-722** Kenneth Brower, "Two Worlds of the Harp Seal: Above and Beneath the Arctic Ice," *Smithsonian* (July 1979), pp. 47-48. **726** From *The New York Times,* September 24, 1985. Adaptation of editorial "The Panda Solution." **766** *The World Almanac & Book of Facts,* 1980 Edition, copyright © Newspaper Enterprise Association, Inc., 1979, New York, NY 10166. **767** (map) *Rand McNally Cosmopolitan World Atlas* © RAND McNALLY & COMPANY, R.L. 81-y-3. **769-770** Subentries listed under the word "exciting" (857.22, 858.7) in ROGET'S INTERNATIONAL THESAURUS, Fourth Edition, Revised by Robert L. Chapman (Thomas Y. Crowell Company). Copyright © 1977 by Harper & Row, Publishers, Inc. Reprinted by permission of the publisher. **771-772** From *Current Biography 1984.* Copyright © 1984 by the H.W. Wilson Company. **772** (second item) Marquis Who's Who, Inc. *Who's Who in America,* 41st Edition, 1980-1981. **773** By permission. From *Webster's Biographical Dictionary* © 1980 by G. & C. Merriam Co., Publishers of the Merriam-Webster® Dictionaries. **777** *The New York Times Index* © 1984 by The New York Times Company. Reprinted by permission. **777** *Reader's Guide to Periodical Literature,* 1984 Volume, by the H.W. Wilson Company. Material reproduced by permission of the publisher. **778** *Reader's Guide to Periodical Literature* Copyright © 1984 by the H.W. Wilson Company. Material reproduced by permis-

831

sion of the publishers. **781** (first item) **784, 785** (third item), **786** (first, third, fourth items), **787, 788, 789** (third item) With permission. From *Webster's New World Dictionary, Students Edition.* Copyright © 1981 by Simon & Schuster, Inc. **781** (second item) By permission. From *Webster's Third New International Dictionary* © 1985 by Merriam-Webster Inc., publisher of the Merriam-Webster® Dictionaries. **785** (first item), **786** (second item), **789** (first item) From THORNDIKE-BARNHART ADVANCED DICTIONARY by E.L. Thorndike and Clarence L. Barnhart. Copyright © 1974 by Scott, Foresman and Company. Reprinted by permission. **785** (fourth item) With permission. From *Webster's New World Dictionary,* Second College Edition. Copyright © 1980 by Simon & Schuster, Inc. **789** (second item) *Macmillan Dictionary.* Copyright © 1981 Macmillan Publishing Co., Inc.

Art Acknowledgments. **Pages 429** Ann Hagem Griffiths, DPI. **507** Rebuffat, Photo Researchers. **508** Ylla, Photo Researchers. **509** King Features Syndicate, Inc., © 1985. **534** Carl Frank, Photo Researchers. **536**, NASA. **564** Jim Anderson, Woodfin Camp. **566** David M. Grossman, Photo Researchers; Monkmeyer Press. **587** Julian E. Caraballo, Monkmeyer Press; Michal Heron, Woodfin Camp. **588** The Granger Collection. **611** Scala, Art Resource; Giraudon, Art Resource. **622** Conklin, Monkmeyer Press. **623** Scala New York, Florence, Art Resource. **638** Culver Pictures. **640** Charles Addams, *The New Yorker,* 1969. **658** Booth, *The New Yorker,* 1972. **664** Rogert Werth, Woodfin Camp.

GRAMMAR USAGE MECHANICS